COMPACT
WORLD
ATLAS

W9-APS-624

470 Lakeview Drive
Noblesville, In 46060
(317)776-4186

PROPERTY OF NCS LIBRARY

LONDON, NEW YORK, MUNICH,
MELBOURNE, DELHI

DK

A DORLING KINDERSLEY PUBLISHING BOOK
www.dk.com

EDITOR-IN-CHIEF
Andrew Heritage

SENIOR MANAGING ART EDITOR
Philip Lord

SENIOR CARTOGRAPHIC MANAGER
David Roberts

SENIOR CARTOGRAPHIC EDITOR
Simon Mumford

PROJECT CARTOGRAPHER
Iorwerth Watkins

PROJECT DESIGNER
Karen Gregory

PROJECT EDITOR
Debra Clapson

SYSTEMS CO-ORDINATOR
Philip Rowles

PRODUCTION
Wendy Penn

First American edition 2001
Published in the United States by Dorling Kindersley Publishing, Inc.,
375 Hudson Street
New York, New York 10014

Copyright © 2001, 2002, 2003 Dorling Kindersley Limited, London
Reprinted 2002, Reprinted with revisions 2003.

A Penguin Company

All rights reserved. No part of this publication may be reproduced, stored in a retrieval system,
or transmitted in any form or by any other means, electronic, mechanical, photocopying, recording
or otherwise, without the written permission of the copyright owner.

A CIP catalog record for this book is available from the Library of Congress

ISBN 0-7894-9357-8

Reproduced by GRB, Italy

Printed and bound in Spain by Artes Gráficas Toledo

For the very latest information, visit:
www.dk.com and click on the Maps & Atlases icon

KEY TO MAP SYMBOLS

PHYSICAL FEATURES

Elevation

	4,000m / 13,124ft
	2,000m / 6,562ft
	1,000m / 3,281ft
	500m / 1,640ft
	250m / 820ft
	100m / 328ft
	0
	Below sea level

△   Mountain

▽   Depression

⌀   Volcano

)(Pass / tunnel

    Sandy desert

DRAINAGE FEATURES

—————   Major perennial river

—————   Minor perennial river

— — —   Seasonal river

    Canal

| Waterfall

    Perennial lake

    Seasonal lake

    Wetland

ICE FEATURES

    Permanent ice cap / ice shelf

    Winter limit of pack ice

    Summer limit of pack ice

BORDERS

—————   Full international border

- - - - -   Disputed *de facto* border

· · · · · ·   Territorial claim border

✕ ✕ ✕   Cease-fire line

— — —   Undefined boundary

—————   Internal administrative boundary

COMMUNICATIONS

—————   Major road

—————   Minor road

—————   Rail

✈   International airport

SETTLEMENTS

◉   Over 500,000

◉   100,000 - 500,000

○   50,000 - 100,000

○   Less than 50,000

●   National capital

●   Internal administrative capital

MISCELLANEOUS FEATURES

+   Site of interest

⊓⊔⊓⊔   Ancient wall

GRATICULE FEATURES

—————   Line of latitude / longitude / Equator

— — —   Tropic / Polar circle

25°   Degrees of latitude / longitude

NAMES

Physical features

Andes

Sahara   Landscape features

Ardennes

Land's End   Headland

Mont Blanc 4,807m   Elevation / volcano / pass

Blue Nile   River / canal / waterfall

Ross Ice Shelf   Ice feature

PACIFIC OCEAN

Sulu Sea   Sea features

Palk Strait

Chile Rise   Undersea feature

Regions

FRANCE   Country

JERSEY (to UK)   Dependent territory

KANSAS   Administrative region

Dordogne   Cultural region

Settlements

PARIS   Capital city

SAN JUAN   Dependent territory capital city

Chicago

Kettering   Other settlements

Burke

INSET MAP SYMBOLS

    Urban area

    City

    Park

■   Place of interest

□   Suburb / district

PROPERTY OF NCS LIBRARY

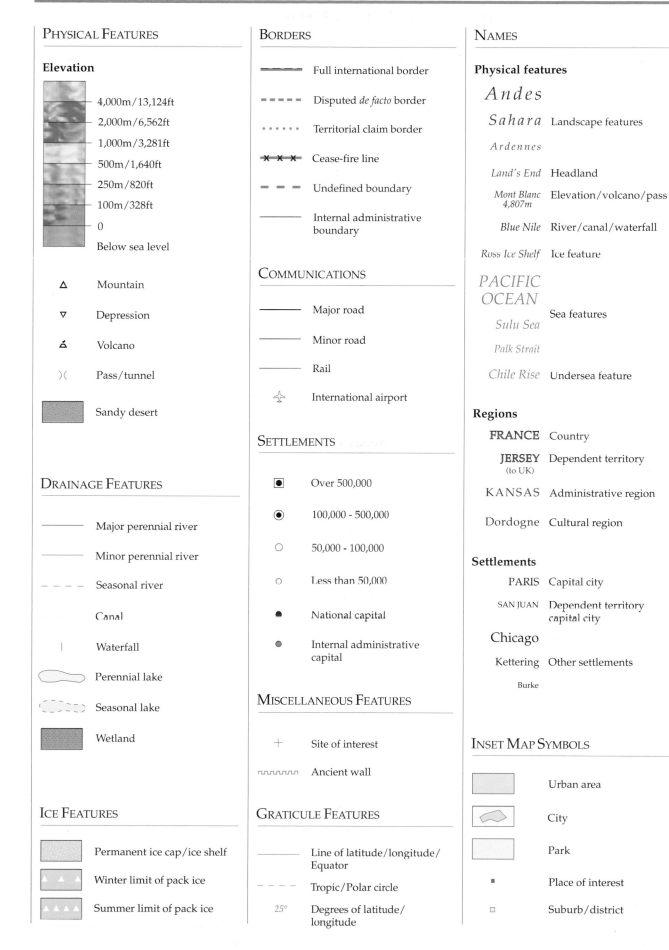

CONTENTS

THE
WORLD ATLAS

NORTH &
CENTRAL AMERICA

SOUTH AMERICA

AFRICA

EUROPE

INDEX – GAZETTEER

THE POLITICAL WORLD

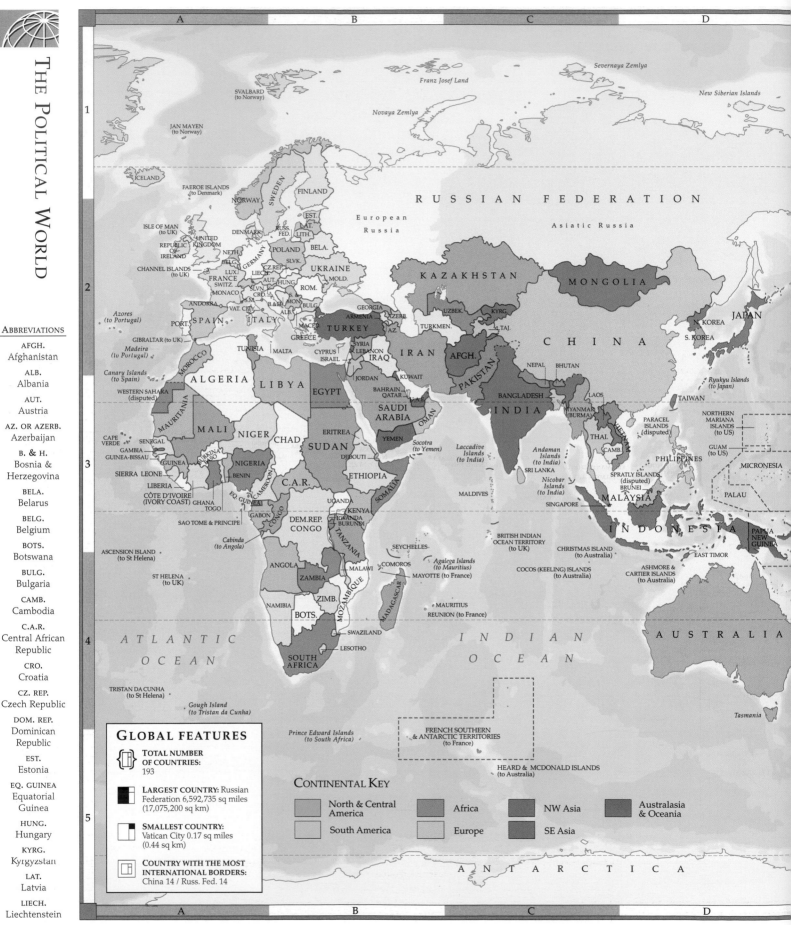

GLOBAL FEATURES

**TOTAL NUMBER
OF COUNTRIES:**
193

LARGEST COUNTRY: Russian
Federation 6,592,735 sq miles
(17,075,200 sq km)

SMALLEST COUNTRY:
Vatican City 0.17 sq miles
(0.44 sq km)

**COUNTRY WITH THE MOST
INTERNATIONAL BORDERS:**
China 14 / Russ. Fed. 14

CONTINENTAL KEY

- North & Central America
- South America
- Africa
- Europe
- NW Asia
- SE Asia
- Australasia & Oceania

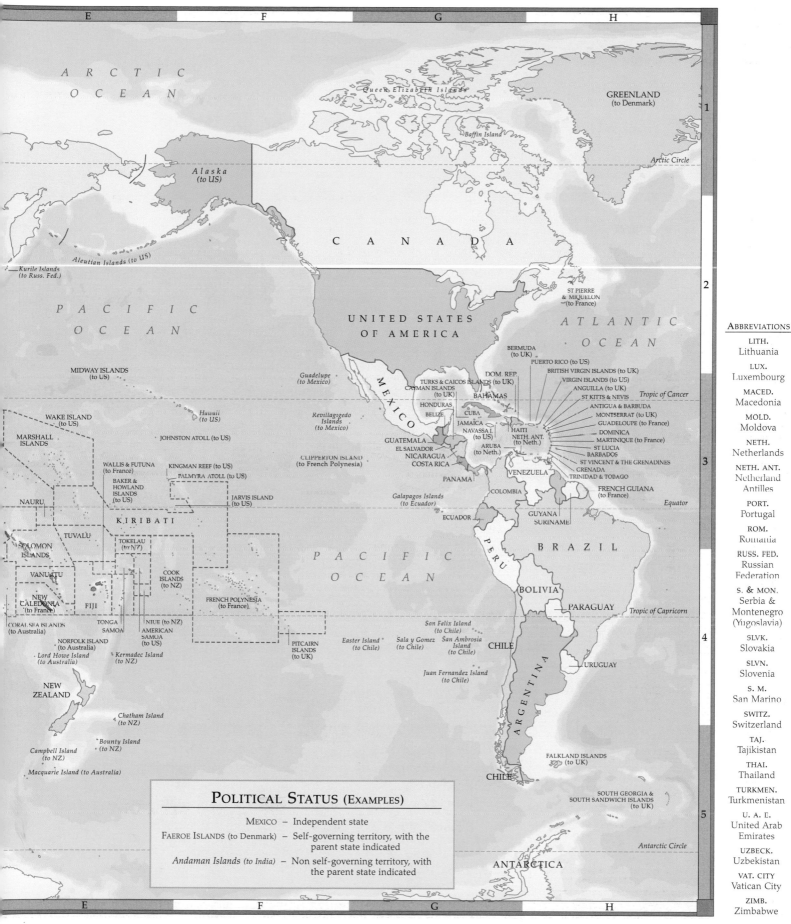

E F G H

ARCTIC OCEAN

Queen Elizabeth Islands

GREENLAND
(to Denmark)

1

Baffin Island

Arctic Circle

*Alaska
(to US)*

C A N A D A

Aleutian Islands (to US)

*Kurile Islands
(to Russ. Fed.)*

2

ST PIERRE
& MIQUELON
(to France)

PACIFIC
OCEAN

UNITED STATES
OF AMERICA

ATLANTIC
OCEAN

BERMUDA
(to UK)

PUERTO RICO (to US)

MIDWAY ISLANDS
(to US)

*Guadelupe
(to Mexico)*

DOM. REP.

BRITISH VIRGIN ISLANDS (to UK)

VIRGIN ISLANDS (to US)

TURKS & CAICOS ISLANDS (to UK)

ANGUILLA (to UK)

CAYMAN ISLANDS
(to UK)

BAHAMAS

ST KITTS & NEVIS

Tropic of Cancer

*Hawaii
(to US)*

*Revillagigedo
Islands
(to Mexico)*

HONDURAS

ANTIGUA & BARBUDA

WAKE ISLAND
(to US)

JOHNSTON ATOLL (to US)

BELIZE

CUBA

MONTSERRAT (to UK)

JAMAICA

GUADELOUPE (to France)

MARSHALL
ISLANDS

HAITI

DOMINICA

NAVASSA I.
(to US)

MARTINIQUE (to France)

WALLIS & FUTUNA
(to France)

KINGMAN REEF (to US)

*CLIPPERTON ISLAND
(to French Polynesia)*

GUATEMALA

NETH. ANT.
(to Neth.)

ST LUCIA

NAURU

BAKER &
HOWLAND
ISLANDS
(to US)

PALMYRA ATOLL (to US)

EL SALVADOR

ARUBA
(to Neth.)

BARBADOS

NICARAGUA

ST VINCENT & THE GRENADINES

COSTA RICA

GRENADA

JARVIS ISLAND
(to US)

PANAMA

VENEZUELA

TRINIDAD & TOBAGO

3

K I R I B A T I

*Galapagos Islands
(to Ecuador)*

COLOMBIA

FRENCH GUIANA
(to France)

Equator

TUVALU

ECUADOR

GUYANA

SURINAME

SOLOMON
ISLANDS

TOKELAU
(to NZ)

VANUATU

COOK
ISLANDS
(to NZ)

PERÚ

B R A Z I L

NEW
CALEDONIA
(to France)

FIJI

FRENCH POLYNESIA
(to France)

*CORAL SEA ISLANDS
(to Australia)*

TONGA

NIUE (to NZ)

BOLIVIA

SAMOA

AMERICAN
SAMOA
(to US)

PARAGUAY

Tropic of Capricorn

*San Felix Island
(to Chile)*

NORFOLK ISLAND
(to Australia)

PITCAIRN
ISLANDS
(to UK)

*Easter Island
(to Chile)*

*Sala y Gomez
(to Chile)*

*San Ambrosia
Island
(to Chile)*

CHILE

4

*Lord Howe Island
(to Australia)*

*Kermadec Island
(to NZ)*

*Juan Fernandez Island
(to Chile)*

A R G E N T I N A

URUGUAY

NEW
ZEALAND

*Chatham Island
(to NZ)*

*Campbell Island
(to NZ)*

*Bounty Island
(to NZ)*

Macquarie Island (to Australia)

FALKLAND ISLANDS
(to UK)

CHILE

SOUTH GEORGIA &
SOUTH SANDWICH ISLANDS
(to UK)

5

POLITICAL STATUS (EXAMPLES)

MEXICO – Independent state

FAEROE ISLANDS (to Denmark) – Self-governing territory, with the
parent state indicated

Andaman Islands (to India) – Non self-governing territory, with
the parent state indicated

Antarctic Circle

ANTARCTICA

E F G H

ABBREVIATIONS

LITH.
Lithuania

LUX.
Luxembourg

MACED.
Macedonia

MOLD.
Moldova

NETH.
Netherlands

NETH. ANT.
Netherland
Antilles

PORT.
Portugal

ROM.
Romania

RUSS. FED.
Russian
Federation

S. & MON.
Serbia &
Montenegro
(Yugoslavia)

SLVK.
Slovakia

SLVN.
Slovenia

S. M.
San Marino

SWITZ.
Switzerland

TAJ.
Tajikistan

THAI.
Thailand

TURKMEN.
Turkmenistan

U. A. E.
United Arab
Emirates

UZBECK.
Uzbekistan

VAT. CITY
Vatican City

ZIMB.
Zimbabwe

THE PHYSICAL WORLD

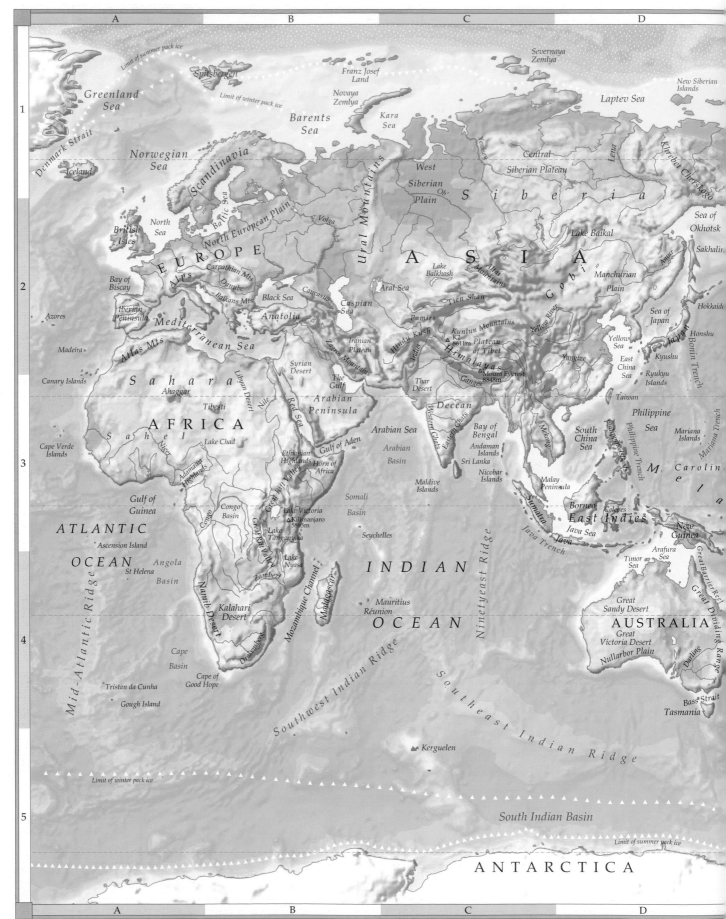

Limit of summer pack ice
Limit of winter pack ice

Spitsbergen
Franz Josef Land
Severnaya Zemlya
New Siberian Islands
Greenland Sea
Novaya Zemlya
Kara Sea
Barents Sea
Laptev Sea
Norwegian Sea
Iceland
Denmark Strait
Scandinavia
Central Siberian Plateau
West Siberian Plain
Ob
Yenisey
Lena
Khrebet Cherskogo
British Isles
North Sea
Baltic Sea
North European Plain
Volga
Ural Mountains
SIBERIA
ASIA
Lake Baikal
Sea of Okhotsk
EUROPE
Alps
Carpathian Mts
Danube
Balkans Mts
Caucasus
Black Sea
Aral Sea
Lake Balkhash
Altai Mountains
Gobi
Amur
Manchurian Plain
Sakhalin
Bay of Biscay
Azores
Iberian Peninsula
Mediterranean Sea
Anatolia
Caspian Sea
Tien Shan
Pamirs
Hindu Kush
Kunlun Mountains
Plateau of Tibet
Yellow River
Yellow Sea
Sea of Japan
Hokkaido
Honshu
Madeira
Atlas Mts
Iranian Plateau
Zagros Mountains
K2 8611m
Himalayas
Mount Everest 8848m
Yangtze
East China Sea
Kyushu
Ryukyu Islands
Japan
Bonin Trench
Canary Islands
Sahara
Libyan Desert
Nile
Syrian Desert
The Gulf
Red Sea
Arabian Peninsula
Thar Desert
Deccan
Taiwan
Ahaggar
Tibesti
AFRICA
Sahel
Niger
Lake Chad
Gulf of Aden
Arabian Sea
Western Ghats
Eastern Ghats
Bay of Bengal
Andaman Islands
South China Sea
Philippine Sea
Mariana Islands
Mariana Trench
Cape Verde Islands
Adamawa Highlands
Ethiopian Highlands
Horn of Africa
Arabian Basin
Sri Lanka
Nicobar Islands
Maldive Islands
Mekong
Philippine Trench
Ma
Caroline
Gulf of Guinea
Congo
Congo Basin
Great Rift Valley
Lake Victoria
Kilimanjaro 5895m
Somali Basin
Malay Peninsula
Borneo
Celebes
East Indies
New Guinea
ATLANTIC OCEAN
Ascension Island
St Helena
Angola Basin
Lake Tanganyika
Zambezi
Lake Nyasa
Seychelles
INDIAN
Sumatra
Java Trench
Java
Java Sea
Arafura Sea
Timor Sea
Mid-Atlantic Ridge
Namib Desert
Kalahari Desert
Mozambique Channel
Madagascar
Mauritius
Réunion
OCEAN
Ninetyeast Ridge
AUSTRALIA
Great Sandy Desert
Great Dividing Range
Great Barrier Reef
Cape Basin
Drakensberg
Cape of Good Hope
Great Victoria Desert
Nullarbor Plain
Darling
Tristan da Cunha
Gough Island
Southwest Indian Ridge
Southeast Indian Ridge
Bass Strait
Tasmania
Kerguelen
Limit of winter pack ice
South Indian Basin
Limit of summer pack ice
ANTARCTICA

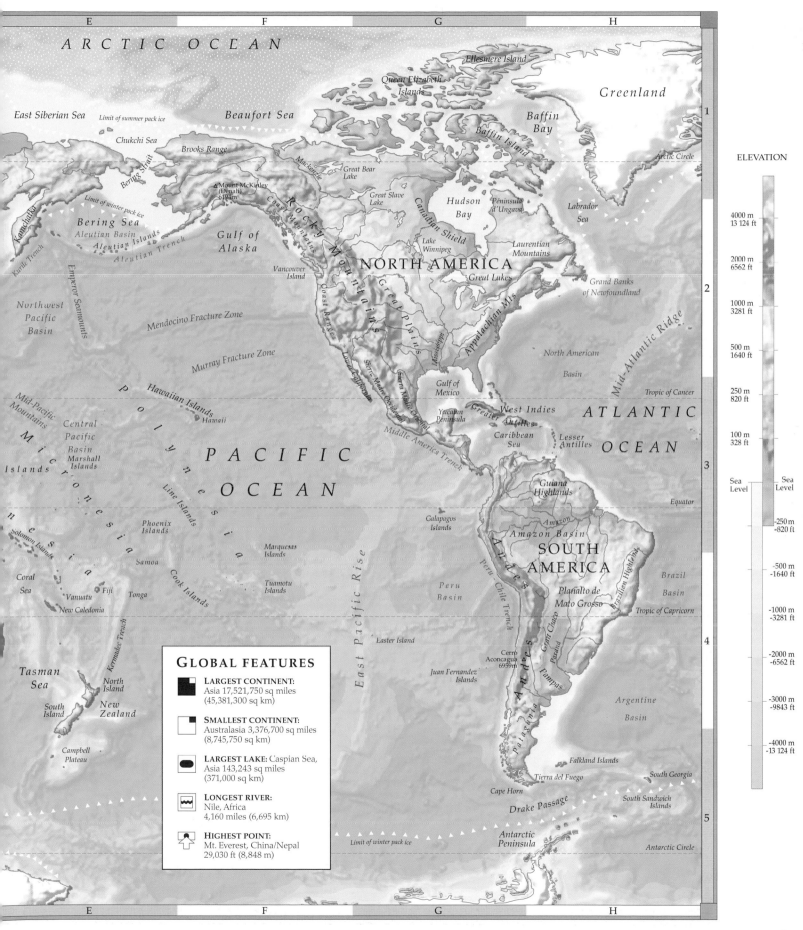

ARCTIC OCEAN

East Siberian Sea
Limit of summer pack ice
Chukchi Sea
Beaufort Sea

Queen Elizabeth
Islands

Ellesmere Island

Greenland

Baffin
Bay

Baffin
Island

1

Brooks Range
Mackenzie
Great Bear
Lake

Arctic Circle

Bering Strait
Kamchatka
Limit of winter pack ice
△ Mount McKinley
(Denali)
6194m
Coast Mountains

Great Slave
Lake

Hudson
Bay

Péninsula
d'Ungava

Labrador
Sea

Bering Sea
Aleutian Basin
Aleutian Islands
Aleutian Trench

Gulf of
Alaska

Canadian Shield

Lake
Winnipeg

NORTH AMERICA

Laurentian
Mountains

Northwest
Pacific
Basin

Emperor Seamounts

Kurile Trench

Vancouver
Island

Rocky Mountains

Coast Ranges

Great Plains

Great Lakes

Appalachian Mts

Grand Banks
of Newfoundland

Mid-Atlantic Ridge

2

Mendocino Fracture Zone

Murray Fracture Zone

Mississippi

North American

Basin

4000 m
13 124 ft

2000 m
6562 ft

1000 m
3281 ft

Mid-Pacific
Mountains

Hawaiian Islands

Hawaii

Sierra Madre Occidental
Sierra Madre Oriental
Lower California

Gulf of
Mexico
Yucatán
Peninsula

Greater
Antilles

West Indies

Tropic of Cancer

ATLANTIC

500 m
1640 ft

Central
Pacific
Basin
Marshall
Islands

PACIFIC
OCEAN

Middle America Trench

Caribbean
Sea

Lesser
Antilles

OCEAN

250 m
820 ft

Micronesia
Islands

Polynesia

Line Islands

Guiana
Highlands

100 m
328 ft

Solomon Islands

Phoenix
Islands

Galapagos
Islands

Amazon

Equator

Sea
Level

Sea
Level

Marquesas
Islands

Samoa

Cook Islands

Tuamotu
Islands

East Pacific Rise

Peru
Basin

Amazon Basin

SOUTH
AMERICA

Andes

Planalto de
Mato Grosso

Brazilian Highlands

Brazil
Basin

−250 m
−820 ft

Coral
Sea
Vanuatu
Fiji
Tonga

New Caledonia

Easter Island

Juan Fernandez
Islands

Cerro
Aconcagua
6959m

Peru–Chile Trench

Gran Chaco
Pantanal

Tropic of Capricorn

−500 m
−1640 ft

−1000 m
−3281 ft

Tasman
Sea

Kermadec Trench

North
Island

New
Zealand

Andes

Pampas

Argentine
Basin

−2000 m
−6562 ft

South
Island

Patagonia

−3000 m
−9843 ft

Campbell
Plateau

Falkland Islands

South Georgia

−4000 m
−13 124 ft

Tierra del Fuego

Cape Horn

South Sandwich
Islands

Drake Passage

Limit of winter pack ice

Antarctic
Peninsula

Antarctic Circle

5

ELEVATION

GLOBAL FEATURES

LARGEST CONTINENT:
Asia 17,521,750 sq miles
(45,381,300 sq km)

SMALLEST CONTINENT:
Australasia 3,376,700 sq miles
(8,745,750 sq km)

LARGEST LAKE: Caspian Sea,
Asia 143,243 sq miles
(371,000 sq km)

LONGEST RIVER:
Nile, Africa
4,160 miles (6,695 km)

HIGHEST POINT:
Mt. Everest, China/Nepal
29,030 ft (8,848 m)

TIME ZONES

The numbers represented thus: +2/-2, indicate the number of hours ahead or behind GMT (Greenwich Mean Time) of each time zone.

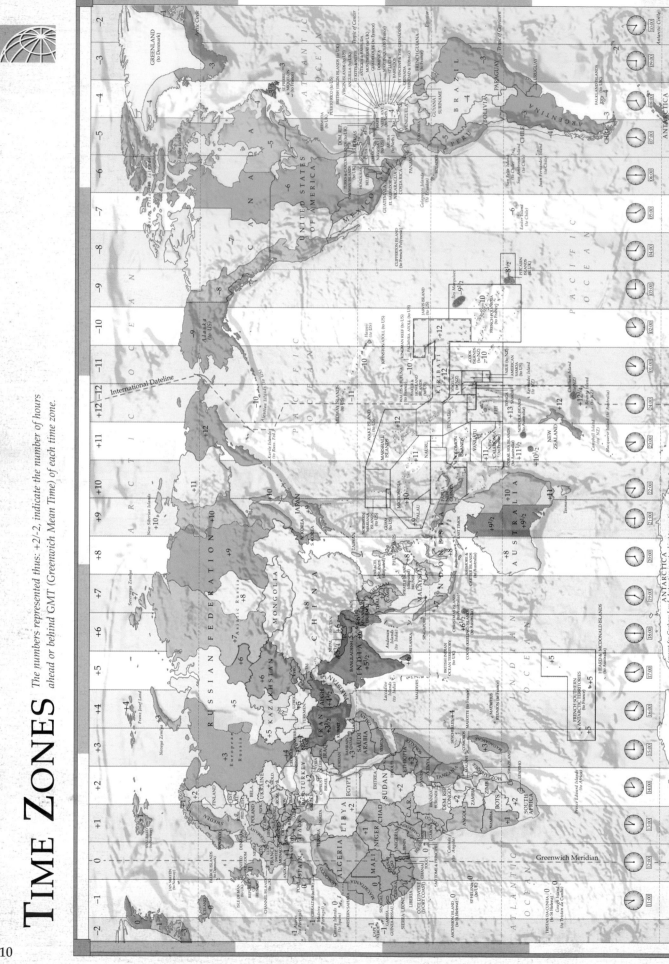

THE

WORLD
ATLAS

THE WORLD ATLAS

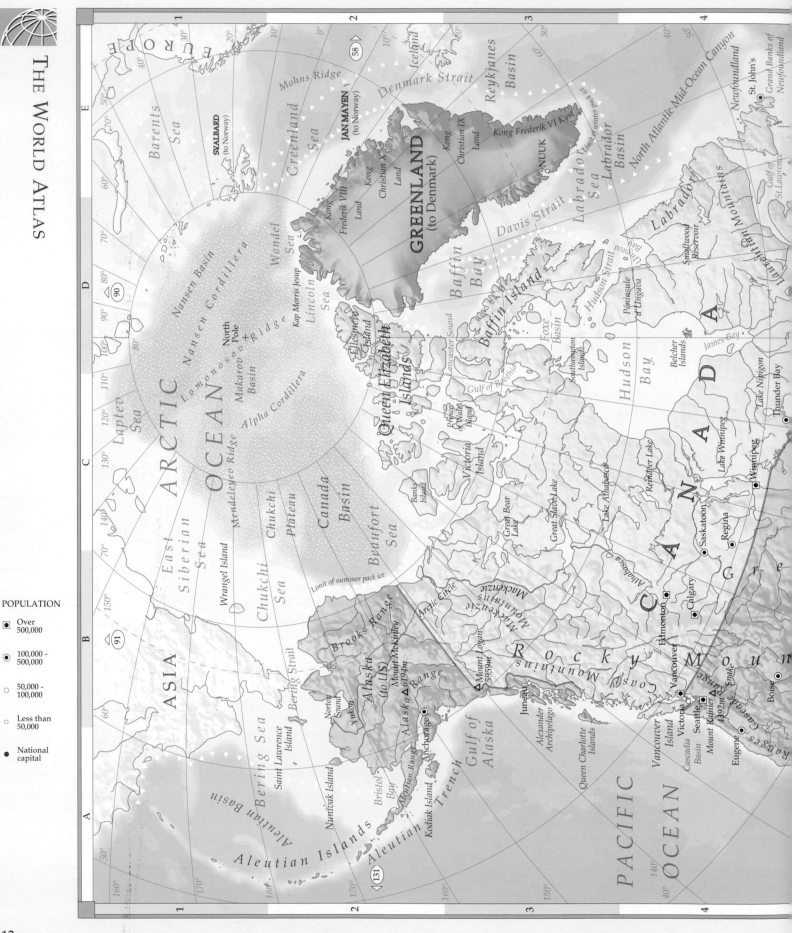

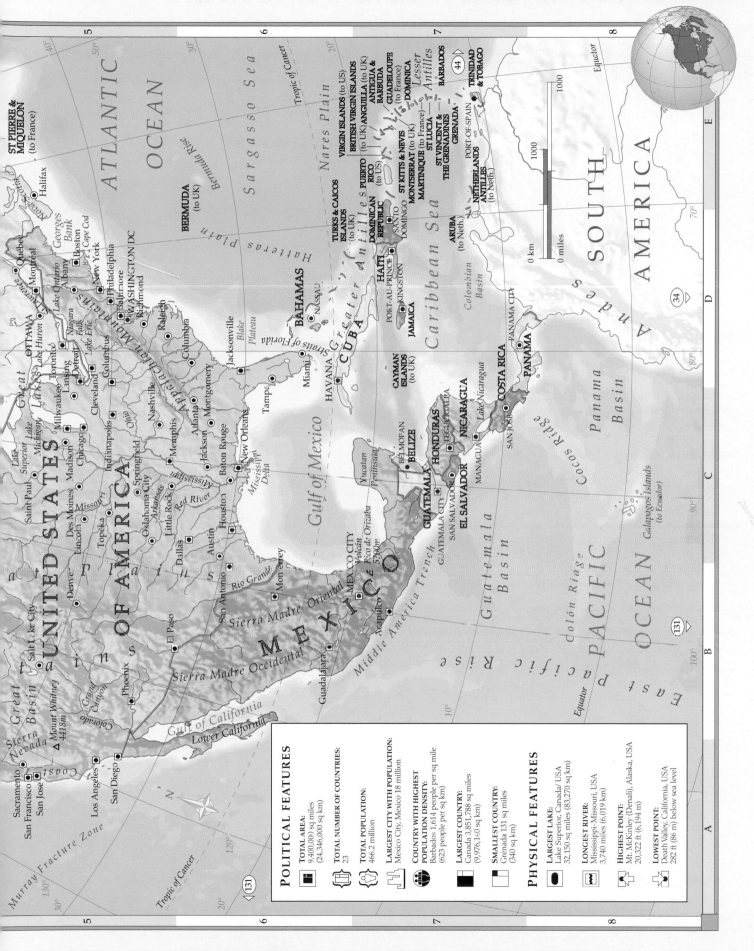

POLITICAL FEATURES

TOTAL AREA:
9,400,000 sq miles
(24,346,000 sq km)

TOTAL NUMBER OF COUNTRIES: 23

TOTAL POPULATION:
466.2 million

LARGEST CITY WITH POPULATION:
Mexico City, Mexico 18 million

COUNTRY WITH HIGHEST POPULATION DENSITY:
Barbados 1,614 people per sq mile
(623 people per sq km)

LARGEST COUNTRY:
Canada 3,851,788 sq miles
(9,976,140 sq km)

SMALLEST COUNTRY:
Grenada 131 sq miles
(340 sq km)

PHYSICAL FEATURES

LARGEST LAKE:
Lake Superior, Canada / USA
32,150 sq miles (83,270 sq km)

LONGEST RIVER:
Mississippi-Missouri, USA
3,740 miles (6,019 km)

HIGHEST POINT:
Mt McKinley (Denali), Alaska, USA
20,322 ft (6,194 m)

LOWEST POINT:
Death Valley, California, USA
282 ft (86 m) below sea level

13

WESTERN CANADA & ALASKA

RUSSIAN FEDERATION

ARCTIC

Poluostrov Kamchatka

Ostrov Vrangelya

Chukchi Sea

Wevok
Point Lay
Barrow
Kivalina

Bering Sea

Gambell
Wales
Deering
Prudhoe Bay
Umiat
Kaktovik

Saint Lawrence Island

Brooks Range

Colville River

Attu Island

Near Islands

Norton Sound

Alakanuk
Grayling
Yukon River
Kokrines
Fort Yukon
Aklavik

Rat Islands

Amchitka Island

Nunivak Island

Pribilof Islands

Kwigillingok

ALASKA (to US)

Fairbanks

Fort McPherson

Aleutian Islands

Andreanof Islands

Atka

Platinum

Kuskokwim Mts

Alaska Range

△ Mount McKinley 6194m

McKinley Park

YUKON

Mackenzie

Umnak Island
Unalaska Island
Dutch Harbor
Unimak Island
Belkofski

Bristol Bay

Iliamna Lake

Susitna

Anchorage
Hope
Valdez
Gulkana
Chitina

TERRITORY

Alaska Peninsula

Kodiak
Cordova
Katalla

△ Mount Logan 5959m

Shumagin Islands

Kodiak Island

Yakutat

Whitehorse

Gulf of Alaska

Haines
Gustavus
Atlin

BRITISH

Juneau
Kake

Alexander Archipelago

PACIFIC

OCEAN

Port Alexander
Ketchikan

Prince Rupert
Kitimat

Queen Charlotte Islands

Ocean Falls

Queen Charlotte Sound

△ Mount Waddington 4016m

Port Hardy
Campbell River

Vancouver Island

Nanaimo
Victoria

POPULATION

- ⬤ Over 500,000
- ◉ 100,000 - 500,000
- ○ 50,000 - 100,000
- ○ Less than 50,000
- ● Internal administrative capital

0 km   400

0 miles   400

N

E F G H

OCEAN

Alert

△133

Knud Rasmussen Land

GREENLAND
(to Denmark)

Axel Heiberg
Island

Ellesmere Island

Nares Strait

Ellef Ringnes
Island
Isachsen

Amund
Ringnes
Island

Arctic Circle

Prince Patrick
Island

Queen Elizabeth Islands

Devon Island

**Baffin
Bay**

Mould Bay

Bathurst
Island Cornwallis
Island

Davis Strait

Melville
Island

Lancaster Sound

60

**Beaufort
Sea**

Viscount Melville
Sound

Resolute

Banks
Island

Somerset
Island

Brodeur
Peninsula

Baffin Island

McClintock Channel

Sachs Harbour

Prince of
Wales Island

Cumberland Sound

Tuktoyaktuk Amundsen Holman
Gulf

**Victoria
Island**

Boothia
Peninsula

Gulf of Boothia

Igloolik

Nettilling
Lake

Inuvik

Iqaluit

Paulatuk

King William
Island

Pelly Bay

Melville
Peninsula

**Foxe
Basin**

Amadjuak
Lake

Fort
Good Hope

Kugluktuk

Cambridge Bay

Gjoa Haven

Repulse Bay

**Southampton
Island**

Hudson Strait

Great
Bear
Lake

Echo Bay

Burnside

NUNAVUT

Garry Lake

Coral
Harbour

**Péninsule
d'Ungava**

**NORTHWEST
TERRITORIES**

Back

Baker Lake

Mansel
Island

Tungsten

Dubawnt

Rankin Inlet

Coats
Island

Edzo Yellowknife Reliance

Whale Cove

QUEBEC

Fort Simpson

Great Slave
Lake

Lutselk'e

Arviat

**Hudson
Bay**

Fort Providence

Fort Liard

Hay River

Fort Smith

Churchill

Fort Nelson

Lake Athabasca

COLUMBIA

Ware

Fort Vermilion

Wollaston Lake

Reindeer Lake

Belcher
Islands

C

Fort St. John

Fort
McMurray

A

Fox Mine

Southern
Indian Lake

N

Nelson

A

**James
Bay**

D

A

ALBERTA

Buffalo
Narrows

Thompson

Grande Prairie

Athabasca

SASKATCHEWAN

Flin Flon

Prince George

Lake
Winnipeg

ONTARIO

Mount Robson
3954 m

Athabasca

North Saskatchewan

The Pas

MANITOBA

Edmonton

Saskatchewan

Leduc

Prince Albert

Red Deer

Saskatoon

Lake
Manitoba

Kamloops

Calgary

Kindersley Yorkton

Lake
Winnipeg

Kelowna

Regina

Qu'Appelle

Winnipeg

Medicine Hat

Brandon

Cranbrook

Lethbridge

Weyburn

Lake
of the Woods

Lake Superior

Vancouver

Milk River

Estevan Melita

Lake
Michigan

Lake Huron

△23

U N I T E D   S T A T E S   O F   A M E R I C A

E F G H

ELEVATION

4000 m 13 124 ft
2000 m 6562 ft
1000 m 3281 ft
500 m 1640 ft
250 m 820 ft
100 m 328 ft
Sea Level
-250 m -820 ft
-500 m -1640 ft
-1000 m -3281 ft
-2000 m -6562 ft
-3000 m -9843 ft
-4000 m -13 124 ft

Eastern Canada

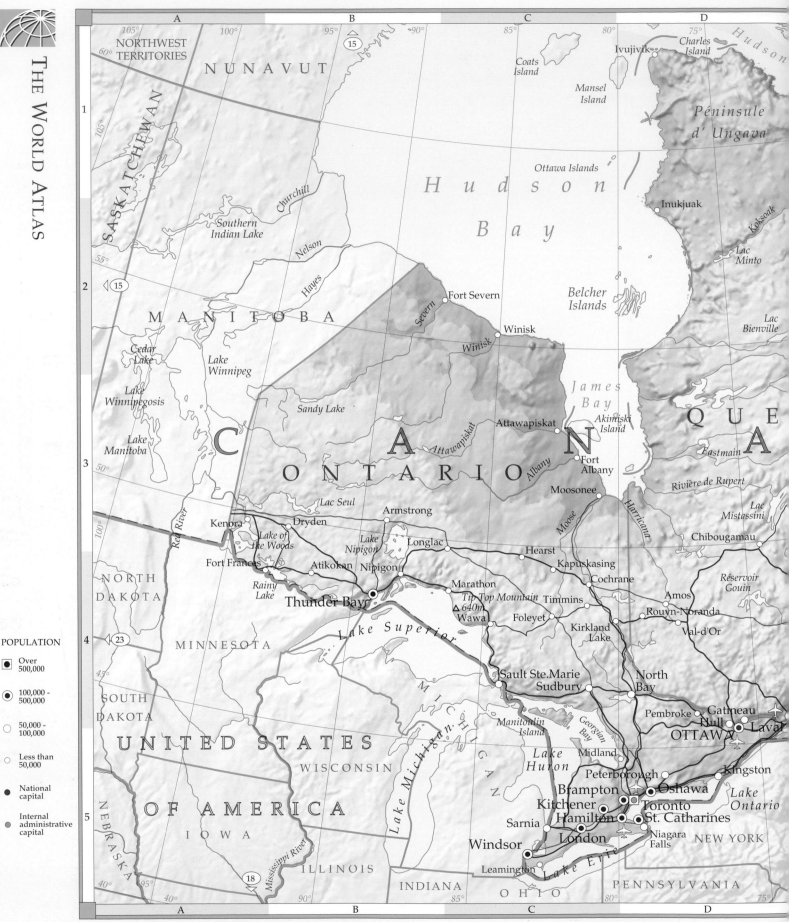

POPULATION

- Over 500,000
- 100,000 – 500,000
- 50,000 – 100,000
- Less than 50,000
- National capital
- Internal administrative capital

NORTH & CENTRAL AMERICA

ELEVATION

4000 m	13 124 ft
2000 m	6562 ft
1000 m	3281 ft
500 m	1640 ft
250 m	820 ft
100 m	328 ft
Sea Level	Sea Level
-250 m	-820 ft
-500 m	-1640 ft
1000 m	-3281 ft
-2000 m	-6562 ft
-3000 m	-9843 ft
-4000 m	-13 124 ft

17

USA: THE NORTHEAST

THE WORLD ATLAS

POPULATION

- ◉ Over 500,000
- ◎ 100,000 – 500,000
- ○ 50,000 – 100,000
- ○ Less than 50,000
- ● National capital
- ● Internal administrative capital

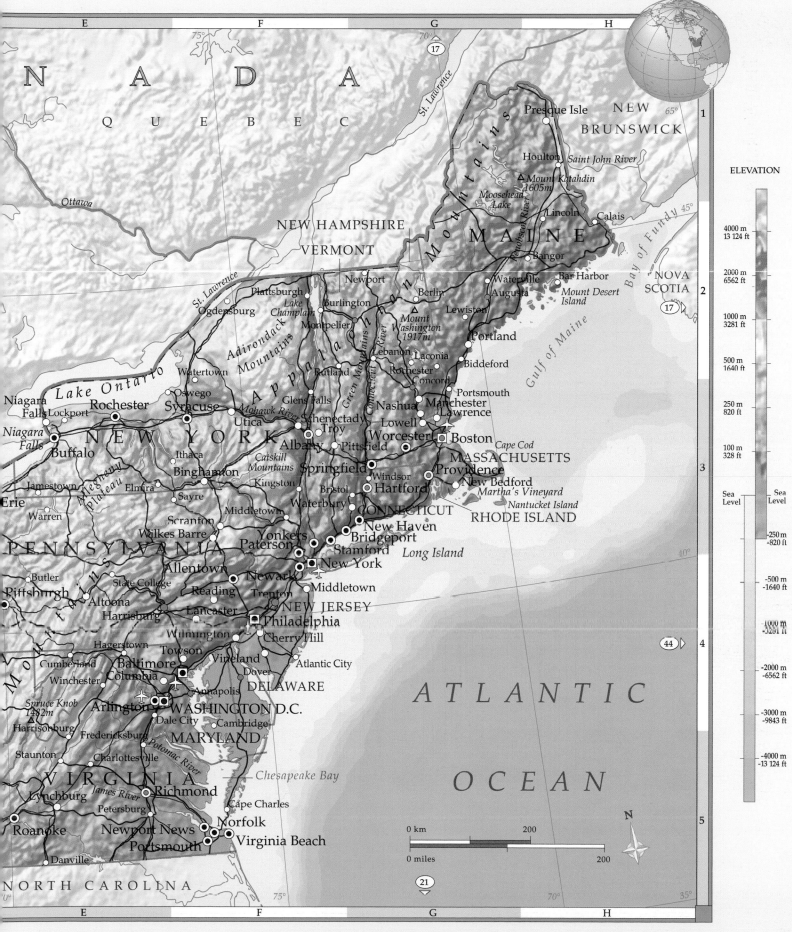

North & Central America

ELEVATION

4000 m
13 124 ft

2000 m
6562 ft

1000 m
3281 ft

500 m
1640 ft

250 m
820 ft

100 m
328 ft

Sea Level

Sea Level

-250 m
-820 ft

-500 m
-1640 ft

-1000 m
-3281 ft

-2000 m
-6562 ft

-3000 m
-9843 ft

-4000 m
-13 124 ft

CANADA
QUEBEC
NEW BRUNSWICK
Ottawa
St. Lawrence
Presque Isle
Houlton
Saint John River
Mount Katahdin 1605m
Moosehead Lake
Lincoln
Calais
MAINE
Penobscot River
Bangor
NOVA SCOTIA
Bay of Fundy
NEW HAMPSHIRE
VERMONT
Newport
Berlin
Waterville
Bar Harbor
Augusta
Mount Desert Island
Gulf of Maine
Plattsburgh
Ogdensburg
Lake Champlain
Burlington
Montpelier
Mount Washington 1917m
Lebanon
Lewiston
Portland
Biddeford
St. Lawrence
Adirondack Mountains
Appalachian Mountains
Connecticut River
Green Mountains
Rutland
Rochester
Laconia
Concord
Portsmouth
Watertown
Glens Falls
Nashua
Manchester
Lawrence
Niagara Falls
Lockport
Rochester
Oswego
Syracuse
Mohawk River
Utica
Schenectady
Troy
Lowell
Worcester
Boston
Cape Cod
Niagara Falls
Buffalo
NEW YORK
Albany
Pittsfield
MASSACHUSETTS
Ithaca
Catskill Mountains
Springfield
Providence
New Bedford
Jamestown
Allegheny Plateau
Binghamton
Kingston
Bristol
Hartford
Martha's Vineyard
Nantucket Island
Erie
Elmira
Sayre
Middletown
Waterbury
CONNECTICUT
RHODE ISLAND
Warren
Scranton
Yonkers
New Haven
Bridgeport
Long Island
PENNSYLVANIA
Wilkes Barre
Paterson
Stamford
Butler
State College
Allentown
Newark
New York
Pittsburgh
Altoona
Reading
Trenton
Middletown
Harrisburg
Lancaster
NEW JERSEY
Hagerstown
Wilmington
Philadelphia
Cherry Hill
Cumberland
Towson
Vineland
Atlantic City
Spruce Knob 1482m
Winchester
Baltimore
Columbia
Dover
DELAWARE
Harrisonburg
Annapolis
Cambridge
Arlington
WASHINGTON D.C.
Dale City
Staunton
Charlottesville
Fredericksburg
MARYLAND
Potomac River
Chesapeake Bay
ATLANTIC OCEAN
VIRGINIA
James River
Richmond
Lynchburg
Petersburg
Cape Charles
Norfolk
Roanoke
Newport News
Virginia Beach
Danville
Portsmouth
NORTH CAROLINA

0 km   200
0 miles   200

N

19

USA: THE SOUTHEAST

THE WORLD ATLAS

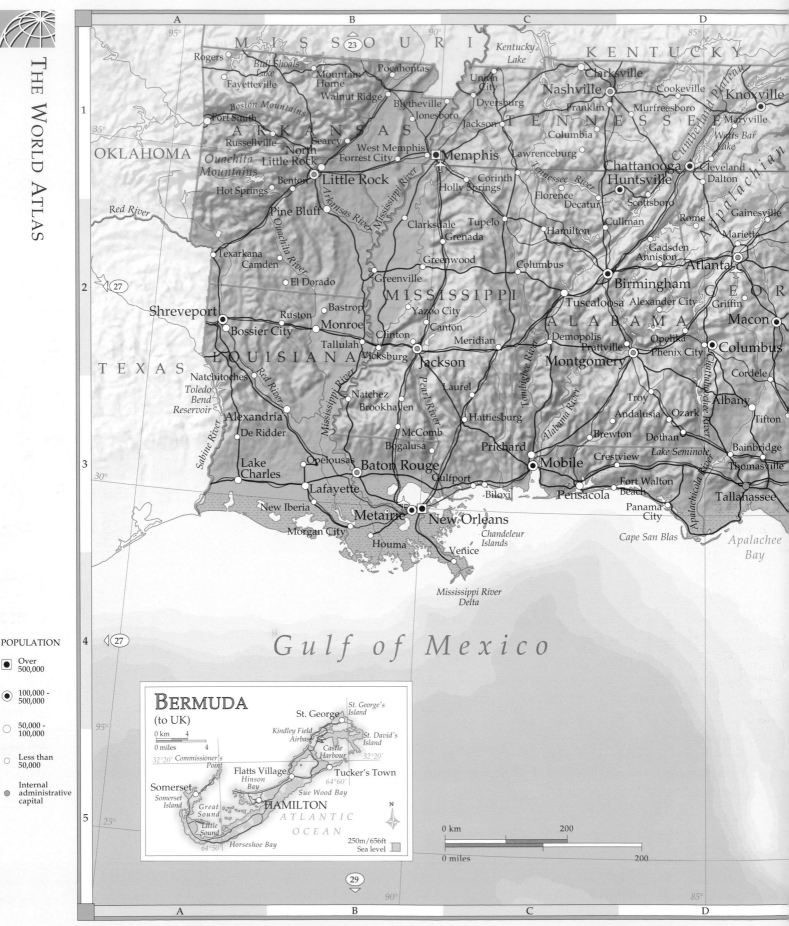

POPULATION

- ● Over 500,000
- ◉ 100,000 – 500,000
- ○ 50,000 – 100,000
- ○ Less than 50,000
- ● Internal administrative capital

BERMUDA
(to UK)

0 km 4
0 miles 4

Commissioner's Point

St. George
St. George's Island

Kindley Field Airbase

St. David's Island

Castle Harbour

Flatts Village
Hinson Bay

Tucker's Town

Somerset

Somerset Island

HAMILTON

Great Sound

Sue Wood Bay

Little Sound

ATLANTIC OCEAN

Horseshoe Bay

250m/656ft
Sea level

32°20'
64°60'
64°50'

0 km 200
0 miles 200

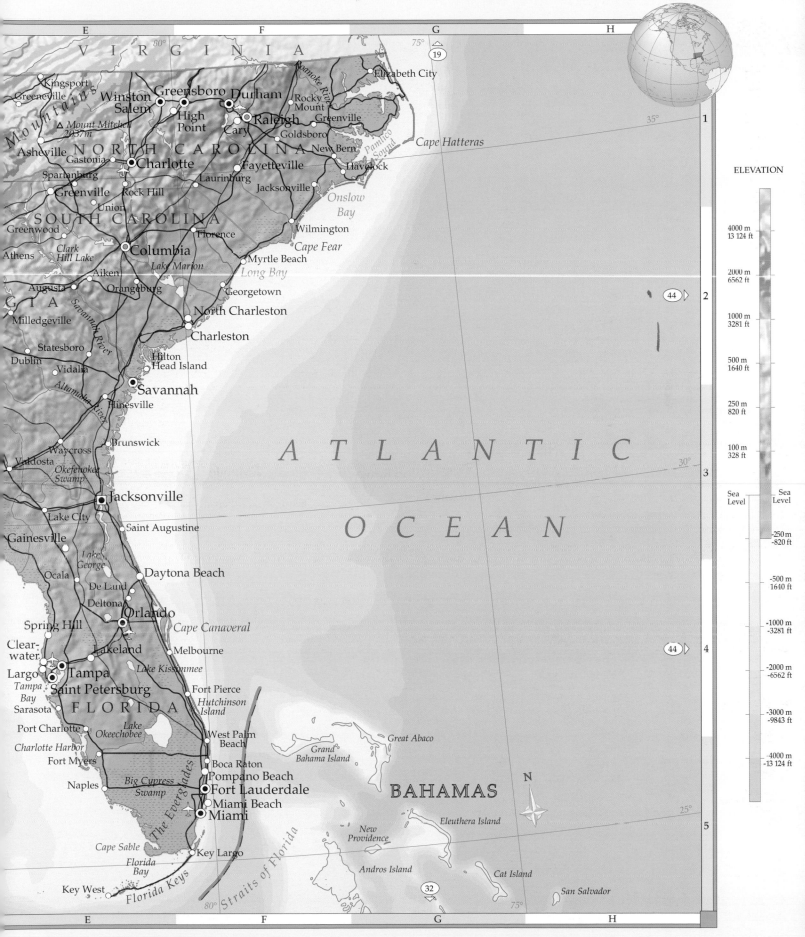

ELEVATION

4000 m
13 124 ft

2000 m
6562 ft

1000 m
3281 ft

500 m
1640 ft

250 m
820 ft

100 m
328 ft

Sea Level   Sea Level

-250 m
-820 ft

-500 m
1640 ft

-1000 m
-3281 ft

-2000 m
-6562 ft

-3000 m
-9843 ft

-4000 m
-13 124 ft

VIRGINIA

Kingsport
Greeneville
Mountains
Winston Salem
Greensboro
Durham
High Point
Raleigh
Cary
Mount Mitchell 2037m
Asheville
NORTH CAROLINA
Gastonia
Charlotte
Spartanburg
Greenville
Rock Hill
Union
SOUTH CAROLINA
Greenwood
Clark Hill Lake
Columbia
Athens
Aiken
Augusta
Orangeburg
GIA
Milledgeville
North Charleston
Savannah River
Statesboro
Charleston
Dublin
Vidalia
Hilton Head Island
Altamaha River
Savannah
Hinesville
Waycross
Brunswick
Valdosta
Okefenokee Swamp
Jacksonville
Lake City
Saint Augustine
Gainesville
Lake George
Ocala
Daytona Beach
De Land
Deltona
Orlando
Spring Hill
Cape Canaveral
Clear-water
Lakeland
Melbourne
Largo
Tampa
Lake Kissimmee
Saint Petersburg
Tampa Bay
Sarasota
FLORIDA
Fort Pierce
Hutchinson Island
Port Charlotte
Lake Okeechobee
Charlotte Harbor
West Palm Beach
Fort Myers
Boca Raton
Naples
Big Cypress Swamp
Pompano Beach
Fort Lauderdale
Miami Beach
The Everglades
Miami
Cape Sable
Key Largo
Florida Bay
Key West
Florida Keys
Straits of Florida

Roanoke River
Elizabeth City
Rocky Mount
Greenville
Goldsboro
New Bern
Fayetteville
Havelock
Laurinburg
Jacksonville
Wilmington
Florence
Cape Fear
Myrtle Beach
Long Bay
Georgetown

Pamlico Sound
Cape Hatteras
Onslow Bay

ATLANTIC

OCEAN

Grand Bahama Island
Great Abaco

BAHAMAS

New Providence
Eleuthera Island

Andros Island
Cat Island
San Salvador

N

21

USA: CENTRAL STATES

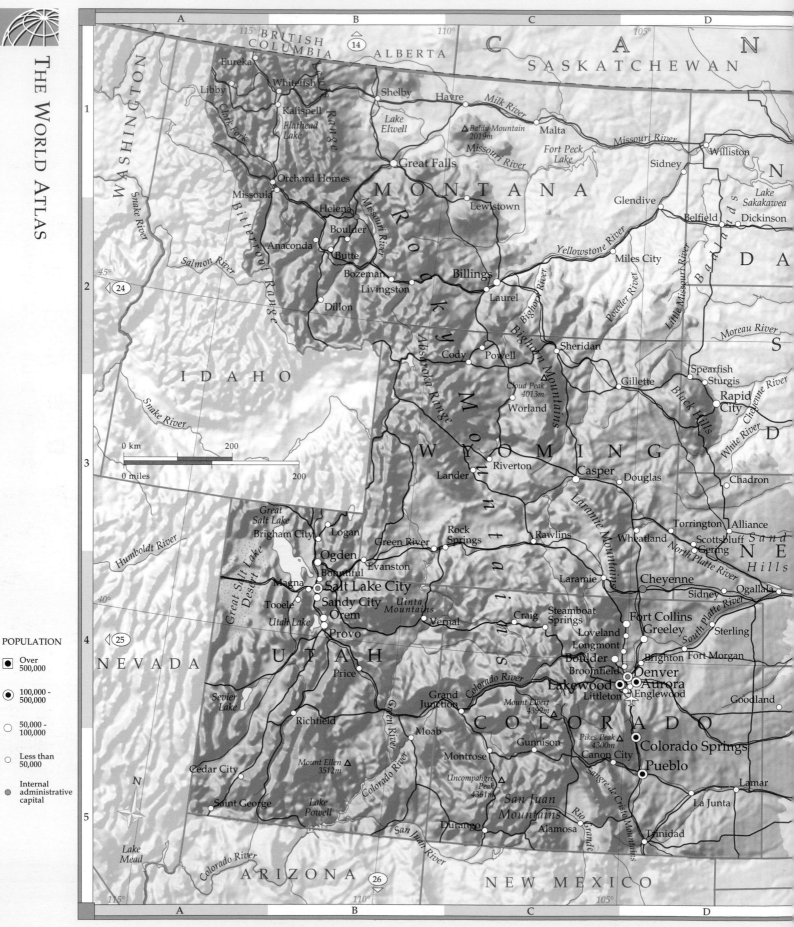

POPULATION

- ▣ Over 500,000
- ◉ 100,000 - 500,000
- ○ 50,000 - 100,000
- ○ Less than 50,000
- ● Internal administrative capital

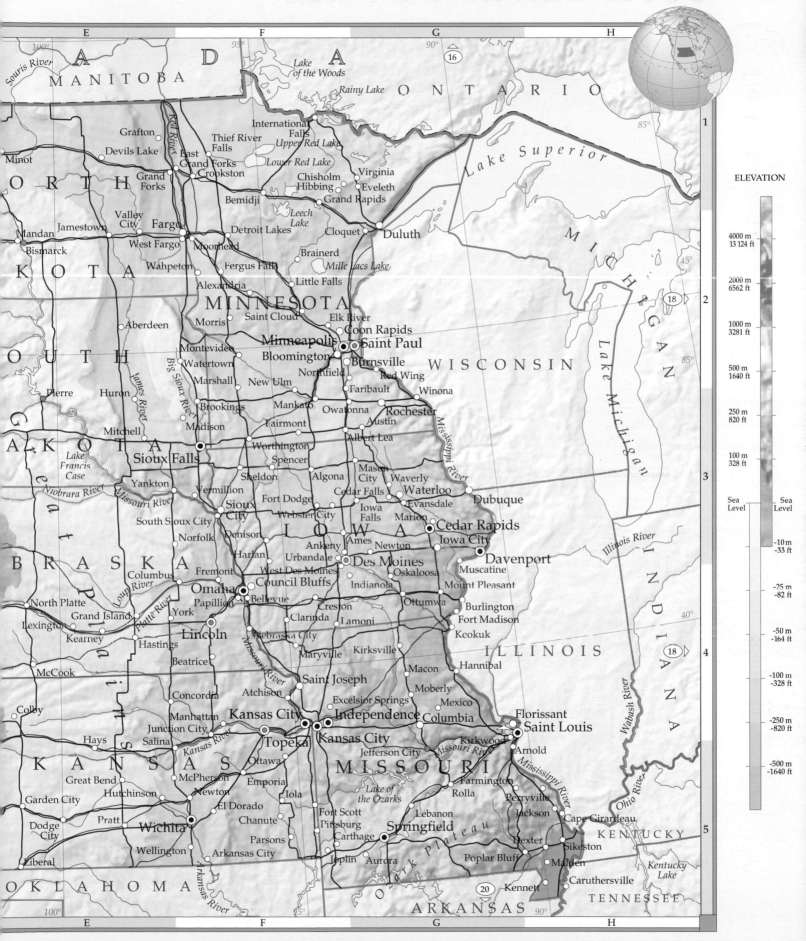

CANADA

MANITOBA

ONTARIO

Lake of the Woods

Rainy Lake

Lake Superior

ELEVATION

4000 m
13 124 ft

2000 m
6562 ft

1000 m
3281 ft

500 m
1640 ft

250 m
820 ft

100 m
328 ft

Sea Level — Sea Level

-10 m
-33 ft

-25 m
-82 ft

-50 m
-164 ft

-100 m
-328 ft

-250 m
-820 ft

-500 m
-1640 ft

Souris River

Minot

Grafton

Devils Lake

NORTH DAKOTA

Mandan
Bismarck

Jamestown
Valley City

Red River

East Grand Forks
Grand Forks
Crookston

Thief River Falls

International Falls

Upper Red Lake
Lower Red Lake

Virginia
Chisholm
Hibbing
Eveleth
Grand Rapids

Fargo
West Fargo
Moorhead

Detroit Lakes

Bemidji

Leech Lake

Cloquet

Duluth

Wahpeton
Fergus Falls

Brainerd

Mille Lacs Lake

MICHIGAN

SOUTH DAKOTA

Aberdeen

Alexandria
Little Falls

MINNESOTA

Morris
Saint Cloud

Elk River
Coon Rapids

Minneapolis
Saint Paul

Lake Michigan

Pierre

Huron

Montevideo
Watertown

Marshall

Bloomington
Burnsville

Northfield
Red Wing

WISCONSIN

James River

Big Sioux River

New Ulm
Faribault
Winona

Mankato
Owatonna
Rochester

Mitchell

Madison
Fairmont
Austin

Albert Lea

Lake Francis Case

Sioux Falls

Worthington
Spencer

Mississippi River

Yankton

Niobrara River

Missouri River

Vermillion

Sheldon
Algona

Mason City
Waverly

Cedar Falls
Waterloo
Evansdale
Dubuque

Sioux City
South Sioux City

Fort Dodge

Webster City

IOWA

Iowa Falls

Marion
Cedar Rapids
Iowa City

Norfolk
Denison
Ames
Newton
Davenport

NEBRASKA

Harlan
Ankeny
Urbandale
Des Moines

Muscatine

Columbus

Loup River

Fremont
West Des Moines
Oskaloosa

Illinois River

North Platte

Grand Island

Platte River

Papillion

Omaha
Bellevue
Council Bluffs

Indianola
Ottumwa

Mount Pleasant

Burlington
Fort Madison

York
Creston
Lamoni
Keokuk

Lexington
Clarinda

Kearney
Lincoln

Hastings
Nebraska City
Maryville
Kirksville
Hannibal

ILLINOIS

McCook
Beatrice

Macon

INDIANA

Saint Joseph
Moberly

Colby
Atchison
Excelsior Springs
Mexico

Concordia
Columbia
Florissant

Manhattan
Kansas City
Independence
Saint Louis

Junction City
Kirkwood
Arnold

Hays
Salina
Topeka
Kansas City

Kansas River
Jefferson City
Missouri River

Great Bend
Ottawa
MISSOURI
Farmington

KANSAS
McPherson
Emporia
Lake of the Ozarks
Rolla

Garden City
Hutchinson
Newton
Iola
Perryville

Jackson
Cape Girardeau

Pratt
El Dorado
Chanute
Lebanon

Dodge City
Wichita
Fort Scott
Springfield
Dexter
Sikeston

KENTUCKY

Liberal
Wellington
Arkansas City
Parsons
Pittsburg
Carthage

Ozark Plateau

Poplar Bluff
Malden

Kentucky Lake

Joplin
Aurora
Caruthersville

OKLAHOMA

Arkansas River

Kennett

TENNESSEE

ARKANSAS

Ohio River

Wabash River

Kentucky

USA: THE WEST

Los Angeles

Valencia
Santa Clarita
San Fernando
San Gabriel Mountains
Burbank
Pasadena
Glendale
Universal Studios
Hollywood
Beverly Hills
Santa Monica
Downey
Inglewood
Venice
Getty Museum
Torrance
Long Beach
Riverside
Buena Park
Anaheim
Disneyland
Santa Ana
Santa Ana Mountains
Costa Mesa

0 km   20
0 miles   20

POPULATION

■ Over 500,000

◉ 100,000 - 500,000

○ 50,000 - 100,000

○ Less than 50,000

● Internal administrative capital

24

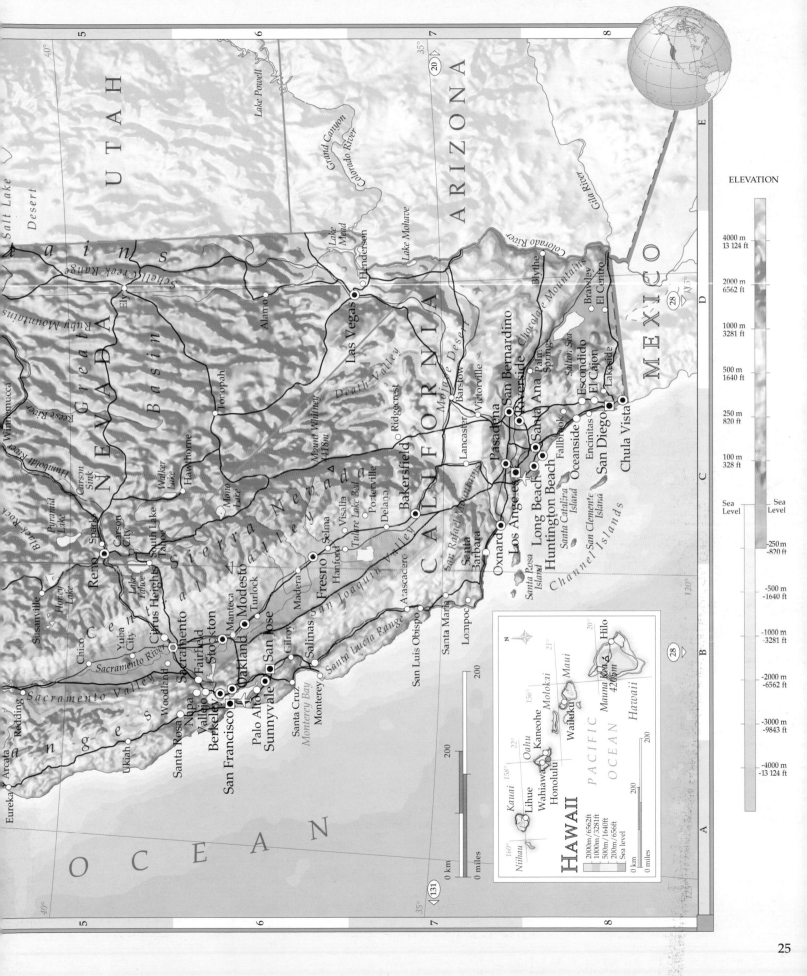

ELEVATION

4000 m
13 124 ft

2000 m
6562 ft

1000 m
3281 ft

500 m
1640 ft

250 m
820 ft

100 m
328 ft

Sea Level

Sea Level

-250 m
-820 ft

-500 m
-1640 ft

-1000 m
-3281 ft

-2000 m
-6562 ft

-3000 m
-9843 ft

-4000 m
-13 124 ft

UTAH

ARIZONA

NEVADA

CALIFORNIA

MEXICO

Salt Lake Desert

Great Basin

Schell Creek Range

Ruby Mountains

Reese River

Winnemucca

Humboldt River

Black Rock

Pyramid Lake

Honey Lake

Susanville

Eureka   Areata

Redding

Ukiah

Santa Rosa

Napa
Vallejo
Berkeley
San Francisco
Palo Alto
Sunnyvale

Sacramento Valley

Woodland

Chico

Yuba City

Citrus Heights
Sacramento
Fairfield
Stockton
Oakland
San Jose

Sacramento River

Manteca
Modesto
Turlock
Madera

Gilroy
Salinas
Santa Cruz
Monterey Bay
Monterey

Santa Lucia Range

San Joaquin Valley

Central Valley

Sierra Nevada

Carson Sink

Carson City
Sparks
Reno
South Lake Tahoe
Lake Tahoe

Walker Lake

Mono Lake

Hawthorne

Toropah

Alamo

Las Vegas

Henderson

Lake Mead

Lake Mohave

Lake Powell

Grand Canyon

Colorado River

Death Valley

Mohave Desert

Mount Whitney 4418m

Ridgecrest

Barstow

Victorville

Lancaster

Bakersfield

Tulare Lake Bed

Delano

Porterville

Visalia

Hanford

Selma

Fresno

Atascadero

San Luis Obispo

Santa Maria

Lompoc

Sur Rafael Mountains

Santa Barbara

Oxnard

Los Angeles

Long Beach

Huntington Beach

Pasadena

San Bernardino

Riverside

Santa Ana

Palm Spring

Salton Sea

Fallbrook

Oceanside

Encinitas

Escondido

El Cajon

Lakeside

San Diego

Chula Vista

Brawley

El Centro

Blythe

Colorado River

Chocolate Mountains

Gila River

Santa Catalina Island

Santa Rosa Island

San Clemente Island

Channel Islands

PACIFIC OCEAN

200

200

200

200

0 km

0 miles

20
28
28
131

40°

40°

35°

35°

120°

115°

125°

5   6   7   8

E
D
C
B
A

HAWAII

Kauai
Niihau
Lihue
Wahiawa
Honolulu
Oahu
Kaneohe
Molokai
Maui
Wailuku
Lanai
Hilo
Mauna Kea 4205m
Hawaii

PACIFIC OCEAN

2000m/6562ft
1000m/3281ft
500m/1640ft
200m/656ft
Sea level

0 km
0 miles

200

N

160°   158°   156°

22°   21°   20°

USA: The Southwest

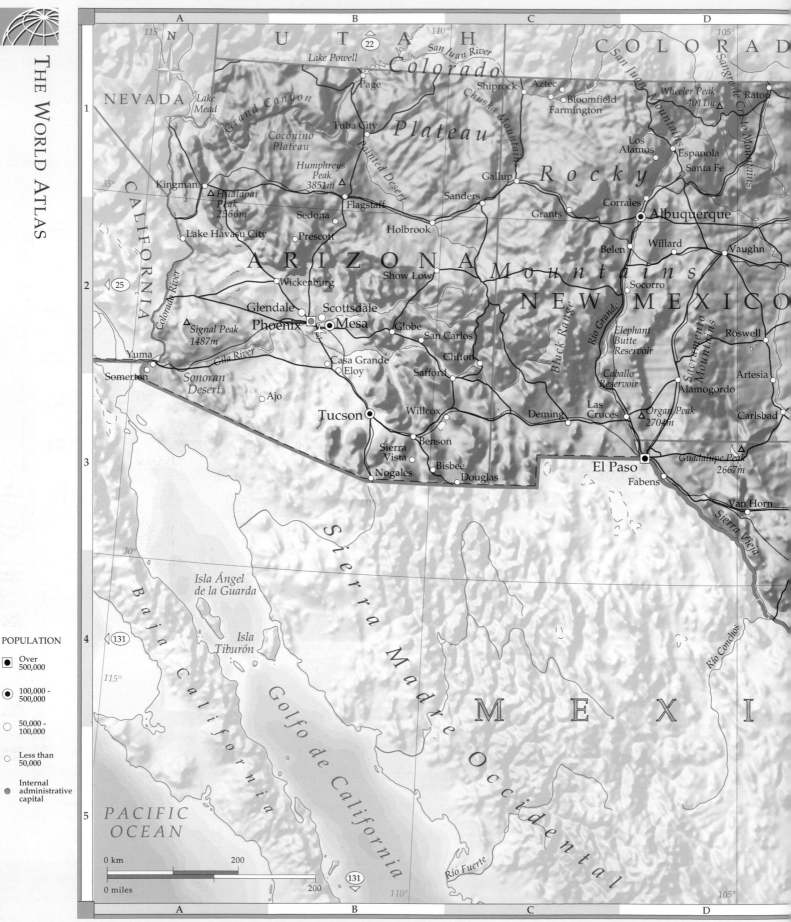

POPULATION

- Over 500,000
- 100,000 – 500,000
- 50,000 – 100,000
- Less than 50,000
- Internal administrative capital

UTAH

COLORADO

NEVADA

CALIFORNIA

ARIZONA

NEW MEXICO

MEXICO

Lake Powell
San Juan River
Colorado
Page
Shiprock
Aztec
Bloomfield
Farmington
Wheeler Peak 4011m
Raton
Tuba City
Coconino Plateau
Painted Desert
Plateau
Los Alamos
Espanola
Santa Fe
Grand Canyon
Humphreys Peak 3851m
Gallup
Rocky
Corrales
Albuquerque
Kingman
Hualapai Peak 2566m
Flagstaff
Sanders
Grants
Sedona
Holbrook
Belen
Willard
Vaughn
Lake Havasu City
Prescott
Show Low
Mountains
Socorro
Wickenburg
Glendale
Scottsdale
Phoenix
Mesa
Globe
San Carlos
Elephant Butte Reservoir
Roswell
Signal Peak 1487m
Gila River
Casa Grande
Eloy
Clifton
Safford
Caballo Reservoir
Artesia
Yuma
Somerton
Sonoran Desert
Ajo
Willcox
Deming
Las Cruces
Organ Peak 2704m
Alamogordo
Carlsbad
Tucson
Benson
Sierra Vista
Bisbee
Nogales
Douglas
El Paso
Fabens
Guadalupe Peak 2667m
Van Horn

Colorado River
Black Range
Rio Grande
Sacramento Mountains
Chuska Mountains
Sangre de Cristo Mountains

Isla Ángel de la Guarda
Isla Tiburón
Baja California
Golfo de California
Sierra Madre Occidental
Río Fuerte
Río Conchos
Sierra Vieja

PACIFIC OCEAN

0 km 200
0 miles 200

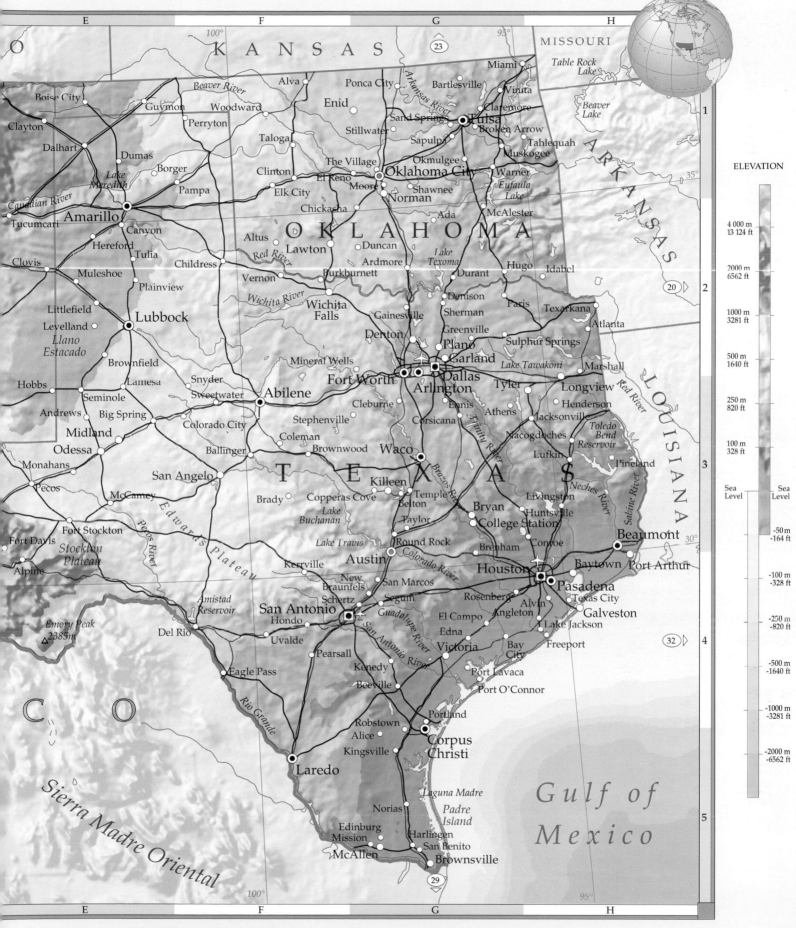

MEXICO

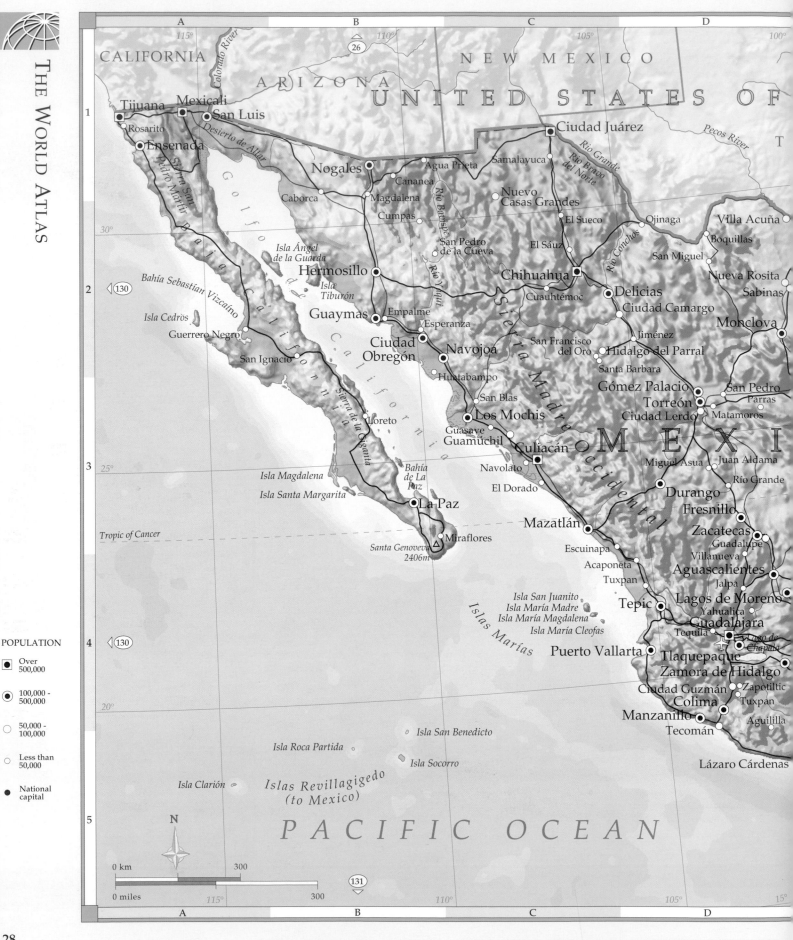

CALIFORNIA

ARIZONA

NEW MEXICO

UNITED STATES OF

Colorado River

Pecos River

1

Tijuana
Rosarito
Ensenada
Mexicali
San Luis
Nogales
Agua Prieta
Cananea
Caborca
Magdalena
Cumpas
Ciudad Juárez
Samalayuca
Río Grande del Norte
Nuevo
Casas Grandes
El Sueco
Ojinaga
Villa Acuña
Boquillas

Desierto de Altar

Sierra San Pedro Mártir

Golfo de California

2

Bahía Sebastián Vizcaíno
Isla Ángel de la Guarda
Isla Cedrös
Isla Tiburón
Isla
Hermosillo
San Pedro de la Cueva
El Sáuz
San Miguel
Nueva Rosita
Sabinas
Chihuahua
Cuauhtémoc
Delicias
Ciudad Camargo
Monclova

Guerrero Negro
Guaymas
Empalme
Esperanza
San Francisco del Oro
Jiménez
Hidalgo del Parral
Santa Barbara

San Ignacio
Ciudad Obregón
Navojoa
Huatabampo
Gómez Palacio
San Pedro
Parras

Baja California

Río Yaqui
Río Bavispe
Río Conchos

Sierra Madre Occidental

3

Isla Magdalena
Isla Santa Margarita
Loreto
San Blas
Los Mochis
Guasave
Guamúchil
Culiacán
Navolato
El Dorado
M E X I
Torreón
Ciudad Lerdo
Matamoros
Miguel Asua
Juan Aldama
Río Grande
Durango
Fresnillo

Bahía de La Paz
La Paz

Tropic of Cancer

Santa Genoveva 2406m
Miraflores

Sierra de la Giganta

Mazatlán
Escuinapa
Zacatecas
Guadalupe
Villanueva
Aguascalientes
Jalpa

4

Islas Marías
Isla San Juanito
Isla María Madre
Isla María Magdalena
Isla María Cleofas
Acaponeta
Tuxpan
Tepic
Yahualica
Lagos de Moreno
Tequila
Guadalajara
Lago de Chapala

Puerto Vallarta
Tlaquepaque
Zamora de Hidalgo
Ciudad Guzmán
Zapotiltic
Colima
Tuxpan
Manzanillo
Aguililla
Tecomán

Isla San Benedicto
Isla Roca Partida
Isla Socorro
Lázaro Cárdenas

5

Isla Clarión
Islas Revillagigedo
(to Mexico)

PACIFIC OCEAN

N

POPULATION

⬤ Over
500,000

◉ 100,000 –
500,000

○ 50,000 –
100,000

○ Less than
50,000

● National
capital

0 km   300
0 miles   300

ALABAMA
FLORIDA
MISSISSIPPI
LOUISIANA
AMERICA
T E X A S
Brazos River
Colorado River
Red River
Sabine River
Mississippi River
Mississippi River Delta

Gulf of Mexico

Piedras Negras
Río Grande
Nuevo Laredo
Padre Island
Sabinas Hidalgo
Ciudad Miguel Alemán
Reynosa
Río Bravo
Matamoros
Monterrey
Saltillo
Montemorelos
Linares
Laguna Madre
C O
Sierra Madre Oriental
Ciudad Victoria
Ciudad Mante
Ciudad Madero
San Luis Potosí
Pánuco
Tampico
Ciudad Valles
Río Verde
Laguna de Tamiahua
Dolores Hidalgo
Tamazunchale
León
Tuxpán
Bahía de Campeche
Guanajuato
Poza Rica
Querétaro
Papantla
Irapuato
Pachuca
Tulancingo
Morelia
Tezutlán
Xalapa
MÉXICO
(MEXICO CITY)
Perote
Veracruz
Tlaxcala
Toluca
Puebla
Alvarado
Cuernavaca
Popocatépetl 5452m
Córdoba
Zacatepec
Cuautla
Tehuacán
Coatzacoalcos
Uruapan
Taxco
San Andrés Tuxtla
Presa del Infiernillo
Iguala
Tuxtepec
Minatitlán
Río Balsas
Sierra Madre del Sur
Chilpancingo
Oaxaca
Istmo de Tehuantepec
Ixtapa
Tecpan
Ixtepec
Matías Romero
Acapulco
Pinotepa Nacional
Tehuantepec
Juchitán
Miahuatlán
Salina Cruz
Arriaga
Pijijiapán
Puerto Escondido
Puerto Angel
Golfo de Tehuantepec
Escuintla
Huixtla
Tapachula
Ciudad Hidalgo

Yucatan Channel
Río Lagartos
Tizimín
Cancún
Progreso
Motul
Isla Cozumel
Mérida
Umán
Valladolid
Ticul
Peto
Oxkutzcab
Teká
Felipe Carrillo Puerto
Campeche
Yucatan Peninsula
Champotón
Chetumal
Laguna de Términos
Fransisco Escárcega
Frontera
Carmen
Comalcalco
Villahermosa
BELIZE
Macuspana
Río Usumacinta
Teapa
San Cristóbal de Las Casas
Tuxtla
Chiapa de Corzo
Comitán
Ocozocuautla
Presa de la Angostura
GUATEMALA
HONDURAS
Gulf of Honduras
EL SALVADOR

Tropic of Cancer

ELEVATION

4000 m 13 124 ft
2000 m 6562 ft
1000 m 3281 ft
500 m 1640 ft
250 m 820 ft
100 m 328 ft
Sea Level — Sea Level
-250 m -820 ft
-500 m -1640 ft
-1000 m -3281 ft
-2000 m -6562 ft
-3000 m -9843 ft
-4000 m -13 124 ft

95°
90°
85°
30°
25°
85°
20°
15°
100°
95°
90°

20
44
30
131

E F G H
1 2 3 4 5

CENTRAL AMERICA

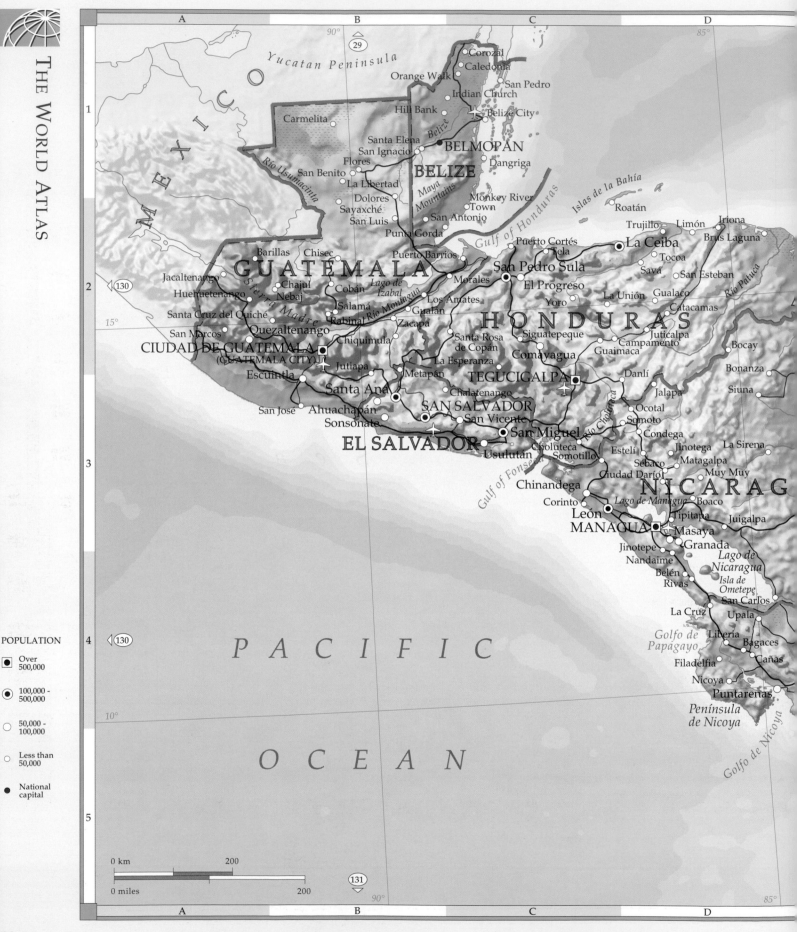

POPULATION

- ◉ Over 500,000
- ◉ 100,000 – 500,000
- ○ 50,000 – 100,000
- ○ Less than 50,000
- ● National capital

0 km   200

0 miles   200

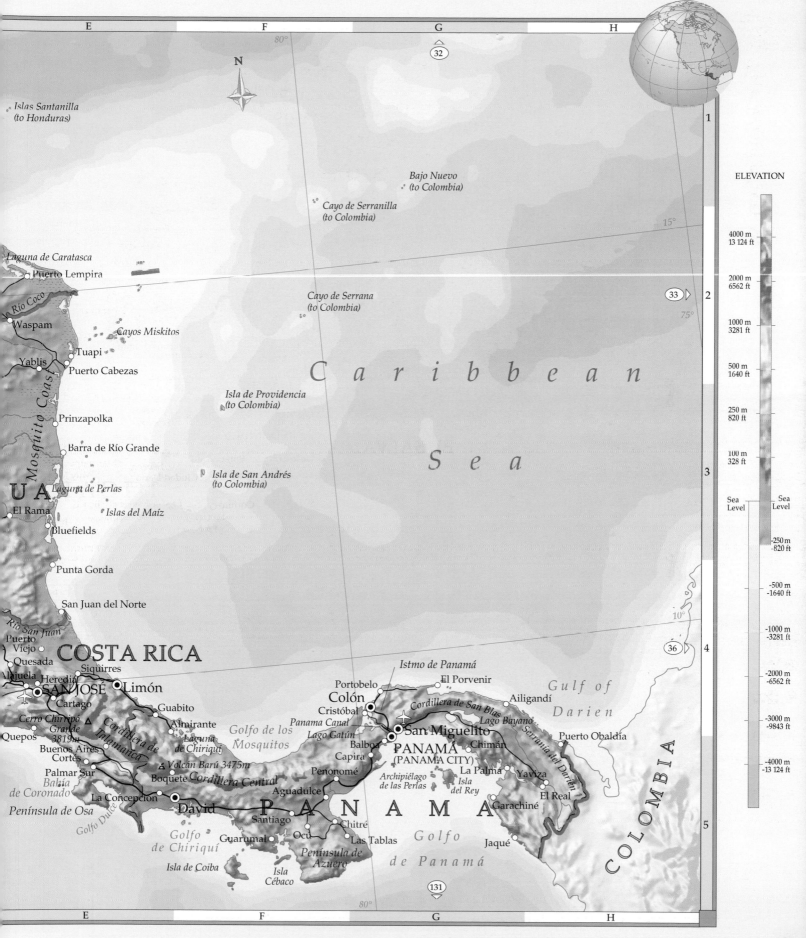

E   F   G   H

32

N

80°

*Islas Santanilla
(to Honduras)*

15°

*Bajo Nuevo
(to Colombia)*

*Cayo de Serranilla
(to Colombia)*

ELEVATION

4000 m
13 124 ft

Laguna de Caratasca

Puerto Lempira

*Cayo de Serrana
(to Colombia)*

33

75°

2000 m
6562 ft

Río Coco

Waspam

Cayos Miskitos

1000 m
3281 ft

C a r i b b e a n

Tuapi

Yablis
Puerto Cabezas

*Isla de Providencia
(to Colombia)*

500 m
1640 ft

Prinzapolka

S e a

250 m
820 ft

Barra de Río Grande

Isla de San Andrés
(to Colombia)

100 m
328 ft

U A

Laguna de Perlas

El Rama

Islas del Maíz

Sea
Level

Sea
Level

Bluefields

-250 m
-820 ft

Punta Gorda

-500 m
-1640 ft

San Juan del Norte

10°

-1000 m
-3281 ft

Río San Juan

Puerto
Viejo

36

4

Quesada

Istmo de Panamá

*Gulf of
Darien*

-2000 m
-6562 ft

Alajuela
Heredia

Siquirres

Portobelo

El Porvenir

SAN JOSÉ
Limón

Colón

Ailigandí

-3000 m
-9843 ft

Cartago

Guabito

Cristóbal

Cordillera de San Blas

*Cerro Chirripó
Grande
3819m*

Almirante

*Golfo de los
Mosquitos*

Panama Canal

Lago Bayano

Puerto Obaldía

-4000 m
-13 124 ft

Quepos

*Laguna
de Chiriquí*

Lago Gatún

Balboa

San Miguelito

Buenos Aires
Cortés

Volcán Barú 3475m

Capira

PANAMÁ
(PANAMA CITY)

Chimán

Palmar Sur

Boquete

Cordillera Central

Penonomé

*Archipiélago
de las Perlas*

La Palma

Yaviza

*Bahía
de Coronado*

La Concepción

David

Aguadulce

*Isla
del Rey*

El Real

Península de Osa

Golfo Dulce

P A N A M A

Santiago

Garachiné

*Golfo
de Chiriquí*

Guarumal

Ocú

Chitré

Golfo

Jaqué

Las Tablas

de Panamá

Isla de Coiba

*Isla
Cébaco*

*Península de
Azuero*

131

80°

E   F   G   H

COSTA RICA

PANAMÁ

C O L O M B I A

THE CARIBBEAN

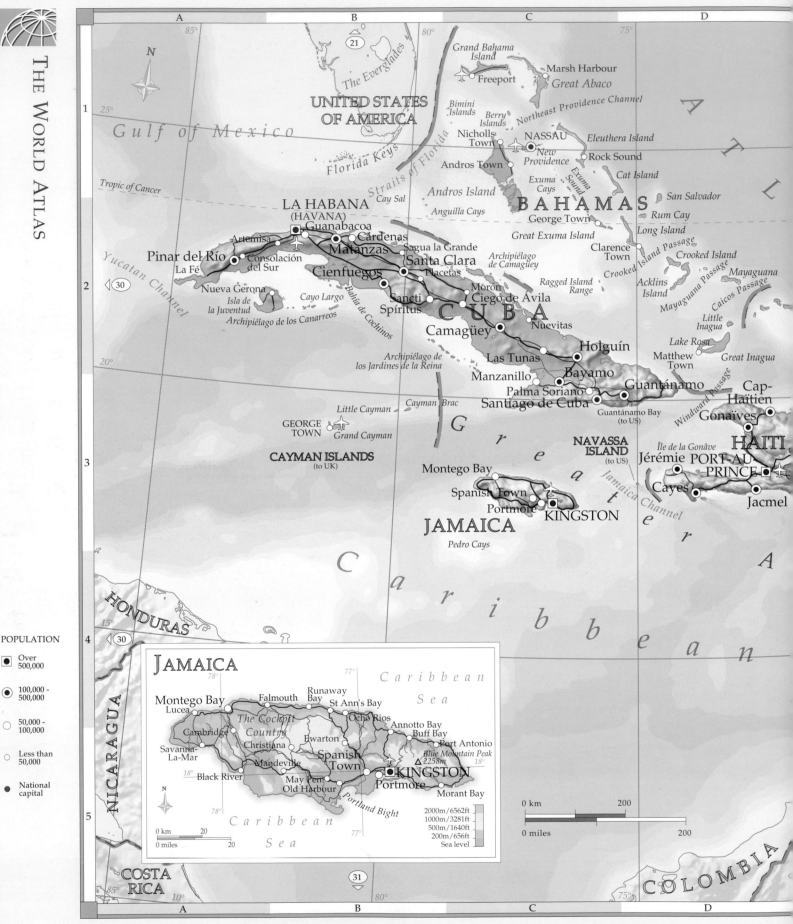

POPULATION

- ● Over 500,000
- ◉ 100,000 – 500,000
- ○ 50,000 – 100,000
- ○ Less than 50,000
- ● National capital

A B C D

N

85° 80° 75°

UNITED STATES OF AMERICA

Gulf of Mexico

The Everglades

21

Grand Bahama Island
Freeport Marsh Harbour
Great Abaco

Bimini Islands
Berry Islands
Northeast Providence Channel

Nicholls Town NASSAU
New Providence Eleuthera Island
Rock Sound

1 25°

Florida Keys
Straits of Florida

Cay Sal
Andros Town
Andros Island

Tropic of Cancer

LA HABANA (HAVANA)
Guanabacoa Cárdenas
Artemisa Matanzas Sagua la Grande
Pinar del Río Santa Clara
Consolación del Sur
La Fé Cienfuegos Placetas
Nueva Gerona Sancti Spíritus
Isla de la Juventud Cayo Largo
Archipiélago de los Canarreos

BAHAMAS

Exuma Cays
Exuma Sound
Cat Island
San Salvador
Rum Cay
George Town
Great Exuma Island
Archipiélago de Camagüey
Ragged Island Range

Long Island
Clarence Town Crooked Island
Crooked Island Passage
Acklins Island
Mayaguana Passage
Mayaguana
Little Inagua
Caicos Passage

Yucatán Channel

30

Bahía de Cochinos

CUBA
Morón
Ciego de Ávila
Camagüey Nuevitas
Holguín
Las Tunas
Manzanillo Bayamo
Palma Soriano Guantánamo
Santiago de Cuba
Guantánamo Bay (to US)

Lake Rosa
Matthew Town Great Inagua
Cap-Haïtien
Gonaïves
HAITI

Windward Passage

2 20°

Archipiélago de los Jardines de la Reina

Little Cayman
Cayman Brac
GEORGE TOWN
Grand Cayman

CAYMAN ISLANDS (to UK)

G r e a t e r

NAVASSA ISLAND (to US)

Jérémie PORT-AU-PRINCE
Cayes
Jacmel

Île de la Gonâve

3

Montego Bay
Spanish Town
Portmore
KINGSTON
JAMAICA

Pedro Cays

Jamaica Channel

C a r i b b e a n

HONDURAS

30

NICARAGUA

4 15°

JAMAICA

78° 77° Caribbean Sea

Montego Bay Falmouth Runaway Bay St Ann's Bay
Lucea Ocho Rios
Cambridge The Cockpit Country Annotto Bay
Christiana Ewarton Buff Bay
Savanna-La-Mar Mandeville Spanish Town Port Antonio
Black River May Pen Blue Mountain Peak
Old Harbour △ 2258m
Portmore KINGSTON
Portland Bight Morant Bay

N

Caribbean Sea

0 km 20
0 miles 20

2000m/6562ft
1000m/3281ft
500m/1640ft
200m/656ft
Sea level

0 km 200
0 miles 200

5 10°

85° 80° 75°

A B C D

COSTA RICA

31

COLOMBIA

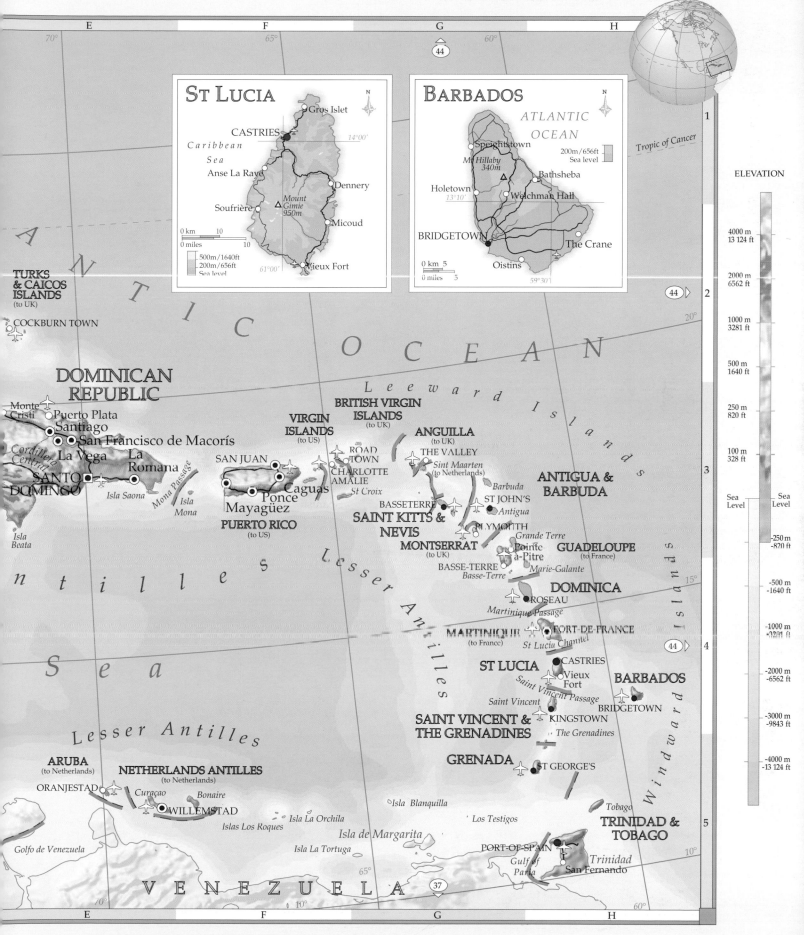

ST LUCIA

N

Gros Islet

CASTRIES

Caribbean
Sea

14°00'

Anse La Raye

Dennery

Soufrière

△ *Mount*
Gimie
950m

Micoud

0 km   10

0 miles

500m/1640ft

200m/656ft

Sea level

61°00'

Vieux Fort

BARBADOS

N

ATLANTIC
OCEAN

Speightstown

Mt Hillaby
340m

200m/656ft
Sea level

Holetown

Bathsheba

13°10'

Welchman Hall

BRIDGETOWN

The Crane

0 km   5

0 miles   5

Oistins

59°30'

E   F   △ 44   G   60°   H

70°   65°

14°00'

ELEVATION

4000 m
13 124 ft

2000 m
6562 ft

1000 m
3281 ft

500 m
1640 ft

250 m
820 ft

100 m
328 ft

Sea   Sea
Level   Level

-250 m
-820 ft

-500 m
-1640 ft

-1000 m
-3281 ft

-2000 m
-6562 ft

-3000 m
-9843 ft

-4000 m
-13 124 ft

TURKS
& CAICOS
ISLANDS
(to UK)

COCKBURN TOWN

L e e w a r d   I s l a n d s

Tropic of Cancer

44

20°

**DOMINICAN
REPUBLIC**

Monte
Cristi   Puerto Plata

Santiago

San Francisco de Macorís

Cordillera
Central   La Vega   La Romana

**SANTO
DOMINGO**   *Isla Saona*

*Isla
Beata*   *Mona Passage*   *Isla*
Mona

VIRGIN
ISLANDS
(to US)

**BRITISH VIRGIN
ISLANDS**
(to UK)

SAN JUAN

Caguas   CHARLOTTE
AMALIE
Ponce   *St Croix*
Mayagüez

PUERTO RICO
(to US)

ROAD
TOWN

ANGUILLA

THE VALLEY

Sint Maarten
(to Netherlands)

BASSETERRE

**SAINT KITTS &
NEVIS**

MONTSERRAT
(to UK)

PLYMOUTH

Pointe
à-Pitre

BASSE-TERRE
Basse-Terre

Barbuda

ST JOHN'S
Antigua

**ANTIGUA &
BARBUDA**

GUADELOUPE
(to France)

Marie-Galante

DOMINICA

ROSEAU

Martinique Passage

MARTINIQUE
(to France)

FORT-DE-FRANCE

St Lucia Channel

ST LUCIA

CASTRIES

Vieux
Fort

Saint Vincent Passage

Saint Vincent

BARBADOS

BRIDGETOWN

**SAINT VINCENT &
THE GRENADINES**

KINGSTOWN

The Grenadines

GRENADA

ST GEORGE'S

ARUBA
(to Netherlands)

ORANJESTAD

NETHERLANDS ANTILLES
(to Netherlands)

Curaçao   *Bonaire*

WILLEMSTAD

Islas Los Roques

Isla La Orchila

Isla Blanquilla

Los Testigos

Tobago

**TRINIDAD &
TOBAGO**

Lesser Antilles

Golfo de Venezuela   *Isla La Tortuga*

Isla de Margarita

PORT-OF-SPAIN

Gulf of
Paria   *Trinidad*

San Fernando

V E N E Z U E L A   37

A N T I L L E S

A T L A N T I C   O C E A N

Lesser   Antilles

n t i l l e s

S e a

W i n d w a r d   I s l a n d s

15°

44

10°

70°   65°   10°   60°

E   F   G   H

SOUTH AMERICA

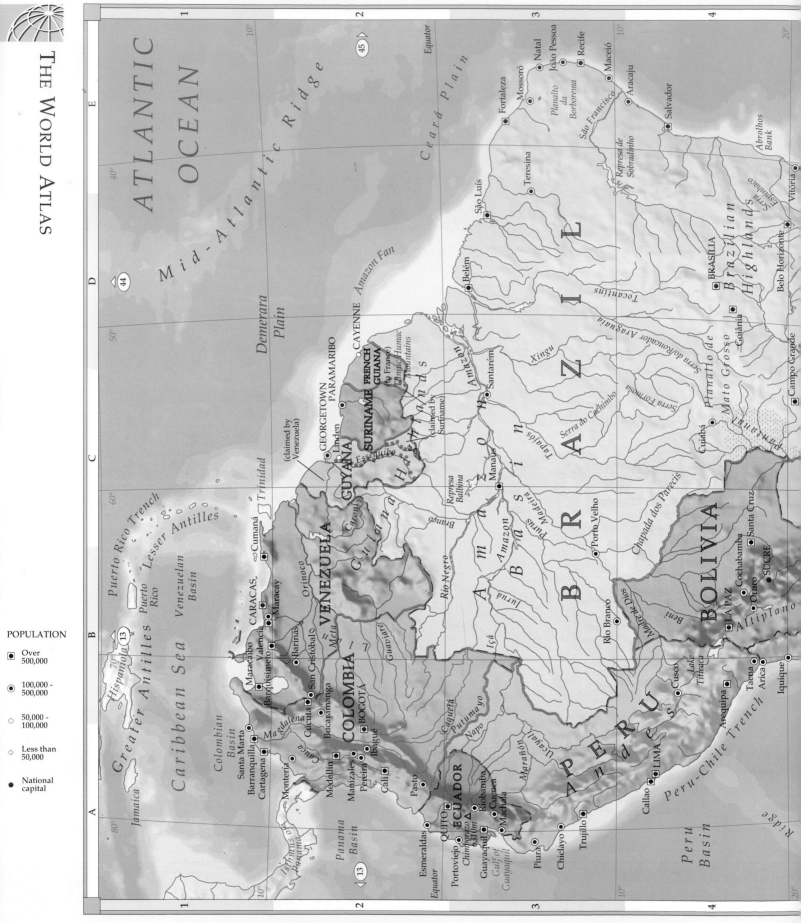

POPULATION

- Over 500,000
- 100,000 - 500,000
- 50,000 - 100,000
- Less than 50,000
- National capital

ATLANTIC OCEAN

Mid-Atlantic Ridge

Demerara Plain

Ceará Plain

Amazon Fan

Equator

Puerto Rico Trench

Greater Antilles

Lesser Antilles

Caribbean Sea

Colombian Basin

Venezuelan Basin

Jamaica

Hispaniola

Trinidad

Puerto Rico

Cumaná

CARACAS

Maracay

Valencia

Barquisimeto

Maracaibo

VENEZUELA

Barinas

San Cristóbal

Cúcuta

Bucaramanga

COLOMBIA

Santa Marta

Barranquilla

Cartagena

Montería

Medellín

Manizales

Pereira

Ibagué

BOGOTÁ

Cali

Pasto

Orinoco

Meta

Guaviare

Caquetá

Putumayo

Napo

Magdalena

Cauca

GEORGETOWN

Linden

PARAMARIBO

CAYENNE

GUYANA

SURINAME

FRENCH GUIANA (to France)

(claimed by Venezuela)

Essequibo

(claimed by Suriname)

Guiana Highlands

Caroní

Branco

Rio Negro

Amazon

Santarém

Manaus

Represa Balbina

Icá

Iça

Japurá

Putumayo

Juruá

Purus

Madeira

BRAZIL

BRASÍLIA

Belém

São Luís

Teresina

Fortaleza

Mossoró

Natal

João Pessoa

Recife

Maceió

Aracaju

Salvador

Vitória

Belo Horizonte

Goiânia

Campo Grande

Cuiabá

Porto Velho

Tocantins

Araguaia

Xingu

Tapajós

Serra do Cachimbo

Serra Formosa

Planalto de Mato Grosso

Chapada dos Parecis

Pantanal

Serra do Roncador

Brazilian Highlands

Planalto da Borborema

São Francisco

Represa de Sobradinho

Abrolhos Bank

Serra Espinhaço

ECUADOR

QUITO

Portoviejo

Esmeraldas

Guayaquil

Gulf of Guayaquil

Cuenca

Machala

Riobamba

Chimborazo 6310m

Equator

Piura

Chiclayo

Trujillo

Marañón

Ucayali

Huallaga

PERU

LIMA

Callao

Cusco

Arequipa

Tacna

Arica

Iquique

Andes

Peru-Chile Trench

Peru Basin

Lake Titicaca

BOLIVIA

LA PAZ

SUCRE

Oruro

Cochabamba

Santa Cruz

Altiplano

Beni

Madre de Dios

Río Branco

Panama Basin

Isthmus of Panama

Madeira

Amazon Basin

44

45

13

13

Equator

34

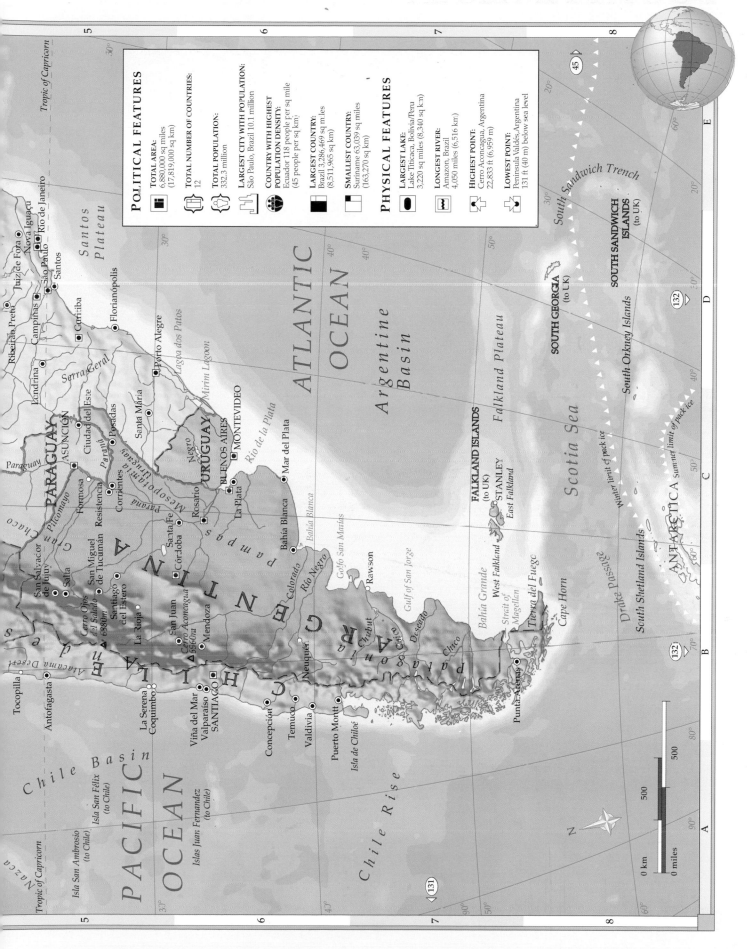

POLITICAL FEATURES

TOTAL AREA:
6,880,000 sq miles
(17,819,000 sq km)

TOTAL NUMBER OF COUNTRIES:
12

TOTAL POPULATION:
332.3 million

LARGEST CITY WITH POPULATION:
São Paulo, Brazil 10.1 million

COUNTRY WITH HIGHEST POPULATION DENSITY:
Ecuador 118 people per sq mile
(45 people per sq km)

LARGEST COUNTRY:
Brazil 3,286,469 sq miles
(8,511,965 sq km)

SMALLEST COUNTRY:
Suriname 63,039 sq miles
(163,270 sq km)

PHYSICAL FEATURES

LARGEST LAKE:
Lake Titicaca, Bolivia/Peru
3,220 sq miles (8,340 sq km)

LONGEST RIVER:
Amazon, Brazil
4,050 miles (6,516 km)

HIGHEST POINT:
Cerro Aconcagua, Argentina
22,833 ft (6,959 m)

LOWEST POINT:
Peninsula Valdés, Argentina
131 ft (40 m) below sea level

NORTHERN SOUTH AMERICA

THE WORLD ATLAS

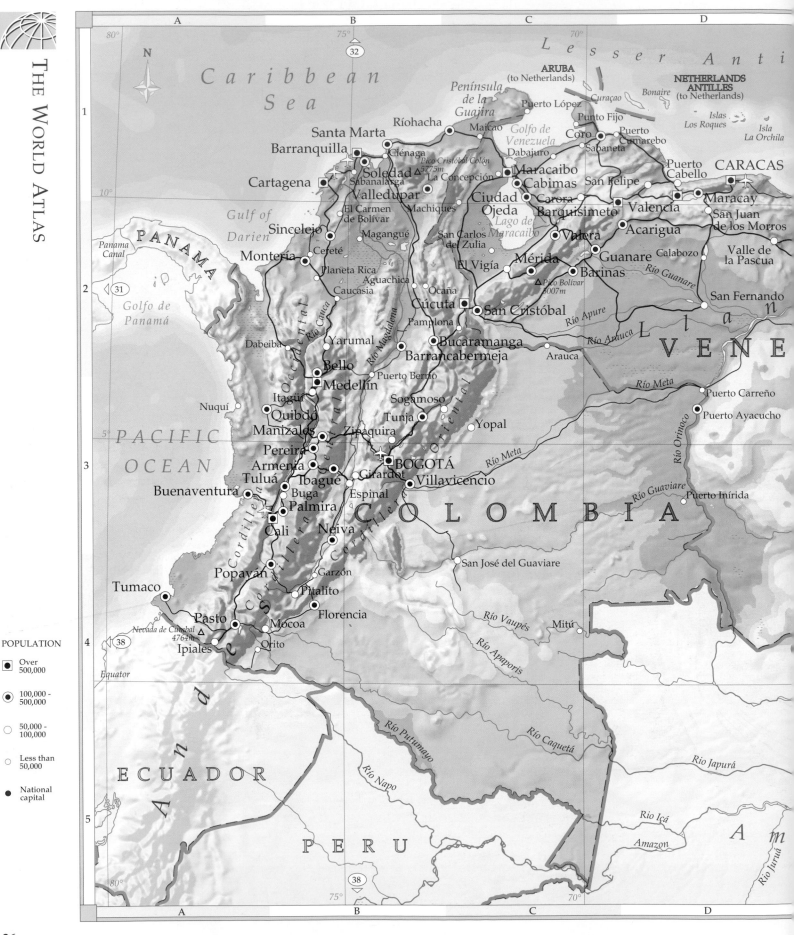

POPULATION

- ■ Over 500,000
- ◉ 100,000 - 500,000
- ○ 50,000 - 100,000
- ○ Less than 50,000
- ● National capital

ATLANTIC

OCEAN

ELEVATION

4000 m 13 124 ft	
2000 m 6562 ft	
1000 m 3281 ft	
500 m 1640 ft	
250 m 820 ft	
100 m 328 ft	
Sea Level	Sea Level
-250 m -820 ft	
-500 m -1640 ft	
-1000 m -3281 ft	
-2000 m -6562 ft	
-3000 m -9843 ft	
-4000 m -13 124 ft	

SAINT VINCENT & THE GRENADINES

BARBADOS

GRENADA

Isla Blanquilla
Isla de Margarita
Islas Los Testigos
Tobago
Isla La Tortuga
La Asunción
Porlamar
Carúpano
TRINIDAD & TOBAGO
Cumaná
Cariaco
Güiria
Gulf of Paria
Puerto La Cruz
Trinidad
Barcelona
The Serpent's Mouth
San Mateo
Maturín
Anaco
Zaraza
Cantaura
Tucupita
El Tigre
Río Orinoco
Ciudad Guayana
ZUELA
Ciudad Bolívar
Upata
Embalse de Guri
Matthews Ridge
Charity
El Callao
Spring Garden
GEORGETOWN
El Dorado
Cuyuni River
Aurora
Parika
New Amsterdam
Río Paragua
Peters Mine
Bartica
PARAMARIBO
Río Caura
Salto Ángel
Rockstone
Totness
Nieuw Amsterdam
St-Laurent-du-Maroni
Kamarang
Linden
GUYANA
Nieuw Nickerie
Sinnamary
Río Caroní
Mount Roraima 2810m
Orealla
Kaaimanston
Kourou
Apoera
CAYENNE
Kurupukari
W. J. van Blommesteinmeer
Montagnes de la Trinité
Ouanary
Guiana Highlands
Pukaraima Mountains
SURINAME
Juliana Top 1230m
Grand-Santi
Montagne Tortue
St-Georges
Río Orinoco
(Venezuela claims all of Guyana west of Essequibo River)
Lethem
FRENCH GUIANA (to France)
Camopi
Essequibo River
Courantyne River
Maroni River
Tumuc Humac Mountains
(claimed by Suriname)
Acarai Mountains
(claimed by Suriname)
Equator

BRAZIL
Río Negro
Amazon
Amazon Basin
Amazon
Amazon
Río Purus
Río Tapajós

WESTERN SOUTH AMERICA

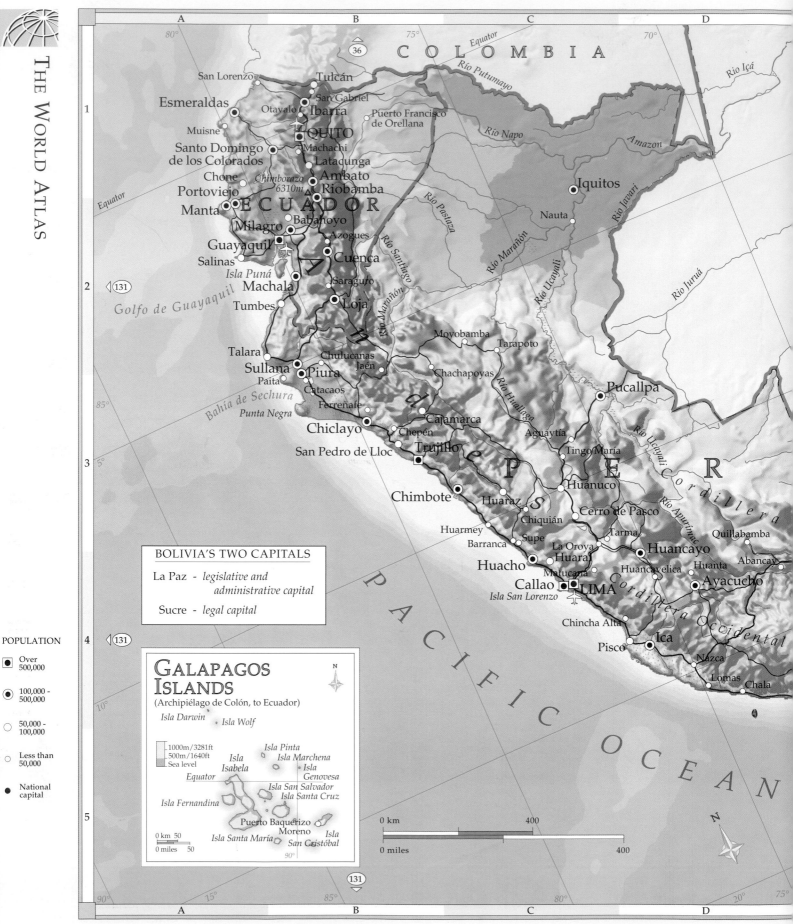

BOLIVIA'S TWO CAPITALS

La Paz - *legislative and administrative capital*

Sucre - *legal capital*

GALAPAGOS ISLANDS

(Archipiélago de Colón, to Ecuador)

Isla Darwin • Isla Wolf

	1000m/3281ft
	500m/1640ft
	Sea level

Isla Pinta
Isla Marchena
Isla Genovesa
Isla Isabela
Isla San Salvador
Isla Santa Cruz
Isla Fernandina
Puerto Baquerizo Moreno
Isla Santa María
Isla San Cristóbal

0 km 50
0 miles 50

POPULATION

- ◉ Over 500,000
- ◉ 100,000 - 500,000
- ○ 50,000 - 100,000
- ○ Less than 50,000
- ● National capital

Map labels:

COLOMBIA
San Lorenzo
Tulcán
San Gabriel
Esmeraldas
Otavalo
Ibarra
Muisne
QUITO
Machachi
Santo Domingo de los Colorados
Latacunga
Chone
Chimborazo 6310m
Ambato
Portoviejo
Riobamba
Manta
ECUADOR
Milagro
Babahoyo
Guayaquil
Azogues
Salinas
Cuenca
Isla Puná
Saraguro
Machala
Tumbes
Loja
Talara
Chulucanas
Jaén
Sullana
Piura
Paita
Catacaos
Ferreñafe
Chiclayo
Chepén
Cajamarca
San Pedro de Lloc
Trujillo
Chimbote
Huaraz
Chiquián
Huarmey
Barranca
Supe
Huaura
Huacho
Matucana
Callao
LIMA
Isla San Lorenzo
Chincha Alta
Pisco
Ica
Nazca
Lomas
Chala

Puerto Francisco de Orellana
Iquitos
Nauta
Moyobamba
Tarapoto
Chachapoyas
Pucallpa
Aguaytía
Tingo María
Huánuco
Cerro de Pasco
Tarma
La Oroya
Huancayo
Huancavelica
Huanta
Quillabamba
Abancay
Ayacucho

PERU
Cordillera Occidental

Río Putumayo
Río Napo
Amazon
Río Içá
Río Javari
Río Pastaza
Río Santiago
Río Marañón
Río Juruá
Río Ucayali
Río Huallaga
Río Apurímac

Golfo de Guayaquil
Bahía de Sechura
Punta Negra
PACIFIC OCEAN

0 km 400
0 miles 400

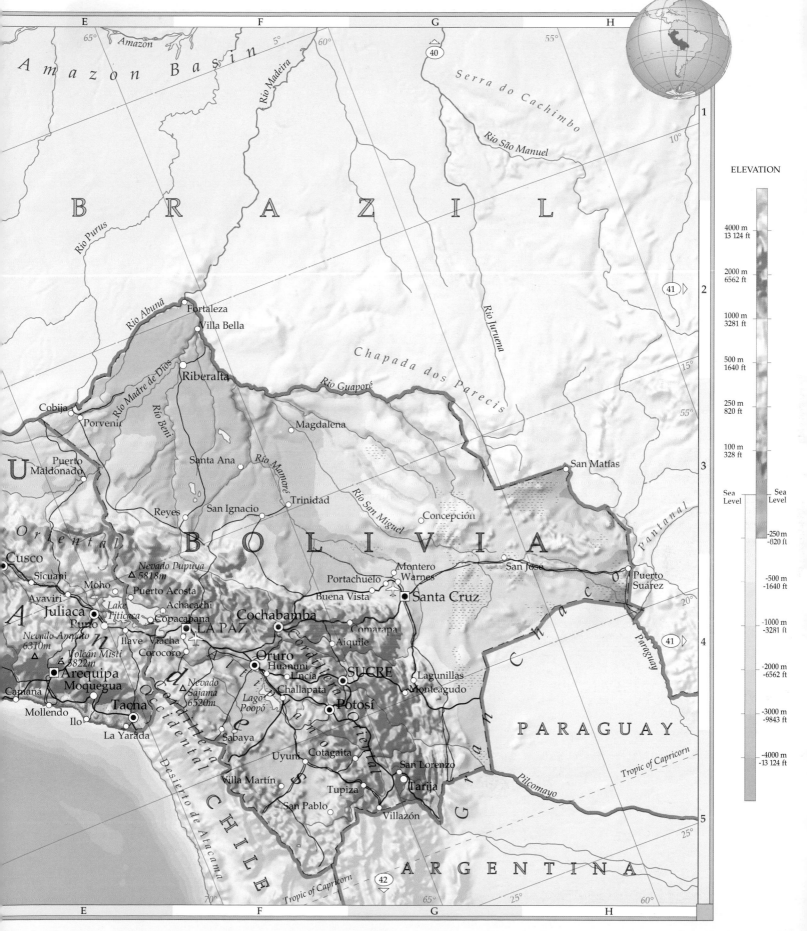

E   F   G   H

65°   Amazon   5°   60°   55°

Amazon Basin

Rio Madeira

Rio São Manuel

Serra do Cachimbo

40

10°   1

B   R   A   Z   I   L

Rio Purus

Rio Iuruena

41   2

Rio Abunã   Fortaleza

Villa Bella

Chapada dos Parecis

15°

Riberalta   Rio Guaporé

Cobija

Porvenir   Rio Madre de Dios

Rio Beni

Magdalena

55°

Puerto   Santa Ana   Rio Mamoré

Maldonado   San Matías   3

U

Reyes   San Ignacio   Trinidad

Rio San Miguel

Pantanal

Concepción

Orienta l   B   O   L   I   V   I   A

Cusco   Nevado Pupuya
                              5818m   Montero   San José
Sicuani   Warnes   Puerto
Moho   Puerto Acosta   Portachuelo   Suárez
Ayaviri   Achacachi   Buena Vista   Santa Cruz   20°
A   Juliaca   Lake   Copacabana   Chaco
          Puno   Titicaca   Cochabamba   Comarapa   41
Nevado Ampato   Paraguay
6310m   Ilave Viacha LA PAZ   Aiquile
n   Corocoro   Cordillera   4
Volcán Misti   Oruro   Comarapa
5822m   Huanuni   SUCRE   Lagunillas
Arequipa   Uncía   Monteagudo
Moquegua   Nevado   Challapata   Potosí
Camaná   Sajama   Lago   P   A   R   A   G   U   A   Y
          6520m   Poopó   Sabaya
Mollendo   Tacna   Tropic of Capricorn
Ilo   Villa Martín   Uyuni   Cotagaita
          La Yarada   San Lorenzo
                    San Pablo   Tupiza   Tarija   25°
CHILE   Desierto de Atacama   Villazón   5

Tropic of Capricorn   42

          A   R   G   E   N   T   I   N   A

70°   65°   25°   60°

E   F   G   H

BRAZIL

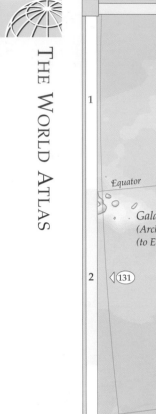

THE WORLD ATLAS

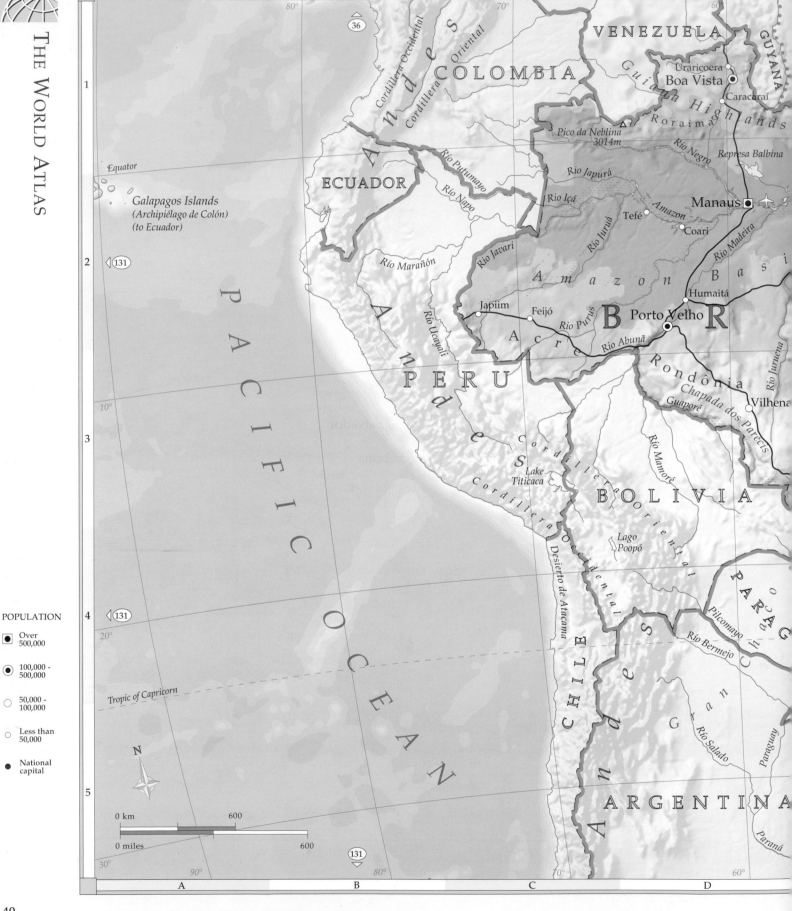

POPULATION

- ⬤ Over 500,000
- ◉ 100,000 – 500,000
- ○ 50,000 – 100,000
- ○ Less than 50,000
- ● National capital

A

VENEZUELA

GUYANA

COLOMBIA

Uraricoera

Boa Vista

Caracaraí

Guiana Highlands

Roraima

Pico da Neblina 3014m

Rio Negro

Represa Balbina

ECUADOR

Rio Putumayo

Rio Napo

Rio Japurá

Rio Içá

Amazon

Manaus

Tefé

Coari

Galapagos Islands
(Archipiélago de Colón)
(to Ecuador)

Equator

Rio Marañón

Rio Javari

Rio Juruá

Rio Madeira

Amazon Basin

Rio Ucayali

Japiim

Feijó

Rio Purus

Rio Abunã

Humaitá

Porto Velho

PERU

Acre

Rondônia

Rio Iurena

Chapada dos Parecis

Guaporé

Vilhena

PACIFIC OCEAN

Cordillera Occidental

Lake Titicaca

Cordillera Oriental

Rio Mamoré

BOLIVIA

Lago Poopó

PARAG

Desierto de Atacama

Pilcomayo

Rio Bermejo

Tropic of Capricorn

CHILE

Gran Cha

Rio Salado

Paraguay

N

0 km   600

0 miles   600

ARGENTINA

Paraná

SURINAME

FRENCH GUIANA (to France)

Tumuc Humac Mountains

Amapá

ATLANTIC OCEAN

Mouths of the Amazon

Ilha Caviana de Fora

Macapá

Ilha de Marajó

Baía de Marajó

Baía de São Marco

Belém

Equator

São Luís

Parnaíba

Alenquer

Amazon

Santarém

Altamira

Bacabal

Camocim

Fortaleza

Atol das Rocas

San Fernando de Noronha (to Brazil)

Itaituba

Represa de Tucuruí

Piripiri

Teresina

Mossoró

Cabo de São Roque

Rio Tapajós

Rio Xingu

Marabá

Imperatriz

Maranhão

Ceará

Açu

Natal

P *a* *r* *á*

Serra do Cachimbo

Serra dos Gradaús

Carolina

Floriano

Rio Grande do Norte

Juazeiro do Norte

João Pessoa

Campina Grande

Serra Formosa

Rio Tocantins

Balsas

Picos

Piauí

Pará

Pernambuco

Recife

Rio São Manuel

B *R* *A* *Z* *I* *L*

Represa de Sobradinho

Alagoas

Maceió

Mato Grosso

Rio Araguaia

Tocantins

Rio São Francisco

Juazeiro

Chapada Diamantina

Aracaju

Rio São Manuel

Goiás

Taguatinga

Estância

Bahia

Feira de Santana

Cuiabá

Planalto

BRASÍLIA

Janaúba

Salvador

Baía de Todos os Santos

Anápolis

Central

Itabuna

Vitória da Conquista

Rondonópolis

Jataí

Goiânia

Minas

Montes Claros

Canavieiras

Mato Grosso do Sul

Pantanal

Araguari

Araçuaí

Governador Valadares

Uberlândia

Uberaba

Gerais

Espírito Santo

Campo Grande

Belo Horizonte

Aquidauana

Ribeirão Preto

Divinópolis

Vitória

Presidente Epitácio

Juiz de Fora

Campos

Marília

Campinas

Londrina

São Paulo

Nova

Maringá

São Paulo

Iguaçu

Rio de Janeiro

Paraná

Santos

Represa de Itaipú

Ponta Grossa

Tropic of Capricorn

Salto do Iguaçu

Rio Iguaçu

Curitiba

Joinville

Paraná

Blumenau

Santa Catarina

Florianópolis

Passo Fundo

Santa Maria

Canoas

Rio Grande

do Sul

Porto Alegre

Bagé

Lagoa dos Patos

Rio Negro

Rio Grande

Mirim Lagoon

URUGUAY

ATLANTIC OCEAN

ELEVATION

4000 m	13 124 ft
2000 m	6562 ft
1000 m	3281 ft
500 m	1640 ft
250 m	820 ft
100 m	328 ft
Sea Level	Sea Level
-250 m	820 ft
-500 m	1640 ft
-1000 m	3201 ft
-2000 m	6562 ft
-3000 m	9843 ft
-4000 m	13 124 ft

SOUTHERN SOUTH AMERICA

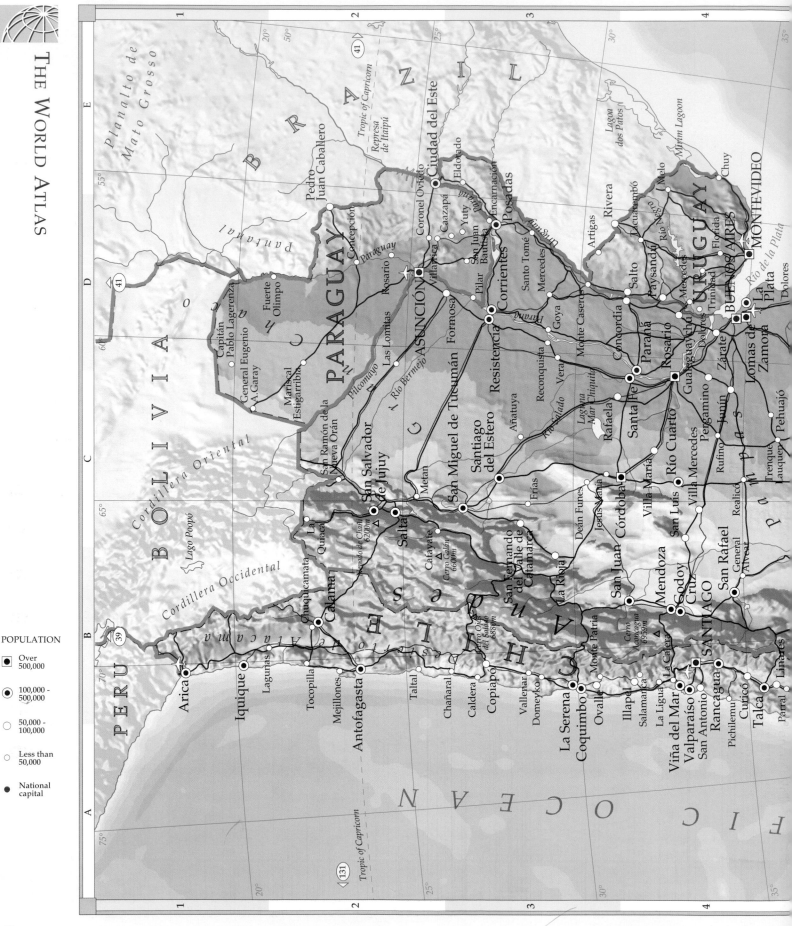

POPULATION

- ● Over 500,000
- ◉ 100,000 – 500,000
- ○ 50,000 – 100,000
- ○ Less than 50,000
- ● National capital

Planalto de Mato Grosso

B R A Z I L

Tropic of Capricorn
Represa de Itaipú

Lagoa dos Patos

Mirim Lagoon

P E R U

B O L I V I A

Lago Poopó

Cordillera Oriental

Cordillera Occidental

Pantanal

C h a c o

P A R A G U A Y

Pedro Juan Caballero

Concepción

Paraguay

Fuerte Olimpo

Capitán Pablo Lagerenza

General Eugenio A. Garay

Mariscal Estigarribia

Pilcomayo

Río Bermejo

Las Lomitas

ASUNCIÓN

Villarrica

Coronel Oviedo

Ciudad del Este

Eldorado

Caazapá

Yuty

San Juan Bautista

Encarnación

Posadas

Pilar

Formosa

Corrientes

Santo Tomé

Mercedes

Artigas

Rivera

Melo

U R U G U A Y

MONTEVIDEO

Chuy

Paysandú

Salto

Concordia

Paraná

Santa Fe

Rosario

Rafaela

San Ramón de la Nueva Orán

San Salvador de Jujuy

Salta

La Quiaca

Nevado de Chañi 6200m

Catavate

Cerro Galán 6600m

San Miguel de Tucumán

Metán

Santiago del Estero

Añatuya

Reconquista

Vera

Goya

Monte Caseros

A N D E S

San Fernando del Valle de Catamarca

La Rioja

Frías

Deán Funes

Jesús María

Villa María

Río Cuarto

Rufino

Junín

Pergamino

Zárate

BUENOS AIRES

La Plata

Río de la Plata

Lomas de Zamora

Trenque Lauquen

Pehuajó

Córdoba

San Luis

Villa Mercedes

San Juan

Mendoza

Godoy Cruz

Cerro Aconcagua 6959m

SANTIAGO

San Rafael

General Alvear

C H I L E

P E R U

Arica

Iquique

Lagunas

Tocopilla

Mejillones

Antofagasta

Taltal

Chañaral

Caldera

Copiapó

Vallenar

Domeyko

La Serena

Coquimbo

Ovalle

Illapel

Salamanca

La Ligua

Monte Patria

Cerro Ojos del Salado 6888m

Viña del Mar

Valparaíso

San Antonio

Rancagua

Pichilemu

Curicó

Talca

Parral

Linares

Tropic of Capricorn

P A C I F I C   O C E A N

42

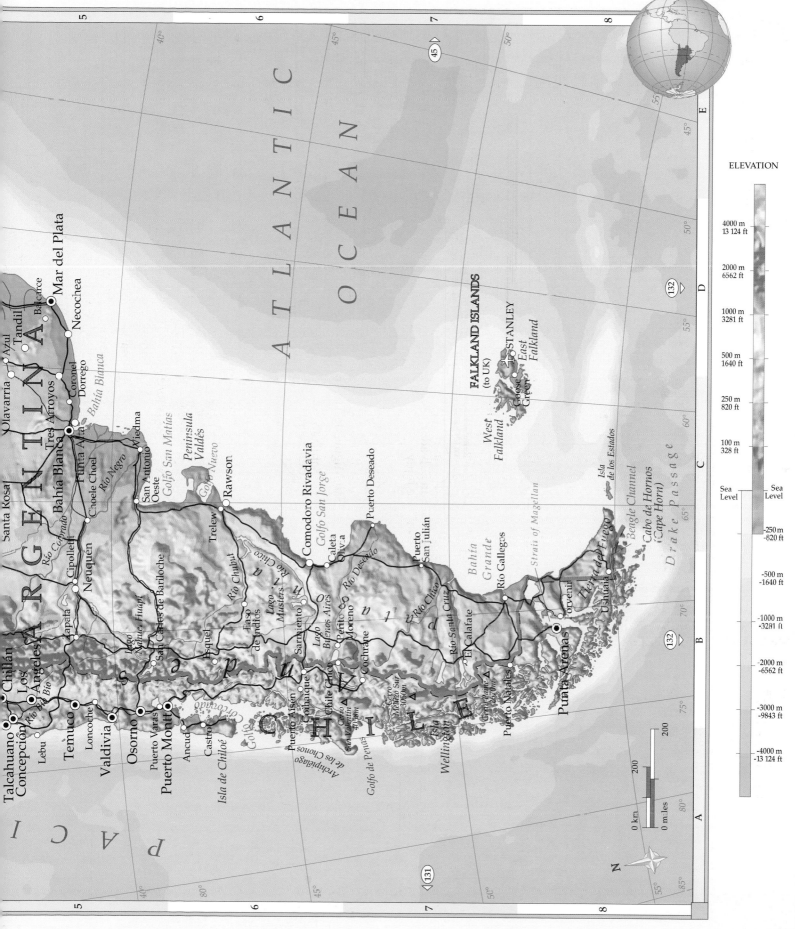

SOUTHERN SOUTH AMERICA

ELEVATION

4000 m	13 124 ft
2000 m	6562 ft
1000 m	3281 ft
500 m	1640 ft
250 m	820 ft
100 m	328 ft
Sea Level	Sea Level
-250 m	-820 ft
-500 m	-1640 ft
-1000 m	-3281 ft
-2000 m	-6562 ft
-3000 m	-9843 ft
-4000 m	-13 124 ft

ATLANTIC OCEAN

PACIFIC

ARGENTINA

CHILE

FALKLAND ISLANDS
(to UK)

STANLEY
East Falkland
Goose Green
West Falkland

Mar del Plata
Balcarce
Azul
Olavarría
Tandil
Necochea
Santa Rosa
Coronel Dorrego
Tres Arroyos
Bahía Blanca
Punta Alta
Bahía Blanca
Viedma
Golfo San Matías
Península Valdés
San Antonio Oeste
Choele Choel
Río Negro
Río Colorado
Cipolletti
Neuquén
Zapala
Rawson
Golfo Nuevo
Trelew
Río Chubut
San Carlos de Bariloche
Lago Nahuel Huapi
Esquel
Paso de Indios
Lago Musters
Sarmiento
Lago Buenos Aires
Comodoro Rivadavia
Golfo San Jorge
Caleta Olivia
Río Deseado
Puerto Deseado
Puerto San Julián
Río Chico
Río Chubut
Perito Moreno
Cochrane
Chile Chico
Coihaique
Puerto Aisén
Cerro San Valentín 4058m
Cerro Murallón Sur 3050m
Río Santa Cruz
Río Chico
El Calafate
Bahía Grande
Río Gallegos
Cerro Paine 2670m
Puerto Natales
Strait of Magellan
Punta Arenas
Porvenir
Tierra del Fuego
Ushuaia
Beagle Channel
Isla de los Estados
Cabo de Hornos (Cape Horn)
Drake Passage

Talcahuano
Concepción
Chillán
Los Ángeles
Lebu
Río Bío Bío
Temuco
Loncoche
Valdivia
Osorno
Puerto Varas
Puerto Montt
Ancud
Castro
Isla de Chiloé
Golfo Corcovado
Archipiélago de los Chonos
Golfo de Peñas
Isla Wellington

131
132
132
45

N

0 km 200
0 miles 200

43

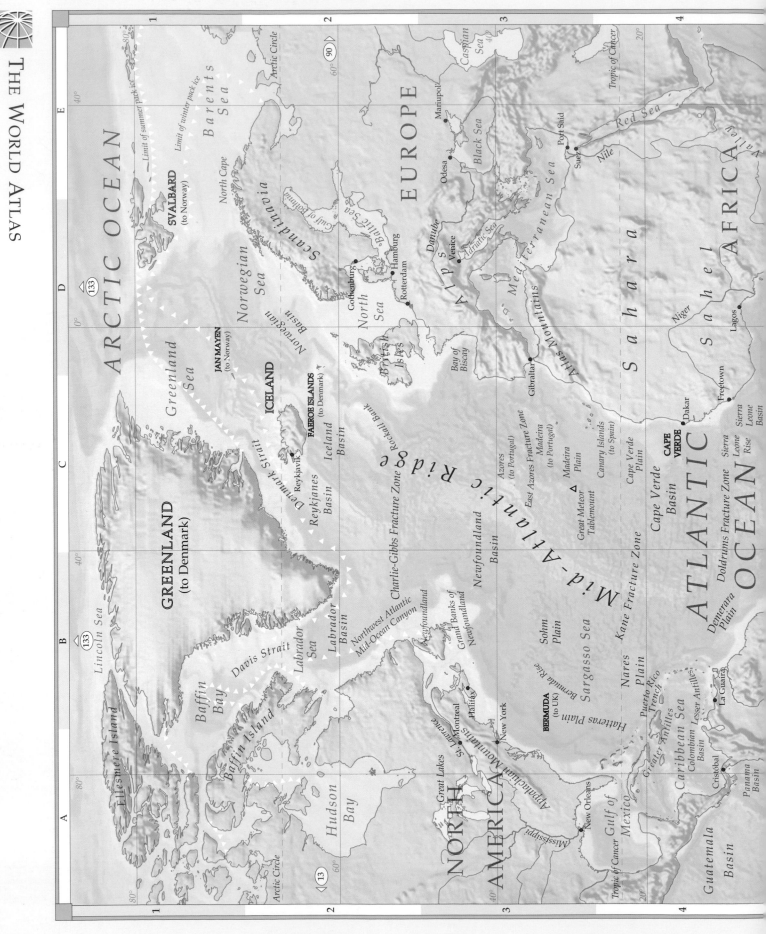

ARCTIC OCEAN

EUROPE

AFRICA

NORTH
AMERICA

ATLANTIC
OCEAN

Barents
Sea

Svalbard
(to Norway)

North Cape

Scandinavia

Norwegian
Sea

Norwegian
Basin

JAN MAYEN
(to Norway)

ICELAND

Greenland
Sea

FAROE ISLANDS
(to Denmark)

Iceland
Basin

Reykjanes
Basin

Reykjavik

Denmark Strait

GREENLAND
(to Denmark)

Labrador
Basin

Labrador
Sea

Davis Strait

Baffin
Bay

Baffin Island

Ellesmere Island

Lincoln Sea

Hudson
Bay

Great Lakes

St. Lawrence

Montreal

Halifax

New York

Appalachian Mountains

Mississippi

New Orleans

Gulf of
Mexico

Tropic of Cancer

Guatemala
Basin

Cristobal

Panama
Plain

Caribbean Sea
Colombian
Basin

Greater Antilles

Lesser Antilles

La Guaira

Puerto Rico
Trench

Demerara
Plain

Nares
Plain

Kane Fracture Zone

Hatteras Plain

Bermuda Rise

BERMUDA
(to UK)

Sohm
Plain

Sargasso Sea

Newfoundland
Basin

Grand Banks of
Newfoundland

Newfoundland

Northwest Atlantic
Mid-Ocean Canyon

Charlie-Gibbs Fracture Zone

Rockall Bank

British
Isles

North
Sea

Gothenburg

Hamburg

Rotterdam

Bay of
Biscay

Gibraltar

Atlas Mountains

Mediterranean Sea

Azores
(to Portugal)

East Azores Fracture Zone

Madeira
(to Portugal)

Madeira
Plain

Canary Islands
(to Spain)

Great Meteor
Tablemount

Cape Verde
Plain

Cape Verde
Basin

CAPE
VERDE

Dakar

Sierra
Leone
Rise

Sierra
Leone
Basin

Freetown

Doldrums Fracture Zone

Mid-Atlantic Ridge

Sahara

Sahel

Nile

Red Sea

Suez

Port Said

Black Sea

Caspian
Sea

Mariupol

Odesa

Danube

Alps

Venice

Adriatic Sea

Baltic Sea

Gulf of Bothnia

Arctic Circle

Niger

Lagos

Tropic of Cancer

Limit of summer pack ice

Limit of winter pack ice

Arctic Circle

133

133

13

90

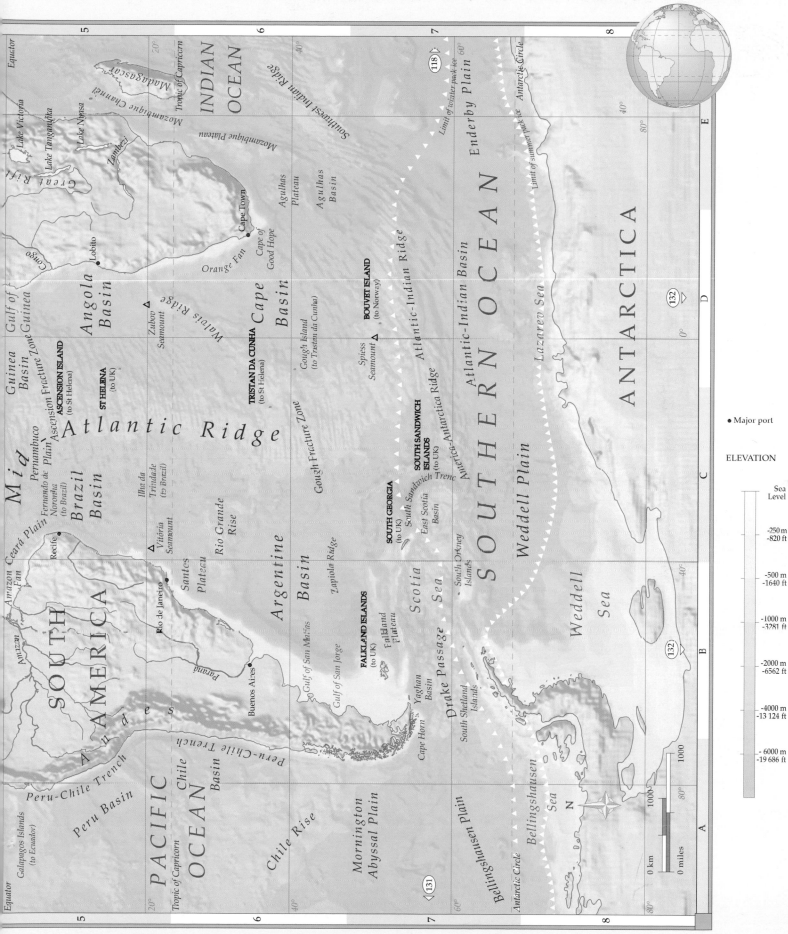

INDIAN
OCEAN

Tropic of Capricorn

20°

40°

Madagascar

Mozambique Channel

Lake Victoria
Lake Tanganyika
Lake Nyasa
Zambezi

Great Rift

Congo

Gulf of
Guinea

Guinea
Basin

Angola
Basin

Lobito

Cape Town
Cape of
Good Hope

Orange Fan

Mozambique Plateau

Southwest Indian Ridge

Agulhas
Plateau

Agulhas
Basin

Limit of winter pack ice

Antarctic Circle

118

Enderby Plain

80°

40°

E

D

132

0°

Lazarev Sea

ANTARCTICA

Limit of summer pack ice

SOUTHERN OCEAN

Atlantic-Indian Basin

Atlantic-Indian Ridge

BOUVET ISLAND
(to Norway)

Spiess
Seamount

Gough Island
(to Tristan da Cunha)

Cape
Basin

Walvis Ridge

Zubov
Seamount

TRISTAN DA CUNHA
(to St Helena)

ST HELENA
(to UK)

ASCENSION ISLAND
(to St Helena)

Ascension Fracture Zone

Guinea
Basin

Mid

Atlantic Ridge

Pernambuco

Fernando de
Noronha
(to Brazil)

Brazil
Basin

Recife

Amazon
Ceará Plain

Amazon
Fan

SOUTH

AMERICA

Ilha da
Trindade
(to Brazil)

Vitória
Seamount

Rio de Janeiro

Santos
Plateau

Rio Grande
Rise

Zapiola Ridge

Argentine

Basin

Paraná

Buenos Aires

Gulf of San Matías

Gulf of San Jorge

FALKLAND ISLANDS
(to UK)

Falkland
Plateau

Yaghan
Basin

Cape Horn

Gough Fracture Zone

SOUTH GEORGIA
(to UK)

SOUTH SANDWICH
ISLANDS
(to UK)

South Sandwich Trench

East Scotia
Basin

Scotia

Sea

South Orkney
Islands

Drake Passage

South Shetland
Islands

America-Antarctica Ridge

Weddell Plain

Weddell
Sea

40°

60°

132

B

ELEVATION

Sea
Level

• Major port

-250 m
-820 ft

-500 m
-1640 ft

-1000 m
-3281 ft

-2000 m
-6562 ft

-4000 m
-13 124 ft

- 6000 m
-19 686 ft

C

Andes

PACIFIC

OCEAN

Tropic of Capricorn

20°

40°

Galapagos Islands
(to Ecuador)

Equator

Peru Basin

Peru-Chile Trench

Chile
Basin

Chile Rise

Mornington
Abyssal Plain

Peru-Chile Trench

Bellingshausen Plain

Antarctic Circle

131

Bellingshausen
Sea

N

Antarctic Circle

80°

60°

1000

0 km

0 miles

1000

A

Equator

5

6

7

8

AFRICA

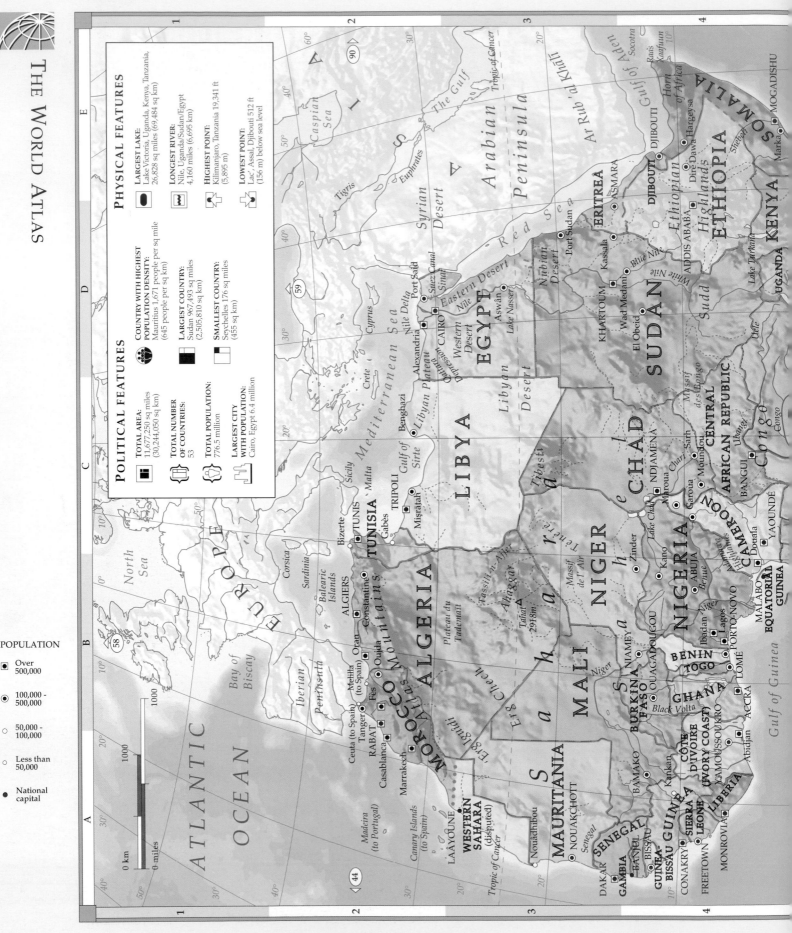

PHYSICAL FEATURES

LARGEST LAKE:
Lake Victoria, Uganda, Kenya, Tanzania, 26,828 sq miles (69,484 sq km)

LONGEST RIVER:
Nile, Uganda/Sudan/Egypt 4,160 miles (6,695 km)

HIGHEST POINT:
Kilimanjaro, Tanzania 19,341 ft (5,895 m)

LOWEST POINT:
Lac' Assal, Djibouti 512 ft (156 m) below sea level

POLITICAL FEATURES

TOTAL AREA:
11,677,250 sq miles (30,244,050 sq km)

TOTAL NUMBER OF COUNTRIES:
53

TOTAL POPULATION:
776.5 million

LARGEST CITY WITH POPULATION:
Cairo, Egypt 6.4 million

COUNTRY WITH HIGHEST POPULATION DENSITY:
Mauritius 1,671 people per sq mile (645 people per sq km)

LARGEST COUNTRY:
Sudan 967,493 sq miles (2,505,810 sq km)

SMALLEST COUNTRY:
Seychelles 176 sq miles (455 sq km)

POPULATION

- Over 500,000
- 100,000 – 500,000
- 50,000 – 100,000
- Less than 50,000
- National capital

46

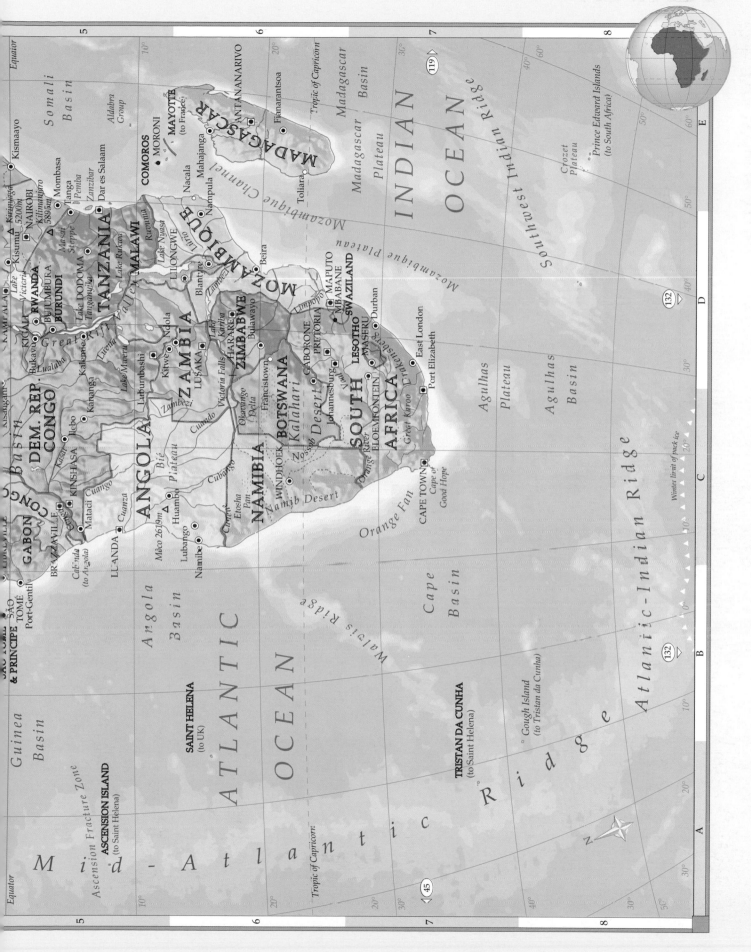

NORTHWEST AFRICA

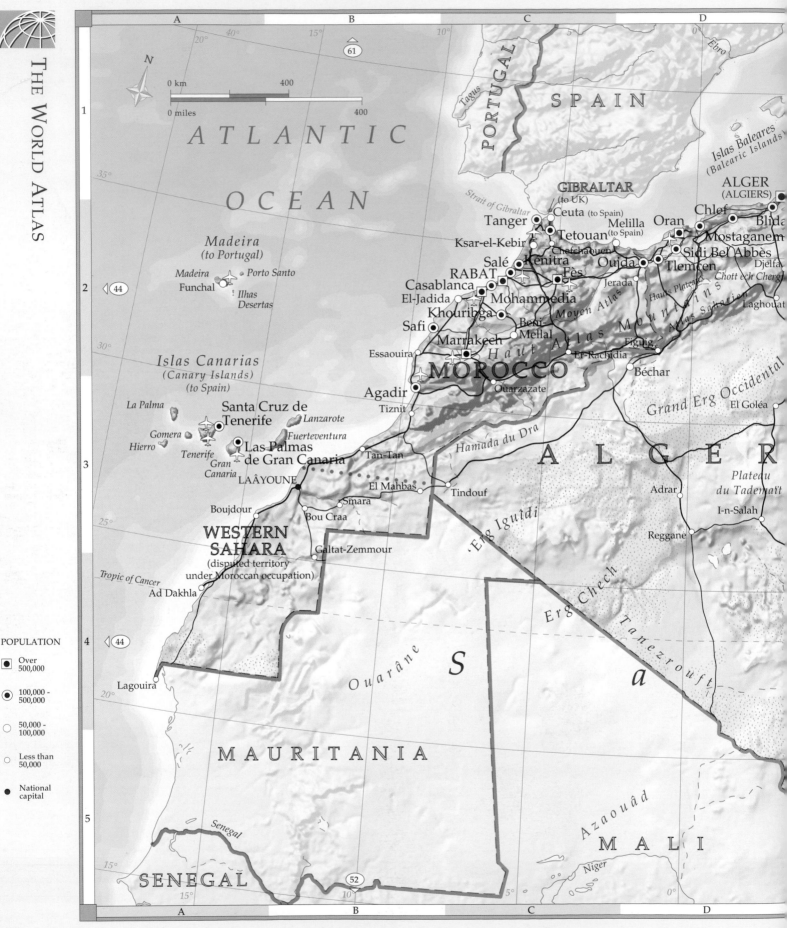

THE WORLD ATLAS

POPULATION

- ⊙ Over 500,000
- ◉ 100,000 – 500,000
- ○ 50,000 – 100,000
- ○ Less than 50,000
- ● National capital

ATLANTIC

OCEAN

Madeira (to Portugal)

Madeira · Porto Santo
Funchal · *Ilhas Desertas*

Islas Canarias (Canary Islands) (to Spain)

La Palma
Gomera · Lanzarote
Hierro · *Tenerife* · *Fuerteventura*
Gran Canaria
Santa Cruz de Tenerife
Las Palmas de Gran Canaria

LAÂYOUNE

Boujdour

WESTERN SAHARA
(disputed territory under Moroccan occupation)

Tropic of Cancer
Ad Dakhla

Lagouira

MAURITANIA

SENEGAL
Senegal

PORTUGAL

SPAIN

Tagus

Islas Baleares (Balearic Islands)

Ebro

GIBRALTAR (to UK)
Ceuta (to Spain)
Strait of Gibraltar
Tanger
Tetouan
Melilla (to Spain)
Ksar-el-Kebir
Chefchaouen
Salé · Kenitra
RABAT · Fès · Oujda
Casablanca
El-Jadida · Mohammedia
Khouribga · Beni-Mellal
Safi
Essaouira · Marrakech
MOROCCO
Agadir
Ouarzazate
Tiznit

Tan-Tan

El Mahbas
Smara
Bou Craa
Galtat-Zemmour

Tindouf

ALGER (ALGIERS)
Oran · Chlef · Blida
Mostaganem
Sidi Bel Abbès
Tlemcen · Djelfa
Jerada
Hauts Plateaux
Chott ech Cherg
Laghouat
Er-Rachidia
Béchar
Grand Erg Occidental
El Goléa

ALGER

Plateau du Tademaït
Adrar
I-n-Salah
Reggane

Hamáda du Dra
Erg Iguîdi
Erg Chech
Tanezrouft

S a h a r a

Ouarâne

Azaouâd

MALI
Niger

Moyen Atlas
Haut Atlas
Atlas Mountains
Atlas Saharien
Figuig

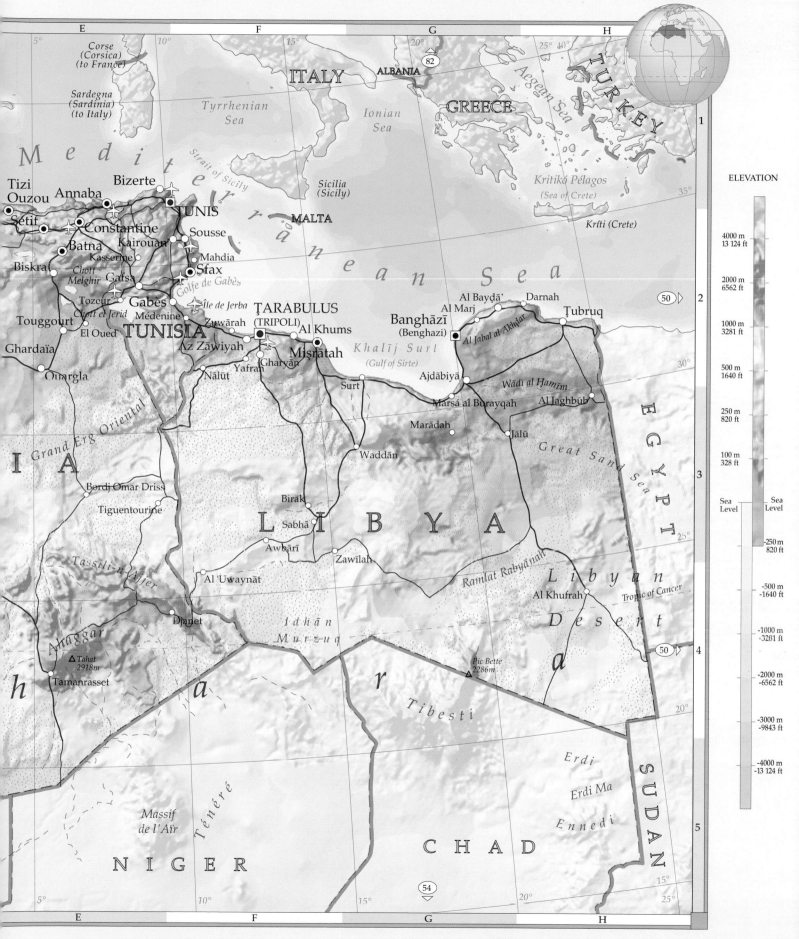

Corse
(Corsica)
(to France)

Sardegna
(Sardinia)
(to Italy)

ITALY

ALBANIA

GREECE

TURKEY

Tyrrhenian
Sea

Ionian
Sea

Aegean Sea

Kritikó Pélagos
(Sea of Crete)

Kríti (Crete)

82

50

Mediterranean Sea

Strait of Sicily

Sicilia
(Sicily)

MALTA

Tizi
Ouzou
Annaba
Bizerte
Sétif
TUNIS
Constantine
Sousse
Batna
Kairouan
Mahdia
Kasserine
Sfax
Biskra
Gafsa
Chott
Melghir
Golfe de Gabès
Tozeur
Gabès
Île de Jerba
Touggourt
Chott el Jerid
Médenine
Zuwārah
ȚARABULUS
(TRIPOLI)
Al Khums
Banghāzī
(Benghazi)
Al Bayḍā'
Darnah
Al Marj
Ţubruq
El Oued
TUNISIA
Az Zāwiyah
Yafran
Gharyān
Miṣrātah
Al Jabal al Akhḍar
Ghardaïa
Nālūt
Khalīj Surt
(Gulf of Sirte)
Ouargla
Surt
Ajdābiyā
Wādī al Ḥamīm
Al Jaghbūb
Marsá al Burayqah
Marādah
Jālū
Grand Erg Oriental
Waddān
Great Sand Sea
EGYPT
Bordj Omar Driss
Tiguentourine
Birāk
Sabḥā
L I B Y A
Tassili-n-Ajjer
Awbārī
Zawīlah
Al 'Uwaynāt
Ramlat Rabyānah
Libyan
Al Khufrah
Tropic of Cancer
Djanet
Idhān
Murzuq
Desert
Ahaggar
△Tahat
2918m
Pic Bette
△2286m
Tamanrasset
Tibesti
Erdi
Erdi Ma
Massif
de l'Aïr
Ténéré
Ennedi
SUDAN
N I G E R
C H A D
54
50

ELEVATION

4000 m
13 124 ft

2000 m
6562 ft

1000 m
3281 ft

500 m
1640 ft

250 m
820 ft

100 m
328 ft

Sea
Level
Sea
Level

-250 m
820 ft

-500 m
-1640 ft

-1000 m
-3281 ft

-2000 m
-6562 ft

-3000 m
-9843 ft

-4000 m
-13 124 ft

THE WORLD ATLAS

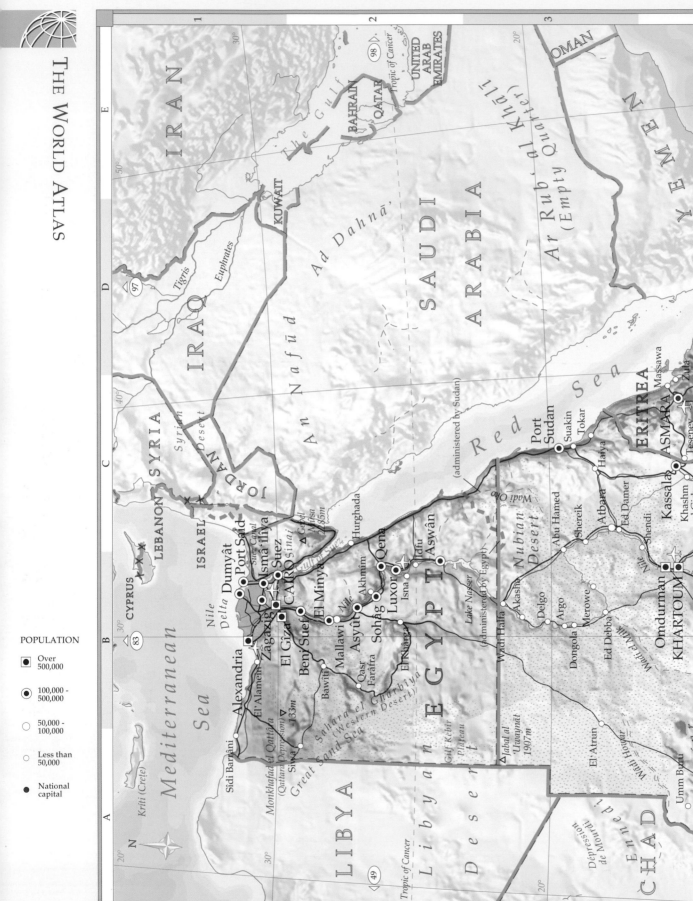

POPULATION

◉ Over
500,000

◉ 100,000 –
500,000

○ 50,000 –
100,000

○ Less than
50,000

● National
capital

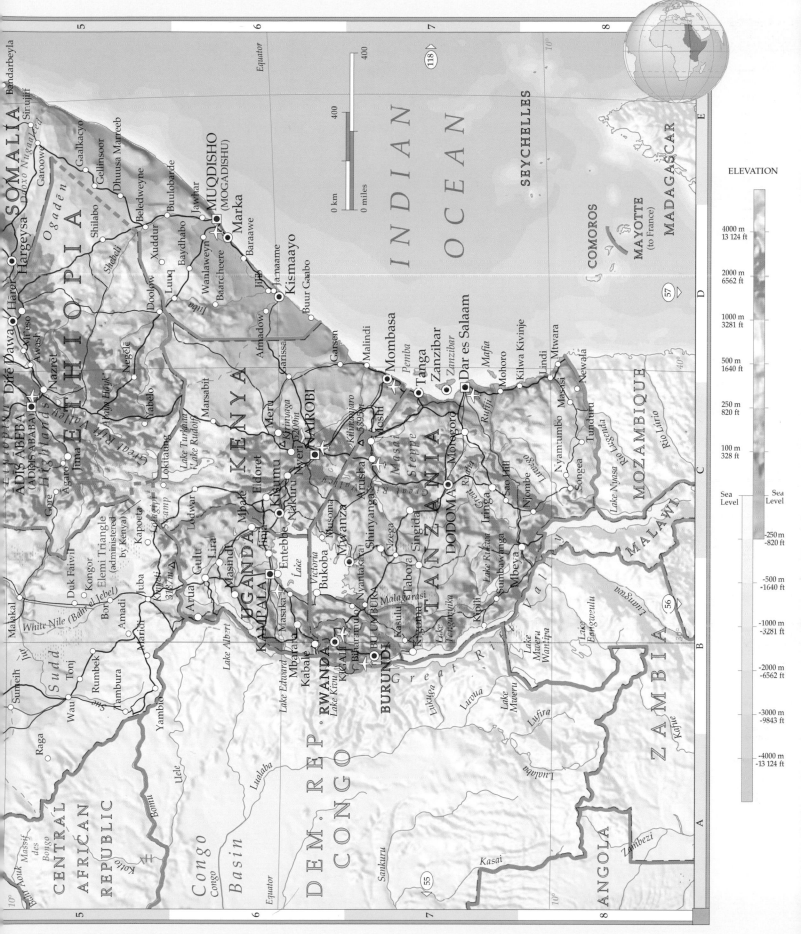

Bandarbeyla
Siirujiif
Dioxo Nugaaleed
SOMALIA
Hargeysa
Garoowe
Gaalkacyo
Gellinsoor
Shilabo
Dhuusa Marreeb
Beledweyne
Buulobarde
Buuloburde
Jawhar
MUQDISHO (MOGADISHU)
Marka
Baraawe
Janaame
Kismaayo
Buur Gaabo

Ogadén

ETHIOPIA
Harēr
Dirē Dawa
Mēso
Awash
Nazrēt
ADĪS ĀBEBA (ADDIS ABABA)
Jima
Agaro
Gore
Negēlē
Ārba Mīnch
Kabelo
Doolow
Xuddur
Baydhabo
Luuq
Wanlaweyn
Baarcheere
Jilib
Afmadow

Shebeli
Juba

Great Rift Valley

Ethiopian Highlands

INDIAN OCEAN

400
400
0 km
0 miles

118
10°

SEYCHELLES

COMOROS

MAYOTTE (to France)

MADAGASCAR

57

KENYA
Marsabit
Meru
Kitinyaga 5200m
Mt Kenya
NAIROBI
Eldoret
Nakuru
Nyeri
Kisumu
Lake Turkana Lake Rudolf
Lokitaung
Lodwar
Moyale

Carissa
Garsen
Malindi
Mombasa
Pemba
Tanga
Zanzibar
Zanzibar
Dar es Salaam
Mafia
Mohoro
Kilwa Kivinje
Lindi
Mtwara
Newala

Kilimanjaro 5895m
Moshi
Arusha
Masai Steppe
Monogoro
Rufiji
Sao Hill
Njombe
Songea
Tunduru
Masasi
Nyamtumbo
Lukuledi

TANZANIA
DODOMA
Singida
Iringa
Great Ruaha
Mbeya
Sumbawanga
Lake Rukwa

Shinyanga
Nzega
Tabora
Nyantakara
Kasulu
Uvinza
Kigoma
Lake Tanganyika
Kipili

UGANDA
KAMPALA
Entebbe
Masindi
Gulu
Arua
Lira
Soroti
Jinja
Tororo
Mbale
Musoma
Mwanza
Bukoba
Lake Victoria
Masaka
Mbarara
Kabale

RWANDA
KIGALI
Lake Kivu
BURUNDI
BUJUMBURA
Biharamulo
Malagarasi

DEM. REP. CONGO
Congo Basin
Lualaba
Luvua
Lake Mweru
Lufira
Luapula
Lake Bangweulu

CENTRAL AFRICAN REPUBLIC
Massif des Bongo
Bongo
Bomu
Uele
Kotto
Bahr Aouk

Sudd
White Nile (Bahr el Jebel)
Malakal
Sumeih
Tonj
Rumbek
Wau
Tambura
Raga
Yambio
Bor
Amadi
Marīdi
Juba
Torit
Kapoeta
Kongor
Duk Faiwil
Elemi Triangle (administered by Kenya)
3187 m

ZAMBIA
ANGOLA
MALAWI
MOZAMBIQUE
Lake Nyasa
Rio Lúrio
Rio Ligonha

Sankuru
Kasai
Lualaba
Zambezi
Kafue

55
56
57
118

Equator
10°
40°
30°
10°

ELEVATION
4000 m 13 124 ft
2000 m 6562 ft
1000 m 3281 ft
500 m 1640 ft
250 m 820 ft
100 m 328 ft
Sea Level — Sea Level
-250 m -820 ft
-500 m -1640 ft
-1000 m -3281 ft
-2000 m -6562 ft
-3000 m -9843 ft
-4000 m -13 124 ft

WEST AFRICA

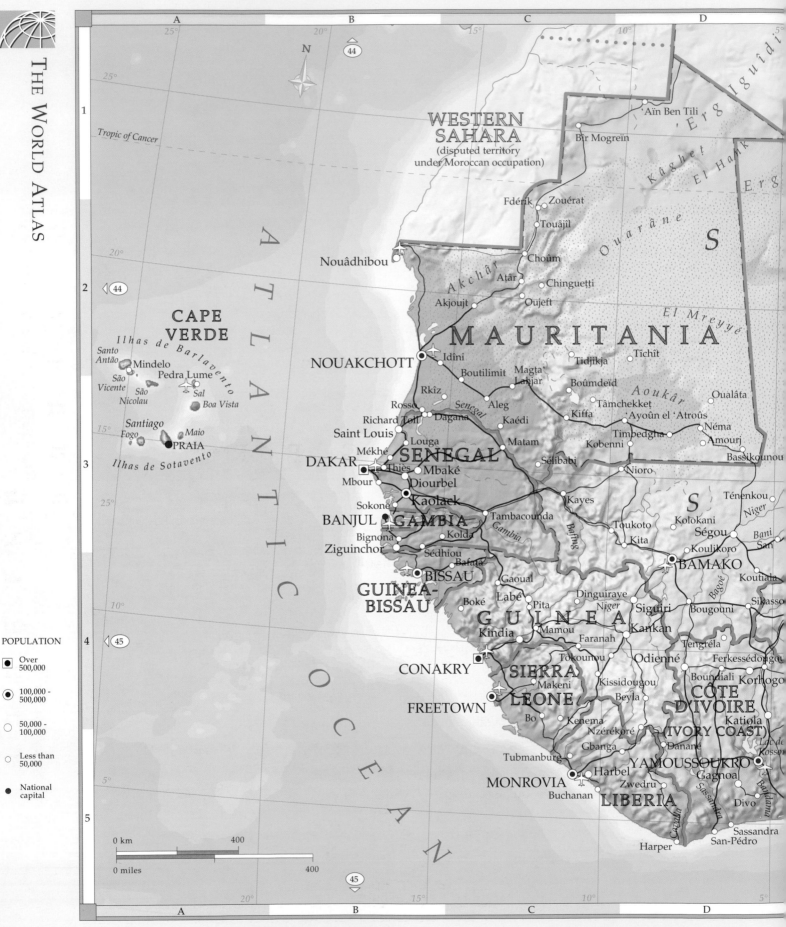

WESTERN SAHARA
(disputed territory
under Moroccan occupation)

Aïn Ben Tili

Bîr Mogreïn

Fdérik   Zouérat

Touâjîl

Choûm

CAPE VERDE

Ilhas de Barlavento

Santo Antão
Mindelo
São Vicente   Pedra Lume
São Nicolau   Sal
Boa Vista

Santiago
Fogo   Maio
●PRAIA

Ilhas de Sotavento

Nouâdhibou

Atâr   Chinguetti

Akjoujt   Oujeft

MAURITANIA

El Mreyyé

NOUAKCHOTT   Idîni

Rkîz   Boutilimit   Magta   Tidjikja   Tîchît
Lahjar   Boûmdeïd   *Aoukâr*   Oualâta
Rosso   Aleg   Tâmchekket
Richard Toll   Dagana   Kaédi   Kiffa   'Ayoûn el 'Atroûs   Néma
Saint Louis   Louga   Matam   Sélibabi   Kobenni   Timbedgha   Amourj
Mékhé   **SENEGAL**   Nioro   Bassikounou
DAKAR   Thiès   Mbaké
Mbour   Diourbel   Kayes   Ténenkou
Kaolack   Koïokani   *Niger*
Sokone   Tambacounda   Toukoto   Ségou
BANJUL   **GAMBIA**   Kolda   Kita   Koulikoro   *Bani*
Bignona   Sédhiou   *Gambia*   San
Ziguinchor   Bafatá   BAMAKO
BISSAU   Gaoual   Koutiala
GUINEA-BISSAU   Labé   Dinguiraye   Siguiri   Bougouni   Sikasso
Boké   Pita   *Niger*   Bougouni
Kindia   Mamou   Kankan   Tengréla
CONAKRY   Tokounou   Odienné   Ferkessédougou
SIERRA   Faranah   Kissidougou   Boundiali   Korhogo
Makeni   Beyla   **CÔTE**
FREETOWN   **LEONE**   Bo   Kenema   Katiola   **D'IVOIRE**
Nzérékoré   Danané   **(IVORY COAST)**
Gbanga
Tubmanburg   Gbanga   **YAMOUSSOUKRO**   Gagnoa
MONROVIA   Harbel   Zwedru   Divo
Buchanan   **LIBERIA**   San-Pédro
Harper   Sassandra

ATLANTIC

OCEAN

Tropic of Cancer

N

POPULATION

◉ Over
500,000

◉ 100,000 -
500,000

○ 50,000 -
100,000

○ Less than
50,000

● National
capital

0 km   400

0 miles   400

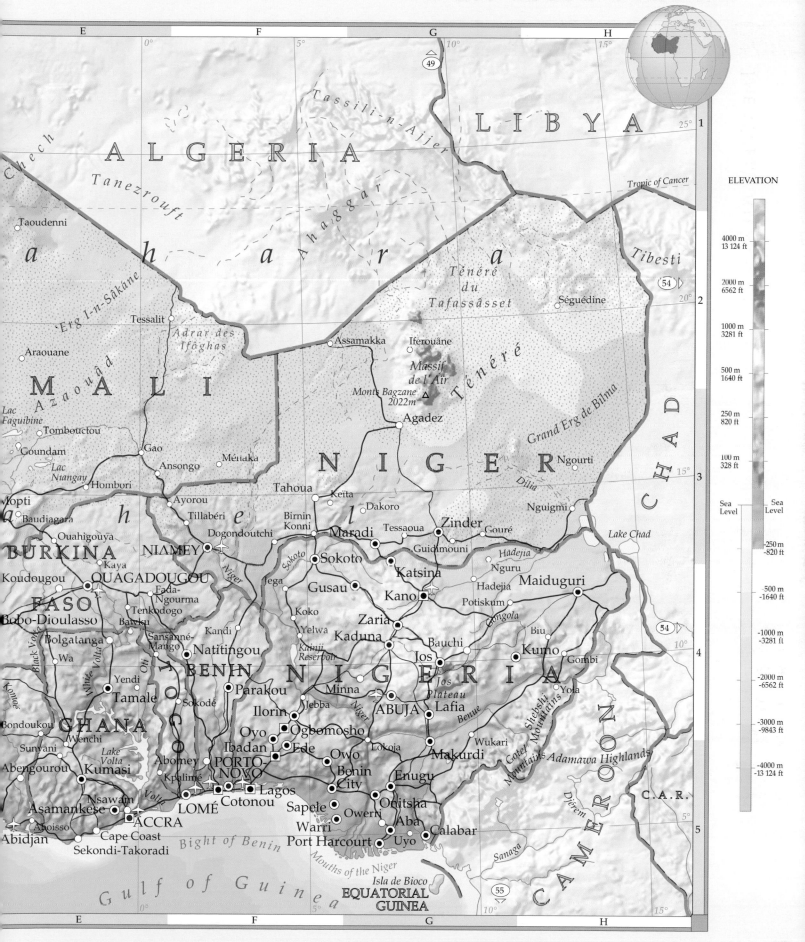

ELEVATION

4000 m	13 124 ft
2000 m	6562 ft
1000 m	3281 ft
500 m	1640 ft
250 m	820 ft
100 m	328 ft
Sea Level	Sea Level
-250 m	-820 ft
-500 m	-1640 ft
-1000 m	-3281 ft
-2000 m	-6562 ft
-3000 m	-9843 ft
-4000 m	-13 124 ft

LIBYA

ALGERIA

Tropic of Cancer

Tassili-n-Ajjer

Ahaggar

Tibesti

Taoudenni

Tanezrouft

Sahara

Ténéré du Tafassâsset

Séguédine

Erg In-Sâkâne

Tessalit

Adrar des Ifôghas

Assamakka

Iferouâne

Ténéré

Araouane

MALI

Azaouâd

Massif de l'Aïr

Monts Bagzane 2022m

Agadez

Grand Erg de Bilma

CHAD

Lac Faguibine

Tombouctou

Gao

Ansongo

Méttaka

NIGER

Ngourti

Goundam

Lac Niangay

Hombori

Ayorou

Tillabéri

Tahoua

Keïta

Dakoro

Nguigmi

Dilia

Mopti

Baudiagara

Dogondoutchi

Birnin Konni

Maradi

Tessaoua

Zinder

Gouré

Nguru

Lake Chad

Ouahigouya

NIAMEY

Hadejia

BURKINA

Kaya

Sokoto

Katsina

Hadejia

Maiduguri

Koudougou

OUAGADOUGOU

Jega

Gusau

Kano

Potiskum

FASO

Fada-Ngourma

Koko

Zaria

Gongola

Biu

Bobo-Dioulasso

Tenkodogo

Bawku

Kandi

Yelwa

Kaduna

Bauchi

Kumo

Bolgatanga

Sansanné-Mango

Kainji Reservoir

Jos

Gombi

Wa

Natitingou

Jos Plateau

Yola

BENIN

NIGERIA

Yendi

Tamale

Parakou

Minna

ABUJA

Lafia

Adamawa Highlands

Sokodé

Ilorin

Jebba

Benue

GHANA

Bondoukou

Wenchi

Oyo

Ogbomosho

Lokoja

Makurdi

Wukari

Shebshi Mountains

Sunyani

Ibadan

Ede

Owo

Gotel Mountains

Abengourou

Kumasi

Abomey

PORTO-NOVO

Benin City

Enugu

C.A.R.

Asamankese

Kpalimé

Lagos

Onitsha

Djerem

Abidjan

Aboisso

ACCRA

LOMÉ

Cotonou

Sapele

Owerri

Aba

Calabar

Cape Coast

Warri

Port Harcourt

Uyo

Sekondi-Takoradi

Bight of Benin

Mouths of the Niger

Sanaga

CAMEROON

Gulf of Guinea

Isla de Bioco

EQUATORIAL GUINEA

CENTRAL AFRICA

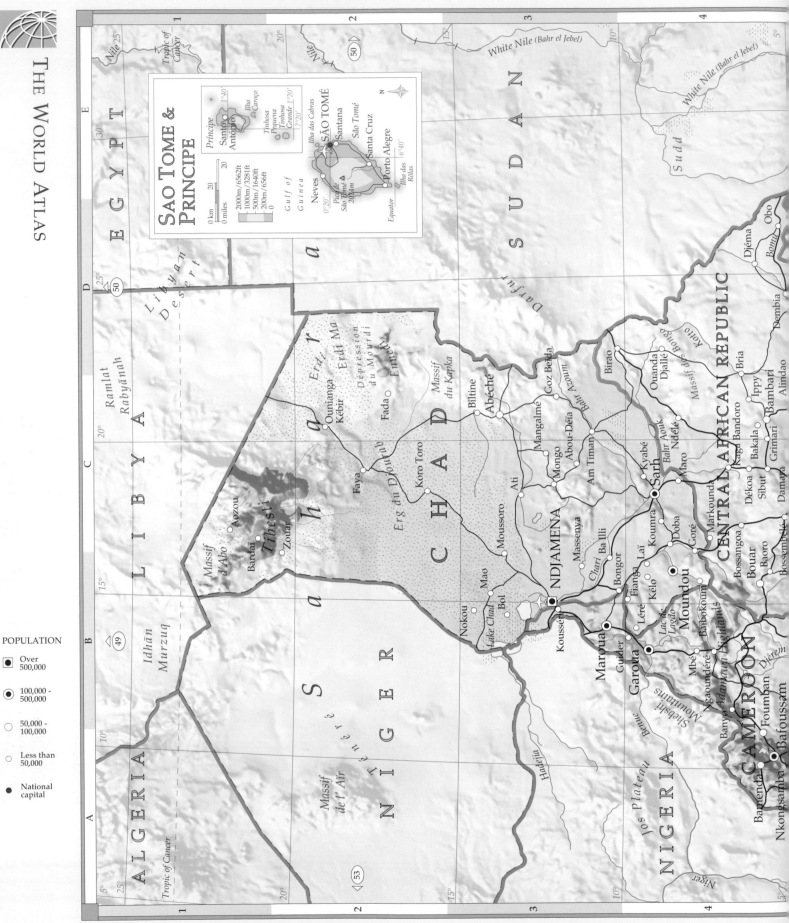

SAO TOME & PRINCIPE

Príncipe
Santo António
Ilha Caroço
Tinhosa Pequena
Tinhosa Grande
1°40'
1°20'
Ilha das Cabras
SÃO TOMÉ
Santana
Gulf of Guinea
São Tomé
Santa Cruz
7°20'
Neves
Picode São Tomé 2024m
Porto Alegre
Ilha das Rôlas
Equator
6°40'
0°20'

0 km 20
0 miles 20
2000m/6562ft
1000m/3281ft
500m/1640ft
200m/656ft

POPULATION

- ▣ Over 500,000
- ◉ 100,000 – 500,000
- ○ 50,000 – 100,000
- ○ Less than 50,000
- ● National capital

EGYPT
SUDAN
LIBYA
Libyan Desert
Ramlat Rabyānah
Idhān Murzuq
Massif d'Abo
Tibesti
Bardaï
Zouar
Aozou
Massif de l'Aïr
Ténéré
NIGER
Sahara
Erdi Ma
Erdi
Ounianga Kébir
Fada
Depression du Mourdi
Ennedi
Massif du Kapka
Faya
Koro Toro
Erg du Djourab
Ati
Moussoro
Mao
Bol
Nokou
Lake Chad
Biltine
Abéché
Mangalme
Goz Beïda
Mongo
Abou-Déïa
Am Timan
Bahr Azoum
Massenya
Chari
Ba Illi
Bongor
Fianga
Léré
Lac de Lagdo
NDJAMENA
Kousséri
Massenya
CHAD
Birao
Ouanda Djallé
Ndélé
Bahr Aouk
Kyabé
Maro
Sarh
Koumra
Doba
Goré
Moundou
Kélo
Baïbokoum
Bossangoa
Bouar
Baoro
Bossembélé
Bozoum
Bamingui
Kaga Bandoro
Bakala
Bria
Ippy
Bambari
Grimari
Damara
Dékoa
Sibut
Alindao
Dembia
Bonnyé
Obo
Djéma
Kotto
Massif des Bongo
CENTRAL AFRICAN REPUBLIC
Darfur
White Nile (Bahr el Jebel)
Sudd
Nile
Tropic of Cancer
ALGERIA
Hadejia
Jos Plateau
NIGERIA
Niger
Maroua
Guider
Garoua
Mbé
Ngaoundéré
Banyo
Foumban
Bamenda
Nkongsamba
Bafoussam
CAMEROON
Shebshi Mountains
Adamawa Highlands
Benue
Djérem
Mambéré

SOUTHERN AFRICA

THE WORLD ATLAS

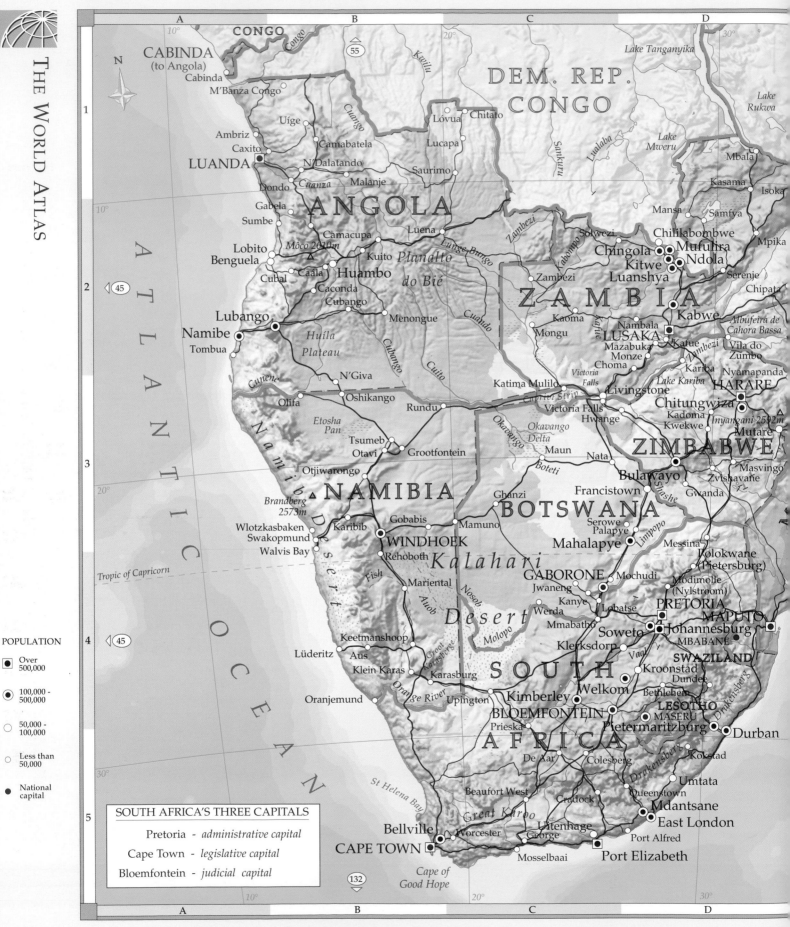

POPULATION

- ◉ Over 500,000
- ◉ 100,000 – 500,000
- ○ 50,000 – 100,000
- ○ Less than 50,000
- ● National capital

SOUTH AFRICA'S THREE CAPITALS

Pretoria - *administrative capital*

Cape Town - *legislative capital*

Bloemfontein - *judicial capital*

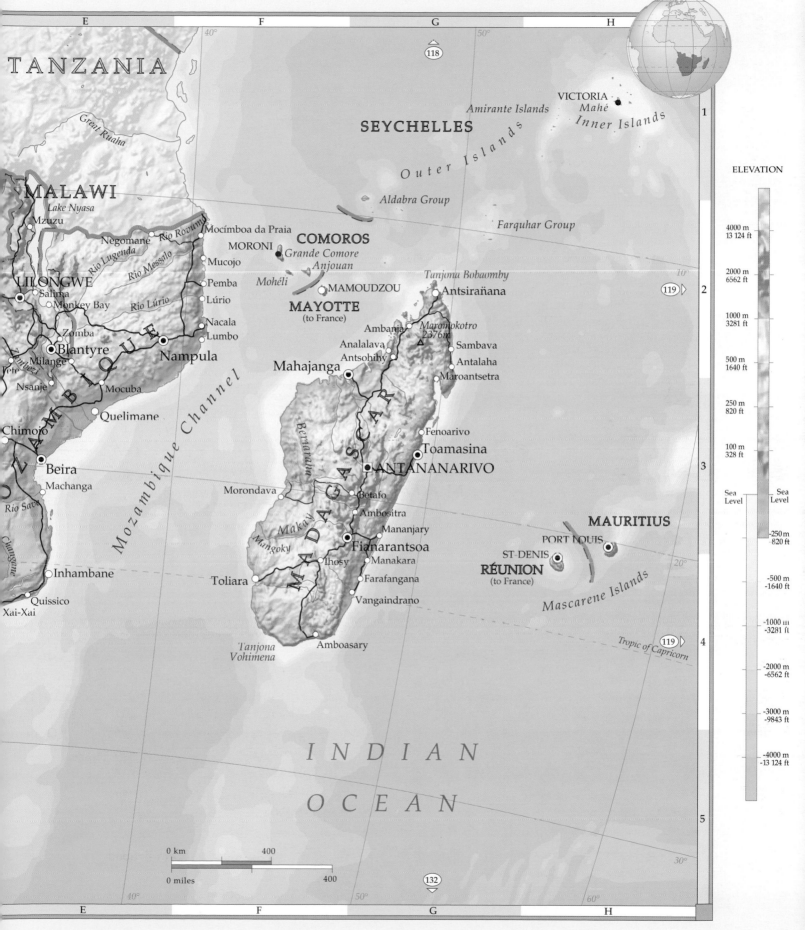

EUROPE

POLITICAL FEATURES

TOTAL AREA:
4,809,200 sq miles
(12,456,000 sq km)

TOTAL NUMBER OF COUNTRIES:
43

TOTAL POPULATION:
582.5

LARGEST CITY WITH POPULATION:
Moscow, European Russia 9 million

**COUNTRY WITH HIGHEST
POPULATION DENSITY:**
Monaco 42,104 people per sq mile
(16,256 people per sq km)

LARGEST COUNTRY:
European Russia 1,527,341 sq miles
(3,955,818 sq km)

SMALLEST COUNTRY:
Vatican City, Italy 0.17 sq miles
(0.44 sq km)

PHYSICAL FEATURES

LARGEST LAKE:
Lagoda, European Russia
7,100 sq miles (18,390 sq km)

LONGEST RIVER:
Volga, European Russia
2,290 miles (3,688 km)

HIGHEST POINT:
El'brus, Caucasus Mts, European Russia
18,510ft (5,642 m)

LOWEST POINT:
Volga Delta, Caspian Sea, European
Russia 92 ft (28m) below sea level

POPULATION

◉ Over
500,000

◉ 100,000 -
500,000

○ 50,000 -
100,000

○ Less than
50,000

● National
capital

Barents Sea

E 20°   30°   40°   F 50°   70°   60°   70°   G 70°   80°   H

North Cape

Ostrov Kolguyev

Arctic Circle

Ob'

Ural Mountains

Irtysh

1

Murmansk

Kola Peninsula

80°

FINLAND

White Sea

Archangel

RUSSIAN

Northern Dvina

Perm'

90

2

Lake Onega

FEDERATION

70°

Tampere

Lake Ladoga

Vologda

Ufa

50°

Turku   HELSINKI

Yaroslavl'

Kazan'

Åland

Uppsala

Saint Petersburg

Nizhniy Novgorod

Orenburg

STOCKHOLM   TALLINN

Ul'yanovsk

Aral Sea

Gotland

ESTONIA

MOSCOW

Samara

Ural

Syr Darya

Baltic Sea

LATVIA

European Plain

Volga Uplands

Volga

3

RĪGA

Central Russian Upland

Amu Darya

LITHUANIA

KALININGRAD (to Russ.Fed).

Kaliningrad   Kaunas   Vitsyebsk

Gdańsk

VILNIUS

MINSK

Voronezh

Ural

Bydgoszcz

Babruysk   Homyel'

WARSAW

BELARUS

Don

Brest   Pripet Marshes

Łódź

POLAND

Dnieper Lowlands

Kharkiv

Volgograd

Wisła   Bug

KIEV

Dnieper

Astrakhan'

Kraków

L'viv   Dniester

UKRAINE

Dnipropetrovs'k

Donets'k

SLOVAKIA   Carpathian Mountains

Chernivtsi

Rostov-na-Donu

40°

BUDAPEST

MOLDOVA

Stavropol'

Caspian Sea

4

HUNGARY   Cluj-Napoca

CHIŞINĂU

Sea of Azov

90

60°

Tisza

ROMANIA

Odesa

Braşov

Crimea

Caucasus

Danube

Simferopol'

El'brus 5642m

BELGRADE

BUCHAREST

SERB. & MON. (YUGO.)

Constanţa

Black Sea

BULGARIA   Varna

SOFIA   Burgas

Balkan Mountains

TURKEY

SKOPJE

MACED.

TIRANA

Anatolia

ASIA

ALBANIA

Aegean Sea

Zagros Mountains

5

Pindus Mountains

GREECE

30°

ATHENS

Piraeus

Peloponnese

Tigris

96

Sea

Irákleio

Cyprus

Euphrates

50°

20°   Crete   30°   40°   G   H

E   F

59

THE NORTH ATLANTIC

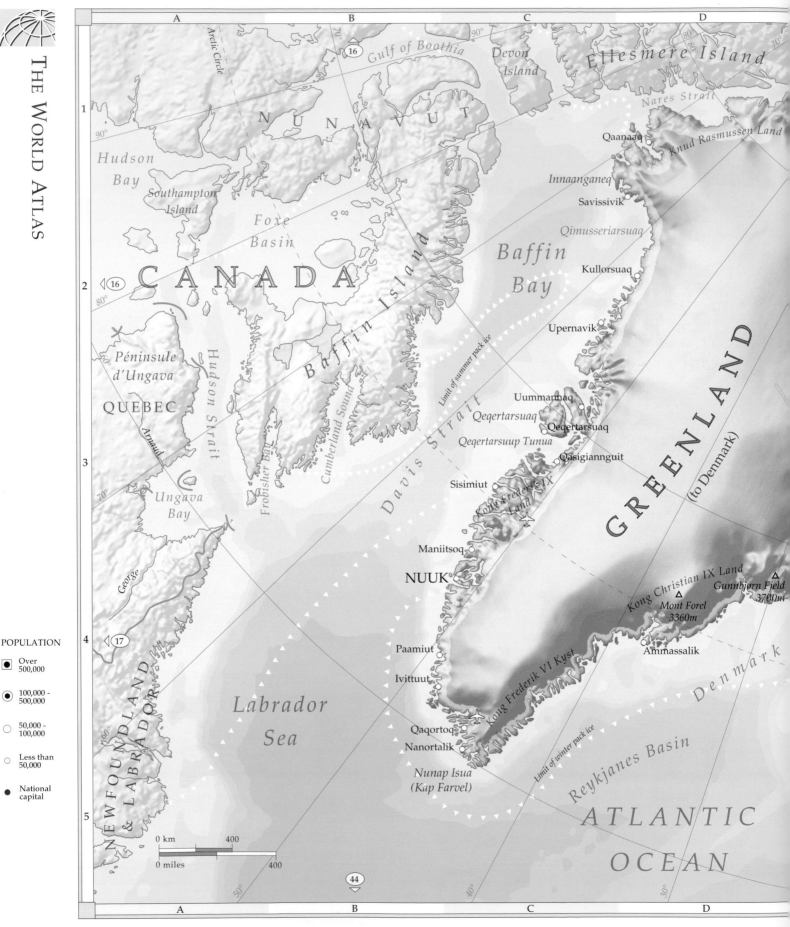

Arctic Circle

Gulf of Boothia

Devon Island

Ellesmere Island

Nares Strait

NUNAVUT

Qaanaaq

Knud Rasmussen Land

Hudson Bay

Innaanganeq

Southampton Island

Savissivik

Foxe Basin

Qimusseriarsuaq

CANADA

Baffin Bay

Kullorsuaq

Baffin Island

Upernavik

Péninsule d'Ungava

Limit of summer pack ice

Uummannaq

Hudson Strait

QUEBEC

Qeqertarsuaq

Qeqertarsuaq

Arnaud

Qeqertarsuup Tunua

GREENLAND (to Denmark)

Qasigiannguit

Cumberland Sound

Sisimiut

Kong Frederik IX Land

Ungava Bay

Davis Strait

Frobisher Bay

Kong Christian IX Land

Gunnbjørn Field 3700m

Maniitsoq

Mont Forel 3360m

George

NUUK

Ammassalik

Denmark

Paamiut

Ivittuut

Labrador Sea

Kong Frederik VI Kyst

NEWFOUNDLAND & LABRADOR

Qaqortoq

Nanortalik

Reykjanes Basin

Limit of winter pack ice

Nunap Isua (Kap Farvel)

ATLANTIC OCEAN

POPULATION

- ◉ Over 500,000
- ◉ 100,000 - 500,000
- ○ 50,000 - 100,000
- ○ Less than 50,000
- ● National capital

0 km 400

0 miles 400

ARCTIC

OCEAN

*Lincoln
Sea*

Kap Morris Jesup

*Zemlya
Frantsa-Iosifa*

*Wandel
Sea*

Kvitøya

*Novaya
Zemlya*

SVALBARD
(to Norway)

Nordaustlandet

Independence Fjord

Nord

Kong Karls Land

Spitsbergen

Barentsøya

*Barents
Sea*

LONGYEARBYEN

Edgeøya

Barentsberg

Storfjorden

*Greenland
Sea*

Limit of winter pack ice

Kong Frederik VIII Land

*Bjørnøya
(to Norway)*

*Nordkapp
(North Cape)*

Limit of summer pack ice

*Kong Christian X
Land*

△ *Petermann Bjerg
2940m*

Daneborg

FINLAND

Mohns Ridge

Kong Oscar Fjord

Kangertittivaq

Ittoqqortoormiit

JAN MAYEN
(to Norway)

Arctic Circle

Kangikajik

Vestfjorden

*Norwegian
Sea*

Strait

Norwegian Basin

S
W
E
D
E
N

*Gulf
of
Bothnia*

ICELAND

Bolungarvík

Siglufjördhur

Raufarhöfn

Ísafjördhur

Húsavík

Akureyri

Seydhisfjördhur

Stykkishólmur

Neskaupstadhur

Faxaflói

REYKJAVÍK

Vatnajökull

Selfoss

Djúpivogur

Thorlákshöfn

*Hvannadalshnúkur
2119m*

Surtsey

Vestmannaeyjar

N

FAEROE ISLANDS
(to Denmark)

TÓRSHAVN

N
O
R
W
A
Y

*Shetland
Islands*

133
88 ▷
62 ▷
63 ▽

ELEVATION

4000 m 13 124 ft	
2000 m 6562 ft	
1000 m 3281 ft	
500 m 1640 ft	
250 m 820 ft	
100 m 328 ft	
Sea Level	Sea Level
-250 m -820 ft	
-500 m -1640 ft	
-1000 m -3281 ft	
-2000 m -6562 ft	
-3000 m -9843 ft	
-4000 m -13 124 ft	

SCANDINAVIA & FINLAND

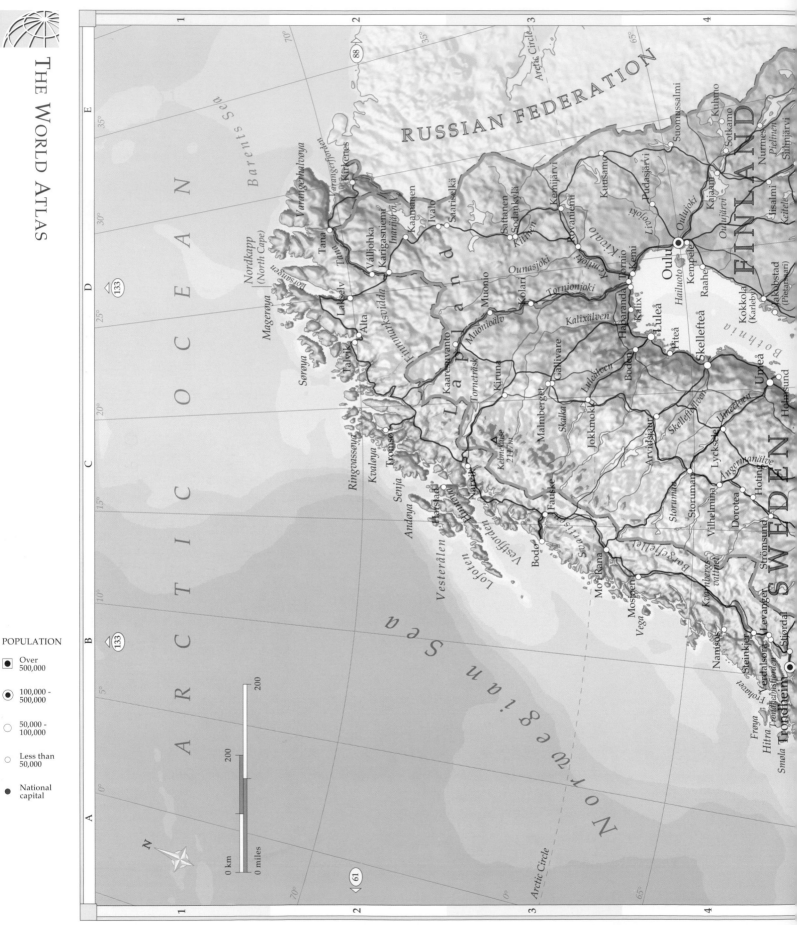

POPULATION

- ● Over 500,000
- ◉ 100,000 - 500,000
- ○ 50,000 - 100,000
- ○ Less than 50,000
- ● National capital

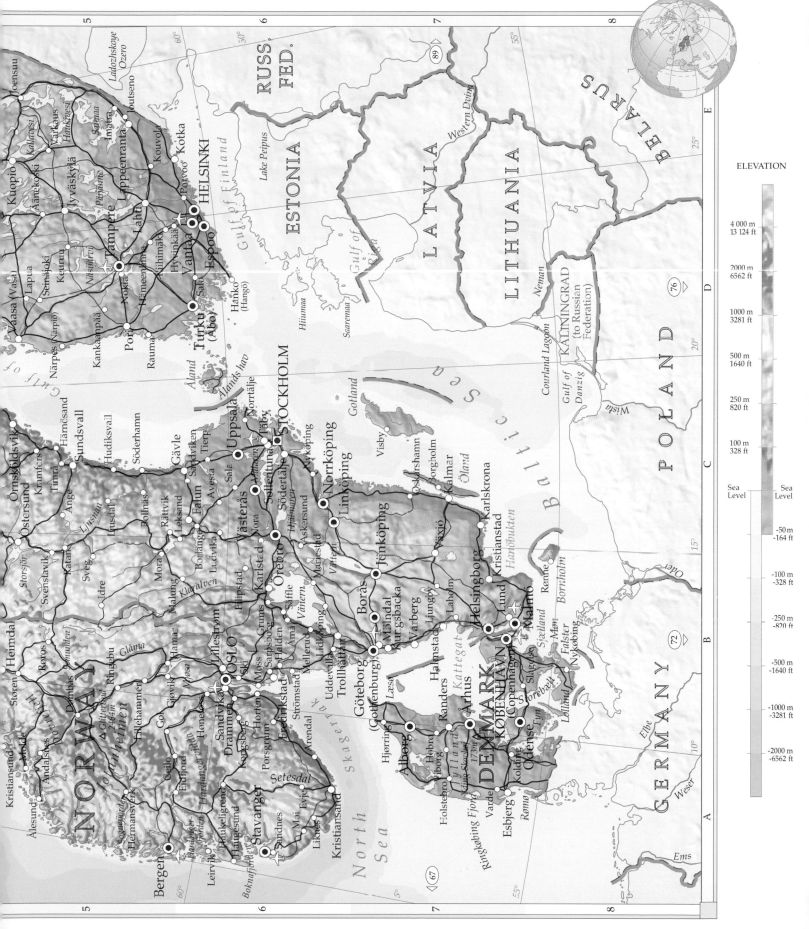

THE LOW COUNTRIES

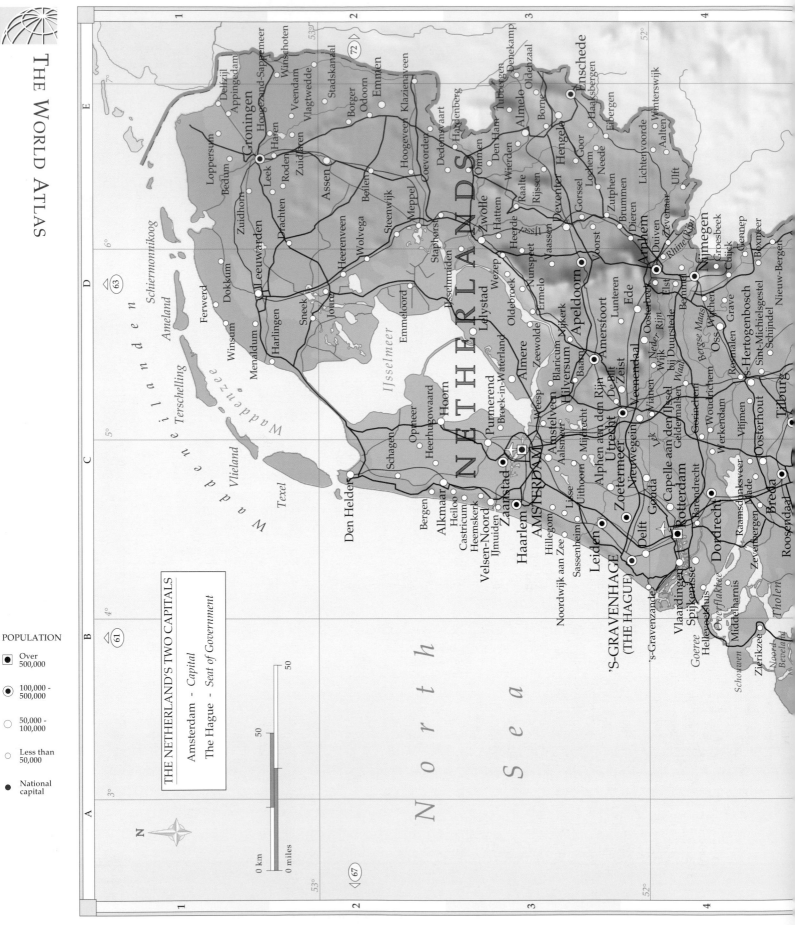

THE NETHERLAND'S TWO CAPITALS

Amsterdam - *Capital*

The Hague - *Seat of Government*

POPULATION

- Over 500,000
- 100,000 - 500,000
- 50,000 - 100,000
- Less than 50,000
- National capital

N

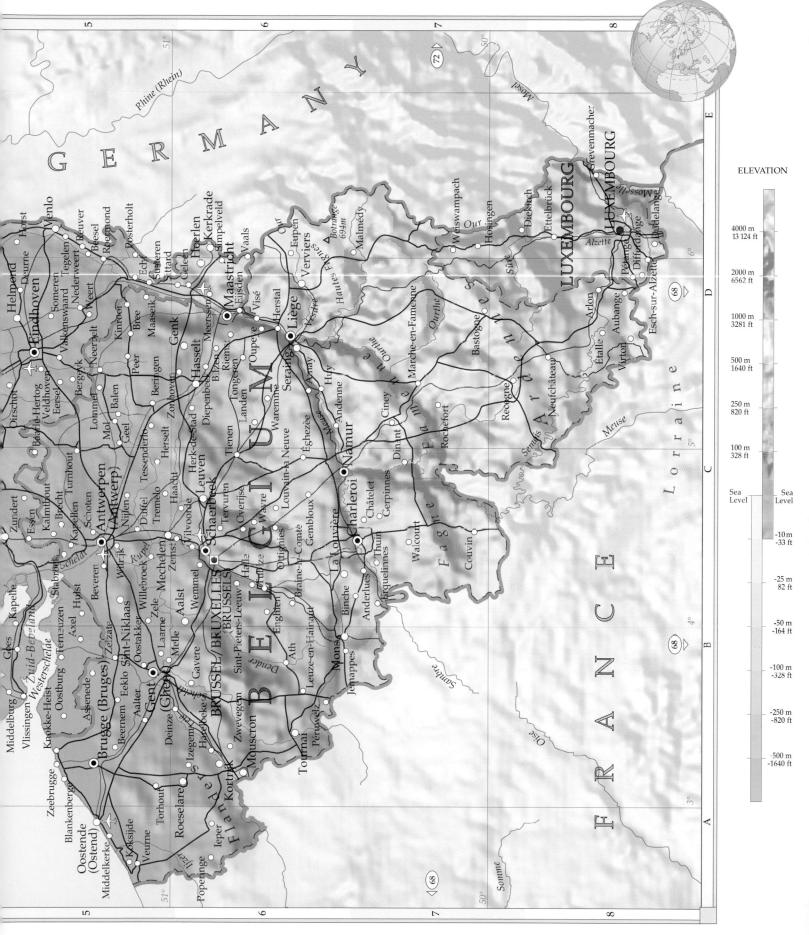

THE WORLD ATLAS

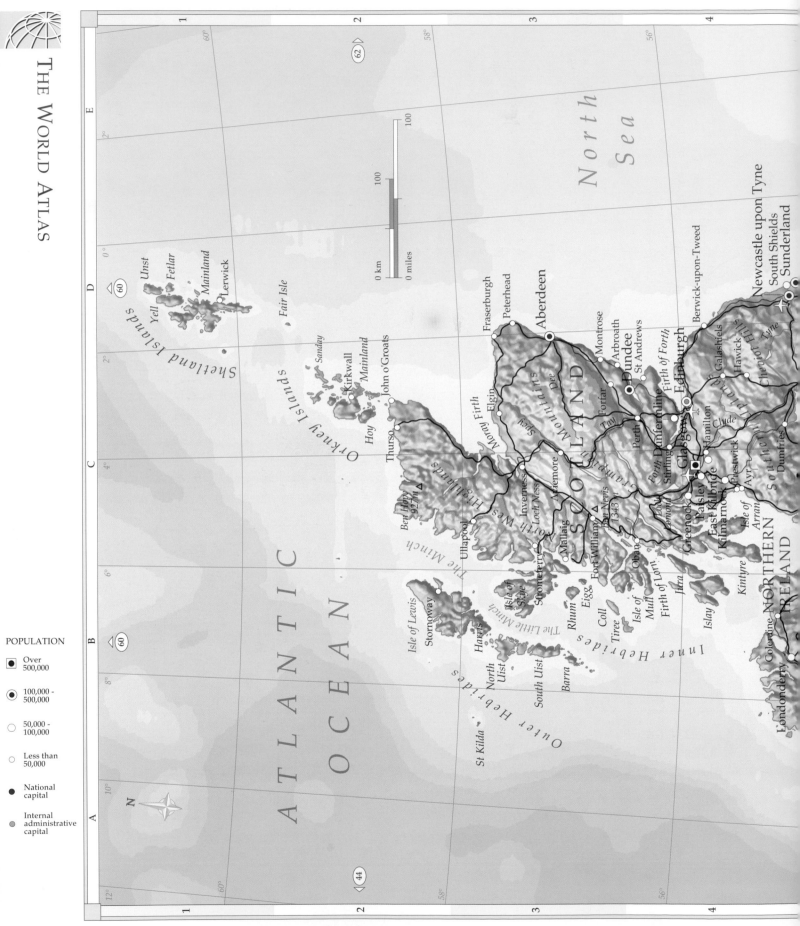

POPULATION

- Over 500,000
- 100,000 – 500,000
- 50,000 – 100,000
- Less than 50,000
- National capital
- Internal administrative capital

North Sea

ATLANTIC OCEAN

Shetland Islands

Unst
Fetlar
Mainland
Yell
Lerwick

Fair Isle

Orkney Islands

Sanday
Kirkwall
Mainland
Hoy

John o'Groats
Thurso

Ben Hope 927 m

Moray Firth
Elgin
Spey
Dee

Fraserburgh
Peterhead
Aberdeen

Montrose
Arbroath
Forfar
Dundee
St Andrews

Firth of Forth
Edinburgh

Berwick-upon-Tweed

Galashiels
Hawick
Cheviot Hills

Newcastle upon Tyne
South Shields
Sunderland

Tyne

Inverness
Loch Ness
Aviemore

Grampian Mountains
SCOTLAND

Tay
Perth

Forth
Stirling
Dumfermline
Glasgow
Hamilton
Clyde

Ullapool

Highlands
North West

Mallaig
Fort William
Ben Nevis 1343 m

Loch Lomond

Paisley
Greenock
East Kilbride
Prestwick
Ayr
Kilmarnock

Southern Uplands
Dumfries

The Minch

Stromeferry

Isle of Skye
Rhum
Eigg
Coll
Tiree

Oban
Firth of Lorn

Isle of Mull

Jura
Islay

Isle of Arran
Kintyre

Stornoway
Isle of Lewis

Harris

The Little Minch

North Uist
South Uist
Barra

Outer Hebrides

Inner Hebrides

St Kilda

NORTHERN IRELAND
Coleraine
Londonderry

60
62

60

60

44

N

THE WORLD ATLAS

66

ELEVATION

4 000 m 13 124 ft	
2000 m 6562 ft	
1000 m 3281 ft	
500 m 1640 ft	
250 m 820 ft	
100 m 328 ft	
Sea Level	Sea Level
-50 m -164 ft	
-100 m -328 ft	
-250 m -820 ft	
-500 m -1640 ft	
-1000 m -3281 ft	
-2000 m -6562 ft	

FRANCE

Seine

English Channel

Channel Tunnel

CHANNEL ISLANDS (to UK)
Guernsey ST PETER PORT
Alderney
Sark
Jersey ST HELIER

UNITED KINGDOM

ENGLAND

WALES

REPUBLIC OF IRELAND

ISLE OF MAN (to UK)
DOUGLAS

Irish Sea

Celtic Sea

St George's Channel

LONDON
(London inset map)
M1, M11, M20, M25, M26, M40, M4, M3, M2, M23, A1, A10, A12, A13, A40, A41, A3
Enfield, Barnet, Finchley, Hampstead, Edgware, Wembley, Heathrow, Watford, Wimbledon, Richmond, Kingston upon Thames, Epsom, Croydon, Orpington, Bromley, Bexley, Dartford, Dagenham, Walthamstow, Greenwich, City, St Paul's Cathedral, Trafalgar Square, Houses of Parliament, Buckingham Palace
Thames
Places of interest
Regions/suburbs
0 km
0 miles

67

FRANCE, ANDORRA & MONACO

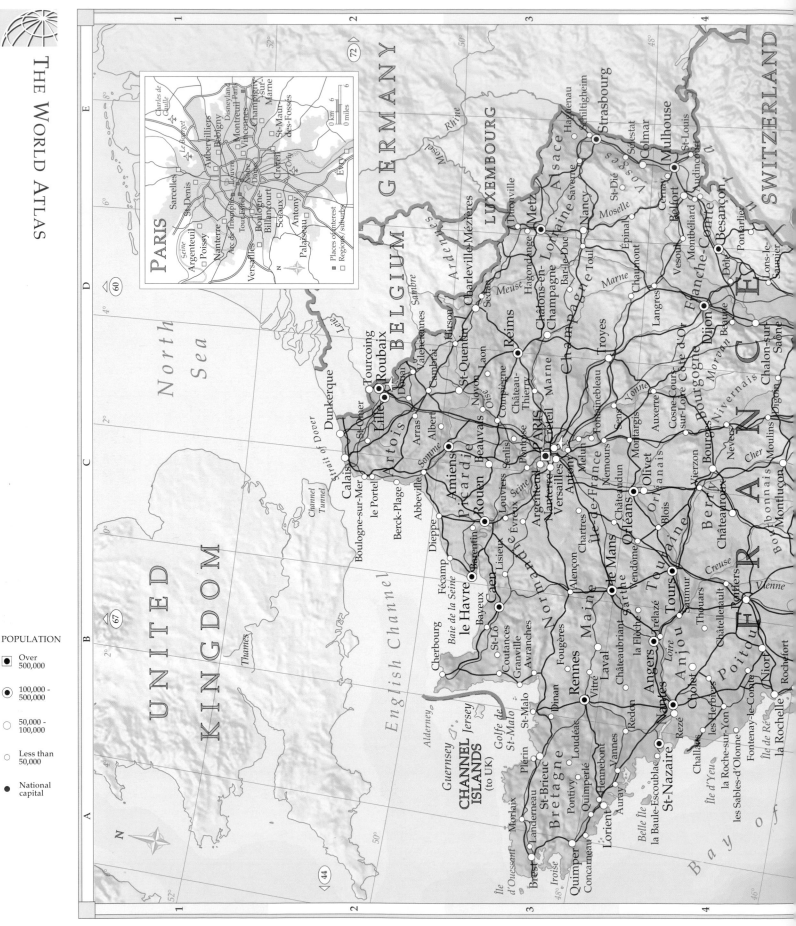

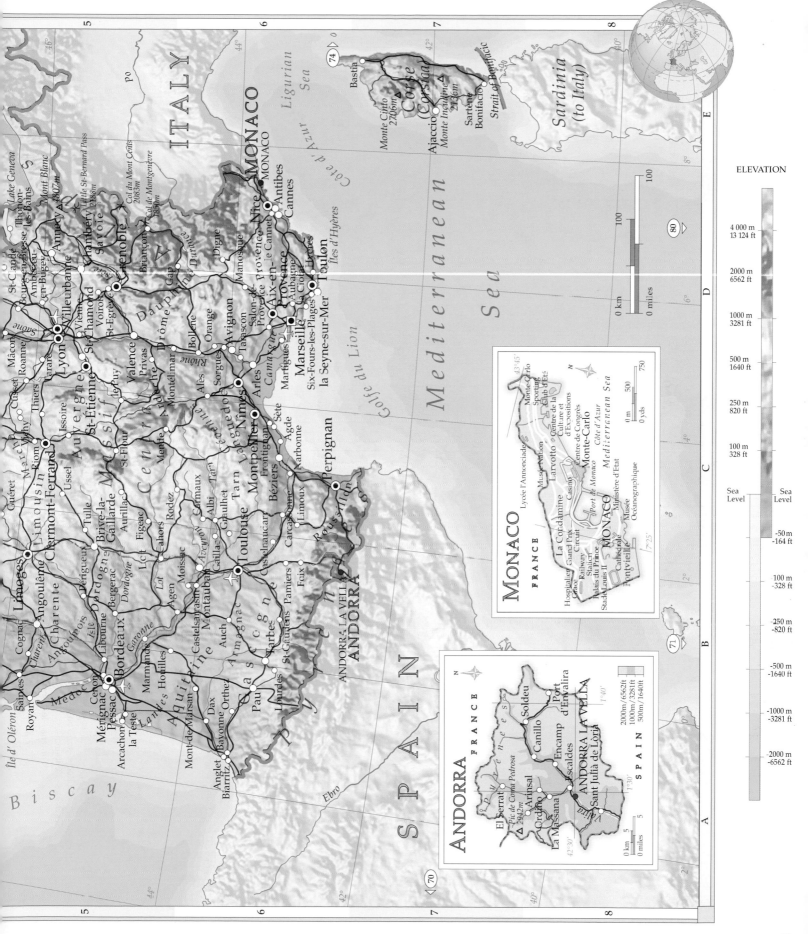

ITALY

MONACO

Ligurian Sea

Bastia

Corse (Corsica)

Monte Cinto 2706m △
Monte Incudine 2136m △

Ajaccio
Sartène
Bonifacio

Strait of Bonifacio

Sardinia (to Italy)

74

42°

40°

Lake Geneva
Thonon-les-Bains
St-Claude
Oyonnax
Bourg-en-Bresse
Bellegarde
Ambérieu
Lyon-Bugey
Mont Blanc 4807m △
Annecy
Col du Petit St-Bernard Pass
Chambéry
Savoie
Col du Mont Cenis 2083m
Briançon
Col de Montgenèvre 1850m

MONACO

Monaco

Nice
Antibes
Cannes

Côte d'Azur

Villeurbanne
Vienne
St-Chamond
Voiron
St-Égrève
Grenoble

Dauphiné

Digne

Provence

Aix-en-Provence
Le Cannet
Aubagne
La Ciotat
Toulon

Îles d'Hyères

Lyon
Tarare
Mâcon
Roanne
Cusset
Vichy
Thiers

Auvergne

St-Étienne
Le Puy
Privas
Valence
Montélimar
Drôme
Ardèche

Provence

Salon-de-Provence
Tarascon
Avignon
Orange
Bollène
Sorgues
Marseille
Martigues
Six-Fours-les-Plages
la Seyne-sur-Mer

Mediterranean Sea

Arles
Sète
Agde

Issoire
Riom
Clermont-Ferrand
Ussel
St-Flour
Mende

Central

Alès
Nîmes

Montpellier
Frontignan
Béziers
Narbonne

Golfe du Lion

Guéret
Marche
Tulle
Brive-la-Gaillarde
Aurillac
Rodez

Massif

Limousin

Figeac
Cahors
Albi
Carmaux
Gaillac

Tarn

Languedoc

Carcassonne
Limoux

Perpignan

Limoges
Périgueux
Bergerac
Dordogne
Montauban
Castelsarrasin
Moissac
Agen
Villeneuve

Aveyron

Gascogne

Castelnaudary
Pamiers
Foix

ANDORRA LA VELLA
ANDORRA

Angoulême
Charente
Libourne
Bordeaux
Pessac
Mérignac
Arcachon
la Teste

Aquitaine

Marmande
Auch
Montauban
Toulouse
Muret
St-Gaudens

Lourdes
Pau
Tarbes

Pyrénées

SPAIN

Cognac
Saintes
Royan

Île d'Oléron

Médoc
Cérons

Landes

Mont-de-Marsan
Dax
Orthez

Anglet
Bayonne
Biarritz

Ebro

B i s c a y

ELEVATION

4 000 m	13 124 ft
2000 m	6562 ft
1000 m	3281 ft
500 m	1640 ft
250 m	820 ft
100 m	328 ft
Sea Level	Sea Level
-50 m	-164 ft
100 m	-328 ft
250 m	-820 ft
500 m	-1640 ft
1000 m	-3281 ft
2000 m	-6562 ft

MONACO

FRANCE

Monte-Carlo
Sporting Club d'Été
Musée National
Larvotto
Centre de la Culture et d'Expositions
Casino
Monte-Carlo
Côte d'Azur
La Condamine
Grand Prix Circuit
Port de Monaco
Ministère d'Etat
MONACO
Hospitaller
Grace Railway
Stade Louis II
Palais du Prince
Cathédrale
Fontvieille
Musée Océanographique

Mediterranean Sea

ANDORRA

FRANCE

Soldeu
Port d'Envalira
El Serrat
Canillo
Pic de Coma Pedrosa 2942m △
Ordino
Arinsal
Encamp
La Massana
Escaldes
ANDORRA LA VELLA
Sant Julià de Lòria

Pyrénées

SPAIN

2000m / 6562ft
1000m / 3281ft
500m / 1640ft

SPAIN & PORTUGAL

THE WORLD ATLAS

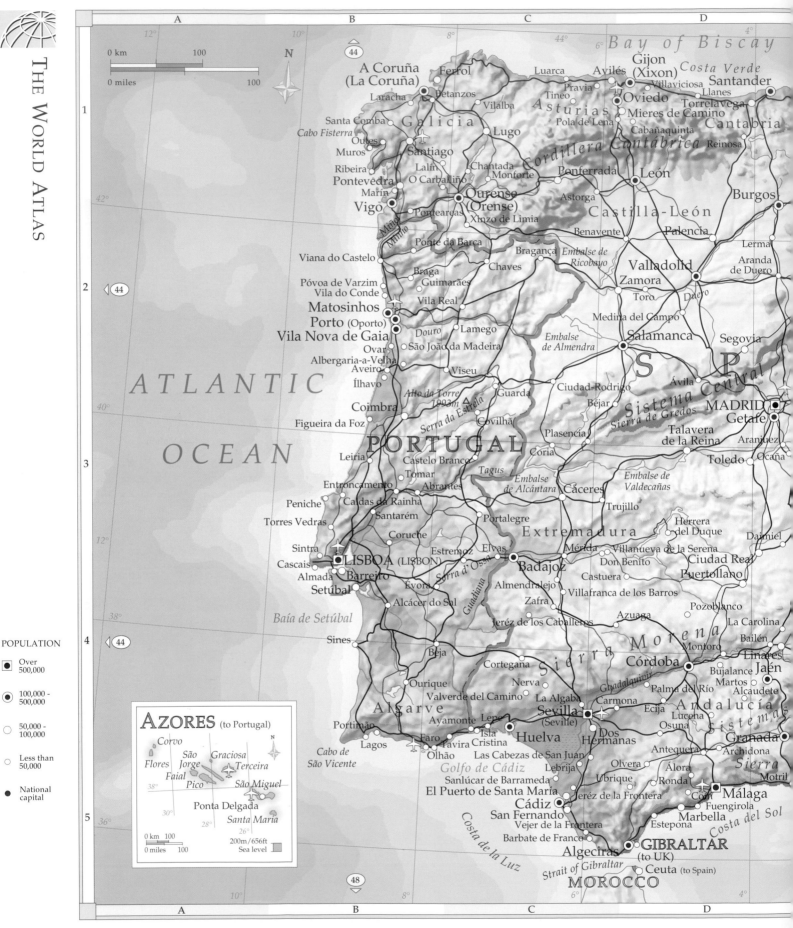

POPULATION

- ● Over 500,000
- ◉ 100,000 – 500,000
- ○ 50,000 – 100,000
- ○ Less than 50,000
- ● National capital

AZORES (to Portugal)

Corvo
Flores
São Jorge Graciosa
Faial   Terceira
Pico   São Miguel
Ponta Delgada
Santa Maria

0 km 100
0 miles 100
200m/656ft
Sea level

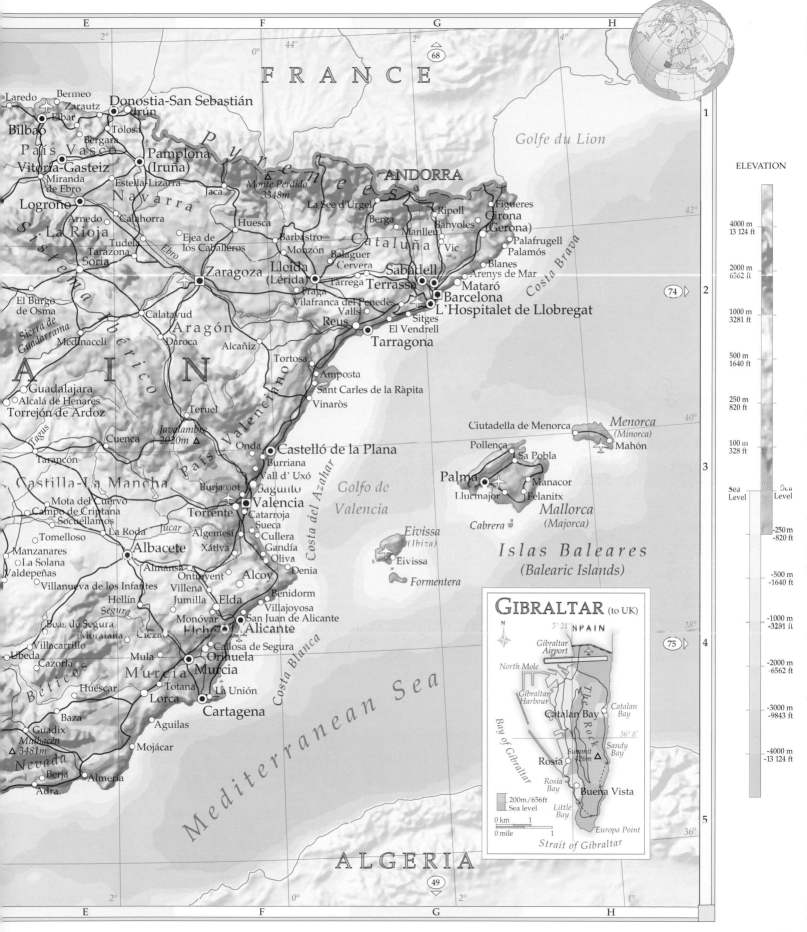

E   F   G   H

FRANCE

Laredo Bermeo
Zarautz Donostia-San Sebastián
Bilbao Eibar Irún
País Vasco Bergara Tolosa
Vitoria-Gasteiz Pamplona
Miranda (Iruña)
de Ebro Estella-Lizarra
Logroño Navarra Jaca
Arnedo Calahorra
La Rioja Tudela
Tarazona Huesca
Soria Barbastro
El Burgo Monzón
de Osma Ejea de
los Caballeros
Zaragoza Lleida
(Lérida)
Calatayud Fraga
Aragón Tàrrega
Daroca
Sierra de Alcañiz
Guadarrama
Medinaceli Teruel
Guadalajara
Alcalá de Henares
Torrejón de Ardoz Cuenca
Tarancón
Castilla-La Mancha
Mota del Cuervo
Campo de Criptana La Roda
Socuéllamos
Tomelloso
Manzanares Albacete
La Solana
Valdepeñas Almansa
Villanueva de los Infantes Villena
Hellín Jumilla Elda
Monóvar
Elche Alicante
Cieza
San Juan de Alicante
Villacarrillo Callosa de Segura
Úbeda Mula
Cazorla Murcia Orihuela
Murcia
Huéscar Totana
Lorca La Unión
Baza Cartagena
Guadix Aguilas
Mulhacén
△3481m Mojácar
Nevada Berja
Adra Almería

Pyrenees
Monte Perdido
3348m
La Seo d'Urgel
Berga Ripoll
Manlleu Banyoles
Cataluña Vic
Balaguer
Cervera Sabadell
Tàrrega Terrassa
Vilafranca del Penedès Barcelona
Valls L'Hospitalet de Llobregat
Reus Sitges
El Vendrell
Tarragona
Tortosa
Amposta
Sant Carles de la Ràpita
Vinaròs

ANDORRA
Figueres
Girona
(Gerona)
Palafrugell
Palamós
Blanes
Arenys de Mar
Costa Brava

Golfe du Lion

País Valenciano
Javalambre
2020m △
Onda
Castelló de la Plana
Burriana
Vall d' Uxó
Sagunto
Burjassot
Valencia
Torrente Catarroja
Sueca
Algemesí Cullera
Xàtiva Gandía
Oliva
Ontinyent Denia
Alcoy
Benidorm
Villajoyosa

Golfo do
Valencia

Costa del Azahar

Ciutadella de Menorca
Menorca
(Minorca)
Mahón

Pollença
Sa Pobla
Palma Manacor
Llucmajor Felanitx
Mallorca
(Majorca)
Cabrera

Islas Baleares
(Balearic Islands)

Eivissa
(Ibiza)
Eivissa
Formentera

Costa Blanca

Mediterranean Sea

ALGERIA

ELEVATION

4000 m
13 124 ft

2000 m
6562 ft

1000 m
3281 ft

500 m
1640 ft

250 m
820 ft

100 m
328 ft

Sea
Level

Sea
Level

-250 m
-820 ft

-500 m
-1640 ft

-1000 m
-3281 ft

-2000 m
-6562 ft

-3000 m
-9843 ft

-4000 m
-13 124 ft

GIBRALTAR (to UK)

SPAIN
Gibraltar
Airport
North Mole
Gibraltar
Harbour
Catalan Bay
Catalan
Bay
The Rock
Rosia
Summit
426m △
Sandy
Bay
Rosia
Bay Buena Vista
Little
Bay
Europa Point
Strait of Gibraltar
Bay of Gibraltar

200m/656ft
Sea level
0 km   1
0 mile   1

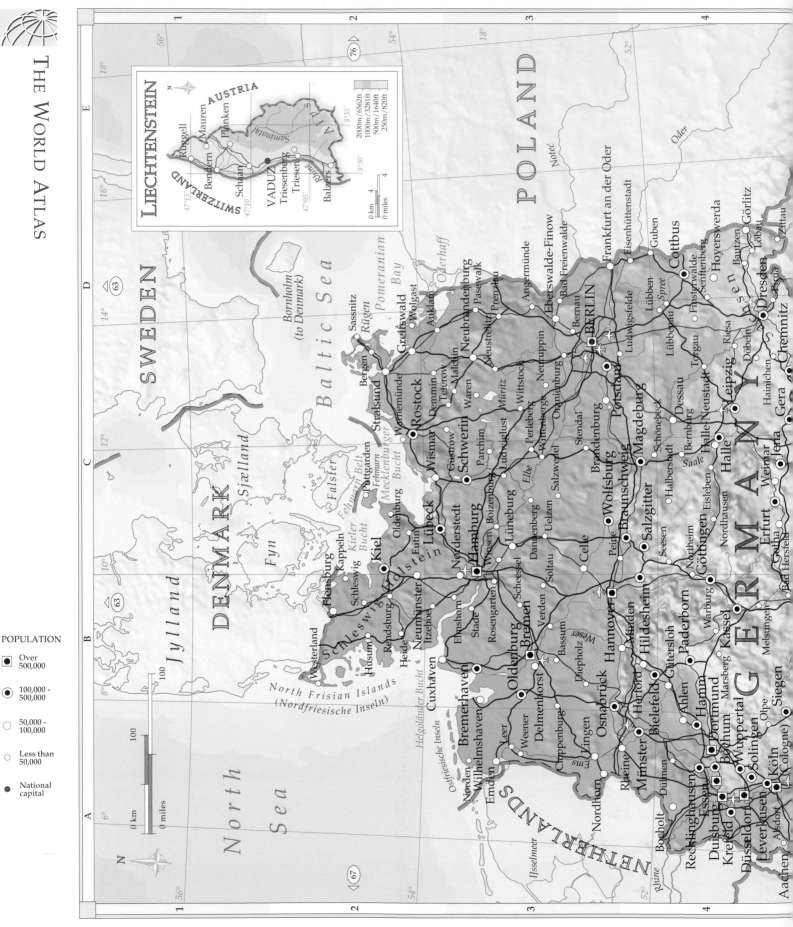

LIECHTENSTEIN

AUSTRIA

SWITZERLAND

Ruggell
Mauren
Planken
Schellenberg
Gamprin
Bendern
Eschen
Schaan
VADUZ
Triesenberg
Triesen
Balzers
Rhine
Saminatal

2000m/6562ft
1000m/3281ft
500m/1640ft
250m/820ft

SWEDEN

DENMARK

Jylland
Sjælland
Fyn
Falster

North Sea

Baltic Sea

Bornholm (to Denmark)

POLAND

NETHERLANDS

GERMANY

POPULATION

● Over 500,000

◉ 100,000 - 500,000

○ 50,000 - 100,000

○ Less than 50,000

● National capital

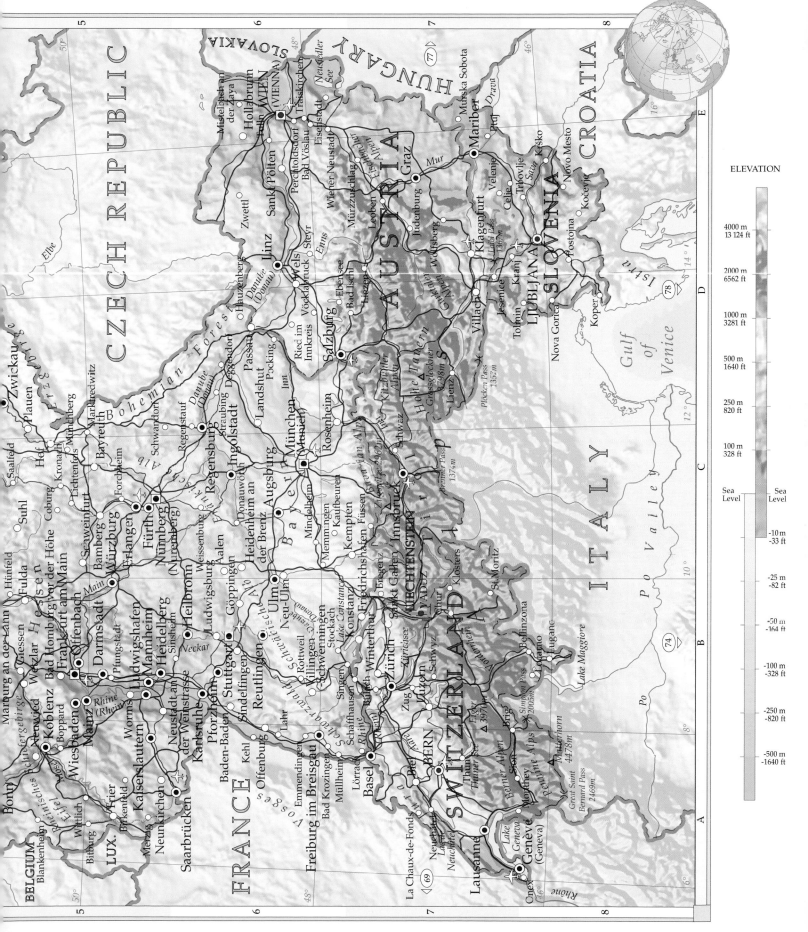

ELEVATION

4000 m
13 124 ft

2000 m
6562 ft

1000 m
3281 ft

500 m
1640 ft

250 m
820 ft

100 m
328 ft

Sea Level   Sea Level

-10 m
-33 ft

-25 m
-82 ft

-50 m
-164 ft

-100 m
-328 ft

-250 m
-820 ft

-500 m
-1640 ft

ITALY

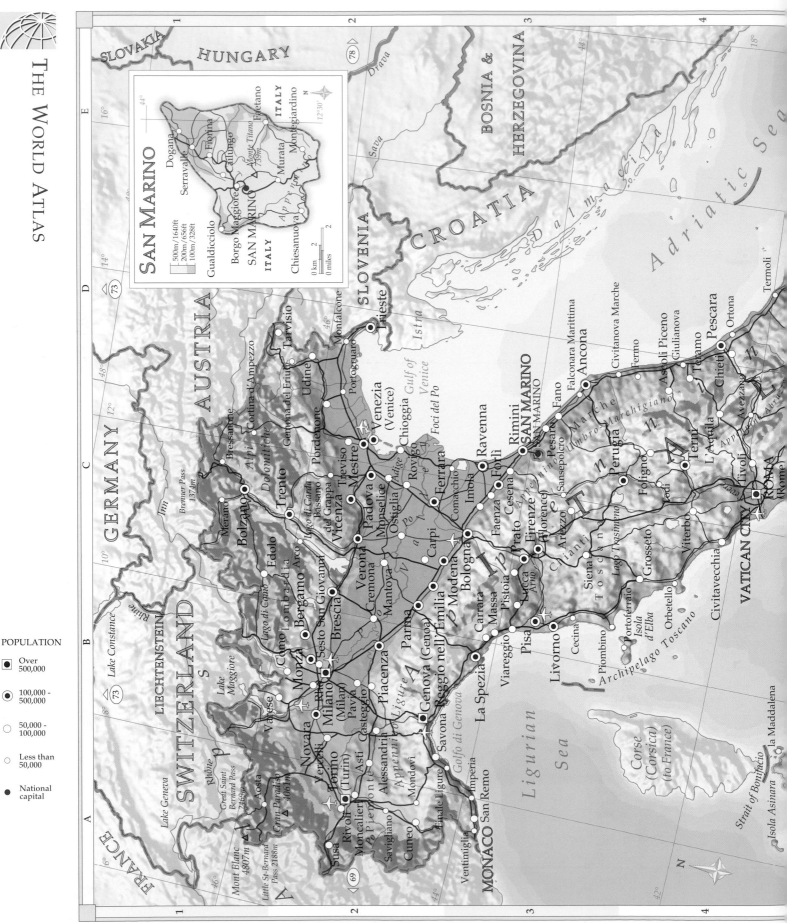

SAN MARINO

Dogana
Serravalle
Fiorina
Gualdicciolo
Borgo Maggiore
Faetano
Montegiardino
Monte Titano 739m
Murata
SAN MARINO
Chiesanuova

ITALY

500m/1640ft
200m/656ft
100m/328ft

0 km   2
0 miles   2

POPULATION

- Over 500,000
- 100,000 – 500,000
- 50,000 – 100,000
- Less than 50,000
- National capital

SLOVAKIA   HUNGARY   Drava

BOSNIA & HERZEGOVINA

CROATIA   Dalmacija   Adriatic Sea

Sava

SLOVENIA

GERMANY   AUSTRIA

SWITZERLAND

FRANCE

Trieste   Istra

Monfalcone

Tarvisio

Udine   Gulf of Venice

Cortina d'Ampezzo
Gemona del Friuli
Portogruaro
Pordenone

Bressanone
Alpi   Dolomitiche

Merano   Trento
Bolzano

Treviso   Venezia (Venice)
Mestre   Chioggia   Foci del Po
Vicenza   Padova   Monselice   Rovigo
Verona   Ostiglia   Adige
Brescia   Mantova   Carpi
Cremona   Modena
Parma   Reggio nell'Emilia
Bergamo   San Giovanni
Monza   Sesto   Como
Milano (Milan)   Lombardia
Pavia   Piacenza
Casteggio   Alessandria

Ferrara   Comacchio
Bologna   Imola
Faenza   Forlì   Ravenna
Cesena   Rimini   SAN MARINO
Firenze (Florence)   Fano   Pesare
Prato   Sansepolcro
Pistoia   Arezzo
Lucca   Chianti
Carrara   Massa
Viareggio   Pisa
Livorno   Cecina

Lago di Garda
Arco   Bassano del Grappa
Lago di Como
Lago Maggiore

Torino (Turin)   Asti
Rivoli   Moncalieri   Piemonte
Savigliano   Cuneo
Mondovì
Finale Ligure   Imperia
Ventimiglia   San Remo
MONACO   San Remo

Genova (Genoa)
Savona   Golfo di Genova
La Spezia

Ligurian Sea

Corse (Corsica) (to France)
Archipelago Toscano
Isola d'Elba   Portoferraio
Piombino   Orbetello
Grosseto   Civitavecchia
Siena   Toscana
Perugia   Foligno
Terni   L'Aquila
Ancona   Civitanova Marche
Falconara Marittima
Pesaro   Marche
Ascoli Piceno   Giulianova
Teramo   Pescara   Ortona
Chieti   Avezzano
Tivoli   ROMA (Rome)
VATICAN CITY
Termoli

Lake Geneva   Rhône
Mont Blanc 4807m
Great Saint Bernard Pass 2469m
Little St-Bernard Pass 2188m
Gran Paradiso 4061m
Aosta   Susa
Lake Constance
Inn   Brenner Pass 1374m
Rhine

Novara   Vercelli
Edolo

73   73   69   78

74

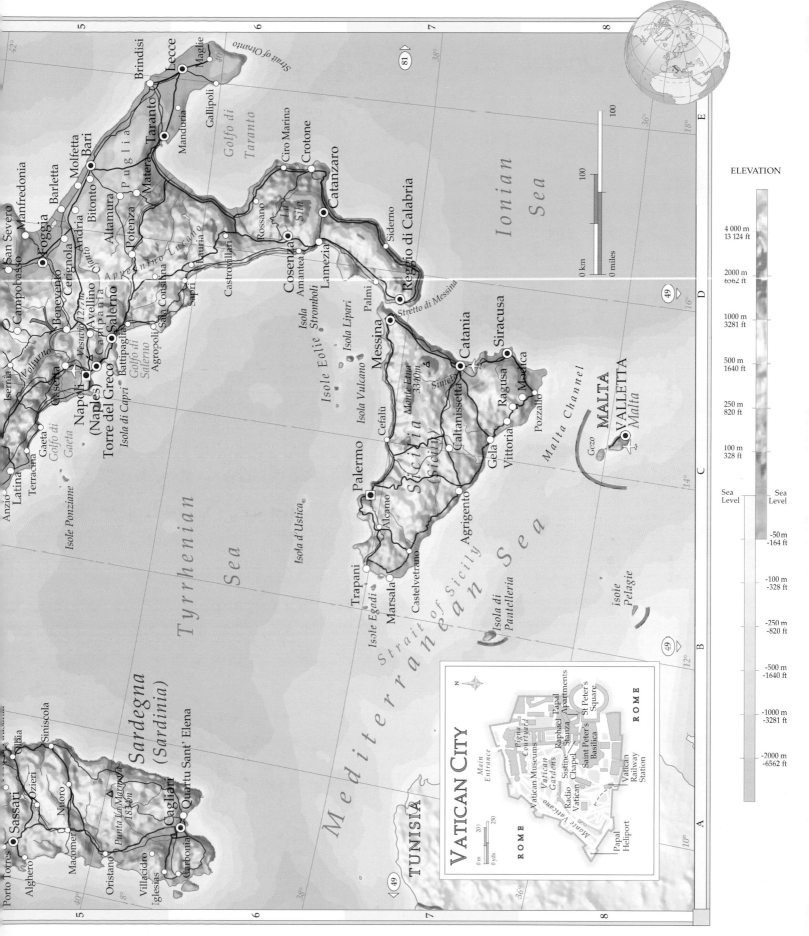

ELEVATION

4 000 m
13 124 ft

2000 m
6562 ft

1000 m
3281 ft

500 m
1640 ft

250 m
820 ft

100 m
328 ft

Sea Level | Sea Level

-50 m
-164 ft

-100 m
-328 ft

-250 m
-820 ft

-500 m
-1640 ft

-1000 m
-3281 ft

-2000 m
-6562 ft

Brindisi
Lecce
Maglie
Taranto
Manduria
Gallipoli
Golfo di Taranto
Strait of Otranto
Molfetta
Bari
Bitonto
Barletta
Manfredonia
Andria
Altamura
Matera
San Severo
Foggia
Cerignola
Puglia
Potenza
Campobasso
Benevento
Avellino
Campania
Salerno
Isernia
Caserta
Napoli (Naples)
Torre del Greco
Vesuvio 1277m
Battipaglia
Golfo di Salerno
Agropoli
Volturno
Gaeta
Golfo di Gaeta
Terracina
Latina
Anzio
Isole Ponziane
Isola di Capri
Sapri
Sagia Costana
Aquila
Apesnino Lucano
Appennino
Castrovillari
Rossano
La Sila
Cosenza
Amantea
Lamezia
Ciro Marino
Crotone
Catanzaro
Siderno
Reggio di Calabria
Stretto di Messina
Palmi
Isola Stromboli
Isola Lipari
Isole Eolie
Isola Vulcano
Messina
Cefalù
Monte Etna 3340m
Simeto
Catania
Siracusa
Augusta
Ragusa
Modica
Caltanissetta
Caltagirone
Sicilia (Sicily)
Gela
Vittoria
Pozzallo
Palermo
Alcamo
Isola d'Ustica
Trapani
Isole Egadi
Marsala
Castelvetrano
Agrigento
Strait of Sicily
Isola di Pantelleria
Isole Pelagie
Malta Channel
Gozo
MALTA
VALLETTA
Malta

Ionian Sea

Tyrrhenian Sea

Mediterranean Sea

Sardegna (Sardinia)
Sassari
Porto Torres
Alghero
Ozieri
Nuoro
Macomer
Oristano
Iglesias
Villacidro
Carbonia
Punta La Marmora 1834m
Olbia
Siniscola
Quartu Sant' Elena
Cagliari

TUNISIA

81
49

Vatican City

ROME

N

Main Entrance
Pigna Courtyard
Vatican Museums
Vatican Gardens
Radio Vatican
Sistine Chapel
Raphael Stanza
Papal Apartments
Saint Peter's Basilica
St Peter's Square
Vatican Railway Station
Papal Heliport
Monte Vaticano

ROME

0 m
0 yds

75

CENTRAL EUROPE

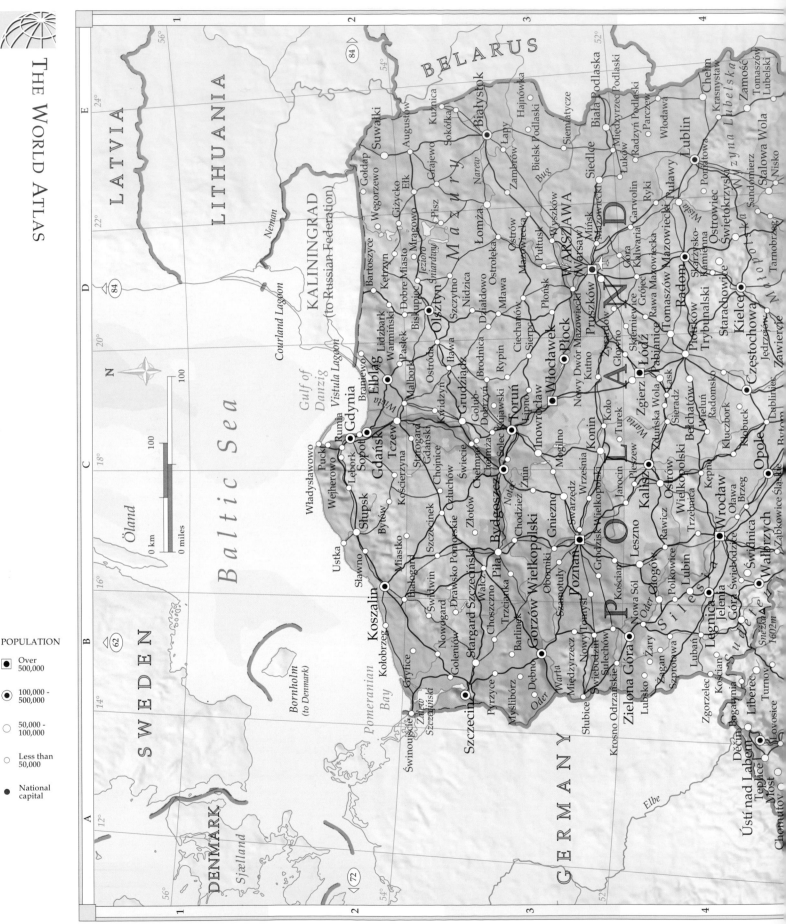

POPULATION

- ◉ Over 500,000
- ◉ 100,000 – 500,000
- ○ 50,000 – 100,000
- ○ Less than 50,000
- ● National capital

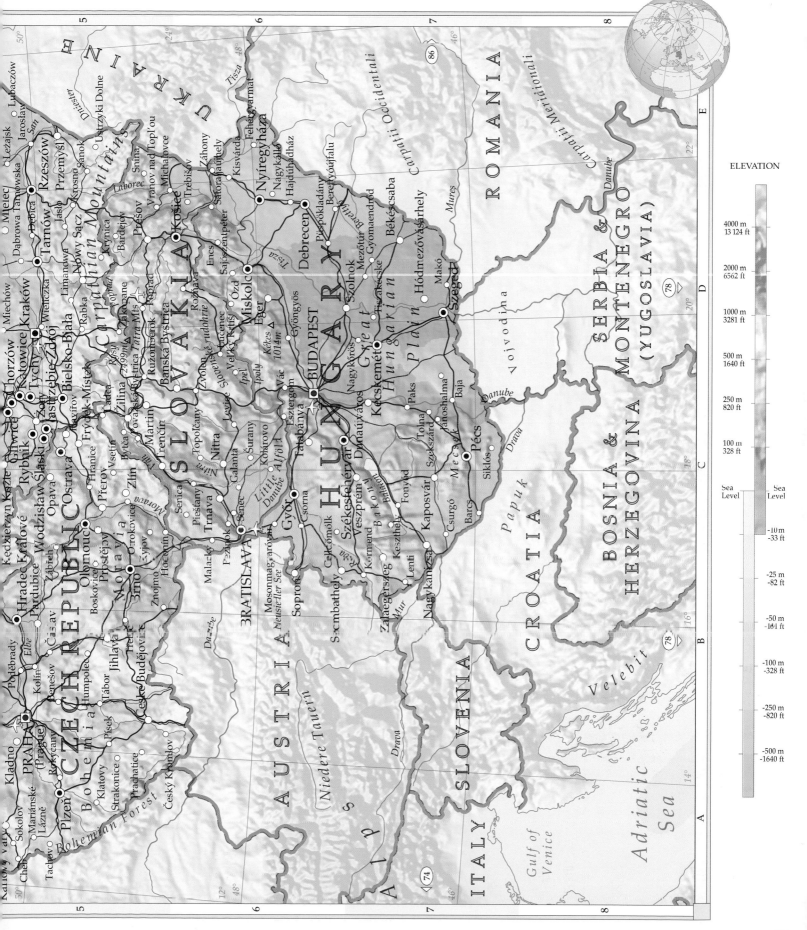

ELEVATION

4000 m 13 124 ft	
2000 m 6562 ft	
1000 m 3281 ft	
500 m 1640 ft	
250 m 820 ft	
100 m 328 ft	
Sea Level	Sea Level
-10 m -33 ft	
-25 m -82 ft	
-50 m -164 ft	
-100 m -328 ft	
-250 m -820 ft	
-500 m -1640 ft	

UKRAINE

ROMANIA

SERBIA & MONTENEGRO (YUGOSLAVIA)

BOSNIA & HERZEGOVINA

CROATIA

SLOVENIA

ITALY

AUSTRIA

SLOVAKIA

HUNGARY

CZECH REPUBLIC

Carpathian Mountains

Great Hungarian Plain

Bohemia

Moravia

Alps

Niedere Tauern

Adriatic Sea

Gulf of Venice

Velebit

PRAHA (Prague)
BUDAPEST
BRATISLAVA

Debrecen
Miskolc
Nyíregyháza
Szeged
Pécs
Szolnok
Kecskemét
Győr
Brno
Kraków
Košice
Tarnów
Rzeszów

SOUTHEAST EUROPE

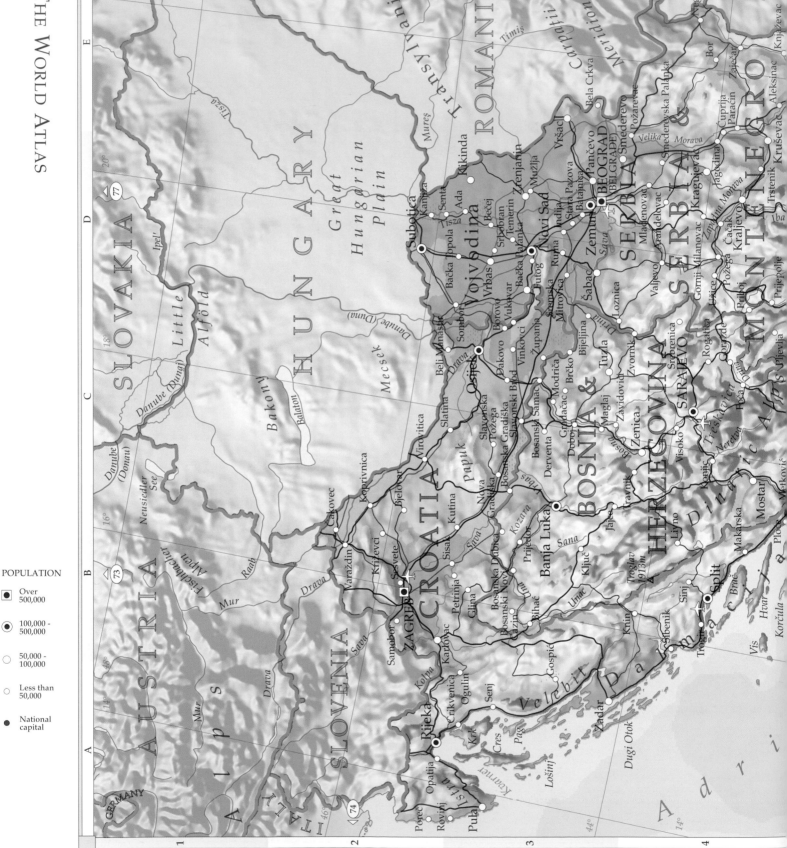

POPULATION

- ◙ Over 500,000
- ◉ 100,000 – 500,000
- ○ 50,000 – 100,000
- ○ Less than 50,000
- ● National capital

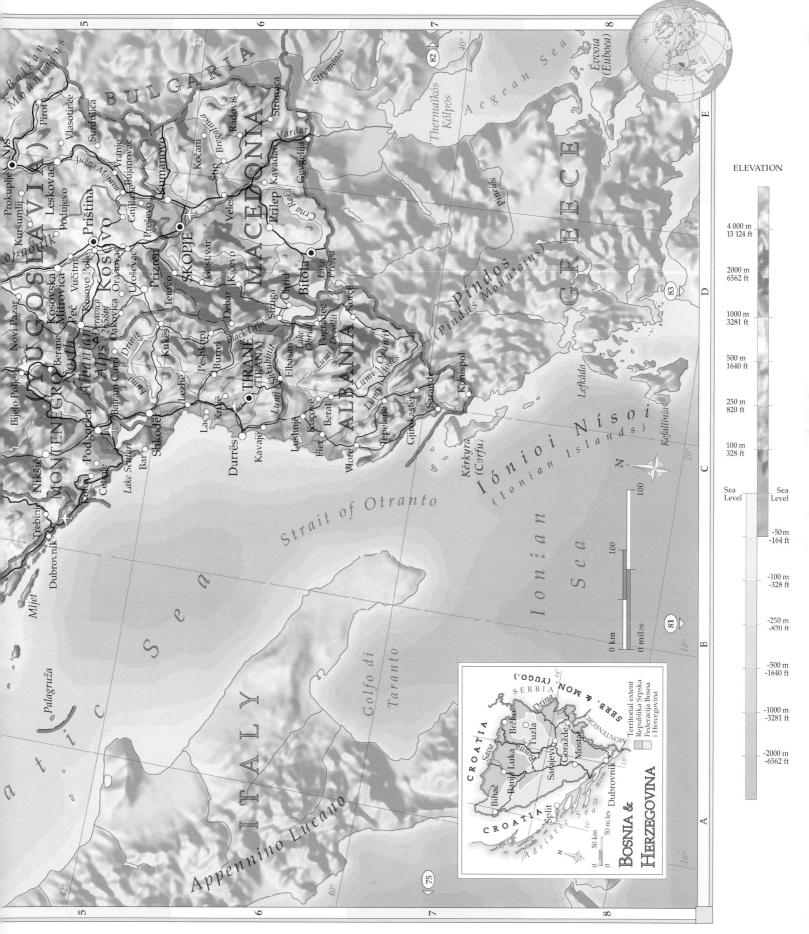

ELEVATION

4 000 m 13 124 ft	
2000 m 6562 ft	
1000 m 3281 ft	
500 m 1640 ft	
250 m 820 ft	
100 m 328 ft	
Sea Level	Sea Level
-50 m -164 ft	
-100 m -328 ft	
-250 m -820 ft	
-500 m -1640 ft	
-1000 m -3281 ft	
-2000 m -6562 ft	

BOSNIA & HERZEGOVINA

Territorial extent
Republika Srpska
Federacija Bosna i Hercegovina

THE MEDITERRANEAN

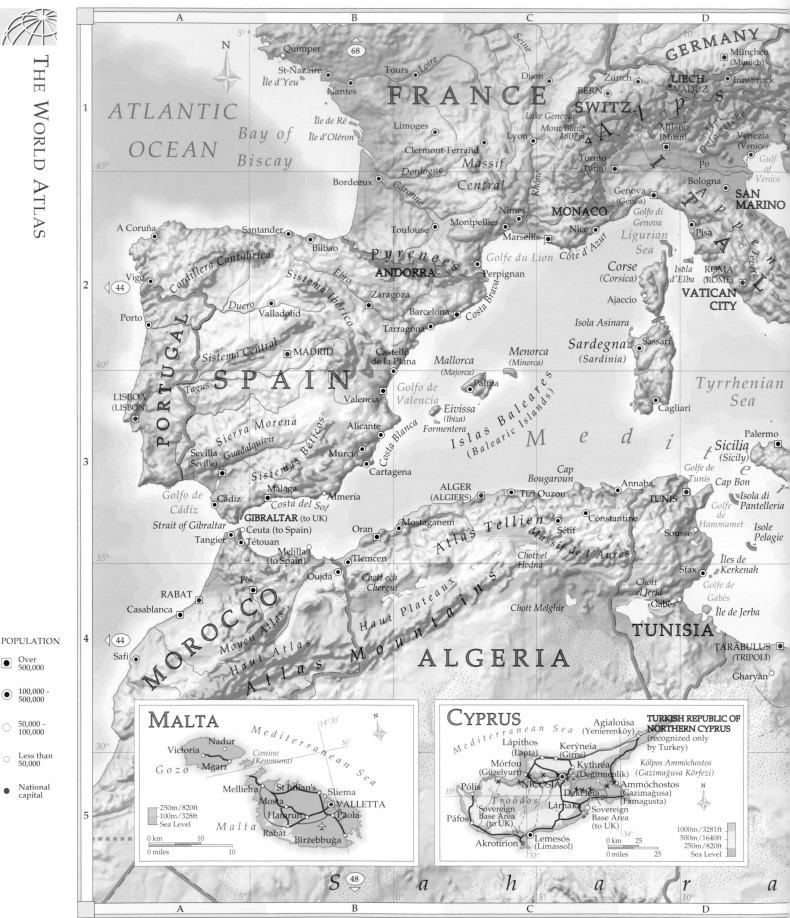

POPULATION

- ▣ Over 500,000
- ◉ 100,000 – 500,000
- ○ 50,000 – 100,000
- ○ Less than 50,000
- ● National capital

MALTA

Mediterranean Sea

Victoria · Nadur
Gozo · Mgarr
Comino (Kemmuna)

Mellieha · St Julian's · Sliema
Mosta · VALLETTA
Hamrun · Paola
Rabat
Birżebbuġa

Malta

250m/820ft
100m/328ft
Sea Level

0 km 10
0 miles 10

CYPRUS

Mediterranean Sea

TURKISH REPUBLIC OF NORTHERN CYPRUS (recognized only by Turkey)

Agialoúsa (Yenierenköy)
Lápithos (Lapta) · Kerýneia (Girne)
Mórfou (Güzelyurt) · Kythréa (Değirmenlik)
Pólis · NICOSIA · Ammóchostos (Gazimağusa) (Famagusta)
Kólpos Ammóchostos (Gazimağusa Körfezi)
Dekéleia · Lárnaka
Sovereign Base Area (to UK)
Páfos · *Tróodos* · Sovereign Base Area (to UK)
Akrotírion · Lemesós (Limassol)

1000m/3281ft
500m/1640ft
250m/820ft
Sea Level

0 km 25
0 miles 25

THE WORLD ATLAS

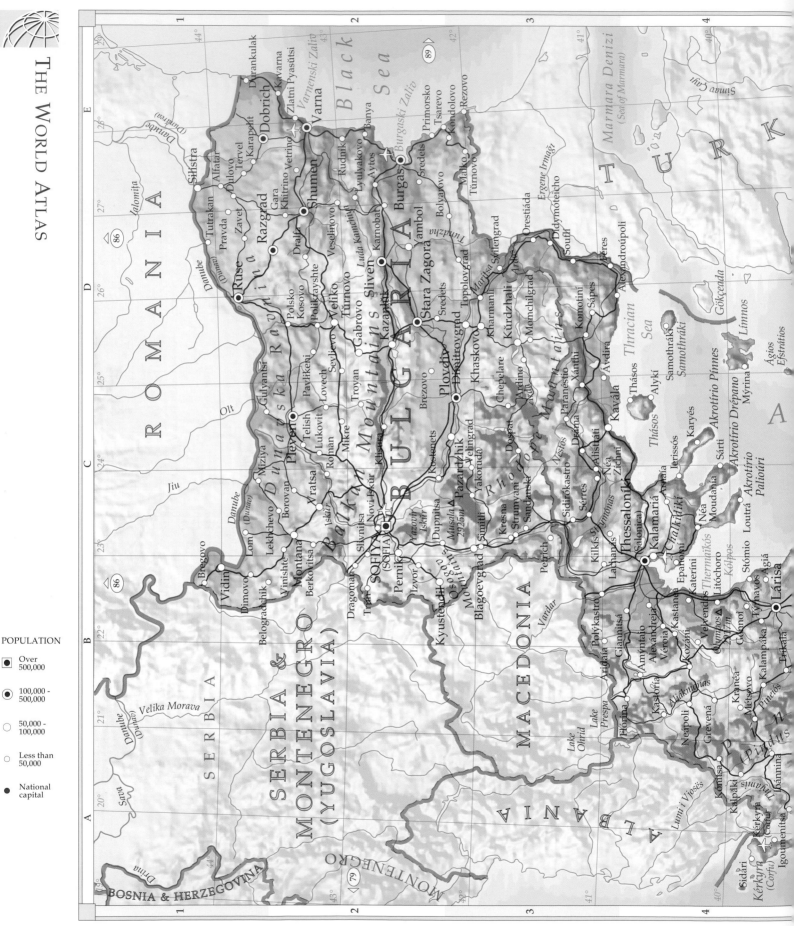

POPULATION

- ◉ Over 500,000
- ◉ 100,000 - 500,000
- ○ 50,000 - 100,000
- ○ Less than 50,000
- ● National capital

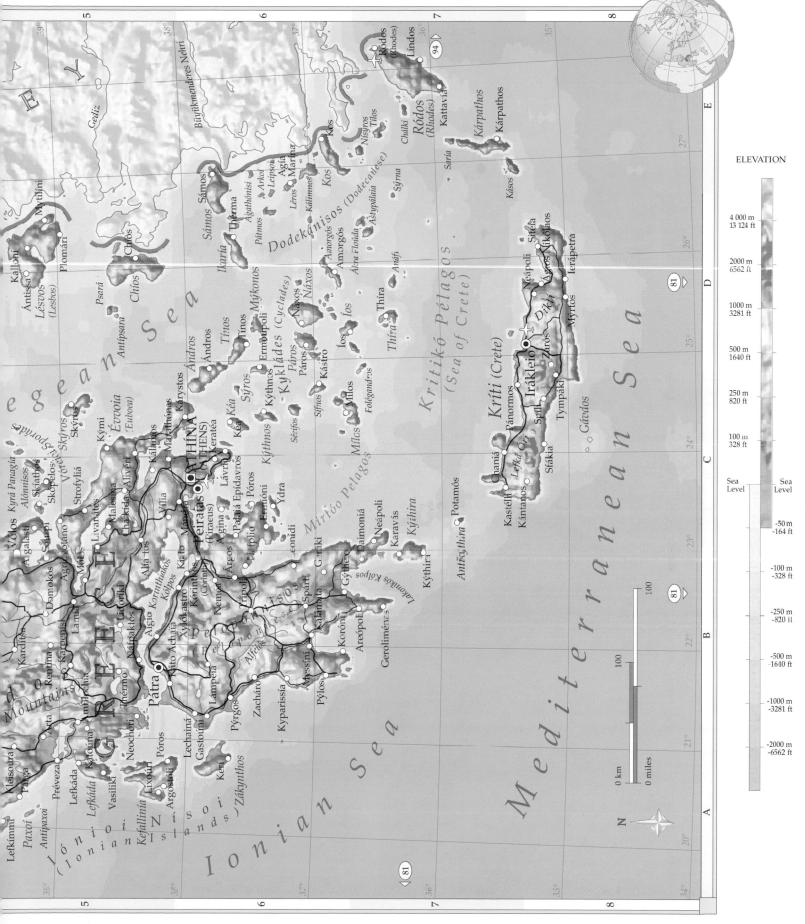

ELEVATION

4 000 m	13 124 ft
2000 m	6562 ft
1000 m	3281 ft
500 m	1640 ft
250 m	820 ft
100 m	328 ft
Sea Level	Sea Level
-50 m	-164 ft
-100 m	-328 ft
-250 m	-820 ft
-500 m	-1640 ft
-1000 m	-3281 ft
-2000 m	-6562 ft

Mediterranean Sea

Ionian Sea

Aegean Sea

Kritikó Pélagos (Sea of Crete)

Mirtóo Pelagos

Dodekánisos (Dodecanese)

Kykládes (Cyclades)

Iónioi Nísoi (Ionian Islands)

GREECE

Kríti (Crete)

Ródos (Rhodes)

Athína (ATHENS)

Pátra

Iráklio

Pindus Mountains

Peloponnese

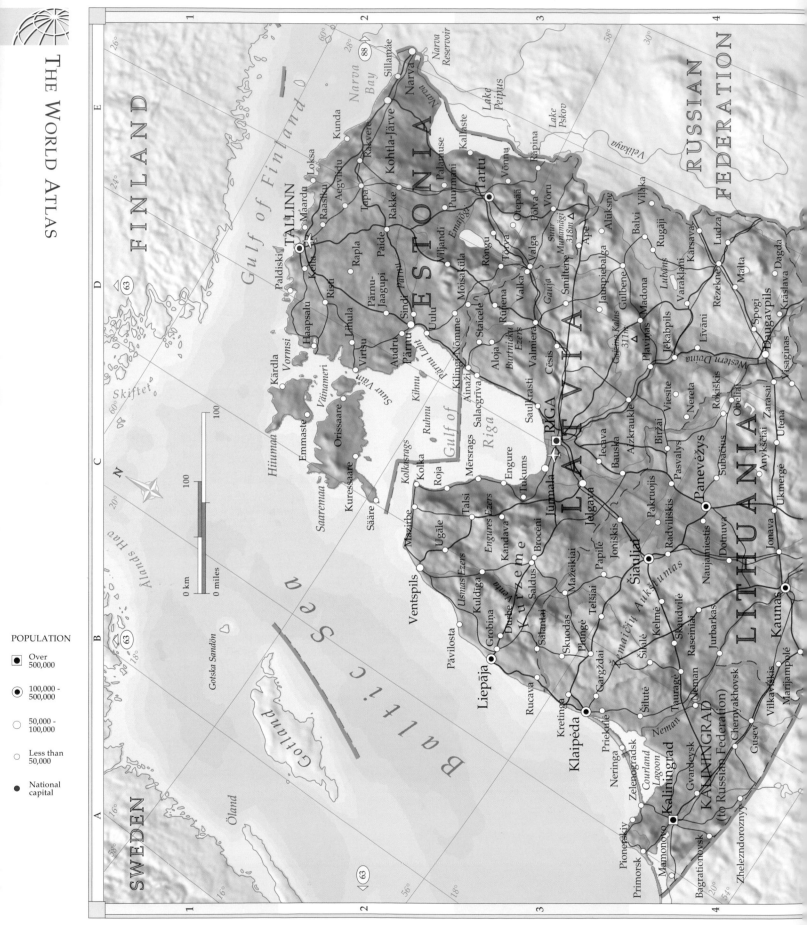

POPULATION

- ◉ Over 500,000
- ◉ 100,000 – 500,000
- ○ 50,000 – 100,000
- ○ Less than 50,000
- ● National capital

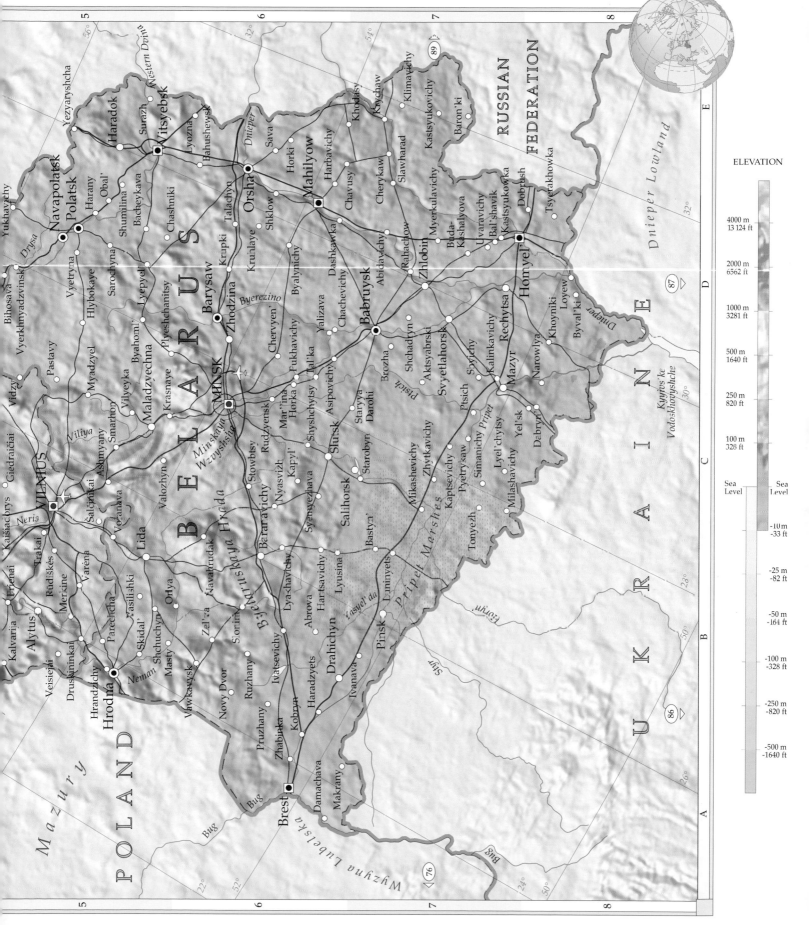

ELEVATION

4000 m 13 124 ft	
2000 m 6562 ft	
1000 m 3281 ft	
500 m 1640 ft	
250 m 820 ft	
100 m 328 ft	
Sea Level	Sea Level
−10 m −33 ft	
−25 m −82 ft	
−50 m −164 ft	
−100 m −328 ft	
−250 m −820 ft	
−500 m −1640 ft	

UKRAINE, MOLDOVA & ROMANIA

POPULATION

- ◉ Over 500,000
- ◉ 100,000 – 500,000
- ○ 50,000 – 100,000
- ○ Less than 50,000
- ● National capital

RUSSIAN FEDERATION

RUSSIAN FEDERATION

A I N E

KYYIV (KIEV)

Chernihiv

Horodnya
Shostka
Shchors
Krolevets'
Hlukhiv
Konotop
Nizhyn
Bakhmach
Nosivka
Romny
Sumy
Brovary
Pryluky
Lebedyn
Boyarka
Yahotyn
Pyryatyn
Okhtyrka
Vasyl'kiv
Hrebinka
Lubny
Myrhorod
Zolochiv
Fastiv
Derhachi
Bila Tserkva
Kaniv
Lyubotyn
Kharkiv
Bohuslav
Merefa
Kup''yans'k
Horodyshche
Zolotonosha
Cherkasy
Hlobyne
Poltava
Zvenyhorodka
Smila
Chyhyryn
Starobil's'k
Shpola
Izyum
Tal'ne
Oleksandrivka
Svitlovods'k
Kremenchuk
Kreminna
Rubizhne
Uman'
Mala Vyska
Znam''yanka
Oleksandriya
Slov''yans'k
Syeverodonets'k
Holovanivs'k
Dniprodzerzhyns'k
Kramators'k
Lysychans'k
Kirovohrad
Zhovti Vody
P''yatykhatky
Novomoskovs'k
Kostyantynivka
Zolote
Luhans'k
Ulyanivka
Dolyns'ke
Dnipropetrovs'k
Pavlohrad
Horlivka
Stakhanov
Vil'shanka
Synel'nykove
Yenakiyeve
Krasnodon
Pervomays'k
Bobrynets
Kryvyy Rih
Pokrovs'ke
Makiyivka
Krasnyy Luch
Kryve Ozero
Arbyzynka
Inhulets'
Donets'k
Torez
Novyy Buh
Zaporizhzhya
Ambrosiyivka
Voznesens'k
Nikopol'
Orikhiv
Volnovakha
Dokuchayevs'k
Ordzhonikidze
Marhanets'
Polohy
Kam''yanka-Dniprovs'ka
Dniprorudne
Don
Tokmak
Mariupol'
Novoazovs'k
Mykolayiv
Molochans'k
Melitopol'
Gulf of Taganrog
Zhovtneve
Kakhovka
Yeya
Ochakiv
Kherson
Akinovka
Prymors'k
Berdyans'k
Odesa
Hola Prystan'
Tsyurupyns'k
Illichivs'k
Chaplynka
Novotroyits'ke
Kalanchak
Heniches'k
Sea of Azov
Armyans'k
Krasnoperekops'k
Karkinits'ka Zatoka
Rozdol'ne
Dzhankoy
Kerch Strait
Chornomors'ke
Krasnohvardiys'ke
Zatoka Syvash
Kerch
Kuban'
Nyzhn'ohirs'kyy
Yevpatoriya
Kryms'kyy Pivostriv
Lenine
Saky
Feodosiya
Simferopol'
Bakhchysaray
Kryms'ki Hory
Sevastopol'
Alushta
Yalta
Alupka

Kyyivs'ke Vodoskhovyshche
Kanivs'ke Vodoskhovyshche
Kremenchuts'ke Vodoskhovyshche
Dniprodzerzhyns'ke Vodoskhovyshche
Kakhovs'ka Vodoskhovyshche

Dnieper (Dnyapro)
Desna
Dnieper Lowland
Psel
Donets
Oskil
Don
Srednerusskaya Vozvyshennost'
Pivdennyy Buh
Dnieper (Dnipro)
B l a c k   S e a
L o w l a n d
B l a c k   S e a

0 km   100
0 miles   100

ELEVATION

4 000 m
13 124 ft

2000 m
6562 ft

1000 m
3281 ft

500 m
1640 ft

250 m
820 ft

100 m
328 ft

Sea Level

-50 m
-164 ft

-100 m
-328 ft

-250 m
820 ft

-500 m
-1640 ft

-1000 m
-3281 ft

-2000 m
-6562 ft

Sea Level

88

94

THE WORLD ATLAS

POPULATION

- ◉ Over 500,000
- ◉ 100,000 – 500,000
- ○ 50,000 – 100,000
- ○ Less than 50,000
- ● National capital

ARCTIC OCEAN

Nordkapp (North Cape)

Barents Sea

Karskoye More

Novaya Zemlya

Pechorskoye More

Prolivy Karskiye Vorota

Ostrov Vaygach

Ostrov Kolguyev

Pomorskiy Proliv

Vorkuta
Severnyy
Promyshlennyy
Inta
Usa
Usinsk
Nar'yan-Mar
Pechora
Nizhniy Odes
Pechora
Solikamsk
Kama

Bol'shezemel'skaya Tundra
Malozemel'skaya Tundra

Timanskiy Kryazh

Ukhta
Yarega
Syktyvkar
Yemva
Mikun'
Koryazhma
Luza
Kotlas
Vel'sk
Sukhona

Ural Mountains

Arctic Circle

RUSSIAN FEDERATION

Severnaya Dvina
Pinega
Mezen'

Nordkapp
Zapolyarnyy
Polyarnyy
Severomorsk
Murmansk
Nikel
Murmashi
Monchegorsk
Olenegorsk
Apatity
Kandalaksha
Zelenoborskiy

Kol'skiy Poluostrov

Beloye More (White Sea)

Arkhangel'sk
(Archangel)
Severodvinsk
Novodvinsk
Onega
Savinskiy
Plesetsk
Nyandoma
Konosha
Belozersk

Kem'
Belomorsk
Nadvoitsy
Segezha
Kondopoga
Medvezh'yegorsk
Petrozavodsk

Onezhskoye Ozero

Vologda
Sokol
Cherepovets
Rybinsk
Yaroslavl'
Kostroma
Tver'

Lapland

NORWAY

SWEDEN

Norwegian Sea

Gulf of Bothnia

FINLAND

Ladozhskoye Ozero
Suoyarvi
Sortavala
Olonets

Baltic Sea
Gulf of Finland

Sankt-Peterburg
(Saint Petersburg)
Petrodvorets
Vyborg
Kolpino
Gatchina
Volkhov
Kirishi
Tikhvin
Novgorod
Babayevo
Borovichi
Uglovka
Valday
Torzhok
Rzhev

ESTONIA
LATVIA
Pskov
Ostrov
Opochka
Velikiye Luki
Zapadnaya Dvina

Luga
Soltsy
Porkhov

Arctic Circle

N

0 km   400
0 miles 400

88

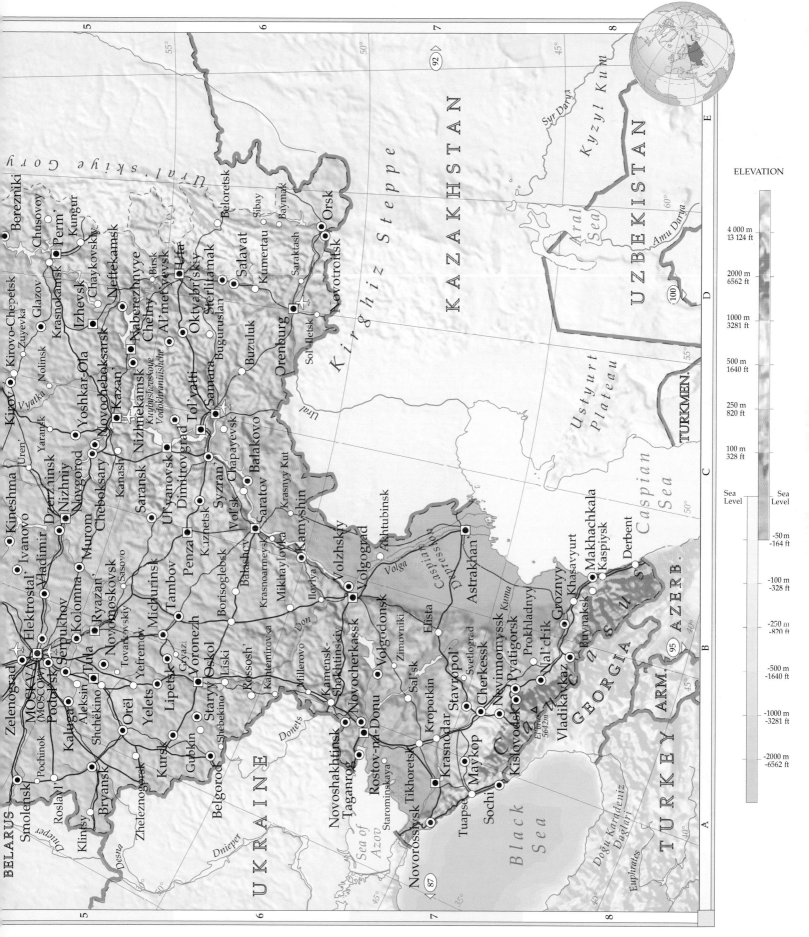

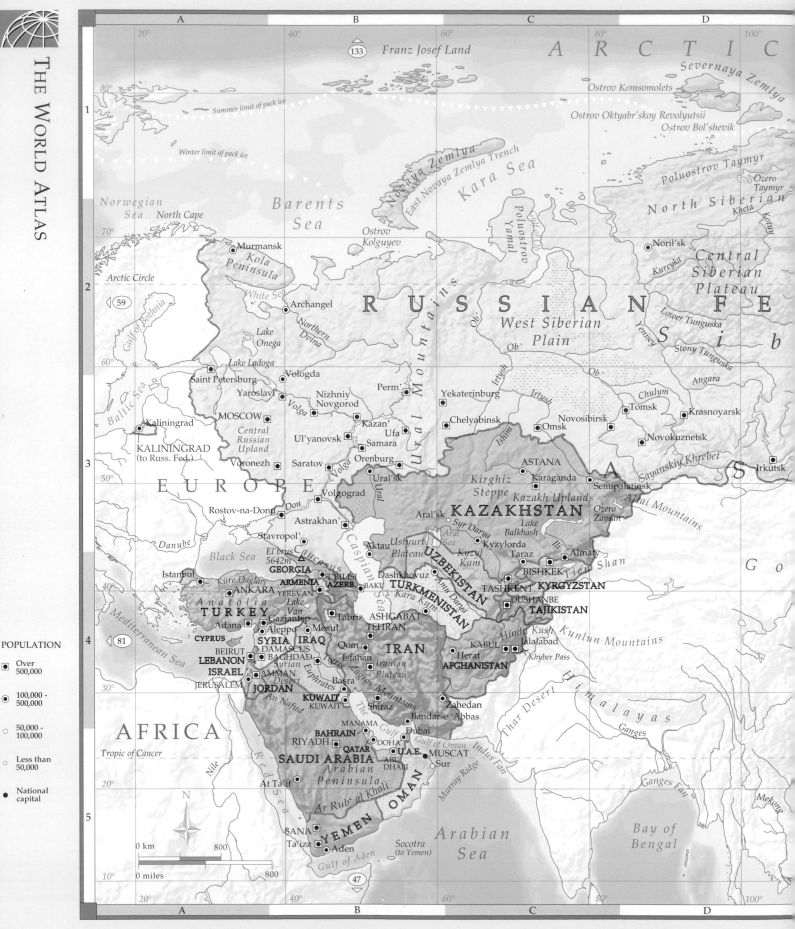

POPULATION

- ▣ Over 500,000
- ◉ 100,000 - 500,000
- ○ 50,000 - 100,000
- ○ Less than 50,000
- ● National capital

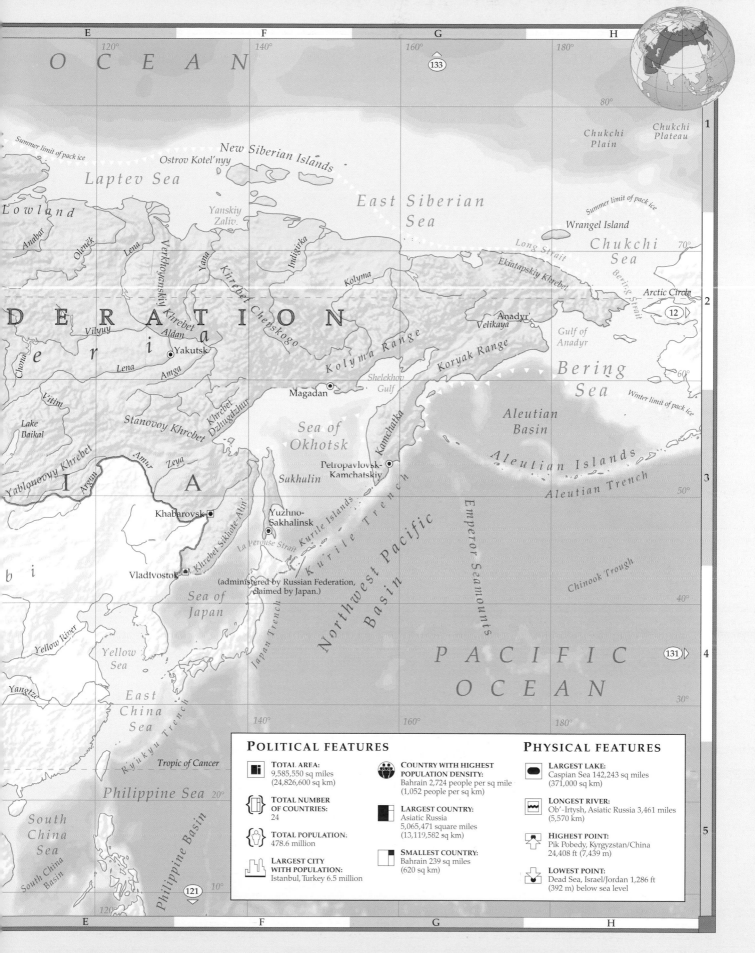

O C E A N

E · 120° · F · 140° · G · 160° · H · 180° · 80°

Summer limit of pack ice

Chukchi
Plain

Chukchi
Plateau

New Siberian Islands

Ostrov Kotel'nyy

Laptev Sea

East Siberian
Sea

Wrangel Island

Lowland

Anabar

Yanskiy
Zaliv.

Long Strait

Chukchi
Sea

70°

Summer limit of pack ice

Olenëk

Lena

Verkhoyanskiy Khrebet

Yana

Indigirka

Kolyma

Ekiatapskiy Khrebet

Bering Strait

Arctic Circle

12

D E R A T I O N

e r i a

Vilyuy

Aldan

Khrebet Cherskogo

Kolyma Range

Anadyr'

Velikaya

Gulf of
Anadyr

60°

Chona

Yakutsk

Koryak Range

Bering
Sea

Lena

Amga

Kolyma Range

Shelekhov
Gulf

V'itim

Stanovoy Khrebet

Magadan

Aleutian
Basin

Winter limit of pack ice

Lake
Baikal

Khrebet Dzhugdzhur

Sea of
Okhotsk

Kamchatka

Aleutian Islands

50°

Yablonovyy Khrebet

Amur

Zeya

Petropavlovsk-
Kamchatskiy

Aleutian Trench

3

Argun

I A

Khabarovsk

Sukhulin

Kurile Islands

Kurile Trench

Northwest Pacific

Emperor Seamounts

Chinook Trough

b i

Yuzhno-
Sakhalinsk

Basin

40°

Vladivostok

La Perouse Strait

Khrebet Sikhote-Alin'

(administered by Russian Federation,
claimed by Japan.)

Sea of
Japan

P A C I F I C

131

4

Yellow River

Yellow
Sea

Japan Trench

O C E A N

30°

Yangtze

East
China
Sea

E · 140° · F · 160° · G · 180° · H

Ryukyu Trench

Tropic of Cancer

Philippine Sea · 20°

South
China
Sea

South China
Basin

Philippine Basin

121

10°

E · 120° · F · G · H

POLITICAL FEATURES

TOTAL AREA:
9,585,550 sq miles
(24,826,600 sq km)

**TOTAL NUMBER
OF COUNTRIES:**
24

TOTAL POPULATION:
478.6 million

**LARGEST CITY
WITH POPULATION:**
Istanbul, Turkey 6.5 million

**COUNTRY WITH HIGHEST
POPULATION DENSITY:**
Bahrain 2,724 people per sq mile
(1,052 people per sq km)

LARGEST COUNTRY:
Asiatic Russia
5,065,471 square miles
(13,119,582 sq km)

SMALLEST COUNTRY:
Bahrain 239 sq miles
(620 sq km)

PHYSICAL FEATURES

LARGEST LAKE:
Caspian Sea 142,243 sq miles
(371,000 sq km)

LONGEST RIVER:
Ob'-Irtysh, Asiatic Russia 3,461 miles
(5,570 km)

HIGHEST POINT:
Pik Pobedy, Kyrgyzstan/China
24,408 ft (7,439 m)

LOWEST POINT:
Dead Sea, Israel/Jordan 1,286 ft
(392 m) below sea level

RUSSIA & KAZAKHSTAN

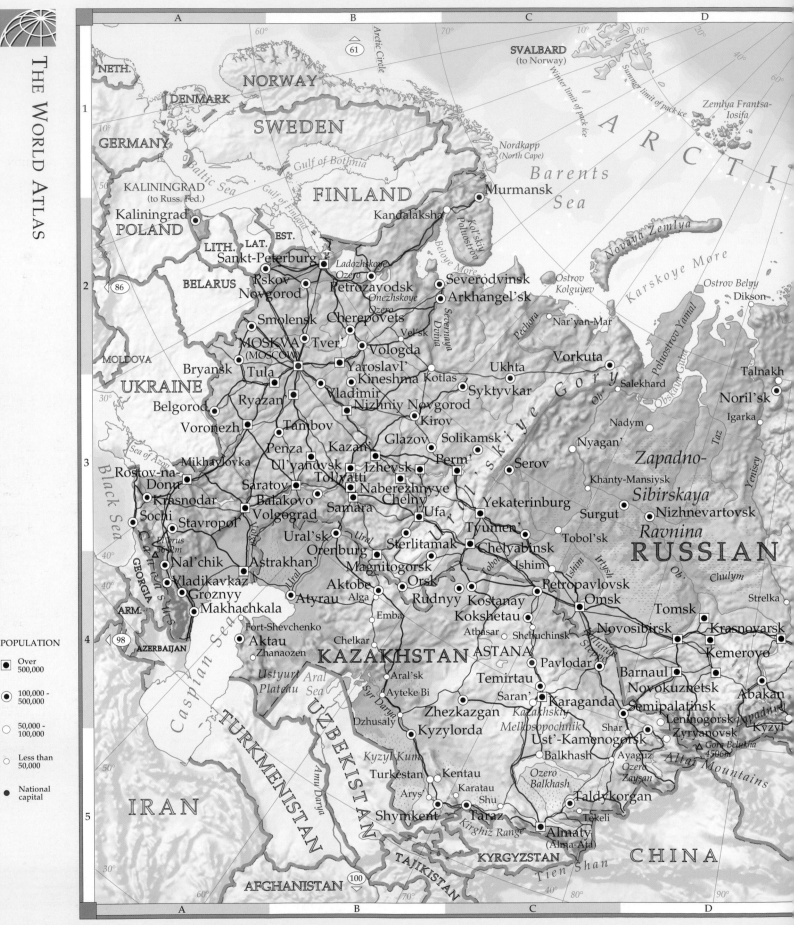

POPULATION

- ■ Over 500,000
- ◉ 100,000 - 500,000
- ○ 50,000 - 100,000
- ○ Less than 50,000
- ● National capital

ELEVATION

4000 m
13 124 ft

2000 m
6562 ft

1000 m
3281 ft

500 m
1640 ft

250 m
820 ft

100 m
328 ft

Sea Level

Sea Level

-250 m
-820 ft

-500 m
-1640 ft

-1000 m
-3281 ft

-2000 m
-6562 ft

-3000 m
-9843 ft

-4000 m
-13 124 ft

ARCTIC OCEAN

Ostrov Komsomolets

Ostrov Oktyabr'skoy Revolyutsii

Severnaya Zemlya

Ostrov Bol'shevik

Poluostrov Taymyr

Ozero Taymyr

Severo-Sibirskaya Nizmennost'

Kheta

Kotuy

Plato Putorana

Srednesibirskoye Ploskogor'ye

Nizhnyaya Tunguska

SIBIR (SIBERIA)

Chunya

Mirnyy

FEDERATION

Angara

Ust'-Ilimsk

Kansk

Bratsk

Tulun

Usol'ye-Sibirskoye

Eastern Sayan

Angarsk

Irkutsk

Ulan-Ude

Kyakhta

MONGOLIA

Gobi

Novosibirskiye Ostrova

Ostrov Novaya Sibir'

Ostrov Kotel'nyy

Ostrov Bol'shoy Lyakhovskiy

More Laptevykh

Ust'-Olenëk

Tiksi

Kazach'ye

Anabar

Olenëk

Olenëk

Vilyuy

Nyurba

Suntar

Olëkminsk

Lena

Vitim

Bodaybo

Ust'-Kut

Ozero Baykal

Chita

Olovyannaya

Krasnokamensk

Zabaykal'sk

CHINA

Yana

Adycha

Verkhoyanskiy Khrebet

Lena

Aldan

Yakutsk

Amga

Aldan

Lena

Chita

Neryungri

Tynda

Skovorodino

Amur

Blagoveshchensk

Shilka

Yablonovyy Khrebet

Vostochno-Sibirskoye More

Indigirka

Kolyma

Khrebet Cherskogo

Alazeya

Pevek

Ambarchik

Cherskiy

Susuman

Okhotsk

Okhotskoye More

Khrebet Dzhugdzhur

Shantarskiye Ostrova

Komsomol'sk-na-Amure

Svobodnyy

Birobidzhan

Khabarovsk

Khor

Bikin

Amur

Khrebet Sikhote-Alin'

Ussuriysk

Vladivostok

Nakhodka

Sea of Japan

NORTH KOREA

Chukchi Sea

Ostrov Vrangelya

Proliv Longa

Ekiatapskiy Khrebet

Anadyr'

Anadyrskiy Zaliv

Koryakskoye Nagor'ye

Anadyr

Ossora

Ostrov Karaginskiy

Zaliv Shelikhova

Atka

Magadan

Atlasovo

Vulkan Klyucheyskaya Sopka 4750m

Ust'-Kamchatsk

Mil'kovo

Poluostrov Kamchatka

Petropavlovsk-Kamchatskiy

Pervyy Kuril'skiy Proliv

Ostrov Paramushir

Ostrov Urup

Kuril'skiye Ostrova (Kurile Islands)

Ostrov Sakhalin

Ostrov Iturup

Kuril'sk

Yuzhno-Sakhalinsk

La Pérouse Strait

(administered by Russian Federation, claimed by Japan)

JAPAN

ALASKA (to US)

Arctic Circle

Bering Strait

Bering Sea

14

130

130

106

TURKEY & THE CAUCASUS

ROMANIA

UKRAINE

Lacul Razim
Lacul Sinoie

Kryms'kyy
Pivostriv

Danube

BULGARIA

Varnenski
Zaliv

B l a c k   S e a

Burgaski
Zaliv

Maritsa

Kırklareli

Edirne

Ergene Nehri

Çorlu

Tekirdag

İstanbul

İzmit
Adapazarı

Yalova
İznik Gölü

Marmara Denizi
(Sea of Marmara)

Bandırma

Çanakkale

Çanakkale
Boğazı
(Dardanelles)

Bursa

Bilecik

Balıkesir

Bozüyük

Eskişehir

ANKARA

Edremit
Ayvalık

Lésvos

Kütahya

Simav

Gediz

Akhisar

Chios

Manisa

Menemen
Gediz Nehri

Uşak

Afyon

İzmir

Ödemiş

Nazilli

Aydın

Sámos

Söke
Büyükmenderes Nehri

Denizli

Dinar

Milas

Burdur

Tavas

Muğla

Burdur
Gölü

Bodrum

Isparta

Marmaris

Dalaman

Antalya

Fethiye

Kaş

Finike

Antalya
Körfezi

Dodekánisos
(Dodecánese)

Ródos
(Rhodes)

Kárpathos

Zonguldak

Küre Dağları

Cide
İnebolu

Bartın

Sinop
Gerze

Bafra

Samsun

Devrek

Karabük

Kastamonu

Kargı

Ünye
Ordu

Çerkeş

Bolu
Gerede

Çankırı

Kızıl Irmak

Merzifon

Çorum

Alaca

Kalecik

Tokat
Yıldızeli
Zara

Kırıkkale

Polatlı

Sorgun

Boğazlıyan

Sivas
Şarkışla

Hirfanlı
Barajı

Kulu

Akşehir

Cihanbeyli

Tuz Gölü

Aksaray

Nevşehir

İncesu

Bünyan

Gürün

Hekimhan

Kayseri

Anatolia

Beyşehir
Gölü

Konya

Ereğli

Nigde

Göksun

Sugla Gölü

Karaman

Toros Dağları

Kahramanmaraş

Manavgat

Mersin
Tarsus

Ceyhan

Adana

Gaziantep

Osmaniye

Alanya

Mut

İskenderun

Kilis

Anamur

Silifke

Antakya

Kırıkhan

Mediterranean

CYPRUS

TURKISH REPUBLIC OF
NORTHERN CYPRUS
(recognised only by Turkey)

Orantes

S e a

LEBANON

POPULATION

● Over
500,000

◉ 100,000 -
500,000

○ 50,000 -
100,000

○ Less than
50,000

● National
capital

0 km   200

0 miles   200

RUSSIAN

FEDERATION

Caspian

Sea

ELEVATION

C a u c a s u s

Gagra
Gudaut'a
Sokhumi
Och'amch'ire
Mestia
Kazbek
5047m
Xaçmaz

Abkhazia *Enguri*

South
Ossetia
K'ut'aisi
Samtredia
GEORGIA
Gori
Tsalka
T'BILISI
Zaqatala
Quba
Siyäzän
Greater Caucasus

P'ot'i
Rust'avi
Şäki
Şamaxı

K'obulet'i
Ajaria
Akhalts'ikhe
Kura
Mingäçevir
Baku
Bat'umi
Hopa
Lesser Caucasus
Vanadzor
Gäncä
Yevlax
Sumqayıt
BAKI
(BAKU)

Trabzon
Rize
Pazar
Artvin
Gyumri
Kars
Sevan
AZERBAIJAN
Imişli
Qazımämmäd
Äli-Bayramı

Giresun
Of
Doğu Karadeniz Dağları
Artik
ARMENIA
Nagornyy
Karabakh

Gümüşhane
İspir
Çoruh Nehri
YEREVAN
Sevana Lich
Xankändi
Bilӓsuvar

Refahiye
Aşkale
Pasinler
Horasan
Aras
Artashat
Goris

Erzincan
Kemah
Tercan
Erzurum
Ağrı
Büyükağrı Dağı
(Mount Ararat)
5137m
Doğubayazıt
AZERBAIJAN
Naxçıvan
Aras
Länkäran

Elâzığ
Malatya
Bingöl
Muş
Van Gölü
Van
Patnos
Erciş
Muradiye
Daryācheh-ye
Orūmīyeh

Silvan
Tatvan
Bitlis
Gevaş

Adıyaman
Diyarbakır
Batman
Siirt
Tigris
IRAN

Silverek
Şırnak

Viranşehir
Mardin

Şanlıurfa
Nusaybin

Buhayrat
al Asad
Ceylanpınar
Al Jazīrah
Kurdistan

Euphrates
Jabal Bishrī
IRAQ

SYRIA
Buhayrat
ath Tharthār

4 000 m
13 124 ft

2000 m
6562 ft

1000 m
3281 ft

500 m
1640 ft

250 m
820 ft

100 m
328 ft

Sea
Level

-50 m
-164 ft

-100 m
-328 ft

-250 m
-820 ft

-500 m
-1640 ft

-1000 m
-3281 ft

-2000 m
-6562 ft

Reshteh-ye Kühhā-ye Alborz
(Elburz Mountains)

Kühhā-ye Zagros
(Zagros Mountains)

THE NEAR EAST

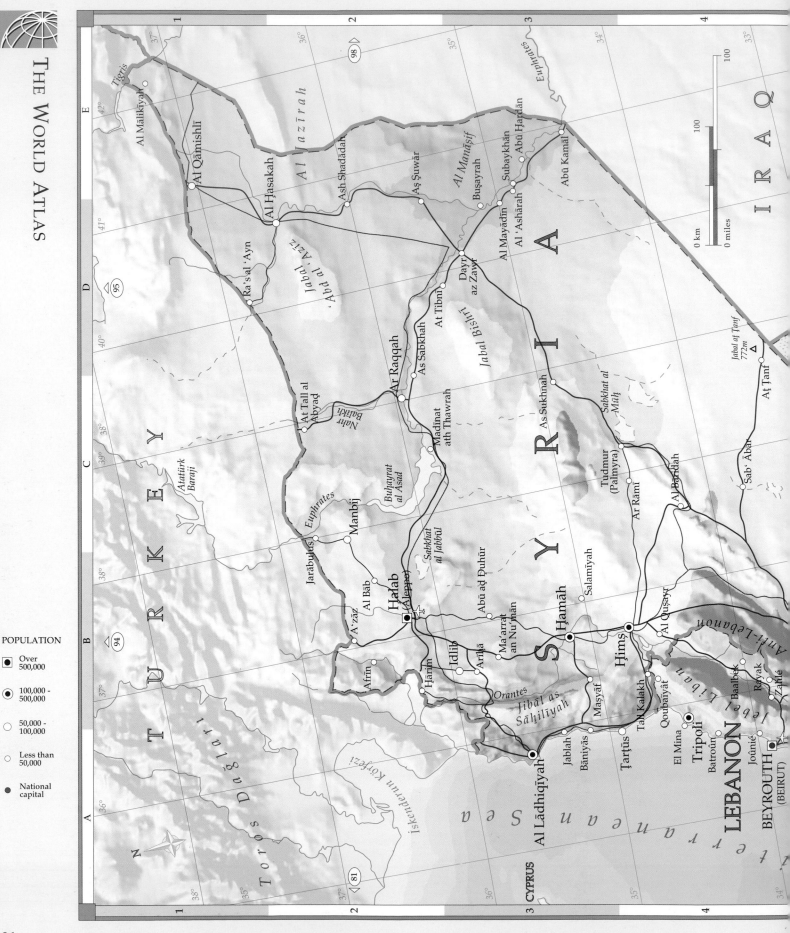

POPULATION

- ● Over 500,000
- ◉ 100,000 - 500,000
- ○ 50,000 - 100,000
- ○ Less than 50,000
- ● National capital

TURKEY

SYRIA

IRAQ

LEBANON

CYPRUS

Mediterranean Sea

Al Mālikīyah
Al Qāmishlī
Al Ḥasakah
Ra's al 'Ayn
At Tall al Abyaḍ
Ash Shadādah
As Suwār
Al Manāṣif
Buşayrah
Subaykhān
Abū Ḥardān
Al 'Ashārah
Al Mayādīn
Abū Kamāl
Dayr az Zawr
At Tibnī
Jabal Bishrī
Jabal 'Abd al 'Azīz
Al Yazīrah
Ar Raqqah
As Sabkhah
Madīnat ath Thawrah
Buḥayrat al Asad
As Sukhnah
Sabkhat al Mūḥ
Tudmur (Palmyra)
Ar Rāmī
Al Bārdah
Sab' Ābar
Jabal aṭ Ṭanf 772m
At Ṭanf
Manbij
Jarābulus
A'zāz
Al Bāb
Ḥalab (Aleppo)
Afrīn
Ḥārim
Idlib
Arīḥā
Abū aḍ Ḍuhūr
Sabkhat al Jabbūl
Ma'arrat an Nu'mān
Ḥamāh
Salamīyah
Ḥimṣ
Al Quşayr
Masyāf
Tall Kalakh
Qoubaiyât
Baalbek
Rayak
Zaḥlé
Al Lādhiqīyah
Jablah
Bāniyās
Tarţūs
El Mina
Tripoli
Batroûn
Jouniê
BEYROUTH (BEIRUT)
Jibāl as Sāḥilīyah
Orantes
Jebel Liban
Anti-Lebanon
Toros Dağları
Atatürk Barajı
Euphrates
Tigris
Nahr Balīkh
İskenderun Körfezi

95
94
81
98

100
0 km
0 miles

N

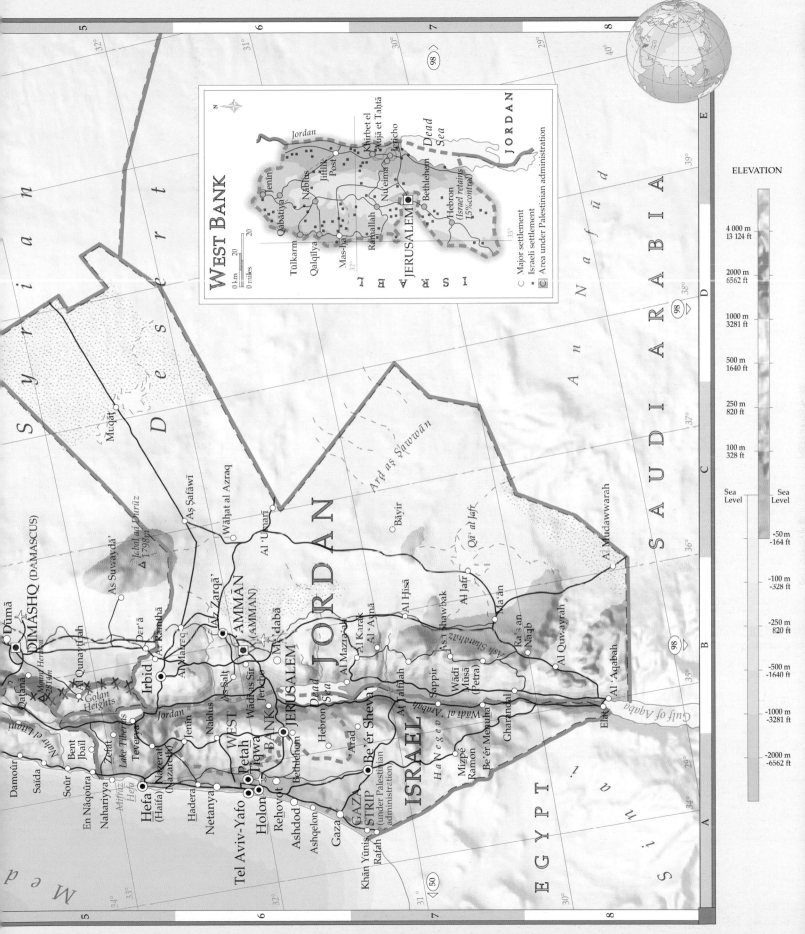

WEST BANK

Jordan

Khirbet el Adja et Tahtā
Jenin
Jiftlik Post
Jericho
Nāblus
Qabātiya
Nu'eima
Ramallah
Bethlehem
JERUSALEM
Tūlkarm
Qalqīlya
Mas-ha
Hebron
(Israel retains
15% control)

ISRAEL

JORDAN

Dead Sea

○ Major settlement
■ Israeli settlement
▨ Area under Palestinian administration

0 km 20
0 miles 20

ELEVATION

4 000 m
13 124 ft

2000 m
6562 ft

1000 m
3281 ft

500 m
1640 ft

250 m
820 ft

100 m
328 ft

Sea Level · Sea Level

-50 m
-164 ft

-100 m
-328 ft

-250 m
820 ft

-500 m
-1640 ft

-1000 m
-3281 ft

-2000 m
-6562 ft

S y r i a n   D e s e r t

Muqat

Aş Şafāwī

Wāhat al Azraq

Al 'Unarī

Bāyir

Qa' al Jafr

Ard as Şawwān

Al Mudawwarah

As Suwaydā'
Jabal ad Durūz
△ 1798 m

Al Hjsā

Al Jafr

Na'ān

Ra's an Naqb

Al Quwayrah

J O R D A N

S A U D I   A R A B I A

A n   N a f ū d

DIMASHQ (DAMASCUS)
Dūmā
Qatanā
Monte Hermon △ 2814 m
Al Quneytra
Der'ā
Ar Ramthā
Irbid
Al Mafraq
Az Zarqā'
AMMAN ('AMMĀN)
As-Salt
Mādabā
Al Mazra'ah
Al Karak
Al 'Ajnā
As Shawbak
Wādī Mūsā (Petra)
Ash Sharāhīz
Sappir
Al Quneytra
Golan Heights
Jordan
Lake Tiberias
Teveryah
Nazerat (Nazareth)
Jenin
Nablus
WEST BANK
Jericho
JERUSALEM
Dead Sea
Hebron
At Tafïlah
Wādī al 'Arabah
Gharandal
Be'ér Menuha
Elat
Al 'Aqabah
Gulf of Aqaba

Damoūr
Saīda
Soūr
Bent Jbaīl
En Naqoūra
Nahariyya
Zefat
Hefa (Haifa)
Hadera
Netanya
Tel Aviv-Yafo
Holon
Rehovot
Ashdod
Ashqelon
Gaza
GAZA STRIP (under Palestinian administration)
Khān Yūnis
Rafah
Petah Tiqwa
Bethlehem
Arad
Be'ér Sheva'
Mizpé Ramon
Ha Negev

I S R A E L

E G Y P T

S i n a i

M e d

Nahr el Litāni
Mifraz Hefa

N A J D

THE MIDDLE EAST

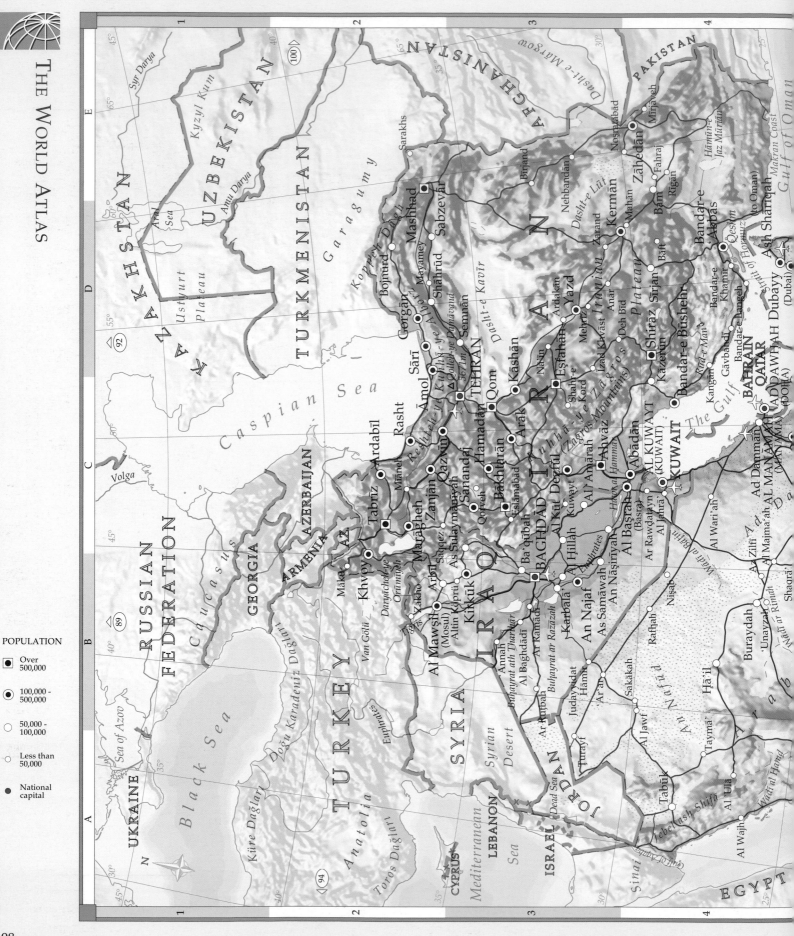

POPULATION

- ◉ Over 500,000
- ◉ 100,000 – 500,000
- ○ 50,000 – 100,000
- ○ Less than 50,000
- ● National capital

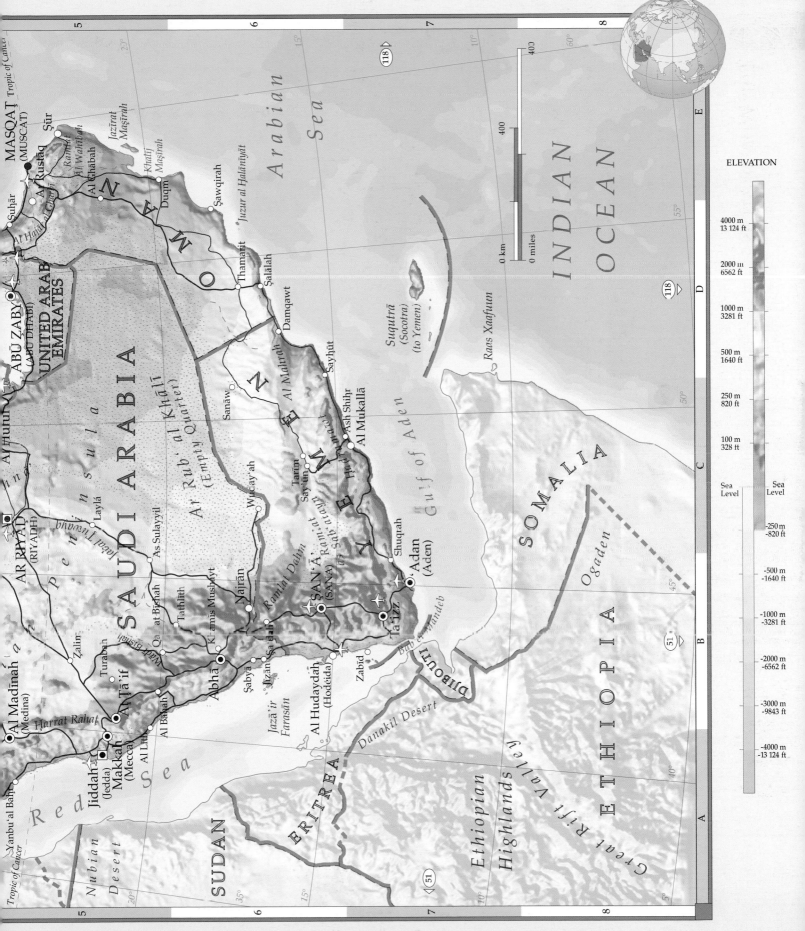

ELEVATION

4000 m	13 124 ft
2000 m	6562 ft
1000 m	3281 ft
500 m	1640 ft
250 m	820 ft
100 m	328 ft
Sea Level	Sea Level
-250 m	-820 ft
-500 m	-1640 ft
-1000 m	-3281 ft
-2000 m	-6562 ft
-3000 m	-9843 ft
-4000 m	-13 124 ft

INDIAN OCEAN

Arabian Sea

OMAN

MASQAT (MUSCAT)
Şūr
Ramlat Al Waḥībah
Jazīrat Maşīrah
Khalīj Maşīrah
Al Khābah
Al Rustāq
Ṣuḥār
Al Ghurbī
Al Ḥajar
Al Wāṭibah
Duqm
Şawqirah

Tropic of Cancer

UNITED ARAB EMIRATES
ABŪ ZABY (ABŪ DHABI)

Al Ḥuṭūf
Liwa
Peninsula
SAUDI ARABIA

Ar Rub' al Khālī (Empty Quarter)

Juzur al Ḥalānīyāt
Thamarīt
Şalālah

Damqawt
Sayḥūt
Al Mahrah

Suquṭrā (Socotra) (to Yemen)

Raas Xaafuun

YEMEN
Sanāw
Wādī Ḥaḍramawt
Tarīm
Sayʼūn
Ash Shiḥr
Al Mukallā

Gulf of Aden

SOMALIA

AR RIYĀD (RIYADH)
Laylā
As Sulayyil
Wādī Dawāsir

Ramlat Dahm
Ramlat as Sab'atayn

Shuqrah
Adan (Aden)

ETHIOPIA

Ogaden

Tathlīth
Khamīs Mushayt
Najrān
ŞAN'Ā' (SANA)
Ta'izz

Bāb el Mandeb

Abḥā
Şabyā
Jīzān
Sa'dah
Al Ḥudaydah (Hodeida)
Zabīd

DJIBOUTI

Zalim
Turabah
Qa'at Bishah
Al Bāḥah
Jazā'ir Farasān
Al Ṭā'if

Danakil Desert

Al Madīnah (Medina)
Ḥarrat Rahaṭ
Al Līth
Al Līth

ERITREA
SUDAN
Ethiopian Highlands
Great Rift Valley

Nubian Desert
Yanbu' al Baḥr
Jiddah (Jedda)
Makkah (Mecca)

Red Sea

Tropic of Cancer

CENTRAL ASIA

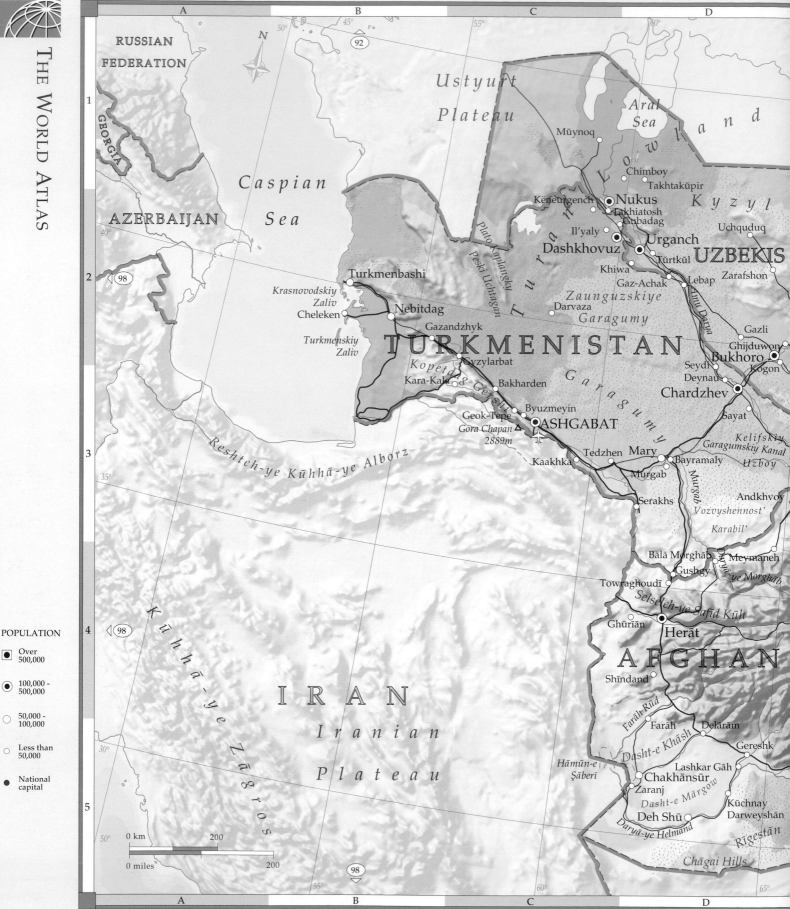

RUSSIAN
FEDERATION

GEORGIA

Caspian
Sea

AZERBAIJAN

Ustyurt
Plateau

Aral
Sea

Mŭynoq

Chimboy

Takhtakŭpir

Kyzyl

Kēŋeurgench
Takhiatosh
Nukus

Il'yaly
Ĝubadag
Urganch

Dashkhovuz

Plato Kaplangsky

Khiwa
Gaz-Achak
Lebap

Tŭrtkŭl
UZBEKIS

Uchquduq

Zarafshon

Peski Uchtagan

Turan

Turkmenbashi

Krasnovodskiy
Zaliv
Cheleken

Nebitdag

Gazandzhyk

Darvaza

Zaunguzskiye
Garagumy

Amu Darya

Gazli

Ghijduwon

Bukhoro
Kogon

Turkmenskiy
Zaliv

Kopeta
Kara-Kala

Gyzylarbat

Bakharden

TURKMENISTAN

Seydi
Deynau

Chardzhev

Sayat

Garagumy

Reshteh-ye Kūhhā-ye Alborz

Geok-Tepe
Gora Chapan
2889m

Byuzmeyin

ASHGABAT

Kaakhka

Tedzhen

Mary

Bayramaly
Murgab

Serakhs

Kelifskiy
Garagumskiy Kanal
Uzboy

Andkhvoy

Murgab

Vozvyshennost'
Karabil'

IRAN

Iranian

Plateau

Kūhhā-ye Zāgros

Bālā Morghāb

Gushgy

Towraghoudī

Daryā-ye Morghāb

Meymaneh

Ghūrīan

Herāt

Selseleh-ye Safīd Kūh

AFGHAN

Shīndand

Farāh Rūd

Farāh
Delārām

Gereshk

Dasht-e Khāsh

Hāmūn-e
Şāberī

Chakhānsūr
Zaranj

Dasht-e Mārgow

Lashkar Gāh

Daryā-ye Helmand

Deh Shū

Kŭchnay
Darweyshān

Rigestān

Chāgai Hills

POPULATION

- ⊙ Over 500,000
- ⊙ 100,000 – 500,000
- ○ 50,000 – 100,000
- ∘ Less than 50,000
- ● National capital

0 km   200

0 miles   200

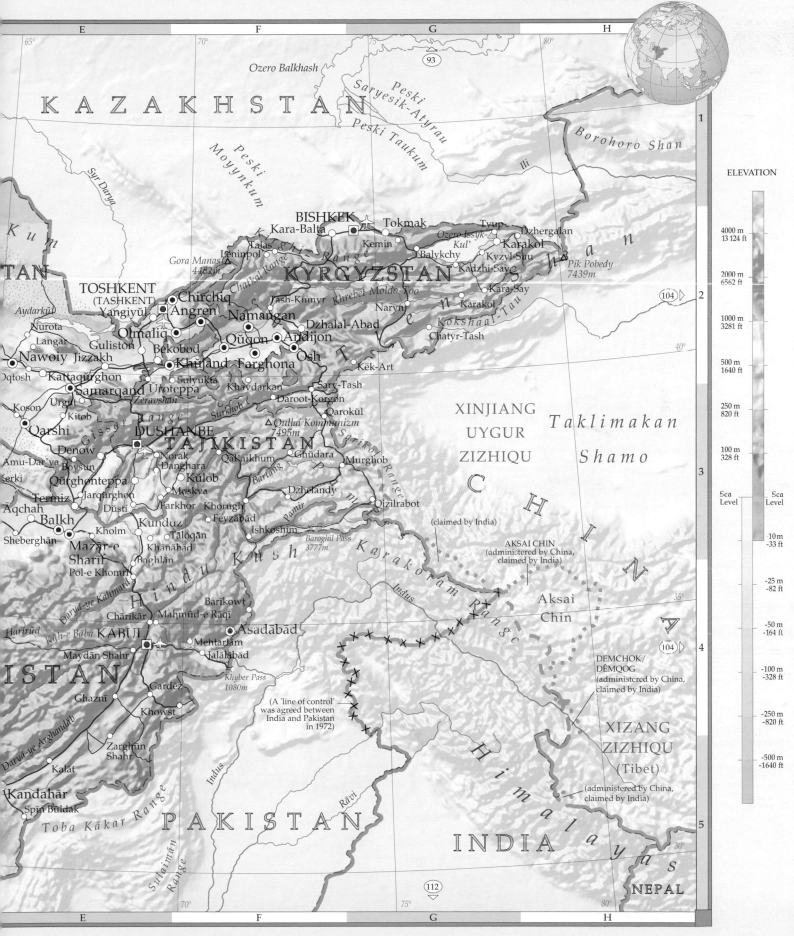

KAZAKHSTAN

Ozero Balkhash

Saryesik-Atyrau

Peski Taukum

Peski Moynkum

Borohoro Shan

Ili

Syr Darya

ELEVATION

4000 m
13 124 ft

BISHKEK
Kara-Balta · Tokmak
Kemin
Ozero Issyk-Kul'
Tyup
Dzhergalan
Karakol
Talas
Leninpol
Gora Manas
4482m
Balykchy
Kyzyl-Suu
Kadzhi-Say
Pik Pobedy
7439m

2000 m
6562 ft

KYRGYZSTAN

TOSHKENT
(TASHKENT)
Chirchiq
Yangiyŭl · Angren
Namangan
Tash-Kumyr
Khrebet Moldo-Too
Naryn
Karakol
Kara-Say

1000 m
3281 ft

Olmaliq
Bekobod
Qŭqon · Andijon
Dzhalal-Abad
Chatyr-Tash

Aydarkŭl
Nurota
Langar
Guliston
Khŭjand · Farghona
Osh
Kokshaal-Tau

500 m
1640 ft

Nawoiy · Jizzakh
Kattaqŭrghon
Sulyukta
Kёk-Art

Qtosh
Samarqand · Uroteppa
Khaydarkan
Sary-Tash

Koson
Urgut
Kitob
Zeravshan
Daroot-Korgon

250 m
820 ft

Qarshi
Gissar Range
DUSHANBE
TAJIKISTAN
Qarokŭl

Denow
Norak
Qal'aikhum
Ghŭdara
Qŭtlai Kommunizm
7495m

XINJIANG
UYGUR
ZIZHIQU

Taklimakan
Shamo

100 m
328 ft

Amu-Dar'ya
Boysun
Danghara
Bartang
Murghob

Qŭrghonteppa
Jarqŭrghon
Kŭlob
Moskva

Termiz
Dŭsti
Farkhor
Khorugh
Dzhelandy

Aqchah
Balkh
Kunduz
Feyzabad
Qizilrabot

Sheberghan
Kholm
Taloqan
Ishkoshim
Baroghil Pass
3777m

Mazar-e
Sharif
Khanabad
Baghlan

Karakoram Range

Indus

C H I N A

(claimed by India)

AKSAI CHIN
(administered by China,
claimed by India)

Aksai
Chin

35°

104

DEMCHOK/
DÊMQOG
(administered by China,
claimed by India)

XIZANG
ZIZHIQU
(Tibet)

(administered by China,
claimed by India)

Pol-e Khomri
Barikowt
Charikar
Mahmud-e Raqi
Asadabad

Hindu Kush
Mehtarlam
Jalalabad

Darya-ye Kahmard
Kŭh-e Baba
KABUL
Maydan Shahr

Hariruda

ISTAN
Ghazni
Gardez

Khowst

Zarghun
Shahr

Kalat
Darya-ye Arghandab
Darya-ye Arghastan

Kandahar
Spin Buldak

Toba Kakar Range

PAKISTAN

Khyber Pass
1080m

(A 'line of control'
was agreed between
India and Pakistan
in 1972)

Himalayas

INDIA

Sulaiman Range
Indus
Ravi

NEPAL

30°

Sea
Level

Sea
Level

-10 m
-33 ft

-25 m
-82 ft

-50 m
-164 ft

-100 m
-328 ft

-250 m
-820 ft

-500 m
-1640 ft

93

104

112

65°
70°
75°
80°

40°

E F G H

1

2

3

4

5

SOUTH & EAST ASIA

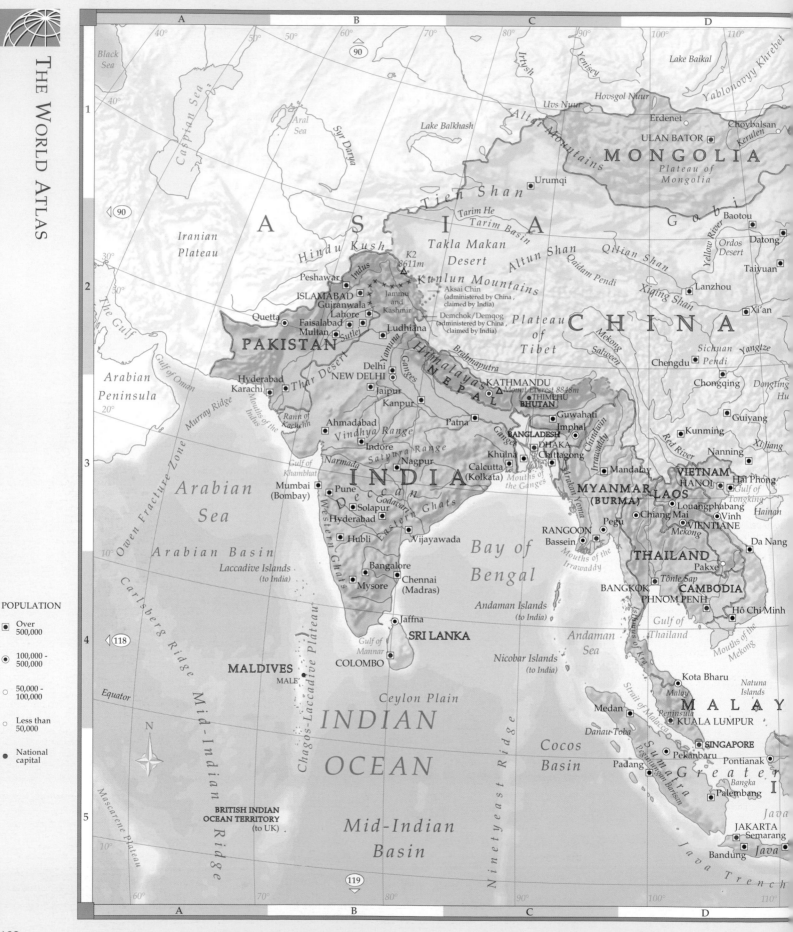

POPULATION

- ▣ Over 500,000
- ◉ 100,000 – 500,000
- ○ 50,000 – 100,000
- ○ Less than 50,000
- ● National capital

POLITICAL FEATURES

TOTAL AREA:
7,936,200 sq miles
(20,554,700 sq km)

TOTAL NUMBER OF COUNTRIES:
24

TOTAL POPULATION:
3,300 million

LARGEST CITY WITH POPULATION:
Tokyo, Japan 18.1 million

COUNTRY WITH HIGHEST POPULATION DENSITY:
Singapore 16,400 people per sq mile
(6,332 people per sq km)

LARGEST COUNTRY:
China 3,705,386 sq miles
(9,596,960 sq km)

SMALLEST COUNTRY:
Maldives 116 sq miles
(300 sq km)

PHYSICAL FEATURES

LARGEST LAKE:
Tônlé Sap, Cambodia
100 sq miles (2,850 sq km)

LONGEST RIVER:
Chang Jiang (Yangtze), China
3,965 miles (6,380 km)

HIGHEST POINT:
Mount Everest, Nepal
29,030 ft (8,848 m)

LOWEST POINT:
Turpan Hami (Turfan Basin), China
505 ft (154 m) below sea level

WESTERN CHINA & MONGOLIA

THE WORLD ATLAS

POPULATION

- ◉ Over 500,000
- ◉ 100,000 - 500,000
- ○ 50,000 - 100,000
- ○ Less than 50,000
- ● National capital
- ● Internal administrative capital

RUSSIAN FED

KAZAKHSTAN

Kazakhskiy Melkosopochnik

Ozero Zaysan

Ozero Balkhash

Kulunda Steppe

Zapadnyy Sayan

Yenisey

Hövsgöl Nuur

Uvs Nuur

Ulaangom

Ölgiy

Möron

Altay

Charus Nuur

Hyargas Nuur

Har Nuur

Hovd

Tsetserleg

MONG

Altay

Bayanhongor

Aj Bogd Uul 3802m

Atas Bogd 2702m

Karamay

Gurbantünggüt Shamo

G o

KYRGYZSTAN

Ozero Issyk-Kul'

Boloro Shan

Kuytun

Shihezi

Fukang

Jimsar

Yining

Ürümqi

Qitai

Turpan

Hami

Tien Shan

Pik Pobedy 7439m

Turpan Pendi

Xingxingxia

Ejin Q

TAJIKISTAN

Kashi

Tarim He

Korla

Bosten Hu

Kuruktag

Lop Nur

GANSU

Qilian Shan

AFGH.

Yengisar

Shache

Tarim Basin

XINJIANG UYGUR

ZIZHIQU

Danghe Nanshan

Yecheng
(claimed by India)

Pishan

Moyu

Taklimakan Shamo

Ruoqiang

Altun Shan

Qaidam Pendi

Qinghai Hu

PAKISTAN

Karakoram Range

Kashmir

Hotan

Qira

Kunlun Shan

Golmud

Burhan Budai Shan

Dulan

C

K2 8611m

Indus

AKSAI CHIN

AKSAI CHIN
(administered by China, claimed by India)

A'nyêmaqên Shan

JAMMU AND KASHMIR

Rutog

Qingzang Gaoyuan (Plateau of Tibet)

Tongtian He

QINGHAI

Bayan Har Shan

CHI

DÊMCHOK/DÊMQOG
(administered by China, claimed by India)

Gar

Zanda

Yamuna

Ganges

Brahmaputra

Himalaya

XIZANG

Nyima

Siling Co

Amdo

Tanggula Shan

Mekong

Yushu

Qamdo

ZIZHIQU

Tangra Yumco

Ngangzê Co

Gyaring Co

Nam Co

Damxung

Nagqu

Saluwen

Jinsha Jiang

(Tibet)

NEPAL

Lhazê

Xigazê

Maizhokunggar

Lhasa

Nyainqêntanglha Shan

ARUNACHAL PRADESH
(claimed by China)

Gonggar

Gyangzê

Mount Everest 8848m

s

BHUTAN

INDIA

MYANMAR
(BURMA)

ELEVATION

4 000 m	13 124 ft
2000 m	6562 ft
1000 m	3281 ft
500 m	1640 ft
250 m	820 ft
100 m	328 ft
Sea Level	Sea Level
-50 m	-164 ft
-100 m	-328 ft
-250 m	-820 ft
-500 m	-1640 ft
-1000 m	-3281 ft
-2000 m	-6562 ft

RUSS. FED.

ERATION

Ozero Baykal

Selenga

Onon

Shilka

Argun (Ergun He)

Amur (Heilong Jiang)

Ergun Zuoqi

Jagdaqi

HEILONGJIANG

Lake Khanka

Sühbaatar

Darhan

Erdenet

Bulgan

Onon Gol

Choybalsan

Hailar

Manzhouli

Hulun Nur

Da Hinggan Ling

ULAANBAATAR
(ULAN BATOR)

Dzuunmod

Öndörhaan

Kerulen

Baruun-Urt

Menengiyn Tal

Hulingol

JILIN

OLIA

Saynshand

Erenhot

Tongliao

Xilinhot

NEI MONGOL ZIZHIQU (Inner Mongolia)

Liao He

Chifeng

LIAONING

Korea Bay

NORTH KOREA

Sea of Japan

Dalandzadgad

Altayn Nuruu

Langshan

Jining

Hohhot

Baotou

Huang He

Wuhai

Mu Us Shamo

BEIJING

TIANJIN

Liaodong Wan

Bo Hai

SOUTH KOREA

JAPAN

Yabrai Shan

Tengger Shamo

NINGXIA HUIZU ZIZHIQU

Great Wall of China

HEBEI

SHANDONG

Yellow Sea

Xining

SHANXI

NA

GANSU

SHAANXI

Han Shui

HENAN

Huang He (Yellow River)

JIANGSU

East China Sea

SICHUAN

HUBEI

ANHUI

SHANGHAI

CHONGQING

Chang Jiang (Yangtze)

ZHEJIANG

Nansei-shotō (to Japan)

HUNAN

JIANGXI

FUJIAN

Tropic of Cancer

YUNNAN

GUIZHOU

TAIWAN

EASTERN CHINA & KOREA

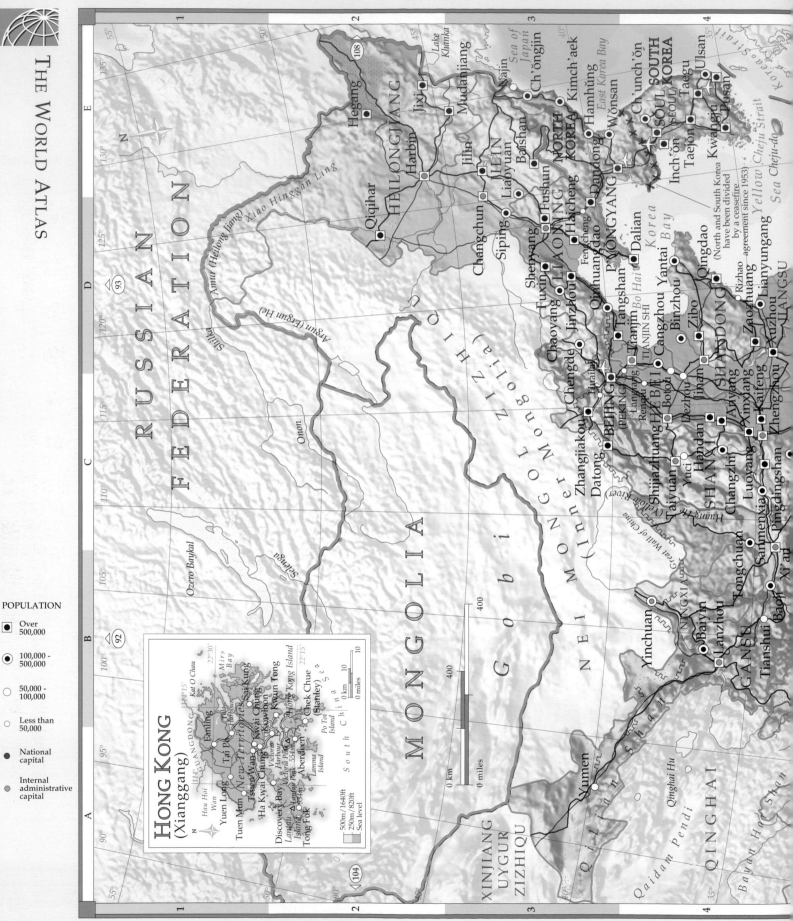

POPULATION

- ▣ Over 500,000
- ◉ 100,000 – 500,000
- ○ 50,000 – 100,000
- ○ Less than 50,000
- ● National capital
- ● Internal administrative capital

HONG KONG (Xianggang)

Kat O Chau
Mirs Bay
Hau Hoi Wan
GUANGDONG
Sha Tau Kok
Fanling
Yuen Long
Tai Po
Tolo Harbour
Sai Kung
Tuen Mun
Kwai Chung
Tsuen Wan
Tsuen Wan
Kowloon
Kwun Tong
Ha Kwai Chung
Hong Kong Island
Victoria
Harbour
Victoria Peak 554m
Aberdeen
Discovery Bay
Lantau Island
Lantau Peak 934m
Chek Chue (Stanley)
Po Toi Island
Lamma Island
Tong Fuk

500m/1640ft
250m/820ft
Sea level

South China Sea

RUSSIAN FEDERATION

MONGOLIA

N E I   M o n g o l   (Inner Mongolia)

Gobi

Ozero Baykal

Selenga

Onon

Stanovoy (Shilka)

Amur (Heilong Jiang)

Argun (Ergun He)

Xiao Hinggan Ling

Qiqihar

HEILONGJIANG

Harbin

Hegang

Jixi

Mudanjiang

Lake Khanka

Sea of Japan

Najin

Ch'ŏngjin

Kimch'aek

Hamhŭng

Wŏnsan

East Korea Bay

NORTH KOREA

PYONGYANG

Nampo

Haeju

Korea Bay

SOUTH KOREA

Ch'unch'ŏn

SOUL (SEOUL)

Inch'ŏn

Suwŏn

Taejŏn

Kwangju

Taegu

Ulsan

Pusan

Cheju-do

Sea
Cheju-do

Korea Strait

Yellow Sea

Jilin

Changchun

JILIN

Baishan

Liaoyuan

Siping

Shenyang

Fushun

LIAONING

Fuxin

Benxi

Haicheng

Fengcheng

Dandong

Dalian

Qinhuangdao

Jinzhou

Chaoyang

Chengde

Bo Hai

Yantai

Qingdao

Yantai

SHANDONG

Jinan

Zibo

Dezhou

Binzhou

Dongying

Rizhao

Lianyungang

Xuzhou

Zhengzhou

Kaifeng

Zhumadian

JIANGSU

Zhangjiakou

Datong

BEIJING (PEKING)

HEBEI

TIANJIN SHI

Tianjin

Langfang

Tangshan

Baoding

Cangzhou

Shijiazhuang

Xingtai

Handan

Anyang

Yuci

Taiyuan

SHANXI

Changzhi

Yangquan

Luoyang

Sanmenxia

Tongchuan

NINGXIA

Yinchuan

Baiyin

Lanzhou

GANSU

Tianshui

Baoji

Xi'an

Pingdingshan

Qilian Shan

Yumen

Qinghai Hu

QINGHAI

Qaidam Pendi

Bayan Har Shan

Huang He (Yellow River)

Great Wall of China

XINJIANG UYGUR ZIZHIQU

JAPAN

East China Sea

Nansei-shoto (land of Japan)

Okinawa

(China and Taiwan claim all of each other's territory)

Tropic of Cancer

TAIWAN

Chilung
TAIPEI
Chungli
T'aichung
Chiai
T'ainan
Kaohsiung

Luzon Strait

Taiwan Strait

PACIFIC OCEAN

PHILIPPINES

130

117

ELEVATION

4 000 m / 13 124 ft	
2000 m / 6562 ft	
1000 m / 3281 ft	
500 m / 1640 ft	
250 m / 820 ft	
100 m / 328 ft	
Sea Level	Sea Level
-50 m / -164 ft	
-100 m / -328 ft	
-250 m / -820 ft	
-500 m / -1640 ft	
-1000 m / -3281 ft	
-2000 m / -6562 ft	

HENAN
Bengbu
Huainan
Nanyang
Xinyang

Yangzhou
Nanjing
Suzhou
Shanghai
Jiaxing
Wuxi
Pei'an
Wuhu
Ningbo
Wenzhou

ANHUI

ZHEJIANG

Hangzhou
Jinhua
Huangshi
Anqing
Jingdezhen
Shangrao
Lishuan

HUBEI
Yichang
Wuhan

JIANGXI
Nanchang
Xiangtan
Hengyang

FUJIAN
Nanping
Yong'an
Fuzhou
Quanzhou
Xiamen

Ganzhou
Longyan
Zhangzhou
Shantou

HUNAN
Changsha
Loudi
Yueyang
Lengshuitan

GUANGDONG
Shaoguan
Guangzhou
Dongguan
Hong Kong (Xianggang)
Macao (Aomen)

Chenzhou
Guilin
Quanzhou

GUANGXI ZHUANGZU ZIZHIQU
Liuzhou
Wuzhou
Zhaoqing
Maoming
Zhanjiang
Haikou

GUIZHOU
Zunyi
Guiyang
Anshun

CHONGQING
Chongqing

SICHUAN
Guangyuan
Nanchong
Neijiang
Zigong

Yulin
Jiangmen
Yulin
Suixi
Beihai
Danzhou
Dongfang

Zhanjiang
Xuwen
Qinzhou
Nanning

Hainan Dao

HAINAN

Gulf of Tongking

PARACEL ISLANDS
(disputed by China, Taiwan and Vietnam)

Amphitrite Group
Crescent Group
Triton Island

SPRATLY ISLANDS
(disputed by China, Malaysia, Philippines, Taiwan and Vietnam)

Flat Island
Nanshan Island
Thitu Island
Loaita Island
Len Dao
Namyit Island
Spratly Island

South China Sea

117

SHAANXI
Hanzhong
Mianyang
Guangyuan

XIZANG ZIZHIQU (Tibet)

INDIA

Hengduan Shan

Chengdu
Ya'an
Leshan
Sichuan Pendi
Dadu Jiang
Utang

Yalong Jiang

Jinsha Jiang

Xichang
Dali
Baoshan

YUNNAN
Kunming
Gejiu
Jinghong

Wuliang Shan

Salween

Mekong

Red River

MYANMAR (BURMA)

Tropic of Cancer

LAOS

THAILAND

VIETNAM

CAMBODIA

Gulf of Thailand

114

114

Dongting Hu
Xiangtan
Zhuzhou

JAPAN

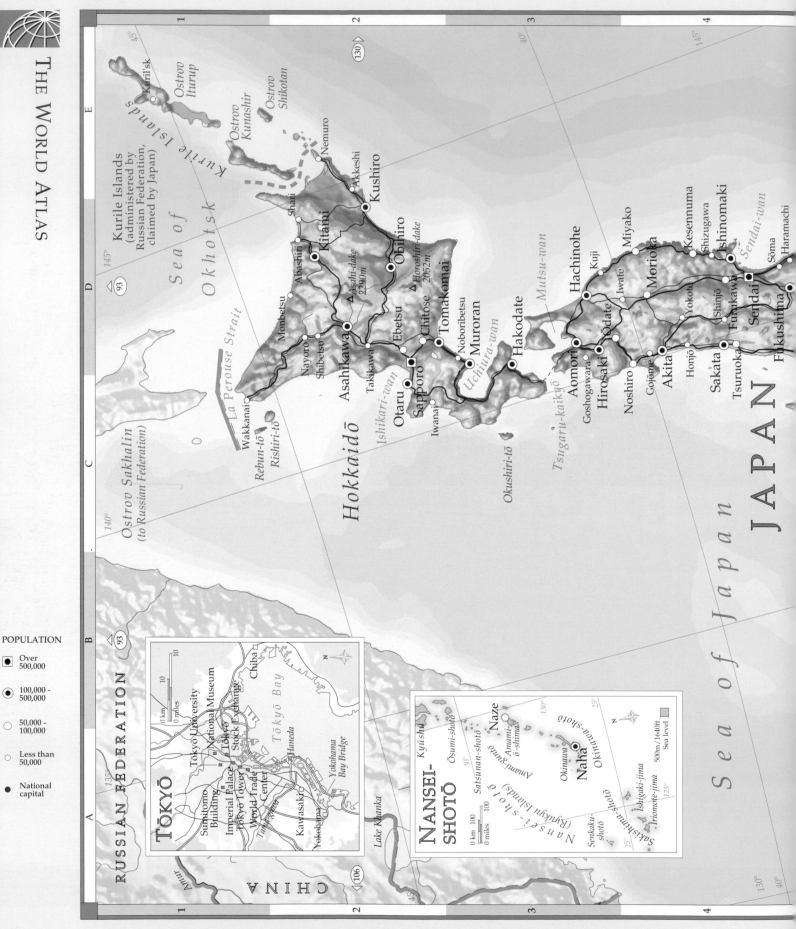

POPULATION

- ■ Over 500,000
- ◉ 100,000 – 500,000
- ○ 50,000 – 100,000
- ○ Less than 50,000
- ● National capital

RUSSIAN FEDERATION

TŌKYŌ

Tōkyō University
National Museum
Tōkyō
Stock Exchange
Chiba
Sumitomo Building
Imperial Palace
Tōkyō Tower
World Trade Center
Kawasaki
Yokohama
Yokohama Bay Bridge
Haneda
Tōkyō Bay

NANSEI-SHOTŌ

Kyūshū
Ōsumi-shotō
Satsunan-shotō
Amami-guntō
Amami-ō-shima
Naze
Okinawa-shotō
Okinawa-jima
Naha
Ryūkyū Islands
Ishigaki-jima
Senkaku-shotō
Sakishima-shotō
Iriomote-jima

Nansei-shotō

500m / 1640ft
Sea level

Kurile Islands (administered by Russian Federation, claimed by Japan)

Kuril'sk
Ostrov Iturup
Ostrov Shikotan
Ostrov Kunashir
Nemuro
Akkeshi
Kushiro
Shari
Kitami
Abashiri
Obihiro
Horoshiri-dake 2052m
Asahi-dake 2290m
Tomakomai
Monbetsu
Asahikawa
Ebetsu
Chitose
Muroran
Nayoro
Shibetsu
Takikawa
Noboribetsu
Hakodate
Otaru
Sapporo
Iwanai
Uchiura-wan
Wakkanai
Rebun-tō
Rishiri-tō
Okushiri-tō
Hokkaidō

Sea of Okhotsk
La Perouse Strait
Ishikari-wan
Tsugaru-kaikyō

Hachinohe
Kuji
Miyako
Morioka
Kesennuma
Shizugawa
Ishinomaki
Iwate
Yokota
Shinjō
Furukawa
Sōma
Haramachi
Ōdate
Sendai
Aomori
Goshogawara
Hirosaki
Yokote
Sakata
Fukushima
Noshiro
Gojōme
Akita
Tsuruoka
Honjō
Mutsu-wan
Sendai-wan

JAPAN
Sea of Japan

Ostrov Sakhalin (to Russian Federation)

Amur
CHINA
Lake Khanka

RUSSIAN FEDERATION

108

Honshū

Kōriyama
Iwaki
Sukagawa
Hitachi
Utsunomiya
Mito
Koyama
Chōshi
Chiba
Kawagoe
TOKYO
Kawasaki
Yokohama
Bōsō-hantō
Maebashi
Matsumoto
Nagano
Toyama
Kōfu
Shizuoka
Fuji
Hamamatsu
Toyota
Sagami-nada
Suruga-wan
O-shima
Nii-jima
Miyake-jima
Mikura-jima
Hachijō-jima
Izu-shotō
Niigata
Nagaoka
Sado
Jōetsu
Shinano-gawa
Itoigawa
Takaoka
Kanazawa
Komatsu
Fukui
Tsuruga
Nakatsugawa
Gifu
Ōgaki
Nagoya
Okazaki
Tsu
Ise
Osaka
Ise-wan
Wakayama
Owase
Shingū
Tanabe
Gobō
Kii-suidō
Shikoku
Tottori
Yonago
Matsue
Oki-shotō
Dōgo
Dōzen
Hamada
Masuda
Gōtsu
Okayama
Kurashiki
Himeji
Akashi
Kōbe
Kyōto
Ōtsu
Awaji-shima
Tokushima
Kōchi
Matsuyama
Mihara
Kure
Tosa-wan
Nakamura
Sukumo
Hiroshima
Iwakuni
Hōfu
Ube
Nobeoka
Ōita
Kyūshū
Miyazaki
Miyakonojō
Matsue
Yamaguchi
Shimonoseki
Kitakyūshū
Fukuoka
Kurume
Ōmuta
Kumamoto
Saga
Sasebo
Nagasaki
Kagoshima
Sendai
Satsushiro
Tanega-shima
Yaku-shima
Kagoshima-wan
Ōsumi-shotō

*Liancourt Rocks
(claimed by Japan
& South Korea)*

SOUTH
KOREA

Korea Strait
Tsushima
Kō-saki
Iki
Gotō-rettō
Kō-saki
Koshikijima-rettō

East
China Sea

P A C I F I C

O C E A N

Amakusa-nada
Bungo-suidō
Iyo-nada
Suō-nada

ELEVATION

4000 m	13 124 ft
2000 m	6562 ft
1000 m	3281 ft
500 m	1640 ft
250 m	820 ft
100 m	328 ft
Sea Level	Sea Level
-250 m	-820 ft
-500 m	-1640 ft
-1000 m	-3281 ft
-2000 m	-6562 ft
-3000 m	-9843 ft
-4000 m	-13 124 ft

N

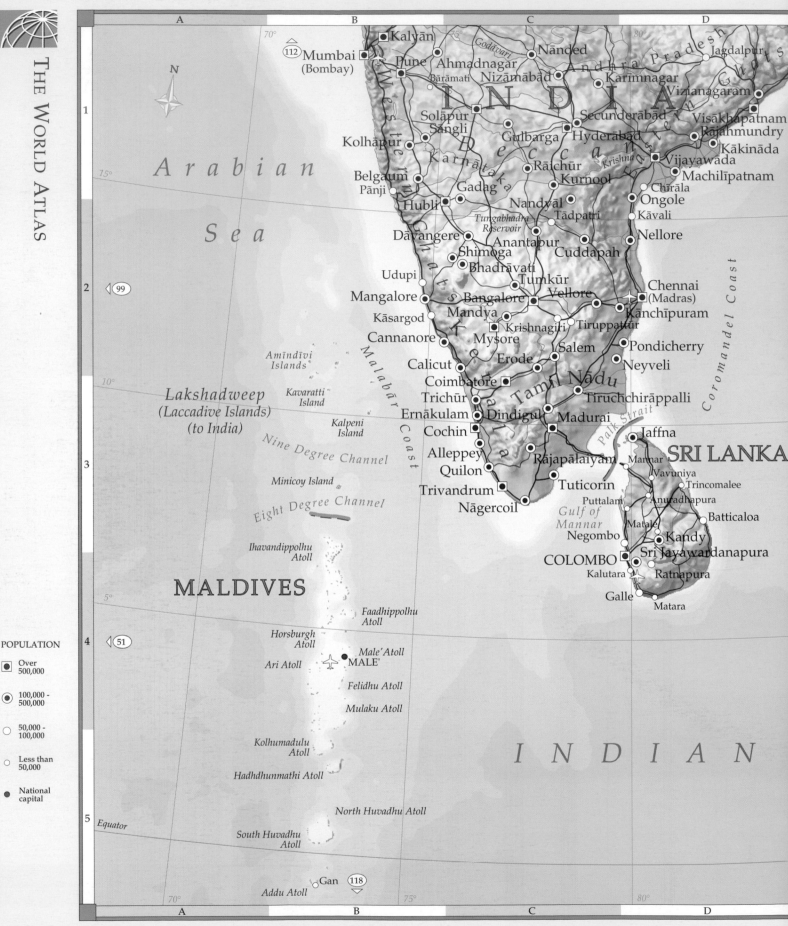

THE WORLD ATLAS

POPULATION

- ◉ Over 500,000
- ◉ 100,000 - 500,000
- ○ 50,000 - 100,000
- ○ Less than 50,000
- ● National capital

A B C D

70° 75° 80°

Kalyān
112 Mumbai (Bombay)
Pune Ahmadnagar
Bārāmati Nizāmābād
Solāpur
Sangli
Kolhāpur
Belgaum
Pānji
Hublī
Gadag

A r a b i a n

S e a

15°

99

Nānded Jagdalpur
Andhra Pradesh
Karīmnagar
Nizāmābād Vizianagaram
Secunderābād Visākhapatnam
Gulbarga Hyderābād Rājahmundry
Raīchūr Krishna Kākināda
Kurnool Vijayawada
Machilīpatnam
Nandyāl Chīrāla
Tādpatri Ongole
Kāvali

I N D I A
D e c c a n
Karnataka

Davangere
Shimoga Anantapur Nellore
Bhadrāvati Cuddapah
Udupi Tumkūr
Mangalore Bangalore Vellore Chennai (Madras)
Kāsargod Mandya Kānchīpuram
Krishnagiri Tiruppattūr
Cannanore Mysore
Calicut Erode Salem Pondicherry
Coimbatore Neyveli
Trichūr *Tamil Nadu*
Ernākulam Dindigul Tiruchchirāppalli
Cochin Madurai
Alleppey Rājapālaiyam Jaffna **SRI LANKA**
Quilon Mannar Vavuniya
Trivandrum Tuticorin Trincomalee
Nāgercoil Puttalam Anurādhapura
Negombo Batticaloa
Matale
COLOMBO Kandy
Sri Jayawardanapura
Kalutara Ratnapura
Galle
Matara

2

10°

Amīndīvi Islands

Lakshadweep (Laccadive Islands) (to India)

Kavaratti Island

Kalpeni Island

Malabār Coast

Coromandel Coast

Tungabhadra Reservoir

Godāvari

West Ghats

Ghats

3

Nine Degree Channel

Minicoy Island

Eight Degree Channel

Palk Strait

Gulf of Mannar

5°

MALDIVES

Ihavandippolhu Atoll

Faadhippolhu Atoll

Horsburgh Atoll

51

Ari Atoll *Male' Atoll*
MALE'

Felidhu Atoll

Mulaku Atoll

I N D I A N

4

Kolhumadulu Atoll

Hadhdhunmathi Atoll

North Huvadhu Atoll

5

Equator

South Huvadhu Atoll

70° 75° 80°

Gan 118
Addu Atoll

A B C D

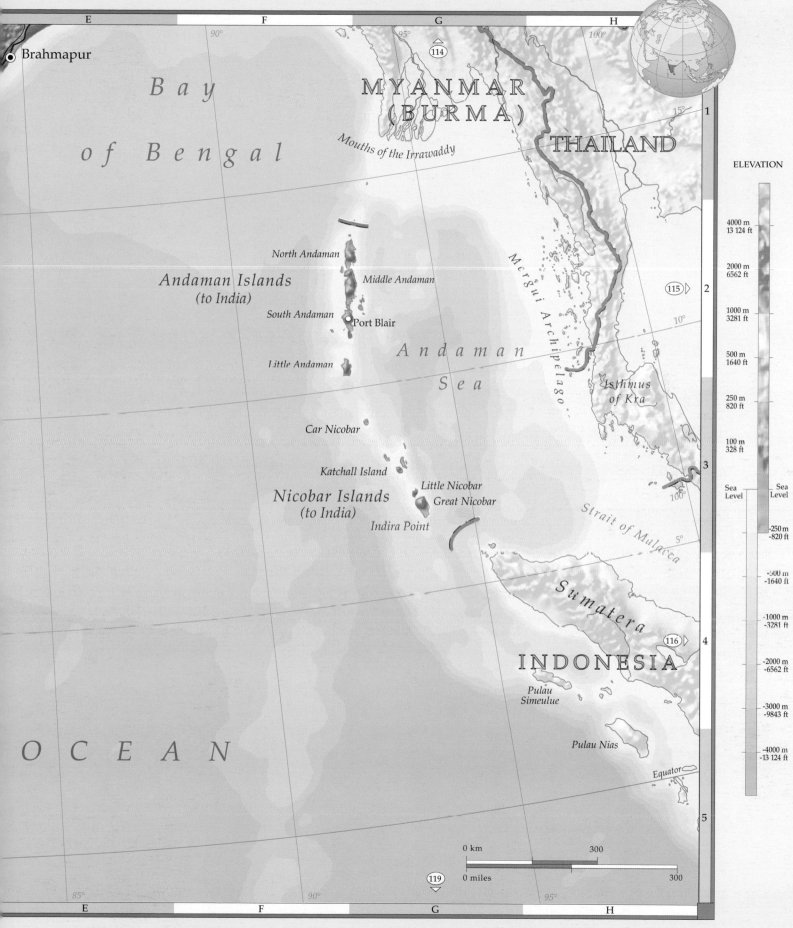

Brahmapur

Bay

of Bengal

MYANMAR
(BURMA)

THAILAND

Mouths of the Irrawaddy

North Andaman

Andaman Islands
(to India)

Middle Andaman

South Andaman

Port Blair

Little Andaman

Andaman

Sea

Mergui Archipelago

*Isthmus
of Kra*

Car Nicobar

Katchall Island

Nicobar Islands
(to India)

Little Nicobar

Great Nicobar

Indira Point

Strait of Malacca

Sumatera

INDONESIA

*Pulau
Simeulue*

Pulau Nias

Equator

OCEAN

ELEVATION

4000 m
13 124 ft

2000 m
6562 ft

1000 m
3281 ft

500 m
1640 ft

250 m
820 ft

100 m
328 ft

Sea
Level

Sea
Level

-250 m
-820 ft

-500 m
-1640 ft

-1000 m
-3281 ft

-2000 m
-6562 ft

-3000 m
-9843 ft

-4000 m
-13 124 ft

0 km   300

0 miles   300

THE WORLD ATLAS

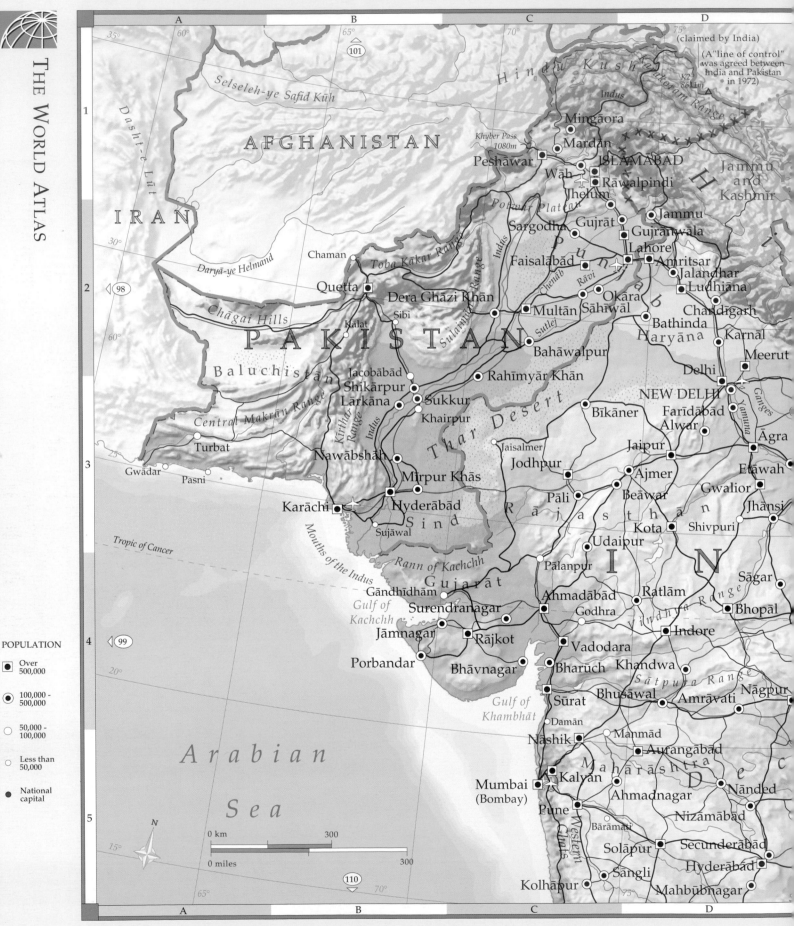

(claimed by India)

(A "line of control" was agreed between India and Pakistan in 1972)

AFGHANISTAN

Selseleh-ye Safid Kūh

Dasht-e Lūt

Hindu Kush

Karakoram Range

K2 8611m

Indus

Jammu and Kashmir

Mingāora

Khyber Pass 1080m

Mardān

IRAN

Peshāwar

Wāh

ISLĀMĀBĀD

Rāwalpindi

Jhelum

Jammu

Potwar Plateau

Sargodha

Gujrāt

Gujrānwāla

Daryā-ye Helmand

Chaman

Toba Kākar Range

Indus

Faisalābād

Lahore

Amritsar

Jalandhar

Quetta

Dera Ghāzi Khān

Sulaimān Range

Chenāb

Rāvi

Okāra

Sāhīwal

Ludhiāna

Kālat

Sibi

Chāgai Hills

Multān

Sutlej

Chandīgarh

Bahāwalpur

Bathinda

Karnāl

Haryāna

PAKISTAN

Baluchistān

Central Makrān Range

Jacobābād

Shikārpur

Larkāna

Kīrthar Range

Indus

Sukkur

Khairpur

Rahīmyār Khān

Thar Desert

Bīkāner

Meerut

Delhi

NEW DELHI

Farīdābād

Alwar

Punjab

Turbat

Nawābshāh

Jaisalmer

Jodhpur

Jaipur

Ajmer

Yamuna

Āgra

Etāwah

Gwalior

Gwādar

Pasni

Mirpur Khās

Hyderābād

Beāwar

Pāli

Rājasthān

Jhānsi

Karāchi

Sind

Kota

Shivpuri

Udaipur

Sujāwal

Mouths of the Indus

Rann of Kachchh

Pālanpur

I N

Tropic of Cancer

Sāgar

Gujarāt

Ahmadābād

Ratlām

Bhopāl

Gāndhīdhām

Godhra

Indore

Surendranagar

Vindhya Range

Gulf of Kachchh

Jāmnagar

Rājkot

Vadodara

Khandwa

Arabian

Porbandar

Bhāvnagar

Bharūch

Sātpura Range

Sea

Sūrat

Bhusāwal

Amrāvati

Nāgpur

Gulf of Khambhāt

Dāmān

Nāshik

Manmād

Aurangābād

D

Maharashtra

Kalyān

Mumbai (Bombay)

Ahmadnagar

Nānded

Pune

Nizāmābad

Western Ghāts

Bārāmati

Solāpur

Secunderābad

Hyderābad

Sāngli

Kolhāpur

Mahbūbnagar

N

POPULATION

- ▣ Over 500,000
- ◉ 100,000 - 500,000
- ○ 50,000 - 100,000
- ○ Less than 50,000
- ● National capital

0 km 300

0 miles 300

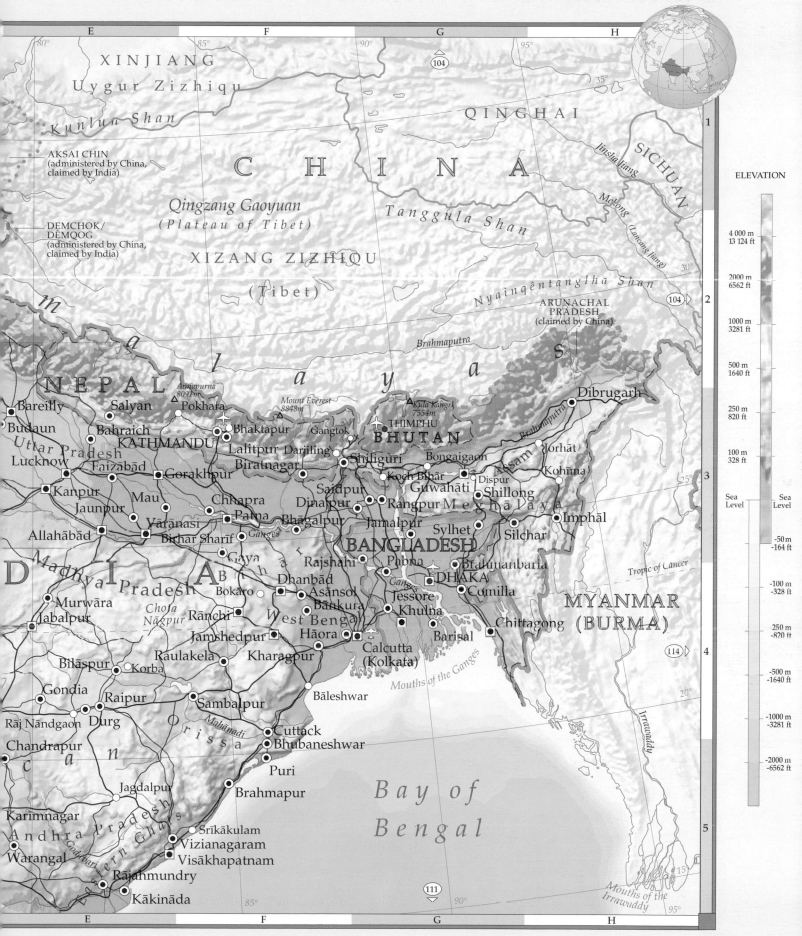

E   F   G   H

XINJIANG
Uygur Zizhiqu

Kunlun Shan

QINGHAI

SICHUAN

C H I N A

Qingzang Gaoyuan
(Plateau of Tibet)

AKSAI CHIN
(administered by China,
claimed by India)

DEMCHOK/
DÊMQOG
(administered by China,
claimed by India)

XIZANG ZIZHIQU

(Tibet)

Tanggula Shan

Jinsha Jiang

Mekong (Lancang Jiang)

Nyainqêntanglha Shan

104

104

ARUNACHAL
PRADESH
(claimed by China)

1

2

Brahmaputra

H   i   m   a   l   a   y   a   s

NEPAL

Annapurna
8091m

Mount Everest
8848m

Kula Kangri
7554m

Dibrugarh

ELEVATION

Bareilly
Budaun
Salyan
Bahraich
Pokhara
Bhaktapur
KATHMANDU
Lalitpur
Gangtok
Darjiling

THIMPHU
BHUTAN

Bongaigaon
Jorhat

Brahmaputra

Assam

4 000 m
13 124 ft

2000 m
6562 ft

1000 m
3281 ft

Uttar Pradesh
Lucknow
Faizabad
Gorakhpur
Biratnagar
Shiliguri
Koch Bihar
Dispur
Guwahati
Shillong
Kohima

500 m
1640 ft

250 m
820 ft

Kanpur
Jaunpur
Mau
Chhapra
Saidpur
Dinajpur
Rangpur
M e g h a l a y a

100 m
328 ft

Allahabad
Varanasi
Patna
Bhagalpur
Jamalpur
Imphal

Sea
Level

Sea
Level

Birhar Sharif
Ganges
Sylhet
Silchar

-50 m
-164 ft

I N D I A
Madhya   Pradesh
Gaya
Rajshahi
BANGLADESH
Pabna
DHAKA
Brahmanbaria
Comilla
Tropic of Cancer

MYANMAR
(BURMA)

-100 m
-328 ft

Murwara
Jabalpur
Chota
Nagpur
Ranchi
Dhanbad
Bokaro
Asansol
Bankura
West Bengal
Haora
Jessore
Khulna
Barisal
Chittagong
Irrawaddy

250 m
-820 ft

Bilaspur
Korba
Raulakela
Jamshedpur
Kharagpur
Calcutta
(Kolkata)

-500 m
-1640 ft

Gondia
Raipur
Sambalpur
Baleshwar
Mouths of the Ganges

-1000 m
-3281 ft

Raj Nandgaon
Durg
Chandrapur
Orissa
Mahanadi
Cuttack
Bhubaneshwar
Puri

-2000 m
-6562 ft

Jagdalpur
Brahmapur

Bay of
Bengal

3

4

5

Karimnagar
Andhra Pradesh
Srikakulam
Vizianagaram
Visakhapatnam
Warangal
Godavari
Eastern Ghats
Rajahmundry
Kakinada

Mouths of the
Irrawaddy

114

111

E   F   G   H

113

THE WORLD ATLAS

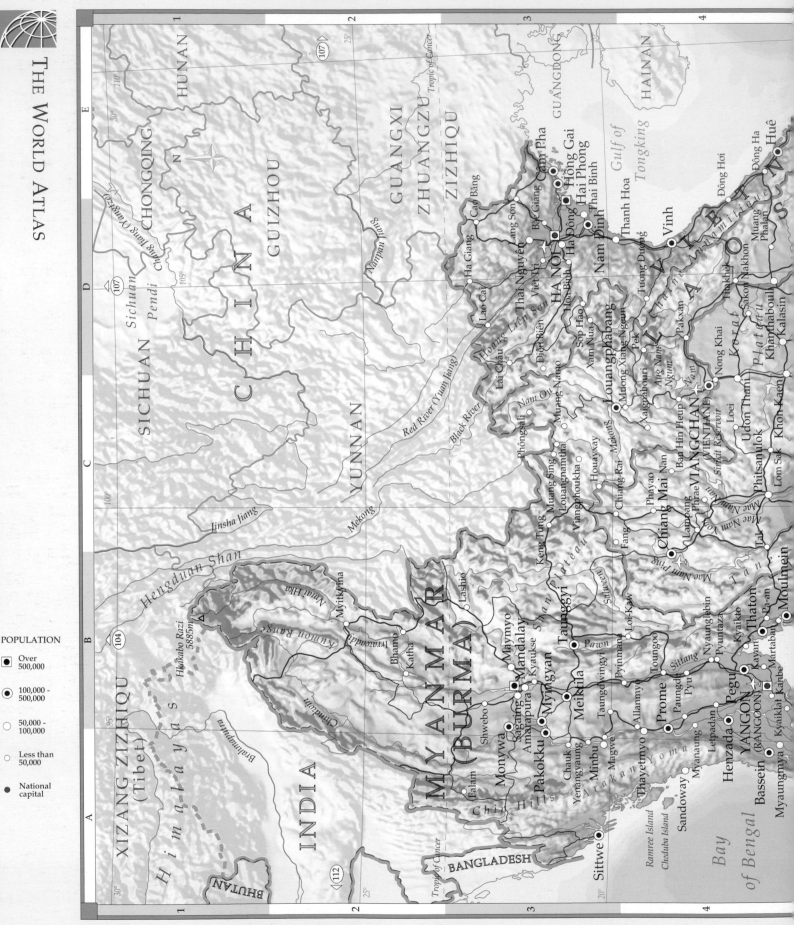

POPULATION

- ◉ Over 500,000
- ◉ 100,000 - 500,000
- ○ 50,000 - 100,000
- ○ Less than 50,000
- ● National capital

MARITIME SOUTHEAST ASIA

SINGAPORE

MALAYSIA

Johore Strait

0 km   10
0 miles   10

Causeway

Lim Chu Kang
Pulau Ubin
Hougang New Town
Pulau Tekong
Bukit Panjang
Changi
Choa Chu Kang
Bukit Timah 176m
Queenstown   City   Bedok New Town
Jurong Industrial Estate
Telok Blangah
Sentosa
Selat Pandan
Pulau Sudong
Pulau Pawai
Strait of Singapore

103°50'
103°40'
104°
1°20'

Urban areas
Open areas
Nature reserves

MYANMAR (BURMA)

LAOS

VIETNAM

THAILAND

CAMBODIA

Gulf of Tongking

Hainan Dao (to China)

PARACEL ISLANDS
(disputed by China, Taiwan and Vietnam)

South China Sea

Mekong

Mouths of the Mekong

SPRATLY ISLANDS
(disputed by China, Malaysia, Philippines, Taiwan and Vietnam)

Andaman Sea

Gulf of Thailand

Nicobar Islands (to India)

Isthmus of Kra

Palawan

Balabac Strait

Gunung Kinabalu 4101m

Bandaaceh   Sigli
George Town   Kota Bharu
Butterworth
Pulau Pinang
Taiping
Ipoh   Dungan
Kuala Terengganu
Kota Kinabalu   Sabah
BANDAR SERI BEGAWAN
BRUNEI
Miri
Tawau

Meulaboh   Langsa
Cukai
Medan   Kuantan
Tebingtinggi   Klang   KUALA LUMPUR
Bintulu
Pematangsiantar
Pulau Simeulue
Strait of Malacca
MALAYSIA
Seremban
Banjaran Tatihak
Kepulauan Banyak
Danau Toba
Melaka   Keluang
Muar   Johor Bahru
Sibu   Batang Raja
Sibolga
Batu Pahat
SINGAPORE
Kuching
Sarawak
Pulau Nias
Sungai Kayan

Equator

Pekanbaru
Kepulauan Lingga
Singkawang   Sidas
Borneo
Samarinda
Solok   Rengat
Pontianak   Sungai Kapuas
Pegunungan Müller
Balikpapan

Padang
Kualatungkal
Selat Karimata
Kalimantan
Sungai Mahakam
Pulau Siberut
Batang Hari
Jambi
Bangka
Sampit
Amuntai
Kandangan
Kepulauan Mentawai
Sungaipenuh
Pangkalpinang
Selat Karimata
Sungai Barito
Palembang
Lahat
Pulau Belitung
Banjarmasin

Bengkulu
INDO
Pulau Laut
Kotabumi
Java Sea
Makassar

Sumatera (Sumatra)
Bandarlampung
Cirebon   Tegal
Pekalongan
Pulau Madura

JAKARTA
Semarang
Serang   Bogor
Kudus   Surabaya
Selat Sunda
Sukabumi   Bandung
Probolinggo   Nu
Tasikmalaya
Kediri   Jember   Mataram
Cilacap
Malang
Denpasar
Jawa (Java)
Magelang
Madiun
Bali   Pulau Lombok
Yogyakarta
Surakarta

INDIAN

OCEAN

POPULATION

- ◉ Over 500,000
- ◉ 100,000 – 500,000
- ○ 50,000 – 100,000
- ○ Less than 50,000
- ● National capital

ELEVATION

4000 m
13 124 ft

2000 m
6562 ft

1000 m
3281 ft

500 m
1640 ft

250 m
820 ft

100 m
328 ft

Sea Level — Sea Level

-250 m
-820 ft

-500 m
-1640 ft

-1000 m
-3281 ft

-2000 m
-6562 ft

-3000 m
-9843 ft

-4000 m
-13 124 ft

Luzon Strait
Babuyan Island
Babuyan Channel

Tuguegarao
Ilagan
Baguio
Luzon
Dagupan
Angeles
Cabanatuan
MANILA
Lucena
PHILIPPINES
Batangas
Naga
Mindoro
Legaspi
Mindoro Strait
Sibuyan Sea
Calbayog
Roxas City
Samar
Cadiz
Panay Island
Tacloban
Iloilo
Leyte
Bacolod City
Cebu
Palawan
Negros
Bohol Sea
Butuan
Puerto Princesa
Iligan
Cagayan de Oro
Bislig
Sulu Sea
Mindanao
Zamboanga
Davao
Basilan
Moro Gulf
Davao Gulf
Sandakan
Lebak
Sulu Archipelago
General Santos

Philippine Sea

PACIFIC

OCEAN

Kepulauan Talaud

Celebes Sea

Kepulauan Sangir

NORTHERN MARIANA ISLANDS (to US)

GUAM (to US)

MICRONESIA

Yap

PALAU

Babeldaob

Equator

Manado
Bitung
Gorontalo
Palu
Gulf of Tomini
Kepulauan Banggai
Sulawesi (Celebes)
Danau Towuti
Parepare
Singkang
Kolaka
Kendari
Watampone
Pulau Buton
Ujungpandang
Bulukumba
Teluk Bone

Pulau Morotai
Pulau Halmahera
Molucca Sea
Halmahera Sea
Selat Dampier
Pulau Waigeo
Sorong
Jazirah Doberai
Pulau Misool
Waflia
Wahai
Tifu
Pulau Buru
Ambon
Pulau Seram
Ceram Sea
Kepulauan Sula
Maluku (Moluccas)
Teluk Berau
Pulau Biak
Pulau Yapen
Teluk Cenderawasih
Sungai Mamberamo
Jayapura
Puncak Jaya 5030m
Pegunungan Maoke
Papua (Irian Jaya)
New Guinea
PAPUA
PAPUA NEW GUINEA
Sungai Digul

NESIA

Kepulauan Kai
Kepulauan Aru
Banda Sea
Kepulauan Tanimbar
Pulau Yamdena

Tenggara
Flores Sea
Flores
Selat Sumba
Savu Sea
Pulau Sumba
Kepulauan Alor
Pulau Wetar
DILI
EAST TIMOR
Timor
Nikiniki
Kupang
Kepulauan Leti

Arafura Sea

Timor Sea

AUSTRALIA

THE INDIAN OCEAN

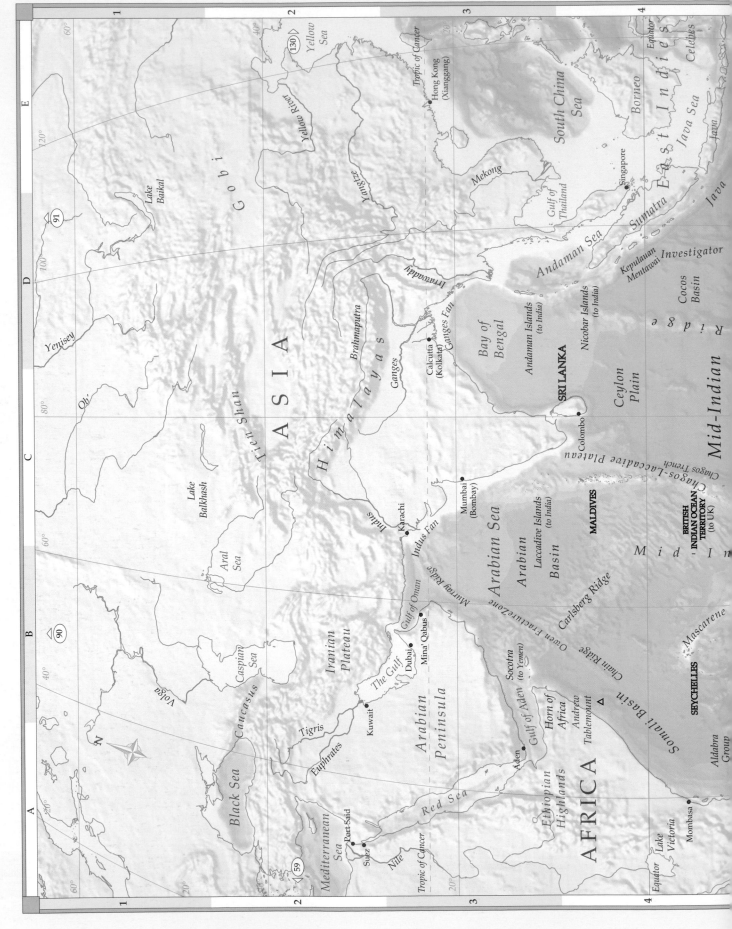

ASIA

AFRICA

Gobi

Lake Baikal

Yenisey

Ob'

Tien Shan

Lake Balkhash

Aral Sea

Caspian Sea

Black Sea

Mediterranean Sea

Volga

Caucasus

Tigris

Euphrates

Iranian Plateau

Arabian Peninsula

Nile

Red Sea

Ethiopian Highlands

Horn of Africa

Gulf of Aden

Socotra (to Yemen)

Aden

Kuwait

The Gulf

Dubai

Mina' Qabus

Gulf of Oman

Murray Ridge

Yellow Sea

Yellow River

Yangtze

Mekong

Hong Kong (Xianggang)

South China Sea

Borneo

Java Sea

Java

Celebes

East Indies

Sumatra

Singapore

Gulf of Thailand

Kepulauan Mentawai

Andaman Sea

Investigator

Cocos Basin

Andaman Islands (to India)

Nicobar Islands (to India)

Bay of Bengal

Ganges Fan

Calcutta (Kolkata)

Ganges

Brahmaputra

Himalayas

Irrawaddy

Indus

Indus Fan

Karachi

Mumbai (Bombay)

SRI LANKA

Colombo

Ceylon Plain

Laccadive Islands (to India)

Arabian Basin

MALDIVES

Arabian Sea

Chagos-Laccadive Plateau

Chagos Trench

BRITISH INDIAN OCEAN TERRITORY (to UK)

Mid-Indian Ridge

Mid-In

Carlsberg Ridge

Owen Fracture Zone

Somali Basin

Chain Ridge

Andrew Tablemount

Mascarene

SEYCHELLES

Aldabra Group

Mombasa

Lake Victoria

Equator

Tropic of Cancer

Port Said

Suez

Tropic of Cancer

60°

120°

100°

80°

60°

40°

20°

40°

20°

20°

130

91

90

59

Page 118

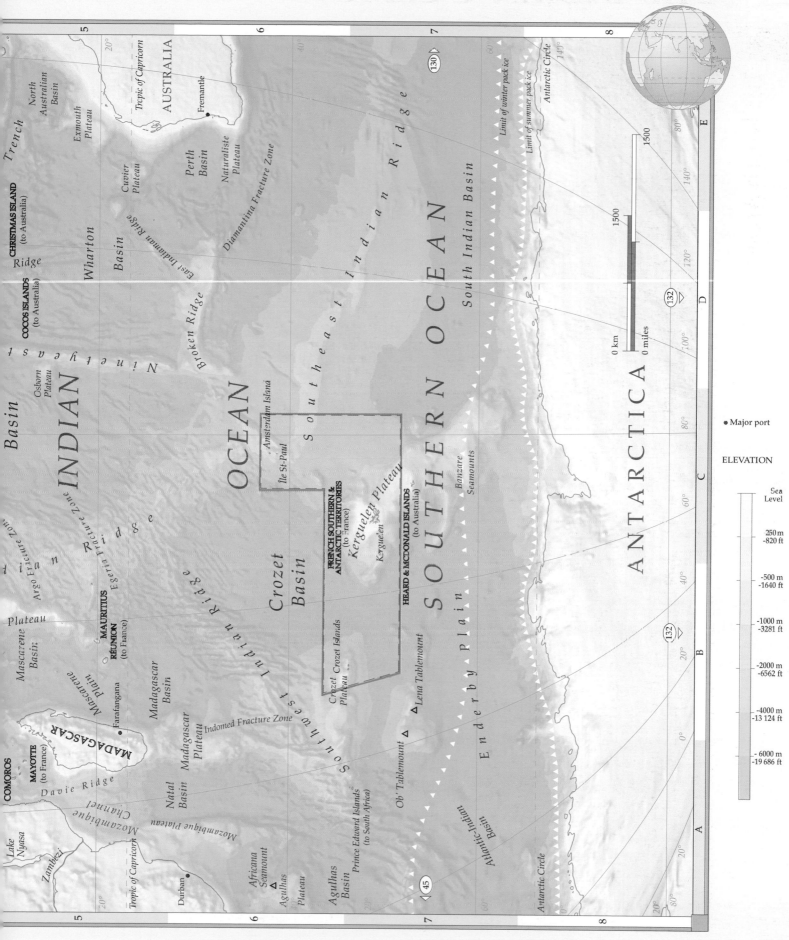

AUSTRALASIA & OCEANIA

THE WORLD ATLAS

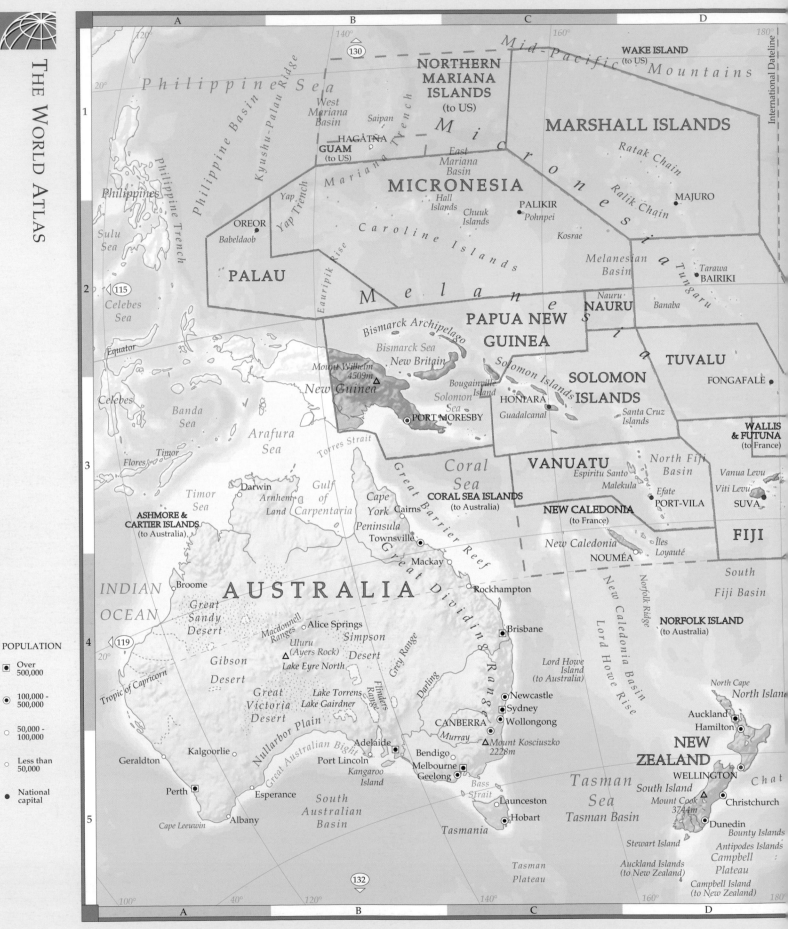

POPULATION

- ▣ Over 500,000
- ◉ 100,000 - 500,000
- ○ 50,000 - 100,000
- ○ Less than 50,000
- ● National capital

Philippine Sea

Philippine Basin

Kyushu-Palau Ridge

NORTHERN MARIANA ISLANDS (to US)

West Mariana Basin

Saipan

WAKE ISLAND (to US)

Mid-Pacific Mountains

Micronesia

MARSHALL ISLANDS

Ratak Chain

Philippine Trench

HAGÅTÑA
GUAM (to US)

East Mariana Basin

Ralik Chain

MAJURO

Philippines

Sulu Sea

MICRONESIA

Yap Trench

Yap

Hall Islands

Chuuk Islands

PALIKIR
Pohnpei

Kosrae

Melanesian Basin

TARAWA
BAIRIKI

Celebes Sea

OREOR
Babeldaob

PALAU

Caroline Islands

Eauripik Rise

Nauru
Banaba

NAURU

TUVALU

FONGAFALE

Equator

Melanesia

Bismarck Archipelago

PAPUA NEW GUINEA

Bismarck Sea
New Britain

Solomon Islands

SOLOMON ISLANDS

Celebes

Mount Wilhelm 4509m △

New Guinea

Bougainville Island
Solomon Sea

HONIARA
Guadalcanal

Santa Cruz Islands

WALLIS & FUTUNA (to France)

Banda Sea

PORT MORESBY

VANUATU

North Fiji Basin

Vanua Levu

Timor
Flores

Arafura Sea

Torres Strait

Coral Sea

CORAL SEA ISLANDS (to Australia)

Espíritu Santo
Malekula

Viti Levu

SUVA

Timor Sea

Darwin
Arnhem Land

Gulf of Carpentaria

Cape York

Cairns

Great Barrier Reef

NEW CALEDONIA (to France)

Efate
PORT-VILA

FIJI

ASHMORE & CARTIER ISLANDS (to Australia)

Peninsula

Townsville

New Caledonia

NOUMÉA
Îles Loyauté

South Fiji Basin

Mackay

Great Dividing Range

New Caledonia Basin

Norfolk Ridge

INDIAN OCEAN

Broome

AUSTRALIA

Rockhampton

Lord Howe Rise

NORFOLK ISLAND (to Australia)

North Cape
North Island

Great Sandy Desert

Macdonnell Ranges
Alice Springs

Simpson Desert

Brisbane

Lord Howe Island (to Australia)

Tropic of Capricorn

Uluru △ (Ayers Rock)
Lake Eyre North

Gibson Desert

Grey Range

Newcastle

Auckland
Hamilton

Great Victoria Desert

Lake Torrens
Lake Gairdner

Flinders Range

Darling

Sydney
Wollongong

CANBERRA
Murray

Mount Kosciuszko 2228m △

NEW ZEALAND

Kalgoorlie

Geraldton

Nullarbor Plain

Adelaide

Bendigo

Melbourne
Geelong

Bass Strait

WELLINGTON
South Island

Mount Cook 3744m △

Chat...

Perth

Port Lincoln
Kangaroo Island

Esperance

Great Australian Bight

Tasman Sea

Christchurch

Albany

Cape Leeuwin

South Australian Basin

Launceston

Hobart

Tasman Basin

Dunedin
Bounty Islands

Stewart Island

Antipodes Islands

Tasmania

Tasman Plateau

Campbell Plateau

Auckland Islands (to New Zealand)

Campbell Island (to New Zealand)

International Dateline

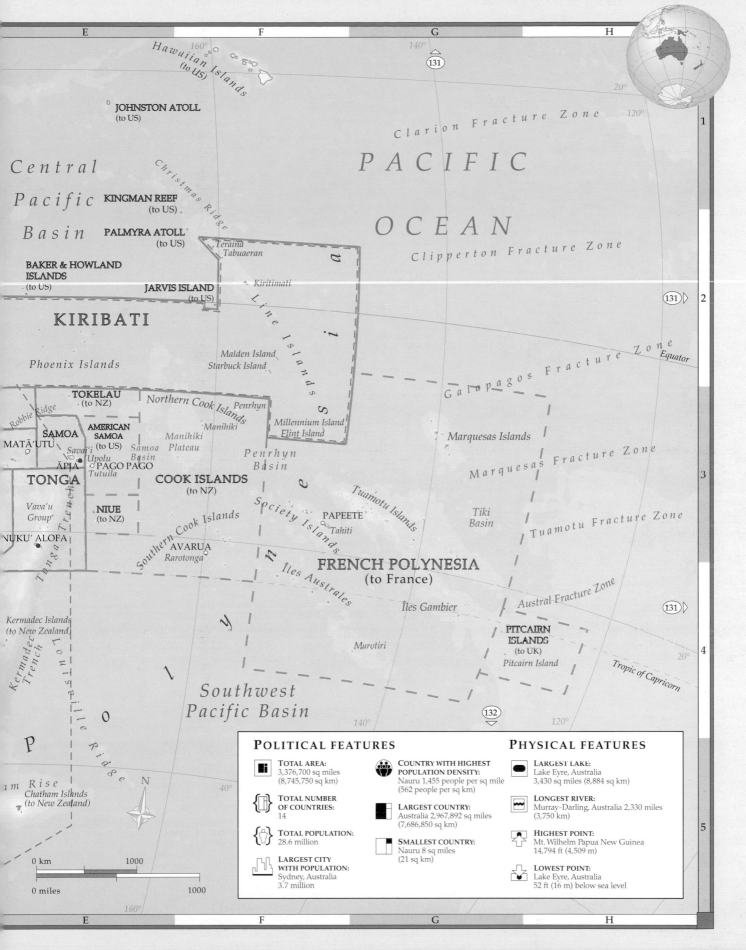

E   F   G   H

160°   140°   120°   20°

Hawaiian Islands (to US)

131

PACIFIC

Clarion Fracture Zone   1

JOHNSTON ATOLL (to US)

Central   **OCEAN**

Pacific

Christmas Ridge

KINGMAN REEF (to US)

Clipperton Fracture Zone

Basin

PALMYRA ATOLL (to US)

Teraina
Tabuaeran

BAKER & HOWLAND ISLANDS (to US)

Kiritimati

JARVIS ISLAND (to US)   131   2

Line Islands   *Equator*

KIRIBATI

Galapagos Fracture Zone

Phoenix Islands

Malden Island
Starbuck Island

Robbie Ridge

TOKELAU (to NZ)

Northern Cook Islands   *Penrhyn*

Marquesas Islands

SAMOA   **AMERICAN SAMOA** (to US)

Manihiki

Millennium Island
Flint Island

Marquesas Fracture Zone   3

MATĀ'UTU

Savai'i   *Manihiki Plateau*

Samoa Basin

ĀPIA   *Upolu*   **PAGO PAGO**
Tutuila

Penrhyn Basin

Tiki Basin

TONGA

COOK ISLANDS (to NZ)

Tuamotu Islands

Tuamotu Fracture Zone

Vava'u Group

NIUE (to NZ)

Society Islands   PAPEETE
Tahiti

NUKU'ALOFA

Southern Cook Islands

AVARUA
Rarotonga

FRENCH POLYNESIA (to France)

Îles Australes

Kermadec Islands (to New Zealand)

Îles Gambier

Austral Fracture Zone   131

Tanga Trench

Louisville Ridge

Murotiri

PITCAIRN ISLANDS (to UK)
Pitcairn Island

20°   *Tropic of Capricorn*   4

Southwest Pacific Basin

... Rise   N

Chatham Islands (to New Zealand)

140°   120°

132

0 km   1000

0 miles   1000

POLITICAL FEATURES

TOTAL AREA:
3,376,700 sq miles
(8,745,750 sq km)

TOTAL NUMBER OF COUNTRIES:
14

TOTAL POPULATION:
28.6 million

LARGEST CITY WITH POPULATION:
Sydney, Australia
3.7 million

COUNTRY WITH HIGHEST POPULATION DENSITY:
Nauru 1,455 people per sq mile
(562 people per sq km)

LARGEST COUNTRY:
Australia 2,967,892 sq miles
(7,686,850 sq km)

SMALLEST COUNTRY:
Nauru 8 sq miles
(21 sq km)

PHYSICAL FEATURES

LARGEST LAKE:
Lake Eyre, Australia
3,430 sq miles (8,884 sq km)

LONGEST RIVER:
Murray-Darling, Australia 2,330 miles
(3,750 km)

HIGHEST POINT:
Mt. Wilhelm Papua New Guinea
14,794 ft (4,509 m)

LOWEST POINT:
Lake Eyre, Australia
52 ft (16 m) below sea level

E   F   G   H

160°

5

THE SOUTHWEST PACIFIC

THE WORLD ATLAS

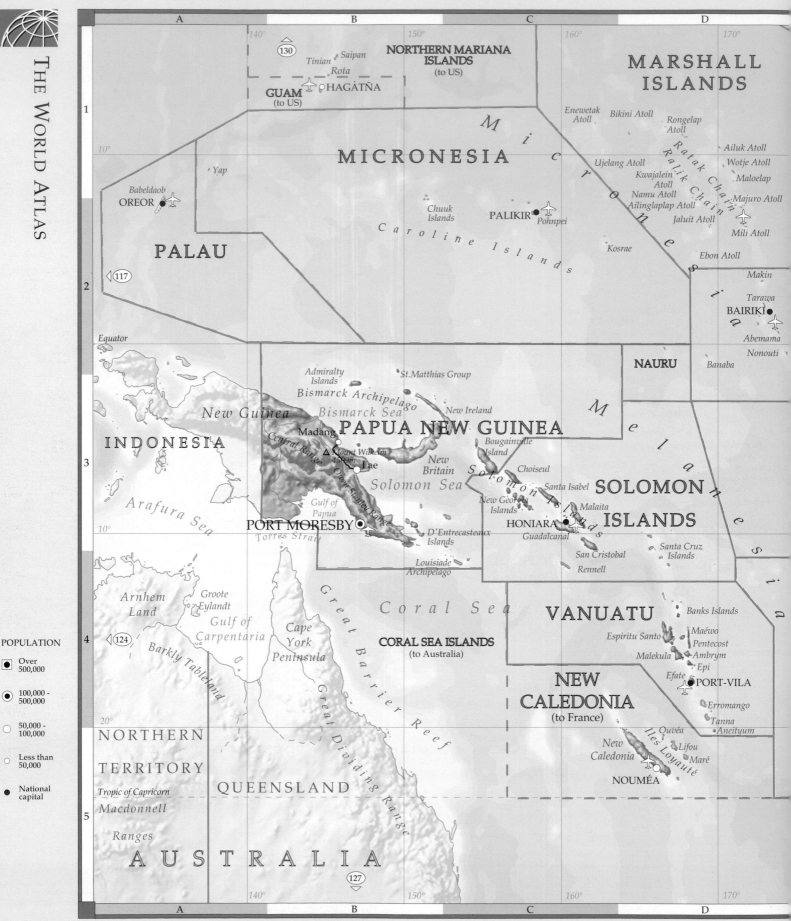

POPULATION

- ● Over 500,000
- ◉ 100,000 – 500,000
- ○ 50,000 – 100,000
- ○ Less than 50,000
- ● National capital

140° 150° 160° 170°

NORTHERN MARIANA ISLANDS
(to US)

MARSHALL ISLANDS

Tinian Saipan
Rota
GUAM HAGÅTÑA
(to US)

MICRONESIA

Enewetak Atoll Bikini Atoll Rongelap Atoll Ailuk Atoll
Ujelang Atoll Wotje Atoll Maloelap
Kwajalein Atoll Majuro Atoll
Namu Atoll Ailinglaplap Atoll Jaluit Atoll Mili Atoll
Kosrae Ebon Atoll

Yap
Babeldaob
OREOR

PALAU

Chuuk Islands PALIKIR Pohnpei

Caroline Islands

Ratak Chain
Ralik Chain

Makin
Tarawa
BAIRIKI
Abemama
Nonouti

Equator

NAURU
Banaba

Admiralty Islands St.Matthias Group
Bismarck Archipelago
New Guinea Bismarck Sea New Ireland
INDONESIA Madang PAPUA NEW GUINEA
Central Range △ Mount Wilhelm 4509m Bougainville Island
Lae New Britain Choiseul
Owen Stanley Range New Georgia Islands Santa Isabel SOLOMON ISLANDS
Solomon Sea Malaita
Arafura Sea Gulf of Papua D'Entrecasteaux Islands HONIARA
PORT MORESBY Guadalcanal
Torres Strait Louisiade Archipelago San Cristobal Santa Cruz Islands
Rennell

Melanesia

Coral Sea

VANUATU Banks Islands
Espiritu Santo Maéwo
Pentecost
Malekula Ambrym
Epi
Efate PORT-VILA
NEW CALEDONIA Erromango
(to France) Tanna
Ouvéa Aneityum
New Caledonia Lifou
Îles Loyauté Maré
NOUMÉA

CORAL SEA ISLANDS
(to Australia)

Arnhem Land
Groote Eylandt
Gulf of Carpentaria
Barkly Tableland
Cape York Peninsula
Great Dividing Range
Great Barrier Reef

NORTHERN TERRITORY
QUEENSLAND
Tropic of Capricorn
Macdonnell Ranges

AUSTRALIA

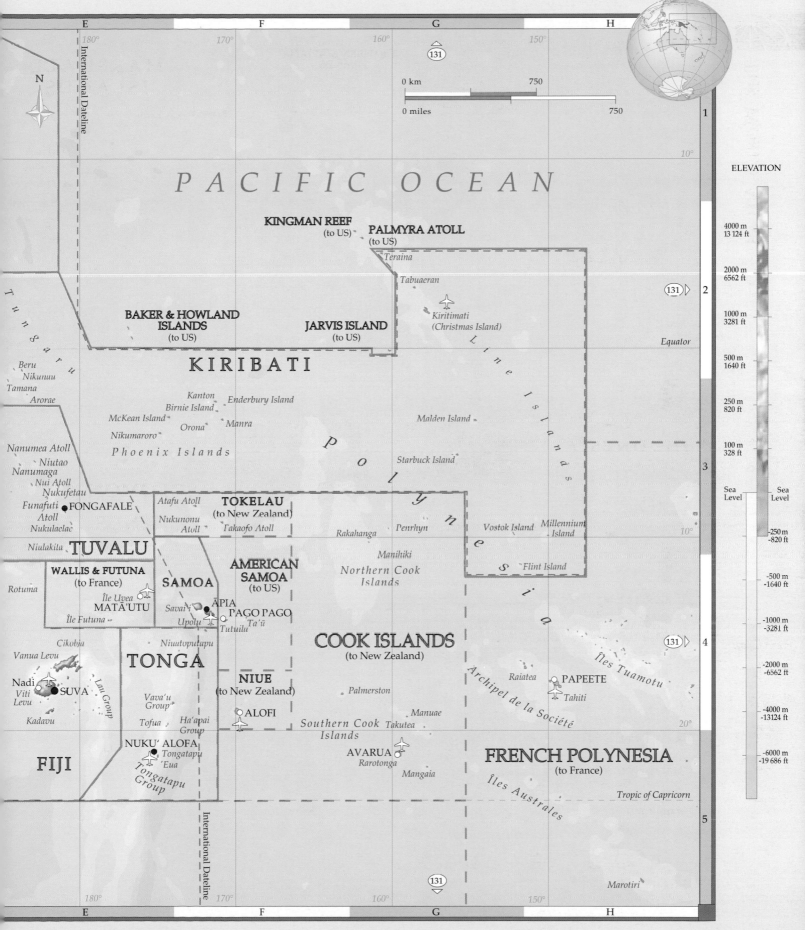

E   F   G   H

180°   170°   160°   150°

131

0 km   750

0 miles   750

N

International Dateline

1

10°

ELEVATION

PACIFIC OCEAN

KINGMAN REEF
(to US)

PALMYRA ATOLL
(to US)

Teraina

Tabuaeran

131   2

BAKER & HOWLAND
ISLANDS
(to US)

JARVIS ISLAND
(to US)

Kiritimati
(Christmas Island)

Equator

4000 m
13 124 ft

2000 m
6562 ft

1000 m
3281 ft

500 m
1640 ft

Tungaru

Beru
Nikunau
Tamana
Arorae

KIRIBATI

Kanton
Birnie Island
McKean Island
Nikumaroro   Orona   Manra

Enderbury Island

Malden Island

Line Islands

250 m
820 ft

Nanumea Atoll
Niutao
Nanumaga
Nui Atoll
Nukufetau
Funafuti   ● FONGAFALE
Atoll
Nukulaelae

Phoenix Islands

Starbuck Island

P
o
l
y
n
e

Atafu Atoll

Nukunonu
Atoll

Takaofo Atoll

TOKELAU
(to New Zealand)

Rakahanga   Penrhyn

Vostok Island   Millennium
Island

Flint Island

100 m
328 ft

3

10°

Sea
Level

Sea
Level

Niulakita   **TUVALU**

WALLIS & FUTUNA
(to France)

Rotuma

Île Uvea
MATÁ'UTU
Île Futuna

SAMOA

Savai'i
Upolu

ĀPIA
PAGO PAGO
Tutuila
Ta'ū

AMERICAN
SAMOA
(to US)

Manihiki

*Northern Cook
Islands*

s
i
a

COOK ISLANDS
(to New Zealand)

131   4

Raiatea   ● PAPEETE

Îles Tuamotu

-250 m
-820 ft

-500 m
-1640 ft

Cikobia
Vanua Levu

Nadi
Viti
Levu   ● SUVA

Lau Group

Niuatoputapu

TONGA

Vava'u
Group

NIUE
(to New Zealand)

Palmerston

ALOFI

Tahiti

Archipel de la Société

-1000 m
-3281 ft

-2000 m
-6562 ft

Kadavu   Tofua

Ha'apai
Group

Southern Cook   Takutea
Islands

Manuae

FRENCH POLYNESIA
(to France)

20°

-4000 m
-13124 ft

FIJI

NUKU' ALOFA

Tongatapu
'Eua
*Tongatapu
Group*

AVARUA
Rarotonga

Mangaia

Îles Australes

Tropic of Capricorn

-6000 m
-19 686 ft

International Dateline

131

5

180°   170°   160°   150°

Marotiri

E   F   G   H

WESTERN AUSTRALIA

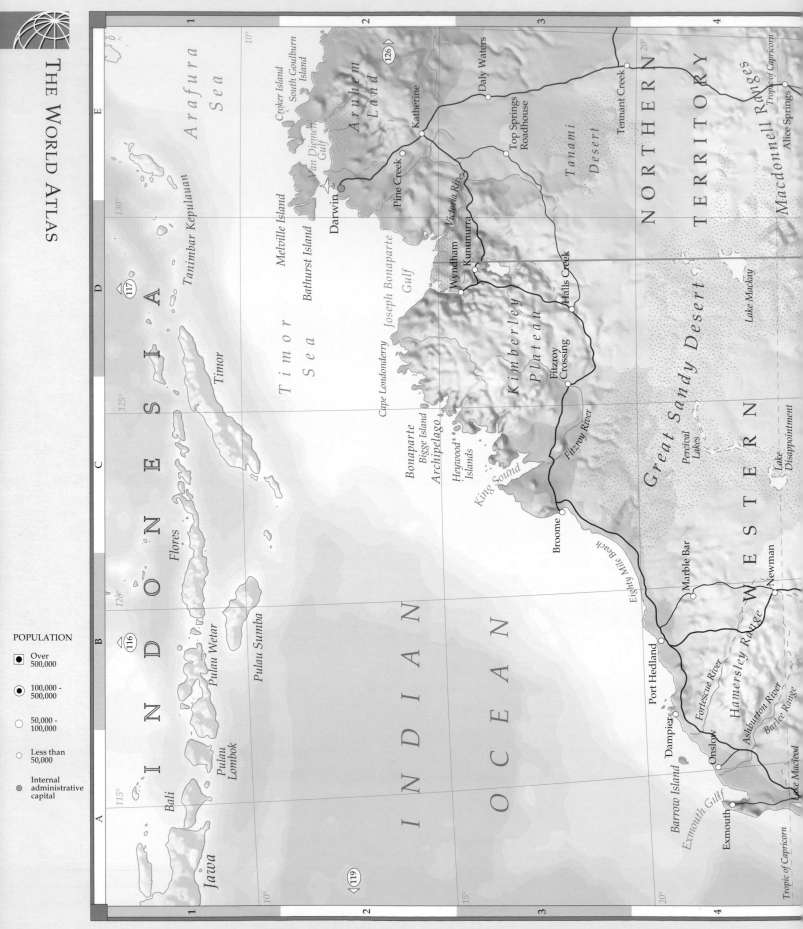

POPULATION

- ● Over 500,000
- ◉ 100,000 – 500,000
- ○ 50,000 – 100,000
- ○ Less than 50,000
- ● Internal administrative capital

AUSTRALIA

SOUTH

Lake Amadeus

Musgrave Ranges

Uluru (Ayers Rock)
862m

Great Victoria Desert

AUSTRALIA

SOUTH
AUSTRALIA

Coober Pedy

Tarcoola

Lake Everard
Penong
Lake Gairdner
Ceduna

Elliston

Port Lincoln

ELEVATION

Nullarbor Plain

Eucla

Reid

Great Australian Bight

INDIAN OCEAN

Gibson Desert

Lake Carnegie
Lake Wells

Robinson Range

Meekatharra

Mount Magnet

Lake Carey

Lake Barlee

Lake Moore

Lake Rebecca

Zanthus

Kalgoorlie
Coolgardie

Lake Cowan

Norseman
Balladonia

Esperance

Southern Cross

Merredin

Northam
Brookton
Narrogin
Wagin
Katanning
Manjimup

Albany

AUSTRALIA

Murchison River

Gascoyne River

Carnarvon

Bernier Island
Dorre Island
Shark Bay
Dirk Hartog
Island

Denham

Kalbarri

Geraldton

Moora

Gingin
Perth
Fremantle
Rockingham
Mandurah
Bunbury
Busselton
Augusta

Collie

4000 m
13 124 ft

2000 m
6562 ft

1000 m
3281 ft

500 m
1640 ft

250 m
820 ft

100 m
328 ft

Sea
Level

Sea
Level

-250 m
-820 ft

-500 m
-1640 ft

-1000 m
-3281 ft

-2000 m
-6562 ft

-3000 m
-9843 ft

-4000 m
-13 124 ft

0 km

0 miles

N

Eastern Australia

SYDNEY

Broken Bay
Palm Beach
Manly
Ku-ring-gai Chase
Ku-ring-gai National Park
Port Jackson
Harbour Bridge
Opera House
Central Station
Hornsby
Windsor
Ryde
Sydney University
Botany
Bondi Beach
Penrith
St Marys
Parramatta
Strathfield
Rockwood Smith
Botany Bay
Liverpool
Bankstown
Sutherland
Rockdale
Hurstville
Kogarah
Port Hacking
Georges River
Campbelltown
Royal National Park

Site of 2000 Olympics
- Places of interest
- Regions/suburbs

0 km 10
0 miles 10

POPULATION

- ● Over 500,000
- ◉ 100,000 – 500,000
- ○ 50,000 – 100,000
- ○ Less than 50,000
- ● National capital
- ● Internal administrative capital

INDONESIA
PAPUA NEW GUINEA

CORAL SEA ISLANDS
(to Australia)

Coral Sea

Arafura Sea

Van Diemen Gulf
Darwin
Croker Island
South Goulburn Island
Wessel Islands
Groote Eylandt
Pine Creek
Katherine
Arnhem Land

Torres Strait
Moa Island
Badu Island
Prince of Wales Island
Endeavour Str
Cape York
Cape York Peninsula

Princess Charlotte Bay
Cooktown
Port Douglas
Cairns
Mareeba
Atherton
Innisfail
Tully
Hinchinbrook Island
Townsville
Bowen
Whitsunday Group
Mackay

Great Barrier Reef

Marlborough
Yeppon
Rockhampton
Curtis Island
Gladstone
Biloela
Bundaberg
Fraser Island

Tropic of Capricorn

Bloomsbury
Charters Towers
Clermont
Emerald
Springsure
Great Dividing Range
Barcaldine
Blackall

Hughenden
Winton
Longreach
Windorah
Cooper Creek

Great Dividing Range
Mitchell River
Gilbert River
Normanton
Flinders River
Gregory Range
Flinders River

Gulf of Carpentaria
Mornington Island
Wellesley Islands
Burketown
Cloncurry
Selwyn Range
Mount Isa

Sir Edward Pellew Group

Barkly Tableland

NORTHERN TERRITORY

Tennant Creek
Tanami Desert

Daly Waters
Top Springs Roadhouse

Alice Springs
Macdonnell Ranges
Tropic of Capricorn
Lake Amadeus
Uluru (Ayers Rock) 867m

Simpson

AUSTRALIA

QUEENSLAND

New Zealand

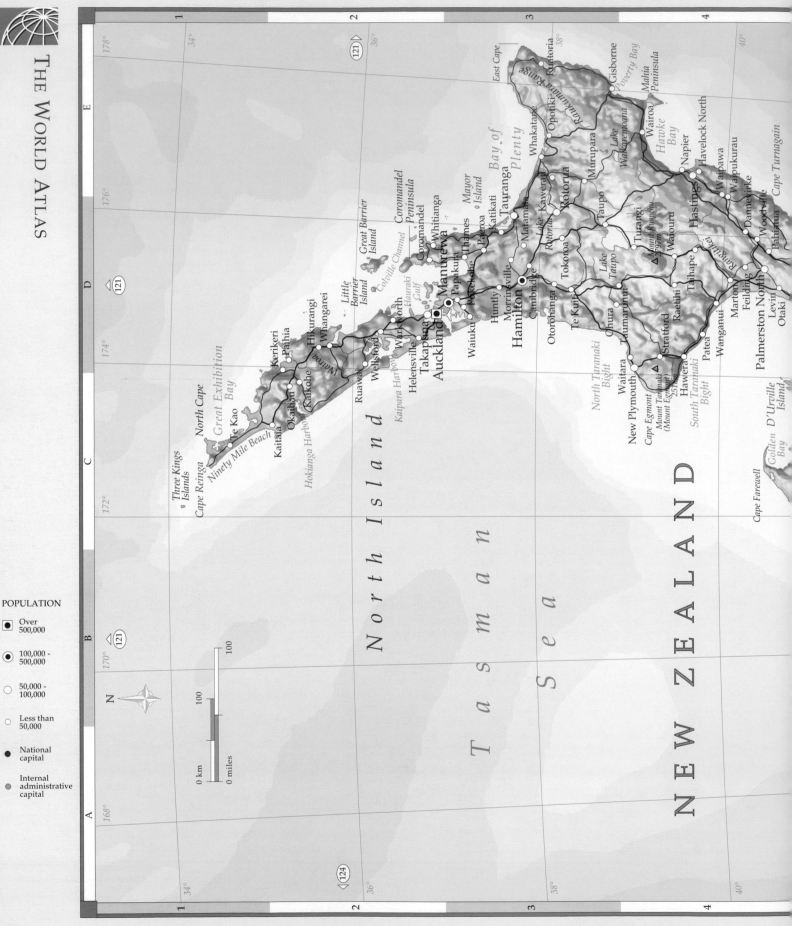

POPULATION

- Over 500,000
- 100,000 – 500,000
- 50,000 – 100,000
- Less than 50,000
- National capital
- Internal administrative capital

N

100
100
0 km
0 miles

Tasman Sea

North Island

NEW ZEALAND

Three Kings Islands
Cape Reinga
North Cape
Great Exhibition Bay
Te Kao
Ninety Mile Beach
Kaitaia
Okaihau
Kaikohe
Hokianga Harbour
Kerikeri
Pahia
Hikurangi
Whangarei
Wairoa
Ruawai
Wellsford
Kaipara Harbour
Helensville
Warkworth
Takapuna
Auckland
Waiuku
Pukekohe
Manurewa
Papakura
Hauraki Gulf
Great Barrier Island
Little Barrier Island
Coville Channel
Coromandel
Coromandel Peninsula
Whitianga
Mayor Island
Thames
Paeroa
Katikati
Tauranga
Matamata
Kawerau
Opotiki
Whakatane
Bay of Plenty
Raukumara Range
East Cape
Ruatoria
Gisborne
Poverty Bay
Mahia Peninsula
Huntly
Morrinsville
Cambridge
Hamilton
Te Kuiti
Otorohanga
Lake Rotorua
Rotorua
Tokoroa
Lake Taupo
Murupara
Lake Waikaremoana
Wairoa
Hawke Bay
Napier
Hastings
Havelock North
Waipawa
Waipukurau
Danneyirke
Woodville
Pahiatua
Cape Turnagain
Taupo
Turangi
Mount Ruapehu 2797m
Waiouru
Taihape
Raetihi
Ohura
Taumarunui
North Taranaki Bight
New Plymouth
Waitara
Stratford
Cape Egmont
Mount Taranaki (Mount Egmont) 2518m
Hawera
Patea
South Taranaki Bight
Wanganui
Rangitikei
Marton
Feilding
Palmerston North
Levin
Otaki
Cape Farewell
Golden Bay
D'Urville Island

172° 174° 176° 178°
170° 168°
34° 36° 38° 40°

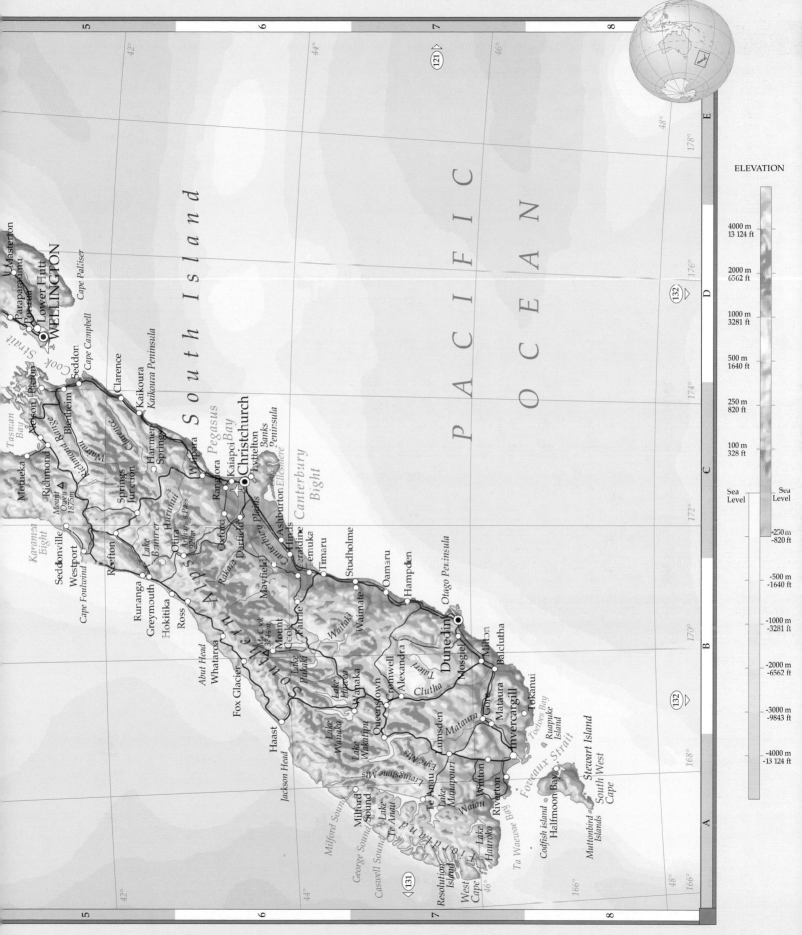

ELEVATION

4000 m	13 124 ft
2000 m	6562 ft
1000 m	3281 ft
500 m	1640 ft
250 m	820 ft
100 m	328 ft
Sea Level	Sea Level
-250 m	-820 ft
-500 m	-1640 ft
-1000 m	-3281 ft
-2000 m	-6562 ft
-3000 m	-9843 ft
-4000 m	-13 124 ft

South Island

PACIFIC OCEAN

Cook Strait

Wellington
Lower Hutt
Petone
Porirua
Paraparaumu
Masterton
Cape Palliser

Seddon
Blenheim
Nelson
Picton
Cape Campbell
Clarence
Kaikoura
Kaikoura Peninsula

Motueka
Richmond
Mount Owen
1875m
Richmond Range
Wairau
Springs Junction
Hanmer Springs
Waipara
Rangiora
Kaiapoi
Pegasus Bay
Christchurch
Lyttelton
Banks Peninsula
Lake Ellesmere

Karamea Bight
Seddonville
Westport
Cape Foulwind
Reefton
Ruranga
Greymouth
Hokitika
Ross

Lake Brunner
Otira
Arthur's Pass
920m
Hurunui
Oxford
Darfield
Rakaia
Ashburton
Canterbury Plains
Hinds
Mayfield
Geraldine
Temuka
Timaru

Canterbury Bight

Abut Head
Whataroa
Fox Glacier
M. Cook
3744m
Mount Cook
Haast
Jackson Head

Lake Pukaki
Lake Tekapo
Fairlie
Waitaki
Waimate
Studholme
Oamaru
Hampden

Lake Wanaka
Lake Hawea
Wanaka
Cromwell
Alexandra
Clutha
Taieri

Otago Peninsula
Dunedin
Mosgiel
Milton
Balclutha

Lake Wakatipu
Queenstown
Lumsden
Mataura
Gore
Mataura

Milford Sound
George Sound
Caswell Sound
Lake Te Anau
Te Anau
Lake Manapouri
Lake Hauroka
Waiau
Eyre Mts
Winton
Riverton
Invercargill
Tokanui

Foveaux Strait
Ruapuke Island
Toetoes Bay
Te Waewae Bay
Codfish Island
Halfmoon Bay
Muttonbird Islands
Stewart Island
South West Cape

Resolution Island
West Cape
Livingstone Mts
Puysegur Point

Tasman Bay

THE PACIFIC OCEAN

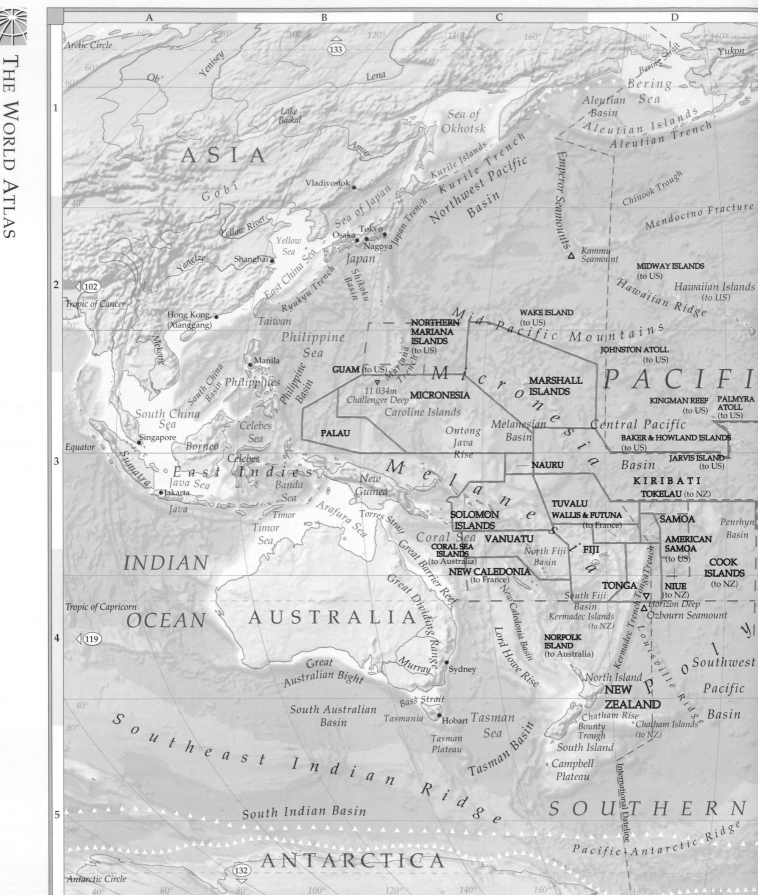

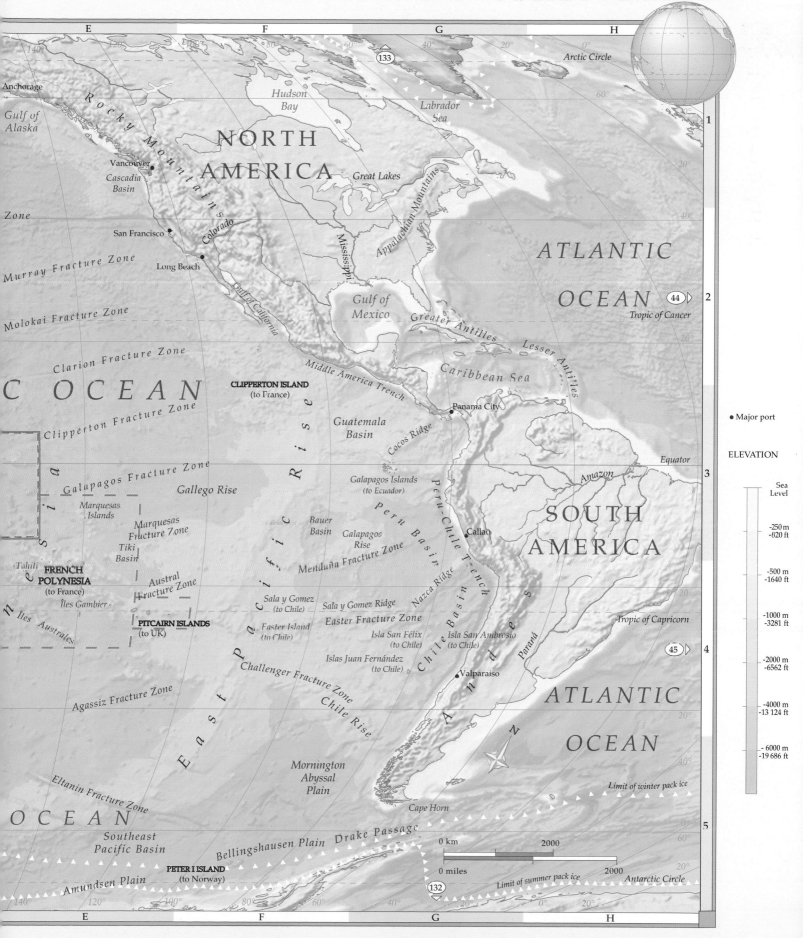

E F G H

133

Arctic Circle

Anchorage

Gulf of Alaska

Rocky Mountains

Hudson Bay

Labrador Sea

NORTH AMERICA

Vancouver

Cascadia Basin

Great Lakes

60°

Zone

40°

San Francisco

Colorado

ATLANTIC

Murray Fracture Zone

Long Beach

Gulf of California

Mississippi

Appalachian Mountains

OCEAN

44

20°

Molokai Fracture Zone

Gulf of Mexico

Greater Antilles

Tropic of Cancer

Clarion Fracture Zone

CLIPPERTON ISLAND (to France)

Middle America Trench

Lesser Antilles

Caribbean Sea

20°

C OCEAN

Clipperton Fracture Zone

Guatemala Basin

Panama City

s i a

Galapagos Fracture Zone

Cocos Ridge

Gallego Rise

Galapagos Islands (to Ecuador)

Amazon

Equator

Marquesas Islands

Bauer Basin

Galapagos Rise

SOUTH AMERICA

Marquesas Fracture Zone

Peru Basin

Tiki Basin

Menduña Fracture Zone

Peru Chile Trench

Callao

Tahiti

FRENCH POLYNESIA (to France)

Nazca Ridge

Îles Gambier

Austral Fracture Zone

Sala y Gomez (to Chile)

Sala y Gomez Ridge

Tropic of Capricorn

PITCAIRN ISLANDS (to UK)

Easter Island (to Chile)

Easter Fracture Zone

Isla San Félix (to Chile)

Isla San Ambrosio (to Chile)

Paraná

45

Îles Australes

Islas Juan Fernández (to Chile)

Chile Basin

A n d e s

East Pacific Rise

Challenger Fracture Zone

Valparaiso

Agassiz Fracture Zone

Chile Rise

ATLANTIC

Eltanin Fracture Zone

Mornington Abyssal Plain

N

OCEAN

Cape Horn

Limit of winter pack ice

OCEAN

Southeast Pacific Basin

Bellingshausen Plain

Drake Passage

0 km   2000

Amundsen Plain

PETER I ISLAND (to Norway)

0 miles   2000

Limit of summer pack ice

Antarctic Circle

132

E F G H

• Major port

ELEVATION

Sea Level

-250 m
-820 ft

-500 m
-1640 ft

-1000 m
-3281 ft

-2000 m
-6562 ft

-4000 m
-13 124 ft

-6000 m
-19 686 ft

ANTARCTICA

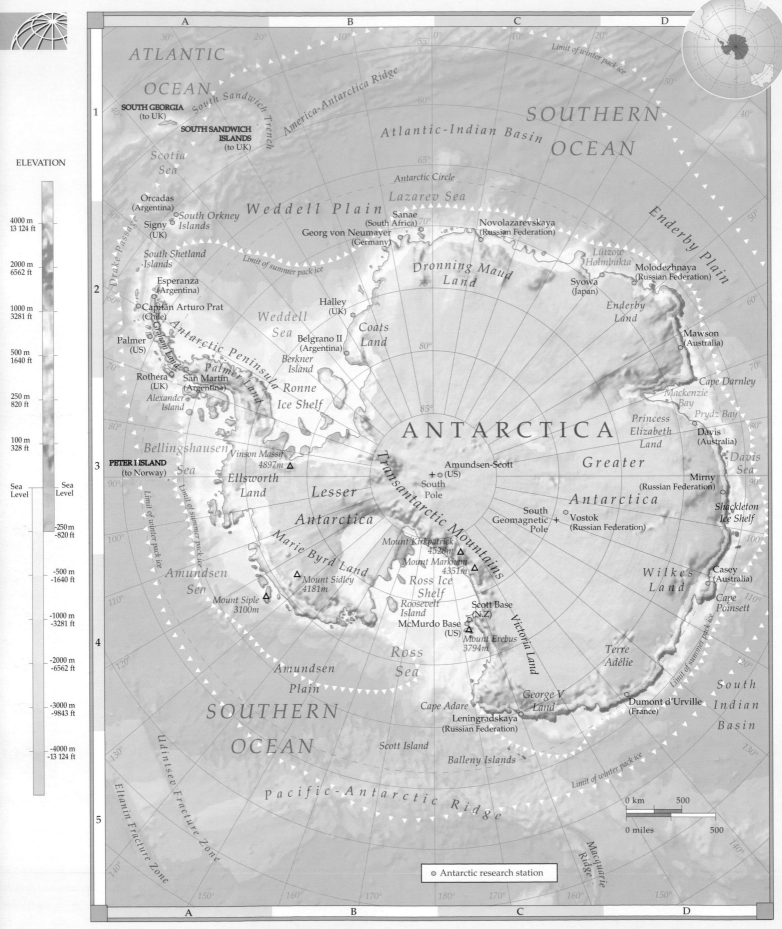

ELEVATION

4000 m
13 124 ft

2000 m
6562 ft

1000 m
3281 ft

500 m
1640 ft

250 m
820 ft

100 m
328 ft

Sea Level — Sea Level

-250 m
-820 ft

-500 m
-1640 ft

-1000 m
-3281 ft

-2000 m
-6562 ft

-3000 m
-9843 ft

-4000 m
-13 124 ft

ATLANTIC OCEAN

SOUTHERN OCEAN

Scotia Sea

SOUTH GEORGIA (to UK)

SOUTH SANDWICH ISLANDS (to UK)

South Sandwich Trench

America-Antarctica Ridge

Limit of winter pack ice

Atlantic-Indian Basin

Antarctic Circle

Lazarev Sea

Enderby Plain

Orcadas (Argentina)

Signy (UK)

South Orkney Islands

Weddell Plain

Sanae (South Africa)

Georg von Neumayer (Germany)

Novolazarevskaya (Russian Federation)

Lützow Holmbukta

Molodezhnaya (Russian Federation)

Drake Passage

South Shetland Islands

Limit of summer pack ice

Dronning Maud Land

Syowa (Japan)

Enderby Land

Esperanza (Argentina)

Capitán Arturo Prat (Chile)

Weddell Sea

Halley (UK)

Antarctic Peninsula

Graham Land

Palmer (US)

Belgrano II (Argentina)

Coats Land

Mawson (Australia)

Rothera (UK)

San Martín (Argentina)

Palmer Land

Berkner Island

Ronne Ice Shelf

Cape Darnley

Alexander Island

Mackenzie Bay

Prydz Bay

Princess Elizabeth Land

Davis (Australia)

ANTARCTICA

Bellingshausen Sea

Vinson Massif 4897m

PETER I ISLAND (to Norway)

Ellsworth Land

Lesser Antarctica

Transantarctic Mountains

Amundsen-Scott (US)

South Pole

Greater Antarctica

Davis Sea

Mirny (Russian Federation)

South Geomagnetic Pole

Vostok (Russian Federation)

Shackleton Ice Shelf

Limit of winter pack ice

Limit of summer pack ice

Amundsen Sea

Mount Sidley 4181m

Marie Byrd Land

Mount Kirkpatrick 4528m

Mount Markham 4351m

Ross Ice Shelf

Wilkes Land

Casey (Australia)

Mount Siple 3100m

Roosevelt Island

Scott Base (N.Z)

McMurdo Base (US)

Mount Erebus 3794m

Victoria Land

Cape Poinsett

Amundsen Plain

Ross Sea

Terre Adélie

SOUTHERN OCEAN

Cape Adare

Leningradskaya (Russian Federation)

George V Land

Dumont d'Urville (France)

South Indian Basin

Udintsev Fracture Zone

Eltanin Fracture Zone

Scott Island

Balleny Islands

Pacific-Antarctic Ridge

Limit of winter pack ice

Macquarie Ridge

0 km — 500

0 miles — 500

○ Antarctic research station

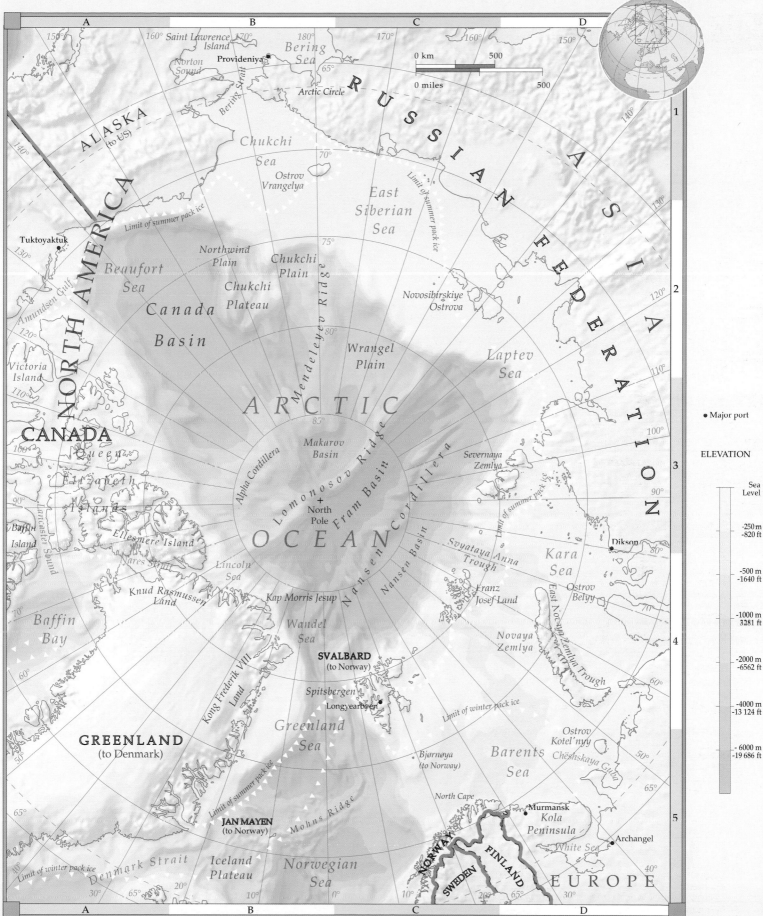

ALASKA (to US)

RUSSIAN FEDERATION

Saint Lawrence Island

Norton Sound

Provid…niya

Bering Sea

Arctic Circle

Bering Strait

Chukchi Sea

Ostrov Vrangelya

East Siberian Sea

Limit of summer pack ice

NORTH AMERICA

Tuktoyaktuk

Limit of summer pack ice

Beaufort Sea

Northwind Plain

Chukchi Plain

Chukchi Plateau

Canada Basin

Novosibirskiye Ostrova

Wrangel Plain

Laptev Sea

Amundsen Gulf

Mendeleyev Ridge

CANADA

Victoria Island

A R C T I C

Makarov Basin

Severnaya Zemlya

Queen

Alpha Cordillera

Lomonosov Ridge

Fram Basin

+ North Pole

Svyataya Anna Trough

Elizabeth Islands

Nansen Cordillera

Dikson

Baffin Island

Lancaster Sound

Ellesmere Island

O C E A N

Nansen Basin

Kara Sea

Ostrov Belyy

Nares Strait

Lincoln Sea

Kap Morris Jesup

Franz Josef Land

East Novaya Zemlya Trough

Knud Rasmussen Land

Wandel Sea

Limit of summer pack ice

Baffin Bay

Kong Frederik VIII Land

SVALBARD (to Norway)

Novaya Zemlya

Ostrov Kotel'nyy

Spitsbergen

Longyearbyen

Chëshskaya Guba

GREENLAND (to Denmark)

Greenland Sea

Bjørnøya (to Norway)

Barents Sea

Limit of winter pack ice

North Cape

Limit of summer pack ice

Mohns Ridge

Murmansk

Kola Peninsula

Archangel

JAN MAYEN (to Norway)

NORWAY

White Sea

Limit of winter pack ice

Denmark Strait

Iceland Plateau

Norwegian Sea

SWEDEN

FINLAND

EUROPE

Legend

● Major port

ELEVATION

Sea Level

-250 m / -820 ft

-500 m / -1640 ft

-1000 m / 3281 ft

-2000 m / -6562 ft

-4000 m / -13 124 ft

-6000 m / -19 686 ft

OVERSEAS TERRITORIES AND DEPENDENCIES

DESPITE THE RAPID PROCESS of decolonization since the end of the Second World War, around 10 million people in more than 50 territories around the world continue to live under the protection of France, Australia, the Netherlands, Denmark, Norway, New Zealand, the United Kingdom or the USA. These remnants of former colonial empires may have persisted for economic, strategic or political reasons, and are administered in a variety of ways.

AUSTRALIA

ASHMORE & CARTIER ISLANDS
Indian Ocean
Status External territory
Claimed 1978
Capital not applicable
Population None
Area 2 sq miles (5.2 sq km)

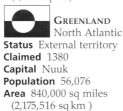
CHRISTMAS ISLAND
Indian Ocean
Status External territory
Claimed 1958
Capital Flying Fish Cove
Population 1,275
Area 52 sq miles (134.6 sq km)

COCOS ISLANDS
Indian Ocean
Status External territory
Claimed 1955
Capital No official capital
Population 670
Area 5.5 sq miles (14.24 sq km)

CORAL SEA ISLANDS
South Pacific
Status External territory
Claimed 1969
Capital None
Population 8 (meteorologists)
Area Less than 1.16 sq miles (3 sq km)

HEARD & McDONALD ISLANDS
Indian Ocean
Status External territory
Claimed 1947
Capital not applicable
Population None
Area 161 sq miles (417 sq km)z

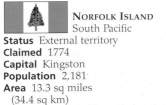
NORFOLK ISLAND
South Pacific
Status External territory
Claimed 1774
Capital Kingston
Population 2,181
Area 13.3 sq miles (34.4 sq km)

DENMARK

FAEROE ISLANDS
North Atlantic
Status External territory
Claimed 1380
Capital Tórshavn
Population 43,382
Area 540 sq miles (1,399 sq km)

GREENLAND
North Atlantic
Status External territory
Claimed 1380
Capital Nuuk
Population 56,076
Area 840,000 sq miles (2,175,516 sq km)

FRANCE

CLIPPERTON ISLAND
East Pacific
Status Dependency of French Polynesia
Claimed 1930
Capital not applicable
Population None
Area 2.7 sq miles (7 sq km)

FRENCH GUIANA South America
Status Overseas department
Claimed 1817
Capital Cayenne
Population 152,300
Area 35,135 sq miles (90,996 sq km)

FRENCH POLYNESIA
South Pacific
Status Overseas territory
Claimed 1843
Capital Papeete
Population 219,521
Area 1,608 sq miles (4,165 sq km)

GUADELOUPE West Indies
Status Overseas department
Claimed 1635
Capital Basse-Terre
Population 419,500
Area 687 sq miles (1,780 sq km)

MARTINIQUE West Indies
Status Overseas department
Claimed 1635
Capital Fort-de-France
Population 381,200
Area 425 sq miles (1,100 sq km)

MAYOTTE Indian Ocean
Status Territorial collectivity
Claimed 1843
Capital Mamoudzou
Population 131,320
Area 144 sq miles (374 sq km)

NEW CALEDONIA South Pacific
Status Overseas territory
Claimed 1853
Capital Nouméa
Population 196,836
Area 7,374 sq miles (19,103 sq km)

RÉUNION Indian Ocean
Status Overseas department
Claimed 1638
Capital Saint-Denis
Population 697,000
Area 970 sq miles (2,512 sq km)

ST. PIERRE & MIQUELON
North America
Status Territorial collectivity
Claimed 1604
Capital Saint-Pierre
Population 6,600
Area 93.4 sq miles (242 sq km)

WALLIS & FUTUNA
South Pacific
Status Overseas territory
Claimed 1842
Capital Matā'Utu
Population 15,000
Area 106 sq miles (274 sq km)

NETHERLANDS

ARUBA
West Indies
Status Autonomous part of the Netherlands
Claimed 1643
Capital Oranjestad
Population 88,000
Area 75 sq miles (194 sq km)

NETHERLANDS ANTILLES
West Indies
Status Autonomous part of the Netherlands
Claimed 1816
Capital Willemstad
Population 207,175
Area 308 sq miles (800 sq km)

NEW ZEALAND

COOK ISLANDS
South Pacific
Status Associated territory
Claimed 1901
Capital Avarua
Population 20,200
Area 113 sq miles (293 sq km)

NIUE
South Pacific
Status Associated territory
Claimed 1901
Capital Alofi
Population 2,080
Area 102 sq miles (264 sq km)

TOKELAU
South Pacific
Status Dependent territory
Claimed 1926
Capital not applicable
Population 1,577
Area 4 sq miles (10.4 sq km)

NORWAY

BOUVET ISLAND
South Atlantic
Status Dependency
Claimed 1928
Capital not applicable
Population None
Area 22 sq miles (58 sq km)**JAN**

MAYEN
North Atlantic
Status Dependency
Claimed 1929
Capital not applicable
Population None
Area 147 sq miles (381 sq km)

PETER I ISLAND
Southern Ocean
Status Dependency
Claimed 1931
Capital not applicable
Population None
Area 69 sq miles (180 sq km)

SVALBARD Arctic Ocean
Status Dependency
Claimed 1920
Capital Longyearbyen
Population 3,231
Area 24,289 sq miles (62,906 sq km)

UNITED KINGDOM

ANGUILLA
West Indies
Status Dependent territory
Claimed 1650
Capital The Valley
Population 10,300
Area 37 sq miles (96 sq km)

ASCENSION ISLAND
South Atlantic
Status Dependency of St. Helena
Claimed 1673
Capital Georgetown
Population 1,099
Area 34 sq miles (88 sq km)

BERMUDA
North Atlantic
Status Crown colony
Claimed 1612
Capital Hamilton
Population 60,144
Area 20.5 sq miles (53 sq km)

BRITISH INDIAN OCEAN TERRITORY Indian Ocean
Status Dependent territory
Claimed 1814
Capital Diego Garcia
Population 930
Area 23 sq miles (60 sq km)

 BRITISH VIRGIN ISLANDS West Indies
Status Dependent territory
Claimed 1672
Capital Road Town
Population 17,896
Area 59 sq miles (153 sq km)

 CAYMAN ISLANDS West Indies
Status Dependent territory
Claimed 1670
Capital George Town
Population 35,000
Area 100 sq miles (259 sq km)

 FALKLAND ISLANDS South Atlantic
Status Dependent territory
Claimed 1832
Capital Stanley
Population 2,564
Area 4,699 sq miles (12,173 sq km)

 GIBRALTAR Southwest Europe
Status Crown colony
Claimed 1713
Capital Gibraltar
Population 27,086
Area 2.5 sq miles (6.5 sq km)

GUERNSEY Channel Islands
Status Crown dependency
Claimed 1066
Capital St Peter Port
Population 56,681
Area 25 sq miles (65 sq km)

 **ISLE OF MAN** British Isles
Status Crown dependency
Claimed 1765
Capital Douglas
Population 71,714
Area 221 sq miles (572 sq km)

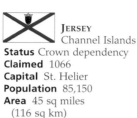 **JERSEY** Channel Islands
Status Crown dependency
Claimed 1066
Capital St. Helier
Population 85,150
Area 45 sq miles (116 sq km)

 MONTSERRAT West Indies
Status Dependent territory
Claimed 1632
Capital Plymouth (uninhabited)
Population 2,850
Area 40 sq miles (102 sq km)

 PITCAIRN ISLANDS South Pacific
Status Dependent territory
Claimed 1887
Capital Adamstown
Population 55
Area 1.35 sq miles (3.5 sq km)

 **ST. HELENA** South Atlantic
Status Dependent territory
Claimed 1673
Capital Jamestown
Population 6,472
Area 47 sq miles (122 sq km)

SOUTH GEORGIA &

THE SOUTH SANDWICH ISLANDS South Atlantic
Status Dependent territory
Capital *not applicable*
Claimed 1775
Population No permanent residents
Area 1,387 sq miles (3,592 sq km)

TRISTAN DA CUNHA South Atlantic
Status Dependency of St. Helena
Claimed 1612
Capital Edinburgh
Population 297
Area 38 sq miles (98 sq km)

  **TURKS & CAICOS ISLANDS** West Indies
Status Dependent territory
Claimed 1766
Capital Cockburn Town
Population 13,800
Area 166 sq miles (430 sq km)

UNITED STATES OF AMERICA

 **AMERICAN SAMOA** South Pacific
Status Unincorporated territory
Claimed 1900
Capital Pago Pago
Population 60,000
Area 75 sq miles (195 sq km)

BAKER & HOWLAND ISLANDS South Pacific
Status Unincorporated territory
Claimed 1856
Capital *not applicable*
Population None
Area 0.54 sq miles (1.4 sq km)

 GUAM West Pacific
Status Unincorporated territory
Claimed 1898
Capital Hagåtña
Population 149,249
Area 212 sq miles (549 sq km)

JARVIS ISLAND South Pacific
Status Unincorporated territory
Claimed 1856
Capital *not applicabl*
Population None
Area 1.7 sq miles (4.5 sq km)

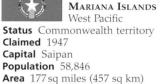 **NORTHERN MARIANA ISLANDS** West Pacific
Status Commonwealth territory
Claimed 1947
Capital Saipan
Population 58,846
Area 177 sq miles (457 sq km)

PALMYRA ATOLL Central Pacific
Status Unincorporated territory
Claimed 1898
Capital *not applicable*
Population None
Area 5 sq miles (12 sq km)

 PUERTO RICO West Indies
Status Commonwealth territory
Claimed 1898
Capital San Juan
Population 3.8 million
Area 3,458 sq miles (8,959 sq km)

 **VIRGIN ISLANDS** West Indies
Status Unincorporated territory
Claimed 1917
Capital Charlotte Amalie
Population 101,809
Area 137 sq miles (355 sq km)

WAKE ISLAND Central Pacific
Status Unincorporated territory
Claimed 1898
Capital *not applicable*
Population 302
Area 2.5 sq miles (6.5 sq km)

COUNTRY PROFILES

THIS FACTFILE IS INTENDED as a guide to a world that is continually changing as political fashions and personalities come and go. Nevertheless, all the material in these factfiles has been researched from the most up-to-date and authoritative sources to give an incisive portrait of the geographical, political, and social characteristics that make each country so unique.

There are currently 193 independent countries in the world - more than at any previous time - and 59 dependencies. Antarctica is the only land area on Earth that is not officially part of, and does not belong to, any single country.

AFGHANISTAN

Page 100 D4

In 2001, following a US-led offensive, the hard-line Muslim taliban militia was replaced by a new interim government under Hamid Karazi

Official name Islamic State of Afghanistan
Formation 1919
Capital Kabul
Population 22.5 million / 90 people per sq mile (35 people per sq km)
Total area 250,000 sq miles (647,500 sq km)
Languages Pashtu, Tajik, Dari, Farsi
Religions Sunni Muslim 84%, Shi'a Muslim 15%, other 1%
Ethnic mix Pashtun 38%, Tajik 25%, Hazara 19%, other 18%
Government Transitional regime
Currency Afghani = 100 puls
Literacy rate 37.3%
Calorie consumption 1,539 kilocalories

135

ALBANIA

Page 79 C6

Lying at the southeastern end of the Adriatic Sea, Albania held its first multiparty elections in 1991, after nearly five decades of communism.

Official name Republic of Albania
Formation 1912
Capital Tiranë
Population 3.1 million/ 279 people per sq mile (108 people per sq km)
Total area 11,100 sq miles (28,748 sq km)
Languages Albanian, Greek
Religions Sunni Muslim 70%, Orthodox Christian 20%, Roman Catholic 10%
Ethnic mix Albanian 86%, Greek 12%, other 2%
Government Multiparty republic
Currency Lek = 100 qindars
Literacy rate 84.7%
Calorie consumption 2,864 kilocalories

ANGOLA

Page 56 B2

Located in southwest Africa, Angola has been in a state of civil war following its independence from Portugal, except for a brief period from 1994–98.

Official name Republic of Angola
Formation 1975
Capital Luanda
Population 13.5 million /28 people per sq mile (11 people per sq km)
Total area 481,351 sq miles (1,246,700 sq km)
Languages Portuguese, Umbundu, Kimbundu, Kikongo
Religions Roman Catholic 50%, other 30%, Protestant 20%
Ethnic mix Ovimbundu 37%, other 25%, Kimbundu 25%, Bakongo 13%
Government Presidential regime
Currency Readjusted kwanza = 100 lwei
Literacy rate 40%
Calorie consumption 1,903 kilocalories

ARMENIA

Page 95 F3

Smallest of the former USSR's republics, Armenia lies in the Lesser Caucasus mountains. Territorial war with Azerbaijan ended in a 1994 ceasefire.

Official name Republic of Armenia
Formation 1991
Capital Yerevan
Population 3.8 million/ 330 people per sq mile (128 people per sq km)
Total area 11,506 sq miles (29,800 sq km)
Languages Armenian, Russian
Religions The Armenian Apostolic Church 94%, other 6%
Ethnic mix Armenian 93%, Azeri 3%, Russian 2%, other 2%
Government Multiparty republic
Currency Dram = 100 louma
Literacy rate 98.4%
Calorie consumption 1,944 kilocalories

AZERBAIJAN

Page 95 G2

Situated on the western coast of the Caspian Sea, Azerbaijan was the first Soviet republic to declare independence from Moscow in 1991.

Official name Republic of Azerbaijan
Formation 1991
Capital Baku
Population 8.1 million / 242 people per sq mile (94 people per sq km)
Total area 33,436 sq miles (86,600 sq km)
Languages Azeri, Russian
Religions Shi'a ithna Muslims 61%, Sunni Muslims 26%, Armenian and Russian Orthodox 11%, other 2%
Ethnic mix Azeri 90%, Russian 3%, Daghestani 3%, Armenian 2%, other 2%
Government Multiparty republic
Currency Manat = 100 gopik
Literacy rate 96%
Calorie consumption 2,468 kilocalories

ALGERIA

Page 48 C3

Algeria achieved independence from France in 1962. Today, its military-dominated government faces a severe challenge from Islamic extremists.

Official name People's Democratic Republic of Algeria
Formation 1962
Capital Algiers
Population 30.8 million / 33 people per sq mile (13 people per sq km)
Total area 919,590 sq miles (2,381,740 sq km)
Languages Arabic, Tamazight, French
Religions Sunni Muslim 99%, other 1%
Ethnic mix Arab 75%, Berber 24%, European 1%
Government Multiparty republic
Currency Algerian dinar = 100 centimes
Literacy rate 67.8%
Calorie consumption 2,944 kilocalories

ANTIGUA & BARBUDA

Page 33 H3

Lying on the Atlantic edge of the Leeward Islands, Antigua and Barbuda's area includes the uninhabited islet of Redonda.

Official name Antigua and Barbuda
Formation 1981
Capital St. John's
Population 66,400 / 389 people per sq mile (150 people per sq km)
Total area 171 sq miles (442 sq km)
Languages English, English patois
Religions Anglican 45%, other Protestant 42%, Roman Catholic 10%, Rastafarian 1%, other 2%
Ethnic mix Black African 95%, other 5%
Government Parliamentary democracy
Currency Eastern Caribbean dollar = 100 cents
Literacy rate 95%
Calorie consumption 2,396 kilocalories

AUSTRALIA

Page 120 A4

An island continent located between the Indian and Pacific oceans, Australia was settled by Europeans 200 years ago, but now has many Asian immigrants.

Official name Commonwealth of Australia
Formation 1901
Capital Canberra
Population 19.3 million / 7 people per sq mile (3 people per sq km)
Total area 2,967,893 sq miles (7,686,893 sq km)
Languages English, Vietnamese, Greek, Arabic, Italian, Aboriginal languages
Religions Christian 64%, other 34%
Ethnic mix European 95%, Asian 4%, Aboriginal and other 1%
Government Parliamentary democracy
Currency Australian dollar = 100 cents
Literacy rate 99%
Calorie consumption 3,176 kilocalories

BAHAMAS

Page 32 C1

Located in the western Atlantic, off the Florida coast, the Bahamas comprise some 700 islands and 2,400 cays, only 30 of which are inhabited.

Official name Commonwealth of the Bahamas
Formation 1973
Capital Nassau
Population 308,000 / 57 people per sq mile (22 people per sq km)
Total area 5,382 sq miles (13,940 sq km)
Languages English, English Creole, French Creole
Religions Baptist 32%, Anglican 20%, Roman Catholic 19%, Church of God 6%, Methodist 6%, other 17%
Ethnic mix Black African 85%, Other 15%
Government Parliamentary democracy
Currency Bahamian dollar = 100 cents
Literacy rate 95.7%
Calorie consumption 2,443 kilocalories

ANDORRA

Page 69 B6

A tiny landlocked principality, Andorra lies high in the eastern Pyrenees between France and Spain. It held its first full elections in 1993.

Official name Principality of Andorra
Formation 1278
Capital Andorra la Vella
Population 66,800 / 370 people per sq mile (143 people per sq km)
Total area 181 sq miles (468 sq km)
Languages Catalan, Spanish, French, Portuguese
Religions Roman Catholic 94%, other 6%
Ethnic mix Spanish 46%, Andorrian 28%, other 18%, French 8%
Government Parliamentary democracy
Currency Euro (French franc and Spanish peseta until 2002)
Literacy rate 99%
Calorie consumption not available

ARGENTINA

Page 43 B5

Most of the southern half of South America is occupied by Argentina. The country returned to civilian rule in 1983 after a series of military coups.

Official name Republic of Argentina
Formation 1816
Capital Buenos Aires
Population 37.5 million / 35 people per sq mile (14 people per sq km)
Total area 1,068,296 sq miles (2,766,890 sq km)
Languages Spanish, Italian, Amerindian languages
Religions Roman Catholic 90%, Jewish 2%, Protestant 2%, other 6%
Ethnic mix Indo European 85%, Mestizo 14%, Amerindian 1%
Government Presidential democracy
Currency Peso = 100 centavos
Literacy rate 96.8%
Calorie consumption 3,181 kilocalories

AUSTRIA

Page 73 D7

Bordering eight countries in the heart of Europe, Austria was created in 1920 after the collapse of the Austro-Hungarian Empire the previous year.

Official name Republic of Austria
Formation 1918
Capital Vienna
Population 8.1 million / 250 people per sq mile (97 people per sq km)
Total area 32,378 sq miles (83,858 sq km)
Languages German, Croatian, Slovenian
Religions Roman Catholic 78%, non-religious 9%, Protestant 5%, other (including Muslim and Jewish) 8%
Ethnic mix German 93%, Croat, Slovene, Hungarian 6%, other 1%
Government Parliamentary democracy
Currency Euro (Austrian schilling until 2002)
Literacy rate 99%
Calorie consumption 3,757 kilocalories

BAHRAIN

Page 98 C4

Bahrain is an archipelago of 33 islands between the Qatar peninsula and the Saudi Arabian mainland. Only three of these islands are inhabited.

Official name State of Bahrain
Formation 1971
Capital Manama
Population 652,000 / 2,724 people per sq mile (1,052 people per sq km)
Total area 239 sq miles (620 sq km)
Languages Arabic
Religions Muslim (mainly Shi'a) 99%, other 1%
Ethnic mix Bahraini 70%, Iranian, Indian, Pakistani 24%, other Arab 4%, European 2%
Government Constitutional monarchy
Currency Bahraini dinar = 1,000 fils
Literacy rate 87.6%
Calorie consumption not available

BANGLADESH

Page 113 G3

Bangladesh lies at the north of the Bay of Bengal. It seceded from Pakistan in 1971 and, after much political instability, returned to democracy in 1991.

Official name People's Republic of Bangladesh
Formation 1971
Capital Dhaka
Population 140.4 million /2,525 people per sq mile (975 people per sq km)
Total area 55,598 sq miles (144,000 sq km)
Languages Bengali, Urdu, Chakma, Marma (Magh), Garo, Khasi, Santhali, Tripuri, Mro
Religions Muslim (mainly Sunni) 87%, Hindu 12%, other 1%
Ethnic mix Bengali 98%, other 2%
Government Parliamentary democracy
Currency Taka = 100 paisa
Literacy rate 41.4%
Calorie consumption 2,103 kilocalories

BELGIUM

Page 65 B6

Located in northwestern Europe, Belgium's history has been marked by the division between its Flemish- and French-speaking communities.

Official name Kingdom of Belgium
Formation 1830
Capital Brussels
Population 10.3 million / 874 people per sq mile (338 people per sq km)
Total area 11,780 sq miles 30,510 sq km)
Languages Dutch, French, German
Religions Roman Catholic 88%, Muslim 2%, other 10%
Ethnic mix Fleming 58%, Walloon 33%, Italian 2%, Moroccan 1%, other 6%
Government Parliamentary democracy
Currency Euro (Belgian franc until 2002)
Literacy rate 99%
Calorie consumption 3,701 kilocalories

BHUTAN

Page 113 G3

The landlocked Buddhist kingdom of Bhutan is perched in the eastern Himalayas between India and China. Gradual reforms protect its cultural identity.

Official name Kingdom of Bhutan
Formation 1656
Capital Thimpu
Population 2.1 million / 116 people per sq mile (45 people per sq km)
Total area 18,147 sq miles (47,000 sq km)
Languages Dzongkha, Nepali, Assamese
Religions Mahayana Buddhist 70%, Hindu 24%, other 6%
Ethnic mix Bhote 50%, Nepalese 25%, other 25%
Government Monarchy
Currency Ngultrum – 100 chetrum
Literacy rate 47.3%
Calorie consumption not available

BOTSWANA

Page 56 C3

Once the British protectorate of Bechuanaland, Botswana lies landlocked in southern Africa. Diamonds provide it with a prosperous economy.

Official name Republic of Botswana
Formation 1966
Capital Gaborone
Population 1.6 million / 7 people per sq mile (3 people per sq km)
Total area 231,803 sq miles (600,370 sq km)
Languages English, Tswana, Shona, San, Khoikhoi, Ndebele
Religions Traditional beliefs 50%, Christian (mainly Protestant) 30%, other (including Muslim) 20%
Ethnic mix Tswana 98% other 2%
Government Presidential democracy
Currency Pula = 100 thebe
Literacy rate 77.2%
Calorie consumption 2,255 kilocalories

BARBADOS

Page 33 H4

Barbados is the most easterly of the Caribbean Windward Islands. Under British rule for 339 years, it became fully independent in 1966.

Official name Barbados
Formation 1966
Capital Bridgetown
Population 268,000 /1,614 people per sq mile (623 people per sq km)
Total area 166 sq miles (430 sq km)
Languages English, Bajan (Barbadian English)
Religions Anglican 40%, other 24%, non-religious 17%, Pentecostal 8%, Methodist 7%, Roman Catholic 4%
Ethnic mix Black African 90%, other 10%
Government Parliamentary democracy
Currency Barbados dollar = 100 cents
Literacy rate 98%
Calorie consumption 3,022 kilocalories

BELIZE

Page 30 B1

The last Central American country to gain independence, this former British colony lies on the eastern shore of the Yucatan Peninsula.

Official name Belize
Formation 1981
Capital Belmopan
Population 200,000 /23 people per sq mile (9 people per sq km)
Total area 8,867 sq miles (22,966 sq km)
Languages English, English Creole, Spanish, Mayan, Garifuna (Carib)
Religions Roman Catholic 62%, Anglican 12%, Mennonite 4%, Methodist 6%, other 16%
Ethnic mix Mestizo 44%, Creole 30%, Maya 11%, Garifuna 7%, Asian Indian 4%, other 4%
Government Parliamentary democracy
Currency Belizean dollar = 100 cents
Literacy rate 93.2%
Calorie consumption 2,888 kilocalories

BOLIVIA

Page 39 F3

Bolivia lies landlocked high in central South America. Mineral riches once made it the region's wealthiest state. Today, it is the poorest.

Official name Republic of Bolivia
Formation 1825
Capital Sucre (judicial)/La Paz (administrative)
Population 8.5 million / 20 people per sq mile (8 people per sq km)
Total area 424,162 sq miles (1,098,580 sq km)
Languages Spanish, Aymara, Quechua
Religions Roman Catholic 93%, other 7%
Ethnic mix Quechua 37%, Aymara 32%, mixed 13%, European 10%, other 8%
Government Presidential democracy
Currency Boliviano = 100 centavos
Literacy rate 85.6%
Calorie consumption 2,218 kilocalories

BRAZIL

Page 40 C2

Brazil covers more than half of South America and is the site of the world's largest rain forest. The country has immense natural resources.

Official name Federative Republic of Brazil
Formation 1822
Capital Brasilia
Population 172.6 million / 53 people per sq mile (20 people per sq km)
Total area 3,286,470 sq miles (8,511,965 sq km)
Languages Portuguese, German, Italian, Spanish, Polish, Japanese
Religions Roman Catholic 74%, Protestant 15%, Atheist 7%, other 4%
Ethnic mix Black 53%, Mixed 40%, White 6%, other 1%
Government Presidential democracy
Currency Real = 100 centavos
Literacy rate 85.2%
Calorie consumption 2,985 kilocalories

BELARUS

Page 85 B6

Formerly known as White Russia, Belarus lies landlocked in eastern Europe. The country reluctantly became independent of the USSR in 1991.

Official name Republic of Belarus
Formation 1991
Capital Minsk
Population 10.1 million / 126 people per sq mile (49 people per sq km)
Total area 80,154 sq miles (207,600 sq km)
Languages Belorussian, Russian
Religions Russian Orthodox 60%, other (including Muslim, Jews and Protestant) 32% Roman Catholic 8%
Ethnic mix Belorussian 78%, Russian 13%, Polish 4%, Ukrainian 3%, other 2%
Government Presidential regime
Currency Belorussian rouble = 100 kopeks
Literacy rate 99%
Calorie consumption 2,902 kilocalories

BENIN

Page 53 F4

Stretching north from the West African coast, Benin became one of the pioneers of African democratization in 1990, ending years of military rule.

Official name Republic of Benin
Formation 1960
Capital Porto-Novo
Population 6.4 million / 147 people per sq mile (57 people per sq km)
Total area 43,483 sq miles (112,620 sq km)
Languages French, Fon, Bariba, Yoruba, Adja, Houeda, Somba
Religions Indigenous beliefs 70%, Muslim 15%, Christian 15%
Ethnic mix Fon 47%, Baraba 10%, Adja 12%, other 31%
Government Presidential democracy
Currency CFA franc = 100 centimes
Literacy rate 40.3%
Calorie consumption 2,558 kilocalories

BOSNIA & HERZEGOVINA

Page 78 B3

At the heart of the western Balkans, Bosnia and Herzegovina was the focus of the bitter conflict surrounding the breakup of former Yugoslavia.

Official name Bosnia and Herzegovina
Formation 1992
Capital Sarajevo
Population 4.1 million /208 people per sq mile (80 people per sq km)
Total area 19,741 sq miles (51,129 sq km)
Languages Serbo-Croat
Religions Muslim (mainly Sunni) 40%, Serbian Orthodox 31%, Roman Catholic 15%, Protestant 4%, other 10%
Ethnic mix Bosniak 44%, Serb 31%, Croat 17%, other 8%
Government Multiparty republic
Currency Marka = 100 pfenniga
Literacy rate 93%
Calorie consumption 2,661 kilocalories

BRUNEI

Page 116 D3

Lying on the northwestern coast of the island of Borneo, Brunei is surrounded and divided in two by the Malaysian state of Sarawak.

Official name Sultanate of Brunei
Formation 1984
Capital Bandar Seri Begawan
Population 335,000 / 150 people per sq mile (58 people per sq km)
Total area 2,228 sq miles (5,770 sq km)
Languages Malay, English, Chinese
Religions Muslim 66%, Buddhist 14%, Christian 10%, other 10%
Ethnic mix Malay 67%, Chinese 16%, Indigenous 6%, other 11%
Government Monarchy
Currency Brunei dollar = 100 cents
Literacy rate 91.5%
Calorie consumption 2,832 kilocalories

BULGARIA

Page 82 C2

Located in southeastern Europe, Bulgaria has made slow progress toward democracy since the fall of its communist regime in 1990.

Official name Republic of Bulgaria
Formation 1908
Capital Sofia
Population 7.9 million / 184 people per sq mile (71 people per sq km)
Total area 42,822 sq miles (110,910 sq km)
Languages Bulgarian, Turkish, Macedonian, Romany
Religions Bulgarian Orthodox 84%, Muslim 13%, Jewish 1%, Roman Catholic 1%, other 1%
Ethnic mix Bulgarian 85%, Turkish 9%, Macedonian 3%, Romany 3%
Government Multiparty republic
Currency Lev = 100 stoninki
Literacy rate 98.4%
Calorie consumption 2,467 kilocalories

CAMBODIA

Page 115 D5

Located in mainland Southeast Asia, Cambodia has emerged from two decades of civil war and invasion from Vietnam.

Official name Kingdom of Cambodia
Formation 1953
Capital Phnom Penh
Population 13.4 million / 192 people per sq mile (74 people per sq km)
Total area 69,900 sq miles (181,040 sq km)
Languages Khmer, French, Chinese, Vietnamese, Cham
Religions Buddhist 93%, Muslim 6%, Christian 1%
Ethnic mix Khmer 90%, Vietnamese 4%, Chinese 1%, other 5%
Government Constitutional monarchy
Currency Riel = 100 sen
Literacy rate 37.4%
Calorie consumption 2,070 kilocalories

CAPE VERDE

Page 52 A2

Off the west coast of Africa, in the Atlantic Ocean, lies the group of islands that make up Cape Verde, a Portuguese colony until 1975.

Official name Republic of Cape Verde
Formation 1975
Capital Praia
Population 437,000 / 281 people per sq mile (108 people per sq km)
Total area 1,557 sq miles (4,033 sq km)
Languages Portuguese Creole, Portuguese
Religions Roman Catholic 97%, Protestant (Church of Nazarene) 1%, other 2%
Ethnic mix Mestico 60%, African 30%, other 10%
Government Multiparty republic
Currency Cape Verde escudo = 100 centavos
Literacy rate 74.2%
Calorie consumption 3,278 kilocalories

CHILE

Page 42 B3

Chile extends in a ribbon down the west coast of South America. It returned to democracy in 1989 after a referendum rejected its military dictator.

Official name Republic of Chile
Formation 1818
Capital Santiago
Population 15.4 million / 53 people per sq mile (20 people per sq km)
Total area 292,258 sq miles (756,950 sq km)
Languages Spanish, Amerindian languages
Religions Roman Catholic 80%, other and non-religious 20%
Ethnic mix Mixed and European 90%, Amerindian 10%
Government Multiparty republic
Currency Chilean peso = 100 centavos
Literacy rate 95.7%
Calorie consumption 2,882 kilocalories

BURKINA FASO

Page 53 E4

Known as Upper Volta until 1984, the West African state of Burkina Faso has been under military rule for most of its post-independence history.

Official name Burkina Faso
Formation 1960
Capital Ouagadougou
Population 11.9 million / 112 people per sq mile (43 people per sq km)
Total area 105,869 sq miles (274,200 sq km)
Languages French, Mossi, Fulani, Tuareg, Dyula, Songhai
Religions Traditional beliefs 55%, Muslim 35%, Roman Catholic 9%, other Christian 1%
Ethnic mix Mossi 50%, other 50%
Government Multiparty republic
Currency CFA franc = 100 centimes
Literacy rate 23.9%
Calorie consumption 2,293 kilocalories

CAMEROON

Page 54 A4

Situated on the central West African coast, Cameroon was effectively a one-party state for 30 years. Multiparty elections were held in 1992.

Official name Republic of Cameroon
Formation 1960
Capital Yaoundé
Population 15.2 million / 83 people per sq mile (32 people per sq km)
Total area 183,567 sq miles (475,440 sq km)
Languages English, French, Bamileke, Fang, Fulani
Religions Traditional beliefs 25%, Christian 53%, Muslim 22%
Ethnic mix Cameroon highlanders 31%, Bantu 19%, Kirdi 11%, other 39%
Government Presidential democracy
Currency CFA franc = 100 centimes
Literacy rate 75.9%
Calorie consumption 2,255 kilocalories

CENTRAL AFRICAN REPUBLIC

Page 54 C4

This landlocked country lies between the basins of the Chad and Congo rivers. Its arid north sustains less than 2% of the population.

Official name Central African Republic
Formation 1960
Capital Bangui
Population 3.8 million / 16 people per sq mile (6 people per sq km)
Total area 240,534 sq miles (622,984 sq km)
Languages French, Sango, Banda, Gbaya
Religions Traditional beliefs 60%, Christian 35%, Muslim 5%
Ethnic mix Baya 34%, Banda 27%, Mandjia 21%, Sara 10%, other 8%
Government Multiparty republic
Currency CFA franc = 100 centimes
Literacy rate 46.7%
Calorie consumption 1,946 kilocalories

CHINA

Page 104 C4

This vast East Asian country was dominated by Mao Zedong, who founded the Communist republic, and Deng Xiaoping, his successor (1976–1997).

Official name People's Republic of China
Formation 960
Capital Beijing
Population 1.29 billion / 348 people per sq mile (134 people per sq km)
Total area 3,705,386 sq miles (9,596,960 sq km)
Languages Mandarin, Wu, Cantonese, Hsiang, Min, Hakka, Kan
Religions Non-religious 59%, Traditional beliefs 20%, other 21%
Ethnic mix Han 93%, other 7%
Government One-party state
Currency Yuan (Renminbi) = 10 jiao
Literacy rate 84.2%
Calorie consumption 3,029 kilocalories

BURUNDI

Page 51 B7

Small, landlocked Burundi lies just south of the Equator, on the Nile-Congo watershed in Central Africa. Since 1993 it has been marked by violent ethnic conflict.

Official name Republic of Burundi
Formation 1962
Capital Bujumbura
Population 6.5 million / 605 people per sq mile (234 people per sq km)
Total area 10,745 sq miles (27,830 sq km)
Languages Kirundi, French, Kiswahili
Religions Christian 60%, Traditional beliefs 39%, Muslim 1%
Ethnic mix Hutu 85%, Tutsi 14%, Twa 1%
Government Transitional regime
Currency Burundi franc = 100 centimes
Literacy rate 48.3%
Calorie consumption 1,605 kilocalories

CANADA

Page 15 E4

Canada extends from its US border norh to the Arctic Ocean. In recent years, French-speaking Quebec has sought independence from the rest of the country.

Official name Canada
Formation 1867
Capital Ottawa
Population 3.1 million /8 people per sq mile (3 people per sq km)
Total area 3,851,788 sq miles (9,976,140 sq km)
Languages English, French, Chinese, Italian, German, Ukranian, Inuktitut
Religions Roman Catholic 47%, Protestant 41%, non-religious 12%
Ethnic mix British origin 44%, French origin 25%, Other European 20%, other 11%
Government Parlimentary democracy
Currency Canadian dollar = 100 cents
Literacy rate 99%
Calorie consumption 3,174 kilocalories

CHAD

Page 54 C3

Landlocked in north central Africa, Chad has been torn by intermittent periods of civil war since it gained independence from France in 1960.

Official name Republic of Chad
Formation 1960
Capital N'Djamena
Population 8.1 million / 16 people per sq mile (6 people per sq km)
Total area 495,752 sq miles (1,284,000 sq km)
Languages French, Arabic, Sara, Maba
Religions Muslim 50%, Traditional beliefs 43%, Christian 7%
Ethnic mix Nomads (Tuareg and Toubou) 38%, Sara 30, Arab 15%, Other 17%
Government Presidential democracy
Currency CFA franc = 100 centimes
Literacy rate 42.6%
Calorie consumption 2,046 kilocalories

COLOMBIA

Page 36 B3

Lying in northwest South America, Colombia is one of the world's most violent countries, with powerful drugs cartels and guerrilla activity.

Official name Republic of Columbia
Formation 1819
Capital Bogotá
Population 42.8 million /97 people per sq mile (38 people per sq km)
Total area 439,733 sq miles (1,138,910 sq km)
Languages Spanish, Amerindian languages, English Creole
Religions Roman Catholic 95%, other 5%
Ethnic mix Mestizo 58%, White 20%, other 22%
Government Presidential democracy
Currency Colombian peso = 100 centavos
Literacy rate 91.8%
Calorie consumption 2,597 kilocalories

COMOROS

Page 57 F2

In the Indian Ocean, between Mozambique and Madagascar, lie the Comoros, comprising three main islands, and a number of smaller islets.

Official name Federal Islamic Republic of the Comoros
Formation 1975
Capital Moroni
Population 727,000 / 868 people per sq mile (335 people per sq km)
Total area 838 sq miles (2,170 sq km)
Languages Arabic, French, Comoran
Religions Muslim (mainly Sunni) 98%, Roman Catholic 1%, other 1%
Ethnic mix Comorian 97%, other 3%
Government Presidential democracy
Currency Comoros franc = 100 centimes
Literacy rate 59.6%
Calorie consumption 1,753 kilocalories

COSTA RICA

Page 31 E4

Costa Rica is the most stable country in Central America. Its neutrality in foreign affairs is long-standing, but it has very strong ties with the US.

Official name Republic of Costa Rica
Formation 1838
Capital San José
Population 4.1 million / 208 people per sq mile (80 people per sq km)
Total area 19,730 sq miles (51,100 sq km)
Languages Spanish, English Creole, Bribri, Cabecar
Religions Roman Catholic 76%, other (including Protestant) 24%
Ethnic mix Mesitzo and European 96%, Black 2%, Indian 1%, Chinese 1%
Government Presidential democracy
Currency Costa Rican colón = 100 centimes
Literacy rate 95.6%
Calorie consumption 2,783 kilocalories

CUBA

Page 32 C

Cuba is the largest island in the Caribbean and the only Communist country in the Americas. It has been led by Fidel Castro since 1959.

Official name Republic of Cuba
Formation 1902
Capital Havana
Population 11.2 million / 262 people per sq mile (101 people per sq km)
Total area 42,803 sq miles (110,860 sq km)
Languages Spanish
Religions Non-religious 49%, Roman Catholic 40%, Atheist 6%, Protestant 1%, other 4%
Ethnic mix White 66%, European-African 22%, Black 12%
Government One-party state
Currency Cuban peso = 100 centavos
Literacy rate 96.7%
Calorie consumption 2,564 kilocalories

DENMARK

Page 63 A7

The country occupies the Jutland peninsula and over 400 islands in Scandinavia. Greenland and the Faeroe Islands are self-governing associated territories.

Official name Kingdom of Denmark
Formation AD 950
Capital Copenhagen (Koebenhavn)
Population 5.3 million / 319 people per sq mile (123 people per sq km)
Total area 16,639 sq miles (43,094 sq km)
Languages Danish
Religions Evangelical Lutheran 89%, Roman Catholic 1%, other 10%
Ethnic mix Danish 96%, Faeroe and Inuit 1%, other (including Scandinavian) 3%
Government Parliamentary democracy
Currency Danish krone = 100 ore
Literacy rate 99%
Calorie consumption 3,396 kilocalories

CONGO

Page 55 B5

Astride the Equator in west central Africa, this former French colony emerged from 26 years of Marxist-Leninist rule in 1990.

Official name Republic of the Congo
Formation 1960
Capital Brazzaville
Population 3.1 million / 23 people per sq mile (9 people per sq km)
Total area 132,046 sq miles (342,000 sq km)
Languages French, Kongo, Teke, Lingala
Religions Traditional beliefs 50%, Christian 48%, Muslim 2%
Ethnic mix Bakongo 48%, Sangha 20%, Teke 17%, Mbochi 12%, other 3%
Government Presidential democracy
Currency CFA franc = 100 centimes
Literacy rate 80.7%
Calorie consumption 2,223 kilocalories

CÔTE D'IVOIRE

Page 52 D4

One of the larger nations along the coast of West Africa, Côte d'Ivoire remains under the influence of its former colonial ruler, France.

Official name Republic of Côte d'Ivoire
Formation 1960
Capital Yamoussoukro
Population 16.3 million / 131 people per sq mile (51 people per sq km)
Total area 124,502 sq miles (322,460 sq km)
Languages French, Akan, Kru, Voltaic
Religions Traditional beliefs 23%, Muslim 25%, Roman Catholic 23%, Protestant 6%, other 23%
Ethnic mix Baoule 23%, Bete 18%, Senufo 15% Agni-Ashanti 14%, Mandinka 11%, other 19%
Government Multiparty republic
Currency CFA franc = 100 centimes
Literacy rate 47.1%
Calorie consumption 2,590 kilocalories

CYPRUS

Page 80 C5

Cyprus lies in the eastern Mediterranean. Since 1974, it has been partitioned between the Turkish-occupied north and the Greek south.

Official name Republic of Cyprus
Formation 1960
Capital Nicosia
Population 790,000 / 221 people per sq mile (85 people per sq km)
Total area 3,571 sq miles (9,250 sq km)
Languages Greek, Turkish, English
Religions Greek Orthodox 73%, Muslim 23%, other 4%
Ethnic mix Greek 77%, Turkish 18%, other (mainly British) 5%
Government Presidential democracy
Currency Cyprus pound / Turkish lira
Literacy rate 97.1%
Calorie consumption 3,259 kilocalories

DJIBOUTI

Page 50 D4

A city state with a desert hinterland, Djibouti lies in northeast Africa. Once known as French Somaliland, its economy relies on its port.

Official name Republic of Djibouti
Formation 1977
Capital Djibouti
Population 644,000 / 76 people per sq mile (29 people per sq km)
Total area 8,490 sq miles (22,000 sq km)
Languages French, Arabic, Somali, Afar
Religions Muslim 94%, Christian 6%
Ethnic mix Issa 60%, Afar 35%, other 5%
Government Presidential democracy
Currency Djibouti franc = 100 centimes
Literacy rate 64.6%
Calorie consumption 2,050 kilocalories

CONGO, DEM. REP.

Page 55 C6

Straddling the Equator in east central Africa, Dem. Rep. Congo is one of Africa's largest countries. It achieved independence from Belgium in 1960.

Official name Democratic Republic of the Congo
Formation 1960
Capital Kinshasa
Population 52.5 million / 58 people per sq mile (22 people per sq km)
Total area 905,563 sq miles (2,345,410 sq km)
Languages French, Kiswahili, Tshiluba
Religions Traditional beliefs 50%, Roman Catholic 37%, Protestant 13%
Ethnic mix Bantu and Hamitic 45%, other 55%
Government Military-based regime
Currency franc = 100 centimes
Literacy rate 61.4%
Calorie consumption 1,514 kilocalories

CROATIA

Page 78 B2

Post-independence fighting in this former Yugoslav republic, thwarted its plans to capitalize on its prime location along the east Adriatic coast.

Official name Republic of Croatia
Formation 1991
Capital Zagreb
Population 4.7 million / 215 people per sq mile (83 people per sq km)
Total area 21,831 sq miles (56,542 sq km)
Languages Croatian
Religions Roman Catholic 76%, Orthodox 11%, Muslim 1%, other 12%
Ethnic mix Croat 78%, Serb 12%, Yugoslav 2%, other 8%
Government Parliamentary democracy
Currency Kuna = 100 lipa
Literacy rate 98.3%
Calorie consumption 2,843 kilocalories

CZECH REPUBLIC

Page 77 A5

Once part of Czechoslovakia in eastern Europe, it became independent in 1993, after peacefully dissolving its federal union with Slovakia.

Official name Czech Republic
Formation 1993
Capital Prague
Population 10.3 million / 338 people per sq mile (131 people per sq km)
Total area 30,450 sq miles (78,866 sq km)
Languages Czech, Slovak, Hungarian
Religions Atheist 38%, Roman Catholic 39%, Protestant 3%, Hussites 2%, other 18%
Ethnic mix Czech 81%, Moravian 13%, Slovak 6%
Government Parliamentary democracy
Currency Czech koruna = 100 halura
Literacy rate 99%
Calorie consumption 3,104 kilocalories

DOMINICA

Page 33 H4

The Caribbean island Dominica resisted European colonization until the 18th century, when it first came under the French, and then, the British

Official name Commonwealth of Dominica
Formation 1978
Capital Roseau
Population 73,000 / 251 people per sq mile (97 people per sq km)
Total area 291 sq miles (754 sq km)
Languages English, French Creole
Religions Roman Catholic 77%, Protestant 15%, other 8%
Ethnic mix Black 91%, Mixed 6%, Indian 2%, other 1%
Government Parliamentary democracy
Currency East Caribbean dollar = 100 cents
Literacy rate 94%
Calorie consumption 2,994 kilocalories

DOMINICAN REPUBLIC

Page 33 E2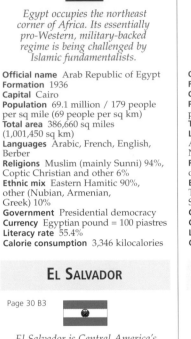

The republic occupies the eastern two-thirds of the island of Hispaniola in the Caribbean. Frequent coups and a strong US influence mark its recent past.

Official name Dominican Republic
Formation 1865
Capital Santo Domingo
Population 8.5 million /
452 people per sq mile (174 people per sq km)
Total area 18,815 sq miles
(48,730 sq km)
Languages Spanish, French Creole
Religions Roman Catholic 92%, other and non-religious 8%
Ethnic mix Mixed 75%, White 15%, Black 10%
Government Presidential democracy
Currency Dominican Republic peso = 100 centavos
Literacy rate 83.6%
Calorie consumption 2,325 kilocalories

EGYPT

Page 50 B2

Egypt occupies the northeast corner of Africa. Its essentially pro-Western, military-backed regime is being challenged by Islamic fundamentalists.

Official name Arab Republic of Egypt
Formation 1936
Capital Cairo
Population 69.1 million / 179 people per sq mile (69 people per sq km)
Total area 386,660 sq miles
(1,001,450 sq km)
Languages Arabic, French, English, Berber
Religions Muslim (mainly Sunni) 94%, Coptic Christian and other 6%
Ethnic mix Eastern Hamitic 90%, other (Nubian, Armenian, Greek) 10%
Government Presidential democracy
Currency Egyptian pound = 100 piastres
Literacy rate 55.4%
Calorie consumption 3,346 kilocalories

ERITREA

Page 50 C3

Lying on the shores of the Red Sea, Eritrea effectively seceded from Ethopia in 1993, following a 30-year war for independence.

Official name State of Eritrea
Formation 1993
Capital Asmara
Population 3.8 million / 81 people per sq mile (31 people per sq km)
Total area 46,842 sq miles (121,320 sq km)
Languages Tigrinya, English, Tigre, Afar, Arabic, Bilen, Kunama, Nara, Saho, Hadareb
Religions Christian 45%, Muslim 45%, other 10%
Ethnic mix Tigray and Kunama 40%, Tigray 50%, Afar 4%, Saho 3%, other 4%
Government Transitional regime
Currency Nafka = 100 cents
Literacy rate 55.7%
Calorie consumption 1,665 kilocalories

FIJI

Page 123 E5

A volcanic archipelago, Fiji comprises 882 islands in the southern Pacific Ocean. Ethnic Fijians and Indo-Fijians have been in conflict since 1987.

Official name Republic of the Fiji Islands
Formation 1970
Capital Suva
Population 823,000 / 117 people per sq mile (45 people per sq km)
Total area 7,054 sq miles
(18,270 sq km)
Languages Fijian, English, Hindi, Urdu, Tamil, Telegu
Religions Hindu 38%, Methodist 37%, Roman Catholic 9%, other 16%
Ethnic mix Melanesian 48%, Indian 46%, other 6%
Government Multiparty republic
Currency Fiji dollar = 100 cents
Literacy rate 92.9%
Calorie consumption 2,861 kilocalories

EAST TIMOR

Page 116 F5

This new nation occupies the eastern half of the island of Timor. Invaded by Indonesia in 1975, it declared independence in 1999.

Official name East Timor
Formation 2002
Capital Dili
Population 737,811 /196 people per sq mile (49 per sq km)
Total area 3,756 sq miles (14, 874 sq km)
Languages Tetum (Portuguese/ Austronesian), Bahasa Indonesia, Portuguese
Religions Roman Catholic 93%, other 7%
Ethnic mix Various Papuan groups; 2% Chinese. In the 1990's Indonesian settlers became numerous, accounting for 20% of the population by 1999.
Government Multiparty republic
Currency US dollar
Literacy rate 41 %
Calorie consumption not available

EL SALVADOR

Page 30 B3

El Salvador is Central America's smallest state. A 12-year war between US-backed government troops and left-wing guerrillas ended in 1992.

Official name Republic of El Salvador
Formation 1841
Capital San Salvador
Population 6.4 million / 788 people per sq mile (304 people per sq km)
Total area 8,124 sq miles
(21,040 sq km)
Languages Spanish
Religions Roman Catholic 80%, Evangelical 18%, other 2%
Ethnic mix Mestizo 94%, Indian 5%, White 1%
Government Presidential democracy
Currency Salvadorean colón = 100 centavos
Literacy rate 78.8%
Calorie consumption 2,503 kilocalories

ESTONIA

Page 84 D2

Estonia is the smallest and most developed of the three Baltic states. It has the highest standard of living of any of the former Soviet republics.

Official name Republic of Estonia
Formation 1991
Capital Tallinn
Population 1.4 million / 80 people per sq mile (31 people per sq km)
Total area 17,462 sq miles
(45,226 sq km)
Languages Estonian, Russian
Religions Evangelical Lutheran 56%, Russian Orthodox 25%, Other 19%
Ethnic mix Estonian 62%, Russian 30%, other 8%
Government Parliamentary democracy
Currency Kroon = 100 cents
Literacy rate 99%
Calorie consumption 3 376 kilocalories

FINLAND

Page 62 D4

Finland's distinctive language and national identity have been influenced by both its Scandinavian and its Russian neighbors.

Official name Republic of Finland
Formation 1917
Capital Helsinki
Population 5.2 million / 40 people per sq mile (15 people per sq km)
Total area 130,127 sq miles
(337,030 sq km)
Languages Finnish, Swedish, Sami
Religions Evangelical Lutheran 89%, Finnish Orthodox 1%, Roman Catholic 1%, other 9%
Ethnic mix Finnish 93%, other (including Sami) 7%
Government Paliamentary democracy
Currency Euro (Markka until 2002)
Literacy rate 99%
Calorie consumption 3,227 kilocalories

ECUADOR

Page 38 A2

Ecuador sits high on South America's western coast. Once part of the Inca heartland, its territory includes the Galapagos Islands, to the west.

Official name Republic of Ecuador
Formation 1830
Capital Quito
Population 12.9 million / 118 people per sq mile (45 people per sq km)
Total area 109,483 sq miles
(283,560 sq km)
Languages Spanish, Quechua, other Amerindian languages
Religions Roman Catholic 93%, Protestant, Jewish and other 7%
Ethnic mix Mestizo 55%, Indian 25%, Black 10%, White 10%
Government Presidential democracy
Currency US dollar
Literacy rate 91.3%
Calorie consumption 2,693 kilocalories

EQUATORIAL GUINEA

Page 55 A5

The country comprises the Rio Muni mainland and five islands on the west coast of central Africa. Free elections were first held in 1988.

Official name Republic of Equatorial Guinea
Formation 1968
Capital Malabo
Population 470,000 / 43 people per sq mile (17 people per sq km)
Total area 10,830 sq miles
(28,051 sq km)
Languages Spanish, Fang, Bubi
Religions Roman Catholic 90%, other 10%
Ethnic mix Fang 85%, Bubi 4%, other 11%
Government Presidential regime
Currency CFA franc = 100 centimes
Literacy rate 83.2%
Calorie consumption not available

ETHIOPIA

Page 51 C5

Located in northeast Africa, Ethiopia was a Marxist regime from 1974–91. It has suffered a series of economic, civil, and natural crises.

Official name Federal Democratic Republic of Ethiopia
Formation 1896
Capital Addis Ababa
Population 64.5 million / 148 people per sq mile (57 people per sq km)
Total area 435,184 sq miles
(1,127,127 sq km)
Languages Amharic, Tigrinya, Galla
Religions Muslim 40%, Ethopian Orthodox 40%, other 20%
Ethnic mix Oromo 40%, Amhara 25%, Sidamo 9%, Somali 6%, Berta 6%, other 14%
Government Multiparty republic
Currency Ethopian birr = 100 cents
Literacy rate 38.4%
Calorie consumption 2,023 kilocalories

FRANCE

Page 68 B4

Straddling Western Europe from the English Channel to the Mediterranean Sea, France, is one of the world's leading industrial powers.

Official name French Republic
Formation 987
Capital Paris
Population 59.5 million / 282 people per sq mile (109 people per sq km)
Total area 211,208 sq miles
(547,030 sq km)
Languages French, Provenial, German, Breton, Catalan, Basque
Religions Roman Catholic 88%, Muslim 8%, Protestant 2%, other 2%
Ethnic mix French 90%, North African 6%, German 2%, other 2%
Government Multiparty republic
Currency Euro (French franc until 2002)
Literacy rate 99%
Calorie consumption 3,591 kilocalories

GABON

Page 55 A5

A former French colony straddling the Equator on Africa's west coast, it returned to multiparty politics in 1990, after 22 years of one-party rule.

Official name Gabonese Republic
Formation 1960
Capital Libreville
Population 1.3 million / 13 people per sq mile (5 people per sq km)
Total area 103,346 sq miles (267,667 sq km)
Languages French, Fang, Punu, Sira, Nzebi, Mpongwe
Religions Christian 55%, Traditional beliefs 40%, Muslim 1%, other 4%
Ethnic mix Fang 35%, other Bantu 29%, Eshira 25%, other 11%
Government Multiparty republic
Currency CFA franc = 100 centimes
Literacy rate 70.8%
Calorie consumption 2,564 kilocalories

GERMANY

Page 72 B4

Europe's strongest economic power, Germany's democratic west and Communist east were re-unified in 1990, after the fall of the east's regime.

Official name Federal Republic of Germany
Formation 1871
Capital Berlin
Population 82 million / 595 people per sq mile (230 people per sq km)
Total area 137,846 sq miles (357,021 sq km)
Languages German, Turkish
Religions Protestant 34%, Roman Catholic 33%, Muslim 3%, other 30%
Ethnic mix German 92%, other 8%
Government Parliamentary democracy
Currency Euro (Deutsche Mark until 2002)
Literacy rate 99%
Calorie consumption 3,451 kilocalories

GRENADA

Page 33 G5

The Windward island of Grenada became a focus of attention in 1983, when the US mounted an invasion to sever its growing links with Cuba.

Official name Grenada
Formation 1974
Capital St. George's
Population 98,000 / 747 people per sq mile (288 people per sq km)
Total area 131 sq miles (340 sq km)
Languages English, English Creole
Religions Roman Catholic 68%, Anglican 17%, other 15%
Ethnic mix Black 82%, Mulatto 13%, Indian 3%, other 2%
Government Parliamentary democracy
Currency East Caribbean dollar = 100 cents
Literacy rate 96%
Calorie consumption 2,764 kilocalorie

GUINEA-BISSAU

Page 52 B4

Known as Portuguese Guinea during its days as a colony, Guinea-Bissau is situated on Africa's west coast, bordered by Senegal and Guinea.

Official name Republic of Guinea-Bissau
Formation 1974
Capital Bissau
Population 1.2 million / 86 people per sq mile (33 people per sq km)
Total area 13,946 sq miles (36,120 sq km)
Languages Portuguese Creole, Fulani Balante, Malinke, Portuguese
Religions Indigenous beliefs 52%, Muslim 40%, Christian 8%
Ethnic mix Balante 25%, Madinka 12%, Fila 20%, Mandyako 11%, other 32%
Government Presidential democracy
Currency CFA franc = 100 centimes
Literacy rate 38.8%
Calorie consumption 2,333 kilocalories

GAMBIA

Page 52 B3

A narrow state on the west coast of Africa, The Gambia was renowned for its stability until its government was overthrown in a coup in 1994.

Official name Republic of The Gambia
Formation 1965
Capital Banjul
Population 1.34 million / 307 people per sq mile (119 people per sq km)
Total area 4,363 sq miles (11,300 sq km)
Languages English, Mandinka, Fulani, Wolof, Jola, Soninke
Religions Sunni Muslim 90%, Christian 9%, Indigenous beliefs 1%
Ethnic mix Mandinka 42%, Fulani 18%, Wolof 16%, Jola 10%, Serahuli 9%, other 5%
Government Multiparty republic
Currency Dalasi = 100 butut
Literacy rate 36.6%
Calorie consumption 2,474 kilocalories

GHANA

Page 53 E5

Once known as the Gold Coast, Ghana in West Africa has experienced intermittent periods of military rule since independence in 1957.

Official name Republic of Ghana
Formation 1957
Capital Accra
Population 19.7 million / 214 people per sq mile (83 people per sq km)
Total area 92,100 sq miles (238,540 sq km)
Languages English, Twi, Fanti, Ewe, Ga, Adangbe, Gurma, Dagomba
Religions Christian 43%, Traditional beliefs 38%, Muslim 11%, other 8%
Ethnic mix Ashanti and Fanti 52%, Moshi-Dagomba 16%, Ewe 12%, Ga 8%, Yoruba 1%, other 11%
Government Presidential democracy
Currency Cedi = 100 pesewas
Literacy rate 71.5%
Calorie consumption 2,699 kilocalories

GUATEMALA

Page 30 A2

The largest state on the Central American isthmus, Guatemala returned to civilian rule in 1986, after 32 years of repressive military rule.

Official name Republic of Guatemala
Formation 1838
Capital Guatemala City
Population 11.7 million / 278 people per sq mile (107 people per sq km)
Total area 42,042 sq miles (108,890 sq km)
Languages Spanish, Quiché, Mam, Cakchiquel, Kekchí
Religions Roman Catholic 65%, Protestant 33%, other 2%
Ethnic mix Amerindian 60%, Mestizo 30%, other 10%
Government Presidential democracy
Currency Quetzal = 100 centavos
Literacy rate 68.8%
Calorie consumption 2,171 kilocalories

GUYANA

Page 37 F3

The only English-speaking country in South America, Guyana gained independence from Britain in 1966, and became a republic in 1970.

Official name Cooperative Republic of Guyana
Formation 1966
Capital Georgetown
Population 763,000 / 9 people per sq mile (4 people per sq km)
Total area 83,000 sq miles (214,970 sq km)
Languages English, English Creole, Hindi, Tamil, Amerindian languages
Religions Christian 57%, Hindu 33%, Muslim 9%, other 1%
Ethnic mix East Indian 52%, Black African 38%, other 10%
Government Presidential democracy
Currency Guyana dollar = 100 cents
Literacy rate 98.5%
Calorie consumption 2,582 kilocalories

GEORGIA

Page 95 F2

Located on the eastern shore of the Black Sea, Georgia's northern provinces have been torn by civil war since independence from the USSR in 1991.

Official name Georgia
Formation 1991
Capital Tbilisi
Population 5.2 million / 193 people per sq mile (75 people per sq km)
Total area 26,911 sq miles (69,700 sq km)
Languages Georgian, Russian
Religions Georgian Orthodox 65%, Muslim 11%, Russian Orthodox 10%, Amenian Orthodox 8%, Unknown 6%
Ethnic mix Georgian 70%, Armenian 8%, Russian 6%, Azeri 6%, Ossetian 3%, other 7%
Government Presidential democracy
Currency Lari = 100 tetri
Literacy rate 99%
Calorie consumption 2,412 kilocalories

GREECE

Page 83 A5

Greece is the southernmost Balkan nation. Surrounded by the Mediterranean, Aegean, and Ionian Seas, it has a strong seafaring tradition.

Official name Hellenic Republic
Formation 1829
Capital Athens
Population 10.6 million / 208 people per sq mile (80 people per sq km)
Total area 50,942 sq miles (131,940 sq km)
Languages Greek, Turkish, Macedonian, Albanian
Religions Greek Orthodox 98%, Muslim 1%, other 1%
Ethnic mix Greek 98%, other 2%
Government Presidential democracy
Currency Euro (Drachma until 2002)
Literacy rate 97.3%
Calorie consumption 3,705 kilocalories

GUINEA

Page 52 C4

Facing the Atlantic Ocean, on the west coast of Africa, Guinea became the first French colony in Africa to gain independence, in 1958.

Official name Republic of Guinea
Formation 1958
Capital Conakry
Population 8.3 million / 87 people per sq mile (34 people per sq km)
Total area 94,925 sq miles (245,857 sq km)
Languages French, Fulani, Malinke, Soussou
Religions Muslim 65%, Traditional beliefs 33%, Christian 2%,
Ethnic mix Fila (Fulani) 30%, Malinke 30%, Soussou 15%, Kissi 10%, other tribes 10%, other 25%
Government Multiparty republic
Currency Guinea franc = 100 centimes
Literacy rate 41.1%
Calorie consumption 2,353 kilocalories

HAITI

Page 32 D3

Haiti shares the Caribbean island of Hispaniola with the Dominican Republic. At independence, in 1804, it became the world's first Black republic.

Official name Republic of Haiti
Formation 1804
Capital Port-au-Prince
Population 8.3 million / 775 people per sq mile (299 people per sq km)
Total area 10,714 sq miles (27,750 sq km)
Languages English, French Creole
Religions Roman Catholic 80%, Protestant 16%, non-religious 1%, other 3%
Ethnic mix Black African 95%, Mulatto and European 5%
Government Multiparty republic
Currency Gourde = 100 centimes
Literacy rate 49.8%
Calorie consumption 2,056 kilocalories

COUNTRY FACTFILE • DOMINICAN REPUBLIC – HAITI

HONDURAS

Page 30 C2

Honduras straddles the Central American isthmus. The country returned to full democratic civilian rule in 1984, after a succession of military regimes.

Official name Republic of Honduras
Formation 1838
Capital Tegucigalpa
Population 6.6 million / 153 people per sq mile (59 people per sq km)
Total area 43,278 sq miles (112,090 sq km)
Languages Spanish, Black Carib, English Creole
Religions Roman Catholic 97%, Protestant minority 3%
Ethnic mix Mestizo 90%, Black African 5%, Amerindian 4%, White 1%
Government Presidential democracy
Currency Lempira = 100 centavos
Literacy rate 74.6%
Calorie consumption 2,395 kilocalories

INDIA

Page 112 D4

Separated from the rest of Asia by the Himalayan mountain ranges, India forms a subcontinent. It is the world's second most populous country.

Official name Republic of India
Formation 1947
Capital New Delhi
Population 1.03 billion / 790 people per sq mile (305 people per sq km)
Total area 1,269,339 sq miles (3,287,590 sq km)
Languages Hindi, English, and 16 regional languages
Religions Hindu 83%, Muslim 11%, Christian 2%, Sikh 2%, other 2%
Ethnic mix Indo-Aryan 72%, Dravidian 25%, Mongoloid and other 3%
Government Parliamentary democracy
Currency Indian rupee = 100 paisa
Literacy rate 57.2%
Calorie consumption 2,428 kilocalories

IRAQ

Page 98 B3

Oil-rich Iraq is situated in the central Middle East. Since the removal of the monarchy in 1958, it has experienced considerable political turmoil.

Official name Republic of Iraq
Formation 1932
Capital Baghdad
Population 23.6 million / 140 people per sq mile (54 people per sq km)
Total area 168,753 sq miles (437,072 sq km)
Languages Arabic, Kurdish, Armenian, Assyrian, Turkic languages
Religions Shi'a ithna Muslim 62%, Sunni Muslim 33%, other 5%
Ethnic mix Arab 79%, Kurdish 16%, Persian 3%, Turkman 2%
Government One-party republic
Currency Iraqi dinar = 1,000 fils
Literacy rate 55.9%
Calorie consumption 2,197 kilocalories

ITALY

Page 74 B3

Projecting into the Mediterranean Sea in Southern Europe, Italy is an ancient land, but also one of the continent's newest unified states.

Official name Italian Republic
Formation 1861
Capital Rome
Population 57.5 million / 494 people per sq mile (191 people per sq km)
Total area 116,305 sq miles (301,230 sq km)
Languages Italian, German, French, Rhaeto-Romanic, Sardinian
Religions Roman Catholic 83%, other and non-religious 17%
Ethnic mix Italian 94%, Sardinian 2%, other 4%
Government Parliamentary democracy
Currency Euro (Italian lira until 2002)
Literacy rate 98.4%
Calorie consumption 3,661 kilocalories

HUNGARY

Page 77 C6

Hungary is bordered by seven states in Central Europe. It has changed its economic and political policies to develop closer ties with the EU.

Official name Republic of Hungary
Formation 1918
Capital Budapest
Population 9.9 million / 276 people per sq mile (106 people per sq km)
Total area 35,919 sq miles (93,030 sq km)
Languages Hungarian
Religions Roman Catholic 64%, Calvinist 20%, non-religious 7%, Lutheran 4%, other 5%
Ethnic mix Magyar 90%, German 2%, Romany 1%, Slovak 1%, other 6%
Government Parliamentary democracy
Currency Forint = 100 filler
Literacy rate 99%
Calorie consumption 3,458 kilocalories

INDONESIA

Page 116 C4

Formerly the Dutch East Indies, Indonesia, the world's largest archipelago, stretches over 5,000 km (3,100 miles), from the Indian Ocean to the Pacific Ocean.

Official name Republic of Indonesia
Formation 1949
Capital Jakarta
Population 214 million / 289 people per sq mile (111 people per sq km)
Total area 741,096 sq miles (1,919,440 sq km)
Languages Bahasa Indonesia, Javanese, Madurese, Sundanese, Dutch
Religions Muslim 87%, Protestant 6%, Roman Catholic 3%, other 4%
Ethnic mix Javanese 45%, Sundanese 14%, Coastal Malays 8%, Madurese 8%, other 25%
Government Multiparty republic
Currency Rupiah = 100 sen
Literacy rate 86.9%
Calorie consumption 2,902 kilocalories

IRELAND

Page 67 A6

The Republic of Ireland occupies about 85% of the island of Ireland, with the remainder (Northern Ireland) being part of the United Kingdom.

Official name Ireland
Formation 1922
Capital Dublin
Population 3.8 million / 140 people per sq mile (54 people per sq km)
Total area 27,135 sq miles (70,280 sq km)
Languages English, Irish Gaelic
Religions Roman Catholic 88%, Anglican 3%, other and non-religious 9%
Ethnic mix Irish 95%, other 5%
Government Parliamentary democracy
Currency Euro (Punt until 2002)
Literacy rate 99%
Calorie consumption 3,613 kilocalories

JAMAICA

Page 32 C3

First colonized by the Spanish and then, from 1655, by the English, Jamaica was the first of the Caribbean island nations to achieve independence, in 1962.

Official name Jamaica
Formation 1962
Capital Kingston
Population 2.6 million / 613 people per sq mile (237 people per sq km)
Total area 4,243 sq miles (10,990 sq km)
Languages English, English Creole
Religions Christian (Church of God, Baptist, Anglican, other Protestant) 55%, other and non-religious 45%
Ethnic mix Black African 75%, Mulatto 13%, European and Chinese 11%, Indian 1%
Government Parliamentary democracy
Currency Jamaican dollar = 100 cents
Literacy rate 86.8%
Calorie consumption 2,693 kilocalories

ICELAND

Page 61 E4

Europe's westernmost country, Iceland lies in the North Atlantic, straddling the mid-Atlantic ridge. Its spectacular, volcanic landscape is largely uninhabited.

Official name Republic of Iceland
Formation 1944
Capital Reykjavik
Population 281,000 / 7 people per sq mile (3 people per sq km)
Total area 39,768 sq miles (103,000 sq km)
Languages Icelandic
Religions Evangelical Lutheran 93%, non-religious 6%, other Christian 1%
Ethnic mix Icelandic 94%, Danish 1%, other 5%
Government Parliamentary democracy
Currency Icelandic króna = 100 aurar
Literacy rate 99%
Calorie consumption 3,342 kilocalories

IRAN

Page 98 B3

Since the 1979 revolution led by Ayatollah Khomeini, which sent Iran's Shah into exile, this Middle Eastern country has become the world's largest theocracy.

Official name Islamic Republic of Iran
Formation 1502
Capital Tehran
Population 71.4 million / 112 people per sq mile (43 people per sq km)
Total area 636,406 sq miles (1,648,293 sq km)
Languages Farsi, Azeri, Gilaki, Baluchi, Mazanderani, Kurdish, Arabic
Religions Shi'a Muslim 95%, Sunni Muslim 4%, other 1%
Ethnic mix Persian 50%, Azeri 24%, Lur and Bakhtiari 8%, Kurd 8%, other 10%
Government Islamic theocracy
Currency Iranian rial = 100 dinars
Literacy rate 76.8%
Calorie consumption 2,913 kilocalories

ISRAEL

Page 97 A7

Israel was created as a new state in 1948 on the east coast of the Mediterranean. Following wars with its Arab neighbors, it has extended its boundaries.

Official name State of Israel
Formation 1948
Capital Jerusalem
Population 6.2 million / 773 people per sq mile (305 people per sq km)
Total area 8,019 sq miles (20,770 sq km)
Languages Hebrew, Arabic, Yiddish, German, Russian, Polish, Romanian, Persian
Religions Jewish 82%, Muslim (mainly Sunni) 14%, other (including Druze) 4%
Ethnic mix Jewish 82%, other (mostly Arab) 18%
Government Parliamentary democracy
Currency Shekel = 100 agorot
Literacy rate 96%
Calorie consumption 3,562 kilocalories

JAPAN

Page 108 C4

Japan comprises four principal islands and over 3,000 smaller ones. With the emperor as constitutional head, it is now the world's most powerful economy.

Official name Japan
Formation 1590
Capital Tokyo
Population 127.3 million / 873 people per sq mile (337 people per sq km)
Total area 145,882 sq miles (377,835 sq km)
Languages Japanese, Korean, Chinese
Religions Shinto and Buddhist 76%, Buddhist 16%, other (including Christian) 8%
Ethnic mix Japanese 99%, other (mainly Korean) 1%
Government Parliamentary democracy
Currency Yen = 100 sen
Literacy rate 99%
Calorie consumption 2,762 kilocalories

JORDAN

Page 97 B6

The kingdom of Jordan lies east of Israel. In 1993, King Hussein responded to calls for greater democracy by agreeing to multiparty elections.

Official name Hashemite Kingdom of Jordan
Formation 1946
Capital Amman
Population 5.1 million / 143 people per sq mile (55 people per sq km)
Total area 35,637 sq miles (92,300 sq km)
Languages Arabic
Religions Muslim (mainly Sunni) 92%, other (mostly Christian) 8%
Ethnic mix Arab 98% (Palestinian 40%), Armenian 1%, Circassian 1%
Government Constitutional monarchy
Currency Jordanian dinar = 1,000 fils
Literacy rate 89.2%
Calorie consumption 2,749 kilocalories

KAZAKHSTAN

Page 92 B4

Second largest of the former Soviet republics, mineral-rich Kazakhstan has the potential to become the major Central Asian economic power.

Official name Republic of Kazakhstan
Formation 1991
Capital Astana
Population 16.1 million / 15 people per sq mile (6 people per sq km)
Total area 1,049,150 sq miles (2,717,300 sq km)
Languages Kazakh, Russian, German, Uighur, Korean
Religions Muslim (mainly Sunni) 50%, Russian Orthodox 13%, other 37%
Ethnic mix Kazakh 53%, Russian 30%, Ukranian 4%, German 2%, Tartar 2%, other 9%
Government Presidential democracy
Currency Tenge = 100 tein
Literacy rate 99%
Calorie consumption 2,991 kilocalories

KENYA

Page 51 C6

Kenya straddles the Equator on Africa's east coast. It became a multiparty democracy in 1992 and has been led by President Moi since 1978.

Official name Republic of Kenya
Formation 1963
Capital Nairobi
Population 31.3 million / 139 people per sq mile (54 people per sq km)
Total area 224,961 sq miles (582,650 sq km)
Languages Kiswahili, English, Kikuyu, Luo, Kamba
Religions Christian 60%, Traditional beliefs 25%, Muslim 6%, other 9%
Ethnic mix Kikuyu 21%, Luhya 14%, Luo 13%, Kamba 11%, Kalenjin 11%, other 30%
Government Presidential democracy
Currency Kenya shilling = 100 cents
Literacy rate 82.4%
Calorie consumption 1,965 kilocalories

KIRIBATI

Page 123 F3

Part of the British colony of the Gilbert and Ellice Islands until independence in 1979, Kiribati comprises 33 islands in the mid-Pacific Ocean.

Official name Republic of Kiribati
Formation 1979
Capital Bairiki (Tarawa Atoll)
Population 92,000 / 332 people per sq mile (128 people per sq km)
Total area 277 sq miles (717 sq km)
Languages English, Micronesian dialect
Religions Roman Catholic 53%, Kiribati Protestant Church 39%, other 8%
Ethnic mix Micronesian 96%, other 4%
Government Non-party democracy
Currency Australian dollar = 100 cents
Literacy rate 98%
Calorie consumption 2,957 kilocalories

KUWAIT

Page 98 C4

Kuwait lies on the northwest extreme of the Persian Gulf. The state was a British protectorate from 1914 until 1961, when full independence was granted.

Official name State of Kuwait
Formation 1961
Capital Kuwait City
Population 2 million / 291 people per sq mile (112 people per sq km)
Total area 6880 sq miles (17,820 sq km)
Languages Arabic, English
Religions Muslim (mainly Sunni) 85%, Christian, Hindu and other 15%
Ethnic mix Kuwaiti 45%, other Arab 35%, South Asian 9%, Iranian 4%, other 7%
Government Constitutional monarchy
Currency Kuwaiti dinar = 1,000 fils
Literacy rate 82.6%
Calorie consumption 3,132 kilocalories

KYRGYZSTAN

Page 101 F2

A mountainous, landlocked state in Central Asia. The most rural of the ex-Soviet republics, it only gradually developed its own cultural nationalism.

Official name Kyrgyz Republic
Formation 1991
Capital Bishkek
Population 5 million / 65 people per sq mile (25 people per sq km)
Total area 76,641 sq miles (198,500 sq km)
Languages Kyrgyz, Russian
Religions Muslim (mainly Sunni) 70%, Russian Orthodox 30%
Ethnic mix Kyrgyz 57%, Russian 19%, Uzbek 13%, Tartar 2%, Ukranian 2%, other 7%
Government Presidential democracy
Currency Som = 100 teen
Literacy rate 97%
Calorie consumption 2,871 kilocalories

LAOS

Page 114 D4

A former French colony, independent in 1953, Laos lies landlocked in Southeast Asia. It has been under communist rule since 1975.

Official name Lao People's Democratic Republic
Formation 1953
Capital Vientiane
Population 5.4 million / 59 people per sq mile (23 people per sq km)
Total area 91,428 sq miles (236,800 sq km)
Languages Lao, Mon-Khmer, Chinese, Yao, Vietnamese, French
Religions Buddhist 85%, other (including Animist) 15%
Ethnic mix Lao Loum 66%, Lao Theung 30%, Lao Soung 2%, other 2%
Government One-party republic
Currency New kip = 100 cents
Literacy rate 48.7%
Calorie consumption 2,266 kilocalories

LATVIA

Page 84 C3

Situated on the east coast of the Baltic Sea, Lativa, like its Baltic neighbors, became independent in 1991. It retains a large Russian population.

Official name Republic of Latvia
Formation 1991
Capital Riga
Population 2.4 million / 96 people per sq mile (37 people per sq km)
Total area 24,938 sq miles (64,589 sq km)
Languages Latvian, Russian
Religions Lutheran 55%, Roman Catholic 24%, Russian Orthodox 9%, other 12%
Ethnic mix Latvian 57%, Russian 32%, Belarussian 4%, Ukranian 3%, Polish 2%, other 2%
Government Presidential democracy
Currency Lat = 100 santimi
Literacy rate 99%
Calorie consumption 2,855 kilocalories

LEBANON

Page 96 A4

Lebanon is dwarfed by its two powerful neighbors, Syria and Israel. The state started rebuilding in 1989, after 14 years of intense civil war.

Official name Republic of Lebanon
Formation 1941
Capital Beirut
Population 3.6 million / 897 people per sq mile (346 people per sq km)
Total area 4,015 sq miles (10,400 sq km)
Languages Arabic, French, Armenian, Assyrian
Religions Muslim 70%, Christian 30%
Ethnic mix Arab 94%, Armenian 4%, other 2%
Government Multiparty republic
Currency Lebanese pound = 100 piastres
Literacy rate 86%
Calorie consumption 3,155 kilocalories

LESOTHO

Page 56 D4

The landlocked kingdom of Lesotho is entirely surrounded by South Africa, which provides all its land transportation links with the outside world.

Official name Kingdom of Lesotho
Formation 1966
Capital Maseru
Population 2.1 million / 179 people per sq mile (69 people per sq km)
Total area 11,720 sq miles (30,355 sq km)
Languages English, Sesotho, Zulu
Religions Traditional beliefs 10% Christian 90%
Ethnic mix Sotho 97%, European and Asian 3%
Government Constitutional monarchy
Currency Loti = 100 lisente
Literacy rate 83.3%
Calorie consumption 2,300 kilocalories

LIBERIA

Page 52 C5

Liberia faces the Atlantic Ocean in equatorial West Africa. Africa's oldest republic, it was established in 1847. Today, it is torn by civil war.

Official name Republic of Liberia
Formation 1847
Capital Monrovia
Population 3.1 million / 72 people per sq mile (28 people per sq km)
Total area 43,000 sq miles (111,370 sq km)
Languages English, Kpelle, Vai, Bassa, Kru, Grebo, Kissi, Gola, Loma
Religions Christian 68%, Traditional beliefs 18%, Muslim 14%
Ethnic mix Indigenous tribes (16 main groups) 95%, Americo-Liberians 5%
Government Multiparty republic
Currency Liberian dollar = 100 cents
Literacy rate 54%
Calorie consumption 2,076 kilocalories

LIBYA

Page 49 F3

Situated on the Mediterranean coast of North Africa, Libya is a Muslim dictatorship, politically marginalized by the West for its terrorist links.

Official name Great Socialist People's Libyan Arab Jamahariyah
Formation 1951
Capital Tripoli
Population 5.4 million / 8 people per sq mile (3 people per sq km)
Total area 679,358 sq miles (1,759,540 sq km)
Languages Arabic, Tuareg
Religions Muslim (mainly Sunni) 97%, other 3%
Ethnic mix Arab and Berber 95%, other 5%
Government One-party state
Currency Libyan dinar = 1,000 dirhams
Literacy rate 80.1%
Calorie consumption 3,305 kilocalories

LIECHTENSTEIN

Page 73 B7

Tucked in the Alps between Switzerland and Austria, Liechtenstein became an independent principality of the Holy Roman Empire in 1719.

Official name Principality of Liechtenstein
Formation 1719
Capital Vaduz
Population 32,200/ 521 people per sq mile (201 people per sq km)
Total area 62 sq miles (160 sq km)
Languages German, Alemannish dialect, Italian
Religions Roman Catholic 81%, Protestant 7%, other 12%
Ethnic mix Liechtensteiner 63%, Foreign residents 37%
Government Parliamentary democracy
Currency Swiss franc = 100 centimes
Literacy rate 99%
Calorie consumption not available

LITHUANIA

Page 84 B4

The largest, most powerful and stable of the Baltic states, Lithuania was the first Baltic country to declare independence from Moscow, in 1991.

Official name Republic of Lithuania
Formation 1991
Capital Vilnius
Population 3.7 million / 147 people per sq mile (57 people per sq km)
Total area 25,174 sq miles (65,200 sq km)
Languages Lithuanian, Russian
Religions Roman Catholic 83%, Protestant 5%, other 12%
Ethnic mix Lithuanian 80%, Russian 9%, Polish 7%, Belarussian 2%, other 2%
Government Parliamentary democracy
Currency Litas = 100 centas
Literacy rate 99%
Calorie consumption 3,040 kilocalories

LUXEMBOURG

Page 65 D8

Making up part of the plateau of the Ardennes in Western Europe, Luxembourg is Europe's last independent duchy and one of its richest states.

Official name Grand Duchy of Luxembourg
Formation 1867
Capital Luxembourg
Population 442,000/ 433 people per sq mile (171 people per sq km)
Total area 998 sq miles (2,586 sq km)
Languages French, German, Luxembourgish
Religions Roman Catholic 97%, other 3%
Ethnic mix Luxembourger 73%, Foreign residents 27%
Government Parliamentary democracy
Currency Euro (Luxembourg and Belgian Franc until 2002)
Literacy rate 99%
Calorie consumption 3,701 kilocalories

MACEDONIA

Page 79 D6

Landlocked in the southern Balkans, Macedonia has been affected by sanctions imposed on its northern trading partners and by Greek antagonism.

Official name Former Yugoslav Republic of Macedonia
Formation 1991
Capital Skopje
Population 2 million / 204 people per sq mile (79 people per sq km)
Total area 9,781 sq miles (25,333 sq km)
Languages Macedonian, Albania, Serbo-Croat
Religions Christian 74%, Muslim 26%
Ethnic mix Macedonian 67%, Albanian 23%, Turkish 4%, other 6%
Government Multiparty republic
Currency Macedonian denar = 100 deni
Literacy rate 94%
Calorie consumption 3,006 kilocalories

MADAGASCAR

Page 57 F4

Lying in the Indian Ocean, Madagascar is the world's fourth largest island. Free elections in 1993 ended 18 years of radical socialist government.

Official name Republic of Madagascar
Formation 1960
Capital Antananarivo
Population 16.4 million / 72 people per sq mile (28 people per sq km)
Total area 226,656 sq miles (587,040 sq km)
Languages French, Malagasy
Religions Traditional beliefs 52%, Christian 41%, Muslim 7%
Ethnic mix Merina 26%, Betsilio 12%, Betsimisaraka 15%, other 47%
Government Presidential democracy
Currency Malagasy franc = 100 centimes
Literacy rate 66.5%
Calorie consumption 2,007 kilocalories

MALAWI

Page 57 E1

A former British colony, Malawi lies landlocked in southeast Africa. Its name means "the land where the sun is reflected in the water like fire."

Official name Republic of Malawi
Formation 1964
Capital Lilongwe
Population 11.6 million / 254 people per sq mile (98 people per sq km)
Total area 45,745 sq miles (118,480 sq km)
Languages English, Chewa, Lomwe, Yao, Ngoni
Religions Protestant 55%, Roman Catholic 20%, Muslim 20%, other 5%
Ethnic mix Bantu 99%, other 1%
Government Presidential democracy
Currency Malawi kwacha = 100 tambala
Literacy rate 60.1%
Calorie consumption 2,181 kilocalories

MALAYSIA

Page 116 B3

Malaysia's three separate territories include Malaya, Sarawak, and Sabah. A financial crisis in 1997 ended a decade of spectacular financial growth.

Official name Federation of Malaysia
Formation 1963
Capital Kuala Lumpur
Population 22.6 million / 178 people per sq mile (69 people per sq km)
Total area 127,316 sq miles (329,750 sq km)
Languages English, Bahasa Malaysia, Malay, Chinese, Tamil
Religions Muslim 53%, Buddhist 19%, Chinese faiths 12%, other 16%
Ethnic mix Malay 48%, Chinese 29%, Indigenous tribes 12%, other 11%
Government Presidential democracy
Currency Ringgit = 100 cents
Literacy rate 87.5%
Calorie consumption 2,919 kilocalories

MALDIVES

Page 110 A4

Only 200 of the more than 1,000 Maldivian small coral islands in the Indian Ocean, are inhabited. Government rests in the hands of a few influential families.

Official name Republic of Maldives
Formation 1965
Capital Malé
Population 300,000 / 2,590 people per sq mile (1000 people per sq km)
Total area 116 sq miles (300 sq km)
Languages Dhivehi (Maldivian),
Religions Sunni Muslim 100%
Ethnic mix Mixed Arab, Sinhalese, Malay 100%
Government Non-party democracy
Currency Rufiyaa (Maldivian rupee) = 100 laari
Literacy rate 96.4%
Calorie consumption 2,592 kilocalories

MALI

Page 53 E2

Landlocked in the heart of West Africa, Mali held its first free elections in 1992, more than 30 years after it gained independence from France.

Official name Republic of Mali
Formation 1960
Capital Bamako
Population 11.7 million / 24 people per sq mile (9 people per sq km)
Total area 478,764 sq miles (1,240,000 sq km)
Languages French, Bambara, Fulani, Senufo, Soninké
Religions Muslim (mainly Sunni) 80%, Traditional beliefs 18%, other 2%
Ethnic mix Bambara 32%, Fula 14%, Senufu 12%, Soninka 9%, other 33%
Government Multiparty republic
Currency CFA franc = 100 centimes
Literacy rate 41.4%
Calorie consumption 2,403 kilocalories

MALTA

Page 80 A5

The Maltese archipelago lies off southern Sicily, midway between Europe and North Africa. The only inhabited islands are Malta, Gozo, and Kemmuna.

Official name Republic of Malta
Formation 1964
Capital Valletta
Population 392,000 / 3,213 people per sq mile (1,241 people per sq km)
Total area 122 sq miles (316 sq km)
Languages Maltese, English
Religions Roman Catholic 98%, other and non-religious 2%
Ethnic mix Maltese (mixed Arab, Sicilian, Norman, Spanish, Italian, English) 96%, other 4%
Government Parliamentary democracy
Currency Maltese lira = 100 cents
Literacy rate 92.1%
Calorie consumption 3,543 kilocalories

MARSHALL ISLANDS

Page 122 D1

A group of 34 atolls, the Marshall Islands were under US rule as part of the UN Trust Territory of the Pacific Islands until 1986. The economy depends on US aid.

Official name Republic of the Marshall Islands
Formation 1986
Capital Majuro
Population 68,100 / 973 people per sq mile (376 people per sq km)
Total area 70 sq miles (181 sq km)
Languages Marshallese, English, Japanese, German
Religions Protestant 90%, Roman Catholic 8%, other 2%
Ethnic mix Micronesian 97%, other 3%
Government Parliamentary democracy
Currency US dollar = 100 cents
Literacy rate 91%
Calorie consumption not available

MAURITANIA

Page 52 C2

Situated in northwest Africa, two-thirds of Mauritania's territory is desert. A former French colony, it achieved independence in 1960.

Official name Islamic Republic of Mauritania
Formation 1960
Capital Nouakchott
Population 2.7 million / 7 people per sq mile (3 people per sq km)
Total area 397,953 sq miles (1,030,700 sq km)
Languages Hassaniyah Arabic, French, Wolof
Religions Muslim (Sunni) 100%
Ethnic mix Maure 81%, Wolof 7%, Tukolor 5%, Soninka 3%, other 4%
Government Multiparty republic
Currency Ouguiya = 5 khoums
Literacy rate 42.3%
Calorie consumption 2,638 kilocalories

MAURITIUS

Page 57 H3

Located to the east of Madagascar in the Indian Ocean, Mauritius became a republic 25 years after it gained independence. Tourism is a mainstay of its economy.

Official name Mauritius
Formation 1968
Capital Port Louis
Population 1.2 million / 1,671 people per sq mile (645 people per sq km)
Total area 718 sq miles (1,860 sq km)
Languages English, French, French Creole, Hindi, Urdu, Tamil, Chinese
Religions Hindu 52%, Muslim 17%, Roman Catholic 26%, other 5%
Ethnic mix Indo-Mauritian 68%, Creole 27%, Sino Mauritian 3%, Franco-Mauritian 2%
Government Parliamentary democracy
Currency Mauritian rupee = 100 cents
Literacy rate 84.6%
Calorie consumption 2,985 kilocalories

MOLDOVA

Page 86 D3

The smallest and most densely populated of the ex-Soviet republics, Moldova has strong linguistic and cultural links with Romania to the west.

Official name Republic of Moldova
Formation 1991
Capital Chisinau
Population 4.3 million / 329 people per sq mile (127 people per sq km)
Total area 13,067 sq miles (33,843 sq km)
Languages Romanian, Moldovan, Russian
Religions Eastern Orthodox 98%, Jewish 2%
Ethnic mix Moldovan 65%, Ukranian 14%, Russian 13%, Gagauzi 4%, other 4%
Government Parliamentary democracy
Currency Moldovan leu = 100 bani
Literacy rate 99%
Calorie consumption 2,764 kilocalories

MOROCCO

Page 48 C2

A former French colony in northwest Africa, independent in 1956, Morocco has occupied the disputed territory of Western Sahara since 1975.

Official name Kingdom of Morocco
Formation 1956
Capital Rabat
Population 30.4 million / 176 people per sq mile (68 people per sq km)
Total area 172,316 sq miles (446,300 sq km)
Languages Arabic, Berber (Shluh, Tamazight, Riffian), French, Spanish
Religions Muslim 99%, other 1%
Ethnic mix Arab 70%, Berber 29%, European 1%
Government Constitutional monarchy
Currency Moroccan dirham = 100 centimes
Literacy rate 48.9%
Calorie consumption 2,964 kilocalories

NAMIBIA

Page 56 B3

Located in southwestern Africa, Namibia became free of South African control in 1990, after years of uncertainty and guerrilla activity.

Official name Republic of Namibia
Formation 1990
Capital Windhoek
Population 1.8 million / 6 people per sq mile (2 people per sq km)
Total area 318,694 sq miles (825,418 sq km)
Languages English, Ovambo, Kavango, Bergdama, German, Afrikaans
Religions Christian 90%, other 10%
Ethnic mix Ovambo 50%, other tribes 16%, Kavango 9%, Herero 8%, Damara 8%, other 9%
Government Parliamentary democracy
Currency Namibian dollar = 100 cents
Literacy rate 82%
Calorie consumption 2,649 kilocalories

MEXICO

Page 28 D3

Located between the United States of America and the Central American states, Mexico was a Spanish colony for 300 years until 1836.

Official name United States of Mexico
Formation 1836
Capital Mexico City
Population 100.4 million / 132 people per sq mile (51 people per sq km)
Total area 761,602 sq miles (1,972,550 sq km)
Languages Spanish, Nahuatl, Mayan, Zapotec, Mixtec, Otomi, Totonac, Tzotzil, Tzeltal
Religions Roman Catholic 95%, Protestant 1%, other 4%
Ethnic mix Mestizo 55%, Amerindian 20%, European 16%, other 9%
Government Presidential democracy
Currency Mexican peso = 100 centavos
Literacy rate 91.3%
Calorie consumption 3,165 kilocalories

MONACO

Page 69 E6

A jet-set image and a thriving service sector define the modern identity of this tiny enclave on the Côte d'Azur in southeastern France.

Official name Principality of Monaco
Formation 1861
Capital Monaco
Population 31,700 / 42,104 people per sq mile (16,256 people per sq km)
Total area 0.75 sq miles (1.95 sq km)
Languages French, Italian, Monégasque, English
Religions Roman Catholic, 89%, Protestant 6%, other 5%
Ethnic mix French 47%, Monégasque 17%, Italian 16%, other 20%
Government Constitutional monarchy
Currency Euro (French franc until 2002)
Literacy rate 99%
Calorie consumption not available

MOZAMBIQUE

Page 57 E3

Mozambique lies on the southeast African coast. It was torn by a civil war between the Marxist government and a rebel group from 1977–1992.

Official name Republic of Mozambique
Formation 1975
Capital Maputo
Population 18.6 million / 60 people per sq mile (23 people per sq km)
Total area 309,494 sq miles (801,590 sq km)
Languages Portuguese, Makua, Tsonga, Sena, Lomwe
Religions Traditional beliefs 60%, Christian 30%, Muslim 10%
Ethnic mix Makua Lomwe 47%, Tsonga 23%, Malawi 12%, Shona 11%, Yao 4%, other 3%
Government Multiparty republic
Currency Metical = 100 centavos
Literacy rate 44%
Calorie consumption 1,927 kilocalories

NAURU

Page 122 D3

Nauru lies in the Pacific, 4,000 km (2,480 miles) northeast of Australia. Phosphate deposits have made its citizens among the richest in the world.

Official name Republic of Nauru
Formation 1968
Capital No official capital
Population 11,800 / 1,455 people per sq mile (562 people per sq km)
Total area 8 sq miles (21 sq km)
Languages Nauruan, English, Kiribati, Chinese, Tuvaluan
Religions Nauruan Congregational Church 60%, Roman Catholic 35, other 5%
Ethnic mix Nauruan 62%, other Pacific islanders 25%, Chinese and Vietnamese 8%, European 5%
Government Non-party democracy
Currency Australian dollar = 100 cents
Literacy rate 99%
Calorie consumption not available

MICRONESIA

Page 122 B1

The Federated States of Micronesia, situated in the western Pacific, comprise 607 islands and atolls grouped into four main island states.

Official name Federated States of Micronesia
Formation 1986
Capital Palikir (Pohnpei island)
Population 133,000 / 490 people per sq mile (189 people per sq km)
Total area 271 sq miles (702 sq km)
Languages English, Trukese, Pohnpeian, Mortlockese, Losrean
Religions Roman Catholic 50%, Protestant 48%, other 2%
Ethnic mix Micronesian 100%
Government Non-party democracy
Currency US dollar = 100 cents
Literacy rate 89%
Calorie consumption not available

MONGOLIA

Page 104 D2

Lying between Russia and China, Mongolia is a vast and isolated country with a small population. Over two-thirds of the country is desert.

Official name Mongolia
Formation 1924
Capital Ulan Bator
Population 2.6 million / 4 people per sq mile (2 people per sq km)
Total area 604,247 sq miles (1,565,000 sq km)
Languages Khalkha Mongolian, Kazakh, Chinese, Russian
Religions Tibetan Buddhist 96%, Muslim 4%
Ethnic mix Mongol 90%, Kazakh 4%, Chinese 2%, Russian 2%, other 2%
Government Multiparty republic
Currency Tugrik (togrog) = 100 möngös
Literacy rate 99%
Calorie consumption 1,981 kilocalories

MYANMAR (BURMA)

Page 114 A3

Myanmar forms the eastern shores of the Bay of Bengal and the Andaman Sea in Southeast Asia. Since 1988 it has been ruled by a repressive military regime.

Official name Union of Myanmar
Formation 1948
Capital Rangoon (Yangoon)
Population 48.4 million / 185 people per sq mile (71 people per sq km)
Total area 261,969 sq miles (678,500 sq km)
Languages Burmese, Karen, Shan, Chin, Kachin, Mon, Palaung, Wa
Religions Buddhist 87%, Christian 6%, Muslim 4%, Hindu 1%, other 2%
Ethnic mix Burman (Bamah) 68%, Shan 9%, Karen 6%, Rakhine 4%, other 13%
Government Military-based regime
Currency Kyat = 100 pyas
Literacy rate 84.7%
Calorie consumption 2,842 kilocalories

NEPAL

Page 113 E3

Nepal lies between India and China, on the shoulder of the southern Himalayas. The elections of 1991 ended a period of absolute monarchy.

Official name Kingdom of Nepal
Formation 1769
Capital Kathmandu
Population 23.6 million / 434 people per sq mile (168 people per sq km)
Total area 54,363 sq miles (140,800 sq km)
Languages Nepali, Maithili, Bhojpuri
Religions Hindu 90%, Buddhist 5%, Muslim 3%, other 2%
Ethnic mix Nepalese 52%, Maithili 11%, Tibeto-Burmese 10%, Bhojpuri 8%, other 19%
Government Constitutional monarchy
Currency Nepalese rupee = 100 paisa
Literacy rate 41.5%
Calorie consumption 2,436 kilocalories

NETHERLANDS

Page 64 C3

Astride the delta of five major rivers in northwest Europe, the Netherlands has a long trading tradition. Rotterdam is the world's largest port.

Official name Kingdom of the Netherlands
Formation 1648
Capital Amsterdam, The Hague
Population 16.2 million / 1,010 people per sq mile (390 people per sq km)
Total area 16,033 sq miles (41,526 sq km)
Languages Dutch, Frisian
Religions Roman Catholic 36%, Protestant 27%, Muslim 3%, other 34%
Ethnic mix Dutch 82%, other 18%
Government Parliamentary democracy
Currency Euro (Netherlands guilder until 2002)
Literacy rate 99%
Calorie consumption 3,294 kilocalories

NIGER

Page 53 F3

Niger lies landlocked in West Africa, but it is linked to the sea by the River Niger. Since 1973 it has suffered civil unrest and two major droughts.

Official name Republic of Niger
Formation 1960
Capital Niamey
Population 11.2 million / 23 people per sq mile (9 people per sq km)
Total area 489,189 sq miles (1,267,000 sq km)
Languages French, Hausa, Djerma
Religions Muslim 85%, Traditional beliefs 14%, other 1%
Ethnic mix Hausa 54%, Djerma and Songhai 21%, Fulani 10%, Tuareg 9%, other 6%
Government Multiparty republic
Currency CFA franc = 100 centimes
Literacy rate 15.9%
Calorie consumption 2,089 kilocalories

NORWAY

Page 63 A5

The Kingdom of Norway traces the rugged western coast of Scandinavia. Settlements are largely restricted to southern and coastal areas.

Official name Kingdom of Norway
Formation 1905
Capital Oslo
Population 4.5 million / 36 people per sq mile (14 people per sq km)
Total area 125,181 sq miles (324,220 sq km)
Languages Norwegian, Sami
Religions Evangelical Lutheran 89%, Roman Catholic 1%, other and non-religious 10%
Ethnic mix Norwegian 93%, Sami 1%, other 6%
Government Parliamentary democracy
Currency Norwegian krone = 100 ore
Literacy rate 99%
Calorie consumption 3,414 kilocalories

PALAU

Page 122 A2

The Palau archipelago, a group of over 200 islands, lies in the western Pacific Ocean. In 1994, it became the world's newest independent state.

Official name Republic of Palau
Formation 1994
Capital Koror
Population 19,100 / 108 people per sq mile (42 people per sq km)
Total area 177 sq miles (458 sq km)
Languages Palauan, English, Japanese, Angaur, Tobi, Sonsorolese
Religions Christian 66%, Modekngei 34%
Ethnic mix Micronesian 87%, Filipino 8%, Chinese 5%
Government Non-party democracy
Currency US dollar = 100 cents
Literacy rate 92%
Calorie consumption not available

NEW ZEALAND

Page 128 A4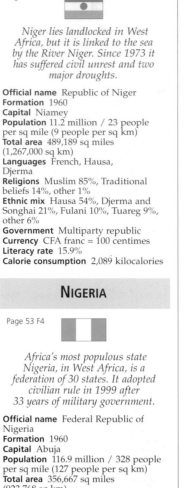

One of the Pacific Rim countries, New Zealand lies southeast of Australia, and comprises the North and South Islands, separated by the Cook Strait.

Official name Dominion of New Zealand
Formation 1947
Capital Wellington
Population 3.8 million / 37 people per sq mile (14 people per sq km)
Total area 103,737 sq miles (268,680 sqkm)
Languages English, Maori
Religions Methodist 24%, Presbyterian 18%, non-religious 16%, Roman Catholic 15%, Methodist 5%, other 22%
Ethnic mix European 77%, Maori 12%, Pacific Islanders 5%, other 6%
Government Parliamentary democracy
Currency New Zealand dollar = 100 cents
Literacy rate 99%

NIGERIA

Page 53 F4

Africa's most populous state Nigeria, in West Africa, is a federation of 30 states. It adopted civilian rule in 1999 after 33 years of military government.

Official name Federal Republic of Nigeria
Formation 1960
Capital Abuja
Population 116.9 million / 328 people per sq mile (127 people per sq km)
Total area 356,667 sq miles (923,768 sq km)
Languages English, Hausa, Yoruba, Ibo
Religions Muslim 50%, Christian 40%, Traditional beliefs 10%
Ethnic mix Hausa 21%, Yoruba 21%, Ibo 18%, Fulani 11%, other 29%
Government Multiparty republic
Currency Naira = 100 kobo
Literacy rate 63.9%
Calorie consumption 2,850 kilocalories

OMAN

Page 99 D6

Situated on the eastern coast of the Arabian Peninsula, Oman is the least developed of the Gulf states, despite modest oil exports.

Official name Sultanate of Oman
Formation 1951
Capital Muscat
Population 2.6 million / 32 people per sq mile (12 people per sq km)
Total area 82,031 sq miles (212,460 sq km)
Languages Arabic, Baluchi
Religions Ibadi Muslim 75%, other Muslim and Hindu 25%
Ethnic mix Arab 88%, Baluch 4%, Persian 3%, Indian and Pakistani 3%, African 2%
Government Monarchy
Currency Omani rial = 1,000 baizas
Literacy rate 71.8%
Calorie consumption not available

PANAMA

Page 31 F5

Southernmost of the Central American countries. The Panama Canal (returned to Panama from US control in 2000) links the Pacific and Atlantic oceans.

Official name Republic of Panama
Formation 1903
Capital Panama City
Population 2.9 million / 96 people per sq mile (37 people per sq km)
Total area 30,193 sq miles (78,200 sq km)
Languages Spanish, English Creole, Amerindian languages, Chibchan
Religions Roman Catholic 86%, Protestant 6%, other 8%
Ethnic mix Mestizo 60%, White 14%, Black 12%, Amerindian 8%, Asian 4%, other 2%
Government Presidential democracy
Currency Balboa = 100 centesimos
Literacy rate 91.9%
Calorie consumption 2,488 kilocalories

NICARAGUA

Page 30 D3

Nicaragua lies at the heart of Central America. An 11-year war between left-wing Sandinistas and right-wing US-backed Contras ended in 1989.

Official name Republic of Nicaragua
Formation 1838
Capital Managua
Population 5.2 million / 104 people per sq mile (40 people per sq km)
Total area 49,998 sq miles (129,494 sq km)
Languages Spanish, English Creole, Miskito
Religions Protestant Evangelicals 17%, Roman Catholic 80%, Zambos 3%
Ethnic mix Mestizo 69%, White 14%, Black 8%, Amerindian 5%, Zambos 4%
Government Presidential democracy
Currency Córdoba oro = 100 pence
Literacy rate 68.6%
Calorie consumption 2,227 kilocalories

NORTH KOREA

Page 106 E3

North Korea comprises the northern half of the Korean peninsula. A communist state since 1948, it is largely isolated from the outside world.

Official name Democratic People's Republic of Korea
Formation 1948
Capital Pyongyang
Population 22.4 million / 481 people per sq mile (186 people per sq km)
Total area 46,540 sq miles (120,540 sq km)
Languages Korean, Chinese
Religions Atheist 100%
Ethnic mix Korean 100%
Government One-party republic
Currency N Korean won = 100 chon
Literacy rate 95%
Calorie consumption 2,185 kilocalories

PAKISTAN

Page 112 B2

Once a part of British India, Pakistan was created in 1947 as an independent Muslim state. Today, the country is divided into four provinces.

Official name Islamic Republic of Pakistan
Formation 1947
Capital Islamabad
Population 145 million / 467 people per sq mile (180 people per sq km)
Total area 310,401 sq miles (803,940 sq km)
Languages Urdu, Punjabi, Sindhi
Religions Sunni Muslim 77%, Shi'a Muslim 20%, Hindu 2%, Christian 1%
Ethnic mix Punjabi 50%, Sindhi 15%, Pashto 15%, Mohajir 8%, other 12%
Government Military-based regime
Currency Pakistani rupee = 100 paisa
Literacy rate 46.1%
Calorie consumption 2,452 kilocalories

PAPUA NEW GUINEA

Page 122 B3

Achieving independence from Australia in 1975, PNG occupies the eastern section of the island of New Guinea and several other island groups.

Official name Independent State of Papua New Guinea
Formation 1975
Capital Port Moresby
Population 5.2 million / 29 people per sq mile (11 people per sq km)
Total area 178,703 sq miles (462,840 sq km)
Languages English, Pidgin English, Papuan, Motu, c.750 native languages
Religions Protestant 60%, Roman Catholic 37%, other 3%
Ethnic mix Melanesian and mixed 100%
Government Multiparty republic
Currency Kina = 100 toea
Literacy rate 63.9%
Calorie consumption 2,175 kilocalories

PARAGUAY

Page 42 D2

Landlocked in central South America. Its post-independence history has included periods of military rule. Free elections were held in 1993.

Official name Republic of Paraguay
Formation 1811
Capital Asunción
Population 5.6 million /
36 people per sq mile (14 people per sq km)
Total area 157,046 sq miles
(406,750 sq km)
Languages Spanish, Guaraní
Religions Roman Catholic 96%, Protestant (including Mennonite) 4%
Ethnic mix Mestizo 90%, Amerindian 2%, other 8%
Government Presidential democracy
Currency Guaraní =
100 centimos
Literacy rate 93.3%
Calorie consumption 2,533 kilocalories

PERU

Page 38 C3

Once the heart of the Inca empire, before the Spanish conquest in the 16th century, Peru lies on the Pacific coast of South America.

Official name Republic of Peru
Formation 1824
Capital Lima
Population 26.1 million /
53 people per sq mile (20 people per sq km)
Total area 496,223 sq miles
(1,285,220 sq km)
Languages Spanish, Quechua, Aymará
Religions Roman Catholic 95%, other 5%
Ethnic mix Amerindian 54%, Mestizo 32%, White 12%, other 2%
Government Presidential democracy
Currency New sol = 100 centimos
Literacy rate 89.9%
Calorie consumption 2,624 kilocalories

PHILIPPINES

Page 117 E1

An archipelago of 7,107 islands between the South China Sea and the Pacific. After 21 years of dictatorship, democracy was restored in 1986.

Official name Republic of the Philippines
Formation 1946
Capital Manila
Population 77.1 million / 666 people per sq mile (257 people per sq km)
Total area 115,830 sq miles
(300,000 sq km)
Languages Filipino, English, Cebuano
Religions Roman Catholic 83%, Protestant 9%, Muslim 5%, other 3%
Ethnic mix Filipino 50%, Indonesian and Polynesian 30%, other 20%
Government Presidential democracy
Currency Peso = 100 centavos
Literacy rate 95.3%
Calorie consumption 2,379 kilocalories

POLAND

Page 76 B3

With its seven international borders and strategic location in the heart of Europe, Poland has always played an important role in European affairs.

Official name Republic of Poland
Formation 1918
Capital Warsaw
Population 38.6 million /
320 people per sq mile (123 people per sq km)
Total area 120,728 sq miles
(312,685 sq km)
Languages Polish
Religions Roman Catholic 93%, Eastern Orthodox 2%, other and non-religious 5%
Ethnic mix Polish 98%, German 1%, other 1%
Government Parliamentary democracy
Currency Zloty – 100 groszy
Literacy rate 99%
Calorie consumption 3,376 kilocalories

PORTUGAL

Page 70 B3

Facing the Atlantic on the western side of the Iberian Peninsula, Portugal is the most westerly country on the European mainland.

Official name Republic of Portugal
Formation 1139
Capital Lisbon
Population 10 million /
280 people per sq mile (108 people per sq km)
Total area 35,672 sq miles
(92,391 sq km)
Languages Portuguese
Religions Roman Catholic 97%, Protestant 1%, other 2%
Ethnic mix Portuguese 98%, African and other 2%
Government Parliamentary democracy
Currency Euro (Portuguese escudo until 2002)
Literacy rate 92.3%
Calorie consumption 3,716 kilocalories

QATAR

Page 98 C4

Projecting north from the Arabian Peninsula into the Persian Gulf, Qatar's reserves of oil and gas make it one of the region's wealthiest states.

Official name State of Qatar
Formation 1971
Capital Doha
Population 575,000 /
130 people per sq mile (50 people per sq km)
Total area 4,416 sq miles
(11,437 sq km)
Languages Arabic
Religions Muslim (mainly Sunni) 95%, other 5%
Ethnic mix Arab 40%, Pakistani 18%, Indian 18%, Iranian 10%, other 14%
Government Monarchy
Currency Qatar riyal = 100 dirhams
Literacy rate 81.2%
Calorie consumption not available

ROMANIA

Page 86 B4

Romania lies on the Black Sea coast. Since the overthrow of its communist regime in 1989, it has been slowly converting to a free-market economy.

Official name Romania
Formation 1878
Capital Bucharest
Population 21.7 million /
237 people per sq mile (91 people per sq km)
Total area 91,699 sq miles
(237,500 sq km)
Languages Romanian, Hungarian, German, Romany
Religions Romanian Orthodox 87%, Roman Catholic 5%, other 8%
Ethnic mix Romanian 89%, Magyar 9%, Romany 1%, other 1%
Government Multiparty republic
Currency Romanian Leu = 100 bani
Literacy rate 98.1%
Calorie consumption 3,274 kilocalories

RUSSIAN FEDERATION

Page 92 D4

Still the world's largest state, despite the breakup of the USSR in 1991, the Russian Federation is struggling to capitalize on its diversity.

Official name Russian Federation
Formation 1991
Capital Moscow
Population 144.7 million /
22 people per sq mile (8 people per sq km)
Total area 6,592,735 sq miles
(17,075,200 sq km)
Languages Russian
Religions Russian Orthodox 75%, other 25%
Ethnic mix Russian 82%, Tatar 4%, Ukranian 3%, Chavash 1%, other 10%
Government Presidential democracy
Currency Rouble = 100 kopeks
Literacy rate 99%
Calorie consumption 2,917 kilocalories

RWANDA

Page 51 B6

Rwanda lies just south of the Equator in east central Africa. Since independence from France in 1962, ethnic tensions have dominated politics.

Official name Republic of Rwanda
Formation 1962
Capital Kigali
Population 7.9 million / 777 people per sq mile (300 people per sq km)
Total area 10,169 sq miles
(26,338 sq km)
Languages French, Kinyarwanda, Kiswahili, English
Religions Roman Catholic 65%, Traditional beliefs 25%, Protestant 9%, Muslim 1%
Ethnic mix Hutu 90%, Tutsi 9%, other (including Twa) 1%
Government Transitional regime
Currency Rwanda franc = 100 centimes
Literacy rate 66.8%
Calorie consumption 2,2077 kilocalories

SAINT KITTS & NEVIS

Page 33 G3

Separated by a channel, the two islands of Saint Kitts and Nevis are part of the Leeward Islands chain in the Caribbean. Nevis is the less developed of the two.

Official name Federation of Saint Christopher and Nevis
Formation 1983
Capital Basseterre
Population 41,000 / 407 people per sq mile (157 people per sq km)
Total area 101 sq miles (261 sq km)
Languages English, English Creole
Religions Anglican 33%, Methodist 29%, Moravian 9%, Roman Catholic 7%, other 22%
Ethnic mix Black 94%, Mixed 3%, Other and Amerindian 2%, other 1%
Government Parliamentary democracy
Currency Eastern Caribbean dollar = 100 cents
Literacy rate 90%
Calorie consumption 2,685 kilocalories

SAINT LUCIA

Page 33 G4

Among the most beautiful of the Caribbean Windward Islands, Saint Lucia retains both French and British influences from its colonial history.

Official name Saint Lucia
Formation 1979
Capital Castries
Population 156,300 /
653 people per sq mile (252 people per sq km)
Total area 239 sq miles
(620 sq km)
Languages English, French Creole
Religions Roman Catholic 90%, other 10%
Ethnic mix Black 90%, Mulatto 6%, Asian 3%, White 1%
Government Parliamentary democracy
Currency Eastern Caribbean dollar = 100 cents
Literacy rate 82%
Calorie consumption 2,838 kilocalories

SAINT VINCENT & THE GRENADINES

Page 33 G4

Formerly ruled by Britain, these volcanic islands form part of the Caribbean Windward Islands.

Official name Saint Vincent and the Grenadines
Formation 1979
Capital Kingston
Population 115,500 / 769 people per sq mile (297 people per sq km)
Total area 150 sq miles (389 sq km)
Languages English, English Creole
Religions Anglican 42%, Methodist 20%, Roman Catholic 19%, other 19%
Ethnic mix Black 66%, Mulatto 19%, Asian 6%, White 4%, other 5%
Government Parliamentary democracy
Currency Eastern Caribbean dollar = 100 cents
Literacy rate 82%
Calorie consumption 2,579 kilocalories

SAMOA

Page 123 F4

The southern Pacific islands of Samoa gained independence from New Zealand in 1962. Four of the nine islands are inhabited.

Official name Independent State of Samoa
Formation 1962
Capital Apia
Population 159,000/ 144 people per sq mile (56 people per sq km)
Total area 1,104 sq miles (2,860 sq km)
Languages Samoan, English
Religions Christian 99%, other 1%
Ethnic mix Polynesian 90%, Euronesian 9%, other 1%
Government Parliamentary democracy
Currency Tala = 100 sene
Literacy rate 80.2%
Calorie consumption not available

SAN MARINO

Page 74 C3

Perched on the slopes of Monte Titano in the Italian Appennino, San Marino has maintained its independence since the 4th century AD.

Official name Republic of San Marino
Formation 1631
Capital San Marino
Population 26,900 / 1,138 people per sq mile (440 people per sq km)
Total area 24 sq miles (61 sq km)
Languages Italian
Religions Roman Catholic 93%, other and non-religious 7%
Ethnic mix Sammarinese 80%, Italian 19%, other 1%
Government Parliamentary democracy
Currency Euro (Lira until 2002)
Literacy rate 99%
Calorie consumption not available

SAO TOME & PRINCIPE

Page 55 A5

A former Portuguese colony off Africa's west coast, comprising two main islands and smaller islets. The 1991 elections ended 15 years of Marxism.

Official name Democratic Republic of São Tomé and Príncipe
Formation 1975
Capital São Tomé
Population 159,900 / 414 people per sq mile (160 people per sq km)
Total area 386 sq miles (1,001 sq km)
Languages Portuguese, Portuguese Creole
Religions Roman Catholic 84%, other Christian 16%
Ethnic mix Black 90%, Portuguese and Creole 10%
Government Multiparty republic
Currency Dobra = 100 centimos
Literacy rate 75%
Calorie consumption 2,390 kilocalories

SAUDI ARABIA

Page 99 B5

Occupying most of the Arabian Peninsula, the desert kingdom of Saudi Arabia, rich in oil and gas, covers an area the size of Western Europe.

Official name Kingdom of Saudi Arabia
Formation 1932
Capital Riyadh
Population 21 million / 28 people per sq mile (11 people per sq km)
Total area 756,981 sq miles (1,960,582 sq km)
Languages Arabic
Religions Sunni Muslim 85%, Shi'a Muslim 15%
Ethnic mix Arab 90%, Afro-Asian 10%
Government Monarchy
Currency Saudi riyal = 100 malalah
Literacy rate 77%
Calorie consumption 2,875 kilocalories

SENEGAL

Page 52 B3

A former French colony, Senegal achieved independence in 1960. Its capital, Dakar, stands on the westernmost cape of Africa.

Official name Republic of Senegal
Formation 1960
Capital Dakar
Population 9.7 million / 128 people per sq mile (49 people per sq km)
Total area 75,749 sq miles (196,190 sq km)
Languages French, Wolof, Fulani, Serer, Diola, Malinke, Soninke, Arabic
Religions Sunni Muslim 90%, Christian (mainly Roman Catholic) 5%, Traditional beliefs 5%
Ethnic mix Wolof 44%, Serer 15%, Fula 12%, Diola 5%, Malinke 4%, other 20%
Government Presidential democracy
Currency CFA franc = 100 centimes
Literacy rate 37.4%
Calorie consumption 2,257 kilocalories

SERBIA & MONTENEGRO (YUGOSLAVIA)

Page 78 D4

Serbia and Montenegro is the successor state to the former Yugoslavia.

Official name Serbia and Montenegro
Formation 1992
Capital Belgrade
Population 10.5 million / 266 people per sq mile (103 people per sq km)
Total area 39,449 sq miles (102,173 sq km)
Languages Serbo-Croat, Albanian, Hungarian
Religions Eastern Orthodox 65, Muslim 19%, Roman Catholic 4%, other 12%
Ethnic mix Serb 62%, Albanian 17%, Montenegrin 5%, other 16%
Government Multiparty republic
Currency Dinar (Euro widely used in Montenegro)
Literacy rate 93.3%
Calorie consumption 2,570 kilocalories

SEYCHELLES

Page 57 G1

A former British colony comprising 115 islands in the Indian Ocean. Under one-party rule for 16 years, it became a multiparty democracy in 1993.

Official name Republic of the Seychelles
Formation 1976
Capital Victoria
Population 79,300/ 451 people per sq mile (174 people per sq km)
Total area 176 sq miles (455 sq km)
Languages French Creole (Seselwa), English, French
Religions Roman Catholic 90%, Anglican 8%, other 2%
Ethnic mix Creole 89%, Indian 5%, Chinese 2%, other 4%
Government Multiparty republic
Currency Seychelles rupee = 100 cents
Literacy rate 84%
Calorie consumption 2,432 kilocalories

SIERRA LEONE

Page 52 C4

The West African state of Sierra Leone achieved independence from the British in 1961. Today, it is one of the world's poorest nations.

Official name Republic of Sierra Leone
Formation 1961
Capital Freetown
Population 4.6 million / 166 people per sq mile (64 people per sq km)
Total area 27,699 sq miles (71,740 sq km)
Languages English, Mende, Temne, Krio
Religions Traditional beliefs 30%, Muslim 30%, Christian 10%, other 30%
Ethnic mix Mende 35%, Temne 32%, Limba 8%, Kuranko 4%, other 21%
Government Multiparty republic
Currency Leone = 100 cents
Literacy rate 36.3%
Calorie consumption 1,863 kilocalories

SINGAPORE

Page 116 A1

A city state linked to the southernmost tip of the Malay Peninsula by a causeway, Singapore is one of Asia's most important commercial centers.

Official name Republic of Singapore
Formation 1965
Capital Singapore
Population 4.1 million / 16,400 people per sq mile (6,332 people per sq km)
Total area 250 sq miles (648 sq km)
Languages Malay, English, Mandarin, Tamil
Religions Buddhist 55%, Taoism 22%, Muslim 16%, Hindu, Christian, Sikh 7%
Ethnic mix Chinese 77%, Malay 14%, Indian 8%, other 1%
Government Parliamentary democracy
Currency Singapore dollar = 100 cents
Literacy rate 92.4%
Calorie consumption not available

SLOVAKIA

Page 77 C6

Landlocked in Central Europe, Slovakia has been independent since 1993. It is the less developed half of the former Czechoslovakia.

Official name Slovak Republic
Formation 1993
Capital Bratislava
Population 5.4 million / 286 people per sq mile (111 people per sq km)
Total area 18,859 sq miles (48,845 sq km)
Languages Slovak, Hungarian, Czech
Religions Roman Catholic 60%, Atheist 10%, Protestant 8%, Orthodox 4%, other 18%
Ethnic mix Slovak 85%, Magyar 11%, Romany 1%, Czech 1%, other 2%
Government Parliamentary democracy
Currency Koruna = 100 halierov
Literacy rate 99%
Calorie consumption 3,133 kilocalories

SLOVENIA

Page 73 D8

Northernmost of the former Yugoslav republics, Slovenia has the closest links with Western Europe. In 1991, it gained independence with little violence.

Official name Republic of Slovenia
Formation 1991
Capital Ljubljana
Population 2 million / 256 people per sq mile (99 people per sq km)
Total area 7820 sq miles (20,253 sq km)
Languages Slovene, Serbo-Croat
Religions Roman Catholic 96%, Muslim 1%, other 3%
Ethnic mix Slovene 88%, Croat 3%, Serb 2%, Muslim 1%, other 6%
Government Parliamentary democracy
Currency Tolar = 100 stotins
Literacy rate 99%
Calorie consumption 3,168 kilocalories

SOLOMON ISLANDS

Page 122 C3

The Solomon archipelago comprises several hundred islands scattered in the southwestern Pacific. Independence from Britain came in 1978.

Official name Solomon Islands
Formation 1978
Capital Honiara
Population 463,000 / 42 people per sq mile (16 people per sq km)
Total area 10,985 sq miles (28,450 sq km)
Languages English, Pidgin English, Melanesian Pidgin
Religions Anglican 34%, Roman Catholic 19%, South Seas Evangelical Church 17%, Methodist 11%, other 19%
Ethnic mix Melanesian 94%, other 6%
Government Parliamentary democracy
Currency Solomon Islands dollar = 100 cents
Literacy rate 62%
Calorie consumption 2,277 kilocalories

Somalia

Page 51 E5

Italian and British Somaliland were united in 1960 to create this semiarid state occupying the horn of Africa. It has suffered years of civil war.

Official name Somali
Formation 1960
Capital Mogadishu
Population 9.2 million / 37 people per sq mile (14 people per sq km)
Total area 246,199 sq miles (637,657 sq km)
Languages Arabic, Somali, English, Italian
Religions Sunni Muslim 98%, other 2%
Ethnic mix Somali 85%, other 15%
Government Transitional regime
Currency Somali shilling = 100 cents
Literacy rate 24.1%
Calorie consumption 1,628 kilocalories

Spain

Page 70 D2

Lodged between mainland Europe and Africa, the Atlantic and the Mediterranean, Spain has occupied a pivotal position since it was united in 1492.

Official name Kingdom of Spain
Formation 1492
Capital Madrid
Population 39.9 million / 205 people per sq mile (79 people per sq km)
Total area 194,896 sq miles (504,782 sq km)
Languages Spanish, Catalan, Galician, Basque
Religions Roman Catholic 96%, other 4%
Ethnic mix Castilian Spanish 72%, Catalan 17%, Galician 6%, other 5%
Government Parliamentary democracy
Currency Euro (pesata until 2002)
Literacy rate 97.7%
Calorie consumption 3,352 kilocalories

Suriname

Page 37 G3

Suriname is a former Dutch colony on the north coast of South America. Democracy was restored in 1991, after almost 11 years of military rule.

Official name Republic of Suriname
Formation 1975
Capital Paramaribo
Population 419,000 / 7 people per sq mile (3 people per sq km)
Total area 63,039 sq miles (163,270 sq km)
Languages Dutch, Sranan, Saramaccan, Javavese, Sarnami Hindi, Chinese
Religions Christian 48%, Hindu 27%, Muslim 20%, other 5%
Ethnic mix South Asian 34%, Creole 34%, Javanese 18%, Black 9%, other 5%
Government Parliamentary democracy
Currency Suriname guilder = 100 cents
Literacy rate 94.2%
Calorie consumption 2,652 kilocalories

Switzerland

Page 73 A7

One of the world's most prosperous countries, with a long tradition of neutrality in foreign affairs, it lies at the center of Western Europe.

Official name Swiss Confederation
Formation 1291
Capital Bern
Population 7.2 million / 469 people per sq mile (174 people per sq km)
Total area 15,942 sq miles (41,290 sq km)
Languages German, French, Italian, Swiss German, Romansch
Religions Roman Catholic 46%, Protestant 40%, other 14%
Ethnic mix German 65%, French 18%, Italian 10%, Romansh 1%, other 6%
Government Parliamentary democracy
Currency Swiss franc = 100 centimes
Literacy rate 99%
Calorie consumption 3,293 kilocalories

South Africa

Page 56 C4

South Africa is the most southerly nation on the African continent. The multiracial elections of 1994 overturned 80 years of white minority rule.

Official name Republic of South Africa
Formation 1934
Capital Pretoria (administrative)
Population 43.8 million / 93 people per sq mile (36 people per sq km)
Total area 471,008 sq miles (1,219,912 sq km)
Languages Afrikaans, English, 9 other African languages
Religions Black Independent 17%, Duthc reformed 11%, Roman Catholic 8%, Methodist 6%, other 58%
Ethnic mix Zulu 23%, other Black 38%, White 16%, Mixed 10%, other 13%
Government Parliamentary democracy
Currency Rand = 100 cents
Literacy rate 85.3%
Calorie consumption 2,886 kilocalories

Sri Lanka

Page 110 D3

The island republic of Sri Lanka is separated from India by the narrow Palk Strait. Since 1983, the Sinhalese and Tamil population have been in conflict.

Official name Democratic Socialist Republic of Sri Lanka
Formation 1948
Capital Colombo
Population 19.1 million / 754 people per sq mile (291 people per sq km)
Total area 25,332 sq miles (65,610 sq km)
Languages Sinhalese, Tamil, English
Religions Buddhist 69%, Hindu 15%, Christian 8%, Muslim 8%
Ethnic mix Sinhalese 74%, Tamil 18%, Moor 7%, other 1%
Government Presidential democracy
Currency Sri Lanka rupee = 100 cents
Literacy rate 91.7%
Calorie consumption 2,405 kilocalories

Swaziland

Page 56 D4

The tiny southern African kingdom of Swaziland gained independence from Britain in 1968. It is economically dependent on South Africa.

Official name Kingdom of Swaziland
Formation 1968
Capital Mbabane
Population 938,000 / 140 people per sq mile (54 people per sq km)
Total area 6,704 sq miles (17,363 sq km)
Languages Siswati, English, Zulu, Tsonga
Religions Christian 60%, Traditional beliefs 40%
Ethnic mix Swazi 97%, other 3%
Government Constitutional monarchy
Currency Lilangeni = 100 cents
Literacy rate 79.6%
Calorie consumption 2,620 kilocalories

Syria

Page 96 B3

Stretching from the eastern Mediterranean to the River Tigris, Syria's borders were created on its independence from France in 1946.

Official name Syrian Arab Republic
Formation 1941
Capital Damascus
Population 16.6 million / 232 people per sq mile (90 people per sq km)
Total area 71,498 sq miles (185,180 sq km)
Languages Arabic, French, Kurdish
Religions Sunni Muslim 74%, other Muslim 16%, Christian 10%
Ethnic mix Arab 89%, Kurdish 6%, Armenian, Turkmen, Circassian 2%, other 3%
Government One-party republic
Currency Syrian pound = 100 piastres
Literacy rate 74.5%
Calorie consumption 3,038 kilocalories

South Korea

Page 106 E4

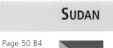

South Korea occupies the southern half of the Korean peninsula. It was separated from the communist North in 1948.

Official name Republic of Korea
Formation 1948
Capital Seoul
Population 47.1 million / 1,239 people per sq mile (478 people per sq km)
Total area 38,023 sq miles (98,480 sq km)
Languages Korean, Chinese
Religions Mahayana Buddhist 47%, Protestant 38%, Roman Catholic 11%, Confucian 3%, other 1%
Ethnic mix Korean 100%
Government Presidential democracy
Currency Korean won = 100 chon
Literacy rate 97.8%
Calorie consumption 3,093 kilocalories

Sudan

Page 50 B4

The largest country in Africa, part of Sudan borders the Red Sea. In 1989, an army coup installed a military Islamic fundamentalist regime.

Official name Republic of the Sudan
Formation 1956
Capital Khartoum
Population 31.8 million / 33 people per sq mile (13 people per sq km)
Total area 967,493 sq miles (2,505,810 sq km)
Languages Arabic, Dinka, Nuer, Zande, Nubian, Beja, Bari, Fur, Shilluk, Lotuko
Religions Muslim (mainly Sunni) 70%, Traditional beliefs 20%, other 10%
Ethnic mix Arab 40%, Tribal 30%, Dinka and Beja 7%, other 23%
Government Presidential regime
Currency Sudanese pound or dinar = 100 piastres
Literacy rate 58%
Calorie consumption 2,348 kilocalories

Sweden

Page 62 B4

The largest Scandinavian country in both population and area, Sweden's strong industrial base helps to fund its extensive welfare system.

Official name Kingdom of Sweden
Formation 1523
Capital Stockholm
Population 8.8 million / 51 people per sq mile (20 people per sq km)
Total area 173,731 sq miles (449,964 sq km)
Languages Swedish, Finnish, Sami
Religions Evangelical Lutheran 89%, Roman Catholic 2%, other 9%
Ethnic mix Swedish 91%, Finnish and Sami 3%, other European 6%
Government Parliamentary democracy
Currency Swedish krona = 100 ore
Literacy rate 99%
Calorie consumption 3,109 kilocalories

Taiwan

Page 107 D6

The island republic of Taiwan lies 130 km (80 miles) off the southeast coast of mainland China. China considers it to be one of its provinces.

Official name Republic of China (Taiwan)
Formation 1949
Capital Taipei
Population 22.2 million / 1,598 people per sq mile (617 people per sq km)
Total area 13,892 sq miles (35,980 sq km)
Languages Mandarin Chinese, Amoy Chinese, Hakka Chinese
Religions Buddhist, Confucian, Taoist 93%, Christian 5%, other 2%
Ethnic mix Indigenous Chinese 84%, Mainland Chinese 14%, Aborigine 2%
Government Multiparty republic
Currency Taiwan dollar = 100 cents
Literacy rate 94%
Calorie consumption not available

COUNTRY FACTFILE • TAJIKISTAN – ZIMBABWE

TAJIKISTAN

Page 101 F3

Tajikistan lies landlocked on the western slopes of the Pamirs in Central Asia. The Tajiks' language and traditions are similar to those of Iran.

Official name Republic of Tajikistan
Formation 1991
Capital Dushanbe
Population 6.1 million / 110 people per sq mile (43 people per sq km)
Total area 55,251 sq miles (143,100 sq km)
Languages Tajik, Russian
Religions Sunni Muslim 80%, Shi'a Muslim 5%, other 15%
Ethnic mix Tajik 62%, Uzbek 24%, Russian 8%, Tatar 1%, Kyrgyz 1%, other 4%
Government Multiparty republic
Currency Somoni
Literacy rate 99%
Calorie consumption 1720 kilocalories

TANZANIA

Page 51 B7

The East African state of Tanzania was formed in 1964 by the union of Tanganyika and Zanzibar. A third of its area is game reserve or national park.

Official name United Republic of Tanzania
Formation 1961
Capital Dodoma
Population 36 million / 99 people per sq mile (38 people per sq km)
Total area 364,898 sq miles (945,087 sq km)
Languages English, Kiswahili, Sukuma
Religions Muslim 33%, Christian 33%, Traditional beliefs 30%, other 4%
Ethnic mix Native African (over 120 tribes) 99%, European and Asian 1%
Government Presidential democracy
Currency Tanzanian shilling = 100 cents
Literacy rate 75.8%
Calorie consumption 1,906 kilocalories

THAILAND

Page 115 C5

Thailand lies at the heart of mainland Southeast Asia. Continuing rapid industrialization has resulted in massive congestion in the capital.

Official name Kingdom of Thailand
Formation 1238
Capital Bangkok
Population 63.6 million / 322 people per sq mile (124 people per sq km)
Total area 197,254 sq miles (510,890 sq km)
Languages Thai, Chinese, Malay, Khmer, Mon, Karen, Miao
Religions Buddhist 95%, Muslim 3%, Christian 1%, other 1%
Ethnic mix Thai 83%, Chinese 12%, Malay 3%, Khmer and other 2%
Government Parliamentary democracy
Currency Baht = 100 stangs
Literacy rate 95.5%
Calorie consumption 2,506 kilocalories

TOGO

Page 53 F4

Togo lies sandwiched between Ghana and Benin in West Africa. The 1993–94 presidential elections were the first since its independence in 1960.

Official name Republic of Togo
Formation 1960
Capital Lomé
Population 4.7 million / 214 people per sq mile (83 people per sq km)
Total area 21,925 sq miles (56,785 sq km)
Languages French, Ewe, Kabye, Gurma
Religions Traditional beliefs 50%, Christian 35%, Muslim 15%
Ethnic mix Ewe 46%, other African 53%, European 1%
Government Presidential regime
Currency CFA franc = 100 centimes
Literacy rate 57.3%
Calorie consumption 2,329 kilocalories

TONGA

Page 123 E4

Northeast of New Zealand, in the South Pacific, Tonga is an archipelago of 170 islands, 45 of which are inhabited. Politics is effectively controlled by the king.

Official name Kingdom of Tonga
Formation 1970
Capital Nuku'alofa
Population 102,200 / 354 people per sq mile (137 people per sq km)
Total area 289 sq miles (748 sq km)
Languages Tongan, English
Religions Free Wesleyan 64%, Roman Catholic 15%, Other 21%
Ethnic mix Polynesian 99%, other Pacific groups and European 1%
Government Monarchy
Currency Pa'anga (Tongan dollar) = 100 seniti
Literacy rate 98.5%
Calorie consumption not available

TRINIDAD & TOBAGO

Page 33 H5

The former British colony of Trinidad and Tobago is the most southerly of the West Indies, lying just 15 km (9 miles) off the coast of Venezuela.

Official name Republic of Trinidad and Tobago
Formation 1962
Capital Port-of-Spain
Population 1.3 million / 657 people per sq mile (254 people per sq km)
Total area 1980 sq miles (5,128 sq km)
Languages English, English Creole, Hindi. French, Spanish
Religions Christian 61%, Hindu 24%, other and non-religious 15%
Ethnic mix Asian 40%, Black 40%, Mixed 19%, White and Chinese 1%
Government Parliamentary democracy
Currency Trinidad and Tobago dollar = 100 cents
Literacy rate 93.8%
Calorie consumption 2,777 kilocalories

TUNISIA

Page 49 E2

Tunisia, in North Africa, has traditionally been one of the more liberal Arab states, but is now facing a challenge from Islamic fundamentalists.

Official name Republic of Tunisia
Formation 1956
Capital Tunis
Population 9.6 million / 152 people per sq mile (59 people per sq km)
Total area 63,170 sq miles (163,610 sq km)
Languages Arabic, French
Religions Muslim (mainly Sunni) 98%, Christian 1%, Jewish 1%
Ethnic mix Arab and Berber 98%, European 1%, other 1%
Government Presidential democracy
Currency Tunisian dinar = 1,000 millimes
Literacy rate 71%
Calorie consumption 3,299 kilocalories

TURKEY

Page 94 B3

Lying partly in Europe, but mostly in Asia, Turkey's position gives it significant influence in the Mediterranean, Black Sea, and Middle East.

Official name Republic of Turkey
Formation 1923
Capital Ankara
Population 67.6 million / 224 people per sq mile (87 people per sq km)
Total area 301,382 sq miles (780,580 sq km)
Languages Turkish, Kurdish, Arabic, Circassian, Armenian, Greek, Georgian
Religions Muslim (mainly Sunni) 99%, other 1%
Ethnic mix Turkish 70%, Kurdish 20%, Arab 2%, other 8%
Government Parliamentary democracy
Currency Turkish lira = 100 krural
Literacy rate 85.1%
Calorie consumption 3,416 kilocalories

TURKMENISTAN

Page 100 B2

Stretching from the Caspian Sea into the deserts of Central Asia, the ex-Soviet state of Turkmenistan has adjusted better than most to independence.

Official name Turkmenistan
Formation 1991
Capital Ashgabat
Population 4.8 million / 25 people per sq mile (10 people per sq km)
Total area 188,455 sq miles (488,100 sq km)
Languages Turkmen, Uzbek, Russian
Religions Sunni Muslim 87%, Eastern Orthodox 11%, other 2%
Ethnic mix Turkmen 73%, Russian 10%, Uzbek 9%, Kazakh 2%, Tatar 1%, other 5%
Government One-party state
Currency Manat = 100 tenge
Literacy rate 98%
Calorie consumption 2,675 kilocalories

TUVALU

Page 123 E3

The former Ellice Islands, linked to the Gilbert Islands as a British colony until 1978, Tuvalu is an isolated chain of nine atolls in the Central Pacific.

Official name Tuvalu
Formation 1978
Capital Fongafale, on Funafuti Atoll
Population 10,800 / 1,076 people per sq mile (415 people per sq km)
Total area 10 sq miles (26 sq km)
Languages English, Tuvaluan, Kiribati
Religions Church of Tuvalu 97%, Seventh-day Adventist 1%, Baha'i 1%, other 1%
Ethnic mix Polynesian 96%, other 4%
Government Non-party democracy
Currency Australian dollar and Tuvaluan dollar = 100 cents
Literacy rate 95%
Calorie consumption not available

UGANDA

Page 51 B6

Uganda lies landlocked in East Africa. It was ruled by one of Africa's more eccentric leaders, the dictator Idi Amin Dada, from 1971–1980.

Official name Republic of Uganda
Formation 1962
Capital Kampala
Population 24 million / 263 people per sq mile (102 people per sq km)
Total area 91,135 sq miles (236,040 sq km)
Languages English, Nkole, Luganda
Religions Roman Catholic 38%, Protestant 33%, Traditional beliefs 13%, Muslim (mainly Sunni) 5%, other 11%
Ethnic mix Bantu Tribes 50%, other 50%
Government Non-party democracy
Currency New Uganda shilling = 100 cents
Literacy rate 67.1%
Calorie consumption 2,359 kilocalories

UKRAINE

Page 86 C2

Bordered by seven states, the former "breadbasket of the Soviet Union" balances assertive nationalism with concerns over its relations with Russia.

Official name Ukraine
Formation 1991
Capital Kiev
Population 48.4 million / 208 people per sq mile (80 people per sq km)
Total area 223,089 sq miles (603,700 sq km)
Languages Ukrainian, Russian, Tartar
Religions Christian (mainly Ukrainian Orthodox) 95%, Jewish 1%, other 4%
Ethnic mix Ukrainian 73%, Russian 22%, Jewish 1%, other 4%
Government Presidential democracy
Currency Hryvnia = 100 kopiykas
Literacy rate 99%
Calorie consumption 2,871 kilocalories

UNITED ARAB EMIRATES

Page 99 D5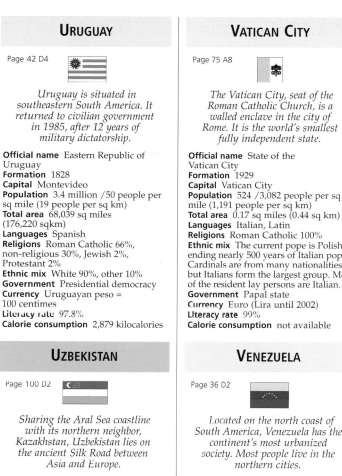

Bordering the Persian Gulf on the northern coast of the Arabian Peninsula, is the United Arab Emirates, a working federation of seven states.

Official name United Arab Emirates
Formation 1971
Capital Abu Dhabi
Population 2.7 million /
84 people per sq mile (33 people per sq km)
Total area 32,000 sq miles
(82,880 sq km)
Languages Arabic, Farsi, English, Indian and Pakistani languages
Religions Muslim (mainly Sunni) 96%, Christian, Hindu and other 4%
Ethnic mix Asian 60%, Emirian 25%, other Arab 12%, European 3%
Government Monarchy
Currency UAE dirham = 100 fils
Literacy rate 75.6%
Calorie consumption 3,192 kilocalories

UNITED KINGDOM

Page 67 B5

Separated from continental Europe by the North Sea and the English Channel, the UK comprises England, Wales, Scotland, and Northern Ireland.

Official name United Kingdom of Great Britain and Northern Ireland
Formation 1707
Capital London
Population 59.5 million / 629 people per sq mile (243 people per sq km)
Total area 94,525 sq miles
(244,820 sq km)
Languages English, Welsh, Scottish
Religions Anglican 47%, Presbyterian 4%, Roman Catholic 9%, other 40%
Ethnic mix English 80%, Scottish 9%, Northern Irish 3%, Welsh 3%, other 5%
Government Parliamentary democracy
Currency Pound sterling = 100 pence
Literacy rate 99%
Calorie consumption 3,334 kilocalories

UNITED STATES OF AMERICA

Page 13 B5

Stretching across the most temperate part of North America, and with many natural resources, the USA is the sole truly global superpower.

Official name United States of America
Formation 1776
Capital Washington DC
Population 281.4 million /76 people per sq mile (29 people per sq km)
Total area 3,717,792 sq miles
(9,629,091 sq km)
Languages English, Spanish, Italian, German, French, Polish, Chinese, Greek
Religions Protestant 61%, Roman Catholic 25%, Jewish 2%, other 12%
Ethnic mix White (including Hispanic) 81%, Native American 2%, Asia 4%, Black American/African 13%
Government Presidential democracy
Currency US dollar = 100 cents
Literacy rate 99%
Calorie consumption 3,772 kilocalories

URUGUAY

Page 42 D4

Uruguay is situated in southeastern South America. It returned to civilian government in 1985, after 12 years of military dictatorship.

Official name Eastern Republic of Uruguay
Formation 1828
Capital Montevideo
Population 3.4 million /50 people per sq mile (19 people per sq km)
Total area 68,039 sq miles
(176,220 sqkm)
Languages Spanish
Religions Roman Catholic 66%, non-religious 30%, Jewish 2%, Protestant 2%
Ethnic mix White 90%, other 10%
Government Presidential democracy
Currency Uruguayan peso = 100 centimes
Literacy rate 97.8%
Calorie consumption 2,879 kilocalories

UZBEKISTAN

Page 100 D2

Sharing the Aral Sea coastline with its northern neighbor, Kazakhstan, Uzbekistan lies on the ancient Silk Road between Asia and Europe.

Official name Republic of Uzbekistan
Formation 1991
Capital Tashkent
Population 25.3 million /
146 people per sq mile (57 people per sq km)
Total area 172,741 sq miles
(447,400 sq km)
Languages Uzbek, Russian
Religions Sunni Muslim 88%, Eastern Orthodox 9%, other 3%
Ethnic mix Uzbek 71%, Russian 8%, Tajik 5%, Kazakh 4%, other 12%
Government Presidential democracy
Currency Som = 100 teen
Literacy rate 88.9%
Calorie consumption 2,317 kilocalories

VANUATU

Page 122 D4

An archipelago of 82 islands and islets in the Pacific Ocean, it was ruled jointly by Britain and France from 1906 until independence in 1980.

Official name Republic of Vanuatu
Formation 1980
Capital Port Vila
Population 200,000 / 42 people per sq mile (16 people per sq km)
Total area 4,710 sq miles
(12,200 sq km)
Languages Bislama, English, French
Religions Presbyterian 37%, Anglican 15%, Roman Catholic 15%, Indigenous beliefs 8%, Seventh-day Adventist 6%, other 19%
Ethnic mix Melanesian 94%, Polynesian 3%, other 3%
Government Parliamentary democracy
Currency Vatu = 100 centimes
Literacy rate 64%
Calorie consumption 2,587 kilocalories

VATICAN CITY

Page 75 A8

The Vatican City, seat of the Roman Catholic Church, is a walled enclave in the city of Rome. It is the world's smallest fully independent state.

Official name State of the Vatican City
Formation 1929
Capital Vatican City
Population 524 /3,082 people per sq mile (1,191 people per sq km)
Total area 0.17 sq miles (0.44 sq km)
Languages Italian, Latin
Religions Roman Catholic 100%
Ethnic mix The current pope is Polish, ending nearly 500 years of Italian popes. Cardinals are from many nationalities, but Italians form the largest group. Most of the resident lay persons are Italian.
Government Papal state
Currency Euro (Lira until 2002)
Literacy rate 99%
Calorie consumption not available

VENEZUELA

Page 36 D2

Located on the north coast of South America, Venezuela has the continent's most urbanized society. Most people live in the northern cities.

Official name Bolivarian Republic of Venezuela
Formation 1830
Capital Caracas
Population 24.6 million /70 people per sq mile (27 people per sq km)
Total area 352,143 sq miles
(912,050 sq km)
Languages Spanish, Amerindian languages
Religions Roman Catholic 89%, Protestant and other 11%
Ethnic mix Mestizo 69%, White 20%, Black 9%, Amerindian 2%
Government Presidential democracy
Currency Bolivar = 100 centimos
Literacy rate 92.6%
Calorie consumption 2,256 kilocalories

VIETNAM

Page 114 D4

Situated in the far east of mainland Southeast Asia, the country is still rebuilding after the devastating 1962–1975 Vietnam War.

Official name Socialist Republic of Vietnam
Formation 1976
Capital Hanoi
Population 79.2 million / 622 people per sq mile (240 people per sq km)
Total area 127,243 sq miles
(329,560 sq km)
Languages Vietnamese, Chinese, Thai, Khmer, Muong, Nung, Miao, Yao
Religions Buddhist 55%, Christian 7%, other and non-religious 38%
Ethnic mix Vietnamese 88%, Chinese 4%, Thai 2%, other 6%
Government One-party republic
Currency Dông = 10 hao = 100 xu
Literacy rate 93.4%
Calorie consumption 2,583 kilocalories

YEMEN

Page 99 C7

Located in southern Arabia, Yemen was formerly two countries – a socialist regime in the south, and a republic in the north. Both united in 1990.

Official name Republic of Yemen
Formation 1990
Capital Sana
Population 19.1 million /
94 people per sq mile (36 people per sq km)
Total area 203,849 sq miles
(527,970 sq km)
Languages Arabic
Religions Shi'a Muslim 42%, Sunni Muslim 55%, Christian, Hindu and Jewish 3%
Ethnic mix Arab 95%, Afro-Arab 3%, Indian, Somali and European 2%
Government Multiparty republic
Currency Yemeni Rial
Literacy rate 46.3%
Calorie consumption 2,038 kilocalories

ZAMBIA

Page 56 C2

Zambia lies landlocked at the heart of southern Africa. In 1991, it made a peaceful transition from single-party rule to multiparty democracy.

Official name Republic of Zambia
Formation 1964
Capital Lusaka
Population 10.6 million /
36 people per sq mile (14 people per sq km)
Total area 290,584 sq miles
(752,612 sq km)
Languages English, Bemba, Nyanja, Tonga, Kaonde, Lunda, Luvale, Lozi
Religions Christian 63%, Indigenous beliefs 36%, other 1%
Ethnic mix Bemba 34%, European 1%, other African 65%
Government Presidential democracy
Currency Zambian kwacha = 100 ngwee
Literacy rate 78.1%
Calorie consumption 1,912 kilocalories

ZIMBABWE

Page 56 D3

The former British colony of Southern Rhodesia became fully independent as Zimbabwe in 1980, after 15 years of troubled white minority rule.

Official name Republic of Zimbabwe
Formation 1980
Capital Harare
Population 12.9 million / 86 people per sq mile (33 people per sq km)
Total area 150,803 sq miles
(390,580 sq km)
Languages English, Shona, Ndebele
Religions Syncretic (Christian and traditional beliefs) 50%, Christian 25%, Traditional beliefs 24%, other 1%
Ethnic mix Shona 71%, Ndebele 16%, other African 11%, Asian 1%, White 1%
Government Presidential regime
Currency Zimbabwe dollar = 100 cents
Literacy rate 88.7%
Calorie consumption 2,117 kilocalories

GEOGRAPHICAL COMPARISONS

LARGEST COUNTRIES

Russ. Fed.	6,592,735 sq miles	(17,075,200 sq km)
Canada	3,851,788 sq miles	(9,976,140 sq km)
USA	3,717,792 sq miles	(9,629,091 sq km)
China	3,705,386 sq miles	(9,596,960 sq km)
Brazil	3,286,470 sq miles	(8,511,965 sq km)
Australia	2,967,893 sq miles	(7,686,893 sq km)
India	1,269,339 sq miles	(3,287,590 sq km)
Argentina	1,068,296 sq miles	(2,766,890 sq km)
Kazakhstan	1,049,150 sq miles	(2,717,300 sq km)
Sudan	967,493 sq miles	(2,505,810 sq km)

SMALLEST COUNTRIES

Vatican City	0.17 sq miles	(0.44 sq km)
Monaco	0.75 sq miles	(1.95 sq km)
Nauru	8 sq miles	(21 sq km)
Tuvalu	10 sq miles	(26 sq km)
San Marino	24 sq miles	(61 sq km)
Liechtenstein	62 sq miles	(160 sq km)
Marshall Islands	70 sq miles	(181 sq km)
St. Kitts & Nevis	101 sq miles	(261 sq km)
Maldives	116 sq miles	(300 sq km)
Malta	122 sq miles	(316 sq km)

LARGEST ISLANDS

(TO THE NEAREST 1,000 - OR 100,000 FOR THE LARGEST)

Greenland	849,400 sq miles	(2,200,000 sq km)
New Guinea	312,000 sq miles	(808,000 sq km)
Borneo	292,222 sq miles	(757,050 sq km)
Madagascar	229,300 sq miles	(594,000 sq km)
Sumatra	202,300 sq miles	(524,000 sq km)
Baffin Island	183,800 sq miles	(476,000 sq km)
Honshu	88,800 sq miles	(230,000 sq km)
Britain	88,700 sq miles	(229,800 sq km)

RICHEST COUNTRIES

(GNP PER CAPITA, IN US$)

Luxembourg	42,930
Liechtenstein	40,000
Switzerland	38,380
Norway	33,470
Denmark	32,050
Japan	32,030
USA	31,910
Germany	25,620
Austria	25,430
Singapore	24,150

POOREST COUNTRIES

(GNP PER CAPITA, IN US$)

Somalia	100
Ethiopia	100
Congo, Dem. Rep.	110
Sierra Leone	130
Malawi	180
Niger	190
Mozambique	220
Burundi	240
Rwanda	250
Tanzania	260

MOST POPULOUS COUNTRIES

China	1,290,000,000
India	1,030,000,000
USA	281,400,000
Indonesia	214,000,000
Brazil	172,600,000
Pakistan	145,000,000
Russian Federation	144,700,000

MOST POPULOUS COUNTRIES continued

Bangladesh	140,400,000
Nigeria	116,900,000
Japan	127,300,000

LEAST POPULOUS COUNTRIES

Vatican City	524
Tuvalu	10,800
Nauru	11,800
Palau	19,100
San Marino	26,900
Liechtenstein	32,200
Monaco	31,700
St. Kitts & Nevis	41,000
Andorra	66,800
Marshall Islands	68,100

MOST DENSELY POPULATED COUNTRIES

Monaco	42,104 people per sq mile	(16,256 per sq km)
Singapore	16,400 people per sq mile	(6,332 per sq km)
Malta	3,213 people per sq mile	(1,241 per sq km)
Vatican City	3,084 people per sq mile	(1,191 per sq km)
Bahrain	2,724 people per sq mile	(1,052 per sq km)
Maldives	2,590 people per sq mile	(1,000 per sq km)
Bangladesh	2,525 people per sq mile	(975 per sq km)
Mauritius	1,671 people per sq mile	(645 per sq km)
Barbados	1,614 people per sq mile	(623 per sq km)
Taiwan	1,598 people per sq mile	(617 per sq km)

MOST SPARSELY POPULATED COUNTRIES

Mongolia	4 people per sq mile	(2 per sq km)
Namibia	6 people per sq mile	(2 per sq km)
Australia	7 people per sq mile	(3 per sq km)
Suriname	7 people per sq mile	(3 per sq km)
Mauritania	7 people per sq mile	(3 per sq km)
Botswana	7 people per sq mile	(3 per sq km)
Iceland	7 people per sq mile	(3 per sq km)
Libya	8 people per sq mile	(3 per sq km)
Canada	8 people per sq mile	(3 per sq km)
Guyana	9 people per sq mile	(4 per sq km)

MOST WIDELY SPOKEN LANGUAGES

1. Chinese (Mandarin)	6. Arabic
2. English	7. Bengali
3. Hindi	8. Portuguese
4. Spanish	9. Malay-Indonesian
5. Russian	10. French

COUNTRIES WITH THE MOST LAND BORDERS

14: China (*Afghanistan, Bhutan, Myanmar, India, Kazakhstan, Kyrgyzstan, Laos, Mongolia, Nepal, North Korea, Pakistan, Russian Federation, Tajikistan, Vietnam*)

14: Russ. Fed. (*Azerbaijan, Belarus, China, Estonia, Finland, Georgia, Kazakhstan, Latvia, Lithuania, Mongolia, North Korea, Norway, Poland, Ukraine*)

10: Brazil (*Argentina, Bolivia, Colombia, French Guiana, Guyana, Paraguay, Peru, Suriname, Uruguay, Venezuela*)

9: Congo, Dem. Rep. (*Angola, Burundi, Central African Republic, Congo, Rwanda, Sudan, Tanzania, Uganda, Zambia*)

9: Germany (*Austria, Belgium, Czech Republic, Denmark, France, Luxembourg, Netherlands, Poland, Switzerland*)

9: Sudan (*Central African Republic, Chad, Congo, Dem. Rep., Egypt, Eritrea, Ethiopia, Kenya, Libya, Uganda*)

8: Austria (*Czech Republic, Germany, Hungary, Italy, Liechtenstein, Slovakia, Slovenia, Switzerland*)

8: France (*Andorra, Belgium, Germany, Italy, Luxembourg, Monaco, Spain, Switzerland*)

8: Tanzania (*Burundi, Congo, Dem. Rep., Kenya, Malawi, Mozambique, Rwanda, Uganda, Zambia*)

8: Turkey (*Armenia, Azerbaijan, Bulgaria, Georgia, Greece, Iran, Iraq, Syria*)

LONGEST RIVERS

Nile (NE Africa)	.4,160 miles	(6,695 km)
Amazon (South America)	.4,049 miles	(6,516 km)
Yangtze (China)	.3,915 miles	(6,299 km)
Mississippi/Missouri (US)	.3,710 miles	(5,969 km)
Ob'-Irtysh (Russ. Fed.)	.3,461 miles	(5,570 km)
Yellow River (China)	.3,395 miles	(5,464 km)
Congo (Central Africa)	.2,900 miles	(4,667 km)
Mekong (Southeast Asia)	.2,749 miles	(4,425 km)
Lena (Russian Federation)	.2,734 miles	(4,400 km)
Mackenzie (Canada)	.2,640 miles	(4,250 km)

HIGHEST MOUNTAINS

(HEIGHT ABOVE SEA LEVEL)

Everest	.29,030 ft	(8,848 m)
K2	.28,253 ft	(8,611 m)
Kanchenjunga I	.28,210 ft	(8,598 m)
Makalu I	.27,767 ft	(8,463 m)
Cho Oyu	.26,907 ft	(8,201 m)
Dhaulagiri I	.26,796 ft	(8,167 m)
Manaslu I	.26,783 ft	(8,163 m)
Nanga Parbat I	.26,661 ft	(8,126 m)
Annapurna I	.26,547 ft	(8,091 m)
Gasherbrum I	.26,471 ft	(8,068 m)

LARGEST BODIES OF INLAND WATER

(WITH AREA AND DEPTH)

Caspian Sea	.143,243 sq miles (371,000 sq km)	.3,215 ft (980 m)
Lake Superior	.32,150 sq miles (83,270 sq km)	.1,289 ft (393 m)
Lake Victoria	.26,828 sq miles (69,484 sq km)	.328 ft (100 m)
Lake Huron	.23,436 sq miles (60,700 sq km)	.751 ft (229 m)
Lake Michigan	22,402 sq miles (58,020 sq km)	.922 ft (281 m)
Lake Tanganyika	.12,703 sq miles (32,900 sq km)	.4,700 ft (1,435 m)
Great Bear Lake	.12,274 sq miles (31,790 sq km)	.1,047 ft (319 m)
Lake Baikal	.11,776 sq miles (30,500 sq km)	.5,712 ft (1,741 m)
Great Slave Lake	.10,981 sq miles (28,440 sq km)	.459 ft (140 m)
Lake Erie	.9,915 sq miles (25,680 sq km)	.197 ft (60 m)

DEEPEST OCEAN FEATURES

Challenger Deep, Marianas Trench (Pacific)	.36,201 ft	(11,034 m)
Vityaz III Depth, Tonga Trench (Pacific)	.35,704 ft	(10,882 m)
Vityaz Depth, Kurile-Kamchatka Trench (Pacific)	.34,588 ft	(10,542 m)
Cape Johnson Deep, Philippine Trench (Pacific)	.34,441 ft	(10,497 m)
Kermadec Trench (Pacific)	.32,964 ft	(10,017 m)
Ramapo Deep, Japan Trench (Pacific)	.32,758 ft	(9,984 m)
Milwaukee Deep, Puerto Rico Trench (Atlantic)	.30,185 ft	(9,200 m)
Argo Deep, Torres Trench (Pacific)	.30,070 ft	(9,165 m)
Meteor Depth, South Sandwich Trench (Atlantic)	.30,000 ft	(9,144 m)
Planet Deep, New Britain Trench (Pacific)	.29,988 ft	(9,140 m)

GREATEST WATERFALLS

(MEAN FLOW OF WATER)

Boyoma (Congo, Dem. Rep.)	600,400 cu. ft/sec	(17,000 cu.m/sec)
Khône (Laos/Cambodia)	.410,000 cu. ft/sec	(11,600 cu.m/sec)
Niagara (USA/Canada)	.195,000 cu. ft/sec	(5,500 cu.m/sec)
Grande (Uruguay)	.160,000 cu. ft/sec	(4,500 cu.m/sec)
Paulo Afonso (Brazil)	.100,000 cu. ft/sec	(2,800 cu.m/sec)
Urubupunga (Brazil)	.97,000 cu. ft/sec	(2,750 cu.m/sec)
Iguaçu (Argentina/Brazil)	.62,000 cu. ft/sec	(1,700 cu.m/sec)
Maribondo (Brazil)	.53,000 cu. ft/sec	(1,500 cu.m/sec)
Victoria (Zimbabwe)	.39,000 cu. ft/sec	(1,100 cu.m/sec)
Kabalega (Uganda)	.42,000 cu. ft/sec	(1,200 cu.m/sec)

HIGHEST WATERFALLS

Angel (Venezuela)	.3,212 ft	(979 m)
Tugela (South Africa)	.3,110 ft	(948 m)
Utigard (Norway)	.2,625 ft	(800 m)
Mongefossen (Norway)	.2,539 ft	(774 m)
Mtarazi (Zimbabwe)	.2,500 ft	(762 m)
Yosemite (USA)	.2,425 ft	(739 m)
Ostre Mardola Foss (Norway)	.2,156 ft	(657 m)
Tyssestrengane (Norway)	.2,119 ft	(646 m)
*Cuquenan (Venezuela)	.2,001 ft	(610 m)
Sutherland (New Zealand)	.1,903 ft	(580 m)

indicates that the total height is a single leap

LARGEST DESERTS

Sahara	.3,450,000 sq miles	(9,065,000 sq km)
Gobi	.500,000 sq miles	(1,295,000 sq km)
Ar Rub al Khali	.289,600 sq miles	(750,000 sq km)
Great Victorian	.219,800 sq miles	(647,000 sq km)
Sonoran	.120,000 sq miles	(311,000 sq km)
Kalahari	.120,000 sq miles	(310,800 sq km)
Kara Kum	.115,800 sq miles	(300,000 sq km)
Takla Makan	.100,400 sq miles	(260,000 sq km)
Namib	.52,100 sq miles	(135,000 sq km)
Thar	.33,670 sq miles	(130,000 sq km)

NB – Most of Antarctica is a polar desert, with only
50 mm of precipitation annually

HOTTEST INHABITED PLACES

Djibouti (Djibouti)	.86° F	(30 °C)
Timbouctou (Mali)	.84.7° F	(29.3 °C)
Tirunelveli (India)		
Tuticorin (India)		
Nellore (India)	.84.5° F	(29.2 °C)
Santa Marta (Colombia)		
Aden (Yemen)	.84° F	(28.9 °C)
Madurai (India)		
Niamey (Niger)		
Hodeida (Yemen)	.83.8° F	(28.8 °C)

DRIEST INHABITED PLACES

Aswân (Egypt)	.0.02 in	(0.5 mm)
Luxor (Egypt)	.0.03 in	(0.7 mm)
Arica (Chile)	.0.04 in	(1.1 mm)
Ica (Peru)	.0.1 in	(2.3 mm)
Antofagasta (Chile)	.0.2 in	(4.9 mm)
El Minya (Egypt)	.0.2 in	(5.1 mm)
Asyût (Egypt)	.0.2 in	(5.2 mm)
Callao (Peru)	.0.5 in	(12.0 mm)
Trujillo (Peru)	.0.55 in	(14.0 mm)
El Faiyûm (Egypt)	.0.8 in	(19.0 mm)

WETTEST INHABITED PLACES

Buenaventura (Colombia)	.265 in	(6,743 mm)
Monrovia (Liberia)	.202 in	(5,131 mm)
Pago Pago (American Samoa)	.196 in	(4,990 mm)
Moulmein (Myanmar)	.191 in	(4,852 mm)
Lae (Papua New Guinea)	.183 in	(4,645 mm)
Baguio (Luzon Island, Philippines)	180 in	(4,573 mm)
Sylhet (Bangladesh)	.176 in	(4,457 mm)
Padang (Sumatra, Indonesia)	.166 in	(4,225 mm)
Bogor (Java, Indonesia)	.166 in	(4,225 mm)
Conakry (Guinea)	.171 in	(4,341 mm)

Aachen – Alexandria

INDEX

Glossary of Abbreviations

This Glossary provides a comprehensive guide to the abbreviations used in this Atlas, and in the Index.

A
abbrev. abbreviated
Afr. Afrikaans
Alb. Albanian
Amh. Amharic
anc. ancient
Ar. Arabic
Arm. Armenian
Az. Azerbaijani

B
Basq. Basque
Bel. Belorussian
Ben. Bengali
Bibl. Biblical
Bret. Breton
Bul. Bulgarian
Bur. Burmese

C
Cam. Cambodian
Cant. Cantonese
Cast. Castilian
Cat. Catalan
Chin. Chinese
Cro. Croat
Cz. Czech

D
Dan. Danish
Dut. Dutch

E
Eng. English
Est. Estonian
est. estimated

F
Faer. Faeroese
Fij. Fijian
Fin. Finnish
Flem. Flemish
Fr. French
Fris. Frisian

G
Geor. Georgian
Ger. German
Gk. Greek
Guj. Gujarati

H
Haw. Hawaiian
Heb. Hebrew
Hind. Hindi
hist. historical
Hung. Hungarian

I
Icel. Icelandic
Ind. Indonesian
Ir. Irish
It. Italian

J
Jap. Japanese

K
Kaz. Kazakh
Kir. Kirghiz
Kor. Korean
Kurd. Kurdish

L
Lao. Laotian
Lapp. Lappish
Lat. Latin
Latv. Latvian
Lith. Lithanian
Lus. Lusatian

M
Mac. Macedonian
Mal. Malay
Malg. Malagasy
Malt. Maltese
Mong. Mongolian

N
Nepali. Nepali
Nor. Norwegian

O
off. officially

P
Pash. Pashtu
Per. Persian
Pol. Polish
Port. Portuguese
prev. previously

R
Rmsch. Romansch
Roman. Romanian
Rus. Russian

S
SCr. Serbo-Croatian
Serb. Serbian
Slvk. Slovak
Slvn. Slovene
Som. Somali
Sp. Spanish
Swa. Swahili
Swe. Swedish

T
Taj. Tajik
Th. Thai
Tib. Tibetan
Turk. Turkish
Turkm. Turkmenistan

U
Uigh. Uighur
Ukr. Ukrainian
Uzb. Uzbek

V
var. variant
Vtn. Vietnamese

W
Wel. Welsh

X
Xh. Xhosa

Y
Yugo. Yugoslavia

INDEX

Index

A

Aachen 72 A4 *Dut.* Aken, *Fr.*Aix-la-Chapelle; *anc.* Aquae Grani, Aquisgranum. Nordrhein-Westfalen, W Germany
Aaiún *see* Laâyoune
Aalborg *see* Ålborg
Aalen 73 B6 Baden-Württemberg, S Germany
Aalsmeer 64 C3 Noord-Holland, C Netherlands
Aalst 65 B6 *Fr.* Alost. Oost-Vlaanderen, C Belgium
Aalten 64 E4 Gelderland, E Netherlands
Aalter 65 B5 Oost-Vlaanderen, NW Belgium
Äänekoski 63 D5 Länsi-Suomi, W Finland
Aar *see* Aare
Aare 73 A7 *var.* Aar. *River* W Switzerland
Aarhus *see* Århus
Aat *see* Ath
Aba 53 G5 Abia, S Nigeria
Aba 55 E5 Orientale, NE Dem. Rep. Congo
Abā as Su'ūd *see* Najrān
Abaco Island *see* Great Abaco
Ābādān 98 C4 Khūzestān, SW Iran
Abai *see* Blue Nile
Abakan 92 D4 Respublika Khakasiya, S Russian Federation
Abancay 38 D4 Apurímac, SE Peru
Abariringa *see* Kanton
Abashiri 108 D2 *var.* Abasiri. Hokkaidō, NE Japan
Abasiri *see* Abashiri
Ābaya Hāyk' 51 C5 *Eng.* Lake Margherita, *It.* Abbaia. *Lake* SW Ethiopia
Ābay Wenz *see* Blue Nile
Abbeville 68 C2 *anc.* Abbatis Villa. Somme, N France
'Abd al 'Azīz, Jabal 96 D2 *mountain range* NE Syria
Abéché 54 C3 *var.* Abécher, Abeshr. Ouaddaï, SE Chad
Abécher *see* Abéché
Abela *see* Ávila
Abemama 122 D2 *var.* Apamama; *prev.* Roger Simpson Island. *Atoll* Tungaru, W Kiribati
Abengourou 53 E5 E Côte d'Ivoire
Aberdeen 66 D3 *anc.* Devana. NE Scotland, UK
Aberdeen 23 E2 South Dakota, N USA
Aberdeen 24 B2 Washington, NW USA
Abergwaun *see* Fishguard
Abertawe *see* Swansea
Aberystwyth 67 C6 W Wales, UK
Abeshr *see* Abéché
Abhā 99 B6 'Asīr, SW Saudi Arabia
Abidavichy 85 D7 *Rus.* Obidovichi. Mahilyowskaya Voblasts', E Belarus
Abidjan 53 E5 S Côte d'Ivoire
Abilene 27 F3 Texas, SW USA
Abingdon *see* Pinta, Isla
Abkhazia 95 E1 *autonomous republic* NW Georgia
Åbo 63 D6 Länsi-Suomi, W Finland
Aboisso 53 E5 SE Côte d'Ivoire
Abo, Massif d' 54 B1 *mountain range* NW Chad
Abomey 53 F5 S Benin
Abou-Déïa 54 C3 Salamat, SE Chad
Abrantes 70 B3 *var.* Abrántes. Santarém, C Portugal
Abrolhos Bank 34 E4 *undersea feature* W Atlantic Ocean
Abrova 85 B6 *Rus.* Obrovo. Brestskaya Voblasts', SW Belarus
Abrud 86 B4 *Ger.* Gross-Schlatten, *Hung.* Abrudbánya. Alba, SW Romania
Abruzzese, Appennino 74 C4 *mountain range* C Italy
Absaroka Range 22 B2 *mountain range* Montana/Wyoming, NW USA
Abū aḍ Ḍuhūr 96 B3 *Fr.* Aboudouhour. Idlib, NW Syria
Abu Dhabi *see* Abū Ẓaby
Abu Hamed 50 C3 River Nile, N Sudan
Abū Ḥardān 96 E3 *var.* Hajîne. Dayr az Zawr, E Syria
Abuja 53 G4 *country capital* (Nigeria) Federal Capital District, C Nigeria
Abū Kamāl 96 E3 *Fr.* Abou Kémal. Dayr az Zawr, E Syria
Abula *see* Ávila
Abunã, Rio 40 C2 *var.* Río Abuná. *River* Bolivia/Brazil
Abut Head 129 B6 *headland* South Island, NZ
Ābuyē Mēda 50 D4 *mountain* C Ethiopia
Abū Ẓabī *see* Abū Ẓaby
Abū Ẓaby 99 C5 *var.* Abū Ẓabī, *Eng.* Abu Dhabi. *Country capital* (UAE) Abū Ẓaby, C UAE
Abyla *see* Ávila
Acalayong 55 A5 SW Equatorial Guinea
Acaponeta 28 D4 Nayarit, C Mexico
Acapulco 29 E5 *var.* Acapulco de Juárez. Guerrero, S Mexico
Acapulco de Juárez *see* Acapulco
Acarai Mountains 37 F5 *Sp.* Serra Acaraí. *Mountain range* Brazil/Guyana
Acarigua 36 D2 Portuguesa, N Venezuela
Accra 53 E5 *country capital* (Ghana) SE Ghana
Achacachi 39 E4 La Paz, W Bolivia
Acklins Island 32 C2 *island* SE Bahamas
Aconcagua, Cerro 42 B4 *mountain* W Argentina
Açores *see* Azores
A Coruña 70 B1 *Cast.* La Coruña, *Eng.* Corunna; *anc.* Caronium. Galicia, NW Spain
Acre 40 C2 *off.* Estado do Acre. *State* W Brazil
Açu 41 G2 *var.* Assu. Rio Grande do Norte, E Brazil
Ada 27 G2 Oklahoma, C USA
Ada 78 D3 Serbia, N Serbia and Montenegro (Yugo.)
Adalia, Gulf of *see* Antalya Körfezi
Adama *see* Nazrēt
Adamawa Highlands 54 B4 *plateau* NW Cameroon
'Adan 99 B7 *Eng.* Aden. SW Yemen
Adana 94 D4 *var.* Seyhan. Adana, S Turkey
Adapazarı 94 B2 *prev.* Ada Bazar. Sakarya, NW Turkey
Adare, Cape 132 B4 *headland* Antarctica
Ad Dahnā' 98 C4 *desert* E Saudi Arabia
Ad Dakhla 48 A4 *var.* Dakhla. SW Western Sahara
Ad Dalanj *see* Dilling
Ad Damar *see* Ed Damer
Ad Damazīn *see* Ed Damazin
Ad Dāmir *see* Ed Damer
Ad Dammān 98 C4 *var.* Dammām. Ash Sharqīyah, NE Saudi Arabia
Ad Dāmūr *see* Damoûr
Ad Dawḥah 98 C4 *Eng.* Doha. *Country capital* (Qatar) C Qatar
Aḍ Ḍiffah *see* Libyan Plateau
Addis Ababa *see* Ādīs Ābeba
Addu Atoll 110 A5 *atoll* S Maldives
Adelaide 127 B6 *state capital* South Australia
Aden *see* 'Adan
Aden, Gulf of 99 C7 *gulf* SW Arabian Sea
Adige 74 C2 *Ger.* Etsch. *River* N Italy
Adirondack Mountains 19 F2 *mountain range* New York, NE USA
Ādīs Ābeba 51 C5 *Eng.* Addis Ababa. *Country capital* (Ethiopia) C Ethiopia
Adıyaman 95 E4 Adıyaman, SE Turkey
Adjud 86 C4 Vrancea, E Romania
Admiralty Islands 122 B3 *island group* N PNG
Adra 71 E5 Andalucía, S Spain
Adrar 48 D3 C Algeria
Adrar des Iforas *see* Ifôghas, Adrar des
Adrian 18 C3 Michigan, N USA
Adriatic Sea 81 E2 *Alb.* Deti Adriatik, *It.* Mare Adriatico, *SCr.* Jadransko More, *Slvn.* Jadransko Morje. *Sea* N Mediterranean Sea
Adycha 93 F2 *river* NE Russian Federation
Aegean Sea 83 C5 *Gk.* Aigaíon Pélagos, Aigaío Pélagos, *Turk.* Ege Denizi. *Sea* NE Mediterranean Sea
Aegviidu 84 D2 *Ger.* Charlottenhof. Harjumaa, NW Estonia
Aelana *see* Al 'Aqabah
Aelok *see* Ailuk Atoll
Aelōnlaplap *see* Ailinglaplap Atoll
Aeolian Islands *see* Eolie, Isole
Afar Depression *see* Danakil Desert
Afghanistan 100 C4 *off.* Islamic State of Afghanistan, *Per.* Dowlat-e Eslāmī-ye Afghānestān; *prev.* Republic of Afghanistan. *Country* C Asia
Afmadow 51 D6 Jubbada Hoose, S Somalia
Africa 46 *continent*
Africa, Horn of 46 E4 *physical region* Ethiopia/Somalia
Africana Seamount 119 A6 *undersea feature* SW Indian Ocean
'Afrīn 96 B2 Ḥalab, N Syria
Afyon 94 B3 *prev.* Afyonkarahisar. Afyon, W Turkey
Agadez 53 G3 *prev.* Agadès. Agadez, C Niger
Agadir 48 B3 SW Morocco
Agana/Agaña *see* Hagåtña
Āgaro 51 C5 C Ethiopia
Agassiz Fracture Zone 121 G5 *tectonic feature* S Pacific Ocean
Agathónisi 83 D6 *island* Dodekánisos, Greece, Aegean Sea
Agde 69 C6 *anc.* Agatha. Hérault, S France
Agedabia *see* Ajdābiyā
Agen 69 B5 *anc.* Aginnum. Lot-et-Garonne, SW France
Aghri Dagh *see* Büyükağrı Dağı
Agiá 82 B4 *var.* Ayiá. Thessalía, C Greece
Agialoúsa 80 D4 *var.* Yenierenköy. NE Cyprus
Agía Marína 83 E6 Léros, Dodekánisos, Greece, Aegean Sea
Ágios Nikólaos 83 D8 *var.* Áyios Nikólaos. Kríti, Greece, E Mediterranean Sea
Āgra 112 D3 Uttar Pradesh, N India
Agram *see* Zagreb
Ağrı 95 F3 *var.* Karaköse; *prev.* Karakılısse. Ağrı, NE Turkey
Agri Dagi *see* Büyükağrı Dağı
Agrigento 75 C7 *Gk.* Akragas; *prev.* Girgenti. Sicilia, Italy, C Mediterranean Sea
Agriovótano 83 C5 Évvoia, C Greece
Agropoli 75 D5 Campania, S Italy
Aguachica 36 B2 Cesar, N Colombia
Aguadulce 31 F5 Coclé, S Panama
Agua Prieta 28 B1 Sonora, NW Mexico
Aguascalientes 28 D4 Aguascalientes, C Mexico
Aguaytía 38 C3 Ucayali, C Peru
Aguilas 71 E4 Murcia, SE Spain
Aguililla 28 D4 Michoacán de Ocampo, SW Mexico
Agulhas Basin 47 D8 *undersea feature* SW Indian Ocean
Agulhas Plateau 45 D6 *undersea feature* SW Indian Ocean
Ahaggar 53 F2 *high plateau region* SE Algeria
Ahlen 72 B4 Nordrhein-Westfalen, W Germany
Ahmadābād 112 C4 *var.* Ahmedabad. Gujarāt, W India
Ahmadnagar 112 C5 *var.* Ahmednagar. Mahārāshtra, W India
Ahmedabad *see* Ahmadābād
Ahmednagar *see* Ahmadnagar
Ahuachapán 30 B3 Ahuachapán, W El Salvador
Ahvāz 98 C3 *var.* Ahwāz; *prev.* Nāsiri. Khūzestān, SW Iran
Ahvenanmaa *see* Åland
Ahwāz *see* Ahvāz
Aïdin *see* Aydın
Aígina 83 C6 *var.* Aíyina, Egina. Aígina, C Greece
Aígio 83 B5 *var.* Egio; *prev.* Aíyion. Dytikí Ellás, S Greece
Aiken 21 E2 South Carolina, SE USA
Ailigandí 31 G4 San Blas, NE Panama
Ailinglaplap Atoll 122 D2 *var.* Aelōnlaplap. *Atoll* Ralik Chain, S Marshall Islands
Ailuk Atoll 122 D1 *var.* Aelok. *Atoll* Ratak Chain, NE Marshall Islands
Ainaži 84 D3 *Est.* Heinaste, *Ger.* Hainasch. Limbaži, N Latvia
'Aïn Ben Tili 52 D1 Tiris Zemmour, N Mauritania
Aintab *see* Gaziantep
Aïoun el Atrous *see* 'Ayoûn el 'Atroûs
Aïoun el Atroûss *see* 'Ayoûn el 'Atroûs
Aiquile 39 F4 Cochabamba, C Bolivia
Aïr *see* Aïr, Massif de l'
Air du Azbine *see* Aïr, Massif de l'
Aïr, Massif de l' 53 G2 *var.* Aïr, Air du Azbine, Asben. *Mountain range* NC Niger
Aiud 86 B4 *Ger.* Strassburg, *Hung.* Nagyenyed; *prev.* Engeten. Alba, SW Romania
Aix *see* Aix-en-Provence
Aix-en-Provence 69 D6 *var.* Aix; *anc.* Aquae Sextiae. Bouches-du-Rhône, SE France
Aíyina *see* Aígina
Aíyion *see* Aígio
Aizkraukle 84 C4 Aizkraukle, S Latvia
Ajaccio 69 E7 Corse, France, C Mediterranean Sea
Ajaria 95 F2 *autonomous republic* SW Georgia
Aj Bogd Uul 104 D2 *mountain* SW Mongolia
Ajdābiyā 49 G2 *var.* Agedabia, Ajdābiyah. NE Libya
Ajdābiyah *see* Ajdābiyā
Ajjinena *see* El Geneina
Ajmer 112 D3 *var.* Ajmere. Rājasthān, N India
Ajmere *see* Ajmer
Ajo 26 A3 Arizona, SW USA
Akaba *see* Al 'Aqabah
Akamagaseki *see* Shimonoseki
Akasha 50 B3 Northern, N Sudan
Akchâr 52 C2 *desert* W Mauritania
Akhalts'ikhe 95 F2 SW Georgia
Akhisar 94 A3 Manisa, W Turkey
Akhmîm 50 B2 *anc.* Panopolis. C Egypt
Akhtubinsk 89 C7 Astrakhanskaya Oblast', SW Russian Federation
Akimiski Island 16 C3 *island* Northwest Territories, C Canada
Akinovka 87 F4 Zaporiz'ka Oblast', S Ukraine
Akita 108 D4 Akita, Honshū, C Japan
Akjoujt 52 C2 *prev.* Fort-Repoux. Inchiri, W Mauritania
Akkeshi 108 E2 Hokkaidō, NE Japan
Aklavik 14 D3 Northwest Territories, NW Canada
Akmola *see* Astana
Akpatok Island 17 E1 *island* Northwest Territories, E Canada
Akra Dhrepanon *see* Drépano, Akrotírio
Akra Kanestron *see* Palioúri, Akrotírio
Akron 18 D4 Ohio, N USA
Akrotiri *see* Akrotírion
Akrotírion 80 C5 *var.* Akrotiri. *UK air base* S Cyprus
Aksai Chin 102 B2 *Chin.* Aksayqin. *Disputed region* China/India
Aksaray 94 C4 Aksaray, C Turkey
Akşehir 94 B4 Konya, W Turkey
Aktau 92 A4 *Kaz.* Aqtaū; *prev.* Shevchenko. Mangistau, W Kazakhstan
Aktobe 92 B4 *Kaz.* Aqtöbe. *prev.* Aktyubinsk. Aktyubinsk, NW Kazakhstan
Aktsyabrski 85 C7 *Rus.* Oktyabr'skiy; *prev.* Karpilovka. Homyel'skaya Voblasts', SE Belarus
Aktyubinsk *see* Aktobe
Akula 55 C5 Equateur, NW Dem. Rep. Congo
Akureyri 61 E4 Nordhurland Eystra, N Iceland
Akyab *see* Sittwe
Alabama 29 G1 *off.* State of Alabama; also known as Camellia State, Heart of Dixie, The Cotton State, Yellowhammer State. *State* S USA
Alabama River 20 C3 *river* Alabama, S USA
Alaca 94 C3 Çorum, N Turkey
Alagoas 41 G2 *off.* Estado de Alagoas. *State* E Brazil
Alajuela 31 E4 Alajuela, C Costa Rica
Alakanuk 14 C2 Alaska, USA
Al 'Alamayn *see* El 'Alamein
Al 'Amārah 98 C3 *var.* Amara. E Iraq
Alamo 25 D6 Nevada, W USA
Alamogordo 26 D3 New Mexico, SW USA
Alamosa 22 C5 Colorado, C USA
Åland 63 C6 *var.* Aland Islands, *Fin.* Ahvenanmaa. *Island group* SW Finland
Aland Islands *see* Åland
Aland Sea *see* Ålands Hav
Ålands Hav 63 C6 *var.* Aland Sea. *Strait* Baltic Sea/Gulf of Bothnia
Alanya 94 C4 Antalya, S Turkey
Alappuzha *see* Alleppey
Al 'Aqabah 97 B8 *var.* Akaba, Aqaba, 'Aqaba; *anc.* Aelana, Elath. Ma'ān, SW Jordan
Alasca, Golfo de *see* Alaska, Gulf of
Alaşehir 94 A4 Manisa, W Turkey
Al 'Ashārah 96 E3 *var.* Ashara. Dayr az Zawr, E Syria
Alaska 14 C3 *off.* State of Alaska; also known as Land of the Midnight Sun, The Last Frontier, Seward's Folly; *prev.* Russian America. *State* NW USA
Alaska, Gulf of 14 C4 *var.* Golfo de Alasca. *Gulf* Canada/USA
Alaska Peninsula 14 C3 *peninsula* Alaska, USA
Alaska Range 12 B2 *mountain range* Alaska, USA
Al-Asnam *see* Chlef
Al Awaynāt *see* Al 'Uwaynāt
Al 'Aynā 97 B7 Al Karak, W Jordan
Alazeya 93 G2 *river* NE Russian Federation
Al Bāb 96 B2 Ḥalab, N Syria
Albacete 71 E3 Castilla-La Mancha, C Spain
Al Baghdādī 98 B3 *var.* Khān al Baghdādī. SW Iraq
Al Bāha *see* Al Bāḥah
Al Bāḥah 99 B5 *var.* Al Bāha. Al Bāḥah, SW Saudi Arabia
Al Baḥr al Mayyit *see* Dead Sea
Alba Iulia 86 B4 *Ger.* Weissenburg, *Hung.* Gyulafehérvár; *prev.* Bălgrad, Karlsburg, Károly-Fehérvár. Alba, W Romania
Albania 79 C7 *off.* Republic of Albania, *Alb.* Republika e Shqipërisë, Shqipëria; *prev.* People's Socialist Republic of Albania. *Country* SE Europe
Albany 16 C3 *river* Ontario, S Canada
Albany 19 F3 *state capital* New York, NE USA
Albany 20 D3 Georgia, SE USA
Albany 24 B3 Oregon, NW USA
Albany 125 B7 Western Australia
Al Bāridah 96 C4 *var.* Bāridah. Ḥimş, C Syria
Al Başrah 98 C3 *Eng.* Basra; *hist.* Busra, Bussora. SE Iraq
Al Batrūn *see* Batroûn
Al Bayḍā' 49 G2 *var.* Beida. NE Libya
Albemarle Island *see* Isabela, Isla
Albemarle Sound 21 G1 *inlet* W Atlantic Ocean
Albergaria-a-Velha 70 B2 Aveiro, N Portugal
Albert 68 C3 Somme, N France
Alberta 15 E4 *province* SW Canada
Albert Edward Nyanza *see* Edward, Lake
Albert, Lake 51 B6 *var.* Albert Nyanza, Lac Mobutu Sese Seko. *Lake* Uganda/Dem. Rep. Congo
Albert Lea 23 F3 Minnesota, N USA
Albert Nyanza *see* Albert, Lake
Albi 69 C6 *anc.* Albiga. Tarn, S France
Ålborg 58 D3 *var.* Aalborg, Ålborg-Nørresundby; *anc.* Alburgum. Nordjylland, N Denmark
Ålborg-Nørresundby *see* Ålborg
Alborz, Reshteh-ye Kūhhā-ye 98 C2 *Eng.* Elburz Mountains. *Mountain range* N Iran
Albuquerque 26 D2 New Mexico, SW USA
Al Burayqah *see* Marsá al Burayqah
Alburgum *see* Ålborg
Albury 127 C7 New South Wales, SE Australia
Alcácer do Sal 70 B4 Setúbal, W Portugal
Alcalá de Henares 71 E3 *Ar.* Alkal'a; *anc.* Complutum. Madrid, C Spain
Alcamo 75 C7 Sicilia, Italy, C Mediterranean Sea
Alcañiz 71 F2 Aragón, NE Spain
Alcántara, Embalse de 70 C3 *reservoir* W Spain
Alcaudete 70 D4 Andalucía, S Spain
Alcázar *see* Ksar-el-Kebir
Alcoi *see* Alcoy
Alcoy 71 F4 *var.* Alcoi. País Valenciano, E Spain
Aldabra Group 57 G2 *island group* SW Seychelles
Aldan 93 F3 *river* NE Russian Federation
al Dar al Baida *see* Rabat
Alderney 68 A2 *island* Channel Islands
Aleg 52 C3 Brakna, SW Mauritania
Aleksandropol' *see* Gyumri
Aleksin 89 B5 Tul'skaya Oblast', W Russian Federation
Aleksinac 78 E4 Serbia, SE Serbia and Montenegro (Yugo.)
Alençon 68 B3 Orne, N France
Alenquer 41 E2 Pará, NE Brazil
Aleppo *see* Ḥalab
Alert 15 F1 Ellesmere Island, Nunavut, N Canada
Alès 69 C6 *prev.* Alais. Gard, S France
Aleşd 86 B3 *Hung.* Élesd. Bihor, SW Romania
Alessandria 74 B2 *Fr.* Alexandrie. Piemonte, N Italy
Ålesund 63 A5 Møre og Romsdal, S Norway
Aleutian Basin 91 G3 *undersea feature* Bering Sea
Aleutian Islands 14 A3 *island group* Alaska, USA
Aleutian Range 12 A2 *mountain range* Alaska, USA
Aleutian Trench 91 H3 *undersea feature* S Bering Sea
Alexander Archipelago 14 D4 *island group* Alaska, USA
Alexander City 20 D2 Alabama, S USA
Alexander Island 132 A3 *island* Antarctica
Alexandra 129 B7 Otago, South Island, NZ
Alexándreia 82 B4 *var.* Alexándria. Kentrikí Makedonía, N Greece
Alexandria 50 B1 *Ar.* Al Iskandarīyah. N Egypt

Alexándria – Aquila degli Abruzzo

Alexándria see Alexándreia
Alexandria 20 B3 Louisiana, S USA
Alexandria 23 F2 Minnesota, N USA
Alexandria 86 C5 Teleorman, S Romania
Alexandroúpoli 82 D3 var. Alexandroupolis, Turk. Dedeagaç, Dedeagach. Anatolikí Makedonía kai Thráki, NE Greece
Alexandroupolis see Alexandroúpoli
Al Fāshir see El Fasher
Alfatar 82 E1 Silistra, NE Bulgaria
Alfeiós 83 B6 prev. Alfiós, anc. Alpheius, Alpheus. River S Greece
Alföld see Great Hungarian Plain
Alga 92 B4 Kaz. Algha. Aktyubinsk, NW Kazakhstan
Algarve 70 B4 cultural region S Portugal
Algeciras 70 C5 Andalucía, SW Spain
Algemesí 71 F3 País Valenciano, E Spain
Al-Genain see El Geneina
Alger 49 E1 var. Algiers, El Djazaïr, Al Jazair. Country capital (Algeria) N Algeria
Algeria 48 C3 off. Democratic and Popular Republic of Algeria. Country N Africa
Algerian Basin 58 C5 var. Balearic Plain undersea feature W Mediterranean Sea
Al Ghābah 99 E5 var. Ghaba. C Oman
Alghero 75 A5 Sardegna, Italy, C Mediterranean Sea
Al Ghurdaqah see Hurghada
Algiers see Alger
Al Golea see El Goléa
Algona 23 F3 Iowa, C USA
Al Ḥajar al Gharbī 99 D5 mountain range N Oman
Al Ḥasakah 96 D2 var. Al Hasijah, El Haseke, Fr. Hasseché. Al Ḥasakah, NE Syria
Al Hasijah see Al Ḥasakah
Al Ḥillah 98 B3 var. Hilla. C Iraq
Al Ḥisā 97 B7 At Ṭafilah, W Jordan
Al Ḥudaydah 99 B6 Eng. Hodeida. W Yemen
Al Hufūf 98 C4 var. Hofuf. Ash Sharqīyah, NE Saudi Arabia
Aliákmonas 82 B4 prev. Aliákmon, anc. Haliacmon. River N Greece
Alíartos 83 C5 Stereá Ellás, C Greece
Alicante 71 F4 Cat. Alacant;. País Valenciano, SE Spain
Alice 27 G5 Texas, SW USA
Alice Springs 126 A4 Northern Territory, C Australia
Aliki see Alykí
Alima 55 B6 river C Congo
Alindao 54 C4 Basse-Kotto, S Central African Republic
Aliquippa 18 D4 Pennsylvania, NE USA
Alistráti 82 C3 Kentrikí Makedonía, NE Greece
Alivéri 83 C5 var. Alivérion. Évvoia, C Greece
Alivérion see Alivéri
Al Jabal al Akhḑar 49 G2 mountain range NE Libya
Al Jabal ash Sharqī see Anti-Lebanon
Al Jafr 97 B7 Ma'ān, S Jordan
Al Jaghbūb 49 H3 NE Libya
Al Jahrā' 98 C4 var. Al Jahrah, Jahra. C Kuwait
Al Jahrah see Al Jahrā'
Al Jawf 98 B4 var. Jauf. Al Jawf, NW Saudi Arabia
Al Jazair see Alger
Al Jazīrah 96 E2 physical region Iraq/Syria
Al Jīzah see El Giza
Al Junaynah see El Geneina
Al Karak 97 B7 var. El Kerak, Karak, Kerak; anc. Kir Moab, Kir of Moab. Al Karak, W Jordan
Al Kaṣr al Kebir see Ksar-el-Kebir
Al Khalīl see Hebron
Al Khārijah see El Khârga
Al Khufrah 49 H4 SE Libya
Al Khums 49 F2 var. Homs, Khoms, Khums. NW Libya
Alkmaar 64 C2 Noord-Holland, NW Netherlands
Al Kūt 98 C3 var. Kūt al 'Amārah, Kut al Imara. E Iraq
Al-Kuwait see Al Kuwayt
Al Kuwayt 98 C4 var. Al-Kuwait, Eng. Kuwait, Kuwait City; prev. Qurein. Country capital (Kuwait) E Kuwait
Al Lādhiqīyah 96 A3 Eng. Latakia, Fr. Lattaquié; anc. Laodicea, Laodicea ad Mare. Al Lādhiqīyah, W Syria
Allahābād 113 E3 Uttar Pradesh, N India
Allanmyo 114 B4 Magwe, C Myanmar
Allegheny Plateau 19 E3 mountain range New York/Pennsylvania, NE USA
Allentown 19 F4 Pennsylvania, NE USA
Alleppey 110 C3 var. Alappuzha; prev. Alleppi. Kerala, SW India
Alleppi see Alleppey
Alliance 22 D3 Nebraska, C USA
Al Līth 99 B5 Makkah, SW Saudi Arabia
Alma-Ata see Almaty
Almada 70 B4 Setúbal, W Portugal
Al Madīnah 99 A5 Eng. Medina. Al Madīnah, W Saudi Arabia
Al Mafraq 97 B6 var. Mafraq. Al Mafraq, N Jordan
Al Mahdīyah see Mahdia
Al Mahrah 99 C6 mountain range E Yemen
Al Majma'ah 98 B4 Ar Riyāḑ, C Saudi Arabia
Al Mālikīyah 96 E1 Al Ḥasakah, NE Syria
Al Manāmah 98 C4 Eng. Manama. Country capital (Bahrain) N Bahrain
Al Manāṣif 96 E3 mountain range E Syria
Almansa 71 F4 Castilla-La Mancha, C Spain
Al Marj 49 G2 var. Barka, It. Barce. NE Libya
Almaty 92 C5 var. Alma-Ata. Almaty, SE Kazakhstan
Al Mawṣil 98 B2 Eng. Mosul. N Iraq
Al Mayādīn 96 D3 var. Mayadin, Fr. Meyadine. Dayr az Zawr, E Syria
Al Mazra' see Al Mazra'ah
Al Mazra'ah 97 B6 var. Al Mazra', Mazra'a. Al Karak, W Jordan
Almelo 64 E3 Overijssel, E Netherlands
Almendra, Embalse de 70 C2 reservoir Castilla-León, NW Spain
Almendralejo 70 C4 Extremadura, W Spain
Almere 64 C3 var. Almere-stad. Flevoland, C Netherlands
Almere-stad see Almere
Almería 71 E5 Ar. Al-Mariyya; anc. Unci, Lat. Portus Magnus. Andalucía, S Spain
Al'met'yevsk 89 D5 Respublika Tatarstan, W Russian Federation
Al Mīnā' see El Mina
Al Minyā see El Minya
Almirante 31 E4 Bocas del Toro, NW Panama
Al Mudawwarah 97 B8 Ma'ān, SW Jordan
Al Mukallā 99 C6 var. Mukalla. SE Yemen
Al Obayyid see El Obeid
Alofi 123 F4 dependent territory capital (Niue) W Niue
Aloja 84 D3 Limbaži, N Latvia
Alónnisos 83 C5 island Vóreioi Sporádes, Greece, Aegean Sea
Álora 70 D5 Andalucía, S Spain
Alor, Kepulauan 117 E5 island group E Indonesia
Al Oued see El Oued
Alpen see Alps
Alpena 18 D2 Michigan, N USA
Alpes see Alps
Alpha Cordillera 133 B3 var. Alpha Ridge. Undersea feature Arctic Ocean
Alpha Ridge see Alpha Cordillera
Alphen see Alphen aan den Rijn
Alphen aan den Rijn 64 C3 var. Alphen. Zuid-Holland, C Netherlands
Alpi see Alps
Alpine 27 E4 Texas, SW USA
Alpi Transilvaniei see Carpații Meridionali
Alps 80 C1 Fr. Alpes, Ger. Alpen, It. Alpi. Mountain range C Europe
Al Qaḑārif see Gedaref
Al Qāmishlī 96 E1 var. Kamishli, Qamishly. Al Ḥasakah, NE Syria
Al Qaṣrayn see Kasserine
Al Qayrawān see Kairouan
Al-Qsar see Ksar-el-Kebir
Al Qubayyāt see Qoubaïyât
Al Qunayṭirah 97 B5 var. El Kuneitra, El Quneitra, Kuneitra, Qunaytra. Al Qunayṭirah, SW Syria
Al Quṣayr 96 B4 var. El Quseir, Quṣayr, Fr. Kousseir. Ḥimṣ, W Syria
Al Quwayrah 97 B8 var. El Quweira. Ma'ān, SW Jordan
Alsace 68 E3 cultural region NE France
Alsdorf 72 A4 Nordrhein-Westfalen, W Germany
Alt see Olt
Alta 62 D2 Fin. Alattio. Finnmark, N Norway
Altai see Altai Mountains
Altai Mountains 104 C2 var. Altai, Chin. Altay Shan, Rus. Altay. Mountain range Asia/Europe
Altamaha River 21 E3 river Georgia, SE USA
Altamira 41 E2 Pará, NE Brazil
Altamura 75 E5 anc. Lupatia. Puglia, SE Italy
Altar, Desierto de 28 A1 var. Sonoran Desert. Desert Mexico/USA see also Sonoran Desert
Altay 104 C2 Chin. A-le-t'ai, Mong. Sharasume; prev. Ch'eng-hua, Chenghwa. Xinjiang Uygur Zizhiqu, NW China
Altay see Altai Mountains
Altay 104 D2 Govĭ-Altay, W Mongolia
Altay Shan see Altai Mountains
Altin Köprü 98 B3 var. Altun Kupri. N Iraq
Altiplano 39 F4 physical region W South America
Alton 18 B5 Illinois, N USA
Alton 18 B4 Missouri, C USA
Altoona 19 E4 Pennsylvania, NE USA
Alto Paraná see Paraná
Altun Kupri see Altin Köprü
Altun Shan 104 C3 var. Altyn Tagh. Mountain range NW China
Altus 27 F2 Oklahoma, C USA
Altyn Tagh see Altun Shan
Al Ubayyiḑ see El Obeid
Alūksne 84 D3 Ger. Marienburg. Alūksne, NE Latvia
Al 'Ulā 98 A4 Al Madīnah, NW Saudi Arabia
Al 'Umarī 97 C6 'Ammān, E Jordan
Alupka 87 F5 Respublika Krym, S Ukraine
Alushta 87 F5 Respublika Krym, S Ukraine
Al 'Uwaynāt 49 F4 var. Al Awaynāt. SW Libya
Alva 27 F1 Oklahoma, C USA
Alvarado 29 F4 Veracruz-Llave, E Mexico
Alvin 27 H4 Texas, SW USA
Al Wajh 98 A4 Tabūk, NW Saudi Arabia
Alwar 112 D3 Rājasthān, N India
Al Wari'ah 98 C4 Ash Sharqīyah, N Saudi Arabia
Alykí 82 C4 var. Aliki. Thásos, N Greece
Alytus 85 B5 Pol. Olita. Alytus, S Lithuania
Alzette 65 D8 river S Luxembourg
Amadeus, Lake 125 D5 seasonal lake Northern Territory, C Australia
Amadi 51 B5 Western Equatoria, SW Sudan
Amadjuak Lake 15 G3 lake Baffin Island, Nunavut, N Canada
Amakusa-nada 109 A7 gulf Kyūshū, SW Japan
Åmål 63 B6 Västra Götaland, S Sweden
Amami guntō 108 A3 island group SW Japan
Amami-Ō-shima 108 A3 island S Japan
Amantea 75 D6 Calabria, SW Italy
Amapá 41 E1 Amapá, NE Brazil
Amara see Al 'Amārah
Amarapura 114 B3 Mandalay, C Myanmar
Amarillo 27 E2 Texas, SW USA
Amay 65 C6 Liège, E Belgium
Amazon 41 E1 Sp. Amazonas. River Brazil/Peru
Amazon Basin 40 D2 basin N South America
Amazon, Mouths of the 41 F1 delta NE Brazil
Ambam 55 B5 Sud, S Cameroon
Ambanja 57 G2 Antsirañana, N Madagascar
Ambarchik 93 G2 Respublika Sakha (Yakutiya), NE Russian Federation
Ambato 38 B1 Tungurahua, C Ecuador
Ambérieu-en-Bugey 69 D5 Ain, E France
Amboasary 57 F4 Toliara, S Madagascar
Ambon 117 F4 prev. Amboina, Amboyna. Pulau Ambon, E Indonesia
Ambositra 57 G3 Fianarantsoa, SE Madagascar
Ambrim see Ambrym
Ambriz 56 A1 Bengo, NW Angola
Ambrym 122 D4 var. Ambrim. Island C Vanuatu
Amchitka Island 14 A2 island Aleutian Islands, Alaska, USA
Amdo 104 C5 Xizang Zizhiqu, W China
Ameland 64 D1 Fris. It Amelân. Island Waddeneilanden, N Netherlands
America-Antarctica Ridge 45 C7 undersea feature S Atlantic Ocean
American Falls Reservoir 24 E4 reservoir Idaho, NW USA
American Samoa 123 E4 US unincorporated territory W Polynesia
Amersfoort 64 D3 Utrecht, C Netherlands
Ames 23 F3 Iowa, C USA
Amfilochía 83 A5 var. Amfilokhía. Dytikí Ellás, C Greece
Amfilokhía see Amfilochía
Amga 93 F3 river NE Russian Federation
Amherst 17 F4 Nova Scotia, SE Canada
Amida see Diyarbakır
Amiens 68 C3 anc. Ambianum, Samarobriva. Somme, N France
Amíndaion see Amýntaio
Amindeo see Amýntaio
Amīndīvi Islands 110 A2 island group Lakshadweep, India, N Indian Ocean
Amirante Islands 57 G1 var. Amirantes Group. Island group C Seychelles
Amirantes Group see Amirante Islands
Amistad Reservoir 27 F4 var. Presa de la Amistad. Reservoir Mexico/USA
'Ammān 97 B6 var. Amman; anc. Philadelphia, Bibl. Rabbah Ammon, Rabbath Ammon. Country capital (Jordan) 'Ammān, NW Jordan
Amman see 'Ammān
Ammassalik 60 D4 var. Angmagssalik. S Greenland
Ammóchostos 80 D5 var. Famagusta, Gazimağusa. E Cyprus
Āmol 98 D2 var. Amul. Māzandarān, N Iran
Amorgós 83 D6 island Kykládes, Greece, Aegean Sea
Amorgós 83 D6 Amorgós, Kykládes, Greece, Aegean Sea
Amos 16 D4 Quebec, SE Canada
Amourj 52 D3 Hodh ech Chargui, SE Mauritania
Amoy see Xiamen
Ampato, Nevado 39 E4 mountain S Peru
Amposta 71 F2 Cataluña, NE Spain
Amrāvati 112 D4 prev. Amraoti. Mahārāshtra, C India
Amritsar 112 D2 Punjab, N India
Amstelveen 64 C3 Noord-Holland, C Netherlands
Amsterdam 64 C3 country capital (Netherlands) Noord-Holland, C Netherlands
Amsterdam Island 119 C6 island NE French Southern and Antarctic Territories
Am Timan 54 C3 Salamat, SE Chad
Amu Darya 100 D2 Rus. Amudar'ya, Taj. Dar"yoi Amu, Turkm. Amyderya, Uzb. Amudaryo; anc. Oxus. River C Asia
Amu Dar'ya 101 E3 Lebapskiy Velayat, NE Turkmenistan
Amul see Amol
Amund Ringnes Island 15 F2 island Nunavut, N Canada
Amundsen Basin see Fram Basin
Amundsen Gulf 15 E2 gulf Northwest Territories, N Canada
Amundsen Plain 132 A4 undersea feature S Pacific Ocean
Amundsen-Scott 132 B3 US research station Antarctica
Amundsen Sea 132 A4 sea S Pacific Ocean
Amuntai 116 D4 prev. Amoentai. Borneo, C Indonesia
Amur 93 G4 Chin. Heilong Jiang. River China/Russian Federation
Amvrosiyivka 87 H3 Rus. Amvrosiyevka. Donets'ka Oblast', SE Ukraine
Amýntaio 82 B4 var. Amindeo; prev. Amíndaion. Dytikí Makedonía, N Greece
Anabar 93 E2 river NE Russian Federation
An Abhainn Mhór see Blackwater
Anaco 37 E2 Anzoátegui, NE Venezuela
Anaconda 22 B2 Montana, NW USA
Anacortes 24 B1 Washington, NW USA
Anadolu Dağları see Doğu Karadeniz Dağları
Anadyr' 93 G1 river NE Russian Federation
Anadyr' 93 H1 Chukotskiy Avtonomnyy Okrug, NE Russian Federation
Anadyr, Gulf of see Anadyrskiy Zaliv
Anadyrskiy Zaliv 93 H1 Eng. Gulf of Anadyr. Gulf NE Russian Federation
Anáfi 83 D7 anc. Anaphe. Island Kykládes, Greece, Aegean Sea
'Anah see 'Annah
Anaheim 24 E2 California, W USA
Anaiza see 'Unayzah
Analalava 57 G2 Mahajanga, NW Madagascar
Anamur 94 C5 İçel, S Turkey
Anantapur 110 C2 Andhra Pradesh, S India
Anápolis 41 F3 Goiás, C Brazil
Anār 98 D3 Kermān, C Iran
Anatolia 94 C4 plateau C Turkey
Anatom see Aneityum
Añatuya 42 C3 Santiago del Estero, N Argentina
An Bhearú see Barrow
Anchorage 14 C3 Alaska, USA
Ancona 74 C3 Marche, C Italy
Ancud 43 B6 prev. San Carlos de Ancud. Los Lagos, S Chile
Åndalsnes 63 A5 Møre og Romsdal, S Norway
Andalucía 70 D4 cultural region S Spain
Andalusia 20 C3 Alabama, S USA
Andaman Islands 102 B4 island group India, NE Indian Ocean
Andaman Sea 102 C4 sea NE Indian Ocean
Andenne 65 C6 Namur, SE Belgium
Anderlues 65 B7 Hainaut, S Belgium
Anderson 18 C4 Indiana, N USA
Andes 42 B3 mountain range W South America
Andhra Pradesh 113 E5 state E India
Andijon 101 F2 Rus. Andizhan. Andijon Wiloyati, E Uzbekistan
Andikíthira see Antikýthira
Andipaxi see Antípaxoi
Andípsara see Antípsara
Ándissa see Ántissa
Andkhvoy 100 D3 Fāryāb, N Afghanistan
Andorra 69 A7 off. Principality of Andorra, Cat. Valls d'Andorra, Fr. Vallée d'Andorre. Country SW Europe
Andorra see Andorra la Vella
Andorra la Vella 69 A8 var. Andorra, Fr. Andorre la Vielle, Sp. Andorra la Vieja. Country capital (Andorra) C Andorra
Andorra la Vieja see Andorra la Vella
Andorre la Vielle see Andorra la Vella
Andover 67 D7 S England, UK
Andøya 62 C2 island C Norway
Andreanof Islands 14 A3 island group Aleutian Islands, Alaska, USA
Andrews 27 E3 Texas, SW USA
Andrew Tablemount 118 A4 var. Gora Andryu. Undersea feature W Indian Ocean
Andria 75 D5 Puglia, SE Italy
An Droichead Nua see Newbridge
Ándros 83 C6 island Kykládes, Greece, Aegean Sea
Ándros 83 D6 Ándros, Kykládes, Greece, Aegean Sea
Andros Island 32 B2 island NW Bahamas
Andros Town 32 C1 Andros Island, NW Bahamas
Aneityum 122 D5 var. Anatom; prev. Kéamu. Island S Vanuatu
Ānewetak see Enewetak Atoll
Angara 93 E4 river C Russian Federation
Angarsk 93 E4 Irkutskaya Oblast', S Russian Federation
Ånge 63 C5 Västernorrland, C Sweden
Ángel de la Guarda, Isla 28 B2 island NW Mexico
Angeles 117 E1 off. Angeles City. Luzon, N Philippines
Angel Falls see Ángel, Salto
Ángel, Salto 37 E3 Eng. Angel Falls. Waterfall E Venezuela
Ångermanälven 62 C1 river N Sweden
Angermünde 72 D3 Brandenburg, NE Germany
Angers 68 B4 anc. Juliomagus. Maine-et-Loire, NW France
Anglesey 67 C5 island NW Wales, UK
Anglet 69 A6 Pyrénées-Atlantiques, SW France
Angleton 27 H4 Texas, SW USA
Angmagssalik see Ammassalik
Ang Nam Ngum 114 C4 lake C Laos
Angola 56 B2 off. Republic of Angola; prev. People's Republic of Angola, Portuguese West Africa. Country SW Africa
Angola Basin 47 B5 undersea feature E Atlantic Ocean
Angostura, Presa de la 29 G5 reservoir SE Mexico
Angoulême 69 B5 anc. Iculisma. Charente, W France
Angoumois 69 B5 cultural region W France
Angren 101 F2 Toshkent Wiloyati, E Uzbekistan
Anguilla 33 G3 UK dependent territory E West Indies
Anguilla Cays 32 B2 islets SW Bahamas
Anhui 106 C5 var. Anhui Sheng, Anhwei, Wan. Admin. region province E China
Anhui Sheng see Anhui
Anhwei see Anhui
Anina 86 A4 Ger. Steierdorf, Hung. Stájerlakanina; prev. Ştaierdorf-Anina, Steierdorf-Anina, Steyerlak-Anina. Caraş-Severin, SW Romania
Anjou 68 B4 cultural region NW France
Anjouan 57 F2 var. Nzwani, Johanna Island. Island SE Comoros
Ankara 94 C3 prev. Angora, anc. Ancyra. Country capital (Turkey) Ankara, C Turkey
Ankeny 23 F3 Iowa, C USA
Anklam 72 D2 Mecklenburg-Vorpommern, NE Germany
Anykščiai 84 C4 Anykščiai, E Lithuania
An Longfort see Longford
An Mhuir Cheilteach see Celtic Sea
Annaba 49 E1 prev. Bône. NE Algeria
An Nafūd 98 B4 desert NW Saudi Arabia
'Annah 98 B3 var. 'Ānah. NW Iraq
An Najaf 98 B3 var. Najaf. S Iraq
Annamitique, Chaîne 114 D4 mountain range C Laos
Annapolis 19 F4 state capital Maryland, NE USA
Annapurna 113 E3 mountain C Nepal
An Nāqūrah see En Nâqoûra
Ann Arbor 18 C3 Michigan, N USA
An Nāṣirīyah 98 C3 var. Nasiriya. SE Iraq
Annecy 69 D5 anc. Anneciacum. Haute-Savoie, E France
An Nīl al Azraq see Blue Nile
Anniston 20 D2 Alabama, S USA
Annotto Bay 32 B4 C Jamaica
An Ómaigh see Omagh
Anqing 106 D5 Anhui, E China
Anse La Raye 33 F1 NW Saint Lucia
Anshun 106 B6 Guizhou, S China
Ansongo 53 E3 Gao, E Mali
An Srath Bán see Strabane
Antakya 94 D4 anc. Antioch, Antiochia. Hatay, S Turkey
Antalaha 57 G2 Antsirañana, NE Madagascar
Antalya 94 B4 prev. Adalia, anc. Attaleia, Bibl. Attalia. Antalya, SW Turkey
Antalya, Gulf of see Antalya Körfezi
Antalya Körfezi 94 B4 var. Gulf of Adalia, Eng. Gulf of Antalya. Gulf SW Turkey
Antananarivo 57 G3 prev. Tananarive. Country capital (Madagascar) Antananarivo, C Madagascar
Antarctica 132 B3 continent
Antarctic Peninsula 132 A2 peninsula Antarctica
Antep see Gaziantep
Antequera 70 D5 anc. Anticaria, Antiquaria. Andalucía, S Spain
Antequera see Oaxaca
Antibes 69 D6 anc. Antipolis. Alpes-Maritimes, SE France
Anticosti, Île d' 17 F3 Eng. Anticosti Island. Island Quebec, E Canada
Antigua 33 G3 island S Antigua and Barbuda, Leeward Islands
Antigua and Barbuda 33 G3 country E West Indies
Antikýthira 83 B7 var. Andikíthira. Island S Greece
Anti-Lebanon 96 B4 var. Jebel esh Sharqi, Ar. Al Jabal ash Sharqī, Fr. Anti-Liban. Mountain range Lebanon/Syria
Anti-Liban see Anti-Lebanon
Antípaxoi 83 A5 var. Andipaxi. Island Iónioi Nísoi, Greece, C Mediterranean Sea
Antipodes Islands 120 D5 island group S NZ
Antípsara 83 D5 var. Andípsara. Island E Greece
Ántissa 83 D5 var. Ándissa. Lésvos, E Greece
An tIúr see Newry
Antofagasta 42 B2 Antofagasta, N Chile
Antony 68 E2 Hauts-de-Seine, N France
Antserana see Antsirañana
An tSionainn see Shannon
Antsirañana 57 G2 var. Antserana; prev. Antsirane, Diégo-Suarez. Antsirañana, N Madagascar
Antsirane see Antsirañana
Antsohihy 57 G2 Mahajanga, NW Madagascar
An-tung see Dandong
Antwerp see Antwerpen
Antwerpen 65 C5 Eng. Antwerp, Fr. Anvers. Antwerpen, N Belgium
Anuradhapura 110 D3 North Central Province, C Sri Lanka
Anyang 106 C4 Henan, C China
A'nyêmaqên Shan 104 D4 mountain range C China
Anzio 75 C5 Lazio, C Italy
Aomen see Macao
Aomori 108 D3 Aomori, Honshū, C Japan
Aóos see Vjosës, Lumi i
Aosta 74 A1 anc. Augusta Praetoria. Valle d'Aosta, NW Italy
Ao Thai see Thailand, Gulf of
Aoukâr 52 D3 var. Aouker. Plateau C Mauritania
Aouk, Bahr 54 C4 river Central African Republic/Chad
Aouker see Aoukâr
Aozou 54 C1 Borkou-Ennedi-Tibesti, N Chad
Apalachee Bay 20 D3 bay Florida, SE USA
Apalachicola River 20 D3 river Florida, SE USA
Apamama see Abemama
Apaporis, Río 36 C4 river Brazil/Colombia
Apatity 88 C2 Murmanskaya Oblast', NW Russian Federation
Ape 84 D3 Alūksne, NE Latvia
Apeldoorn 64 D3 Gelderland, E Netherlands
Apennines see Appennino
Āpia 123 F4 country capital (Samoa) Upolu, SE Samoa
Apoera 37 G3 Sipaliwini, NW Suriname
Apostle Islands 18 B1 island group Wisconsin, N USA
Appalachian Mountains 13 D5 mountain range E USA
Appennino 74 E2 Eng. Apennines. Mountain range Italy/San Marino
Appingedam 64 E1 Groningen, NE Netherlands
Appleton 18 B2 Wisconsin, N USA
Apure, Río 36 C2 river W Venezuela
Apurímac, Río 38 D3 river S Peru
Apuseni, Munţii 86 A4 mountain range W Romania
'Aqaba see Al 'Aqabah
Aqaba, Gulf of 98 A4 var. Gulf of Elat, Ar. Khalīj al 'Aqabah; anc. Sinus Aelaniticus. Gulf NE Red Sea
Āqchah 101 E3 var. Āqcheh. Jowzjān, N Afghanistan
Āqcheh see Āqchah
Aquae Augustae see Dax
Aquae Sextiae see Aix-en-Provence
Aquae Tarbelicae see Dax
Aquidauana 41 E4 Mato Grosso do Sul, S Brazil
Aquila see L'Aquila
Aquila degli Abruzzo see L'Aquila

Bahama Islands – Bemidji

Bahama Islands *see* Bahamas
Bahamas *32 C2 off.* Commonwealth of the Bahamas. *Country* N West Indies
Bahamas *13 D6 var.* Bahama Islands. *Island group* N West Indies
Bahāwalpur *112 C2* Punjab, E Pakistan
Bahía *41 F3 off.* Estado da Bahia. *State* E Brazil
Bahía Blanca *43 C5* Buenos Aires, E Argentina
Bahía, Islas de la *30 C1 Eng.* Bay Islands. *Island group* N Honduras
Bahir Dar *50 C4 var.* Bahr Dar, Bahrdar Giyorgis. NW Ethiopia
Bahraich *113 E3* Uttar Pradesh, N India
Bahrain *98 C4 off.* State of Bahrain, Dawlat al Bahrayn, *Ar.* Al Baḥrayn; *prev.* Bahrein, *anc.* Tylos or Tyros. *Country* SW Asia
Baḥr al Milḥ *see* Razāzah, Buḥayrat ar
Baḥrat Lūṭ *see* Dead Sea
Bahrat Tabariya *see* Tiberias, Lake
Bahr Dar *see* Bahir Dar
Bahrdar Giyorgis *see* Bahir Dar
Bahr el Azraq *see* Blue Nile
Bahr el Jebel *see* White Nile
Bahret Lut *see* Dead Sea
Bahr Tabariya, Sea of *see* Tiberias, Lake
Bahushewsk *85 E6 Rus.* Bogushëvsk. Vitsyebskaya Voblasts', NE Belarus
Baia Mare *86 B3 Ger.* Frauenbach, *Hung.* Nagybánya; *prev.* Neustadt. Maramureș, NW Romania
Baia Sprie *86 B3 Ger.* Mittelstadt, *Hung.* Felsőbánya. Maramureș, NW Romania
Baïbokoum *54 B4* Logone-Oriental, SW Chad
Baidoa *see* Baydhabo
Baie-Comeau *17 E3* Quebec, SE Canada
Baikal, Lake *see* Baykal, Ozero
Baile Átha Luain *see* Athlone
Bailén *70 D4* Andalucía, S Spain
Baile na Mainistreach *see* Newtownabbey
Băilești *86 B5* Dolj, SW Romania
Ba Illi *54 B3* Chari-Baguirmi, SW Chad
Bainbridge *20 D3* Georgia, SE USA
Bā'ir *see* Bāyir
Baireuth *see* Bayreuth
Bairiki *122 D2 country capital* (Kiribati) Tarawa, NW Kiribati
Bairnsdale *127 C7* Victoria, SE Australia
Baishan *107 E3 prev.* Hunjiang. Jilin, NE China
Baiyin *106 B4* Gansu, C China
Baja *77 C7* Bács-Kiskun, S Hungary
Baja California *26 A4 Eng.* Lower California. *Peninsula* NW Mexico
Baja California *28 B2 state* NW Mexico
Bajo Boquete *see* Boquete
Bajram Curri *79 D5* Kukës, N Albania
Bakala *54 C4* Ouaka, C Central African Republic
Bakan *see* Shimonoseki
Baker *24 C3* Oregon, NW USA
Baker and Howland Islands *123 F2 US unincorporated territory* W Polynesia
Baker Lake *15 F3* Nunavut, N Canada
Bakersfield *25 C7* California, W USA
Bakharden *100 C3 Turkm.* Bäherden; *prev.* Bakherden. Akhalskiy Velayat, C Turkmenistan
Bakhchysaray *87 F5 Rus.* Bakhchisaray. Respublika Krym, S Ukraine
Bakhmach *87 F1* Chernihivs'ka Oblast', N Ukraine
Bākhtarān *98 C3 prev.* Kermānshāh, Qahremānshahr. Kermānshāh, W Iran
Bakı *95 H2 Eng.* Baku. *Country capital* (Azerbaijan) E Azerbaijan
Bakony *77 C7 Eng.* Bakony Mountains, *Ger.* Bakonywald. *Mountain range* W Hungary
Baku *see* Bakı
Balabac Island *107 C8 island* W Philippines
Balabac Strait *116 D2 var.* Selat Balabac. *Strait* Malaysia/Philippines
Ba'labakk *see* Baalbek
Balaguer *71 F2* Cataluña, NE Spain
Balakovo *89 C6* Saratovskaya Oblast', W Russian Federation
Bālā Morghāb *100 D4* Laghmān, NW Afghanistan
Balashov *89 B6* Saratovskaya Oblast', W Russian Federation
Balaton *C7 var.* Lake Balaton, *Ger.* Plattensee. *Lake* W Hungary
Balaton, Lake *see* Balaton
Balbina, Represa *40 D1 reservoir* NW Brazil
Balboa *31 G4* Panamá, C Panama
Balcarce *43 D5* Buenos Aires, E Argentina
Balclutha *129 B7* Otago, South Island, NZ
Baldy Mountain *22 C1 mountain* Montana, NW USA
Bâle *see* Basel
Baleares, Islas *71 G3 Eng.* Balearic Islands. *Island group* Spain, W Mediterranean Sea
Balearic Islands *see* Baleares, Islas
Balearic Plain *see* Algerian Basin
Baleine, Rivière à la *17 E2 river* Quebec, E Canada
Balen *65 C5* Antwerpen, N Belgium
Bāleshwar *113 F4 prev.* Balasore. Orissa, E India
Bali *116 D5 island* C Indonesia
Balıkesir *94 A3* Balıkesir, W Turkey
Balīkh, Nahr *96 C2 river* N Syria
Balikpapan *116 D4* Borneo, C Indonesia
Balkan Mountains *82 C2 Bul./SCr.* Stara Planina. *Mountain range* Bulgaria/Serbia and Montenegro (Yugo.)
Balkh *101 E3 anc.* Bactra. Balkh, N Afghanistan
Balkhash *92 C5 Kaz.* Balqash. Karaganda, SE Kazakhstan
Balkhash, Lake *see* Balkhash, Ozero
Balkhash, Ozero *92 C5 Eng.* Lake Balkhash, *Kaz.* Balqash. *Lake* SE Kazakhstan
Balladonia *125 C6* Western Australia
Ballarat *127 C7* Victoria, SE Australia
Balleny Islands *132 B5 island group* Antarctica
Ballinger *27 F3* Texas, SW USA
Balochistān *see* Baluchistān
Balş *86 B5* Olt, S Romania
Balsas *41 F2* Maranhão, E Brazil
Balsas, Río *29 E5 var.* Río Mexcala. *River* S Mexico
Bal'shavik *85 D7 Rus.* Bol'shevik. Homyel'skaya Voblasts', SE Belarus
Balta *86 D3* Odes'ka Oblast', SW Ukraine
Bălți *86 D3 Rus.* Bel'tsy. N Moldova
Baltic Sea *63 C7 Ger.* Ostee, *Rus.* Baltiskoye More. *Sea* N Europe
Baltimore *19 F4* Maryland, NE USA
Baltkrievija *see* Belarus
Baluchistān *112 B3 var.* Balochistān, Beluchistan. *Admin. region province* SW Pakistan
Balvi *84 D4* Balvi, NE Latvia
Balykchy *101 G2 Kir.* Ysyk-Köl; *prev.* Issyk-Kul', Rybach'ye. Issyk-Kul'skaya Oblast', NE Kyrgyzstan
Balzers *72 E2* S Liechtenstein
Bam *98 E4* Kermān, SE Iran
Bamako *52 D4 country capital* (Mali) Capital District, SW Mali
Bambari *54 C4* Ouaka, C Central African Republic
Bamberg *73 C5* Bayern, SE Germany
Bamenda *54 A4* Nord-Ouest, W Cameroon
Banaba *122 D2 var.* Ocean Island. *Island* Tungaru, W Kiribati
Bandaaceh *116 A3 var.* Banda Atjeh; *prev.* Koetaradja, Kutaradja, Kutaraja. Sumatera, W Indonesia
Banda Atjeh *see* Bandaaceh
Bandama *52 D5 var.* Bandama Fleuve. *River* S Côte d'Ivoire
Bandama Fleuve *see* Bandama
Bandar 'Abbās *see* Bandar-e 'Abbās
Bandarbeyla *51 E5 var.* Bender Beila, Bender Beyla. Bari, NE Somalia
Bandar-e 'Abbās *98 D4 var.* Bandar 'Abbās; *prev.* Gombroon. Hormozgān, S Iran
Bandar-e Būshehr *98 C4 var.* Būshehr, *Eng.* Bushire. Būshehr, S Iran
Bandar-e Khamīr *98 D4* Hormozgān, S Iran
Bandar-e Langeh *98 D4 var.* Bandar-e Lengeh, Lingeh. Hormozgān, S Iran
Bandar-e Lengeh *see* Bandar-e Langeh
Bandar Kassim *see* Boosaaso
Bandarlampung *116 C4 prev.* Tanjungkarang, Teloekbetoeng, Telukbetung. Sumatera, W Indonesia
Bandar Maharani *see* Muar
Bandar Masulipatnam *see* Machilīpatnam
Bandar Seri Begawan *116 D3 prev.* Brunei Town. *Country capital* (Brunei) N Brunei
Bandar Sri Aman *see* Sri Aman
Banda Sea *117 F5 var.* Laut Banda. *Sea* E Indonesia
Bandiagara *53 E3* Mopti, C Mali
Bandırma *94 A3 var.* Penderma. Balıkesir, NW Turkey
Bandundu *55 C6 prev.* Banningville. Bandundu, W Dem. Rep. Congo
Bandung *116 C5 prev.* Bandoeng. Jawa, C Indonesia
Bangalore *110 C2* Karnātaka, S India
Bangassou *54 D4* Mbomou, SE Central African Republic
Banggai, Kepulauan *117 E4 island group* C Indonesia
Banghāzī *49 G2 Eng.* Bengazi, Benghazi, *It.* Bengasi. NE Libya
Bangka, Pulau *116 C4 island* W Indonesia
Bangkok *see* Krung Thep
Bangkok, Bight of *see* Krung Thep, Ao
Bangladesh *113 G3 off.* People's Republic of Bangladesh; *prev.* East Pakistan. *Country* S Asia
Bangor *67 B5 Ir.* Beannchar. E Northern Ireland, UK
Bangor *19 G2* Maine, NE USA
Bangor *67 C6* NW Wales, UK
Bangui *55 B5 country capital* (Central African Republic) Ombolla-Mpoko, SW Central African Republic
Bangweulu, Lake *51 B8 var.* Lake Bengweulu. *Lake* N Zambia
Ban Hat Yai *see* Hat Yai
Ban Hin Heup *114 C4* Viangchan, C Laos
Ban Houayxay *see* Houayxay
Ban Houei Sai *see* Houayxay
Ban Hua Hin *115 C6 var.* Hua Hin. Prachuap Khiri Khan, SW Thailand
Bani *52 D3 river* S Mali
Banias *see* Bāniyās
Banī Suwayf *see* Beni Suef
Bāniyās *96 B3 var.* Banias, Baniyas, Paneas. Ṭarṭūs, W Syria
Baniyas *see* Bāniyās
Banja Luka *78 B3* Republika Srpska, NW Bosnia and Herzegovina
Banjarmasin *116 D4 prev.* Bandjarmasin. Borneo, C Indonesia
Banjul *52 B3 prev.* Bathurst. *Country capital* (Gambia) W Gambia
Banks Island *15 E2 island* Banks Island, Northwest Territories, NW Canada
Banks Islands *122 D4 Fr.* Îles Banks. *Island group* N Vanuatu
Banks Lake *24 B1 reservoir* Washington, NW USA
Banks Peninsula *129 C6 peninsula* South Island, NZ
Banks Strait *127 C8 strait* SW Tasman Sea
Bānkura *113 F4* West Bengal, NE India
Ban Mak Khaeng *see* Udon Thani
Banmo *see* Bhamo
Bañolas *see* Banyoles
Ban Pak Phanang *see* Pak Phanang
Ban Sichon *see* Sichon
Banská Bystrica *77 C6 Ger.* Neusohl, *Hung.* Besztercebánya. Banskobystrický Kraj, C Slovakia
Bantry Bay *67 A7 Ir.* Bá Bheanntraí. *Bay* SW Ireland
Banya *82 E2* Burgas, E Bulgaria
Banyak, Kepulauan *116 A3 prev.* Kepulauan Banjak. *Island group* NW Indonesia
Banyo *54 B4* Adamaoua, NW Cameroon
Banyoles *71 G2 var.* Bañolas. Cataluña, NE Spain
Banzare Seamounts *119 C7 undersea feature* S Indian Ocean
Baoji *106 B4 var.* Pao-chi, Paoki. Shaanxi, C China
Baoro *54 B4* Nana-Mambéré, W Central African Republic
Baoshan *106 A6 var.* Pao-shan. Yunnan, SW China
Baotou *105 F3 var.* Pao-t'ou, Paotow. Nei Mongol Zizhiqu, N China
Ba'qūbah *98 B3 var.* Qubba. C Iraq
Baquerizo Moreno *see* Puerto Baquerizo Moreno
Bar *79 C5 It.* Antivari. Montenegro, SW Serbia and Montenegro (Yugo.)
Baraawe *51 D6 It.* Brava. Shabeellaha Hoose, S Somalia
Baraji, Hirfanli *94 C3 lake* C Turkey
Bārāmati *112 C5* Mahārāshtra, W India
Baranavichy *85 B6 Pol.* Baranowicze, *Rus.* Baranovichi. Brestskaya Voblasts', SW Belarus
Barbados *33 G1 country* SE West Indies
Barbastro *71 F2* Aragón, NE Spain
Barbate de Franco *70 C5* Andalucía, S Spain
Barbuda *33 G3 island* N Antigua and Barbuda
Barcaldine *126 C4* Queensland, E Australia
Barce *see* Al Marj
Barcelona *71 G2 anc.* Barcino, Barcinona. Cataluña, E Spain
Barcelona *37 E2* Anzoátegui, NE Venezuela
Barcoo *see* Cooper Creek
Barcs *77 C7* Somogy, SW Hungary
Bardaï *54 C1* Borkou-Ennedi-Tibesti, N Chad
Bardejov *77 D5 Ger.* Bartfeld, *Hung.* Bártfa. Prešovský Kraj, E Slovakia
Bardera *see* Baardheere
Bardere *see* Baardheere
Bareilly *113 E3 var.* Bareli. Uttar Pradesh, N India
Bareli *see* Bareilly
Barendrecht *64 C4* Zuid-Holland, SW Netherlands
Barentin *68 C3* Seine-Maritime, N France
Barentsberg *61 G2* Spitsbergen, W Svalbard
Barentsøya *61 G2 island* E Svalbard
Barents Sea *88 C2 Nor.* Barents Havet, *Rus.* Barentsevo More. *Sea* Arctic Ocean
Barents Trough *59 E1 undersea feature* SW Barents Sea
Bar Harbor *19 H2* Mount Desert Island, Maine, NE USA
Bari *75 E5 var.* Bari delle Puglie; *anc.* Barium. Puglia, SE Italy
Bāridah *see* Al Bāridah
Bari delle Puglie *see* Bari
Barikot *see* Barīkowṭ
Barīkowṭ *101 F4 var.* Barikot. Kunar, NE Afghanistan
Barillas *30 A2 var.* Santa Cruz Barillas. Huehuetenango, NW Guatemala
Barinas *36 C2* Barinas, W Venezuela
Barisal *113 G4* Khulna, S Bangladesh
Barisan, Pegunungan *116 B4 mountain range* Sumatera, W Indonesia
Barito, Sungai *116 D4 river* Borneo, C Indonesia
Barium *see* Bari
Barka *see* Al Marj
Barkly Tableland *126 B3 plateau* Northern Territory/Queensland, N Australia
Bârlad *86 D4 prev.* Bîrlad. Vaslui, E Romania
Barlavento, Ilhas de *52 A2 var.* Windward Islands. *Island group* N Cape Verde
Bar-le-Duc *68 D3 var.* Bar-sur-Ornain. Meuse, NE France
Barlee, Lake *125 B6 lake* Western Australia
Barlee Range *124 A4 mountain range* Western Australia
Barletta *75 D5 anc.* Barduli. Puglia, SE Italy
Barlinek *76 B3 Ger.* Berlinchen. Zachodniopomorskie, NW Poland
Barmouth *67 C6* NW Wales, UK
Barnaul *92 D4* Altayskiy Kray, C Russian Federation
Barnet *67 A7* SE England, UK
Barnstaple *67 C7* SW England, UK
Baroghil Pass *101 F3 var.* Kowtal-e Barowghīl. *Pass* Afghanistan/Pakistan
Baron'ki *85 E7 Rus.* Boron'ki. Mahilyowskaya Voblasts', E Belarus
Barquisimeto *36 C2* Lara, NW Venezuela
Barra *66 B3 island* NW Scotland, UK
Barra de Río Grande *31 E3* Región Autónoma Atlántico Sur, E Nicaragua
Barragem de Sobradinho *see* Sobradinho, Represa de
Barranca *38 C3* Lima, W Peru
Barrancabermeja *36 B2* Santander, N Colombia
Barranquilla *36 B1* Atlántico, N Colombia
Barreiro *70 B4* Setúbal, W Portugal
Barrier Range *127 C6 hill range* New South Wales, SE Australia
Barrow *67 B6 Ir.* An Bhearú. *River* SE Ireland
Barrow *14 D2* Alaska, USA
Barrow-in-Furness *67 C5* NW England, UK
Barrow Island *124 A4 island* Western Australia
Barstow *25 C7* California, W USA
Bar-sur-Ornain *see* Bar-le-Duc
Bartang *101 F3 river* SE Tajikistan
Bartica *37 F3* N Guyana
Bartın *94 C2* Bartın NW Turkey
Bartlesville *27 G1* Oklahoma, C USA
Bartoszyce *76 D2 Ger.* Bartenstein. Warmińsko-Mazurskie, NE Poland
Baruun-Urt *105 F2* Sühbaatar, E Mongolia
Barú, Volcán *31 E5 var.* Volcán de Chiriquí. *Volcano* W Panama
Barwon River *127 D5 river* New South Wales, SE Australia
Barysaw *85 D6 Rus.* Borisov. Minskaya Voblasts', NE Belarus
Basarabeasca *86 D4 Rus.* Bessarabka. SE Moldova
Basel *73 A7 Eng.* Basle, *Fr.* Bâle. Basel-Stadt, NW Switzerland
Basilan *117 E3 island* SW Philippines
Basle *see* Basel
Basra *see* Al Baṣrah
Bassano del Grappa *74 C2* Veneto, NE Italy
Bassein *114 A4 var.* Pathein. Irrawaddy, SW Myanmar
Basse-Terre *33 G4 dependent territory capital* (Guadeloupe) Basse Terre, SW Guadeloupe
Basse Terre *33 G4 island* W Guadeloupe
Basseterre *33 G3 country capital* (Saint Kitts and Nevis) Saint Kitts, Saint Kitts and Nevis
Bassikounou *52 D3* Hodh ech Chargui, SE Mauritania
Bass Strait *127 C7 strait* SE Australia
Bassum *72 B3* Niedersachsen, NW Germany
Bastia *69 E7* Corse, France, C Mediterranean Sea
Bastogne *65 D7* Luxembourg, SE Belgium
Bastrop *20 B2* Louisiana, S USA
Bastyn' *85 B7 Rus.* Bostyn'. Brestskaya Voblasts', SW Belarus
Basuo *see* Dongfang
Bata *55 A5* NW Equatorial Guinea
Batabanó, Golfo de *32 A2 gulf* W Cuba
Batajnica *78 D3* Serbia, N Serbia and Montenegro (Yugo.)
Batangas *117 E2 off.* Batangas City. Luzon, N Philippines
Bătdâmbâng *115 C5 prev.* Battambang. Bătdâmbâng, NW Cambodia
Batéké, Plateaux *55 B6 plateau* S Congo
Bath *67 D7 hist.* Akermanceaster; *anc.* Aquae Calidae, Aquae Solis. SW England, UK
Bathinda *112 D2* Punjab, NW India
Bathsheba *33 G1* E Barbados
Bathurst *17 F4* New Brunswick, SE Canada
Bathurst *127 D6* New South Wales, SE Australia
Bathurst Island *124 D2 island* Northern Territory, N Australia
Bathurst Island *15 F2 island* Parry Islands, Nunavut, N Canada
Bāṭin, Wādī al *136 C4 dry watercourse* SW Asia
Batman *95 E4 var.* Iluh. Batman, SE Turkey
Batna *49 E2* NE Algeria
Baton Rouge *20 B3 state capital* Louisiana, S USA
Batroûn *96 A4 var.* Al Batrūn. N Lebanon
Batticaloa *110 D3* Eastern Province, E Sri Lanka
Battipaglia *75 D5* Campania, S Italy
Bat'umi *95 F2* W Georgia
Batu Pahat *116 B3 prev.* Bandar Penggaram. Johor, Peninsular Malaysia
Bauchi *53 G4* Bauchi, NE Nigeria
Bauer Basin *131 F3 undersea feature* E Pacific Ocean
Bauska *84 C3 Ger.* Bauske. Bauska, S Latvia
Bautzen *72 D4 Lus.* Budyšin. Sachsen, E Germany
Bavarian Alps *73 C7 Ger.* Bayrische Alpen. *Mountain range* Austria/Germany
Bavispe, Río *28 C2 river* NW Mexico
Bawīṭī *50 B2* N Egypt
Bawku *53 E4* N Ghana
Bayamo *32 C3* Granma, E Cuba
Bayan Har Shan *104 D4 var.* Bayan Khar. *Mountain range* C China
Bayanhongor *104 D2* Bayanhongor, C Mongolia
Bayan Khar *see* Bayan Har Shan
Bayano, Lago *31 G4 lake* E Panama
Bay City *18 C3* Michigan, N USA
Bay City *27 G4* Texas, SW USA
Baydhabo *51 D6 var.* Baydhowa, Isha Baydhabo, *It.* Baidoa. Bay, SW Somalia
Baydhowa *see* Baydhabo
Bayern *73 C6 cultural region* SE Germany
Bayeux *68 B3 anc.* Augustodurum. Calvados, N France
Bāyir *97 C7 var.* Bā'ir. Ma'ān, S Jordan
Baykal, Ozero *93 E4 Eng.* Lake Baikal. *Lake* S Russian Federation
Baymak *89 D6* Respublika Bashkortostan, W Russian Federation
Bayonne *69 A6 anc.* Lapurdum. Pyrénées-Atlantiques, SW France
Bayramaly *100 D3 prev.* Bayram-Ali. Maryyskiy Velayat, S Turkmenistan
Bayreuth *73 C5 var.* Baireuth. Bayern, SE Germany
Bayrūt *see* Beyrouth
Baytown *27 H4* Texas, SW USA
Baza *71 E4* Andalucía, S Spain
Beagle Channel *43 C8 channel* Argentina/Chile
Béal Feirste *see* Belfast
Beannchar *see* Bangor
Bear Lake *24 E4 lake* Idaho/Utah, NW USA
Beas de Segura *71 E4* Andalucía, S Spain
Beata, Isla *33 E3 island* SW Dominican Republic
Beatrice *23 F4* Nebraska, C USA
Beaufort Sea *14 D2 sea* Arctic Ocean
Beaufort West *56 C5 Afr.* Beaufort-Wes. Western Cape, SW South Africa
Beaumont *27 H3* Texas, SW USA
Beaune *68 D4* Côte d'Or, C France
Beauvais *68 C3 anc.* Bellovacum, Caesaromagus. Oise, N France
Beaver Island *18 C2 island* Michigan, N USA
Beaver Lake *27 H1 reservoir* Arkansas, C USA
Beaver River *27 F1 river* Oklahoma, C USA
Beāwar *112 C3* Rājasthān, N India
Bečej *78 D3 Ger.* Altbetsche, *Hung.* Óbecse, Rácz-Becse; *prev.* Magyar-Becse, Stari Bečej. Serbia, N Serbia and Montenegro (Yugo.)
Béchar *48 D2 prev.* Colomb-Béchar. W Algeria
Beckley *18 D5* West Virginia, NE USA
Bedford *67 D6* E England, UK
Bedum *64 E1* Groningen, NE Netherlands
Be'er Menuḥa *97 B7 var* Be'er Menukha. Southern, S Israel
Be'er Menukha *see* Be'ér Menuḥa
Beernem *65 A5* West-Vlaanderen, NW Belgium
Beersheba *see* Be'ér Sheva'
Be'ér Sheva' *97 A7 var.* Beersheba, *Ar.* Bir es Saba. Southern, S Israel
Beesel *65 D5* Limburg, SE Netherlands
Beeville *27 G4* Texas, SW USA
Bega *127 D7* New South Wales, SE Australia
Beida *see* Al Bayḍā'
Beihai *106 B6* Guangxi Zhuangzu Zizhiqu, S China
Beijing *106 C3 var.* Pei-ching, *Eng.* Peking; *prev.* Pei-p'ing. *Country/municipality capital* (China) Beijing Shi, E China
Beilen *64 E2* Drenthe, NE Netherlands
Beira *57 E3* Sofala, C Mozambique
Beirut *see* Beyrouth
Beit Leḥm *see* Bethlehem
Beiuș *86 B3 Hung.* Belényes. Bihor, NW Romania
Beja *70 B4 anc.* Pax Julia. Beja, SE Portugal
Béjar *70 C3* Castilla-León, N Spain
Bejraburi *see* Phetchaburi
Békéscsaba *77 D7 Rom.* Bichiș-Ciaba. Békés, SE Hungary
Bekobod *101 E2 Rus.* Bekabad; *prev.* Begovat. Toshkent Wiloyati, E Uzbekistan
Bela Crkva *78 E3 Ger.* Weisskirchen, *Hung.* Fehértemplom. Serbia, W Serbia and Montenegro (Yugo.)
Belarus *85 B6 off.* Republic of Belarus, *var.* Belorussia, *Latv.* Baltkrievija; *prev.* Belorussian SSR, *Rus.* Belorusskaya SSR. *Country* E Europe
Belau *see* Palau
Belchatow *see* Bełchatów
Bełchatów *76 C4 var.* Belchatow. Łódzkie, C Poland
Belcher Islands *16 C2 Fr.* Îles Belcher. *Island group* Northwest Territories, SE Canada
Beledweyne *51 D5 var.* Belet Huen, *It.* Belet Uen. Hiiraan, C Somalia
Belém *41 F1 var.* Pará. *State capital* Pará, N Brazil
Belen *26 D2* New Mexico, SW USA
Belén *30 D4* Rivas, SW Nicaragua
Belet Huen *see* Beledweyne
Belet Uen *see* Beledweyne
Belfast *67 B5 Ir.* Béal Feirste. *Admin capital* E Northern Ireland, UK
Belfield *22 D2* North Dakota, N USA
Belfort *68 E4* Territoire-de-Belfort, E France
Belgaum *110 B1* Karnātaka, W India
Belgium *65 B6 off.* Kingdom of Belgium, *Dut.* België, *Fr.* Belgique. *Country* NW Europe
Belgorod *89 A6* Belgorodskaya Oblast', W Russian Federation
Belgrade *see* Beograd
Belgrano II *132 B2 Argentinian research station* Antarctica
Belice *see* Belize City
Beligrad *see* Berat
Beli Manastir *78 C3 Hung.* Pélmonostor; *prev.* Monostor. Osijek-Baranja, NE Croatia
Bélinga *55 B5* Ogooué-Ivindo, NE Gabon
Belitung, Pulau *116 C4 island* W Indonesia
Belize *30 B1 Sp.* Belice; *prev.* British Honduras, Colony of Belize. *Country* Central America
Belize *30 B1 river* Belize/Guatemala
Belize *see* Belize City
Belize City *30 C1 var.* Belize, *Sp.* Belice. Belize, NE Belize
Belkofski *14 B3* Alaska, USA
Belle Île *68 A4 island* NW France
Belle Isle, Strait of *17 G3 strait* Newfoundland and Labrador, E Canada
Belleville *18 B4* Illinois, N USA
Bellevue *23 F4* Iowa, C USA
Bellevue *24 B2* Washington, NW USA
Bellingham *24 B1* Washington, NW USA
Belling Hausen Mulde *see* Southeast Pacific Basin
Bellingshausen Abyssal Plain *see* Bellingshausen Plain
Bellingshausen Plain *131 F5 var.* Bellingshausen Abyssal Plain. *Undersea feature* SE Pacific Ocean
Bellingshausen Sea *132 A3 sea* Antarctica
Bellinzona *73 B8 Ger.* Bellenz. Ticino, S Switzerland
Bello *36 B2* Antioquia, W Colombia
Bellville *56 B5* Western Cape, SW South Africa
Belmopan *30 C1 country capital* (Belize) Cayo, C Belize
Belogradchik *82 B1* Vidin, NW Bulgaria
Belo Horizonte *41 F4 prev.* Bello Horizonte. *State capital* Minas Gerais, SE Brazil
Belomorsk *88 B3* Respublika Kareliya, NW Russian Federation
Beloretsk *89 D6* Respublika Bashkortostan, W Russian Federation
Belorussia/Belorussian SSR *see* Belarus
Belorusskaya SSR *see* Belarus
Beloye More *88 C3 Eng.* White Sea. *Sea* NW Russian Federation
Belozersk *88 B4* Vologodskaya Oblast', NW Russian Federation
Belton *27 G3* Texas, SW USA
Beluchistan *see* Baluchistān
Belukha, Gora *92 D5 mountain* Kazakhstan/Russian Federation
Belyy, Ostrov *92 D2 island* N Russian Federation
Bemaraha *57 F3 var.* Plateau du Bemaraha. *Mountain range* W Madagascar
Bemidji *23 F1* Minnesota, N USA

INDEX

Chiang Rai – Corpus Christi

Chiang Rai 114 C3 var. Chianpai, Chienrai, Muang Chiang Rai. Chiang Rai, NW Thailand
Chiang-su see Jiangsu
Chian-ning see Nanjing
Chianpai see Chiang Rai
Chianti 74 C3 cultural region C Italy
Chiapa see Chiapa de Corzo
Chiapa de Corzo 29 G5 var. Chiapa. Chiapas, SE Mexico
Chiayi see Chiai
Chiba 108 B1 var. Tiba. Chiba, Honshū, S Japan
Chibougamau 16 D3 Quebec, SE Canada
Chicago 18 B3 Illinois, N USA
Ch'i-ch'i-ha-erh see Qiqihar
Chickasha 27 G2 Oklahoma, C USA
Chiclayo 38 B3 Lambayeque, NW Peru
Chico 25 B5 California, W USA
Chico, Río 43 B6 river S Argentina
Chico, Río 43 B7 river SE Argentina
Chicoutimi 17 E4 Quebec, SE Canada
Chiengmai see Chiang Mai
Chienrai see Chiang Rai
Chiesanuova 74 D2 SW San Marino
Chieti 74 D4 var. Teate. Abruzzo, C Italy
Chifeng 105 G2 var. Ulanhad. Nei Mongol Zizhiqu, N China
Chih-fu see Yantai
Chihli see Hebei
Chihli, Gulf of see Bo Hai
Chihuahua 28 C2 Chihuahua, NW Mexico
Childress 27 F2 Texas, SW USA
Chile 42 B3 off. Republic of Chile. Country SW South America
Chile Basin 35 A5 undersea feature E Pacific Ocean
Chile Chico 43 B6 Aisén, W Chile
Chile Rise 35 A7 undersea feature SE Pacific Ocean
Chililabombwe 56 D2 Copperbelt, C Zambia
Chi-lin see Jilin
Chillán 43 B5 Bío Bío, C Chile
Chillicothe 18 D4 Ohio, N USA
Chiloé, Isla de 43 A6 var. Isla Grande de Chiloé. Island W Chile
Chilpancingo 29 E5 var. Chilpancingo de los Bravos. Guerrero, S Mexico
Chilpancingo de los Bravos see Chilpancingo
Chilung 106 D6 var. Keelung, Jap. Kirun, Kirun'; prev. Sp. Santissima Trinidad. N Taiwan
Chimán 31 G5 Panamá, E Panama
Chimborazo 38 A1 volcano C Ecuador
Chimbote 38 C3 Ancash, W Peru
Chimboy 100 D1 Rus. Chimbay. Qoraqalpoghiston Respublikasi, NW Uzbekistan
Chimoio 57 E3 Manica, C Mozambique
China 102 C2 off. People's Republic of China, Chin. Chung-hua Jen-min Kung-ho-kuo, Zhonghua Renmin Gongheguo; prev. Chinese Empire. Country E Asia
Chi-nan see Jinan
Chinandega 30 C3 Chinandega, NW Nicaragua
Chincha Alta 38 D4 Ica, SW Peru
Chin-chiang see Quanzhou
Chin-chou see Jinzhou
Chinchow see Jinzhou
Chindwin 114 B2 river N Myanmar
Ch'ing Hai see Qinghai Hu
Chingola 56 D2 Copperbelt, C Zambia
Ching-Tao see Qingdao
Chinguetti 52 C2 var. Chinguetti. Adrar, C Mauritania
Chin Hills 114 A3 mountain range W Myanmar
Chinhsien see Jinzhou
Chinnereth see Tiberias, Lake
Chinook Trough 91 H4 undersea feature N Pacific Ocean
Chioggia 74 C2 anc. Fossa Claudia. Veneto, NE Italy
Chíos 83 D5 var. Hios, Khíos, It. Scio, Turk. Sakiz-Adasi. Chíos, E Greece
Chíos 83 D5 var. Khíos. Island E Greece
Chipata 56 D2 prev. Fort Jameson. Eastern, E Zambia
Chiquián 38 C3 Ancash, W Peru
Chiquimula 30 B2 Chiquimula, SE Guatemala
Chīrāla 110 D1 Andhra Pradesh, E India
Chirchiq 101 E2 Rus. Chirchik. Toshkent Wiloyati, E Uzbekistan
Chiriquí, Golfo de 31 E5 Eng. Chiriqui Gulf. Gulf SW Panama
Chiriquí, Laguna de 31 E5 lagoon NW Panama
Chirripó Grande, Cerro 30 D4 var. Cerro Chirripó. Mountain SE Costa Rica
Chisec 30 B2 Alta Verapaz, C Guatemala
Chisholm 23 F1 Minnesota, N USA
Chisimaio see Kismaayo
Chisimayu see Kismaayo
Chişinău 86 D4 Rus. Kishinev. Country capital (Moldova) C Moldova
Chita 93 F4 Chitinskaya Oblast', S Russian Federation
Chitato 56 C1 Lunda Norte, NE Angola
Chitina 14 D3 Alaska, USA
Chitose 108 D2 var. Titose. Hokkaidō, NE Japan
Chitré 31 F5 Herrera, S Panama
Chittagong 113 G4 Ben. Chāttagām. Chittagong, SE Bangladesh
Chitungwiza 56 D3 prev. Chitangwiza. Mashonaland East, NE Zimbabwe
Chlef 48 D2 var. Ech Cheliff, Ech Chleff; prev. Al-Asnam, El Asnam, Orléansville. NW Algeria
Chocolate Mountains 25 D8 mountain range California, W USA
Chodzież 76 C3 Wielkopolskie, C Poland
Choele Choel 43 C5 Río Negro, C Argentina
Choiseul 122 C3 var. Lauru. Island NW Solomon Islands
Chojnice 76 C2 Ger. Knoitz. Pomorskie, N Poland
Ch'ok'ē 50 C4 var. Choke Mountains. Mountain range NW Ethiopia
Choke Mountains see Ch'ok'ē
Cholet 68 B4 Maine-et-Loire, NW France
Choluteca 30 C3 Choluteca, S Honduras
Choluteca, Río 30 C3 river SW Honduras
Choma 56 D2 Southern, S Zambia
Chomutov 76 A4 Ger. Komotau. Ústecký Kraj, NW Czech Republic
Chona 91 E2 river C Russian Federation
Chon Buri 115 C5 prev. Bang Pla Soi. Chon Buri, S Thailand
Chone 38 A1 Manabí, W Ecuador
Ch'ŏngjin 107 E3 NE North Korea
Chongqing 106 B5 var. Ch'ung-ching, Ch'ung-ch'ing, Chungking, Pahsien, Tchongking, Yuzhou. Chongqing, C China
Chongqing 106 B5 Admin. region province C China
Chonos, Archipiélago de los 43 A6 island group S Chile
Chorne More see Black Sea
Chornomors'ke 87 E4 Rus. Chernomorskoye. Respublika Krym, S Ukraine
Chortkiv 86 C2 Rus. Chortkov. Ternopil's'ka Oblast', W Ukraine
Chorum see Çorum
Chorzów 77 C5 Ger. Königshütte; prev. Królewska Huta. Śląskie, S Poland
Chōshi 109 D5 var. Tyôsi. Chiba, Honshū, S Japan
Choszczno 76 B3 Ger. Arnswalde. Zachodniopomorskie, NW Poland
Chota Nāgpur 113 E4 plateau N India
Chott el-Hodna see Hodna, Chott El
Chott Melrhir see Melghir, Chott
Choûm 52 C2 Adrar, C Mauritania
Choybalsan 105 F2 Dornod, E Mongolia
Christchurch 129 C6 Canterbury, South Island, NZ
Christiana 32 B5 C Jamaica
Christiansand see Kristiansand
Christianshåb see Qasigiannguit
Christiansund see Kristiansund
Christmas Island 119 D5 Australian external territory E Indian Ocean
Christmas Ridge 121 E1 undersea feature C Pacific Ocean
Chuan see Sichuan
Ch'uan-chou see Quanzhou
Chubut 35 B7 off. Provincia de Chubut. Admin. region province S Argentina
Chubut, Río 43 B6 river SE Argentina
Ch'u-chiang see Shaoguan
Chūgoku-sanchi 109 B6 mountain range Honshū, SW Japan
Chuí see Chuy
Chukai see Cukai
Chukchi Plain 133 B2 undersea feature Arctic Ocean
Chukchi Plateau 12 C2 undersea feature Arctic Ocean
Chukchi Sea 12 B2 Rus. Chukotskoye More. Sea Arctic Ocean
Chula Vista 25 C8 California, W USA
Chulucanas 38 B2 Piura, NW Peru
Chulym 92 D4 river C Russian Federation
Chumphon 115 C6 var. Jumporn. Chumphon, SW Thailand
Ch'unch'ŏn 107 E4 Jap. Shunsen. N South Korea
Ch'ung-ching see Chongqing
Chungking see Chongqing
Chunya 93 E3 river C Russian Federation
Chuquicamata 42 B2 Antofagasta, N Chile
Chur 73 B7 Fr. Coire, It. Coira, Rmsch. Cuera, Quera; anc. Curia Rhaetorum. Graubünden, E Switzerland
Churchill 16 B2 river Manitoba/Saskatchewan, C Canada
Churchill 17 F2 river Newfoundland and Labrador, E Canada
Churchill 15 G4 Manitoba, C Canada
Chuska Mountains 26 C1 mountain range Arizona/New Mexico, SW USA
Chusovoy 89 D5 Permskaya Oblast', NW Russian Federation
Chuuk Islands 122 B2 var. Hogoley Islands; prev. Truk Islands. Island group Caroline Islands, C Micronesia
Chuy 42 E4 var. Chuí. Rocha, E Uruguay
Chyhyryn 87 E2 Rus. Chigirin. Cherkas'ka Oblast', N Ukraine
Ciadîr-Lunga 86 D4 var. Ceadâr-Lunga, Rus. Chadyr-Lunga. S Moldova
Cide 94 C2 Kastamonu, N Turkey
Ciechanów 76 D3 prev. Zichenau. Mazowieckie, C Poland
Ciego de Ávila 32 C2 Ciego de Ávila, C Cuba
Ciénaga 36 B1 Magdalena, N Colombia
Cienfuegos 32 B2 Cienfuegos, C Cuba
Cieza 71 E4 Murcia, SE Spain
Cihanbeyli 94 C3 Konya, C Turkey
Cikobia 123 E4 prev. Thikombia. Island N Fiji
Cilacap 116 C5 prev. Tjilatjap. Jawa, C Indonesia
Cill Airne see Killarney
Cill Chainnigh see Kilkenny
Cill Mhantáin see Wicklow
Cincinnati 18 C4 Ohio, N USA
Ciney 65 C7 Namur, SE Belgium
Cinto, Monte 69 E7 mountain Corse, France, C Mediterranean Sea
Cipolletti 43 B5 Río Negro, C Argentina
Cirebon 116 C4 prev. Tjirebon. Jawa, S Indonesia
Ciro Marino 75 E6 Calabria, S Italy
Cisnădie 86 B4 Ger. Heltau; Hung. Nagydisznód. Sibiu, SW Romania
Citlaltépetl see Orizaba, Volcán Pico de
Citrus Heights 25 B5 California, W USA
Ciudad Bolívar 37 E2 prev. Angostura. Bolívar, E Venezuela
Ciudad Acuña see Villa Acuña
Ciudad Camargo 28 D2 Chihuahua, N Mexico
Ciudad Cortés see Cortés
Ciudad Darío 30 D3 var. Dario. Matagalpa, W Nicaragua
Ciudad de Dolores Hidalgo see Dolores Hidalgo
Ciudad de Guatemala 30 B2 var. Gautemala City Eng. Guatemala City; prev. Santiago de los Caballeros. Country capital (Guatemala) Guatemala, C Guatemala
Ciudad del Carmen see Carmen
Ciudad del Este 42 E2 prev. Cuidad Presidente Stroessner, Presidente Stroessner, Puerto Presidente Stroessner. Alto Paraná, SE Paraguay
Ciudad Delicias see Delicias
Ciudad de México see México
Ciudad de Panamá see Panamá
Ciudad Guayana 37 E2 prev. San Tomé de Guayana, Santo Tomé de Guayana. Bolívar, NE Venezuela
Ciudad Guzmán 28 D4 Jalisco, SW Mexico
Ciudad Hidalgo 29 G5 Chiapas, SE Mexico
Ciudad Juárez 28 C1 Chihuahua, N Mexico
Ciudad Lerdo 28 D3 Durango, C Mexico
Ciudad Madero 29 E3 var. Villa Cecilia. Tamaulipas, C Mexico
Ciudad Mante 29 E3 Tamaulipas, C Mexico
Ciudad Miguel Alemán 29 E2 Tamaulipas, C Mexico
Ciudad Obregón 28 B2 Sonora, NW Mexico
Ciudad Ojeda 36 C1 Zulia, NW Venezuela
Ciudad Porfirio Díaz see Piedras Negras
Ciudad Quesada see Quesada
Ciudad Real 70 D3 Castilla-La Mancha, C Spain
Ciudad-Rodrigo 70 C3 Castilla-León, N Spain
Ciudad Valles 29 E3 San Luis Potosí, C Mexico
Ciudad Victoria 29 E3 Tamaulipas, C Mexico
Ciutadella see Ciutadella de Menorca
Ciutadella de Menorca 71 H3 var. Ciutadella. Menorca, Spain, W Mediterranean Sea
Civitanova Marche 74 D3 Marche, C Italy
Civitavecchia 74 C4 anc. Centum Cellae, Trajani Portus. Lazio, C Italy
Claremore 27 G1 Oklahoma, C USA
Clarence 129 C5 river South Island, NZ
Clarence 129 C5 Canterbury, South Island, NZ
Clarence Town 32 D2 Long Island, C Bahamas
Clarinda 23 F4 Iowa, C USA
Clarion Fracture Zone 131 E2 tectonic feature NE Pacific Ocean
Clarión, Isla 28 A5 island W Mexico
Clark Fork 22 A1 river Idaho/Montana, NW USA
Clark Hill Lake 21 E2 var. J.Storm Thurmond Reservoir. Reservoir Georgia/South Carolina, SE USA
Clarksburg 18 D4 West Virginia, NE USA
Clarksdale 20 B2 Mississippi, S USA
Clarksville 20 C1 Tennessee, S USA
Clayton 27 E1 New Mexico, SW USA
Clearwater 21 E4 Florida, SE USA
Clearwater Mountains 24 D2 mountain range Idaho, NW USA
Cleburne 27 G3 Texas, SW USA
Clermont 126 D4 Queensland, E Australia
Clermont-Ferrand 69 C5 Puy de Dôme, C France
Cleveland 18 D3 Ohio, N USA
Cleveland 20 D1 Tennessee, S USA
Clifton 26 C2 Arizona, SW USA
Clinton 20 B2 Mississippi, S USA
Clinton 27 F1 Oklahoma, C USA
Clipperton Fracture Zone 131 E3 tectonic feature E Pacific Ocean
Clipperton Island 13 A7 French dependency of French Polynesia E Pacific Ocean
Cloncurry 126 B3 Queensland, C Australia
Clonmel 67 B6 Ir. Cluain Meala. S Ireland
Cloppenburg 72 B3 Niedersachsen, NW Germany
Cloquet 23 G2 Minnesota, N USA
Cloud Peak 22 C3 mountain Wyoming, C USA
Clovis 27 E2 New Mexico, SW USA
Cluain Meala see Clonmel
Cluj-Napoca 86 B3 Ger. Klausenburg, Hung. Kolozsvár; prev. Cluj. Cluj, NW Romania
Clutha 129 B7 river South Island, NZ
Clyde 66 C4 river W Scotland, UK
Coari 40 D2 Amazonas, N Brazil
Coast Mountains 14 D4 Fr. Chaîne Côtière. Mountain range Canada/USA
Coast Ranges 24 A4 mountain range W USA
Coats Island 15 G3 island Nunavut, NE Canada
Coats Land 132 B2 physical region Antarctica
Coatzacoalcos 29 G4 var. Quetzalcoalco; prev. Puerto México. Veracruz-Llave, E Mexico
Cobán 30 B2 Alta Verapaz, C Guatemala
Cobar 127 C6 New South Wales, SE Australia
Cobija 39 E3 Pando, NW Bolivia
Coburg 73 C5 Bayern, SE Germany
Coca see Puerto Francisco de Orellana
Cochabamba 39 F4 hist. Oropeza. Cochabamba, C Bolivia
Cochin 110 C3 var. Kochi. Kerala, SW India
Cochinos, Bahía de 32 B2 Eng. Bay of Pigs. Bay SE Cuba
Cochrane 43 B7 Aisén, S Chile
Cochrane 16 C4 Ontario, S Canada
Cocibolca see Nicaragua, Lago de
Cockburn Town 33 E2 var. Grand Turk. dependent territory capital (Turks and Caicos Islands) Grand Turk Island, SE Turks and Caicos Islands
Cockpit Country, The 32 A4 physical region W Jamaica
Cocobeach 55 A5 Estuaire, NW Gabon
Coconino Plateau 26 B1 plain Arizona, SW USA
Coco, Río 31 E2 var. Río Wanki, Segoviao Wangkí. River Honduras/Nicaragua
Cocos Basin 102 C5 undersea feature E Indian Ocean
Cocos Island Ridge see Cocos Ridge
Cocos Islands 119 D5 island group E Indian Ocean
Cocos Ridge 13 C8 var. Cocos Island Ridge. Undersea feature E Pacific Ocean
Cod, Cape 19 G3 headland Massachusetts, NE USA
Codfish Island 129 A8 island SW NZ
Codlea 86 C4 Ger. Zeiden, Hung. Feketehalom. Braşov, C Romania
Cody 22 C2 Wyoming, C USA
Coeur d'Alene 24 C2 Idaho, NW USA
Coevorden 64 E2 Drenthe, NE Netherlands
Coffs Harbour 127 E6 New South Wales, SE Australia
Cognac 69 B5 anc. Compniacum. Charente, W France
Coiba, Isla de 31 E5 island SW Panama
Coihaique 43 B6 var. Coyhaique. Aisén, S Chile
Coimbatore 110 C3 Tamil Nādu, S India
Coimbra 70 B3 anc. Conimbria, Conimbriga. Coimbra, W Portugal
Coín 70 D5 Andalucía, S Spain
Coirib, Loch see Corrib, Lough
Colby 23 E4 Kansas, C USA
Colchester 67 E6 hist. Colneceaste, anc. Camulodunum. E England, UK
Col du Brenner see Brenner Pass
Coleman 27 F3 Texas, SW USA
Coleraine 66 B4 Ir. Cúil Raithin. N Northern Ireland, UK
Colesberg 56 C5 Northern Cape, C South Africa
Colima 28 D4 Colima, S Mexico
Coll 66 B3 island W Scotland, UK
College Station 27 G3 Texas, SW USA
Collie 125 A7 Western Australia
Colmar 68 E4 Ger. Kolmar. Haut-Rhin, NE France
Cöln see Köln
Cologne see Köln
Colombia 36 B3 off. Republic of Colombia. Country N South America
Colombian Basin 34 A1 undersea feature SW Caribbean Sea
Colombo 110 C4 country capital (Sri Lanka) Western Province, W Sri Lanka
Colón 31 G4 prev. Aspinwall. Colón, C Panama
Colonia Agrippina see Köln
Colón Ridge 13 B8 undersea feature E Pacific Ocean
Colorado 22 C4 off. State of Colorado; also known as Centennial State, Silver State. State C USA
Colorado City 27 F3 Texas, SW USA
Colorado Plateau 26 B1 plateau W USA
Colorado, Río 43 C5 river E Argentina
Colorado, Río see Colorado River
Colorado River 13 B5 var. Río Colorado. River Mexico/USA
Colorado River 27 G4 river Texas, SW USA
Colorado Springs 22 D5 Colorado, C USA
Columbia 24 B3 river Canada/USA
Columbia 21 E2 state capital South Carolina, SE USA
Columbia 19 E4 Maryland, NE USA
Columbia 23 G4 Missouri, C USA
Columbia 20 C1 Tennessee, S USA
Columbia Plateau 24 C3 plateau Idaho/Oregon, NW USA
Columbus 18 D4 state capital Ohio, N USA
Columbus 20 D2 Georgia, SE USA
Columbus 18 C4 Indiana, N USA
Columbus 20 C2 Mississippi, S USA
Columbus 23 F4 Nebraska, C USA
Colville Channel 128 D2 channel North Island, NZ
Colville River 14 D2 river Alaska, USA
Comacchio 74 C3 var. Commachio; anc. Comactium. Emilia-Romagna, N Italy
Comactium see Comacchio
Comalcalco 29 G4 Tabasco, SE Mexico
Coma Pedrosa, Pic de 69 A7 mountain NW Andorra
Comarapa 39 F4 Santa Cruz, C Bolivia
Comayagua 30 C2 Comayagua, W Honduras
Comer See see Como, Lago di
Comilla 113 G4 Ben. Kumillā. Chittagong, E Bangladesh
Comino 80 A5 Malt. Kemmuna. Island C Malta
Comitán 29 G5 var. Comitán de Domínguez. Chiapas, SE Mexico
Comitán de Domínguez see Comitán
Commachio see Comacchio
Commissioner's Point 20 A5 headland W Bermuda
Communism Peak see Kommunizm, Qullai
Como 74 B2 anc. Comum. Lombardia, N Italy
Comodoro Rivadavia 43 B6 Chubut, SE Argentina
Como, Lago di B2 var. Lario, Eng. Lake Como, Ger. Comer See. Lake N Italy
Como, Lake see Como, Lago di
Comoros 57 F2 off. Federal Islamic Republic of the Comoros, Fr. République Fédérale Islamique des Comores. Country W Indian Ocean
Compiègne 68 C3 Oise, N France
Compostella see Santiago
Comrat 86 D4 Rus. Komrat. S Moldova
Conakry 52 C4 country capital (Guinea) Conakry, SW Guinea
Concarneau 68 A3 Finistère, NW France
Concepción 42 D2 var. Villa Concepción. Concepción, C Paraguay
Concepción see La Concepción
Concepción 43 B5 Bío Bío, C Chile
Concepción 39 G3 Santa Cruz, E Bolivia
Concepción de la Vega see La Vega
Conchos, Río 28 D2 river C Mexico
Conchos, Río 26 D4 river NW Mexico
Concord 19 G3 state capital New Hampshire, NE USA
Concordia 42 D4 Entre Ríos, E Argentina
Concordia 23 E4 Kansas, C USA
Côn Đao 115 E7 var. Con Son. Island S Vietnam
Condate see Cosne-Cours-sur-Loire
Condega 30 D3 Estelí, NW Nicaragua
Congo 55 B5 off. Republic of the Congo, Fr. Moyen-Congo; prev. Middle Congo. Country C Africa
Congo 55 C6 off. Democratic Republic of Congo; prev. Zaire, Belgian Congo, Congo (Kinshasa). Country C Africa
Congo 55 C6 var. Kongo, Fr. Zaire. River C Africa
Congo Basin 55 C6 drainage basin W Dem. Rep. Congo
Connacht see Connaught
Connaught 67 A5 var. Connacht, Ir. Chonnacht, Cúige. Cultural region W Ireland
Connecticut 19 F3 off. State of Connecticut; also known as Blue Law State, Constitution State, Land of Steady Habits, Nutmeg State. State NE USA
Connecticut 19 G3 river Canada/USA
Conroe 27 G3 Texas, SW USA
Consolación del Sur 32 A2 Pinar del Río, W Cuba
Côn Son see Côn Đao
Constance see Konstanz
Constance, Lake B7 Ger. Bodensee. Lake C Europe
Constanța 86 D5 var. Küstendje, Eng. Constanza, Ger. Konstanza, Turk. Küstence. Constanța, SE Romania
Constantia see Konstanz
Constantine 49 E2 var. Qacentina, Ar. Qoussantîna. NE Algeria
Constantinople see İstanbul
Constanz see Konstanz
Constanza see Constanța
Coober Pedy 127 A5 South Australia
Cookeville 20 D1 Tennessee, S USA
Cook Islands 123 F4 territory in free association with NZ S Pacific Ocean
Cook, Mount 129 B6 prev. Aoraki, Aorangi. Mountain South Island, NZ
Cook Strait 129 D5 var. Raukawa. Strait NZ
Cooktown 126 D2 Queensland, NE Australia
Coolgardie 125 B6 Western Australia
Cooma 127 D7 New South Wales, SE Australia
Coon Rapids 23 F2 Minnesota, N USA
Cooper Creek 126 C4 var. Barcoo, Cooper's Creek. Seasonal river Queensland/South Australia
Cooper's Creek see Cooper Creek
Coos Bay 24 A3 Oregon, NW USA
Cootamundra 127 D6 New South Wales, SE Australia
Copacabana 39 E4 La Paz, W Bolivia
Copenhagen see København
Copiapó 42 B3 Atacama, N Chile
Copperas Cove 27 G3 Texas, SW USA
Coppermine see Kugluktuk
Coquimbo 42 B3 Coquimbo, N Chile
Corabia 86 B5 Olt, S Romania
Coral Harbour 15 G3 Southampton Island, Nunavut, NE Canada
Coral Sea 120 B3 sea SW Pacific Ocean
Coral Sea Islands 122 B4 Australian external territory SW Pacific Ocean
Corantijn Rivier see Courantyne River
Corcaigh see Cork
Corcovado, Golfo 43 B6 gulf S Chile
Cordele 20 D3 Georgia, SE USA
Cordillera Ibérica see Ibérico, Sistema
Cordoba see Córdoba
Córdoba 70 D4 var. Cordoba, Eng. Cordova; anc. Corduba. Andalucía, SW Spain
Córdoba 42 C3 Córdoba, C Argentina
Córdoba 29 F4 Veracruz-Llave, E Mexico
Cordova see Córdoba
Cordova 14 C3 Alaska, USA
Corduba see Córdoba
Corentyne River see Courantyne River
Corfu see Kérkyra
Coria 70 C3 Extremadura, W Spain
Corinth see Kórinthos
Corinth 20 C1 Mississippi, S USA
Corinth, Gulf of see Korinthiakós Kólpos
Corinthiacus Sinus see Korinthiakós Kólpos
Corinto 30 C3 Chinandega, NW Nicaragua
Cork 67 A6 Ir. Corcaigh. S Ireland
Çorlu 94 A2 Tekirdağ, NW Turkey
Corner Brook 17 G3 Newfoundland, Newfoundland and Labrador, E Canada
Corn Islands see Maíz, Islas del
Cornwallis Island 15 F2 island Nunavut, N Canada
Coro 36 C1 prev. Santa Ana de Coro. Falcón, NW Venezuela
Corocoro 39 F4 La Paz, W Bolivia
Coromandel 128 D2 Waikato, North Island, NZ
Coromandel Coast 110 D2 coast E India
Coromandel Peninsula 128 D2 peninsula North Island, NZ
Coronado, Bahía de 30 D5 bay S Costa Rica
Coronel Dorrego 43 C5 Buenos Aires, E Argentina
Coronel Oviedo 42 D2 Caaguazú, SE Paraguay
Corozal 30 C1 Corozal, N Belize
Corpus Christi 27 G4 Texas, SW USA

INDEX

Di Linh – El Gedaref

Di Linh *115 E6* Lâm Đông, S Vietnam
Dilli *see* Delhi
Dilli *see* Dili
Dillia *see* Dilia
Dilling *50 B4 var.* Ad Dalanj. Southern Kordofan, C Sudan
Dillon *22 B2* Montana, NW USA
Dilly *see* Dili
Dilolo *55 D7* Ngounié, S Gabon
Dimashq *97 B5 var.* Ash Shām, Esh Sham, *Eng.* Damascus, *Fr.* Damas, *It.* Damasco. *Country capital* (Syria) Dimashq, SW Syria
Dimitrovgrad *82 D3* Khaskovo, S Bulgaria
Dimitrovgrad *89 C6* Ul'yanovskaya Oblast', W Russian Federation
Dimovo *82 B1* Vidin, NW Bulgaria
Dinajpur *113 F3* Rajshahi, NW Bangladesh
Dinan *68 B3* Côtes d'Armor, NW France
Dinant *65 C7* Namur, S Belgium
Dinar *94 B4* Afyon, SW Turkey
Dinara *see* Dinaric Alps
Dinaric Alps *78 C4 var.* Dinara. *Mountain range* Bosnia and Herzegovina/Croatia
Dindigul *110 C3* Tamil Nādu, SE India
Dingle Bay *67 A6 Ir.* Bá an Daingin. *Bay* SW Ireland
Dinguiraye *52 C4* Haute-Guinée, N Guinea
Diourbel *52 B3* W Senegal
Dirē Dawa *51 D5* E Ethiopia
Dirk Hartog Island *125 A5 island* Western Australia
Disappointment, Lake *124 C4 salt lake* Western Australia
Dispur *113 G3* Assam, NE India
Divinópolis *41 F4* Minas Gerais, SE Brazil
Divo *52 D5* S Côte d'Ivoire
Diyarbakır *95 E4 var.* Diarbekr; *anc.* Amida. Diyarbakır, SE Turkey
Dizful *see* Dezfūl
Djajapura *see* Jayapura
Djakovica *see* Đakovica
Djakovo *see* Đakovo
Djambala *55 B6* Plateaux, C Congo
Djambi *see* Jambi
Djanet *49 E4 prev.* Fort Charlet. SE Algeria
Djéblé *see* Jablah
Djelfa *48 D2 var.* El Djelfa. N Algeria
Djéma *54 D4* Haut-Mbomou, E Central African Republic
Djérablous *see* Jarābulus
Djerba *see* Jerba, Île de
Djérem *54 B4 river* C Cameroon
Djevdjelija *see* Gevgelija
Djibouti *50 D4 off.* Republicof Djibouti, *var.* Jibuti; *prev.* French Somaliland, French Territory of the Afars and Issas, *Fr.* Côte Française des Somalis, Territoire Français des Afars et des Issas. *Country* E Africa
Djibouti *50 D4 var.* Jibuti. *Country capital* (Djibouti) E Djibouti
Djourab, Erg du *51 C2 dunes* N Chad
Djúpivogur *61 E5* Austurland, SE Iceland
Dnieper *59 F4 Bel.* Dnyapro, *Rus.* Dnepr, *Ukr.* Dnipro. *River* E Europe
Dnieper Lowland *87 E2 Bel.* Prydnyaprowskaya Nizina, *Ukr.* Prydniprovs'ka Nyzovyna. *Lowlands* Belarus/Ukraine
Dniester *59 E4 Rom.* Nistru, *Rus.* Dnestr, *Ukr.* Dnister; *anc.* Tyras. *River* Moldova/Ukraine
Dnipro *see* Dnieper
Dniprodzerzhyns'k *87 F3 Rus.* Dneprodzerzhinsk; *prev.* Kamenskoye. Dnipropetrovs'ka Oblast', E Ukraine
Dniprodzerzhyns'ke Vodoskhovyshche *87 F3 Rus.* Dneprodzerzhinskoye Vodokhranilishche. *Reservoir* C Ukraine
Dnipropetrovs'k *87 F3 Rus.* Dnepropetrovsk; *prev.* Yekaterinoslav. Dnipropetrovs'ka Oblast', E Ukraine
Dniprorudne *87 F3 Rus.* Dneprorudnoye. Zaporiz'ka Oblast', SE Ukraine
Doba *54 C4* Logone-Oriental, S Chad
Döbeln *72 D4* Sachsen, E Germany
Doberai, Jazirah *117 G4 Dut.* Vogelkop. *Peninsula* Irian Jaya, E Indonesia
Doboj *78 C3* Republika Srpska, N Bosnia and Herzegovina
Dobre Miasto *76 D2 Ger.* Guttstadt. Warmińsko-Mazurskie, NE Poland
Dobrich *82 E1 Rom.* Bazargic; *prev.* Tolbukhin. Dobrich, NE Bulgaria
Dobrush *85 D7* Homyel'skaya Voblasts', SE Belarus
Dodecánese *see* Dodekánisos
Dodekánisos *83 D6 var.* Nóties Sporádes, *Eng.* Dodecanese; *prev.* Dhodhekánisos. *Island group* SE Greece
Dodge City *23 E5* Kansas, C USA
Dodoma *47 D5 country capital* (Tanzania) Dodoma, C Tanzania
Dodoma *51 C7 region* C Tanzania
Dogana *74 E1* NE San Marino
Dōgo *109 B6 island* Oki-shotō, SW Japan
Dogondoutchi *53 F3* Dosso, SW Niger
Doğubayazıt *95 F3* Ağrı, E Turkey
Doğu Karadeniz Dağları *95 E3 var.* Anadolu Dağları. *Mountain range* NE Turkey
Doha *see* Ad Dawḩah
Doire *see* Londonderry
Dokkum *64 D1* Friesland, N Netherlands
Dokuchayevs'k *87 G3 var.* Dokuchayevsk. Donets'ka Oblast', SE Ukraine
Dokuchayevsk *see* Dokuchayevs'k
Doldrums Fracture Zone *44 C4 tectonic feature* W Atlantic Ocean
Dôle *68 D4* Jura, E France
Dolisie *55 B6 prev.* Loubomo. Le Niari, S Congo
Dolomites *see* Dolomitiche, Alpi
Dolomiti *see* Dolomitiche, Alpi
Dolomitiche, Alpi *74 C1 var.* Dolomiti, *Eng.* Dolomites. *Mountain range* NE Italy
Dolores *42 D4* Buenos Aires, E Argentina
Dolores *30 B1* Petén, N Guatemala
Dolores *42 D4* Soriano, SW Uruguay
Dolores Hidalgo *29 E4 var.* Ciudad de Dolores Hidalgo. Guanajuato, C Mexico
Dolyna *86 B2 Rus.* Dolina. Ivano-Frankivs'ka Oblast', W Ukraine
Dolyns'ka *87 F3 Rus.* Dolinskaya. Kirovohrads'ka Oblast', S Ukraine
Domachëvo *see* Damachava
Domaczewo *see* Damachava
Dombås *63 B5* Oppland, S Norway
Domel Island *see* Letsôk-aw Kyun
Domeyko *42 B3* Atacama, N Chile
Dominica *33 H4 off.* Commonwealth of Dominica. *Country* E West Indies
Dominica Channel *see* Martinique Passage
Dominican Republic *33 E2 country* C West Indies
Domokós *83 B5 var.* Dhomokós. Stereá Ellás, C Greece
Don *89 B6 var.* Duna, Tanais. *River* SW Russian Federation
Donau *see* Danube
Donauwörth *73 C6* Bayern, S Germany
Don Benito *70 C3* Extremadura, W Spain
Doncaster *67 D5 anc.* Danum. N England, UK
Dondo *56 B1* Cuanza Norte, NW Angola
Donegal *67 B5 Ir.* Dún na nGall. NW Ireland
Donegal Bay *67 A5 Ir.* Bá Dhún na nGall. *Bay* NW Ireland
Donets *87 G2 var.* Sivers'kyy Donets', *Rus.* Severskiy Donets. Serra Acaraí. *river* Russian Federation/Ukraine
Donets'k *87 G3 Rus.* Donetsk; *prev.* Stalino. Donets'ka Oblast', E Ukraine
Dongfang *106 B7 var.* Basuo. Hainan, S China
Dongguan *106 C6* Guangdong, S China
Đông Hà *114 E4* Quang Tri, C Vietnam
Đông Hơi *114 D4* Quang Binh, C Vietnam
Dongliao *see* Liaoyuan
Dongola *50 B3 var.* Donqola, Dunqulah. Northern, N Sudan
Dongou *55 C5* La Likouala, NE Congo
Dongting Hu *106 C5 var.* Tung-t'ing Hu. *Lake* S China
Donji Vakuf *var.* Srbobran, Federacija Bosna I Hercegovina, N Serbia and Montenegro (Yugo.)
Donostia-San Sebastián *71 E1* País Vasco, N Spain
Donqola *see* Dongola
Doolow *51 D5* E Ethiopia
Doornik *see* Tournai
Door Peninsula *18 C2 peninsula* Wisconsin, N USA
Dooxo Nugaaleed *51 E5 var.* Nogal Valley. *Valley* E Somalia
Dordogne *69 B5 cultural region* SW France
Dordogne *69 B5 river* W France
Dordrecht *64 C4 var.* Dordt, Dort. Zuid-Holland, SW Netherlands
Dordt *see* Dordrecht
Dorohoi *86 C3* Botoşani, NE Romania
Dorotea *62 C4* Västerbotten. N Sweden
Dorre Island *125 A5 island* Western Australia
Dort *see* Dordrecht
Dortmund *72 A4* Nordrhein-Westfalen, W Germany
Dos Hermanas *70 C4* Andalucía, S Spain
Dospad Dagh *see* Rhodope Mountains
Dospat *82 C3* Smolyan, S Bulgaria
Dothan *20 D3* Alabama, S USA
Dotnuva *84 B4* Kėdainiai, C Lithuania
Douai *68 C2 prev.* Douay, *anc.* Duacum. Nord, N France
Douala *55 A5 var.* Duala. Littoral, W Cameroon
Douglas *67 C5 dependent territory capital* (Isle of Man) E Isle of Man
Douglas *26 C3* Arizona, SW USA
Douglas *22 D3* Wyoming, C USA
Douro *70 B2 Sp.* Duero. *River* Portugal/Spain *see also* Duero
Dover *67 E7 Fr.* Douvres; *Lat.* Dubris Portus. SE England, UK
Dover *19 F4 state capital* Delaware, NE USA
Dover, Strait of *68 C2 var.* Straits of Dover, *Fr.* Pas de Calais. *Strait* England, UK/France
Dover, Straits of *see* Dover, Strait of
Dovrefjell *63 B5 plateau* S Norway
Downpatrick *67 B5 Ir.* Dún Pádraig. SE Northern Ireland, UK
Dōzen *109 B6 island* Oki-shotō, SW Japan
Drač *see* Durrës
Drachten *64 D2* Friesland, N Netherlands
Drăgăşani *86 B5* Vâlcea, SW Romania
Dragoman *82 B2* Sofiya, W Bulgaria
Dra, Hamada du *48 C3 var.* Hammada du Drâa, Haut Plateau du Dra. *Plateau* W Algeria
Drahichyn *85 B6 Pol.* Drohiczyn Poleski, *Rus.* Drogichin. Brestskaya Voblasts', SW Belarus
Drakensberg *56 D5 mountain range* Lesotho/South Africa
Drake Passage *35 B8 passage* Atlantic Ocean/Pacific Ocean
Dralfa *82 D2* Tŭrgovishte, N Bulgaria
Dráma *82 C3 var.* Dhráma. Anatolikí Makedonía kai Thráki, NE Greece
Drammen *63 B6* Buskerud, S Norway
Drau *see* Drava
Drava *78 C3 var.* Drau, *Eng.* Drave, *Hung.* Dráva. *River* C Europe *see also* Drau
Dráva *see* Drava
Drave *see* Drava
Drawsko Pomorskie *76 B3 Ger.* Dramburg. Zachodniopomorskie, NW Poland
Drépano, Akrotírio *82 C4 var.* Akra Dhrepanon. *Headland* N Greece
Dresden *72 D4* Sachsen, E Germany
Drin *see* Drinit, Lumi i
Drina *78 C3 river* Bosnia and Herzegovina /Serbia and Montenegro (Yugo.)
Drinit, Lumi i *79 D5 var.* Drin. *River* NW Albania
Drobeta-Turnu Severin *86 B5 prev.* Turnu Severin. Mehedinţi, SW Romania
Drogheda *67 B5 Ir.* Droichead Átha. NE Ireland
Drohobych *86 B2 Pol.* Drohobycz, *Rus.* Drogobych. L'vivs'ka Oblast', NW Ukraine
Droichead Átha *see* Drogheda
Drôme *69 D5 cultural region* SE France
Dronning Maud Land *132 B2 physical region* Antarctica
Drummondville *17 E4* Quebec, SE Canada
Druskininkai *85 B5 Pol.* Druskienniki. Druskininkai, S Lithuania
Dryden *16 B3* Ontario, C Canada
Drysa *85 D5 Rus.* Drissa. *River* N Belarus
Duala *see* Douala
Dubai *see* Dubayy
Dubăsari *86 D3 Rus.* Dubossary. NE Moldova
Dubawnt *15 F4 river* Northwest Territories/Nunavut, NW Canada
Dubayy *98 D4 Eng.* Dubai. Dubayy, NE UAE
Dubbo *127 D6* New South Wales, SE Australia
Dublin *67 B5 Ir.* Baile Átha Cliath; *anc.* Eblana. *Country capital* (Ireland), E Ireland
Dublin *21 E2* Georgia, SE USA
Dubno *86 C2* Rivnens'ka Oblast', NW Ukraine
Dubrovnik *79 B5 It.* Ragusa. Dubrovnik-Neretva, SE Croatia
Dubuque *23 G3* Iowa, C USA
Dudelange *65 D8 var.* Forge du Sud, *Ger.* Dudelingen. Luxembourg, S Luxembourg
Dudelingen *see* Dudelange
Duero *70 D2 Port.* Douro. *River* Portugal/Spain *see also* Douro
Duesseldorf *see* Düsseldorf
Duffel *65 C5* Antwerpen, C Belgium
Dugi Otok *78 A4 var.* Isola Grossa, *It.* Isola Lunga. *Island* W Croatia
Duisburg *72 A4 prev.* Duisburg-Hamborn. Nordrhein-Westfalen, W Germany
Duiven *64 D4* Gelderland, E Netherlands
Duk Faiwil *51 B5* Jonglei, SE Sudan
Dulan *104 D4 var.* Qagan Us. Qinghai, C China
Dulce, Golfo *31 E5 gulf* S Costa Rica
Dülmen *72 A4* Nordrhein-Westfalen, W Germany
Dulovo *82 E1* Silistra, NE Bulgaria
Duluth *23 G2* Minnesota, N USA
Dūmā *97 B5 Fr.* Douma. Dimashq, SW Syria
Dumas *27 E1* Texas, SW USA
Dumfries *66 C4* S Scotland, UK
Dumont d'Urville *132 C4 French research station* Antarctica
Dumyâț *50 B1 Eng.* Damietta. N Egypt
Duna *see* Danube
Duna *see* Don
Dunaj *see* Danube
Dunaújváros *77 C7 prev.* Dunapentele, Sztálinváros. Fejér, C Hungary
Dunav *see* Danube
Dunavska Ravnina *82 C2 Eng.* Danubian Plain. *Plain* N Bulgaria
Duncan *27 G2* Oklahoma, C USA
Dundalk *67 B5 Ir.* Dún Dealgan. NE Ireland
Dún Dealgan *see* Dundalk
Dundee *66 C4* E Scotland, UK
Dundee *56 D4* KwaZulu/Natal, E South Africa
Dunedin *129 B7* Otago, South Island, NZ
Dunfermline *66 C4* C Scotland, UK
Dungu *55 E5* Orientale, NE Dem. Rep. Congo
Dungun *116 B3 var.* Kuala Dungun. Terengganu, Peninsular Malaysia
Dunkerque *68 C2 Eng.* Dunkirk, *Flem.* Duinekerke, *prev.* Dunquerque. Nord, N France
Dún Laoghaire *67 B6 Eng.* Dunleary; *prev.* Kingstown. E Ireland
Dún na nGall *see* Donegal
Dún Pádraig *see* Downpatrick
Dunqulah *see* Dongola
Dunărea *see* Danube
Dupnitsa *82 C2 prev.* Marek, Stanke Dimitrov. Kyustendil, W Bulgaria
Duqm *99 E5 var.* Daqm. E Oman
Durance *69 D6 river* SE France
Durango *28 D3 var.* Victoria de Durango. Durango, W Mexico
Durango *22 C5* Colorado, C USA
Durankulak *82 E1 Rom.* Răcari; *prev.* Blatnitsa, Duranulac. Dobrich, NE Bulgaria
Durant *27 G2* Oklahoma, C USA
Durazzo *see* Durrës
Durban *56 D4 var.* Port Natal. KwaZulu/Natal, E South Africa
Durbe *84 B3 Ger.* Durben. Liepāja, W Latvia
Durg *113 E4 prev.* Drug. Madhya Pradesh, C India
Durham *67 D5 hist.* Dunholme. N England, UK
Durham *21 F1* North Carolina, SE USA
Durostorum *see* Silistra
Durrës *79 C6 var.* Durresi, Dursi, *It.* Durazzo, *SCr.* Drač, *Turk.* Draç. Durrës, W Albania
Durrësi *see* Durrës
Dursi *see* Durrës
Durūz, Jabal ad *97 C5 mountain* SW Syria
D'Urville Island *128 C4 island* C NZ
Dusa Mareb *see* Dhuusa Marreeb
Dusa Marreb *see* Dhuusa Marreeb
Dushanbe *101 E3 var.* Dyushambe; *prev.* Stalinabad, *Taj.* Stalinobod. *Country capital* (Tajikistan) W Tajikistan
Düsseldorf *72 A4 var.* Duesseldorf. Nordrhein-Westfalen, W Germany
Dŭsti *101 E3 Rus.* Dusti. SW Tajikistan
Dutch Harbor *14 B3* Unalaska Island, Alaska, USA
Dutch New Guinea *see* Irian Jaya
Duzdab *see* Zāhedān
Dvina *see* Severnaya Dvina
Dvina Bay *see* Cheshskaya Guba
Dyanev *see* Deynau
Dyersburg *20 C1*Tennessee, S USA
Dyushambe *see* Dushanbe
Dza Chu *see* Mekong
Dzerzhinsk *89 C5* Nizhegorodskaya Oblast', W Russian Federation
Dzhalal-Abad *101 F2 Kir.* Jalal-Abad. Dzhalal-Abadskaya Oblast', W Kyrgyzstan
Dzhambul *see* Taraz
Dzhankoy *87 F4* Respublika Krym, S Ukraine
Dzhelandy *101 F3* SE Tajikistan
Dzhergalan *101 G2 Kir.* Jyrgalan. Issyk-Kul'skaya Oblast', NE Kyrgyzstan
Dzhugdzhur, Khrebet *93 G3 mountain range* E Russian Federation
Dzhusaly *92 B4 Kaz.* Zholsaly. Kyzylorda, SW Kazakhstan
Działdowo *76 D3* Warmińsko-Mazurskie, NE Poland
Dzuunmod *105 E2* Töv, C Mongolia

E

Eagle Pass *27 F4* Texas, SW USA
East Açores Fracture Zone *see* East Azores Fracture Zone
East Antarctica *see* Greater Antarctica
East Australian Basin *see* Tasman Basin
East Azores Fracture Zone *44 C3 var.* East Açores Fracture Zone. *Tectonic feature* E Atlantic Ocean
Eastbourne *67 E7* SE England, UK
East Cape *128 E3 headland* North Island, NZ
East China Sea *103 E2 Chin.* Dong Hai. *Sea* W Pacific Ocean
Easter Fracture Zone *131 G4 tectonic feature* E Pacific Ocean
Easter Island *131 F4 var.* Rapa Nui, *island* E Pacific Ocean
Eastern Desert *46 D3 var.* Aş Şahrā' ash Sharqīyah, *Eng.* Arabian Desert, Eastern Desert. *Desert* E Egypt
Eastern Ghats *102 B3 mountain range* SE India
Eastern Sayans *93 E4 Mong.* Dzüün Soyonï Nuruu, *Rus.* Vostochnyy Sayan. *Mountain range* Mongolia/Russian Federation
East Falkland *43 D8 var.* Isla Soledad. *Island* E Falkland Islands
East Grand Forks *23 E1* Minnesota, N USA
East Indiaman Ridge *119 D6 undersea feature* E Indian Ocean
East Indies *130 A3 island group* SE Asia
East Kilbride *66 C4* S Scotland, UK
East Korea Bay *107 E3 bay* E North Korea
Eastleigh *67 D7* S England, UK
East London *56 D5 Afr.* Oos-Londen; *prev.* Emonti, Port Rex. Eastern Cape, S South Africa
Eastmain *16 D3 river* Quebec, C Canada
East Mariana Basin *120 B1 undersea feature* W Pacific Ocean
East Novaya Zemlya Trench *90 C1 var.* Novaya Zemlya Trench. *Undersea feature* W Kara Sea
East Pacific Rise *131 F1 undersea feature* E Pacific Ocean
East Saint Louis *18 B4* Illinois, N USA
East Scotia Basin *45 C7 undersea feature* SE Scotia Sea
East Sea *see* Japan, Sea of
East Siberian Sea *see* Vostochno-Sibirskoye More
East Timor *117 F5 var.* Loro Sae *prev.* Portuguese Timor, Timor Timur, , *Country* SE Asia
Eau Claire *18 A2* Wisconsin, N USA
Eauripik Rise *120 B2 undersea feature* W Pacific Ocean
Ebensee *73 D6* Oberösterreich, N Austria
Eberswalde-Finow *72 D3* Brandenburg, E Germany
Ebetsu *108 D2 var.* Ebetu. Hokkaidō, NE Japan
Ebetu *see* Ebetsu
Ebolowa *55 A5* Sud, S Cameroon
Ebon Atoll *122 D2 var.* Epoon. *Atoll* Ralik Chain, S Marshall Islands
Ebro *71 E2 river* NE Spain
Ebusus *see* Eivissa
Ech Cheliff *see* Chlef
Ech Chleff *see* Chlef
Echo Bay *15 E3* Northwest Territories, NW Canada
Echt *65 D5* Limburg, SE Netherlands
Ecija *70 D4 anc.* Astigi. Andalucía, SW Spain
Ecuador *38 B1 off.* Republic of Ecuador. *Country* NW South America
Ed Da'ein *50 A4* Southern Darfur, W Sudan
Ed Damazin *50 C4 var.* Ad Damazīn. Blue Nile, E Sudan
Ed Damer *50 C3 var.* Ad Damar, Ad Dāmir. River Nile, NE Sudan
Ed Debba *50 B3* Northern, N Sudan
Ede *64 D4* Gelderland, C Netherlands
Ede *53 F5* Osun, SW Nigeria
Edéa *55 A5* Littoral, SW Cameroon
Edeyin Murzuq *see* Murzuq, Idhān
Edfu *see* Idfu
Edgeøya *61 G2 island* S Svalbard
Edgware *67 A7* SE England, UK
Edinburg *27 G5* Texas, SW USA
Edinburgh *66 C4 admin capital* S Scotland, UK
Edirne *94 A2 Eng.* Adrianople; *anc.* Adrianopolis, Hadrianopolis. Edirne, NW Turkey
Edmonds *24 B2* Washington, NW USA
Edmonton *15 E5* Alberta, SW Canada
Edmundston *17 E4* New Brunswick, SE Canada
Edna *27 G4* Texas, SW USA
Edolo *74 B1* Lombardia, N Italy
Edremit *94 A3* Balıkesir, NW Turkey
Edward, Lake *55 E5 var.* Albert Edward Nyanza, Edward Nyanza, Lac Idi Amin, Lake Rutanzige. *Lake* Uganda/Zaire
Edward Nyanza *see* Edward, Lake
Edwards Plateau *27 F3 plain* Texas, SW USA
Eeklo *65 B5 var.* Eekloo. Oost-Vlaanderen, NW Belgium
Edzo *53 E4 prev.* Rae-Edzo. Northwest Territories, NW Canada
Eekloo *see* Eeklo
Eersel *65 C5* Noord-Brabant, S Netherlands
Efate *122 D4 var.* Éfaté *Fr.* Vaté; *prev.* Sandwich Island. *Island* C Vanuatu
Effingham *18 B4* Illinois, N USA
Eforie Sud *86 D5* Constanţa, E Romania
Efstrátios, Ágios *82 D4 var.* Ayios Evstratios. *Island* E Greece
Egadi, Isole *75 B7 island group* S Italy
Eger *77 D6 Ger.* Erlau. Heves, NE Hungary
Egeria Fracture Zone *119 C5 tectonic feature* W Indian Ocean
Éghezèe *65 C6* Namur, C Belgium
Egina *see* Aígina
Egio *see* Aígio
Egmont, Mount *see* Taranaki, Mount
Egmont, Cape *128 C4 headland* North Island, NZ
Egoli *see* Johannesburg
Egypt *50 B2 off.* Arab Republic of Egypt, *Ar.* Jumhūrīyah Mişr al 'Arabīyah; *prev.* United Arab Republic, *anc.* Aegyptus. *Country* NE Africa
Eibar *71 E1* País Vasco, N Spain
Eibergen *64 E3* Gelderland, E Netherlands
Eidfjord *63 A5* Hordaland, S Norway
Eier-Berg *see* Suur Munamägi
Eifel *73 A5 plateau* W Germany
Eiger *73 B7 mountain* C Switzerland
Eigg *66 B3 island* W Scotland, UK
Eight Degree Channel *110 B3 channel* India/Maldives
Eighty Mile Beach *124 B4 beach* Western Australia
Eijsden *65 D6* Limburg, SE Netherlands
Eilat *see* Elat
Eindhoven *65 D5* Noord Brabant, S Netherlands
Eipel *see* Ipel'
Eipel *see* Ipoly
Eisenhüttenstadt *72 D4* Brandenburg, E Germany
Eisenstadt *73 E6* Burgenland, E Austria
Eisleben *72 C4* Sachsen-Anhalt, C Germany
Eivissa *71 G3 var.* Iviza, *Cast.* Ibiza; *anc.* Ebusus. *Island* Islas Baleares, Spain, W Mediterranean Sea
Eivissa *71 G3 var.* Iviza, *Cast.* Ibiza; *anc.* Ebusus. Eivissa, Spain, W Mediterranean Sea
Ejea de los Caballeros *71 E2* Aragón, NE Spain
Ejin Qi *104 D3 var.* Dalain Hob. Nei Mongol Zizhiqu, N China
Ekapa *see* Cape Town
Ekiatapskiy Khrebet *93 G1 mountain range* NE Russian Federation
El 'Alamein *50 B1 var.* Al 'Alamayn. N Egypt
El Asnam *see* Chlef
Elat *97 B8 var.* Eilat, Elath. Southern, S Israel
Elat, Gulf of *see* Aqaba, Gulf of
Elath *see* Al 'Aqabah
Elath *see* Elat
El'Atrun *50 B3* Northern Darfur, NW Sudan
Elâzığ *95 E3 var.* Elaziz. Elâzığ, E Turkey
Elâziz *see* Elâzığ
Elba, Isola d' *74 B4 island* Archipelago Toscano, C Italy
Elbasan *79 D6 var.* Elbasani. Elbasan, C Albania
Elbasani *see* Elbasan
Elbe *58 D3 Cz.* Labe. *River* Czech Republic/Germany
El Beni *see* Beni
Elbert, Mount *22 C4 mountain* Colorado, C USA
Elbing *see* Elbląg
Elbląg *76 C2 var.* Elblag, *Ger.* Elbing. Warmińsko-Mazurskie, NE Poland
El Boulaida *see* Blida
El'brus *89 A8 var.* Gora El'brus. *Mountain* SW Russian Federation
El Burgo de Osma *71 E2* Castilla-León, C Spain
El Cajon *25 C8* California, W USA
El Calafate *43 B7 var.* Calafate. Santa Cruz, S Argentina
El Callao *37 E2* Bolívar, E Venezuela
El Campo *27 G4* Texas, SW USA
El Carmen de Bolívar *36 B2* Bolívar, NW Colombia
El Centro *25 D8* California, W USA
Elche *71 F4 var.* Elx-Elche; *anc.* Ilici, *Lat.* Illicis. País Valenciano, E Spain
Elda *71 F4* País Valenciano, E Spain
El Djazaïr *see* Alger
El Djelfa *see* Djelfa
El Dorado *20 B2* Arkansas, C USA
El Dorado *37 F2* Bolívar, E Venezuela
El Dorado *23 F5* Kansas, C USA
El Dorado *28 C3* Sinaloa, C Mexico
Eldorado *42 E3* Misiones, NE Argentina
Eldoret *51 C6* Rift Valley, W Kenya
Elektrostal' *89 B5* Moskovskaya Oblast', W Russian Federation
Elemi Triangle *51 B5 disputed region* Kenya/Sudan
Elephant Butte Reservoir *26 C2 reservoir* New Mexico, SW USA
Eleuthera Island *32 C1 island* N Bahamas
El Fasher *50 A4 var.* Al Fāshir. Northern Darfur, W Sudan
El Ferrol *see* Ferrol
El Ferrol del Caudillo *see* Ferrol
El Gedaref *see* Gedaref

INDEX

Fontainebleau – Gljøvik

Fontainebleau *68 C3* Seine-et-Marne, N France
Fontenay-le-Comte *68 B4* Vendée, NW France
Fontvieille *69 B8* SW Monaco
Fonyód *77 C7* Somogy, W Hungary
Foochow *see* Fuzhou
Forchheim *73 C5* Bayern, SE Germany
Forel, Mont *60 D4 mountain* SE Greenland
Forfar *66 C3* E Scotland, UK
Forge du Sud *see* Dudelange
Forlì *74 C3 anc.* Forum Livii. Emilia-Romagna, N Italy
Formentera *71 G4 anc.* Ophiusa, *Lat.* Frumentum. *Island* Islas Baleares, Spain, W Mediterranean Sea
Formosa *42 D2* Formosa, NE Argentina
Formosa, Serra *41 E3 mountain range* C Brazil
Formosa Strait *see* Taiwan Strait
Forrest City *20 B1* Arkansas, C USA
Fort Albany *16 C3* Ontario, C Canada
Fortaleza *41 G2 prev.* Ceará. *State capital* Ceará, NE Brazil
Fortaleza *39 F2* Pando, N Bolivia
Fort-Bayard *see* Zhanjiang
Fort-Cappolani *see* Tidjikja
Fort Collins *22 D4* Colorado, C USA
Fort Davis *27 E3* Texas, SW USA
Fort-de-France *33 H4 prev.* Fort-Royal. *Dependent territory capital* (Martinique) W Martinique
Fort Dodge *23 F3* Iowa, C USA
Fortescue River *124 A4 river* Western Australia
Fort Frances *16 B4* Ontario, S Canada
Fort Good Hope *15 E3 var.* Good Hope. Northwest Territories, NW Canada
Fort Gouraud *see* Fdérik
Forth *66 C4 river* C Scotland, UK
Forth, Firth of *66 C4 estuary* E Scotland, UK
Fort-Lamy *see* Ndjamena
Fort Lauderdale *21 F5* Florida, SE USA
Fort Liard *15 E4 var.* Liard. Northwest Territories, W Canada
Fort Madison *23 G4* Iowa, C USA
Fort McMurray *15 E4* Alberta, C Canada
Fort McPherson *11 D3 var.* McPherson. Northwest Territories, NW Canada
Fort Morgan *22 D4* Colorado, C USA
Fort Myers *21 E5* Florida, SE USA
Fort Nelson *15 E4* British Columbia, W Canada
Fort Peck Lake *22 C1 reservoir* Montana, NW USA
Fort Pierce *21 F4* Florida, SE USA
Fort Providence *15 E4 var.* Providence. Northwest Territories, W Canada
Fort St.John *15 E4* British Columbia, W Canada
Fort Scott *23 F5* Kansas, C USA
Fort Severn *16 C2* Ontario, C Canada
Fort-Shevchenko *92 A4* Mangistau, W Kazakhstan
Fort Simpson *15 E4 var.* Simpson. Northwest Territories, W Canada
Fort Smith *15 E4 district capital* Northwest Territories, W Canada
Fort Smith *20 B1* Arkansas, C USA
Fort Stockton *27 E3* Texas, SW USA
Fort-Trinquet *see* Bîr Mogreïn
Fort Vermilion *15 E4* Alberta, W Canada
Fort Walton Beach *20 C3* Florida, SE USA
Fort Wayne *18 C4* Indiana, N USA
Fort William *66 C3* N Scotland, UK
Fort Worth *27 G2* Texas, SW USA
Fort Yukon *14 D3* Alaska, USA
Fougamou *55 A6* Ngounié, C Gabon
Fougères *68 B3* Ille-et-Vilaine, NW France
Fou-hsin *see* Fuxin
Foulwind, Cape *129 B5 headland* South Island, NZ
Foumban *54 A4* Ouest, NW Cameroon
Fou-shan *see* Fushun
Foveaux Strait *129 A8 strait* S NZ
Foxe Basin *15 G3 sea* Nunavut, N Canada
Fox Glacier *129 B6* West Coast, South Island, NZ
Fox Mine *15 F4* Manitoba, C Canada
Fraga *71 F2* Aragón, NE Spain
Fram Basin *133 C3 var.* Amundsen Basin. *Undersea feature* Arctic Ocean
France *68 B4 off.* French Republic, *It./Sp.* Francia; *prev.* Gaul, Gaule, *Lat.* Gallia. *Country* W Europe
Franceville *55 B6 var.* Massoukou, Masuku. Haut-Ogooué, E Gabon
Francfort prev *see* Frankfurt am Main
Franche-Comté *68 D4 cultural region* E France
Francis Case, Lake *23 E3 reservoir* South Dakota, N USA
Francisco Escárcega *29 G4* Campeche, SE Mexico
Francistown *56 D3* North East, NE Botswana
Franconian Jura *see* Fränkische Alb
Frankenalb *see* Fränkische Alb
Frankenstein *see* Ząbkowice Śląskie
Frankenstein in Schlesien *see* Ząbkowice Śląskie
Frankfort *18 C5 state capital* Kentucky, S USA
Frankfort on the Main *see* Frankfurt am Main
Frankfurt *see* Frankfurt am Main
Frankfurt am Main *73 B5 var.* Frankfurt, *Fr.* Francfort; prev. *Eng.* Frankfort on the Main. Hessen, SW Germany
Frankfurt an der Oder *72 D3* Brandenburg, E Germany
Fränkische Alb *73 C6 var.* Frankenalb, *Eng.* Franconian Jura. *Mountain range* S Germany
Franklin *20 C1* Tennessee, S USA
Franklin D.Roosevelt Lake *24 C1 reservoir* Washington, NW USA
Frantsa-Iosifa, Zemlya *92 D1 Eng.* Franz Josef Land. *Island group* N Russian Federation
Franz Josef Land *see* Frantsa-Iosifa, Zemlya
Fraserburgh *66 D3* NE Scotland, UK
Fraser Island *126 E4 var.* Great Sandy Island. *Island* Queensland, E Australia
Fredericksburg *19 E5* Virginia, NE USA
Fredericton *17 F4* New Brunswick, SE Canada
Frederikshåb *see* Paamiut
Fredrikstad *63 B6* Østfold, S Norway
Freeport *32 C1* Grand Bahama Island, N Bahamas
Freeport *27 H4* Texas, SW USA
Freetown *52 C4 country capital* (Sierra Leone) W Sierra Leone
Freiburg *see* Freiburg im Breisgau
Freiburg im Breisgau *73 A6 var.* Freiburg, *Fr.* Fribourg-en-Brisgau. Baden-Württemberg, SW Germany
Fremantle *125 A6* Western Australia
Fremont *23 F4* Nebraska, C USA
French Guiana *37 H3 var.* Guiana, Guyane. *French overseas department* N South America
French Polynesia *121 F4 French overseas territory* C Polynesia
French Southern and Antarctic Territories *119 B7 Fr.* Terres Australes et Antarctiques Françaises. *French overseas territory* S Indian Ocean
Fresnillo *28 D3 var.* Fresnillo de González Echeverría. Zacatecas, C Mexico
Fresnillo de González Echeverría *see* Fresnillo
Fresno *25 C6* California, W USA
Frías *42 C3* Catamarca, N Argentina
Fribourg-en-Brisgau *see* Freiburg im Breisgau
Friedrichshafen *73 B7* Baden-Württemberg, S Germany
Frobisher Bay *60 B3 inlet* Baffin Island, Northwest Territories, NE Canada
Frohavet *62 B4 sound* C Norway
Frome, Lake *127 B6 salt lake* South Australia
Frontera *29 G4* Tabasco, SE Mexico
Frontignan *69 C6* Hérault, S France
Frostviken *see* Kvarnbergsvattnet
Frøya *62 A4 island* W Norway
Frunze *see* Bishkek
Frýdek-Místek *77 C5 Ger.* Friedek-Mistek. Ostravský Kraj, E Czech Republic
Fu-chien *see* Fujian
Fu-chou *see* Fuzhou
Fuengirola *70 D5* Andalucía, S Spain
Fuerte Olimpo *42 D2 var.* Olimpo. Alto Paraguay, NE Paraguay
Fuerte, Río *26 C5 river* C Mexico
Fuerteventura *48 B3 island* Islas Canarias, Spain, NE Atlantic Ocean
Fuhkien *see* Fujian
Fu-hsin *see* Fuxin
Fuji *109 D6 var.* Huzi. Shizuoka, Honshu, S Japan
Fujian *106 D6 var.* Fu-chien, Fuhkien, Fujian Sheng, Fukien, Min. Admin. region *province* SE China
Fujian Sheng *see* Fujian
Fuji-san *109 C6 var.* Fujiyama, *Eng.* Mount Fuji. *Mountain* Honshū, SE Japan
Fujiyama *see* Fuji-san
Fukang *104 C2* Xinjiang Uygur Zizhiqu, W China
Fukien *see* Fujian
Fukui *109 C6 var.* Hukui. Fukui, Honshu, SW Japan
Fukuoka *109 A7 var.* Hukuoka; *hist.* Najima. Fukuoka, Kyūshū, SW Japan
Fukushima *108 D4 var.* Hukusima. Fukushima, Honshū, C Japan
Fulda *73 B5* Hessen, C Germany
Funafuti *see* Fongafale
Funafuti Atoll *123 E3 atoll* C Tuvalu
Funchal *48 A2* Madeira, Portugal, NE Atlantic Ocean
Fundy, Bay of *17 F5 bay* Canada/USA
Furnes *see* Veurne
Fürth *73 C5* Bayern, S Germany
Furukawa *108 D4 var.* Hurukawa. Miyagi, Honshū, C Japan
Fushun *106 D3 var.* Fou-shan, Fu-shun. Liaoning, NE China
Fu-shun *see* Fushun
Fusin *see* Fuxin
Füssen *73 C7* Bayern, S Germany
Futog *78 D3* Serbia, NW Serbia and Montenegro (Yugo.)
Futuna, Île *123 E4 island* S Wallis and Futuna
Fuxin *106 D3 var.* Fou-hsin, Fu-hsin, Fusin. Liaoning, NE China
Fuzhou *106 D6 var.* Foochow, Fu-chou. Fujian, SE China
Fuzhou *see* Linchuan
Fyn *63 B8 Ger.* Fünen. *Island* C Denmark
Fyzabad *see* Feyzābād

G

Gaafu Alifu Atoll *see* North Huvadhu Atoll
Gaafu Dhaalu Atoll *see* South Huvadhu Atoll
Gaalkacyo *51 E5 var.* Galka'yo, *It.* Galcaio. Mudug, C Somalia
Gabela *56 B2* Cuanza Sul, W Angola
Gabès *49 E2 var.* Qābis. E Tunisia
Gabès, Golfe de *49 F2 Ar.* Khalīj Qābis. *Gulf* E Tunisia
Gabon *55 B6 off.* Gabonese Republic. *Country* C Africa
Gaborone *56 C4 prev.* Gaberones. *Country capital* (Botswana) South East, SE Botswana
Gabrovo *82 D2* Gabrovo, N Bulgaria
Gadag *110 C1* Karnātaka, W India
Gadsden *20 D2* Alabama, S USA
Gaeta *75 C5* Lazio, C Italy
Gaeta, Golfo di *75 C5 var.* Gulf of Gaeta. *Gulf* C Italy
Gaeta, Gulf of *see* Gaeta, Golfo di
Gäfle *see* Gävle
Gafsa *49 E2 var.* Qafşah. W Tunisia
Gagnoa *52 D5* C Côte d'Ivoire
Gagra *95 E1* NW Georgia
Gaillac *69 C6 var.* Gaillac-sur-Tarn. Tarn, S France
Gaillac-sur-Tarn *see* Gaillac
Gaillimh *see* Galway
Gainesville *21 E3* Florida, SE USA
Gainesville *20 D2* Georgia, SE USA
Gainesville *27 G2* Texas, SW USA
Gairdner, Lake *127 A6 salt lake* South Australia
Gaiziņ *see* Gaizina Kalns
Gaizina Kalns *84 C3 var.* Gaiziņ. *Mountain* E Latvia
Galán, Cerro *42 B3 mountain* NW Argentina
Galanta *77 C6 Hung.* Galánta. Trnavský Kraj, W Slovakia
Galapagos Fracture Zone *131 E3 tectonic feature* E Pacific Ocean
Galapagos Islands *131 F3 var.* Islas de los Galápagos,*Tortoise Islands. Island group* Ecuador, E Pacific Ocean
Galapagos Rise *131 F3 undersea feature* E Pacific Ocean
Galashiels *66 C4* SE Scotland, UK
Galaţi *86 D4 Ger.* Galatz. Galaţi, E Romania
Galcaio *see* Gaalkacyo
Galesburg *18 B3* Illinois, N USA
Galicia *70 B1 cultural region* NW Spain
Galicia Bank *58 B4 undersea feature* E Atlantic Ocean
Galilee, Sea of *see* Tiberias, Lake
Galka'yo *see* Gaalkacyo
Galle *110 D4 prev.* Point de Galle. Southern Province, SW Sri Lanka
Gallego Rise *131 F3 undersea feature* E Pacific Ocean
Gallegos *see* Río Gallegos
Gallipoli *75 E6* Puglia, SE Italy
Gällivare *62 C3* Norrbotten, N Sweden
Gallup *26 C1* New Mexico, SW USA
Galtat-Zemmour *48 B3* C Western Sahara
Galveston *27 H4* Texas, SW USA
Galway *67 A5 Ir.* Gaillimh. W Ireland
Galway Bay *67 A6 Ir.* Cuan na Gaillimhe. *Bay* W Ireland
Gambell *14 C2* Saint Lawrence Island, Alaska, USA
Gambia *52 C3 Fr.* Gambie. *River* W Africa
Gambia *52 B3 off.* Republic of The Gambia, The Gambia. *Country* W Africa
Gambier, Îles *121 G4 island group* E French Polynesia
Gamboma *55 B6* Plateaux, E Congo
Gan *see* Gansu
Gan *see* Jiangxi
Gan *110 B5* Addu Atoll, C Maldives
Gäncä *95 G2 Rus.* Gyandzha; *prev.* Kirovabad, Yelisavetpol. W Azerbaijan
Gandajika *55 D7* Kasai Oriental, S Dem. Rep. Congo
Gander *17 G3* Newfoundland, Newfoundland and Labrador, SE Canada
Gāndhīdhām *112 C4* Gujarāt, W India
Gandía *71 F3* País Valenciano, E Spain
Ganges *113 F3 Ben.* Padma. *River* Bangladesh/India *see also* Padma
Ganges Cone *see* Ganges Fan
Ganges Fan *118 D3 var.* Ganges Cone. *Undersea feature* N Bay of Bengal
Ganges, Mouths of the *113 G4 delta* Bangladesh/India
Gangra *see* Çankırı
Gangtok *113 F3* Sikkim, N India
Gansu *106 B4 var.* Gan, Gansu Sheng, Kansu. Admin. region *province* N China
Gansu Sheng *see* Gansu
Ganzhou *106 D6* Jiangxi, S China
Gao *53 E3* Gao, E Mali
Gaoual *52 C4* Moyenne-Guinée, N Guinea
Gaoxiong *see* Kaohsiung
Gap *69 D5 anc.* Vapincum. Hautes-Alpes, SE France
Gar *104 A4 var.* Gar Xincun. Xizang Zizhiqu, W China
Garachiné *31 G5* Darién, SE Panama
Garagum *see* Garagumy
Garagum Kanaly *see* Garagumskiy Kanal
Garagumskiy Kanal *100 D3 var.* Kara Kum Canal, Karakumskiy Kanal, *Turkm.* Garagum Kanaly. *Canal* C Turkmenistan
Garagumy *100 C3 var.* Qara Qum, *Eng.* Black Sand Desert, Kara Kum, *Turkm.* Garagum; *prev.* Peski Karakumy. *Desert* C Turkmenistan
Gara Khitrino *82 D2* Shumen, NE Bulgaria
Garda, Lago di *C2 var.* Benaco, *Eng.* Lake Garda, *Ger.* Gardasee. *Lake* NE Italy
Garda, Lake *see* Garda, Lago di
Gardasee *see* Garda, Lago di
Garden City *23 E5* Kansas, C USA
Gardeyz *see* Gardēz
Gardēz *101 E4 var.* Gardeyz, Gordiaz. Paktīā, E Afghanistan
Gargždai *84 B3* Gargždai, W Lithuania
Garissa *51 D6* Coast, E Kenya
Garland *27 G2* Texas, SW USA
Garman, Loch *see* Wexford
Garoe *see* Garoowe
Garonne *69 B5 anc.* Garumna. *River* S France
Garoowe *51 E5 var.* Garoe. Nugaal, N Somalia
Garoua *54 B4 var.* Garua. Nord, N Cameroon
Garrygala *see* Kara-Kala
Garry Lake *15 F3 lake* Nunavut, N Canada
Garsen *51 D6* Coast, S Kenya
Garua *see* Garoua
Garwolin *76 D4* Mazowieckie, C Poland
Gar Xincun *see* Gar
Gary *18 B3* Indiana, N USA
Garzón *36 B4* Huila, S Colombia
Gascogne *69 B6 Eng.* Gascony. *Cultural region* S France
Gascoyne River *125 A5 river* Western Australia
Gaspé *17 F3* Quebec, SE Canada
Gaspé, Péninsule de *17 E4 var.* Péninsule de la Gaspésie. *Peninsula* Quebec, SE Canada
Gastonia *21 E1* North Carolina, SE USA
Gastoúni *83 B6* Dytikí Ellás, S Greece
Gatchina *88 B4* Leningradskaya Oblast', NW Russian Federation
Gatineau *16 D4* Quebec, SE Canada
Gatún, Lago *31 F4 reservoir* C Panama
Gauja *84 D3 Ger.* Aa. *River* Estonia/Latvia
Gauteng *see* Johannesburg
Gāvbandī *98 D4* Hormozgān, S Iran
Gávdos *83 C8 island* SE Greece
Gavere *65 B6* Oost-Vlaanderen, NW Belgium
Gävle *63 C6 var.* Gäfle; *prev.* Gefle. Gävleborg, C Sweden
Gawler *127 B6* South Australia
Gaya *113 F3* Bihār, N India
Gayndah *127 E5* Queensland, E Australia
Gaza *97 A6 Ar.* Ghazzah, *Heb.* 'Azza. NE Gaza Strip
Gaz-Achak *100 D2 Turkm.* Gazojak. Lebapskiy Velayat, NE Turkmenistan
Gazandzhyk *100 B2 Turkm.* Gazanjyk; *prev.* Kazandzhik. Balkanskiy Velayat, W Turkmenistan
Gaza Strip *97 A7 Ar.* Qiţā' Ghazzah. *Disputed region* SW Asia
Gazi Antep *see* Gaziantep
Gaziantep *94 D4 var.* Gazi Antep; *prev.* Aintab, Antep. Gaziantep, S Turkey
Gazimağusa *see* Ammóchostos
Gazimağusa Körfezi *see* Kólpos Ammóchostos
Gazli *100 D2* Bukhoro Wiloyati, C Uzbekistan
Gbanga *52 D5 var.* Gbarnga. N Liberia
Gbarnga *see* Gbanga
Gdańsk *76 C2 Fr.* Dantzig, *Ger.* Danzig. Pomorskie, N Poland
Gdan'skaya Bukhta *see* Danzig, Gulf of
Pomorskie, Gulf of *see* Danzig, Gulf of
Gdynia *76 C2 Ger.* Gdingen. Pomorskie, N Poland
Gedaref *50 C4 var.* Al Qaḍārif, El Gedaref. Gedaref, E Sudan
Gediz *94 B3* Kütahya, W Turkey
Gediz Nehri *94 A3 river* W Turkey
Geel *65 C5 var.* Gheel. Antwerpen, N Belgium
Geelong *127 C7* Victoria, SE Australia
Ge'e'mu *see* Golmud
Gefle *see* Gävle
Geilo *63 A5* Buskerud, S Norway
Gejiu *106 B6 var.* Kochiu. Yunnan, S China
Gëkdepe *see* Geok-Tepe
Gela *75 C7 prev.* Terranova di Sicilia. Sicilia, Italy, C Mediterranean Sea
Geldermalsen *64 C4* Gelderland, C Netherlands
Geleen *65 D6* Limburg, SE Netherlands
Gelinsoor *see* Gellinsoor
Gellinsoor *51 E5 var.* Gelinsoor. Mudug, NE Somalia
Gembloux *65 C6* Namur, Belgium
Gemena *55 C5* Equateur, NW Dem. Rep. Congo
Gemona del Friuli *74 D2* Friuli-Venezia Giulia, NE Italy
Genck *see* Genk
General Alvear *42 B4* Mendoza, W Argentina
General Eugenio A.Garay *42 C1* Guairá, S Paraguay
General Machado *see* Camacupa
General Santos *117 F3 off.* General Santos City. Mindanao, S Philippines
Geneva *see* Genève
Geneva, Lake *A7 Fr.* Lac de Genève, Lac Léman, le Léman, *Ger.* Genfer See. *Lake* France/Switzerland
Genève *73 A7 Eng.* Geneva, *Ger.* Genf, *It.* Ginevra. Genève, SW Switzerland
Genf *see* Genève
Genk *65 D6 var.* Genck. Limburg, NE Belgium
Gennep *64 D4* Limburg, SE Netherlands
Genoa *see* Genova
Genova *80 D1 Eng.* Genoa, *Fr.* Gênes; *anc.* Genua. Liguria, NW Italy
Genova, Golfo di *74 A3 Eng.* Gulf of Genoa. *Gulf* NW Italy
Genovesa, Isla *38 B5 var.* Tower Island. *Island* Galapagos Islands, Ecuador, E Pacific Ocean
Gent *65 B5 Eng.* Ghent, *Fr.* Gand. Oost-Vlaanderen, NW Belgium
Geok-Tepe *100 C3 var.* Gëkdepe, *Turkm.* Gökdepe. Akhalskiy Velayat, C Turkmenistan
George *60 A4 river* Newfoundland and Labrador/Quebec, E Canada
George *56 C5* Western Cape, S South Africa
George, Lake *21 E3 lake* Florida, SE USA
Georges Bank *13 D5 undersea feature* W Atlantic Ocean
George Sound *129 A7 sound* South Island, NZ
Georges River *126 D2 river* New South Wales, SE Australia
George Town *32 B3 var.* Georgetown. *Dependent territory capital* (Cayman Islands) Grand Cayman, SW Cayman Islands
George Town *116 B3 var.* Penang, Pinang. Pinang, Peninsular Malaysia
George Town *32 C2* Great Exuma Island, C Bahamas
Georgetown *37 F2 country capital* (Guyana) N Guyana
Georgetown *21 F2* South Carolina, SE USA
George V Land *132 C4 physical region* Antarctica
Georgia *95 F2 off.* Republic of Georgia, *Geor.* Sak'art'velo, *Rus.* Gruzinskaya SSR, Gruziya; *prev.* Georgian SSR. *Country* SW Asia
Georgia *20 D2 off.* State of Georgia; also known as Empire State of the South, Peach State. *State* SE USA
Georgian Bay *18 D2 lake bay* Ontario, S Canada
Georgia, Strait of *24 A1 strait* British Columbia, W Canada
Georg von Neumayer *132 A2 German research station* Antarctica
Gera *72 C4* Thüringen, E Germany
Geráki *83 B6* Pelopónnisos, S Greece
Geraldine *129 B6* Canterbury, South Island, NZ
Geraldton *125 A6* Western Australia
Geral, Serra *35 D5 mountain range* S Brazil
Gerede *94 C2* Bolu, N Turkey
Gereshk *100 D5* Helmand, SW Afghanistan
Gering *22 D3* Nebraska, C USA
Germanicopolis *see* Çankırı
Germany *72 B4 off.* Federal Republic of Germany, *Ger.* Bundesrepublik Deutschland, Deutschland. *Country* N Europe
Geroliménas *83 B7* Pelopónnisos, S Greece
Gerona *see* Girona
Gerpinnes *65 C7* Hainaut, S Belgium
Gerunda *see* Girona
Gerze *94 D2* Sinop, N Turkey
Gesoriacum *see* Boulogne-sur-Mer
Gessoriacum *see* Boulogne-sur-Mer
Getafe *70 D3* Madrid, C Spain
Gevaş *95 F3* Van, SE Turkey
Gevgeli *see* Gevgelija
Gevgelija *79 E6 var.* Đevđelija, Djevdjelija, *Turk.* Gevgeli. SE FYR Macedonia
Ghaba *see* Al Ghābah
Ghana *53 E5 off.* Republic of Ghana. *Country* W Africa
Ghanzi *56 C3 var.* Khanzi. Ghanzi, W Botswana
Gharandal *97 B7* Ma'ān, SW Jordan
Ghardaïa *48 D2* N Algeria
Gharvān *see* Gharyān
Gharyān *49 F2 var.* Gharvān. NW Libya
Ghaznī *101 E4 var.* Ghazni. Ghaznī, E Afghanistan
Ghazni *see* Ghaznī
Gheel *see* Geel
Gheorgheni *86 C4 prev.* Gheorghieni, Sînt-Miclăuş, *Ger.* Niklasmarkt, *Hung.* Gyergyószentmiklós. Harghita, C Romania
Ghijduwon *100 D2 Rus.* Gizhduvan. Bukhoro Wiloyati, C Uzbekistan
Ghŭdara *101 F3 var.* Gudara, *Rus.* Kudara. SE Tajikistan
Ghurdaqah *see* Hurghada
Ghūriān *100 D4* Herāt, W Afghanistan
Giannitsá *82 D4 var.* Yiannitsá. Kentrikí Makedonía, N Greece
Gibraltar *71 G4 UK dependent territory* SW Europe
Gibraltar, Bay of *71 C5 bay* Gibraltar/Spain
Gibraltar, Strait of *70 C5 Fr.* Détroit de Gibraltar, *Sp.* Estrecho de Gibraltar. *Strait* Atlantic Ocean/Mediterranean Sea
Gibson Desert *125 B5 desert* Western Australia
Giedraičiai *85 C5* Molėtai, E Lithuania
Giessen *73 B5* Hessen, W Germany
Gifu *109 C6 var.* Gihu. Gifu, Honshū, SW Japan
Giganta, Sierra de la *28 B3 mountain range* W Mexico
Gihu *see* Gifu
Gijón *70 D1 var.* Xixón. Asturias, NW Spain
Gilani *see* Gnjilane
Gila River *26 A2 river* Arizona, SW USA
Gilbert River *126 C3 river* Queensland, NE Australia
Gilf Kebir Plateau *50 A2 Ar.* Haḍabat al Jilf al Kabīr. *Plateau* SW Egypt
Gillette *22 D3* Wyoming, C USA
Gilroy *25 B6* California, W USA
Gimie, Mount *33 F1 mountain* C Saint Lucia
Gimma *see* Jīma
Ginevra *see* Genève
Gingin *125 A6* Western Australia
Giohar *see* Jawhar
Girardot *36 B3* Cundinamarca, C Colombia
Giresun *95 E2 var.* Kerasunt; *anc.* Cerasus, Pharnacia. Giresun, NE Turkey
Girin *see* Jilin
Girne *see* Keryneia
Girona *71 G2 var.* Gerona; *anc.* Gerunda. Cataluña, NE Spain
Gisborne *128 E3* Gisborne, North Island, NZ
Gissar Range *101 E3 Rus.* Gissarskiy Khrebet. *Mountain range* Tajikistan/Uzbekistan
Githio *see* Gýtheio
Giulianova *74 D4* Abruzzo, C Italy
Giumri *see* Gyumri
Giurgiu *86 C5* Giurgiu, S Romania
Giza *see* El Gîza
Gizeh *see* El Gîza
Giżycko *76 D2* Warmiùsko-Mazurskie, NE Poland
Gjakovë *see* Đakovica
Gjilan *see* Gnjilane
Gjinokastër *see* Gjirokastër
Gjirokastër *79 C7 var.* Gjirokastra; *prev.* Gjinokastër, *Gk.* Argyrokastron, *It.* Argirocastro. Gjirokastër, S Albania
Gjirokastra *see* Gjirokastër
Gjoa Haven *15 F3* King William Island, Nunavut, NW Canada
Gjøvik *63 B5* Oppland, S Norway

Haguenau – Hsining

Haguenau 68 E3 Bas-Rhin, NE France
Haicheng 106 D3 Liaoning, NE China
Haidarabad see Hyderābād
Haifa see Ḥefa
Haifong see Hai Phong
Haikou 106 C7 var. Hai-k'ou, Hoihow, Fr. Hoï-Hao. Hainan, S China
Hai-k'ou see Haikou
Ḥā'il 98 B4 off. Minṭaqah Ḥā'il. Province N Saudi Arabia
Hai-la-erh see Hailar
Hailar 105 F1 var. Hai-la-erh; prev. Hulun. Nei Mongol Zizhiqu, N China
Hailuoto 62 D4 Swe. Karlö. Island W Finland
Hainan 106 B7 var. Hainan Sheng, Qiong. Admin. region province S China
Hainan Dao 106 C7 island S China
Hainan Sheng see Hainan
Haines 14 D4 Alaska, USA
Hainichen 72 D4 Sachsen, E Germany
Hai Phong 114 D3 var. Haifong, Haiphong. N Vietnam
Haiphong see Hai Phong
Haiti 32 D3 off. Republic of Haiti. Country C West Indies
Haiya 50 C3 Red Sea, NE Sudan
Hajdúhadház 77 D6 Hajdú-Bihar, E Hungary
Hajîne see Abū Ḥardān
Hajnówka 76 E3 Ger. Hermhausen. Podlaskie, NE Poland
Hakodate 108 D3 Hokkaidō, NE Japan
Ḥalab 96 B2 Eng. Aleppo, Fr. Alep; anc. Beroea. Ḥalab, NW Syria
Ḥalāniyāt, Juzur al 137 D6 var. Jazā'ir Bin Ghalfān, Eng. Kuria Muria Islands. Island group S Oman
Halberstadt 72 C4 Sachsen-Anhalt, C Germany
Halden 63 B6 prev. Fredrikshald. Østfold, S Norway
Halfmoon Bay 129 A8 var. Oban. Stewart Island, Southland, NZ
Halifax 17 F4 Nova Scotia, SE Canada
Halkida see Chalkída
Halle 65 B6 Fr. Hal. Vlaams Brabant, C Belgium
Halle 72 C4 var. Halle an der Saale. Sachsen-Anhalt, C Germany
Halle an der Saale see Halle
Halle-Neustadt 72 C4 Sachsen-Anhalt, C Germany
Halley 132 B2 UK research station Antarctica
Hall Islands 120 B2 island group C Micronesia
Halls Creek 124 C3 Western Australia
Halmahera, Pulau 117 F3 prev. Djailolo, Gilolo, Jailolo. Island E Indonesia
Halmahera Sea 117 F4 Ind. Laut Halmahera. Sea E Indonesia
Halmstad 63 B7 Halland, S Sweden
Hama see Ḥamāh
Hamada 109 B6 Shimane, Honshū, SW Japan
Hamadān 98 C3 anc. Ecbatana. Hamadān, W Iran
Ḥamāh 96 B3 var. Hama; anc. Epiphania, Bibl. Hamath. Ḥamāh, W Syria
Hamamatsu 109 D6 var. Hamamatu. Shizuoka, Honshū, S Japan
Hamamatu see Hamamatsu
Hamar 63 B5 prev. Storhammer. Hedmark, S Norway
Hamath see Ḥamāh
Hamburg 72 B3 Hamburg, N Germany
Ḥamḍ, Wādī al 136 A4 dry watercourse W Saudi Arabia
Hämeenlinna 63 D5 Swe. Tavastehus. Etelä-Suomi, S Finland
Hamersley Range 124 A4 mountain range Western Australia
Hamhŭng 107 E3 C North Korea
Hami 104 C3 var. Ha-mi, Uigh. Kumul, Qomul. Xinjiang Uygur Zizhiqu, NW China
Ha-mi see Hami
Hamilton 20 C2 Alabama, S USA
Hamilton 16 D5 Ontario, S Canada
Hamilton 66 C4 S Scotland, UK
Hamilton 128 D3 Waikato, North Island, NZ
Ḥamīm, Wādī al 87 G2 river NE Libya
Hamïs Musait see Khamīs Mushayṭ
Hamiton 20 A5 dependent territory capital (Bermuda) C Bermuda
Hamm 72 B4 var. Hamm in Westfalen. Nordrhein-Westfalen, W Germany
Hammada du Drâa see Dra, Hamada du
Hammamet, Golfe de 80 D3 Ar. Khalīj al Ḥammāmāt. Gulf NE Tunisia
Ḥammār, Hawr al 136 C3 lake SE Iraq
Hamm in Westfalen see Hamm
Hampden 129 B7 Otago, South Island, NZ
Hampstead 67 A7 SE England, UK
Hamrun 80 B5 C Malta
Hâncești see Hîncești
Handan 106 C4 var. Han-tan. Hebei, E China
Haneda 108 A2 international airport (Tōkyō) Tōkyō, Honshū, S Japan
HaNegev 97 A7 Eng. Negev. Desert S Israel
Hanford 25 C6 California, W USA
Hangayn Nuruu 104 D2 mountain range C Mongolia
Hang-chou see Hangzhou
Hangchow see Hangzhou
Hangö see Hanko
Hangzhou 106 D5 var. Hang-chou, Hangchow. Zhejiang, SE China
Hania see Chaniá
Hanka, Lake see Khanka, Lake
Hanko 63 D6 Swe. Hangö. Etelä-Suomi, SW Finland
Han-k'ou see Wuhan
Hankow see Wuhan
Hanmer Springs 129 C5 Canterbury, South Island, NZ
Hannibal 23 G4 Missouri, C USA
Hannover 72 B3 Eng. Hanover. Niedersachsen, NW Germany
Hanöbukten 63 B7 bay S Sweden
Ha Nôi 114 D3 Eng. Hanoi, Fr. Ha noï. Country capital (Vietnam) N Vietnam
Hanoi see Ha Nôi
Han Shui 105 E4 river C China
Han-tan see Handan
Hantsavichy 85 B6 Pol. Hancewicze, Rus. Gantsevichi. Brestskaya Voblasts', SW Belarus
Hanyang see Wuhan
Hanzhong 106 B5 Shaanxi, C China
Hāora 113 F4 prev. Howrah. West Bengal, NE India
Haparanda 62 D4 Norrbotten, N Sweden
Haradok 85 E5 Rus. Gorodok. Vitsyebskaya Voblasts', N Belarus
Haradzyets 85 B6 Rus. Gorodets. Brestskaya Voblasts', SW Belarus
Haramachi 108 D4 Fukushima, Honshū, E Japan
Harany 85 D5 Rus. Gorany. Vitsyebskaya Voblasts', N Belarus
Harare 56 D3 prev. Salisbury. Country capital (Zimbabwe) Mashonaland East, NE Zimbabwe
Harbavichy 85 E6 Rus. Gorbovichi. Mahilyowskaya Voblasts', E Belarus
Harbel 52 C5 W Liberia
Harbin 107 E2 var. Haerbin, Ha-erh-pin, Kharbin; prev. Haerhpin, Pingkiang, Pinkiang. Heilongjiang, NE China
Hardangerfjorden 63 A6 fjord S Norway
Hardangervidda 63 A6 plateau S Norway
Hardenberg 64 E3 Overijssel, E Netherlands
Harelbeke 65 A6 var. Harlebeke. West-Vlaanderen, W Belgium
Harem see Ḥārim
Haren 64 E2 Groningen, NE Netherlands
Hārer 51 D5 E Ethiopia
Hargeisa see Hargeysa
Hargeysa 51 D5 var. Hargeisa. Woqooyi Galbeed, NW Somalia
Hariana see Haryāna
Hari, Batang 116 B4 prev. Djambi. River Sumatera, W Indonesia
Ḥārim 96 B2 var. Harem. Idlib, W Syria
Harima-nada 109 B6 sea S Japan
Harīrūd var. Tedzhen, Turkm. Tejen. River Afghanistan/Iran see also Tedzhen
Harlan 23 F3 Iowa, C USA
Harlebeke see Harelbeke
Harlingen 64 D2 Fris. Harns. Friesland, N Netherlands
Harlingen 27 G5 Texas, SW USA
Harlow 67 E6 E England, UK
Harney Basin 24 B4 basin Oregon, NW USA
Härnösand 63 C5 var. Hernösand. Västernorrland, C Sweden
Har Nuur 104 C2 lake NW Mongolia
Harper 52 D5 var. Cape Palmas. NE Liberia
Harricana 16 D3 river Quebec, SE Canada
Harris 66 B3 physical region NW Scotland, UK
Harrisburg 19 E4 state capital Pennsylvania, NE USA
Harrisonburg 19 E4 Virginia, NE USA
Harrison, Cape 17 F2 headland Newfoundland and Labrador, E Canada
Harris Ridge see Lomonosov Ridge
Harrogate 67 D5 N England, UK
Hârșova 86 D5 prev. Hîrşova. Constanța, SE Romania
Harstad 62 C2 Troms, N Norway
Hartford 19 G3 state capital Connecticut, NE USA
Hartlepool 67 D5 N England, UK
Harunabad see Eslāmābād
Harwich 67 E6 E England, UK
Haryāna 112 D2 var. Hariana. Admin. region state N India
Hasselt 65 C6 Limburg, NE Belgium
Hassetché see Al Ḥasakah
Hastings 128 E4 Hawke's Bay, North Island, NZ
Hastings 23 F4 Nebraska, C USA
Hastings 67 E7 SE England, UK
Hațeg 86 B4 Ger. Wallenthal, Hung. Hátszeg; prev. Hatzeg, Hötzing. Hunedoara, SW Romania
Hatizyô Zima see Hachijō-jima
Hattem 64 D3 Gelderland, E Netherlands
Hatteras, Cape 21 G1 headland North Carolina, SE USA
Hatteras Plain 13 D6 undersea feature W Atlantic Ocean
Hattiesburg 20 C3 Mississippi, S USA
Hatton Bank see Hatton Ridge
Hatton Ridge 58 B2 var. Hatton Bank. Undersea feature N Atlantic Ocean
Hat Yai 115 C7 var. Ban Hat Yai. Songkhla, SW Thailand
Haugesund 63 A6 Rogaland, S Norway
Haukeligrend 63 A6 Telemark, S Norway
Haukivesi 63 E5 lake SE Finland
Hauraki Gulf 128 D2 gulf North Island, NZ
Hauroko, Lake 129 A7 lake South Island, NZ
Haut Atlas 48 B3 Eng. High Atlas. Mountain range C Morocco
Hautes Fagnes 65 D6 Ger. Hohes Venn. Mountain range E Belgium
Haut Plateau du Dra see Dra, Hamada du
Hauts Plateaux 48 D2 plateau Algeria/Morocco
Hauzenberg 73 D6 Bayern, SE Germany
Havana see La Habana
Havana 13 D6 Illinois, N USA
Havant 67 D7 S England, UK
Havelock 21 F1 North Carolina, SE USA
Havelock North 128 E4 Hawke's Bay, North Island, NZ
Haverfordwest 67 C6 SW Wales, UK
Havířov 77 C5 Ostravský Kraj, E Czech Republic
Havre 22 C1 Montana, NW USA
Havre-St-Pierre 17 F3 Quebec, E Canada
Hawaii 25 B8 Haw. Hawai'i. Island Hawaiian Islands, USA, C Pacific Ocean
Hawaii 25 A8 off. State of Hawaii; also known as Aloha State, Paradise of the Pacific. State USA, C Pacific Ocean
Hawaiian Islands 130 D2 prev. Sandwich Islands. Island group Hawaii, USA, C Pacific Ocean
Hawaiian Ridge 91 H4 undersea feature N Pacific Ocean
Hawash see Āwash
Hawea, Lake 129 B6 lake South Island, NZ
Hawera 128 D4 Taranaki, North Island, NZ
Hawick 66 C4 SE Scotland, UK
Hawke Bay 128 E4 bay North Island, NZ
Hawlēr see Arbīl
Hawthorne 25 C6 Nevada, W USA
Hay 127 C6 New South Wales, SE Australia
Hayes 16 B2 river Manitoba, C Canada
Hay River 15 E4 Northwest Territories, W Canada
Hays 23 E5 Kansas, C USA
Haysyn 86 D3 Rus. Gaysin. Vinnyts'ka Oblast', C Ukraine
Heard and McDonald Islands 119 B7 Australian external territory S Indian Ocean
Hearst 16 C4 Ontario, S Canada
Heathrow 67 A8 international airport (London)SE England, UK
Hebei 106 C4 var. Hebei Sheng, Hopeh, Hopei, Ji; prev. Chihli. Admin. region province E China
Hebei Sheng see Hebei
Hebron 97 A6 var. Al Khalīl, El Khalil, Heb. Ḥevron; anc. Kiriath-Arba. S West Bank
Hebrus see Maritsa
Heemskerk 64 C3 Noord-Holland, W Netherlands
Heerde 64 D3 Gelderland, E Netherlands
Heerenveen 64 D2 Fris. It Hearrenfean. Friesland, N Netherlands
Heerhugowaard 64 C2 Noord-Holland, NW Netherlands
Heerlen 65 D6 Limburg, SE Netherlands
Heerwegen see Polkowice
Ḥefa 97 A5 var. Haifa; hist. Caiffa, Caiphas, anc. Sycaminum. Haifa, N Israel
Ḥefa, Mifraẕ 97 A5 Eng. Bay of Haifa. Bay N Israel
Hefei 106 D5 var. Hofei; hist. Luchow. Anhui, E China
Hegang 107 E2 Heilongjiang, NE China
Hei see Heilongjiang
Heide 72 B2 Schleswig-Holstein, N Germany
Heidelberg 73 B5 Baden-Württemberg, SW Germany
Heidenheim see Heidenheim an der Brenz
Heidenheim an der Brenz 73 B6 var. Heidenheim. Baden-Württemberg, S Germany
Heilbronn 73 B6 Baden-Württemberg, SW Germany
Heilongjiang 106 D2 var. Hei, Heilongjiang Sheng, Hei-lung-chiang, Heilungkiang. Admin. region province NE China
Heilongjiang Sheng see Heilongjiang
Heiloo 64 C3 Noord-Holland, NW Netherlands
Hei-lung-chiang see Heilongjiang
Heilungkiang see Heilongjiang
Heimdal 63 B5 Sør-Trøndelag, S Norway
Hekimhan 91 D3 Malatya, C Turkey
Helena 22 B2 state capital Montana, NW USA
Helensville 128 D2 Auckland, North Island, NZ
Helgoland Bay see Helgoländer Bucht
Helgoländer Bucht 72 A2 var. Helgoland Bay, Heligoland Bight. Bay NW Germany
Heligoland Bight see Helgoländer Bucht
Heliopolis see Baalbek
Hellevoetsluis 64 B4 Zuid-Holland, SW Netherlands
Hellín 71 E4 Castilla-La Mancha, C Spain
Helmand, Daryā-ye var. Rūd-e Hīrmand. River Afghanistan/Iran see also Hīrmand, Rūd-e
Helmond 65 D5 Noord-Brabant, S Netherlands
Helsingborg 63 B7 prev. Hälsingborg. Skåne, S Sweden
Helsinki 63 D6 Swe. Helsingfors. Country capital (Finland) Etelä-Suomi, S Finland
Henan 106 C5 var. Henan Sheng, Honan, Yu. Admin. region province C China
Henan Sheng see Henan
Henderson 18 B5 Kentucky, S USA
Henderson 25 D7 Nevada, W USA
Henderson 27 H3 Texas, SW USA
Hengchow see Hengyang
Hengduan Shan 106 A5 mountain range SW China
Hengelo 64 E3 Overijssel, E Netherlands
Hengnan see Hengyang
Hengyang 106 C6 var. Hengnan, Heng-yang; prev. Hengchow. Hunan, S China
Heng-yang see Hengyang
Heniches'k 87 F4 Rus. Genichesk. Khersons'ka Oblast', S Ukraine
Hennebont 68 A3 Morbihan, NW France
Henzada 114 B4 Irrawaddy, SW Myanmar
Herakleion see Irákleio
Herat 100 D4 var. Herat; anc. Aria. Herāt, W Afghanistan
Herat see Herāt
Heredia 31 E4 Heredia, C Costa Rica
Hereford 27 E2 Texas, SW USA
Herford 72 B4 Nordrhein-Westfalen, NW Germany
Herk-de-Stad 65 C6 Limburg, NE Belgium
Hermansverk 63 A5 Sogn Og Fjordane, S Norway
Hermhausen see Hajnówka
Hermiston 24 C2 Oregon, NW USA
Hermon, Mount 97 B5 Ar. Jabal ash Shaykh. Mountain S Syria
Hermosillo 28 B2 Sonora, NW Mexico
Hermoupolis see Ermoúpoli
Hernösand see Härnösand
Herrera del Duque 70 D3 Extremadura, W Spain
Herselt 65 C5 Antwerpen, C Belgium
Herstal 65 D6 Fr. Héristal. Liège, E Belgium
Hessen 73 B5 cultural region C Germany
Ḥevron see Hebron
Heydebrech see Kędzierzyn-Kole
Heywood Islands 124 C3 island group Western Australia
Hibbing 23 F1 Minnesota, N USA
Hidalgo del Parral 28 C2 var. Parral. Chihuahua, N Mexico
Hida-sanmyaku 109 C5 mountain range Honshū, S Japan
Hierro 48 A3 var. Ferro. Island Islas Canarias, Spain, NE Atlantic Ocean
High Plains see Great Plains
High Point 21 E1 North Carolina, SE USA
High Veld see Great Karoo
Hiiumaa 84 C2 Ger. Dagden, Swe. Dagö. Island W Estonia
Hikurangi 128 D2 Northland, North Island, NZ
Hildesheim 72 B4 Niedersachsen, N Germany
Hilla see Al Ḥillah
Hillaby, Mount 33 G1 mountain N Barbados
Hill Bank 30 C1 Orange Walk, N Belize
Hillegom 64 C3 Zuid-Holland, W Netherlands
Hilo 25 B8 Hawaii, USA, C Pacific Ocean
Hilton Head Island 21 E2 South Carolina, SE USA
Hilversum 64 C3 Noord-Holland, C Netherlands
Himalaya see Himalayas
Himalayas 113 E2 var. Himalaya, Chin. Himalaya Shan. Mountain range S Asia
Himalaya Shan see Himalayas
Himeji 109 C6 var. Himezi. Hyōgo, Honshū, SW Japan
Himezi see Himeji
Ḥimş 96 B4 var. Homs; anc. Emesa. Ḥimş, C Syria
Hîncești 86 D4 var. Hâncești; prev. Kotovsk. C Moldova
Hinchinbrook Island 126 D3 island Queensland, NE Australia
Hinds 129 C6 Canterbury, South Island, NZ
Hindu Kush 101 F4 Per. Hendū Kosh. Mountain range Afghanistan/Pakistan
Hinesville 21 E3 Georgia, SE USA
Hinnøya 62 C3 island C Norway
Hinson Bay 20 A5 bay W Bermuda
Hios see Chíos
Hirosaki 108 D3 Aomori, Honshū, C Japan
Hiroshima 109 B6 var. Hirosima. Hiroshima, Honshū, SW Japan
Hirosima see Hiroshima
Hirson 68 D3 Aisne, N France
Hispaniola 34 B1 island Dominion Republic/Haiti
Hitachi 109 D5 var. Hitati. Ibaraki, Honshū, S Japan
Hitati see Hitachi
Hitra 62 A4 prev. Hitteren. Island S Norway
Hjälmaren 63 C6 Eng. Lake Hjalmar. Lake C Sweden
Hjørring 63 B7 Nordjylland, N Denmark
Hkakabo Razi 114 B1 mountain Myanmar/China
Hlobyne 87 F2 Rus. Globino. Poltavs'ka Oblast', NE Ukraine
Hlukhiv 87 F1 Rus. Glukhov. Sums'ka Oblast', NE Ukraine
Hlybokaye 85 D5 Rus. Glubokoye. Vitsyebskaya Voblasts', N Belarus
Hoa Binh 114 D3 Hoa Binh, N Vietnam
Hoang Liên Sơn 114 D3 mountain range N Vietnam
Hobart 127 C8 prev. Hobarton, Hobart Town. State capital Tasmania, SE Australia
Hobbs 27 E3 New Mexico, SW USA
Hobro 63 A7 Nordjylland, N Denmark
Hô Chi Minh 115 E6 var. Ho Chi Minh City; prev. Saigon. S Vietnam
Ho Chi Minh City see Hô Chi Minh
Hódmezővásárhely 77 D7 Csongrád, SE Hungary
Hodna, Chott El 118 C4 var. Chott el-Hodna, Ar. Shatt al-Hodna. Salt lake N Algeria
Hodonín 77 C5 Ger. Göding. Brněnský Kraj, SE Czech Republic
Hoë Karoo see Great Karoo
Hof 73 C5 Bayern, SE Germany
Hofei see Hefei
Hōfu 109 B7 Yamaguchi, Honshū, SW Japan
Hofuf see Al Hufūf
Hogoley Islands see Chuuk Islands
Hohe Tauern 73 C7 mountain range W Austria
Hohhot 105 F3 var. Huhehot, Huhuohaote, Mong. Kukukhoto; prev. Kweisui, Kwesui. Nei Mongol Zizhiqu, N China
Hôi An 115 E5 prev. Faifo. Quang Nam-Đa Nẵng, C Vietnam
Hoï-Hao see Haikou
Hoihow see Haikou
Hokianga Harbour 128 C2 inlet SE Tasman Sea
Hokitika 129 B5 West Coast, South Island, NZ
Hokkaidō 108 C2 prev. Ezo, Yeso, Yezo. Island NE Japan
Hola Prystan' 87 E4 Rus. Golaya Pristan. Khersons'ka Oblast', S Ukraine
Holbrook 26 B2 Arizona, SW USA
Holetown 33 G1 prev. Jamestown. W Barbados
Holguín 32 C2 Holguín, SE Cuba
Hollabrunn 73 E6 Niederösterreich, NE Austria
Hollandia see Jayapura
Holly Springs 20 C1 Mississippi, S USA
Holman 15 E3 Victoria Island, Northwest Territories, N Canada
Holmsund 62 D4 Västerbotten, N Sweden
Holon 97 A6 var. Kholon. Tel Aviv, C Israel
Holovanivs'k 87 E3 Rus. Golovanevsk. Kirovohrads'ka Oblast', C Ukraine
Holstebro 63 A7 Ringkøbing, W Denmark
Holsteinborg see Sisimiut
Holsteinsborg see Sisimiut
Holstenborg see Sisimiut
Holstensborg see Sisimiut
Holyhead 67 C5 Wel. Caer Gybi. NW Wales, UK
Hombori 53 E3 Mopti, S Mali
Homs see Al Khums
Homs see Ḥimş
Homyel' 85 D7 Rus. Gomel'. Homyel'skaya Voblasts', SE Belarus
Honan see Henan
Honan see Luoyang
Hondo see Honshū
Hondo 27 F4 Texas, SW USA
Honduras 30 C2 off. Republic of Honduras. Country Central America
Honduras, Gulf of 30 C2 Sp. Golfo de Honduras. Gulf W Caribbean Sea
Hønefoss 63 B6 Buskerud, S Norway
Honey Lake 25 B5 lake California, W USA
Hon Gai see Hông Gai
Hongay see Hông Gai
Hông Gai 114 E3 var. Hon Gai, Hongay. Quang Ninh, N Vietnam
Hong Kong 106 A1 Chin. Xianggang. S China
Hong Kong Island 106 B2 Chin. Xianggang. Island S China
Honiara 122 C3 country capital (Solomon Islands) Guadalcanal, C Solomon Islands
Honjō 108 D4 var. Honzyô. Akita, Honshū, C Japan
Honolulu 25 A8 admin capital Oahu, Hawaii, USA, C Pacific Ocean
Honshū 109 E5 var. Hondo, Honsyû. Island SW Japan
Honsyû see Honshū
Honzyô see Honjō
Hoogeveen 64 E2 Drenthe, NE Netherlands
Hoogezand-Sappemeer 64 E2 Groningen, NE Netherlands
Hoorn 64 C2 Noord-Holland, NW Netherlands
Hopa 95 E2 Artvin, NE Turkey
Hope 14 C3 British Columbia, SW Canada
Hopedale 17 F2 Newfoundland and Labrador, NE Canada
Hopeh see Hebei
Hopei see Hebei
Hopkinsville 18 B5 Kentucky, S USA
Horasan 95 F3 Erzurum, NE Turkey
Horizon Deep 130 D4 undersea feature W Pacific Ocean
Horki 85 E6 Rus. Gorki. Mahilyowskaya Voblasts', E Belarus
Horlivka 87 G3 Rom. Adâncata, Rus. Gorlovka. Donets'ka Oblast', E Ukraine
Hormuz, Strait of 98 D4 var. Strait of Ormuz, Per. Tangeh-ye Hormoz. Strait Iran/Oman
Hornos, Cabo de 43 C8 Eng. Cape Horn. Headland S Chile
Hornsby 126 E1 New South Wales, SE Australia
Horodnya 87 E1 Rus. Gorodnya. Chernihivs'ka Oblast', NE Ukraine
Horodyshche 87 E2 Rus. Gorodishche. Cherkas'ka Oblast', C Ukraine
Horokok 86 B2 Pol. Gródek Jagielloński, Rus. Gorodok, Gorodok Yagellonski. L'vivs'ka Oblast', NW Ukraine
Horoshiri dake 108 D2 var. Horosiri Dake. Mountain Hokkaidō, N Japan
Horosiri Dake see Horoshiri-dake
Horsburgh Atoll 110 A4 atoll N Maldives
Horseshoe Bay 20 A5 bay W Bermuda
Horseshoe Seamounts 58 A4 undersea feature E Atlantic Ocean
Horsham 127 B7 Victoria, SE Australia
Horst 65 D5 Limburg, SE Netherlands
Horten 63 B6 Vestfold, S Norway
Horyn' 85 B7 Rus. Goryn. River NW Ukraine
Hosingen 65 D7 Diekirch, NE Luxembourg
Hospitalet see L'Hospitalet de Llobregat
Hotan 104 B4 var. Khotan, Chin. Ho-t'ien. Xinjiang Uygur Zizhiqu, NW China
Ho-t'ien see Hotan
Hoting 62 C4 Jämtland, C Sweden
Hot Springs 20 B1 Arkansas, C USA
Houayxay 114 C3 var. Ban Houayxay, Ban Houei Sai. Bokèo, N Laos
Houghton 18 B1 Michigan, N USA
Houilles 69 B5 Yvelines, N France
Houlton 19 H1 Maine, NE USA
Houma 20 B3 Louisiana, S USA
Houston 27 H4 Texas, SW USA
Hovd 104 C2 var. Khovd. Hovd, W Mongolia
Hove 67 E7 SE England, UK
Hoverla, Hora 86 C3 Rus. Gora Goverla. Mountain W Ukraine
Hovsgol, Lake see Hövsgöl Nuur
Hövsgöl Nuur 104 D1 var. Lake Hovsgol. Lake N Mongolia
Howar, Wādi 50 A3 var. Ouadi Howa. River Chad/Sudan see also Howa, Ouadi
Hoy 66 C2 island N Scotland, UK
Hoyerswerda 72 D4 Sachsen, E Germany
Hradec Králové 77 B5 Ger. Königgrätz. Hradecký Kraj, N Czech Republic
Hrandzichy 85 B5 Rus. Grandichi. Hrodzyenskaya Voblasts', W Belarus
Hranice 77 C5 Ger. Mährisch-Weisskirchen. Olomoucký Kraj, E Czech Republic
Hrebinka 87 E2 Rus. Grebenka. Poltavs'ka Oblast', NE Ukraine
Hrodna 85 B5 Pol. Grodno. Hrodzyenskaya Voblasts', W Belarus
Hsia-men see Xiamen
Hsiang-t'an see Xiangtan
Hsi Chiang see Xi Jiang
Hsing-k'ai Hu see Khanka, Lake
Hsining see Xining

INDEX

INDEX

Kitchener – Kurile Trench

Kitchener 16 C5 Ontario, S Canada
Kíthira see Kýthira
Kíthnos see Kýthnos
Kitimat 14 D4 British Columbia, SW Canada
Kitinen 62 D3 river N Finland
Kitob 101 E3 Rus. Kitab. Qashqadaryo Wiloyati, S Uzbekistan
Kitwe 56 D2 var. Kitwe-Nkana. Copperbelt, C Zambia
Kitwe-Nkana see Kitwe
Kitzbühler Alpen 73 C7 mountain range W Austria
Kivalina 14 C2 Alaska, USA
Kivalo 62 D3 ridge C Finland
Kivertsi 86 C1 Pol. Kiwerce, Rus. Kivertsy. Volyns'ka Oblast', NW Ukraine
Kivu, Lake 55 E6 Fr. Lac Kivu. Lake Rwanda/Dem. Rep. Congo
Kızıl Irmak 94 C3 river C Turkey
Kizil Kum see Kyzyl Kum
Kladno 77 A5 Středočesky Kraj, NW Czech Republic
Klagenfurt 73 D7 Slvn. Celovec. Kärnten, S Austria
Klaipėda 84 B3 Ger. Memel. Klaipėda, NW Lithuania
Klamath Falls 24 B4 Oregon, NW USA
Klamath Mountains 24 A4 mountain range California/Oregon, W USA
Klang 116 B3 var. Kelang; prev. Port Swettenham. Selangor, Peninsular Malaysia
Klarälven 63 B6 river Norway/Sweden
Klatovy 77 A5 Ger. Klattau. Plzeňský Kraj, W Czech Republic
Klazienaveen 64 E2 Drenthe, NE Netherlands
Klein Karas 56 B4 Karas, S Namibia
Kleisoúra 83 A5 Ípeiros, W Greece
Klerksdorp 56 D4 North-West, N South Africa
Klimavichy 85 E7 Rus. Klimovichi. Mahilyowskaya Voblasts', E Belarus
Klintsy 89 A5 Bryanskaya Oblast', W Russian Federation
Klisura 82 C2 Plovdiv, C Bulgaria
Ključ 78 B3 Federacija Bosna I Hercegovina, NW Bosnia and Herzegovina
Kłobuck 76 C4 Śląskie, S Poland
Klosters 73 B7 Graubünden, SE Switzerland
Kluang see Keluang
Kluczbork 76 C4 Ger. Kreuzburg, Kreuzburg in Oberschlesien. Opolskie, S Poland
Klyuchevskaya Sopka, Vulkan 93 H3 volcano E Russian Federation
Knin 78 B4 Šibenik-Knin, S Croatia
Knjaževac 78 E4 Serbia, E Serbia and Montenegro (Yugo.)
Knokke-Heist 65 A5 West-Vlaanderen, NW Belgium
Knoxville 20 D1 Tennessee, S USA
Knud Rasmussen Land 60 D1 physical region N Greenland
Kōbe 109 C6 Hyōgo, Honshū, SW Japan
København 63 B7 Eng. Copenhagen; anc. Hafnia. Country capital (Denmark) Sjælland, København, E Denmark
Kobenni 52 D3 Hodh el Gharbi, S Mauritania
Koblenz 73 A5 prev. Coblenz, Fr. Coblence, anc. Confluentes. Rheinland-Pfalz, W Germany
Kobryn 85 A6 Pol. Kobryn, Rus. Kobrin. Brestskaya Voblasts', SW Belarus
K'obulet'i 95 F2 W Georgia
Kočani 79 E6 NE FYR Macedonia
Kočevje 73 D8 Ger. Gottschee. S Slovenia
Koch Bihār 113 G3 West Bengal, NE India
Kōchi 109 B7 var. Kôti. Kōchi, Shikoku, SW Japan
Kochi see Cochin
Kochiu see Gejiu
Kodiak 14 C3 Kodiak Island, Alaska, USA
Kodiak Island 14 C3 island Alaska, USA
Koeln see Köln
Ko-erh-mu see Golmud
Koetai see Mahakam, Sungai
Koetaradja see Bandaaceh
Kōfu 109 D5 var. Kôhu. Yamanashi, Honshū, S Japan
Kogarah 126 E2 New South Wales, SE Australia
Kogon 100 D2 Rus. Kagan. Bukhoro Wiloyati, C Uzbekistan
Kohīma 113 H3 Nāgāland, E India
Koh I Noh see Büyükağrı Dağı
Kohtla-Järve 84 E2 Ida-Virumaa, NE Estonia
Kôhu see Kōfu
Kokand see Qŭqon
Kokkola 62 D4 Swe. Karleby; prev. Swe. Gamlakarleby. Länsi-Suomi, W Finland
Koko see Qinghai Hu
Koko 53 F4 Kebbi, W Nigeria
Kokomo 18 C4 Indiana, N USA
Koko Nor see Qinghai
Kokrines 14 C2 Alaska, USA
Kokshaal-Tau 101 G2 Rus. Khrebet Kakshaal-Too. Mountain range China/Kyrgyzstan
Kokshetau 92 C4 Kaz. Kökshetaū; prev. Kokchetav. Severnyy Kazakhstan, N Kazakhstan
Koksijde 65 A5 West-Vlaanderen, W Belgium
Koksoak 16 D2 river Quebec, E Canada
Kokstad 56 D5 KwaZulu/Natal, E South Africa
Kola see Kol'skiy Poluostrov
Kolaka 117 E4 Sulawesi, C Indonesia
Kolam see Quilon
K'o-la-ma-i see Karamay
Kola Peninsula see Kol'skiy Poluostrov
Kolari 62 D3 Lappi, NW Finland
Kolárovo 77 C6 Ger. Gutta; prev. Guta, Hung. Gúta. Nitriansky Kraj, SW Slovakia
Kolda 52 C3 S Senegal
Kolding 63 A7 Vejle, C Denmark
Kölen 59 E1 Nor. Kjølen. Mountain range Norway/Sweden
Kolguyev, Ostrov 88 C2 island NW Russian Federation
Kolhāpur 110 B1 Mahārāshtra, SW India
Kolhumadulu Atoll 110 A5 var. Kolumadulu Atoll, Thaa Atoll. Atoll S Maldives
Kolín 77 B5 Ger. Kolin. Středočesky Kraj, C Czech Republic
Kolka 84 C2 Talsi, NW Latvia
Kolkasrags 84 C2 prev. Eng. Cape Domesnes. Headland NW Latvia
Kolkata see Calcutta
Kollam see Quilon
Köln 72 A4 var. Koeln, Eng./Fr. Cologne; prev. Cöln, anc. Colonia Agrippina, Oppidum Ubiorum. Nordrhein-Westfalen, W Germany
Koło 76 C3 Wielkopolskie, C Poland
Kołobrzeg 76 B2 Ger. Kolberg. Zachodniopomorskie, NW Poland
Kolokani 52 D3 Koulikoro, W Mali
Kolomna 89 B5 Moskovskaya Oblast', W Russian Federation
Kolomyya 86 C3 Ger. Kolomea. Ivano-Frankivs'ka Oblast', W Ukraine
Kolpa 78 A2 Ger. Kulpa, SCr. Kupa. River Croatia/Slovenia
Kolpino 88 B4 Leningradskaya Oblast', NW Russian Federation
Kólpos Ammóchostos 80 C5 var. Famagusta Bay, bay E Cyprus
Kol'skiy Poluostrov 88 C2 Eng. Kola Peninsula. Peninsula NW Russian Federation
Kolumadulu Atoll see Kolhumadulu Atoll
Kolwezi 55 D7 Shaba, S Dem. Rep. Congo
Kolyma 93 G2 river NE Russian Federation
Kolyma Range 91 G2 var. Khrebet Kolymskiy, Eng. Kolyma Range. Mountain range E Russian Federation
Komatsu 109 C5 var. Komatu. Ishikawa, Honshū, SW Japan
Komatu see Komatsu
Kommunizma Pik see Kommunizm, Qullai
Kommunizm, Qullai 101 F3 var. Qullai Garmo, Eng. Communism Peak, Rus. Kommunizma Pik; prev. Stalin Peak. Mountain E Tajikistan
Komoé 53 E4 var. Komoé Fleuve. River E Côte d'Ivoire
Komoé Fleuve see Komoé
Komotiní 82 D3 var. Gümüljina, Turk. Gümülcine. Anatolikí Makedonía kai Thráki, NE Greece
Komsomolets, Ostrov 93 E1 island Severnaya Zemlya, N Russian Federation
Komsomol'sk-na-Amure 93 G4 Khabarovskiy Kray, SE Russian Federation
Kondolovo 82 E3 Burgas, E Bulgaria
Kondopoga 88 B3 Respublika Kareliya, NW Russian Federation
Kondoz see Kunduz
Kondūz see Kunduz
Kong Christian IX Land 60 D4 Eng. King Christian IX Land. Physical region SE Greenland
Kong Frederik IX Land 60 C3 Eng. King Frederik IX Land. Physical region SW Greenland
Kong Frederik VIII Land 61 E2 Eng. King Frederik VIII Land. Physical region NE Greenland
Kong Frederik VI Kyst 60 C4 Eng. King Frederik VI Coast. Physical region SE Greenland
Kong Karls Land 61 G2 Eng. King Charles Islands. Island group SE Svalbard
Kongo see Congo
Kongolo 55 D6 Shaba, E Dem. Rep. Congo
Kongor 51 B5 Jonglei, SE Sudan
Kong Oscar Fjord 61 E3 fjord E Greenland
Kongsberg 63 B6 Buskerud, S Norway
Kông, Tônle 115 E5 Lao. Xê Kong. River Cambodia/Laos
Konia see Konya
Konieh see Konya
Konin 76 C3 Ger. Kuhnau. Wielkopolskie, C Poland
Konispol 79 C7 var. Konispoli. Vlorë, S Albania
Konispoli see Konispol
Kónitsa 82 A4 Ípeiros, W Greece
Konitz see Chojnice
Konjic 78 C4 Federacija Bosna I Hercegovina, S Bosnia and Herzegovina
Konosha 88 C4 Arkhangel'skaya Oblast', NW Russian Federation
Konotop 87 F1 Sums'ka Oblast', NE Ukraine
Konstanz 73 B7 var. Constanz, Eng. Constance; hist. Kostnitz, anc. Constantia. Baden-Württemberg, S Germany
Konstanza see Constanța
Konya 94 C4 var. Konieh; prev. Konia, anc. Iconium. Konya, C Turkey
Kopaonik 79 D5 mountain range S Serbia and Montenegro (Yugo.)
Koper 73 D8 It. Capodistria; prev. Kopar. SW Slovenia
Kopetdag Gershi 100 C3 mountain range Iran/Turkmenistan
Koppeh Dāgh 98 D2 var. Khrebet Kopetdag. Mountain range Iran/Turkmenistan
Koprivnica 78 B2 Ger. Kopreinitz, Hung. Kaproncza. Koprivnica-Križevci, N Croatia
Korat see Nakhon Ratchasima
Korat Plateau 114 D4 plateau E Thailand
Korba 113 E4 Madhya Pradesh, C India
Korça see Korçë
Korçë 79 D6 var. Korça, Gk. Korytsa, It. Corriza; prev. Koritsa. Korçë, SE Albania
Korčula 78 B4 It. Curzola; anc. Corcyra Nigra. Island S Croatia
Korea Bay 105 G3 bay China/North Korea
Korea Strait 109 A7 Jap. Chōsen-kaikyō, Kor. Taehan-haehyŏp. Channel Japan/South Korea
Korhogo 52 D4 N Côte d'Ivoire
Korinthiakós Kólpos 83 B5 Eng. Gulf of Corinth; anc. Corinthiacus Sinus. Gulf C Greece
Kórinthos 83 B6 Eng. Corinth; anc. Corinthus. Pelopónnisos, S Greece
Koritsa see Korçë
Kōriyama 109 D5 Fukushima, Honshū, C Japan
Korla 104 C3 Chin. K'u-erh-lo. Xinjiang Uygur Zizhiqu, NW China
Körmend 77 B7 Vas, W Hungary
Koróni 83 B6 Pelopónnisos, S Greece
Koror see Oreor
Korosten' 86 D1 Zhytomyrs'ka Oblast', NW Ukraine
Koro Toro 54 C2 Borkou-Ennedi-Tibesti, N Chad
Kortrijk 65 A6 Fr. Courtrai. West-Vlaanderen, W Belgium
Koryak Range see Koryakskoye Nagor'ye
Koryakskiy Khrebet see Koryakskoye Nagor'ye
Koryakskoye Nagor'ye 93 H2 var. Koryakskiy Khrebet, Eng. Koryak Range. Mountain range NE Russian Federation
Koryazhma 88 C4 Arkhangel'skaya Oblast', NW Russian Federation
Korytsa see Korçë
Kos 83 E6 It. Coo; anc. Cos. Island Dodekánisos, Greece, Aegean Sea
Kos 83 E6 Kos, Dodekánisos, Greece, Aegean Sea
Kō-saki 109 A7 headland Nagasaki, Tsushima, SW Japan
Kościan 76 B4 Ger. Kosten. Wielkopolskie, C Poland
Koscian see Lubań
Kościerzyna 76 C2 Pomorskie, NW Poland
Kosciusko, Mount see Kosciuszko, Mount
Kosciuszko, Mount 127 C7 prev. Mount Kosciusko. Mountain New South Wales, SE Australia
Koshikijima-rettō 109 A8 var. Kosikizima Rettô. Island group SW Japan
Košice 77 D6 Ger. Kaschau, Hung. Kassa. Košický Kraj, E Slovakia
Kosikizima Rettô see Koshikijima-rettō
Koson 101 E3 Rus. Kasan. Qashqadaryo Wiloyati, S Uzbekistan
Kosovo 79 D5 prev. Autonomous Province of Kosovo and Metohija. Region S Serbia and Montenegro (Yugo.)
Kosovo Polje 79 D5 Serbia, S Serbia and Montenegro (Yugo.)
Kosovska Mitrovica 79 D5 Alb. Mitrovicë; prev. Mitrovica, Titova Mitrovica. Serbia, S Serbia and Montenegro (Yugo.)
Kosrae 122 C2 prev. Kusaie. Island Caroline Islands, E Micronesia
Kossou, Lac de 52 D5 lake C Côte d'Ivoire
Kostanay 130 C4 var. Kustanay, Kaz. Qostanay. Kostanay, N Kazakhstan
Kosten see Lubań
Kostenets 82 C2 prev. Georgi Dimitrov. Sofiya, W Bulgaria
Kostnitz see Konstanz
Kostroma 88 B4 Kostromskaya Oblast', NW Russian Federation
Kostyantynivka 87 G3 Rus. Konstantinovka. Donets'ka Oblast', SE Ukraine
Koszalin 76 B2 Ger. Köslin. Zachodniopomorskie, NW Poland
Kota 112 D3 prev. Kotah. Rājasthān, N India
Kota Baharu see Kota Bharu
Kota Bahru see Kota Bharu
Kotabaru see Jayapura
Kota Bharu 116 B3 var. Kota Baharu, Kota Bahru. Kelantan, Peninsular Malaysia
Kotabumi 116 B4 prev. Kotaboemi. Sumatera, W Indonesia
Kota Kinabalu 116 D3 prev. Jesselton. Sabah, East Malaysia
Kotel'nyy, Ostrov 93 E2 island Novosibirskiye Ostrova, N Russian Federation
Kôti see Kōchi
Kotka 63 E5 Kymi, S Finland
Kotlas 88 C4 Arkhangel'skaya Oblast', NW Russian Federation
Kotonu see Cotonou
Kotor 79 C5 It. Cattaro. Montenegro, SW Serbia and Montenegro (Yugo.)
Kotovs'k 86 D3 Rus. Kotovsk. Odes'ka Oblast', SW Ukraine
Kotovsk see Hînceşti
Kotte see Sri Jayawardanapura
Kotto 54 D4 river Central African Republic/Dem. Rep. Congo
Kotuy 93 E2 river N Russian Federation
Koudougou 53 E4 C Burkina faso
Koulamoutou 55 B6 Ogooué-Lolo, C Gabon
Koulikoro 52 D3 Koulikoro, SW Mali
Koumra 54 C4 Moyen-Chari, S Chad
Kourou 37 H3 N French Guiana
Kousseir see Al Quşayr
Kousséri 54 B3 prev. Fort-Foureau. Extrême-Nord, NE Cameroon
Koutiala 52 D4 Sikasso, S Mali
Kouvola 63 E5 Kymi, S Finland
Kovel' 86 C1 Pol. Kowel. Volyns'ka Oblast', NW Ukraine
Kowloon 106 A2 Chin. Jiulong. Hong Kong, S China
Kowtal-e Barowghīl see Baroghil Pass
Kowtal-e Khaybar see Khyber Pass
Kozáni 82 B4 Dytikí Makedonía, N Greece
Kozara 78 B3 mountain range NW Bosnia and Herzegovina
Kozarska Dubica see Bosanska Dubica
Kozhikode see Calicut
Kōzu-shima 109 D6 island E Japan
Kozyatyn 86 D2 Rus. Kazatin. Vinnyts'ka Oblast', C Ukraine
Kpalimé 53 E5 var. Palimé. SW Togo
Krâchéh 115 D6 prev. Kratie. Krâchéh, E Cambodia
Kragujevac 78 D4 Serbia, C Serbia and Montenegro (Yugo.)
Kra, Isthmus of 115 B6 isthmus Malaysia/Thailand
Kraków 77 D5 Eng. Cracow, Ger. Krakau; anc. Cracovia. Małopolskie, S Poland
Krâlănh 115 D5 Siĕmréab, NW Cambodia
Kraljevo 78 D4 prev. Rankovićevo. Serbia, C Serbia and Montenegro (Yugo.)
Kramators'k 87 G3 Rus. Kramatorsk. Donets'ka Oblast', SE Ukraine
Kramfors 63 C5 Västernorrland, C Sweden
Kranéa 82 B4 Dytikí Makedonía, N Greece
Kranj 73 D7 Ger. Krainburg. NW Slovenia
Krāslava 84 D4 Krāslava, SE Latvia
Krasnaye 85 C5 Rus. Krasnoye. Minskaya Voblasts', C Belarus
Krasnoarmeysk 89 C6 Saratovskaya Oblast', W Russian Federation
Krasnodar 89 A7 prev. Ekaterinodar, Yekaterinodar. Krasnodarskiy Kray, SW Russian Federation
Krasnodon 87 H3 Luhans'ka Oblast', E Ukraine
Krasnohvardiys'ke 87 F4 Rus. Krasnogvardeyskoye. Respublika Krym, S Ukraine
Krasnokamensk 93 F4 Chitinskaya Oblast', S Russian Federation
Krasnokamsk 89 D5 Permskaya Oblast', W Russian Federation
Krasnoperekops'k 87 F4 Rus. Krasnoperekopsk. Respublika Krym, S Ukraine
Krasnovodskiy Zaliv 100 A2 Turkm. Krasnowodsk Aylagy. Lake gulf W Turkmenistan
Krasnoyarsk 92 D4 Krasnoyarskiy Kray, S Russian Federation
Krasnystaw 76 E4 Rus. Krasnostav. Lubelskie, E Poland
Krasnyy Kut 89 C6 Saratovskaya Oblast', W Russian Federation
Krasnyy Luch 87 H3 prev. Krindachevka. Luhans'ka Oblast', E Ukraine
Krâvanh, Chuŏr Phnum 115 C6 Eng. Cardamom Mountains, Fr. Chaîne des Cardamomes. Mountain range W Cambodia
Krefeld 72 A4 Nordrhein-Westfalen, W Germany
Kremenchuk 87 F2 Rus. Kremenchug. Poltavs'ka Oblast', NE Ukraine
Kremenchuts'ke Vodoskhovyshche 87 F2 Eng. Kremenchuk Reservoir, Rus. Kremenchugskoye Vodokhranilishche. Reservoir C Ukraine
Kremenets' 86 C2 Pol. Krzemieniec, Rus. Kremenets. Ternopil's'ka Oblast', W Ukraine
Kreminna 87 G2 Rus. Kremennaya. Luhans'ka Oblast', E Ukraine
Kresena see Kresna
Kresna 82 C3 var. Kresena. Blagoevgrad, SW Bulgaria
Kretikon Delagos see Kritikó Pélagos
Kretinga 84 B3 Ger. Krottingen. Kretinga, NW Lithuania
Krishna 110 C1 prev. Kistna. River C India
Krishnagiri 110 C2 Tamil Nādu, SE India
Kristiansand 63 A6 var. Christiansand. Vest-Agder, S Norway
Kristianstad 63 B7 Skåne, S Sweden
Kristiansund 62 A4 var. Christiansund. Møre og Romsdal, S Norway
Kríti 83 C7 Eng. Crete. Island Greece, Aegean Sea
Kritikó Pélagos 83 D7 var. Kretikon Delagos, Eng. Sea of Crete; anc. Mare Creticum. Sea Greece, Aegean Sea
Križevci 78 B2 Ger. Kreuz, Hung. Kőrös. Varaždin, NE Croatia
Krk 78 A3 It. Veglia; anc. Curieta. Island NW Croatia
Krolevets' 87 F1 Rus. Krolevets. Sums'ka Oblast', NE Ukraine
Kronach 73 C5 Bayern, E Germany
Kroonstad 56 D4 Free State, C South Africa
Kropotkin 89 A7 Krasnodarskiy Kray, SW Russian Federation
Krosno 77 D5 Ger. Krossen. Podkarpackie, SE Poland
Krosno Odrzańskie 76 B3 Ger. Crossen, Kreisstadt. Lubuskie, W Poland
Krško 73 E8 Ger. Gurkfeld; prev. Videm-Krško. E Slovenia
Kruhlaye 85 D6 Rus. Krugloye. Mahilyowskaya Voblasts', E Belarus
Kruja see Krujë
Krujë 79 C6 var. Kruja, It. Croia. Durrës, C Albania
Krummau see Český Krumlov
Krung Thep 115 C5 var. Krung Thep Mahanakhon, Eng. Bangkok. Country capital (Thailand) Bangkok, C Thailand
Krung Thep, Ao 115 C5 var. Bight of Bangkok. Bay S Thailand
Krung Thep Mahanakhon see Krung Thep
Krupki 85 D6 Rus. Krupki. Minskaya Voblasts', C Belarus
Krychaw 85 E7 Rus. Krichëv. Mahilyowskaya Voblasts', E Belarus
Krym see Crimea
Krymskaya Oblast' see Crimea
Kryms'ki Hory 87 F5 mountain range S Ukraine
Kryms'kyy Pivostriv 87 F5 peninsula S Ukraine
Krynica 77 D5 Ger. Tannenhof. Małopolskie, S Poland
Kryve Ozero 87 E3 Odes'ka Oblast', SW Ukraine
Kryvyy Rih 87 F3 Rus. Krivoy Rog. Dnipropetrovs'ka Oblast', SE Ukraine
Ksar al Kabir see Ksar-el-Kebir
Ksar al Soule see Er-Rachidia
Ksar-el-Kebir 48 C2 var. Alcázar, Ksar al Kabir, Ksar-el-Kébir, Ar. Al-Kasr al-Kebir, Al-Qsar al-Kbir, Sp. Alcazarquivir. NW Morocco
Ksar-el-Kébir see Ksar-el-Kebir
Kuala Dungun see Dungun
Kuala Lumpur 116 B3 country capital (Malaysia) Kuala Lumpur, Peninsular Malaysia
Kuala Terengganu 116 B3 var. Kuala Trengganu. Terengganu, Peninsular Malaysia
Kuala Trengganu see Kuala Terengganu
Kualatungkal 116 B4 Sumatera, W Indonesia
Kuang-chou see Guangzhou
Kuang-hsi see Guangxi Zhuangzu Zizhiqu
Kuang-tung see Guangdong
Kuang-yuan see Guangyuan
Kuantan 116 B3 Pahang, Peninsular Malaysia
Kuban' 87 G5 var. Hypanis. River SW Russian Federation
Kubango see Cubango
Kuching 116 C3 prev. Sarawak. Sarawak, East Malaysia
Kūchnay Darweyshān 100 D5 Helmand, S Afghanistan
Kuçova see Kuçovë
Kuçovë 79 C6 var. Kuçova; prev. Qyteti Stalin. Berat, C Albania
Kudara see Ghŭdara
Kudus 116 C5 prev. Koedoes. Jawa, C Indonesia
Kuei-chou see Guizhou
Kuei-lin see Guilin
Kuei-Yang see Guiyang
Kueyang see Guiyang
Kugluktuk 53 E3 var. Qurlurtuuq prev. Coppermine. Nunavut, NW Canada
Kuhmo 62 E4 Oulu, E Finland
Kühnö see Kihnu
Kuibyshev see Kuybyshevskoye Vodokhranilishche
Kuito 56 B2 Port. Silva Porto. Bié, C Angola
Kuji 108 D3 var. Kuzi. Iwate, Honshū, C Japan
Kukës 79 D5 var. Kukësi. Kukës, NE Albania
Kukësi see Kukës
Kukong see Shaoguan
Kukukhoto see Hohhot
Kula Kangri 113 G3 var. Kulhakangri. Mountain Bhutan/China
Kuldīga 84 B3 Ger. Goldingen. Kuldīga, W Latvia
Kuldja see Yining
Kulhakangri see Kula Kangri
Kullorsuaq 60 D2 var. Kuvdlorssuak. C Greenland
Kulmsee see Chełmża
Kŭlob 101 F3 Rus. Kulyab. SW Tajikistan
Kulu 94 C3 Konya, W Turkey
Kulunda Steppe 92 C4 Kaz. Qulyndy Zhazyghy, Rus. Kulundinskaya Ravnina. Grassland Kazakhstan/Russian Federation
Kum see Qom
Kuma 89 B7 river SW Russian Federation
Kumamoto 109 A7 Kumamoto, Kyūshū, SW Japan
Kumanovo 79 E5 Turk. Kumanova. N FYR Macedonia
Kumasi 53 E5 prev. Coomassie. C Ghana
Kumayri see Gyumri
Kumba 55 A5 Sud Ouest, W Cameroon
Kumertau 89 D6 Respublika Bashkortostan, W Russian Federation
Kumo 53 G4 Gombe, E Nigeria
Kumon Range 114 B2 mountain range N Myanmar
Kumul see Hami
Kunashiri see Kunashir, Ostrov
Kunashir, Ostrov 108 E1 var. Kunashiri Island Kuril'skiye Ostrova, SE Russian Federation
Kunda 84 E2 Lääne-Virumaa, NE Estonia
Kunduz 101 E3 var. Kondoz, Kundūz, Qondūz, Per. Kondūz. Kunduz, NE Afghanistan
Kuneitra see Al Qunayţirah
Kunene see Cunene
Kungsbacka 63 B7 Halland, S Sweden
Kungur 89 D5 Permskaya Oblast', NW Russian Federation
Kunlun Mountains see Kunlun Shan
Kunlun Shan 104 B4 Eng. Kunlun Mountains. Mountain range NW China
Kunming 106 B6 var. K'un-ming; prev. Yunnan. Yunnan, SW China
K'un-ming see Kunming
Kununurra 124 D3 Western Australia
Kuopio 63 E5 Itä-Suomi, C Finland
Kupang 117 E5 prev. Koepang. Timor, C Indonesia
Kup"yans'k 87 G2 Rus. Kupyansk. Kharkivs'ka Oblast', E Ukraine
Kura 95 H3 Az. Kür, Geor. Mtkvari, Turk. Kura Nehri. River SW Asia
Kurashiki 109 B6 var. Kurasiki. Okayama, Honshū, SW Japan
Kurasiki see Kurashiki
Kurdistan 95 F4 cultural region SW Asia
Kŭrdzhali 82 D3 var. Kirdzhali. Kŭrdzhali, S Bulgaria
Kure 109 B7 Hiroshima, Honshū, SW Japan
Küre Dağları 94 C2 mountain range N Turkey
Kuressaare 84 C2 Ger. Arensburg; prev. Kingissepp. Saaremaa, W Estonia
Kureyka 90 D2 river N Russian Federation
Kuria Muria Islands see Ḩalāniyāt, Juzur al
Kurile Islands see Kuril'skiye Ostrova
Kurile-Kamchatka Depression see Kurile Trench
Kurile Trench 91 F3 var. Kurile-Kamchatka Depression. Undersea feature NW Pacific Ocean

INDEX

Lewiston – Macdonnell Ranges

Lewistown *22 C1* Montana, NW USA
Lexington *18 C5* Kentucky, S USA
Lexington *23 E4* Nebraska, C USA
Leyte *117 F2 island* C Philippines
Leżajsk *77 E5* Podkarpackie, SE Poland
Lezha *see* Lezhë
Lezhë *79 C6 var.* Lezha; *prev.* Lesh, Leshi. Lezhë, NW Albania
Lhasa *104 C5 var.* La-sa, Lassa. Xizang Zizhiqu, W China
Lhaviyani Atoll *see* Faadhippolhu Atoll
Lhazê *104 C5* Xizang Zizhiqu, W China
L'Hospitalet de Llobregat *71 G2 var.* Hospitalet. Cataluña, NE Spain
Liancourt Rocks *109 A5 Jap.* Take-shima, *Kor.* Tok-Do. *Island group* Japan/South Korea
Lianyungang *106 D4 var.* Xinpu. Jiangsu, E China
Liao *see* Liaoning
Liaodong Wan *105 G3 Eng.* Gulf of Lantung, Gulf of Liaotung. *Gulf* NE China
Liao He *103 E1 river* NE China
Liaoning *106 D3 var.* Liao, Liaoning Sheng, Shengking; *hist.* Fengtien, Shenking. Admin. region *province* NE China
Liaoyuan *107 E3 var.* Dongliao, Shuang-liao, *Jap.* Chengchiatun. Jilin, NE China
Liard *see* Fort Liard
Liban, Jebel *96 B4 Ar.* Jabal al Gharbt, Jabal Lubnān, *Eng.* Mount Lebanon. *Mountain range* C Lebanon
Libby *22 A1* Montana, NW USA
Liberal *23 E5* Kansas, C USA
Liberec *76 B4 Ger.* Reichenberg. Liberecký Kraj, N Czech Republic
Liberia *52 C5 off.* Republic of Liberia. *Country* W Africa
Liberia *30 D4* Guanacaste, NW Costa Rica
Libian Desert *see* Libyan Desert
Libourne *69 B5* Gironde, SW France
Libreville *55 A5 country capital* (Gabon) Estuaire, NW Gabon
Libya *49 F3 off.* Socialist People's Libyan Arab Jamahiriya, *Ar.* Al Jamāhīrīyah al 'Arabīyah al Lībīyah ash Sha'bīyah al Ishtirākīyah; *prev.* Libyan Arab Republic. *Country* N Africa
Libyan Desert *49 H4 var.* Libian Desert, *Ar.* Aṣ Ṣahrā' al Lībīyah. *Desert* N Africa
Libyan Plateau *81 F4 var.* Aḍ Diffah. *Plateau* Egypt/Libya
Lichtenfels *73 C5* Bayern, SE Germany
Lichtenvoorde *64 E4* Gelderland, E Netherlands
Lichuan *106 C5* Hubei, C China
Lida *85 B5 Rus.* Lida. Hrodzyenskaya Voblasts', W Belarus
Lidköping *63 B6* Västra Götaland, S Sweden
Lidoríki *83 B5 prev.* Lidhorikíon, Lidokhorikion. Stereá Ellás, C Greece
Lidzbark Warmiński *76 D2 Ger.* Heilsberg. Warmińsko-Mazurskie, NE Poland
Liechtenstein *72 D1 off.* Principality of Liechtenstein. *Country* C Europe
Liège *65 D6 Dut.* Luik, *Ger.* Lüttich. Liège, E Belgium
Lienz *73 D7* Tirol, W Austria
Liepāja *84 B3 Ger.* Libau. Liepāja, W Latvia
Liezen *73 D7* Steiermark, C Austria
Liffey *67 B6 river* E Ireland
Lifou *122 D5 island* Îles Loyauté, E New Caledonia
Liger *see* Loire
Ligure, Appennino *74 A2 Eng.* Ligurian Mountains. *Mountain range* NW Italy
Ligurian Sea *74 A3 Fr.* Mer Ligurienne, *It.* Mar Ligure. *Sea* N Mediterranean Sea
Lihue *25 A7 Haw.* Līhu'e. Kauai, Hawaii, USA, C Pacific Ocean
Lihula *84 D2 Ger.* Leal. Läänemaa, W Estonia
Likasi *55 D7 prev.* Jadotville. Shaba, SE Dem. Rep. Congo
Liknes *63 A6* Vest-Agder, S Norway
Lille *68 C2 var.* l'Isle, *Dut.* Rijssel, *Flem.* Ryssel; *prev.* Lisle, *anc.* Insula. Nord, N France
Lillehammer *63 B5* Oppland, S Norway
Lillestrøm *63 B6* Akershus, S Norway
Lilongwe *57 E2 country capital* (Malawi) Central, W Malawi
Lima *38 C4 country capital* (Peru) Lima, W Peru
Limanowa *77 D5* Małopolskie, S Poland
Limassol *see* Lemesós
Limerick *67 A6 Ir.* Luimneach. SW Ireland
Límnos *81 F3 anc.* Lemnos. *Island* E Greece
Limoges *69 C5 anc.* Augustoritum Lemovicensium, Lemovices. Haute-Vienne, C France
Limón *31 E4 var.* Puerto Limón. Limón, E Costa Rica
Limón *30 D2* Colón, NE Honduras
Limousin *69 C5 cultural region* C France
Limoux *69 C6* Aude, S France
Limpopo *56 D3 var.* Crocodile. *River* S Africa
Linares *70 D4* Andalucía, S Spain
Linares *42 B4* Maule, C Chile
Linares *29 E3* Nuevo León, NE Mexico
Linchuan *106 D5 var.* Fuzhou. Jiangxi, S China
Lincoln *67 D5 anc.* Lindum, Lindum Colonia. E England, UK
Lincoln *23 F4 state capital* Nebraska, C USA
Lincoln *19 H2* Maine, NE USA
Lincoln Sea *12 D2 sea* Arctic Ocean
Linden *37 F3* E Guyana
Líndhos *see* Líndos
Lindi *51 D8* Lindi, SE Tanzania
Líndos *83 E7 var.* Líndhos. Ródos, Dodekánisos, Greece, Aegean Sea
Line Islands *123 G3 island group* E Kiribati
Lingeh *see* Bandar-e Langeh
Lingen *72 A3 var.* Lingen an der Ems. Niedersachsen, NW Germany
Lingen an der Ems *see* Lingen
Lingga, Kepulauan *116 B4 island group* W Indonesia
Linköping *63 C6* Östergötland, S Sweden
Linz *73 D6 anc.* Lentia. Oberösterreich, N Austria
Lion, Golfe du *69 C7 Eng.* Gulf of Lion, Gulf of Lions; *anc.* Sinus Gallicus. *Gulf* S France
Lipari Islands *see* Eolie, Isole
Lipari, Isola *75 D6 island* Isole Eolie, S Italy
Lipetsk *89 B5* Lipetskaya Oblast', W Russian Federation
Lipno *76 C3* Kujawsko-pomorskie, C Poland
Lipova *86 A4 Hung.* Lippa. Arad, W Romania
Liqeni i Ohrit *see* Ohrid, Lake
Lira *51 B6* N Uganda
Lisala *55 C5* Equateur, N Dem. Rep. Congo
Lisboa *70 B4 Eng.* Lisbon; *anc.* Felicitas Julia, Olisipo. *Country capital* (Portugal) Lisboa, W Portugal
Lisbon *see* Lisboa
Lisieux *68 B3 anc.* Noviomagus. Calvados, N France
Liski *89 B6 prev.* Georgiu-Dezh. Voronezhskaya Oblast', W Russian Federation
Lisle *see* Lille
l'Isle *see* Lille
Lismore *127 E5* Victoria, SE Australia
Lisse *64 C3* Zuid-Holland, W Netherlands
Litang *106 A5* Sichuan, C China
Līṭānī, Nahr el *135 B5 var.* Nahr al Litant. *River* C Lebanon
Lithgow *127 D6* New South Wales, SE Australia
Lithuania *84 B4 off.* Republic of Lithuania, *Ger.* Litauen, *Lith.* Lietuva, *Pol.* Litwa, *Rus.* Litva; *prev.* Lithuanian SSR, *Rus.* Litovskaya SSR. *Country* NE Europe
Litóchoro *82 B4 var.* Litohoro, Litókhoron. Kentrikí Makedonía, N Greece
Litohoro *see* Litóchoro
Litókhoron *see* Litóchoro
Little Alföld *77 C6 Ger.* Kleines Ungarisches Tiefland, *Hung.* Kisalföld, *Slvk.* Podunajská Rovina. *Plain* Hungary/Slovakia
Little Andaman *111 F2 island* Andaman Islands, India, NE Indian Ocean
Little Barrier Island *128 D2 island* N NZ
Little Bay *71 H5 bay* S Gibraltar
Little Cayman *32 B3 island* E Cayman Islands
Little Falls *23 F2* Minnesota, N USA
Littlefield *27 E2* Texas, SW USA
Little Inagua *32 D2 var.* Inagua Islands. *Island* S Bahamas
Little Minch, The *66 B3 strait* NW Scotland, UK
Little Missouri River *22 D2 river* NW USA
Little Nicobar *111 G3 island* Nicobar Islands, India, NE Indian Ocean
Little Rock *20 B1 state capital* Arkansas, C USA
Little Saint Bernard Pass *69 D5 Fr.* Col du Petit St-Bernard, *It.* Colle di Piccolo San Bernardo. *Pass* France/Italy
Little Sound *20 A5 bay* Bermuda, NW Atlantic Ocean
Littleton *22 D4* Colorado, C USA
Liu-chou *see* Liuzhou
Liuchow *see* Liuzhou
Liuzhou *106 C6 var.* Liu-chou, Liuchow. Guangxi Zhuangzu Zizhiqu, S China
Livanátes *83 B5 prev.* Livanátai. Stereá Ellás, C Greece
Līvāni *84 D4 Ger.* Lievenhof. Preiļi, SE Latvia
Liverpool *126 D2* New South Wales, SE Australia
Liverpool *17 F5* Nova Scotia, SE Canada
Liverpool *67 C5* NW England, UK
Livingston *22 B2* Montana, NW USA
Livingstone *56 C3 var.* Maramba. Southern, S Zambia
Livingstone *27 H3* Texas, SW USA
Livingstone Mountains *129 A7 mountain range* South Island, NZ
Livno *78 B4* Federacija Bosna I Hercegovina, SW Bosnia and Herzegovina
Livojoki *62 D4 river* C Finland
Livonia *18 D3* Michigan, N USA
Livorno *74 B3 Eng.* Leghorn. Toscana, C Italy
Lixoúri *83 A5 prev.* Lixoúrion. Kefallinía, Iónioi Nísoi, Greece, C Mediterranean Sea
Ljubljana *73 D7 Ger.* Laibach, *It.* Lubiana; *anc.* Aemona, Emona. *Country capital* (Slovenia) C Slovenia
Ljungby *63 B7* Kronoberg, S Sweden
Ljusdal *63 C5* Gävleborg, C Sweden
Ljusnan *63 C5 river* C Sweden
Llanelli *67 C6 prev.* Llanelly. SW Wales, UK
Llanes *70 D1* Asturias, N Spain
Llanos *36 D2 physical region* Colombia/Venezuela
Lleida *71 F2 Cast.* Lérida; *anc.* Ilerda. Cataluña, NE Spain
Lluchmayor *see* Llucmajor
Llucmajor *71 G3 var.* Lluchmayor. Mallorca, Spain, W Mediterranean Sea
Loaita Island *106 C8 island* W Spratly Islands
Loanda *see* Luanda
Lobatse *56 C4 var.* Lobatsi. Kgatleng, SE Botswana
Lobatsi *see* Lobatse
Löbau *72 D4* Sachsen, E Germany
Lobito *56 B2* Benguela, W Angola
Lob Nor *see* Lop Nur
Loburi *see* Lop Buri
Locarno *73 B8 Ger.* Luggarus. Ticino, S Switzerland
Lochem *64 E3* Gelderland, E Netherlands
Lockport *19 E3* New York, NE USA
Lodja *55 D6* Kasai Oriental, C Dem. Rep. Congo
Lodwar *51 C6* Rift Valley, NW Kenya
Łódź *76 D4 Rus.* Lodz. Łódzkie, C Poland
Loei *114 C4 var.* Loey, Muang Loei. Loei, C Thailand
Loey *see* Loei
Lofoten *62 B3 var.* Lofoten Islands. *Island group* C Norway
Lofoten Islands *see* Lofoten
Logan *22 B3* Utah, W USA
Logan, Mount *14 D3 mountain* Yukon Territory, W Canada
Logroño *71 E1 anc.* Vareia, *Lat.* Juliobriga. La Rioja, N Spain
Loibl Pass *73 D7 Ger.* Loiblpass, *Slvn.* Ljubelj. *Pass* Austria/Slovenia
Loi-Kaw *114 B4* Kayah State, C Myanmar
Loire *68 B4 var.* Liger. *River* C France
Loja *38 B2* Loja, S Ecuador
Lokitaung *51 C5* Rift Valley, NW Kenya
Lokoja *53 G4* Kogi, C Nigeria
Loksa *84 E2 Ger.* Loxa. Harjumaa, NW Estonia
Lolland *63 B8 prev.* Laaland. *Island* S Denmark
Lom *82 C1 prev.* Lom-Palanka. Montana, NW Bulgaria
Lomami *55 D6 river* C Dem. Rep. Congo
Lomas *38 D4* Arequipa, SW Peru
Lomas de Zamora *42 D4* Buenos Aires, E Argentina
Lombardia *74 B2 cultural region* N Italy
Lombok, Pulau *116 D5 island* Nusa Tenggara, C Indonesia
Lomé *53 F5 country capital* (Togo) S Togo
Lomela *55 D6* Kasai Oriental, C Dem. Rep. Congo
Lommel *65 C5* Limburg, N Belgium
Lomond, Loch *66 B4 lake* C Scotland, UK
Lomonosov Ridge *133 B3 var.* Harris Ridge, *Rus.* Khrebet Lomonsova. *Undersea feature* Arctic Ocean
Lompoc *25 B7* California, W USA
Lom Sak *114 C4 var.* Muang Lom Sak. Phetchabun, C Thailand
Łomża *76 D3 off.* Województwo Łomżyńskie, *Rus.* Lomzha. Podlaskie, NE Poland
Loncoche *43 B5* Araucanía, C Chile
London *67 A7 anc.* Augusta, *Lat.* Londinium. *Country capital* (UK) SE England, UK
London *18 C5* Kentucky, S USA
London *16 C5* Ontario, S Canada
Londonderry *66 B4 var.* Derry, *Ir.* Doire. NW Northern Ireland, UK
Londonderry, Cape *124 C2 headland* Western Australia
Londrina *41 E4* Paraná, S Brazil
Longa, Proliv *93 G1 Eng.* Long Strait. *Strait* NE Russian Federation
Long Bay *21 F2 bay* North Carolina/South Carolina, E USA
Long Beach *25 C7* California, W USA
Longford *67 B5 Ir.* An Longfort. C Ireland
Long Island *32 D2 island* C Bahamas
Long Island *19 G4 island* New York, NE USA
Long Island *see* Bermuda
Longlac *16 C3* Ontario, S Canada
Longmont *22 D4* Colorado, C USA
Longreach *126 C4* Queensland, E Australia
Long Strait *see* Longa, Proliv
Longview *27 H3* Texas, SW USA
Longview *24 B2* Washington, NW USA
Long Xuyên *115 D6 var.* Longxuyen. An Giang, S Vietnam
Longxuyen *see* Long Xuyên
Longyan *106 D6* Fujian, SE China
Longyearbyen *61 G2 dependent territory capital* (Svalbard) Spitsbergen, W Svalbard
Lons-le-Saunier *68 D4 anc.* Ledo Salinarius. Jura, E France
Lop Buri *115 C5 var.* Loburi. Lop Buri, C Thailand
Lop Nor *see* Lop Nur
Lop Nur *104 C3 var.* Lob Nor, Lop Nor, Lo-pu Po. *Seasonal lake* NW China
Loppersum *64 E1* Groningen, NE Netherlands
Lo-pu Po *see* Lop Nur
Lorca *71 E4 Ar.* Lurka; *anc.* Eliocroca, *Lat.* Illur co. Murcia, S Spain
Lord Howe Island *120 C4 island* E Australia
Lord Howe Rise *120 C4 undersea feature* SW Pacific Ocean
Loreto *28 B3* Baja California Sur, W Mexico
Lorient *68 A3 prev.* l'Orient. Morbihan, NW France
Lorn, Firth of *66 B4 inlet* W Scotland, UK
Loro Sae *see* East Timor
Lörrach *73 A7* Baden-Württemberg, S Germany
Lorraine *68 D3 cultural region* NE France
Los Alamos *26 C1* New Mexico, SW USA
Los Amates *30 B2* Izabal, E Guatemala
Los Angeles *25 C7* California, W USA
Los Ángeles *43 B5* Bío Bío, C Chile
Lošinj *78 A3 Ger.* Lussin, *It.* Lussino. *Island* W Croatia
Los Mochis *28 C3* Sinaloa, C Mexico
Los Roques, Islas *36 D1 island group* N Venezuela
Los Testigos, Isla *33 G5 island* NE Venezuela
Lost River Range *24 D3 mountain range* Idaho, C USA
Lot *69 B5 cultural region* C France
Lot *69 B5 river* S France
Lotagipi Swamp *51 C5 wetland* Kenya/Sudan
Louangnamtha *114 C3 var.* Luong Nam Tha. Louang Namtha, N Laos
Louangphabang *102 D3 var.* Louangphrabang, Luang Prabang. Louangphabang, N Laos
Louangphrabang *see* Louangphabang
Loudéac *68 A3* Côtes d'Armor, NW France
Loudi *106 C5* Hunan, S China
Louga *52 B3* NW Senegal
Louisiade Archipelago *122 B4 island group* SE PNG
Louisiana *20 A2 off.* State of Louisiana; also known as Creole State, Pelican State. *State* S USA
Louisville *18 C5* Kentucky, S USA
Louisville Ridge *121 E4 undersea feature* S Pacific Ocean
Loup River *23 E4 river* Nebraska, C USA
Lourdes *69 B6* Hautes-Pyrénées, S France
Louth *67 E5* E England, UK
Loutrá *82 C4* Kentrikí Makedonía, N Greece
Lóuva *56 C1* Lunda Norte, NE Angola
Louvain-la Neuve *65 C6* Wallon Brabant, C Belgium
Louviers *68 C3* Eure, N France
Lovech *82 C2* Lovech, N Bulgaria
Loveland *22 D4* Colorado, C USA
Lovosice *76 A4 Ger.* Lobositz. Ústecký Kraj, NW Czech Republic
Lowell *19 G3* Massachusetts, NE USA
Lower California *see* Baja California
Lower Hutt *129 D5* Wellington, North Island, NZ
Lower Lough Erne *67 A5 lake* SW Northern Ireland, UK
Lower Red Lake *23 F1 lake* Minnesota, N USA
Lower Tunguska *see* Nizhnyaya Tunguska
Lowestoft *67 E6* E England, UK
Lo-yang *see* Luoyang
Loyauté, Îles *122 D5 island group* S New Caledonia
Loyew *85 D8 Rus.* Loyev. Homyel'skaya Voblasts', SE Belarus
Loznica *78 C3* Serbia, W Serbia and Montenegro (Yugo.)
Lu *see* Shandong
Lualaba *55 D6 Fr.* Loualaba. *River* SE Dem. Rep. Congo
Luanda *56 A1 var.* Loanda, *Port.* São Paulo de Loanda. *Country capital* (Angola) Luanda, NW Angola
Luang Prabang *see* Louangphabang
Luang, Thale *115 C7 lagoon* S Thailand
Luangua, Rio *see* Luangwa
Luangwa *51 B8 var.* Aruângua, Rio Luangua. *River* Mozambique/Zambia
Luanshya *56 D2* Copperbelt, C Zambia
Luarca *70 C1* Asturias, N Spain
Lubaczów *77 E5 var.* Lúbaczów. Podkarpackie, SE Poland
Lubań *76 B4 var.* Koscian, *Ger.* Kosten. Dolnośląskie, SW Poland
Lubānas Ezers *see* Lubāns
Lubango *56 B2 Port.* Sá da Bandeira. Huíla, SW Angola
Lubāns *84 D4 var.* Lubānas Ezers. *Lake* E Latvia
Lubao *55 D6* Kasai Oriental, C Dem. Rep. Congo
Lübben *72 D4* Brandenburg, E Germany
Lübbenau *72 D4* Brandenburg, E Germany
Lubbock *27 E2* Texas, SW USA
Lübeck *72 C2* Schleswig-Holstein, N Germany
Lubelska, Wyżyna *76 E4 plateau* SE Poland
Lubin *76 B4 Ger.* Lüben. Dolnośląskie, W Poland
Lublin *76 E4 Rus.* Lyublin. Lubelskie, E Poland
Lubliniec *76 C4* Śląskie, S Poland
Lubny *87 F2* Poltavs'ka Oblast', NE Ukraine
Lubsko *76 B4 Ger.* Sommerfeld. Lubuskie, W Poland
Lubumbashi *55 E8 prev.* Élisabethville. Shaba, SE Dem. Rep. Congo
Lubutu *55 D6* Maniema, E Dem. Rep. Congo
Lucan *67 B5 Ir.* Leamhcán. E Ireland
Lucano, Appennino *75 D5 Eng.* Lucanian Mountains. *Mountain range* S Italy
Lucapa *56 C1 var.* Lukapa. Lunda Norte, NE Angola
Lucca *74 B3 anc.* Luca. Toscana, C Italy
Lucea *32 A4* W Jamaica
Lucena *117 E1 off.* Lucena City. Luzon, N Philippines
Lucena *70 D4* Andalucía, S Spain
Lučenec *77 D6 Ger.* Losontz, *Hung.* Losonc. Banskobystrický Kraj, C Slovakia
Luchow *see* Hefei
Lucknow *113 E3 var.* Lakhnau. Uttar Pradesh, N India
Lüda *see* Dalian
Luda Kamchiya *82 D2 river* E Bulgaria
Lüderitz *56 B4 prev.* Angra Pequena. Karas, SW Namibia
Ludhiāna *112 D2* Punjab, N India
Ludington *18 C2* Michigan, N USA
Luduş *86 B4 Ger.* Ludasch, *Hung.* Marosludas. Mureş, C Romania
Ludvika *63 C6* Kopparberg, C Sweden
Ludwigslust *72 C3* Mecklenburg-Vorpommern, N Germany
Ludwigsburg *73 B6* Baden-Württemberg, SW Germany
Ludwigsfelde *72 D3* Brandenburg, NE Germany
Ludwigshafen *73 B5 var.* Ludwigshafen am Rhein. Rheinland-Pfalz, W Germany
Ludwigshafen am Rhein *see* Ludwigshafen
Ludza *84 D4 Ger.* Ludsan. Ludza, E Latvia
Luebo *55 C6* Kasai Occidental, SW Dem. Rep. Congo
Luena *56 C2 var.* Lwena, *Port.* Luso. Moxico, E Angola
Lufira *55 E7 river* SE Dem. Rep. Congo
Lufkin *27 H3* Texas, SW USA
Luga *88 A4* Leningradskaya Oblast', NW Russian Federation
Lugano *73 B8 Ger.* Lauis. Ticino, S Switzerland
Lugenda, Rio *57 E2 river* N Mozambique
Lugo *70 C1 anc.* Lugus Augusti. Galicia, NW Spain
Lugoj *86 A4 Ger.* Lugosch, *Hung.* Lugos. Timiş, W Romania
Luhans'k *87 H3 Rus.* Lugansk; *prev.* Voroshilovgrad. Luhans'ka Oblast', E Ukraine
Luimneach *see* Limerick
Lukapa *see* Lucapa
Lukenie *55 C6 river* C Dem. Rep. Congo
Lukovit *82 C2* Lovech, NW Bulgaria
Łuków *76 E4 Ger.* Bogendorf. Lubelskie, E Poland
Lukuga *55 D7 river* SE Dem. Rep. Congo
Luleå *62 D4* Norrbotten, N Sweden
Luleälven *62 C3 river* N Sweden
Lulonga *55 C5 river* NW Dem. Rep. Congo
Lulua *55 D7 river* S Dem. Rep. Congo
Lumbo *57 F2* Nampula, NE Mozambique
Lumsden *129 A7* Southland, South Island, NZ
Lund *63 B7* Skåne, S Sweden
Lüneburg *72 C3* Niedersachsen, N Germany
Lungkiang *see* Qiqihar
Lungué-Bungo *56 C2 var.* Lungwebungu. *River* Angola/Zambia *see also* Lungwebungu
Lungwebungu *see* Lungué-Bungo
Luninyets *85 B7 Pol.* Łuniniec, *Rus.* Luninets. Brestskaya Voblasts', SW Belarus
Lunteren *64 D4* Gelderland, C Netherlands
Luong Nam Tha *see* Louangnamtha
Luoyang *106 C4 var.* Honan, Lo-yang. Henan, C China
Lúrio *57 F2* Nampula, NE Mozambique
Lúrio, Rio *57 E2 river* NE Mozambique
Lusaka *56 D2 country capital* (Zambia) Lusaka, SE Zambia
Lushnja *see* Lushnjë
Lushnjë *79 C6 var.* Lushnja. Fier, C Albania
Luso *see* Luena
Lūt, Dasht-e *98 D3 var.* Kavīr-e Lūt. *Desert* E Iran
Luton *67 D6* SE England, UK
Łutselk'e *15 F4 prev.* Snowdrift. Northwest Territories, W Canada
Luts'k *86 C1 Pol.* Łuck, *Rus.* Lutsk. Volyns'ka Oblast', NW Ukraine
Lutzow-Holm Bay *see* Lützow Holmbukta
Lützow Holmbukta *132 C2 var.* Lutzow-Holm Bay. *Bay* Antarctica
Luuq *51 D6 It.* Lugh Ganana. Gedo, SW Somalia
Luvua *55 D7 river* SE Dem. Rep. Congo
Luwego *51 C8 river* S Tanzania
Luxembourg *65 D8 off.* Grand Duchy of Luxembourg, *var.* Lëtzebuerg, Luxemburg. *Country* NW Europe
Luxembourg *65 D8 country capital* (Luxembourg) Luxembourg, S Luxembourg
Luxor *50 B2 Ar.* Al Uqşur. E Egypt
Luza *88 C4* Kirovskaya Oblast', NW Russian Federation
Luz, Costa de la *70 C5 coastal region* SW Spain
Luzern *73 B7 Fr.* Lucerne, *It.* Lucerna. Luzern, C Switzerland
Luzon *117 E1 island* N Philippines
Luzon Strait *103 E3 strait* Philippines/Taiwan
L'viv *86 B2 Ger.* Lemberg, *Pol.* Lwów, *Rus.* L'vov. L'vivs'ka Oblast', W Ukraine
Lwena *see* Luena
Lyakhavichy *85 B6 Rus.* Lyakhovichi. Brestskaya Voblasts', SW Belarus
Lycksele *62 C4* Västerbotten, N Sweden
Lycopolis *see* Asyūt
Lyel'chytsy *85 C7 Rus.* Lel'chitsy. Homyel'skaya Voblasts', SE Belarus
Lyepyel' *85 D5 Rus.* Lepel'. Vitsyebskaya Voblasts', N Belarus
Lyme Bay *67 C7 bay* S England, UK
Lynchburg *19 E5* Virginia, NE USA
Lynn Regis *see* King's Lynn
Lyon *69 D5 Eng.* Lyons; *anc.* Lugdunum. Rhône, E France
Lyozna *85 E6 Rus.* Liozno. Vitsyebskaya Voblasts', NE Belarus
Lypovets' *86 D2 Rus.* Lipovets. Vinnyts'ka Oblast', C Ukraine
Lysychans'k *87 H3 Rus.* Lisichansk. Luhans'ka Oblast', E Ukraine
Lyttelton *129 C6* Canterbury, South Island, NZ
Lyubotyn *87 G2 Rus.* Lyubotin. Kharkivs'ka Oblast', E Ukraine
Lyulyakovo *82 E2 prev.* Keremitlik. Burgas, E Bulgaria
Lyusina *85 B6 Rus.* Lyusino. Brestskaya Voblasts', SW Belarus

M

Ma'ān *97 B7* Ma'ān, SW Jordan
Maardu *84 D2 Ger.* Maart. Harjumaa, NW Estonia
Ma'aret-en-Nu'man *see* Ma'arrat an Nu'mān
Ma'arrat an Nu'mān *96 B3 var.* Ma'aret-en-Nu'man, *Fr.* Maarret enn Naamâne. Idlib, NW Syria
Maarret enn Naamâne *see* Ma'arrat an Nu'mān
Maaseik *65 D5 prev.* Maeseyck. Limburg, NE Belgium
Maastricht *65 D6 var.* Maestricht; *anc.* Traietum ad Mosam, Traiectum Tungorum. Limburg, SE Netherlands
Macao *107 C6 Chin.* Aomen, *Port.* Macau. S China
Macapá *41 E1 state capital* Amapá, N Brazil
Macassar *see* Ujungpandang
MacCluer Gulf *see* Berau, Teluk
Macdonnell Ranges *124 D4 mountain range* Northern Territory, C Australia

Maryland – Mitchell, Mount

Maryland *20 D1* Tennessee, S USA
Maryville *23 F4* Missouri, C USA
Masai Steppe *51 C7 grassland* NW Tanzania
Masaka *51 B6* SW Uganda
Masallı *95 H3 Rus.* Masally. S Azerbaijan
Masasi *51 C8* Mtwara, SE Tanzania
Masawa *see* Massawa
Masaya *30 D3* Masaya, W Nicaragua
Mascarene Basin *119 B5 undersea feature* W Indian Ocean
Mascarene Islands *57 H4 island group* W Indian Ocean
Mascarene Plain *119 B5 undersea feature* W Indian Ocean
Mascarene Plateau *119 B5 undersea feature* W Indian Ocean
Maseru *56 D4 country capital* (Lesotho) W Lesotho
Mas-ha *59 D7* W Bank
Mashhad *98 E2 var.* Meshed. Khorāsān, NE Iran
Masindi *51 B6* W Uganda
Masīra *see* Maşīrah, Jazīrat
Masira, Gulf of *see* Maşīrah, Khalīj
Maşīrah, Jazīrat *99 E5 var.* Masīra. *Island* E Oman
Maşīrah, Khalīj *99 E5 var.* Gulf of Masira. *Bay* E Oman
Masis *see* Büyükağrı Dağı
Maskat *see* Masqaţ
Mason City *23 F3* Iowa, C USA
Masqaţ *99 E5 var.* Maskat, *Eng.* Muscat. *Country capital* (Oman) NE Oman
Massa *74 B3* Toscana, C Italy
Massachusetts *19 G3 off.* Commonwealth of Massachusetts; also known as Bay State, Old Bay State, Old Colony State. *State* NE USA
Massawa *50 C4 var.* Masawa, *Amh.* Mits'iwa. E Eritrea
Massenya *54 B3* Chari-Baguirmi, SW Chad
Massif Central *69 C5 plateau* C France
Massif du Makay *see* Makay
Massoukou *see* Franceville
Masterton *129 D5* Wellington, North Island, NZ
Masty *85 B5 Rus.* Mosty. Hrodzyenskaya Voblasts', W Belarus
Masuda *109 B6* Shimane, Honshū, SW Japan
Masuku *see* Franceville
Masvingo *56 D3 prev.* Fort Victoria, Nyanda, Victoria. Masvingo, SE Zimbabwe
Maşyāf *96 B3 Fr.* Misiaf. Ḩamāh, C Syria
Matadi *55 B6* Bas-Zaïre, W Dem. Rep. Congo
Matagalpa *30 D3* Matagalpa, C Nicaragua
Matale *110 D3* Central Province, C Sri Lanka
Matam *52 C3* NE Senegal
Matamata *128 D3* Waikato, North Island, NZ
Matamoros *28 D3* Coahuila de Zaragoza, NE Mexico
Matamoros *29 E2* Tamaulipas, C Mexico
Matane *17 E4* Quebec, SE Canada
Matanzas *32 B2* Matanzas, NW Cuba
Matara *110 D4* Southern Province, S Sri Lanka
Mataram *116 D5* Pulau Lombok, C Indonesia
Mataró *71 G2 anc.* Illuro. Cataluña, E Spain
Mataura *129 B7 river* South Island, NZ
Mataura *129 B7* Southland, South Island, NZ
Mata Uta *see* Matā'utu
Matā'utu *123 E4 var.* Mata Uta. *Dependent territory capital* (Wallis and Futuna) Île Uvea, Wallis and Futuna
Matera *75 E5* Basilicata, S Italy
Matías Romero *29 F5* Oaxaca, SE Mexico
Mato Grosso *41 F4 prev.* Vila Bela da Santissima Trindade. Mato Grosso, W Brazil
Mato Grosso do Sul *41 E4 off.* Estado de Mato Grosso do Sul. *State* S Brazil
Mato Grosso, Planalto de *34 C4 plateau* C Brazil
Matosinhos *70 B2 prev.* Matozinhos. Porto, NW Portugal
Matsue *109 B6 var.* Matsuye, Matue. Shimane, Honshū, SW Japan
Matsumoto *109 C5 var.* Matumoto. Nagano, Honshū, S Japan
Matsuyama *109 B7 var.* Matuyama. Ehime, Shikoku, SW Japan
Matsuye *see* Matsue
Matterhorn *73 A8 It.* Monte Cervino. *Mountain* Italy/Switzerland *see also* Cervino, Monte
Matthews Ridge *37 F2* N Guyana
Matthew Town *32 D2* Great Inagua, S Bahamas
Matucana *38 C4* Lima, W Peru
Matue *see* Matsue
Matumoto *see* Matsumoto
Maturín *37 E2* Monagas, NE Venezuela
Matuyama *see* Matsuyama
Mau *113 E3 var.* Maunāth Bhanjan. Uttar Pradesh, N India
Maui *25 B8 island* Hawaii, USA, C Pacific Ocean
Maulmain *see* Moulmein
Maun *56 C3* Ngamiland, C Botswana
Maunāth Bhanjan *see* Mau
Mauren *72 E1* NE Liechtenstein
Mauritania *52 C2 off.* Islamic Republic of Mauritania, *Ar.* Mūrītāniyah. *Country* W Africa
Mauritius *57 H3 off.* Republic of Mauritius, *Fr.* Maurice. *Country* W Indian Ocean
Mauritius *119 B5 island* W Indian Ocean
Mawlamyine *see* Moulmein
Mawson *132 D2 Australian research station* Antarctica
Maya *30 B1 river* E Russian Federation
Mayadin *see* Al Mayādīn
Mayaguana *32 D2 island* SE Bahamas
Mayaguana Passage *32 D2 passage* SE Bahamas
Mayagüez *33 F3* W Puerto Rico
Mayamey *98 D2* Semnān, N Iran
Maya Mountains *30 B2 Sp.* Montañas Mayas. *Mountain range* Belize/Guatemala
Maych'ew *50 C4 var.* Mai Chio, *It.* Mai Ceu. N Ethiopia
Maydān Shahr *101 E4* Wardag, E Afghanistan
Mayebashi *see* Maebashi
Mayfield *129 B6* Canterbury, South Island, NZ
Maykop *89 A7* Respublika Adygeya, SW Russian Federation
Maymana *see* Meymaneh
Maymyo *114 B3* Mandalay, C Myanmar
Mayo *see* Maio
Mayor Island *128 D3 island* NE NZ
Mayor Pablo Lagerenza *see* Capitán Pablo Lagerenza
Mayotte *57 F2 French territorial collectivity* E Africa
May Pen *32 B5* C Jamaica
Mazabuka *56 D2* Southern, S Zambia
Mazaca *see* Kayseri
Mazār-e Sharīf *101 E3 var.* Mazār-i Sharif. Balkh, N Afghanistan
Mazār-i Sharif *see* Mazār-e Sharīf
Mazatlán *28 C3* Sinaloa, C Mexico
Mažeikiai *84 B3* Mažeikiai, NW Lithuania
Mazirbe *84 C2* Talsi, NW Latvia
Mazra'a *see* Al Mazra'ah
Mazury *76 D3 physical region* NE Poland
Mazyr *85 C7 Rus.* Mozyr'. Homyel'skaya Voblasts', SE Belarus
Mbabane *56 D4 country capital* (Swaziland) NW Swaziland
Mbacké *see* Mbaké
M'Baiki *see* Mbaïki
Mbaïki *55 C5 var.* M'Baïki. Lobaye, SW Central African Republic
Mbaké *52 B3 var.* Mbacké. W Senegal
Mbala *56 D1 prev.* Abercorn. Northern, NE Zambia
Mbale *51 C6* E Uganda
Mbandaka *55 C5 prev.* Coquilhatville. Equateur, NW Dem. Rep. Congo
M'Banza Congo *56 B1 var.* Mbanza Congo; *prev.* São Salvador, São Salvador do Congo. Zaire, NW Angola
Mbanza-Ngungu *55 B6* Bas-Zaïre, W Dem. Rep. Congo
Mbarara *51 B6* SW Uganda
Mbé *54 B4* Nord, N Cameroon
Mbeya *51 C7* Mbeya, SW Tanzania
Mbomou *see* Bomu
M'Bomu *see* Bomu
Mbour *52 B3* W Senegal
Mbuji-Mayi *55 D7 prev.* Bakwanga. Kasai Oriental, S Dem. Rep. Congo
McAlester *27 G2* Oklahoma, C USA
McAllen *27 G5* Texas, SW USA
McCamey *27 E3* Texas, SW USA
McClintock Channel *15 F2 channel* Nunavut, N Canada
McComb *20 B3* Mississippi, S USA
McCook *23 E4* Nebraska, C USA
McKean Island *123 E3 island* Phoenix Islands, C Kiribati
McKinley, Mount *14 C3 var.* Denali. *Mountain* Alaska, USA
McKinley Park *14 C3* Alaska, USA
McMinnville *24 B3* Oregon, NW USA
McMurdo Base *132 B4 US research station* Antarctica
McPherson *see* Fort McPherson
McPherson *23 E5* Kansas, C USA
Mdantsane *56 D5* Eastern Cape, SE South Africa
Mead, Lake *25 D6 reservoir* Arizona/Nevada, W USA
Mecca *see* Makkah
Mechelen *65 C5 Eng.* Mechlin, *Fr.* Malines. Antwerpen, C Belgium
Mecklenburger Bucht *72 C2 bay* N Germany
Mecsek *77 C7 mountain range* SW Hungary
Medan *116 B3* Sumatera, E Indonesia
Medeba *see* Ma'dabā
Medellín *36 B3* Antioquia, NW Colombia
Médenine *49 F2 var.* Madanīyīn. SE Tunisia
Medford *24 B4* Oregon, NW USA
Medgidia *86 D5* Constanţa, SE Romania
Mediaş *86 B4 Ger.* Mediasch, *Hung.* Medgyes. Sibiu, C Romania
Medicine Hat *15 F5* Alberta, SW Canada
Medinaceli *71 E2* Castilla-León, N Spain
Medina del Campo *70 D2* Castilla-León, N Spain
Mediterranean Sea *80 D3 Fr.* Mer Méditerranée. *Sea* Africa/Asia/Europe
Médoc *69 B5 cultural region* SW France
Medvezh'yegorsk *88 B3* Respublika Kareliya, NW Russian Federation
Meekatharra *125 B5* Western Australia
Meemu Atoll *see* Mulaku Atoll
Meerssen *65 D6 var.* Mersen. Limburg, SE Netherlands
Meerut *112 D2* Uttar Pradesh, N India
Meghālaya *113 G3 state* NE India
Mehdia *see* Mahdia
Meheso *see* Mī'ēso
Me Hka *see* Nmai Hka
Mehrīz *98 D3* Yazd, C Iran
Mehtar Lām *see* Mehtarlām
Mehtarlām *101 F4 var.* Mehtar Lām, Meterlam, Methariam, Metharlam. Laghmān, E Afghanistan
Meiktila *114 B3* Mandalay, C Myanmar
Mejillones *42 B2* Antofagasta, N Chile
Mek'elē *50 C4 var.* Makale. N Ethiopia
Mékhé *52 B3* NW Senegal
Mekong *102 D3 var.* Lan-ts'ang Chiang, *Cam.* Mékôngk, *Chin.* Lancang Jiang, *Lao.* Mènam Khong, *Th.* Mae Nam Khong, *Tib.* Dza Chu, *Vtn.* Sông Tiên Giang. *River* SE Asia
Mékôngk *see* Mekong
Mekong, Mouths of the *115 E6 delta* S Vietnam
Melaka *116 B3 var.* Malacca. Melaka, Peninsular Malaysia
Melanesia *122 D3 island group* W Pacific Ocean
Melanesian Basin *120 C2 undersea feature* W Pacific Ocean
Melbourne *127 C7 state capital* Victoria, SE Australia
Melbourne *21 E4* Florida, SE USA
Melghir, Chott *49 E2 var.* Chott Melrhir. *Salt lake* E Algeria
Melilla *58 B5 anc.* Rusaddir, Russadir. Melilla, Spain, N Africa
Melilla *48 D2 enclave* Spain, N Africa
Melita *15 F5* Manitoba, S Canada
Melitopol' *87 F4* Zaporiz'ka Oblast', SE Ukraine
Melle *65 B5* Oost-Vlaanderen, NW Belgium
Mellerud *63 B6* Västra Götaland, S Sweden
Mellieha *80 B5* E Malta
Mellizo Sur, Cerro *43 A7 mountain* S Chile
Melo *42 E4* Cerro Largo, NE Uruguay
Melsungen *72 B4* Hessen, C Germany
Melun *68 C3 anc.* Melodunum. Seine-et-Marne, N France
Melville Island *124 D2 island* Northern Territory, N Australia
Melville Island *15 E2 island* Parry Islands, Northwest Territories/Nunavut, NW Canada
Melville, Lake *17 F2 lake* Newfoundland and Labrador, E Canada
Melville Peninsula *15 G3 peninsula* Northwest Territories, NE Canada
Membidj *see* Manbij
Memmingen *73 B6* Bayern, S Germany
Memphis *20 C1* Tennessee, S USA
Ménaka *53 F3* Goa, E Mali
Menaldum *64 D1 Fris.* Menaam. Friesland, N Netherlands
Mènam Khong *see* Mekong
Mendaña Fracture Zone *131 F4 tectonic feature* E Pacific Ocean
Mende *69 C5 anc.* Mimatum. Lozère, S France
Mendeleyev Ridge *133 B2 undersea feature* Arctic Ocean
Mendocino Fracture Zone *130 D2 tectonic feature* NE Pacific Ocean
Mendoza *42 B4* Mendoza, W Argentina
Menemen *94 A3* İzmir, W Turkey
Menengiyn Tal *105 F2 plain* E Mongolia
Menongue *56 B2 var.* Vila Serpa Pinto, *Port.* Serpa Pinto. Cuando Cubango, C Angola
Menorca *71 H3 Eng.* Minorca; *anc.* Balearis Minor. *Island* Islas Baleares, Spain, W Mediterranean Sea
Mentawai, Kepulauan *116 A4 island group* W Indonesia
Meppel *64 D2* Drenthe, NE Netherlands
Merano *74 C1 Ger.* Meran. Trentino-Alto Adige, N Italy
Merca *see* Marka
Mercedes *see* Villa Mercedes
Mercedes *42 D3* Corrientes, NE Argentina
Mercedes *42 D4* Soriano, SW Uruguay
Meredith, Lake *27 E1 reservoir* Texas, SW USA
Merefa *87 G2* Kharkivs'ka Oblast', E Ukraine
Mergui *115 B6* Tenasserim, S Myanmar
Mergui Archipelago *115 B6 island group* S Myanmar
Meriç *see* Maritsa
Mérida *70 C4 anc.* Augusta Emerita. Extremadura, W Spain
Mérida *36 C2* Mérida, W Venezuela
Mérida *29 H3* Yucatán, SW Mexico
Meridian *20 C2* Mississippi, S USA
Mérignac *69 B5* Gironde, SW France
Merkinė *85 B5* Varėna, S Lithuania
Merowe *50 B3 desert* W Sudan
Merredin *125 B6* Western Australia
Mersen *see* Meerssen
Mersey *67 D5 river* NW England, UK
Mersin *94 C4* İçel, S Turkey
Mērsrags *84 C3* Talsi, NW Latvia
Meru *51 C6* Eastern, C Kenya
Merzifon *94 D2* Amasya, N Turkey
Merzig *73 A5* Saarland, SW Germany
Mesa *26 B2* Arizona, SW USA
Meshed *see* Mashhad
Mesopotamia *35 C5 var.* Mesopotamia Argentina. *Physical region* NE Argentina
Mesopotamia Argentina *see* Mesopotamia
Messalo, Rio *57 E2 var.* Mualo. *River* NE Mozambique
Messana *see* Messina
Messene *see* Messina
Messina *75 D7 var.* Messana, Messene; *anc.* Zancle. Sicilia, Italy, C Mediterranean Sea
Messina *56 D3* Northern, NE South Africa
Messina, Stretto di *75 D7 Eng.* Strait of Messina. *Strait* SW Italy
Messíni *83 B6* Pelopónnisos, S Greece
Mestghanem *see* Mostaganem
Mestia *95 F1 var.* Mestiya. N Georgia
Mestiya *see* Mestia
Mestre *74 C2* Veneto, NE Italy
Meta *34 B2 off.* Departamento del Meta. *Province* C Colombia
Metairie *20 B3* Louisiana, S USA
Metán *42 C2* Salta, N Argentina
Metapán *30 B2* Santa Ana, NW El Salvador
Meta, Río *36 D3 river* Colombia/Venezuela
Meterlam *see* Mehtarlām
Methariam *see* Mehtarlām
Metharlam *see* Mehtarlām
Metković *78 B4* Dubrovnik-Neretva, SE Croatia
Métsovo *82 B4 prev.* Métsovon. Ípeiros, C Greece
Metz *68 D3 anc.* Divodurum Mediomatricum, Mediomatrica, Metis. Moselle, NE France
Meulaboh *116 A3* Sumatera, W Indonesia
Meuse *65 C6 Dut.* Maas. *River* W Europe *see also* Maas
Meuse *68 D3 department* NE France
Mexcala, Río *see* Balsas, Río
Mexicali *28 A1* Baja California, NW Mexico
Mexico *28 C3 off.* United Mexican States, *var.* Méjico, México, *Sp.* Estados Unidos Mexicanos. *Country* N Central America
Mexico *23 G4* Missouri, C USA
México *29 E4 var.* Ciudad de México, *Eng.* Mexico City. *Country capital* (Mexico) México, C Mexico
Mexico City *see* México
Mexico, Gulf of *29 F2 Sp.* Golfo de México. *Gulf* W Atlantic Ocean
Meyadine *see* Al Mayādīn
Meymaneh *100 D3 var.* Maimāna, Maymana. Fāryāb, NW Afghanistan
Mezen' *88 D3 river* NW Russian Federation
Mezőtúr *77 D7* Jász-Nagykun-Szolnok, E Hungary
Mġarr *80 A5* Gozo, N Malta
Miahuatlán *29 F5 var.* Miahuatlán de Porfirio Díaz. Oaxaca, SE Mexico
Miahuatlán de Porfirio Díaz *see* Miahuatlán
Miami *21 F5* Florida, SE USA
Miami *27 G1* Oklahoma, C USA
Miami Beach *21 F5* Florida, SE USA
Mīāneh *98 C2 var.* Miyāneh. Āžarbāyjān-e Khāvarī, NW Iran
Mianyang *106 B5* Sichuan, C China
Miastko *76 C2 Ger.* Rummelsburg in Pommern. Pomorskie, N Poland
Mi Chai *see* Nong Khai
Michalovce *77 E5 Ger.* Grossmichel, *Hung.* Nagymihály. Košický Kraj, E Slovakia
Michigan *18 C1 off.* State of Michigan; also known as Great Lakes State, Lake State, Wolverine State. *State* N USA
Michigan, Lake *18 C2 lake* N USA
Michurinsk *89 B5* Tambovskaya Oblast', W Russian Federation
Micoud *33 F2* SE Saint Lucia
Micronesia *122 B1 off.* Federated States of Micronesia. *Country* W Pacific Ocean
Micronesia *122 C1 island group* W Pacific Ocean
Mid-Atlantic Cordillera *see* Mid-Atlantic Ridge
Mid-Atlantic Ridge *44 C3 var.* Mid-Atlantic Cordillera, Mid-Atlantic Rise, Mid-Atlantic Swell. *Undersea feature* Atlantic Ocean
Mid-Atlantic Rise *see* Mid-Atlantic Ridge
Mid-Atlantic Swell *see* Mid-Atlantic Ridge
Middelburg *65 B5* Zeeland, SW Netherlands
Middelharnis *64 B4* Zuid-Holland, SW Netherlands
Middelkerke *65 A5* West-Vlaanderen, W Belgium
Middle America Trench *13 B7 undersea feature* E Pacific Ocean
Middle Andaman *111 F2 island* Andaman Islands, India, NE Indian Ocean
Middlesboro *18 C5* Kentucky, S USA
Middlesbrough *67 D5* N England, UK
Middletown *19 F4* New Jersey, NE USA
Middletown *19 F3* New York, NE USA
Mid-Indian Basin *119 C5 undersea feature* N Indian Ocean
Mid-Indian Ridge *119 C5 var.* Central Indian Ridge. *Undersea feature* C Indian Ocean
Midland *18 C3* Michigan, N USA
Midland *16 D5* Ontario, S Canada
Midland *27 E3* Texas, SW USA
Mid-Pacific Mountains *130 C2 var.* Mid-Pacific Seamounts. *Undersea feature* NW Pacific Ocean
Mid-Pacific Seamounts *see* Mid-Pacific Mountains
Midway Islands *130 D2 US territory* C Pacific Ocean
Miechów *77 D5* Małopolskie, S Poland
Międzyrzec Podlaski *76 E3* Lubelskie, E Poland
Międzyrzecz *76 B3 Ger.* Meseritz. Lubuskie, W Poland
Mielec *77 D5* Podkarpackie, SE Poland
Miercurea-Ciuc *86 C4 Ger.* Szeklerburg, *Hung.* Csíkszereda. Harghita, C Romania
Mieres del Camín *see* Mieres del Camino
Mieres del Camino *108 D1 var.* Mieres del Camín. Asturias, NW Spain
Mieresch *see* Mureş
Mī'ēso *51 D5 var.* Meheso, Miesso. C Ethiopia
Miesso *see* Mī'ēso
Miguel Asua *28 D3 var.* Miguel Auza. Zacatecas, C Mexico
Miguel Auza *see* Miguel Asua
Mijdrecht *64 C3* Utrecht, C Netherlands
Mikashevichy *85 C7 Pol.* Mikaszewicze, *Rus.* Mikashevichi. Brestskaya Voblasts', SW Belarus
Mikhaylovka *89 B6* Volgogradskaya Oblast', SW Russian Federation
Míkonos *see* Mýkonos
Mikre *82 C2* Lovech, N Bulgaria
Mikun' *88 D4* Respublika Komi, NW Russian Federation
Mikuni-sanmyaku *109 D5 mountain range* Honshū, N Japan
Mikura-jima *109 D6 island* E Japan
Milagro *38 B2* Guayas, SW Ecuador
Milan *see* Milano
Milange *57 E2* Zambézia, NE Mozambique
Milano *74 B2 Eng.* Milan, *Ger.* Mailand; *anc.* Mediolanum. Lombardia, N Italy
Milas *94 A4* Muğla, SW Turkey
Milashavichy *85 C7 Rus.* Milashevichi. Homyel'skaya Voblasts', SE Belarus
Mildura *127 C6* Victoria, SE Australia
Mile *see* Mili Atoll
Miles *127 D5* Queensland, E Australia
Miles City *22 C2* Montana, NW USA
Milford Haven *67 C6 prev.* Milford. SW Wales, UK
Milford Sound *129 A6 inlet* South Island, NZ
Milford Sound *129 A6* Southland, South Island, NZ
Mili Atoll *122 D2 var.* Mile. *Atoll* Ratak Chain, SE Marshall Islands
Mil'kovo *93 H3* Kamchatskaya Oblast', E Russian Federation
Milk River *22 C1 river* Montana, NW USA
Milk River *15 E5* Alberta, SW Canada
Milk, Wadi el *88 B4 var.* Wadi al Malik. *River* C Sudan
Milledgeville *21 E2* Georgia, SE USA
Mille Lacs Lake *23 F2 lake* Minnesota, N USA
Millennium Island *160 C8 prev.* Caroline Island, Thornton Island. *Atoll* Line Islands, E Kiribati
Millerovo *89 B6* Rostovskaya Oblast', SW Russian Federation
Mílos *83 C7 island* Kykládes, Greece, Aegean Sea
Mílos *83 C6* Mílos, Kykládes, Greece, Aegean Sea
Milton *129 B7* Otago, South Island, NZ
Milton Keynes *67 D6* SE England, UK
Milwaukee *18 B3* Wisconsin, N USA
Min *see* Fujian
Mīnā' Qābūs *118 B3* NE Oman
Minas Gerais *41 F3 off.* Estado de Minas Gerais. *State* E Brazil
Minatitlán *29 F4* Veracruz-Llave, E Mexico
Minbu *114 A3* Magwe, W Myanmar
Minch, The *66 B3 var.* North Minch. *Strait* NW Scotland, UK
Mindanao *117 F2 island* S Philippines
Mindanao Sea *see* Bohol Sea
Mindelheim *73 C6* Bayern, S Germany
Mindello *see* Mindelo
Mindelo *52 A2 var.* Mindello; *prev.* Porto Grande. São Vicente, N Cape Verde
Minden *72 B4 anc.* Minthun. Nordrhein-Westfalen, NW Germany
Mindoro *117 E2 island* N Philippines
Mindoro Strait *117 E2 strait* W Philippines
Mineral Wells *27 F2* Texas, SW USA
Mingäçevir *95 G2 Rus.* Mingechaur, Mingechevir. C Azerbaijan
Mingaora *112 C1 var.* Mingora, Mongora. North-West Frontier Province, N Pakistan
Mingora *see* Mingāora
Minho *70 B2 former province* N Portugal
Minho, Rio *70 B2 Sp.* Miño. *River* Portugal/Spain *see also* Miño
Minicoy Island *110 B3 island* SW India
Minius *see* Miño
Minna *53 G4* Niger, C Nigeria
Minneapolis *23 F2* Minnesota, N USA
Minnesota *23 F2 off.* State of Minnesota; also known as Gopher State, New England of the West, North Star State. *State* N USA
Miño *70 B2 var.* Mino, Minius, *Port.* Rio Minho. *River* Portugal/Spain *see also* Minho, Rio
Mino *see* Miño
Minot *23 E1* North Dakota, N USA
Minsk *85 C6 country capital* (Belarus) Minskaya Voblasts', C Belarus
Minskaya Wzvyshsha *85 C6 mountain range* C Belarus
Mińsk Mazowiecki *76 D3 var.* Nowo-Minsk. Mazowieckie, C Poland
Minto, Lac *16 D2 lake* Quebec, C Canada
Minya *see* El Minya
Miraflores *28 C3* Baja California Sur, W Mexico
Miranda de Ebro *71 E1* La Rioja, N Spain
Miri *116 D3* Sarawak, East Malaysia
Mirim Lagoon *41 E5 var.* Lake Mirim, *Sp.* Laguna Merín. *Lagoon* Brazil/Uruguay
Mirim, Lake *see* Mirim Lagoon
Mírina *see* Mýrina
Mīrjāveh *98 E4* Sīstān va Balūchestān, SE Iran
Mirny *132 C3 Russian research station* Antarctica
Mirnyy *93 F3* Respublika Sakha (Yakutiya), NE Russian Federation
Mīrpur Khās *112 B3* Sind, SE Pakistan
Mirtóo Pélagos *83 C6 Eng.* Mirtoan Sea; *anc.* Myrtoum Mare. *Sea* S Greece
Miskito Coast *see* Mosquito Coast
Miskitos, Cayos *31 E2 island group* NE Nicaragua
Miskolc *77 D6* Borsod-Abaúj-Zemplén, NE Hungary
Misool, Pulau *117 F4 island* Maluku, E Indonesia
Mişrātah *49 F2 var.* Misurata. NW Libya
Mission *27 G5* Texas, SW USA
Mississippi *20 B2 off.* State of Mississippi; also known as Bayou State, Magnolia State. *State* SE USA
Mississippi Delta *20 B4 delta* Louisiana, S USA
Mississippi River *13 C6 river* C USA
Missoula *22 B1* Montana, NW USA
Missouri *23 F5 off.* State of Missouri; also known as Bullion State, Show Me State. *State* C USA
Missouri River *23 E3 river* C USA
Mistassini, Lac *16 D3 lake* Quebec, SE Canada
Mistelbach an der Zaya *73 E6* Niederösterreich, NE Austria
Misti, Volcán *39 E4 mountain* S Peru
Misurata *see* Mişrātah
Mitchell *127 D5* Queensland, E Australia
Mitchell *23 E3* South Dakota, N USA
Mitchell, Mount *21 E1 mountain* North Carolina, SE USA

Nadi – Niuatobutabu

Nadi *123 E4 prev.* Nandi. Viti Levu, W Fiji
Nadur *80 A5* Gozo, N Malta
Nadvirna *86 C3 Pol.* Nadwórna, *Rus.* Nadvornaya. Ivano-Frankivs'ka Oblast', W Ukraine
Nadvoitsy *88 B3* Respublika Kareliya, NW Russian Federation
Nadym *92 C3* Yamalo-Nenetskiy Avtonomnyy Okrug, N Russian Federation
Náfpaktos *83 B5 var.* Návpaktos. Dytikí Ellás, C Greece
Náfplio *83 B6 prev.* Návplion. Pelopónnisos, S Greece
Naga *117 E2 off.* Naga City; *prev.* Nueva Caceres. Luzon, N Philippines
Nagano *109 C5* Nagano, Honshū, S Japan
Nagaoka *109 D5* Niigata, Honshū, C Japan
Nagara Pathom *see* Nakhon Pathom
Nagara Sridharmaraj *see* Nakhon Si Thammarat
Nagara Svarga *see* Nakhon Sawan
Nagasaki *109 A7* Nagasaki, Kyūshū, SW Japan
Nagato *109 A7* Yamaguchi, Honshū, SW Japan
Nāgercoil *110 C3* Tamil Nādu, SE India
Nagorno-Karabakhskaya Avtonomnaya Oblast *see* Nagornyy Karabakh
Nagornyy Karabakh *95 G3 var.* Nagorno-Karabakhskaya Avtonomnaya Oblast , *Arm.* Lerrnayin Gharabakh, *Az.* Dağliq Qarabağ. *Former autonomous region* SW Azerbaijan
Nagoya *109 C6* Aichi, Honshū, SW Japan
Nāgpur *112 D4* Mahārāshtra, C India
Nagqu *104 C5 Chin.* Na-ch'ii; *prev.* Hei-ho. Xizang Zizhiqu, W China
Nagykálló *77 E6* Szabolcs-Szatmár-Bereg, E Hungary
Nagykanizsa *77 C7 Ger.* Grosskanizsa. Zala, SW Hungary
Nagykőrös *77 D7* Pest, C Hungary
Nagyszentmiklós *see* Sânnicolau Mare
Naha *108 A3* Okinawa, Okinawa, SW Japan
Nahariya *see* Nahariyya
Nahariyya *97 A5 var.* Nahariya. Northern, N Israel
Nahr al 'Aṣī *see* Orantes
Nahr al Litant *see* Lītani, Nahr el
Nahr an Nīl *see* Nile
Nahr el Aassi *see* Orantes
Nahuel Huapi, Lago *43 B5 lake* W Argentina
Na'in *98 D3* Eṣfahan, C Iran
Nain *17 F2* Newfoundland and Labrador, NE Canada
Nairobi *47 E5 country capital* (Kenya) Nairobi Area, S Kenya
Nairobi *51 C6 international airport* Nairobi Area, S Kenya
Najaf *see* An Najaf
Najima *see* Fukuoka
Najin *107 E3* NE North Korea
Najrān *99 B6 var.* Abā as Su'ūd. Najrān, S Saudi Arabia
Nakambé *see* White Volta
Nakamura *109 B7* Kōchi, Shikoku, SW Japan
Nakatsugawa *109 C6 var.* Nakatugawa. Gifu, Honshū, SW Japan
Nakatugawa *see* Nakatsugawa
Nakhodka *93 G5* Primorskiy Kray, SE Russian Federation
Nakhon Pathom *115 C5 var.* Nagara Pathom, Nakorn Pathom. Nakhon Pathom, W Thailand
Nakhon Ratchasima *115 C5 var.* Khorat, Korat. Nakhon Ratchasima, E Thailand
Nakhon Sawan *115 C5 var.* Muang Nakhon Sawan, Nagara Svarga. Nakhon Sawan, W Thailand
Nakhon Si Thammarat *115 C7 var.* Nagara Sridharmaraj, Nakhon Sithamnaraj. Nakhon Si Thammarat, SW Thailand
Nakhon Sithamnaraj *see* Nakhon Si Thammarat
Nakorn Pathom *see* Nakhon Pathom
Nakuru *51 C6* Rift Valley, SW Kenya
Nal'chik *89 B8* Kabardino-Balkarskaya Respublika, SW Russian Federation
Nālūt *49 F2* NW Libya
Namakan Lake *18 A1 lake* Canada/USA
Namangan *101 F2* Namangan Wiloyati, E Uzbekistan
Nambala *56 D2* Central, C Zambia
Nam Co *104 C5 lake* W China
Nam Định *114 D3* Nam Ha, N Vietnam
Namib Desert *56 B3 desert* W Namibia
Namibe *56 A2 Port.* Moçâmedes, Mossâmedes. Namibe, SW Angola
Namibia *56 B3 off.* Republic of Namibia, *var.* South West Africa, *Afr.* Suidwes-Afrika, *Ger.* Deutsch-Südwestafrika; *prev.* German Southwest Africa, South-West Africa. *Country* S Africa
Namo *see* Namu Atoll
Nam Ou *114 C3 river* N Laos
Nampa *24 D3* Idaho, NW USA
Nampula *57 E2* Nampula, NE Mozambique
Namsos *62 B4* Nord-Trøndelag, C Norway
Nam Tha *114 C4 river* N Laos
Namu Atoll *122 D2 var.* Namo. *Atoll* Ralik Chain, C Marshall Islands
Namur *65 C6 Dut.* Namen. Namur, SE Belgium
Namyit Island *106 C8 island* S Spratly Islands
Nan *114 C4 var.* Muang Nan. Nan, NW Thailand
Nanaimo *14 D5* Vancouver Island, British Columbia, SW Canada
Nanchang *106 C5 var.* Nan-ch'ang, Nanch'ang-hsien. Jiangxi, S China
Nanch'ang-hsien *see* Nanchang
Nan-ching *see* Nanjing
Nancy *68 D3* Meurthe-et-Moselle, NE France
Nandaime *30 D3* Granada, SW Nicaragua
Nānded *112 D5* Mahārāshtra, C India
Nandyāl *110 C1* Andhra Pradesh, E India
Nanjing *106 D5 var.* Nan-ching, Nanking; *prev.* Chianning, Chian-ning, Kiang-ning. Jiangsu, E China
Nanking *see* Nanjing
Nanning *106 B6 var.* Nan-ning; *prev.* Yung-ning. Guangxi Zhuangzu Zizhiqu, S China
Nan-ning *see* Nanning
Nanortalik *60 C5* S Greenland
Nanpan Jiang *114 D2 river* S China
Nanping *106 D6 var.* Nan-p'ing; *prev.* Yenping. Fujian, SE China
Nansei-Shotō *108 A2 var.* Ryukyu Islands. *Island group* SW Japan
Nansei Syotō Trench *see* Ryukyu Trench
Nansen Basin *133 C4 undersea feature* Arctic Ocean
Nansen Cordillera *133 B3 var.* Arctic-Mid Oceanic Ridge, Nansen Ridge. *Undersea feature* Arctic Ocean
Nansen Ridge *see* Nansen Cordillera
Nanterre *68 D1* Hauts-de-Seine, N France
Nantes *68 B4 Bret.* Naoned; *anc.* Condivincum, Namnetes. Loire-Atlantique, NW France
Nantucket Island *19 G3 island* Massachusetts, NE USA
Nanumaga *123 E3 var.* Nanumanga. *Atoll* NW Tuvalu
Nanumanga *see* Nanumaga
Nanumea Atoll *123 E3 atoll* NW Tuvalu
Nanyang *106 C5 var.* Nan-yang. Henan, C China
Napa *25 B6* California, W USA
Napier *128 E4* Hawke's Bay, North Island, NZ
Naples *58 D5 anc.* Neapolis. Campania, S Italy
Naples *21 E5* Florida, SE USA
Napo *34 A3 province* NE Ecuador
Napo, Río *38 C1 river* Ecuador/Peru
Naracoorte *127 B7* South Australia
Naradhivas *see* Narathiwat
Narathiwat *115 C7 var.* Naradhivas. Narathiwat, SW Thailand
Narbada *see* Narmada
Narbonne *69 C6 anc.* Narbo Martius. Aude, S France
Narborough Island *see* Fernandina, Isla
Nares Abyssal Plain *see* Nares Plain
Nares Plain *13 E6 var.* Nares Abyssal Plain. *Undersea feature* NW Atlantic Ocean
Nares Strait *60 D1 Dan.* Nares Stræde. *Strait* Canada/Greenland
Narew *76 E3 river* E Poland
Narmada *102 B3 var.* Narbada. *River* C India
Narowlya *85 C8 Rus.* Narovlya. Homyel'skaya Voblasts', SE Belarus
Närpes *63 D5 Fin.* Närpiö. Länsi-Suomi, W Finland
Narrabri *127 D6* New South Wales, SE Australia
Narrogin *125 B6* Western Australia
Narva *84 E2 prev.* Narova. *River* Estonia/Russian Federation
Narva *84 E2* Ida-Virumaa, NE Estonia
Narva Bay *84 E2 Est.* Narva Laht, *Ger.* Narwa-Bucht, *Rus.* Narvskiy Zaliv. *Bay* Estonia/Russian Federation
Narva Reservoir *84 E2 Est.* Narva Veehoidla, *Rus.* Narvskoye Vodokhranilishche. *Reservoir* Estonia/Russian Federation
Narvik *62 C3* Nordland, C Norway
Nar'yan-Mar *88 D3 prev.* Beloshchel'ye, Dzerzhinskiy. Nenetskiy Avtonomnyy Okrug, NW Russian Federation
Naryn *101 G2* Narynskaya Oblast', C Kyrgyzstan
Năsăud *86 B3 Ger.* Nussdorf, *Hung.* Naszód. Bistrița-Năsăud, N Romania
Nase *see* Naze
Nāsik *112 C5 prev.* Nāsik. Mahārāshtra, W India
Nashua *19 G3* New Hampshire, NE USA
Nashville *20 C1 state capital* Tennessee, S USA
Näsijärvi *63 D5 lake* SW Finland
Nāsiri *see* Ahvāz
Nasiriya *see* An Nāṣirīyah
Nassau *32 C1 country capital* (Bahamas) New Providence, N Bahamas
Nasser, Lake *50 B3 var.* Buhayrat Nasir, Buḥayrat Nāṣir, Buḥeiret Nâṣir. *Lake* Egypt/Sudan
Nata *56 C3* Central, NE Botswana
Natal *41 G2* Rio Grande do Norte, E Brazil
Natal Basin *119 A6 var.* Mozambique Basin. *Undersea feature* W Indian Ocean
Natanya *see* Netanya
Natchez *20 B3* Mississippi, S USA
Natchitoches *20 A2* Louisiana, S USA
Nathanya *see* Netanya
Natitingou *53 F4* NW Benin
Natsrat *see* Nazerat
Natuna Islands *102 D4 island group* W Indonesia
Naturaliste Plateau *119 E6 undersea feature* E Indian Ocean
Naugard *see* Nowogard
Naujamiestis *84 C4* Panevėžys, C Lithuania
Nauru *122 D2 off.* Republic of Nauru; *prev.* Pleasant Island. *Country* W Pacific Ocean
Nauta *38 C2* Loreto, N Peru
Navahrudak *85 C6 Pol.* Nowogródek, *Rus.* Novogrudok. Hrodzyenskaya Voblasts', W Belarus
Navapolatsk *85 D5 Rus.* Novopolotsk. Vitsyebskaya Voblasts', N Belarus
Navarra *71 E2 cultural region* N Spain
Navassa Island *32 C3 US unincorporated territory* C West Indies
Navojoa *28 C2* Sonora, NW Mexico
Navolat *see* Navolato
Navolato *66 C3 var.* Navolat. Sinaloa, C Mexico
Návpaktos *see* Náfpaktos
Nawabashah *see* Nawābshāh
Nawābshāh *112 B3 var.* Nawabashah. Sind, S Pakistan
Nawoiy *101 E2 Rus.* Navoi. Nawoiy Wiloyati, C Uzbekistan
Naxçıvan *95 G3 Rus.* Nakhichevan'. SW Azerbaijan
Náxos *83 D6 var.* Naxos. Náxos, Kykládes, Greece, Aegean Sea
Náxos *83 D6 island* Kykládes, Greece, Aegean Sea
Nayoro *108 D2* Hokkaidō, NE Japan
Nazca *38 D4* Ica, S Peru
Nazca Ridge *35 A5 undersea feature* E Pacific Ocean
Naze *108 B3 var.* Nase. Kagoshima, Amami-ōshima, SW Japan
Nazerat *97 A5 var.* Natsrat, *Ar.* En Nazira, *Eng.* Nazareth. Northern, N Israel
Nazilli *94 A4* Aydın, SW Turkey
Nazrēt *51 C5 var.* Adama, Hadama. C Ethiopia
N'Dalatando *56 B1 Port.* Salazar, Vila Salazar. Cuanza Norte, NW Angola
Ndélé *54 C4* Bamingui-Bangoran, N Central African Republic
Ndendé *55 B6* Ngounié, S Gabon
Ndindi *55 A6* Nyanga, S Gabon
Ndjamena *54 B3 var.* N'Djamena; *prev.* Fort-Lamy. *Country capital* (Chad) Chari-Baguirmi, W Chad
Ndjolé *55 A5* Moyen-Ogooué, W Gabon
Ndola *56 D2* Copperbelt, C Zambia
Neagh, Lough *67 B5 lake* E Northern Ireland, UK
Néa Moudanía *82 C4 var.* Néa Moudhaniá. Kentrikí Makedonía, N Greece
Néa Moudhaniá *see* Néa Moudanía
Neápoli *82 B4 prev.* Neápolis. Dytikí Makedonía, N Greece
Neápoli *83 D8* Kríti, Greece, E Mediterranean Sea
Neápoli *83 C7* Pelopónnisos, S Greece
Neapolis *see* Nablus
Near Islands *14 A2 island group* Aleutian Islands, Alaska, USA
Néa Zíchni *82 C3 var.* Néa Zíkhni; *prev.* Néa Zíkhna. Kentrikí Makedonía, NE Greece
Néa Zíkhna *see* Néa Zíchni
Néa Zíkhni *see* Néa Zíchni
Nebaj *30 B2* Quiché, W Guatemala
Nebitdag *100 B2* Balkanskiy Velayat, W Turkmenistan
Neblina, Pico da *40 C1 mountain* NW Brazil
Nebraska *22 D4 off.* State of Nebraska; *also known as* Blackwater State, Cornhusker State, Tree Planters State. *State* C USA
Nebraska City *23 F4* Nebraska, C USA
Neches River *27 H3 river* Texas, SW USA
Neckar *73 B6 river* SW Germany
Necochea *43 D5* Buenos Aires, E Argentina
Neder Rijn *64 D4 Eng.* Lower Rhine. *River* C Netherlands
Nederweert *65 D5* Limburg, SE Netherlands
Neede *64 E3* Gelderland, E Netherlands
Neerpelt *65 D5* Limburg, NE Belgium
Neftekamsk *89 D5* Respublika Bashkortostan, W Russian Federation
Negēlē *51 D5 var.* Negelli, *It.* Neghelli. C Ethiopia
Negelli *see* Negēlē
Neghelli *see* Negēlē
Negomane *57 E2 var.* Negomano. Cabo Delgado, N Mozambique
Negomano *see* Negomane
Negombo *110 C3* Western Province, SW Sri Lanka
Negotin *78 E4* Serbia, E Serbia and Montenegro (Yugo.)
Negra, Punta *38 A3 headland* NW Peru
Negrești-Oaș *86 B3 Hung.* Avasfelsőfalu; *prev.* Negrești. Satu Mare, NE Romania
Negro, Río *43 C5 river* E Argentina
Negro, Rio *40 D1 river* N South America
Negro, Río *42 D4 river* Brazil/Uruguay
Negros *117 E2 island* C Philippines
Nehbandān *98 E3* Khorāsān, E Iran
Neijiang *106 B5* Sichuan, C China
Nei Monggol Zizhiqu *see* Inner Mongolia
Nei Mongol *see* Inner Mongolia
Neiva *36 B3* Huila, S Colombia
Nellore *110 D2* Andhra Pradesh, E India
Nelson *15 G4 river* Manitoba, C Canada
Nelson *129 C5* Nelson, South Island, NZ
Néma *52 D3* Hodh ech Chargui, SE Mauritania
Neman *84 A4 Bel.* Nyoman, *Ger.* Memel, *Lith.* Nemunas, *Pol.* Niemen, *Rus.* Neman. *River* NE Europe
Neman *84 B4 Ger.* Ragnit. Kaliningradskaya Oblast', W Russian Federation
Neméa *83 B6* Pelopónnisos, S Greece
Nemours *68 C3* Seine-et-Marne, N France
Nemuro *108 E2* Hokkaidō, NE Japan
Neochóri *83 B5* Dytikí Ellás, C Greece
Nepal *113 E3 off.* Kingdom of Nepal. *Country* S Asia
Nereta *84 C4* Aizkraukle, S Latvia
Neretva *78 C4 river* Bosnia and Herzegovina/Croatia
Neringa *84 A3 Ger.* Nidden; *prev.* Nida. Neringa, SW Lithuania
Neris *85 C5 Bel.* Viliya, *Pol.* Wilia; *prev. Pol.* Wilja. *River* Belarus/Lithuania
Nerva *70 C4* Andalucía, S Spain
Neryungri *93 F4* Respublika Sakha (Yakutiya), NE Russian Federation
Neskaupstadhur *61 E5* Austurland, E Iceland
Ness, Loch *66 C3 lake* N Scotland, UK
Néstos *82 C3 Bul.* Mesta, *Turk.* Kara Su. *River* Bulgaria/Greece *see also* Mesta
Netanya *97 A6 var.* Natanya, Nathanya. Central, C Israel
Netherlands *64 C3 off.* Kingdom of the Netherlands, *var.* Holland, *Dut.* Koninkrijk der Nederlanden, Nederland. *Country* NW Europe
Netherlands Antilles *33 E5 prev.* Dutch West Indies. *Dutch autonomous region* S Caribbean Sea
Netherlands New Guinea *see* Irian Jaya
Nettilling Lake *15 G3 lake* Baffin Island, Nunavut, N Canada
Neubrandenburg *72 D3* Mecklenburg-Vorpommern, NE Germany
Neuchâtel *73 A7 Ger.* Neuenburg. Neuchâtel, W Switzerland
Neuchâtel, Lac de *A7 Ger.* Neuenburger See. *Lake* W Switzerland
Neufchâteau *65 D8* Luxembourg, SE Belgium
Neumünster *72 B2* Schleswig-Holstein, N Germany
Neunkirchen *73 A5* Saarland, SW Germany
Neuquén *43 B5* Neuquén, SE Argentina
Neuruppin *72 C3* Brandenburg, NE Germany
Neusalz an der Oder *see* Nowa Sól
Neusiedler See *73 E6 Hung.* Fertő. *Lake* Austria/Hungary
Neustadt an der Weinstrasse *73 B5 prev.* Neustadt an der Haardt, *hist.* Niewenstat, *anc.* Nova Civitas. Rheinland-Pfalz, SW Germany
Neustrelitz *72 D3* Mecklenburg-Vorpommern, NE Germany
Neu-Ulm *73 B6* Bayern, S Germany
Neuwied *73 A5* Rheinland-Pfalz, W Germany
Neuzen *see* Terneuzen
Nevada *25 C5 off.* State of Nevada; *also known as* Battle Born State, Sagebrush State, Silver State. *State* W USA
Nevada, Sierra *70 D5 mountain range* S Spain
Nevers *68 C4 anc.* Noviodunum. Nièvre, C France
Neves *54 E2* São Tomé, S Sao Tome and Principe
Nevinnomyssk *89 B7* Stavropol'skiy Kray, SW Russian Federation
Nevşehir *94 C3 var.* Nevshehr. Nevşehir, C Turkey
Nevshehr *see* Nevşehir
Newala *51 C8* Mtwara, SE Tanzania
New Albany *18 C5* Indiana, N USA
New Amsterdam *37 G3* E Guyana
Newark *19 F4* New Jersey, NE USA
New Bedford *19 G3* Massachusetts, NE USA
Newberg *24 B3* Oregon, NW USA
New Bern *21 F1* North Carolina, SE USA
New Braunfels *27 G4* Texas, SW USA
Newbridge *67 B6 Ir.* An Droichead Nua. C Ireland
New Britain *122 B3 island* E PNG
New Brunswick *17 E4 Fr.* Nouveau-Brunswick. *Province* SE Canada
New Caledonia *122 D4 var.* Kanaky, *Fr.* Nouvelle-Calédonie. *French overseas territory* SW Pacific Ocean
New Caledonia *122 C5 island* SW Pacific Ocean
New Caledonia Basin *120 C4 undersea feature* W Pacific Ocean
Newcastle *see* Newcastle upon Tyne
Newcastle *127 D6* New South Wales, SE Australia
Newcastle upon Tyne *66 D4 var.* Newcastle; *hist.* Monkchester, *Lat.* Pons Aelii. NE England, UK
New Delhi *112 D3 country capital* (India) Delhi, N India
Newfoundland *17 G3 Fr.* Terre-Neuve. *Island* Newfoundland, SE Canada
Newfoundland and Labrador *17 F2 Fr.* Terre Neuve. *Province* SE Canada
Newfoundland Basin *44 B3 undersea feature* NW Atlantic Ocean
New Georgia Islands *122 C3 island group* NW Solomon Islands
New Glasgow *17 F4* Nova Scotia, SE Canada
New Goa *see* Panji
New Guinea *122 A3 Dut.* Nieuw Guinea, *Ind.* Irian. *Island* Indonesia/PNG
New Hampshire *19 F2 off.* State of New Hampshire; *also known as* The Granite State. *State* NE USA
New Haven *19 G3* Connecticut, NE USA
New Iberia *20 B3* Louisiana, S USA
New Ireland *122 C3 island* NE PNG
New Jersey *19 F4 off.* State of New Jersey; *also known as* The Garden State. *State* NE USA
Newman *124 B4* Western Australia
Newmarket *67 E6* E England, UK
New Mexico *26 C2 off.* State of New Mexico; *also known as* Land of Enchantment, Sunshine State. *State* SW USA
New Orleans *20 B3* Louisiana, S USA
New Plymouth *128 C4* Taranaki, North Island, NZ
Newport *18 C4* Kentucky, S USA
Newport *67 D7* S England, UK
Newport *67 C7* SE Wales, UK
Newport *19 G2* Vermont, NE USA
Newport News *19 F5* Virginia, NE USA
New Providence *32 C1 island* N Bahamas
Newquay *67 C7* SW England, UK
Newry *67 B5 Ir.* An tIúr. SE Northern Ireland, UK
New Sarum *see* Salisbury
New Siberian Islands *see* Novosibirskiye Ostrova
New South Wales *127 C6 state* SE Australia
Newton *23 G3* Iowa, C USA
Newtownabbey *67 B5 Ir.* Baile na Mainistreach. E Northern Ireland, UK
New Ulm *23 F2* Minnesota, N USA
New York *19 F4* New York, NE USA
New York *19 F3 state* NE USA
New Zealand *128 A4 abbrev.* NZ. *Country* SW Pacific Ocean
Neyveli *110 C2* Tamil Nādu, SE India
Ngangzê Co *104 B5 lake* W China
Ngaoundéré *54 B4 var.* N'Gaoundéré. Adamaoua, N Cameroon
N'Giva *56 B3 var.* Ondjiva, *Port.* Vila Pereira de Eça. Cunene, S Angola
Ngo *55 B6* Plateaux, SE Congo
Ngoko *55 B5 river* Cameroon/Congo
Ngourti *53 H3* Diffa, E Niger
Nguigmi *53 H3 var.* N'Guigmi. Diffa, SE Niger
Nguru *53 G3* Yobe, NE Nigeria
Nha Trang *115 E6* Khanh Hoa, S Vietnam
Niagara Falls *18 D3 waterfall* Canada/USA
Niagara Falls *19 E3* New York, NE USA
Niagara Falls *16 D5* Ontario, S Canada
Niamey *53 F3 country capital* (Niger) Niamey, SW Niger
Niangay, Lac *53 E3 lake* E Mali
Nia-Nia *55 E5* Orientale, NE Dem. Rep. Congo
Nias, Pulau *116 A3 island* W Indonesia
Nicaragua *30 D3 off.* Republic of Nicaragua. *Country* Central America
Nicaragua, Lago de *30 D4 var.* Cocibolca, Gran Lago, *Eng.* Lake Nicaragua. *Lake* S Nicaragua
Nicaragua, Lake *see* Nicaragua, Lago de
Nicaria *see* Ikaría
Nice *69 D6 It.* Nizza; *anc.* Nicaea. Alpes-Maritimes, SE France
Nicephorium *see* Ar Raqqah
Nicholas II Land *see* Severnaya Zemlya
Nicholls Town *32 C1* Andros Island, NW Bahamas
Nicobar Islands *102 B4 island group* India, E Indian Ocean
Nicosia *80 C5 Gk.* Lefkosía, *Turk.* Lefkoşa. *Country capital* (Cyprus) C Cyprus
Nicoya *30 D4* Guanacaste, W Costa Rica
Nicoya, Golfo de *30 D5 gulf* W Costa Rica
Nicoya, Península de *30 D4 peninsula* NW Costa Rica
Nidzica *76 D3 Ger.* Niedenburg. Warmińsko-Mazurskie, NE Poland
Niedere Tauern *77 A6 mountain range* C Austria
Nieuw Amsterdam *37 G3* Commewijne, NE Suriname
Nieuw-Bergen *64 D4* Limburg, SE Netherlands
Nieuwegein *64 C4* Utrecht, C Netherlands
Nieuw Nickerie *37 G3* Nickerie, NW Suriname
Niğde *94 C4* Niğde, C Turkey
Niger *53 F3 off.* Republic of Niger. *Country* W Africa
Niger *53 F4 river* W Africa
Nigeria *53 F4 off.* Federal Republic of Nigeria. *Country* W Africa
Niger, Mouths of the *53 F5 delta* S Nigeria
Nihon *see* Japan
Niigata *109 D5* Niigata, Honshū, C Japan
Niihama *109 B7* Ehime, Shikoku, SW Japan
Niʻihau *25 A7 island* Hawaii, USA, C Pacific Ocean
Nii-jima *109 D6 island* E Japan
Nijkerk *64 D3* Gelderland, C Netherlands
Nijlen *65 C5* Antwerpen, N Belgium
Nijmegen *64 D4 Ger.* Nimwegen; *anc.* Noviomagus. Gelderland, SE Netherlands
Nikaria *see* Ikaría
Nikel' *88 C2* Murmanskaya Oblast', NW Russian Federation
Nikiniki *117 E5* Timor, S Indonesia
Nikopol' *87 F3* Pleven, N Bulgaria
Nikšić *79 C5* Montenegro, SW Serbia and Montenegro (Yugo.)
Nikumaroro *123 E3 prev.* Gardner Island, Kemins Island. *Atoll* Phoenix Islands, C Kiribati
Nikunau *123 E3 var.* Nukunau; *prev.* Byron Island. *Atoll* Tungaru, W Kiribati
Nile *46 D3 Ar.* Nahr an Nīl. *River* N Africa
Nile *50 B2 former province* NW Uganda
Nile Delta *50 B1 delta* N Egypt
Nîmes *69 C6 anc.* Nemausus, Nismes. Gard, S France
Nine Degree Channel *110 B3 channel* India/Maldives
Ninetyeast Ridge *119 D5 undersea feature* E Indian Ocean
Ninety Mile Beach *128 C1 beach* North Island, NZ
Ningbo *106 D5 var.* Ning-po, Yin-hsien; *prev.* Ninghsien. Zhejiang, SE China
Ninghsien *see* Ningbo
Ning-po *see* Ningbo
Ningxia *106 B4 off.* Ningxia Huizu Zizhiqu, *var.* Ning-hsia, Ningsia, *Eng.* Ningsia Hui, Ningsia Hui Autonomous Region. Admin. region *autonomous region* N China
Ningxia Huizu Zizhiqu *see* Ningxia
Nio *see* Íos
Niobrara River *23 E3 river* Nebraska/Wyoming, C USA
Nioro *52 D3 var.* Nioro du Sahel. Kayes, W Mali
Nioro du Sahel *see* Nioro
Niort *68 B4* Deux-Sèvres, W France
Nipigon *16 B4* Ontario, S Canada
Nipigon, Lake *16 B3 lake* Ontario, S Canada
Nippon *see* Japan
Niš *79 E5 Eng.* Nish, *Ger.* Nisch; *anc.* Naissus. Serbia, SE Serbia and Montenegro (Yugo.)
Nişab *98 B4* Al Ḥudūd ash Shamālīyah, N Saudi Arabia
Nisibin *see* Nusaybin
Nisiros *see* Nísyros
Nisko *76 E4* Podkarpackie, SE Poland
Nísyros *83 E7 var.* Nisiros. *Island* Dodekánisos, Greece, Aegean Sea
Nitra *77 C6 Ger.* Neutra, *Hung.* Nyitra. *River* W Slovakia
Nitra *77 C6 Ger.* Neutra, *Hung.* Nyitra. Nitriansky Kraj, SW Slovakia
Niuatobutabu *see* Niuatoputapu

INDEX

Opava – Patani

Opava 77 C5 *Ger.* Troppau. Ostravský Kraj, E Czech Republic
Opelika 20 D2 Alabama, S USA
Opelousas 20 B3 Louisiana, S USA
Opmeer 64 C2 Noord-Holland, NW Netherlands
Opochka 88 A4 Pskovskaya Oblast', W Russian Federation
Opole 76 C4 *Ger.* Oppeln. Opolskie, S Poland
Opotiki 128 E3 Bay of Plenty, North Island, NZ
Oppidum Ubiorum *see* Köln
Oqtosh 101 E2 *Rus.* Aktash. Samarqand Wiloyati, C Uzbekistan
Oradea 86 B3 *prev.* Oradea Mare, *Ger.* Grosswardein, *Hung.* Nagyvárad. Bihor, NW Romania
Orahovac 79 D5 *Alb.* Rahovec. Serbia, S Serbia and Montenegro (Yugo.)
Oran 48 D2 *var.* Ouahran, Wahran. NW Algeria
Orange 69 D6 *anc.* Arausio. Vaucluse, SE France
Orange 127 D6 New South Wales, SE Australia
Orangeburg 21 E2 South Carolina, SE USA
Orange Cone *see* Orange Fan
Orange Fan 47 C7 *var.* Orange Cone. *Undersea feature* SW Indian Ocean
Orange Mouth *see* Oranjemund
Orangemund *see* Oranjemund
Orange River 56 B4 *Afr.* Oranjerivier. *River* S Africa
Orange Walk 30 C1 Orange Walk, N Belize
Oranienburg 72 D3 Brandenburg, NE Germany
Oranjemund 56 B4 *var.* Orangemund; *prev.* Orange Mouth. Karas, SW Namibia
Oranjestad 33 E5 *dependent territory capital* (Aruba) W Aruba
Orantes 96 B3 *var.* Ononte, *Ar.* Nahr el Aassi, Nahr al 'Aṣī. *River* SW Asia
Oraviţa 86 A4 *Ger.* Orawitza, *Hung.* Oravicabánya. Caraş-Severin, SW Romania
Orbetello 74 B4 Toscana, C Italy
Orcadas 132 A1 *Argentinian research station* South Orkney Islands, Antarctica
Orchard Homes 22 B1 Montana, NW USA
Ordino 69 A8 NW Andorra
Ordos Desert *see* Mu Us Shamo
Ordu 94 D2 *anc.* Cotyora. Ordu, N Turkey
Ordzhonikidze 87 F3 Dnipropetrovs'ka Oblast', E Ukraine
Orealla 37 G3 E Guyana
Örebro 63 C6 Örebro, C Sweden
Oregon 24 B3 *off.* State of Oregon; also known as Beaver State, Sunset State, Valentine State, Webfoot State. *State* NW USA
Oregon City 24 B3 Oregon, NW USA
Orël 89 B5 Orlovskaya Oblast', W Russian Federation
Orem 22 B4 Utah, W USA
Orenburg 89 D6 *prev.* Chkalov. Orenburgskaya Oblast', W Russian Federation
Orense *see* Ourense
Oreor 122 A2 *var.* Koror. *Country capital* (Palau) Oreor, N Palau
Orestiáda 82 D3 *prev.* Orestiás. Anatolikí Makedonía kai Thráki, NE Greece
Organ Peak 26 D3 *mountain* New Mexico, SW USA
Orgeyev *see* Orhei
Orhei 86 D3 *var.* Orheiu, *Rus.* Orgeyev. N Moldova
Orheiu *see* Orhei
Oriental, Cordillera 38 D3 *mountain range* Bolivia/Peru
Oriental, Cordillera 39 F4 *mountain range* C Bolivia
Oriental, Cordillera 36 B3 *mountain range* C Colombia
Orihuela 71 F4 País Valenciano, E Spain
Orikhiv 87 G3 *Rus.* Orekhov. Zaporiz'ka Oblast', SE Ukraine
Orinoco, Río 37 E2 *river* Colombia/Venezuela
Orissa 113 F4 *state* NE India
Orissaare 84 C2 *Ger.* Orissaar. Saaremaa, W Estonia
Oristano 75 A5 Sardegna, Italy, C Mediterranean Sea
Orito 36 A4 Putumayo, SW Colombia
Orizaba, Volcán Pico de 13 C7 *var.* Citlaltépetl. *Mountain* S Mexico
Orkney *see* Orkney Islands
Orkney Islands 66 C2 *var.* Orkney, Orkneys. *Island group* N Scotland, UK
Orkneys *see* Orkney Islands
Orlando 21 E4 Florida, SE USA
Orléanais 68 C4 *cultural region* C France
Orléans 68 C4 *anc.* Aurelianum. Loiret, C France
Orléansville *see* Chlef
Orly 68 E2 *international airport* (Paris) Essonne, N France
Orlya 85 B6 *Rus.* Orlya. Hrodzyenskaya Voblasts', W Belarus
Ormuz, Strait of *see* Hormuz, Strait of
Örnsköldsvik 63 C5 Västernorrland, C Sweden
Oromocto 17 F4 New Brunswick, SE Canada
Orona 123 F3 *prev.* Hull Island. *Atoll* Phoenix Islands, C Kiribati
Orosirá Rodhópis *see* Rhodope Mountains
Orpington 67 B8 SE England, UK
Orsha 85 E6 *Rus.* Orsha. Vitsyebskaya Voblasts', NE Belarus
Orsk 92 B4 Orenburgskaya Oblast', W Russian Federation
Orşova 86 A4 *Ger.* Orschowa, *Hung.* Orsova. Mehedinţi, SW Romania
Orthez 69 B6 Pyrénées-Atlantiques, SW France
Ortona 74 D4 Abruzzo, C Italy
Oruba *see* Aruba
Oruro 39 F4 Oruro, W Bolivia
Ōsaka 109 C6 *hist.* Naniwa. Ōsaka, Honshū, SW Japan
Osa, Península de 31 E5 *peninsula* S Costa Rica
Osborn Plateau 119 D5 *undersea feature* E Indian Ocean
Osh 101 F2 Oshskaya Oblast', SW Kyrgyzstan
Oshawa 16 D5 Ontario, SE Canada
Oshikango 56 B3 Ohangwena, N Namibia
Ō-shima 109 D6 *island* S Japan
Oshkosh 18 B2 Wisconsin, N USA
Osijek 78 C3 *prev.* Osiek, Osjek, *Ger.* Esseg, *Hung.* Eszék. Osijek-Baranja, E Croatia
Oskaloosa 23 G4 Iowa, C USA
Oskarshamn 63 C7 Kalmar, S Sweden
Oskil 87 G2 *Rus.* Oskol. *River* Russian Federation/Ukraine
Oslo 63 B6 *prev.* Christiania, Kristiania. *Country capital* (Norway) Oslo, S Norway
Osmaniye 94 D4 Osmaniye, admin. region *province* S Turkey
Osnabrück 72 A3 Niedersachsen, NW Germany
Osogov Mountains 120 B3 *var.* Osogovske Planine, Osogovski Planina, *Mac.* Osogovski Planini. *mountain range* Bulgaria/FYR, Macedonia
Osogovske Planine/Osogovski Planina/Osogovski Planini *see* Osogov Mountains
Osorno 43 B5 Los Lagos, C Chile
Oss 64 D4 Noord-Brabant, S Netherlands
Ossa, Serra d' 70 C4 *mountain range* SE Portugal
Ossora 93 H2 Koryakskiy Avtonomnyy Okrug, E Russian Federation
Ostend *see* Oostende
Ostende *see* Oostende
Oster 87 E1 Chernihivs'ka Oblast', N Ukraine
Östersund 63 C5 Jämtland, C Sweden
Ostfriesische Inseln 72 A3 *Eng.* East Frisian Islands. *Island group* NW Germany
Ostiglia 74 C2 Lombardia, N Italy
Ostrava 77 C5 Ostravský Kraj, E Czech Republic
Ostróda 76 D3 *Ger.* Osterode, Osterode in Ostpreussen. Warmińsko-Mazurskie, NE Poland
Ostrołęka 76 D3 *Ger.* Wiesenhof, *Rus.* Ostrolenka. Mazowieckie, C Poland
Ostrov 88 A4 *Latv.* Austrava. Karlovarský Kraj, W Czech Republic
Ostrovets *see* Ostrowiec Świętokrzyski
Ostrów *see* Ostrów Wielkopolski
Ostrowiec *see* Ostrowiec Świętokrzyski
Ostrowiec Świętokrzyski 76 D4 *var.* Ostrowiec, *Rus.* Ostrovets. Świętokrzyskie, C Poland
Ostrów Mazowiecka 76 D3 *var.* Ostrów Mazowiecki. Mazowieckie, C Poland
Ostrów Mazowiecki *see* Ostrów Mazowiecka
Ostrowo *see* Ostrów Wielkopolski
Ostrów Wielkopolski 76 C4 *var.* Ostrów, *Ger.* Ostrowo. Wielkopolskie, C Poland
Osum *see* Osumit, Lumi i
Ōsumi-shotō 109 A8 *island group* SW Japan
Osumit, Lumi i 79 D7 *var.* Osum. *River* SE Albania
Osuna 70 D4 Andalucía, S Spain
Oswego 19 F2 New York, NE USA
Otago Peninsula 129 B7 *peninsula* South Island, NZ
Otaki 128 D4 Wellington, North Island, NZ
Otaru 108 C2 Hokkaidō, NE Japan
Otavalo 38 B1 Imbabura, N Ecuador
Otavi 56 B3 Otjozondjupa, N Namibia
Oţelu Roşu 86 B4 *Ger.* Ferdinandsberg, *Hung.* Nándorhgy. Caras-Severin, SW Romania
Otepää 84 D3 *Ger.* Odenpäh. Valgamaa, SE Estonia
Oti 53 E4 *river* W Africa
Otira 129 C6 West Coast, South Island, NZ
Otjiwarongo 56 B3 Otjozondjupa, N Namibia
Otorohanga 128 D3 Waikato, North Island, NZ
Otranto, Strait of 79 C6 *It.* Canale d'Otranto. *Strait* Albania/Italy
Otrokovice 77 C5 *Ger.* Otrokowitz. Zlínský Kraj, E Czech Republic
Ōtsu 109 C6 *var.* Ôtu. Shiga, Honshū, SW Japan
Ottawa 19 E2 *Fr.* Outaouais. Admin. region *river* Ontario/Quebec, SE Canada
Ottawa 16 D5 *country capital* (Canada) Ontario, SE Canada
Ottawa 18 B3 Illinois, N USA
Ottawa 23 F5 Kansas, C USA
Ottawa Islands 16 C1 *island group* Northwest Territories, C Canada
Ottignies 65 C6 Wallon Brabant, C Belgium
Ottumwa 23 G4 Iowa, C USA
Ôtu *see* Ōtsu
Ouachita Mountains 20 A1 *mountain range* Arkansas/Oklahoma, C USA
Ouachita River 20 B2 *river* Arkansas/Louisiana, C USA
Ouadi Howa *see* Howar, Wādi
Ouagadougou 53 E4 *var.* Wagadugu. *Country capital* (Burkina Faso) C Burkina Faso
Ouahigouya 53 E3 NW Burkina faso
Ouahran *see* Oran
Oualata *see* Oualâta
Oualâta 52 D3 *var.* Oualata. Hodh ech Chargui, SE Mauritania
Ouanary 37 H3 E French Guiana
Ouanda Djallé 54 D4 Vakaga, NE Central African Republic
Ouarâne 52 D2 *desert* C Mauritania
Ouargla 49 E2 *var.* Wargla. NE Algeria
Ouarzazate 48 C3 S Morocco
Oubangui *see* Ubangi
Oubangui-Chari *see* Central African Republic
Ouessant, Île d' 68 A3 *Eng.* Ushant. *Island* NW France
Ouésso 55 B5 La Sangha, NW Congo
Oujda 48 D2 *Ar.* Oudjda, Ujda. NE Morocco
Oujeft 52 C2 Adrar, C Mauritania
Oulu 62 D4 *Swe.* Uleåborg. Oulu, C Finland
Oulujärvi 62 D4 *Swe.* Uleträsk. *Lake* C Finland
Oulujoki 62 D4 *Swe.* Uleälv. *River* C Finland
Ounasjoki 62 D3 *river* N Finland
Ounianga Kébir 54 C2 Borkou-Ennedi-Tibesti, N Chad
Oup *see* Auob
Oupeye 65 D6 Liège, E Belgium
Our 65 D6 *river* NW Europe
Ourense 70 C1 *var.* Cast. Orense; *Lat.* Aurium. Galicia, NW Spain
Ourique 70 B4 Beja, S Portugal
Ourthe 65 D7 *river* E Belgium
Ouse 67 D5 *river* N England, UK
Outer Hebrides 66 B3 *var.* Western Isles. *Island group* NW Scotland, UK
Outer Islands 57 G1 *island group* SW Seychelles
Outes 70 B1 Galicia, NW Spain
Ouvéa 122 D5 *island* Îles Loyauté, NE New Caledonia
Ouyen 127 C6 Victoria, SE Australia
Ovalle 42 B3 Coquimbo, N Chile
Ovar 70 B2 Aveiro, N Portugal
Overflakkee 64 B4 *island* SW Netherlands
Overijse 65 C6 Vlaams Brabant, C Belgium
Oviedo 70 C1 *anc.* Asturias. Asturias, NW Spain
Ovruch 86 D1 Zhytomyrs'ka Oblast', N Ukraine
Owando 55 B5 *prev.* Fort-Rousset. Cuvette, C Congo
Owase 109 C6 Mie, Honshū, SW Japan
Owatonna 23 F3 Minnesota, N USA
Owen Fracture Zone 118 B4 *tectonic feature* W Arabian Sea
Owen, Mount 129 C5 *mountain* South Island, NZ
Owensboro 18 B5 Kentucky, S USA
Owen Stanley Range 122 B3 *mountain range* S PNG
Owerri 53 G5 Imo, S Nigeria
Owo 53 F5 Ondo, SW Nigeria
Owyhee River 24 C4 *river* Idaho/Oregon, NW USA
Oxford 67 D6 *Lat.* Oxonia. S England, UK
Oxford 129 C6 Canterbury, South Island, NZ
Oxkutzcab 29 H4 Yucatán, SE Mexico
Oxnard 25 B7 California, W USA
Oyama 109 D5 Tochigi, Honshū, S Japan
Oyem 55 B5 Woleu-Ntem, N Gabon
Oyo 55 B6 Cuvette, C Congo
Oyo 53 F4 Oyo, W Nigeria
Ozark 20 D3 Alabama, S USA
Ozark Plateau 23 G5 *plain* Arkansas/Missouri, C USA
Ozarks, Lake of the 23 F5 *reservoir* Missouri, C USA
Ozbourn Seamount 130 D4 *undersea feature* W Pacific Ocean
Ózd 77 D6 Borsod-Abaúj-Zemplén, NE Hungary
Ozero Khanka *see* Khanka, Lake
Ozero Ubsu-Nur *see* Uvs Nuur
Ozieri 75 A5 Sardegna, Italy, C Mediterranean Sea

P

Paamiut 60 B4 *var.* Pâmiut, *Dan.* Frederikshåb. S Greenland
Pa-an 114 B4 Karen State, S Myanmar
Pabianice 76 C4 Łodz, C Poland
Pabna 113 G4 Rajshahi, W Bangladesh
Pachuca 29 E4 *var.* Pachuca de Soto. Hidalgo, C Mexico
Pachuca de Soto *see* Pachuca
Pacific-Antarctic Ridge 132 B5 *undersea feature* S Pacific Ocean
Pacific Ocean 130 D3 *ocean*
Padalung *see* Phatthalung
Padang 116 B4 Sumatera, W Indonesia
Paderborn 72 B4 Nordrhein-Westfalen, NW Germany
Padma *see* Brahmaputra
Padova 74 C2 *Eng.* Padua; *anc.* Patavium. Veneto, NE Italy
Padre Island 27 G5 *island* Texas, SW USA
Padua *see* Padova
Paducah 18 B5 Kentucky, S USA
Paeroa 128 D3 Waikato, North Island, NZ
Páfos 80 C5 *var.* Paphos. W Cyprus
Pag 78 A3 *It.* Pago. *Island* Zadar SW Croatia
Page 26 B1 Arizona, SW USA
Pago Pago 123 F4 *dependent territory capital* (American Samoa) Tutuila, W American Samoa
Pahiatua 128 D4 Manawatu-Wanganui, North Island, NZ
Pahsien *see* Chongqing
Paide 84 D2 *Ger.* Weissenstein. Järvamaa, N Estonia
Paihia 128 D2 Northland, North Island, NZ
Päijänne 63 D5 *lake* S Finland
Paine, Cerro 43 A7 *mountain* S Chile
Painted Desert 26 B1 *desert* Arizona, SW USA
Paisley 66 C4 W Scotland, UK
País Valenciano 71 F3 *cultural region* NE Spain
País Vasco 71 E1 *cultural region* N Spain
Paita 38 B3 Piura, NW Peru
Pakanbaru *see* Pekanbaru
Pakaraima Mountains 37 E3 *var.* Serra Pacaraim, Sierra Pacaraima. *Mountain range* N South America
Pakistan 112 A2 *off.* Islamic Republic of Pakistan, *var.* Islami Jamhuriya e Pakistan. *Country* S Asia
Paknam *see* Samut Prakan
Pakokku 114 A3 Magwe, C Myanmar
Pak Phanang 115 C7 *var.* Ban Pak Phanang. Nakhon Si Thammarat, SW Thailand
Pakruojis 84 C4 Pakruojis, N Lithuania
Paks 77 C7 Tolna, S Hungary
Paksé *see* Pakxé
Pakxé 115 D5 *var.* Paksé. Champasak, S Laos
Palafrugell 71 G2 Cataluña, NE Spain
Palagruža 79 B5 *It.* Pelagosa. *Island* SW Croatia
Palaiá Epídavros 83 C6 Pelopónnisos, S Greece
Palaiseau 68 D2 Essonne, N France
Palamós 71 G2 Cataluña, NE Spain
Palamuse 84 E2 *Ger.* Sankt-Bartholomäi. Jõgevamaa, E Estonia
Pālanpur 112 C4 Gujarāt, W India
Palapye 56 D3 Central, SE Botswana
Palau 122 A2 *var.* Belau. *Country* W Pacific Ocean
Palawan 117 E2 *island* W Philippines
Palawan Passage 116 D2 *passage* W Philippines
Paldiski 84 D2 *prev.* Baltiski, *Eng.* Baltic Port, *Ger.* Baltischport. Harjumaa, NW Estonia
Palembang 116 B4 Sumatera, W Indonesia
Palencia 70 D2 *anc.* Palantia, Pallantia. Castilla-León, NW Spain
Palermo 75 C7 *Fr.* Palerme; *anc.* Panhormus, Panormus. Sicilia, Italy, C Mediterranean Sea
Pāli 112 C3 Rajasthan, N India
Palikir 122 C2 *country capital* (Micronesia) Pohnpei, E Micronesia
Palimé *see* Kpalimé
Palioúri, Akrotírio 82 C4 *var.* Akra Kanestron. Headland N Greece
Palk Strait 110 C3 *strait* India/Sri Lanka
Palliser, Cape 129 D5 *headland* North Island, NZ
Palma 71 G3 *var.* Palma de Mallorca. Mallorca, Spain, W Mediterranean Sea
Palma del Río 70 D4 Andalucía, S Spain
Palma de Mallorca *see* Palma
Palmar Sur 31 E5 Puntarenas, SE Costa Rica
Palma Soriano 32 C3 Santiago de Cuba, E Cuba
Palm Beach 126 E1 New South Wales, SE Australia
Palmer 132 A2 *US research station* Antarctica
Palmer Land 132 A3 *physical region* Antarctica
Palmerston 123 F4 *island* S Cook Islands
Palmerston North 128 D4 Manawatu-Wanganui, North Island, NZ
Palmi 75 D7 Calabria, SW Italy
Palmira 36 B3 Valle del Cauca, W Colombia
Palm Springs 25 D7 California, W USA
Palmyra *see* Tudmur
Palmyra Atoll 123 G2 *US privately owned unincorporated territory* C Pacific Ocean
Palo Alto 25 B6 California, W USA
Palu 117 E4 *prev.* Paloe. Sulawesi, C Indonesia
Pamiers 69 B6 Ariège, S France
Pamir *var.* Daryā-ye Pāmīr, *Taj.* Dar"yoi Pomir. *River* Afghanistan/Tajikistan *see also* Pāmīr, Daryā-ye
Pamirs 101 F3 *Pash.* Daryā-ye Pāmīr, *Rus.* Pamir. *Mountain range* C Asia
Pâmiut *see* Paamiut
Pamlico Sound 21 G1 *sound* North Carolina, SE USA
Pampa 27 E1 Texas, SW USA
Pampas 42 C4 *plain* C Argentina
Pamplona 71 E1 *Basq.* Iruña; *prev.* Pampeluna, *anc.* Pompaelo. Navarra, N Spain
Pamplona 36 C2 Norte de Santander, N Colombia
Pānji 110 B1 *var.* Pangim, Panjim, New Goa. Goa, W India
Panama 31 G5 *off.* Republic of Panama. *Country* Central America
Panamá 31 G4 *var.* Ciudad de Panamá, *Eng.* Panama City. *Country capital* (Panama) Panamá, C Panama
Panama Basin 13 C8 *undersea feature* E Pacific Ocean
Panama Canal 31 F4 *canal* E Panama
Panama City *see* Panamá
Panama City 20 D3 Florida, SE USA
Panamá, Golfo de 31 G5 *var.* Gulf of Panama. *Gulf* S Panama
Panama, Gulf of *see* Panamá, Golfo de
Panamá, Isthmus of *see* Panamá, Istmo de
Panamá, Istmo de 31 G4 *Eng.* Isthmus of Panama; *prev.* Isthmus of Darien. *Isthmus* E Panama
Panay Island 117 E2 *island* C Philippines
Pančevo 78 D3 *Ger.* Pantschowa, *Hung.* Pancsova. Serbia, N Serbia and Montenegro (Yugo.)
Paneas *see* Bāniyās
Panevėžys 84 C4 Panevėžys, C Lithuania
Pangim *see* Pānji
Pangkalpinang 116 C4 Pulau Bangka, W Indonesia
Pang-Nga *see* Phang-Nga
Panjim *see* Pānji
Pánormos 83 C7 Kríti, Greece, E Mediterranean Sea
Pantanal 41 E3 *var.* Pantanalmato-Grossense. *Swamp* SW Brazil
Pantanalmato-Grossense *see* Pantanal
Pantelleria, Isola di 75 B7 *island* SW Italy
Pánuco 29 E3 Veracruz-Llave, E Mexico
Pao-chi *see* Baoji
Paoki *see* Baoji
Paola 80 B5 E Malta
Pao-shan *see* Baoshan
Pao-t'ou *see* Baotou
Paotow *see* Baotou
Papagayo, Golfo de 30 C4 *gulf* NW Costa Rica
Papakura 128 D3 Auckland, North Island, NZ
Papantla 29 F4 *var.* Papantla de Olarte. Veracruz-Llave, E Mexico
Papantla de Olarte *see* Papantla
Papeete 123 H4 *dependent territory capital* (French Polynesia) Tahiti, W French Polynesia
Paphos *see* Páfos
Papilė 84 B3 Akmenė, NW Lithuania
Papillion 23 F4 Nebraska, C USA
Papua 117 H4 *var.* Irian Barat, Irian Jaya West Irian, West New Guinea, West Papua; *prev.* Dutch New Guinea, Netherlands New Guinea. Admin. region *province* E Indonesia
Papua, Gulf of 122 B3 *gulf* S PNG
Papua New Guinea 122 B3 *off.* Independent State of Papua New Guinea; *prev.* Territory of Papua and New Guinea, *abbrev.* PNG. *Country* NW Melanesia
Papuk 78 C3 *mountain range* NE Croatia
Pará 41 E2 *off.* Estado do Pará. *State* NE Brazil
Pará *see* Belém
Paracel Islands 103 E3 *disputed territory* SE Asia
Paraćin 78 D4 Serbia, C Serbia and Montenegro (Yugo.)
Paragua, Río 37 E3 *river* SE Venezuela
Paraguay 42 D2 *var.* Río Paraguay. *River* C South America
Paraguay 42 C2 *country* C South America
Paraguay, Río *see* Paraguay
Paraíba 41 G2 *off.* Estado da Paraíba; *prev.* Parahiba, Parahyba. *State* E Brazil
Parakou 53 F4 C Benin
Paramaribo 37 G3 *country capital* (Suriname) Paramaribo, N Suriname
Paramushir, Ostrov 93 H3 *island* SE Russian Federation
Paraná 41 E5 *off.* Estado do Paraná. *State* S Brazil
Paraná 35 C5 *var.* Alto Paraná. *River* C South America
Paraná 41 E4 Entre Ríos, E Argentina
Paranéstio 82 C3 Anatolikí Makedonía kai Thráki, NE Greece
Paraparaumu 129 D5 Wellington, North Island, NZ
Parchim 72 C3 Mecklenburg-Vorpommern, N Germany
Parczew 76 E4 Lubelskie, E Poland
Pardubice 77 B5 *Ger.* Pardubitz. Pardubický Kraj, C Czech Republic
Parechcha 85 B5 *Rus.* Porech'ye. Hrodzyenskaya Voblasts', NE Belarus
Parecis, Chapada dos 40 D3 *var.* Serra dos Parecis. *Mountain range* W Brazil
Parepare 117 E4 Sulawesi, C Indonesia
Párga 83 A5 Ípeiros, W Greece
Paria, Golfo de *see* Paria, Gulf of
Paria, Gulf of 37 E1 *var.* Golfo de Paria. *Gulf* Trinidad and Tobago/Venezuela
Parika 37 F2 NE Guyana
Paris 68 D1 *anc.* Lutetia, Lutetia Parisiorum, Parisii. *Country capital* (France) Paris, N France
Paris 27 G2 Texas, SW USA
Parkersburg 18 D4 West Virginia, NE USA
Parkes 127 D6 New South Wales, SE Australia
Parma 74 B2 Emilia-Romagna, N Italy
Parnahyba *see* Parnaíba
Parnaíba 41 F2 *var.* Parnahyba. Piauí, E Brazil
Pärnu 84 D2 *Ger.* Pernau, *Latv.* Pērnava; *prev.* Rus. Pernov. Pärnumaa, SW Estonia
Pärnu 84 D2 *var.* Parnu Jõgi, *Ger.* Pernau. *River* SW Estonia
Pärnu-Jaagupi 84 D2 *Ger.* Sankt-Jakobi. Pärnumaa, SW Estonia
Parnu Jõgi *see* Pärnu
Pärnu Laht 84 D2 *Ger.* Pernauer Bucht. *Bay* SW Estonia
Páros 83 C6 *island* Kykládes, Greece, Aegean Sea
Páros 83 D6 Páros, Kykládes, Greece, Aegean Sea
Parral *see* Hidalgo del Parral
Parral 42 B4 Maule, C Chile
Parramatta 126 D1 New South Wales, SE Australia
Parras 28 D3 *var.* Parras de la Fuente. Coahuila de Zaragoza, NE Mexico
Parras de la Fuente *see* Parras
Parsons 23 F5 Kansas, C USA
Pasadena 25 C7 California, W USA
Pasadena 27 H4 Texas, SW USA
Paşcani 86 C3 *Hung.* Páskán. Iaşi, NE Romania
Pasco 24 C2 Washington, NW USA
Pas de Calais *see* Dover, Strait of
Pasewalk 72 D3 Mecklenburg-Vorpommern, NE Germany
Pasinler 95 F3 Erzurum, NE Turkey
Pasłęk 76 D2 *Ger.* Preußisch Holland. Warmińsko-Mazurskie, NE Poland
Pasni 112 A3 Baluchistān, SW Pakistan
Paso de Indios 43 B6 Chubut, S Argentina
Passau 73 D6 Bayern, SE Germany
Passo del Brennero *see* Brenner Pass
Passo Fundo 41 E5 Rio Grande do Sul, S Brazil
Pastavy 85 C5 *Pol.* Postawy, *Rus.* Postavy. Vitsyebskaya Voblasts', NW Belarus
Pastaza, Río 38 B2 *river* Ecuador/Peru
Pasto 36 A4 Nariño, SW Colombia
Pasvalys 84 C4 Pasvalys, N Lithuania
Patagonia 35 B7 *physical region* Argentina/Chile
Patalung *see* Phatthalung
Patani *see* Pattani

INDEX

Porterville – Radviliškis

Porterville *25 C7* California, W USA
Port-Gentil *55 A6* Ogooué-Maritime, W Gabon
Port Harcourt *53 G5* Rivers, S Nigeria
Port Hardy *14 D5* Vancouver Island, British Columbia, SW Canada
Port Harrison *see* Inukjuak
Port Hedland *124 B4* Western Australia
Port Huron *18 D3* Michigan, N USA
Portimão *70 B4 var.* Vila Nova de Portimão. Faro, S Portugal
Port Jackson *126 E1 harbour* New South Wales, SE Australia
Port Láirge *see* Waterford
Portland *19 G2* Maine, NE USA
Portland *24 B3* Oregon, NW USA
Portland *27 G4* Texas, SW USA
Portland *127 B7* Victoria, SE Australia
Portland Bight *32 B5 bay* S Jamaica
Portlaoighise *see* Portlaoise
Portlaoise *67 B6 Ir.* Portlaoighise; *prev.* Maryborough. C Ireland
Port Lavaca *27 G4* Texas, SW USA
Port Lincoln *127 A6* South Australia
Port Louis *57 H3 country capital* (Mauritius) NW Mauritius
Port Macquarie *127 E6* New South Wales, SE Australia
Portmore *32 B5* C Jamaica
Port Moresby *122 B3 country capital* (PNG) Central/National Capital District, SW PNG
Port Musgrave *127 B9 bay* Queensland, N Australia
Port Natal *see* Durban
Porto *70 B2 Eng.* Oporto; *anc.* Portus Cale. Porto, NW Portugal
Porto Alegre *41 E5 var.* Pôrto Alegre. *State capital* Rio Grande do Sul, S Brazil
Porto Alegre *54 E2* São Tomé, S Sao Tome and Principe
Porto Bello *see* Portobelo
Portobelo *31 G4 var.* Porto Bello, Puerto Bello. Colón, N Panama
Port O'Connor *27 G4* Texas, SW USA
Porto Edda *see* Sarandë
Portoferraio *74 B4* Toscana, C Italy
Port-of-Spain *33 H5 country capital* (Trinidad and Tobago) Trinidad, Trinidad and Tobago
Porto Grande *see* Mindelo
Portogruaro *74 C2* Veneto, NE Italy
Porto-Novo *53 F5 country capital* (Benin) S Benin
Porto Santo *48 A2 var.* Ilha do Porto Santo. *Island* Madeira, Portugal, NE Atlantic Ocean
Porto Torres *75 A5* Sardegna, Italy, C Mediterranean Sea
Porto Velho *40 D2 var.* Velho. *State capital* Rondônia, W Brazil
Portoviejo *38 A2 var.* Puertoviejo. Manabí, W Ecuador
Port Pirie *127 B6* South Australia
Port Said *50 B1 Ar.* Būr Sa'īd. N Egypt
Portsmouth *19 G3* New Hampshire, NE USA
Portsmouth *18 D4* Ohio, N USA
Portsmouth *67 D7* S England, UK
Portsmouth *19 F5* Virginia, NE USA
Port Stanley *see* Stanley
Port Sudan *50 C3* Red Sea, NE Sudan
Port Swettenham *see* Klang
Port Talbot *67 C7* S Wales, UK
Portugal *70 B3 off.* Republic of Portugal. *Country* SW Europe
Portuguese Timor *see* East Timor
Port-Vila *122 D4 var.* Vila. *Country capital* (Vanuatu) Éfaté, C Vanuatu
Porvenir *43 B8* Magallanes, S Chile
Porvenir *39 E3* Pando, NW Bolivia
Porvoo *63 E6 Swe.* Borgå. Etelä-Suomi, S Finland
Posadas *42 D3* Misiones, NE Argentina
Poschega *see* Požega
Posterholt *65 D5* Limburg, SE Netherlands
Postojna *73 D8 Ger.* Adelsberg, *It.* Postumia. SW Slovenia
Potamós *83 C7* Antikythira, S Greece
Potenza *75 D5 anc.* Potentia. Basilicata, S Italy
P'ot'i *95 F2* W Georgia
Potiskum *53 G4* Yobe, NE Nigeria
Potomac River *19 E5 river* NE USA
Potosí *39 F4* Potosí, S Bolivia
Potsdam *72 D3* Brandenburg, NE Germany
Potwar Plateau *112 C2 plateau* NE Pakistan
Poŭthĭsăt *115 D6 prev.* Pursat. Poŭthĭsăt, W Cambodia
Po Valley *74 C2 It.* Valle del Po. *Valley* N Italy
Považská Bystrica *77 C5 Ger.* Waagbistritz, *Hung.* Vágbeszterce. Trenčiansky Kraj, W Slovakia
Poverty Bay *128 E4 inlet* North Island, NZ
Póvoa de Varzim *70 B2* Porto, NW Portugal
Powder River *22 D2 river* Montana/Wyoming, NW USA
Powell *22 C2* Wyoming, C USA
Powell, Lake *22 B5 lake* Utah, W USA
Požarevac *78 D4 Ger.* Passarowitz. Serbia, NE Serbia and Montenegro (Yugo.)
Poza Rica *29 F4 var.* Poza Rica de Hidalgo. Veracruz-Llave, E Mexico
Poza Rica de Hidalgo *see* Poza Rica
Požega *78 D4 prev.* Slavonska Požega. *Ger.* Poschega, *Hung.* Pozsega. Požega-Slavonija, NE Croatia
Pozsega *see* Požega
Poznań *76 C3 Ger.* Posen, Posnania. Wielkopolskie, C Poland
Pozoblanco *70 D4* Andalucía, S Spain
Pozzallo *75 C8* Sicilia, Italy, C Mediterranean Sea
Prachatice *77 A5 Ger.* Prachatitz. Budějovický Kraj, S Czech Republic
Prado del Ganso *see* Goose Green
Prae *see* Phrae
Prague *58 D3* Oklahoma, C USA
Praha *77 A5 Eng.* Prague, *Ger.* Prag, *Pol.* Praga. *Country capital* (Czech Republic) Středočesky Kraj, NW Czech Republic
Praia *52 A3 country capital* (Cape Verde) Santiago, S Cape Verde
Prato *74 B3* Toscana, C Italy
Pratt *23 E5* Kansas, C USA
Prattville *20 D2* Alabama, S USA
Pravda *82 D1 prev.* Dogrular. Silistra, NE Bulgaria
Pravia *70 C1* Asturias, N Spain
Prenzlau *72 D3* Brandenburg, NE Germany
Přerov *77 C5 Ger.* Prerau. Olomoucký Kraj, E Czech Republic
Presa de la Amistad *see* Amistad Reservoir
Preschau *see* Prešov
Prescott *26 B2* Arizona, SW USA
Preševo *79 D5* Serbia, SE Serbia and Montenegro (Yugo.)
Presidente Epitácio *41 E4* São Paulo, S Brazil
Prešov *77 D5 var.* Preschau, *Ger.* Eperies, *Hung.* Eperjes. Prešouský Kraj, E Slovakia
Prespa, Lake *79 D6 Alb.* Liqen i Prespës, *Gk.* Límni Megáli Préspa, Limni Prespa, *Mac.* Prespansko Ezero, *Serb.* Prespansko Jezero. *Lake* SE Europe
Presque Isle *19 H1* Maine, NE USA
Preston *67 D5* NW England, UK
Prestwick *66 C4* W Scotland, UK
Pretoria *56 D4 var.* Epitoli, Tshwane. *Country capital* (South Africa-administrative capital) Gauteng, NE South Africa
Préveza *83 A5* Ípeiros, W Greece
Pribilof Islands *14 A3 island group* Alaska, USA
Priboj *78 C4* Serbia, W Serbia and Montenegro (Yugo.)
Price *22 B4* Utah, W USA
Prichard *20 C3* Alabama, S USA
Priekulė *84 B3 Ger.* Prökuls. Gargždai, W Lithuania
Prienai *85 B5 Pol.* Preny. Prienai, S Lithuania
Prieska *56 C4* Northern Cape, C South Africa
Prijedor *78 B3* Republika Srpska, NW Bosnia and Herzegovina
Prijepolje *78 D4* Serbia, W Serbia and Montenegro (Yugo.)
Prilep *79 D6 Turk.* Perlepe. S FYR Macedonia
Primorsk *84 A4 Ger.* Fischhausen. Kaliningradskaya Oblast', W Russian Federation
Primorsko *82 E2 prev.* Keupriya. Burgas, E Bulgaria
Prince Albert *15 F5* Saskatchewan, S Canada
Prince Edward Island *17 F4 Fr.* Île-du Prince-Édouard. *Province* SE Canada
Prince Edward Islands *47 E8 island group* S South Africa
Prince George *15 E5* British Columbia, SW Canada
Prince of Wales Island *15 F2 island* Queen Elizabeth Islands, Nunavut, NW Canada
Prince of Wales Island *126 B1 island* Queensland, E Australia
Prince Patrick Island *15 E2 island* Parry Islands, Northwest Territories, NW Canada
Prince Rupert *14 D4* British Columbia, SW Canada
Prince's Island *see* Príncipe
Princess Charlotte Bay *126 C2 bay* Queensland, NE Australia
Princess Elizabeth Land *132 C3 physical region* Antarctica
Príncipe *55 A5 var.* Príncipe Island, *Eng.* Prince's Island. *Island* N Sao Tome and Principe
Príncipe Island *see* Príncipe
Prinzapolka *31 E3* Región Autónoma Atlántico Norte, NE Nicaragua
Pripet *85 C7 Bel.* Prypyats', *Ukr.* Pryp"yat'. *River* Belarus/Ukraine
Pripet Marshes *85 B7 wetland* Belarus/Ukraine
Priština *79 D5 Alb.* Prishtine. Serbia, S Serbia and Montenegro (Yugo.)
Privas *69 D5* Ardèche, E France
Prizren *79 D5 Alb.* Prizreni. Serbia, S Serbia and Montenegro (Yugo.)
Probolinggo *116 D5* Jawa, C Indonesia
Progreso *29 H3* Yucatán, SE Mexico
Prokhladnyy *89 B8* Kabardino-Balkarskaya Respublika, SW Russian Federation
Prokuplje *79 D5* Serbia, SE Serbia and Montenegro (Yugo.)
Prome *114 B4 var.* Pyè. Pegu, C Myanmar
Promyshlennyy *88 E3* Respublika Komi, NW Russian Federation
Prostějov *77 C5 Ger.* Prossnitz, *Pol.* Prościejów. Olomoucký Kraj, E Czech Republic
Provence *69 D6 cultural region* SE France
Providence *see* Fort Providence
Providence *19 G3 state capital* Rhode Island, NE USA
Providencia, Isla de *31 F3 island* NW Colombia
Provideniya *172 B1* Chukotskiy Avtonomnyy Okrug, NE Russian Federation
Provo *22 B4* Utah, W USA
Prudhoe Bay *14 D2* Alaska, USA
Prusa *see* Bursa
Pruszków *76 D3 Ger.* Kaltdorf. Mazowieckie, C Poland
Prut *86 D4 Ger.* Pruth. *River* E Europe
Pruzhany *85 B6 Pol.* Prużana. Brestskaya Voblasts', SW Belarus
Prydz Bay *132 D3 bay* Antarctica
Pryluky *87 E2 Rus.* Priluki. Chernihivs'ka Oblast', NE Ukraine
Prymors'k *87 G4 Rus.* Primorsk; *prev.* Primorskoye. Zaporiz'ka Oblast', SE Ukraine
Przemysl *77 E5 Rus.* Peremyshl. Podkarpackie, SE Poland
Psará *83 D5 island* E Greece
Psël *87 F2 river* Russian Federation/Ukraine
Pskov *92 B2 Ger.* Pleskau, *Latv.* Pleskava. Pskovskaya Oblast', W Russian Federation
Pskov, Lake *E3 Est.* Pihkva Järv, *Ger.* Pleskauer See, *Rus.* Pskovskoye Ozero. *Lake* Estonia/Russian Federation
Ptsich *85 C7 Rus.* Ptich'. *River* SE Belarus
Ptsich *85 C7 Rus.* Ptich'. Homyel'skaya Voblasts', SE Belarus
Ptuj *73 E7 Ger.* Pettau; *anc.* Poetovio. NE Slovenia
Pucallpa *38 C3* Ucayali, C Peru
Puck *76 C2* Pomorskie, N Poland
Pudasjärvi *62 D4* Oulu, C Finland
Puduchcheri *see* Pondicherry
Puebla *29 F4 var.* Puebla de Zaragoza. Puebla, S Mexico
Puebla de Zaragoza *see* Puebla
Pueblo *22 D5* Colorado, C USA
Puerto Acosta *39 E4* La Paz, W Bolivia
Puerto Aisén *43 B6* Aisén, S Chile
Puerto Ángel *29 F5* Oaxaca, SE Mexico
Puerto Argentino *see* Stanley
Puerto Ayacucho *36 D3* Amazonas, SW Venezuela
Puerto Baquerizo Moreno *38 B5 var.* Baquerizo Moreno. Galapagos Islands, Ecuador, E Pacific Ocean
Puerto Barrios *30 C2* Izabal, E Guatemala
Puerto Bello *see* Portobelo
Puerto Berrío *36 B2* Antioquia, C Colombia
Puerto Cabello *36 D1* Carabobo, N Venezuela
Puerto Cabezas *31 E2 var.* Bilwi. Región Autónoma Atlántico Norte, NE Nicaragua
Puerto Carreño *36 D3* Vichada, E Colombia
Puerto Cortés *30 C2* Cortés, NW Honduras
Puerto Cumarebo *36 C1* Falcón, N Venezuela
Puerto Deseado *43 C7* Santa Cruz, SE Argentina
Puerto Escondido *29 F5* Oaxaca, SE Mexico
Puerto Francisco de Orellana *38 B1 var.* Coca. Napo, N Ecuador
Puerto Gallegos *see* Río Gallegos
Puerto Inírida *36 D3 var.* Obando. Guainía, E Colombia
Puerto La Cruz *37 E1* Anzoátegui, NE Venezuela
Puerto Lempira *31 E2* Gracias a Dios, E Honduras
Puerto Limón *see* Limón
Puertollano *70 D4* Castilla-La Mancha, C Spain
Puerto López *36 C1* La Guajira, N Colombia
Puerto Maldonado *39 E3* Madre de Dios, E Peru
Puerto México *see* Coatzacoalcos
Puerto Montt *43 B5* Los Lagos, C Chile
Puerto Natales *43 B7* Magallanes, S Chile
Puerto Obaldía *31 H5* San Blas, NE Panama
Puerto Plata *33 E3 var.* San Felipe de Puerto Plata. N Dominican Republic
Puerto Princesa *117 E2 off.* Puerto Princesa City. Palawan, W Philippines
Puerto Rico *33 F3 off.* Commonwealth of Puerto Rico; *prev.* Porto Rico. *US commonwealth territory* C West Indies
Puerto Rico *34 B1 island* C West Indies
Puerto Rico Trench *34 B1 undersea feature* NE Caribbean Sea
Puerto San José *see* San José
Puerto San Julián *43 B7 var.* San Julián. Santa Cruz, SE Argentina
Puerto Suárez *39 H4* Santa Cruz, E Bolivia
Puerto Vallarta *28 D4* Jalisco, SW Mexico
Puerto Varas *43 B5* Los Lagos, C Chile
Puerto Viejo *31 E4* Heredia, NE Costa Rica
Puertoviejo *see* Portoviejo
Puget Sound *24 B1 sound* Washington, NW USA
Puglia *75 E5 Eng.* Apulia. *Cultural region* SE Italy
Pukaki, Lake *129 B6 lake* South Island, NZ
Pukekohe *128 D3* Auckland, North Island, NZ
Puket *see* Phuket
Pukhavichy *85 C6 Rus.* Pukhovichi. Minskaya Voblasts', C Belarus
Pula *78 A3 It.* Pola; *prev.* Pulj. Istra, NW Croatia
Pulaski *18 D5* Virginia, NE USA
Pulau Butung *see* Buton, Pulau
Puławy *76 D4 Ger.* Neu Amerika. Lublin, E Poland
Pul-i-Khumri *see* Pol-e Khomrī
Pullman *24 C2* Washington, NW USA
Pułtusk *76 D3* Mazowieckie, C Poland
Puná, Isla *38 A2 island* SW Ecuador
Pune *112 C5 prev.* Poona. Mahārāshtra, W India
Punjab *112 C2 prev.* West Punjab, Western Punjab. *Province* E Pakistan
Puno *39 E4* Puno, SE Peru
Punta Alta *43 C5* Buenos Aires, E Argentina
Punta Arenas *43 B8 prev.* Magallanes. Magallanes, S Chile
Punta Gorda *31 E4* Región Autónoma Atlántico Sur, SE Nicaragua
Punta Gorda *30 C2* Toledo, SE Belize
Puntarenas *30 D4* Puntarenas, W Costa Rica
Punto Fijo *36 C1* Falcón, N Venezuela
Pupuya, Nevado *39 E4 mountain* W Bolivia
Puri *113 F5 var.* Jagannath. Orissa, E India
Puriramya *see* Buriram
Purmerend *64 C3* Noord-Holland, C Netherlands
Purus, Rio *40 C2 Sp.* Río Purús. *River* Brazil/Peru
Pusan *107 E4 off.* Pusan-gwangyŏksi, *var.* Busan, *Jap.* Fusan. SE South Korea
Püspökladány *77 D6* Hajdú-Bihar, E Hungary
Putorana Mountains *see* Putorana, Plato
Putorana, Plato *92 D3 var.* Gory Putorana, *Eng.* Putorana Mountains. *Mountain range* N Russian Federation
Puttalam *110 C3* North Western Province, W Sri Lanka
Puttgarden *72 C2* Schleswig-Holstein, N Germany
Putumayo, Río *36 B5 var.* Rio Içá. *River* NW South America *see also* Içá, Rio
Putumayo, Río *see* Içá, Rio
Puurmani *84 D2 Ger.* Talkhof. Jõgevamaa, E Estonia
Pyatigorsk *89 B7* Stavropol'skiy Kray, SW Russian Federation
P"yatykhatky *87 F3 Rus.* Pyatikhatki. Dnipropetrovs'ka Oblast', E Ukraine
Pyè *see* Prome
Pyetrykaw *85 C7 Rus.* Petrikov. Homyel'skaya Voblasts', SE Belarus
Pyinmana *114 B4* Mandalay, C Myanmar
Pýlos *83 B6 var.* Pilos. Pelopónnisos, S Greece
P'yŏngyang *107 E3 var.* P'yŏngyang-si, *Eng.* Pyongyang. *Country capital* (North Korea) SW North Korea
P'yŏngyang-si *see* P'yŏngyang
Pyramid Lake *25 C5 lake* Nevada, W USA
Pyrenees *80 B2 Fr.* Pyrénées, *Sp.* Pirineos; *anc.* Pyrenaei Montes. *Mountain range* SW Europe
Pýrgos *83 B6 var.* Pírgos. Dytikí Ellás, S Greece
Pyryatyn *87 E2 Rus.* Piryatin. Poltavs'ka Oblast', NE Ukraine
Pyrzyce *76 B3 Ger.* Pyritz. Zachodniopomorskie, NW Poland
Pyu *114 B4* Pegu, C Myanmar
Pyuntaza *114 B4* Pegu, SW Myanmar

Q

Qā' al Jafr *97 C7 lake* S Jordan
Qaanaaq *60 D1 var.* Qânâq, *Dan.* Thule. N Greenland
Qābis *see* Gabès
Qacentina *see* Constantine
Qafṣah *see* Gafsa
Qagan Us *see* Dulan
Qahremānshahr *see* Bākhtarān
Qaidam Pendi *104 C4 basin* C China
Qal'aikhum *101 F3 Rus.* Kalaikhum. S Tajikistan
Qal'at Bīshah *99 B5* 'Asīr, SW Saudi Arabia
Qamdo *104 D5* Xizang Zizhiqu, W China
Qamishly *see* Al Qāmishlī
Qânâq *see* Qaanaaq
Qaqortoq *60 C4 Dan.* Julianehåb. S Greenland
Qara Qum *see* Garagumy
Qarkilik *see* Ruoqiang
Qarokŭl *101 F3 Rus.* Karakul'. E Tajikistan
Qars *see* Kars
Qarshi *101 E3 Rus.* Karshi; *prev.* Bek-Budi. Qashqadaryo Wiloyati, S Uzbekistan
Qasigianguit *see* Qasigiannguit
Qasigiannguit *60 C3 var.* Qasigianguit, *Dan.* Christianshåb. C Greenland
Qasr Farâfra *50 B2* W Egypt
Qaṭanā *97 B5 var.* Katana. Dimashq, S Syria
Qatar *98 C4 off.* State of Qatar, *Ar.* Dawlat Qaṭar. *Country* SW Asia
Qattara Depression *see* Qaṭṭâra, Monkhafad el
Qaṭṭâra, Monkhafad el *88 A1 var.* Munkhafaḍ al Qaṭṭārah, *Eng.* Qattara Depression. *Desert* NW Egypt
Qazimämmäd *95 H3 Rus.* Kazi Magomed. SE Azerbaijan
Qazvīn *98 C2 var.* Kazvin. Qazvīn, N Iran
Qena *50 B2 var.* Qinā; *anc.* Caene, Caenepolis. E Egypt
Qeqertarssuaq *see* Qeqertarsuaq
Qeqertarsuaq *60 C3 var.* Qeqertarssuaq, *Dan.* Godhavn. S Greenland
Qeqertarsuaq *60 C3 island* W Greenland
Qeqertarsuup Tunua *60 C3 Dan.* Disko Bugt. *Inlet* W Greenland
Qerveh *see* Qorveh
Qeshm *98 D4 var.* Jazīreh-ye Qeshm, Qeshm Island. *Island* S Iran
Qeshm Island *see* Qeshm
Qian *see* Guizhou
Qilian Shan *104 D3 var.* Kilien Mountains. *Mountain range* N China
Qimusseriarsuaq *60 C2 Dan.* Melville Bugt, *Eng.* Melville Bay. *Bay* NW Greenland
Qinā *see* Qena
Qing *see* Qinghai
Qingdao *106 D4 var.* Ching-Tao, Ch'ing-tao, Tsingtao, Tsintao, *Ger.* Tsingtau. Shandong, E China
Qinghai *104 C4 var.* Chinghai, Koko Nor, Qing, Qinghai Sheng, Tsinghai. *Admin. region province* C China
Qinghai Hu *104 D4 var.* Ch'ing Hai, Tsing Hai, *Mong.* Koko Nor. *lake* C China
Qinghai Sheng *see* Qinghai
Qingzang Gaoyuan *104 B4 var.* Xizang Gaoyuan, *Eng.* Plateau of Tibet. *Plateau* W China
Qinhuangdao *106 D3* Hebei, E China
Qinzhou *106 B6* Guangxi Zhuangzu Zizhiqu, S China
Qiong *see* Hainan
Qiqihar *106 D2 var.* Ch'i-ch'i-ha-erh, Tsitsihar; *prev.* Lungkiang. Heilongjiang, NE China
Qira *104 B4* Xinjiang Uygur Zizhiqu, NW China
Qitai *104 C3* Xinjiang Uygur Zizhiqu, NW China
Qīzān *see* Jīzān
Qizil Orda *see* Kyzylorda
Qizil Qum *see* Kyzyl Kum
Qizilrabot *101 G3 Rus.* Kyzylrabot. SE Tajikistan
Qom *98 C3 var.* Kum, Qum. Qom, N Iran
Qomul *see* Hami
Qondūz *see* Kunduz
Qorveh *98 C3 var.* Qerveh, Qurveh. Kordestān, W Iran
Qostanay *see* Kostanay
Qoubaïyât *96 B4 var.* Al Qubayyāt. N Lebanon
Qoussantîna *see* Constantine
Quang Ngai *115 E5 var.* Quangngai, Quang Nghia. Quang Ngai, C Vietnam
Quangngai *see* Quang Ngai
Quang Nghia *see* Quang Ngai
Quanzhou *106 D6 var.* Ch'uan-chou, Tsinkiang; *prev.* Chin-chiang. Fujian, SE China
Quanzhou *106 C6* Guangxi Zhuangzu Zizhiqu, S China
Qu'Appelle *15 F5 river* Saskatchewan, S Canada
Quarles, Pegunungan *117 E4 mountain range* Sulawesi, C Indonesia
Quarnero *see* Kvarner
Quartu Sant' Elena *75 A6* Sardegna, Italy, C Mediterranean Sea
Quba *95 H2 Rus.* Kuba. N Azerbaijan
Qubba *see* Ba'qūbah
Québec *17 E4 var.* Quebec. Quebec, SE Canada
Quebec *16 D3 var.* Québec. *Admin. region province* SE Canada
Queen Charlotte Islands *14 C5 Fr.* Îles de la Reine-Charlotte. *Island group* British Columbia, SW Canada
Queen Charlotte Sound *14 C5 sea area* British Columbia, W Canada
Queen Elizabeth Islands *15 E2 Fr.* Îles de la Reine-Élisabeth. *Island group* Northwest Territories/Nunavut, N Canada
Queensland *126 B4 state* N Australia
Queenstown *56 D5* Eastern Cape, S South Africa
Queenstown *129 B7* Otago, South Island, NZ
Quelimane *57 E3 var.* Kilimane, Kilmain, Quilimane. Zambézia, NE Mozambique
Quepos *31 E4* Puntarenas, S Costa Rica
Querétaro *29 E4* Querétaro de Arteaga, C Mexico
Quesada *31 E4 var.* Ciudad Quesada, San Carlos. Alajuela, N Costa Rica
Quetta *112 B2* Baluchistān, SW Pakistan
Quetzalcoalco *see* Coatzacoalcos
Quetzaltenango *see* Quezaltenango
Quezaltenango *30 A2 var.* Quetzaltenango. Quezaltenango, W Guatemala
Quibdó *36 A3* Chocó, W Colombia
Quilimane *see* Quelimane
Quillabamba *38 D3* Cusco, C Peru
Quilon *110 C3 var.* Kolam, Kollam. Kerala, SW India
Quimper *68 A3 anc.* Quimper Corentin. Finistère, NW France
Quimperlé *68 A3* Finistère, NW France
Quincy *18 A4* Illinois, N USA
Qui Nhon *see* Quy Nhon
Quissico *57 E4* Inhambane, S Mozambique
Quito *38 B1 country capital* (Ecuador) Pichincha, N Ecuador
Qullai Garmo *see* Kommunizm, Qullai
Qum *see* Qom
Qunaytra *see* Al Qunayṭirah
Qŭqon *101 F2 var.* Khokand, *Rus.* Kokand. Farghona Wiloyati, E Uzbekistan
Qurein *see* Al Kuwayt
Qŭrghonteppa *101 E3 Rus.* Kurgan-Tyube. SW Tajikistan
Qurlurtuuq *see* Kugluktuk
Qurveh *see* Qorveh
Quṣayr *see* Al Quṣayr
Quy Nhon *115 E5 var.* Quinhon, Qui Nhon. Bình Định, C Vietnam
Qyteti Stalin *see* Kuçovë
Qyzylorda *see* Kyzylorda

R

Raab *78 B1 Hung.* Rába. *River* Austria/Hungary *see also* Rába
Raahe *62 D4 Swe.* Brahestad. Oulu, W Finland
Raalte *64 D3* Overijssel, E Netherlands
Raamsdonksveer *64 C4* Noord-Brabant, S Netherlands
Raasiku *84 D2 Ger.* Rasik. Harjumaa, NW Estonia
Rába *77 B7 Ger.* Raab. *River* Austria/Hungary *see also* Raab
Rabat *48 C2 var.* al Dar al Baida. *Country capital* (Morocco) NW Morocco
Rabat *see* Victoria
Rabat *80 B5* W Malta
Rabbah Ammon *see* 'Ammān
Rabbath Ammon *see* 'Ammān
Rabinal *30 B2* Baja Verapaz, C Guatemala
Rabka *77 D5* Małopolskie, S Poland
Râbniţa *see* Rîbniţa
Rabyanāh, Ramlat *49 G4 var.* Rebiana Sand Sea, ṣaḥrā' Rabyanāh. *Desert* SE Libya
Race, Cape *17 H3 headland* Newfoundland, Newfoundland and Labrador, E Canada
Rach Gia *115 D6* Kiên Giang, S Vietnam
Rach Gia, Vinh *115 D6 bay* S Vietnam
Racine *18 B3* Wisconsin, N USA
Rădăuţi *86 C3 Ger.* Radautz, *Hung.* Radóc. Suceava, N Romania
Radom *76 D4* Mazowieckie, C Poland
Radomsko *76 D4 Rus.* Novoradomsk. Łódzkie, C Poland
Radomyshl' *86 D2* Zhytomyrs'ka Oblast', N Ukraine
Radoviš *79 E6 prev.* Radovište. E FYR Macedonia
Radviliškis *84 B4* Radviliškis, N Lithuania

Ruse – San Pedro

Ruse 82 D1 var. Ruschuk, Rustchuk, Turk. Rusçuk. Ruse, N Bulgaria
Rus Krymskaya ASSR see Crimea
Russellville 20 A1 Arkansas, C USA
Russian Federation 90 D2 off. Russian Federation, var. Russia, Latv. Krievija, Rus. Rossiyskaya Federatsiya. Country Asia/Europe
Rustaq see Ar Rustāq
Rust'avi 95 G2 SE Georgia
Rustchuk see Ruse
Ruston 20 B2 Louisiana, S USA
Rutanzige I M, Lake see Edward, Lake
Rutba see Ar Ruṭbah
Rutland 19 F2 Vermont, NE USA
Rutog 104 A4 var. Rutok. Xizang Zizhiqu, W China
Rutok see Rutog
Ruvuma 47 E5 var. Rio Rovuma. River Mozambique/Tanzania see also Rovuma, Rio
Ruvuma see Rovuma, Rio
Ruwenzori 55 E5 mountain range Uganda/Dem. Rep. Congo
Ruzhany 85 B6 Rus. Ruzhany. Brestskaya Voblasts', SW Belarus
Ružomberok 77 C5 Ger. Rosenberg, Hung. Rózsahegy. Žilinsky Kraj, N Slovakia
Rwanda 51 B6 off. Rwandese Republic; prev. Ruanda. Country C Africa
Ryazan' 89 B5 Ryazanskaya Oblast', W Russian Federation
Rybinsk 88 B4 prev. Andropov. Yaroslavskaya Oblast', W Russian Federation
Rybnik 77 C5 Śląskie, S Poland
Rybnitsa see Rîbniţa
Ryde 126 E1 New South Wales, SE Australia
Ryki 76 D4 Lublin, E Poland
Rypin 76 C3 Kujawsko-pomorskie, C Poland
Ryssel see Lille
Rysy 77 C5 mountain S Poland
Ryukyu Islands 103 E3 island group SW Japan
Ryukyu Trench 103 F3 var. Nansei Syotō Trench. Undersea feature S East China Sea
Rzeszów 77 E5 Podkarpackie, SE Poland
Rzhev 88 B4 Tverskaya Oblast', W Russian Federation

S

Saale 72 C4 river C Germany
Saalfeld 73 C5 var. Saalfeld an der Saale. Thüringen, C Germany
Saalfeld an der Saale see Saalfeld
Saarbrücken 73 A6 Fr. Sarrebruck. Saarland, SW Germany
Sääre 84 C2 var. Sjar. Saaremaa, W Estonia
Saaremaa 84 C2 Ger. Oesel, Ösel; prev. Saare. Island W Estonia
Saariselkä 62 D2 Lapp. Suoločielgi. Lappi, N Finland
Sab' Ābār 96 C4 var. Sab'a Biyar, Sa'b Bi'ār. Ḥimṣ, C Syria
Sab'a Biyar see Sab' Ābār
Šabac 78 D3 Serbia, W Serbia and Montenegro (Yugo.)
Sabadell 71 G2 Cataluña, E Spain
Sabah 116 D3 cultural region Borneo, SE Asia
Sabanalarga 36 B1 Atlántico, N Colombia
Sabaneta 36 C1 Falcón, N Venezuela
Sab'atayn, Ramlat as 99 C6 desert C Yemen
Sabaya 39 F4 Oruro, S Bolivia
Sa'b Bi'ār see Sab' Ābār
Şāberī, Hāmūn-e var. Daryācheh-ye Hāmūn, Daryācheh-ye Sīstān. Lake Afghanistan/Iran see also Sīstān, Daryacheh-ye
Sabhā 49 F3 C Libya
Sabi, Rio see Save, Rio
Sabinas 29 E2 Coahuila de Zaragoza, NE Mexico
Sabinas Hidalgo 29 E2 Nuevo León, NE Mexico
Sabine River 27 H3 river Louisiana/Texas, SW USA
Sabkha see As Sabkhah
Sable, Cape 21 E5 headland Florida, SE USA
Sable Island 17 G4 island Nova Scotia, SE Canada
Şabyā 99 B6 Jīzān, SW Saudi Arabia
Sabzawar see Sabzevār
Sabzevār 98 D2 var. Sabzawar. Khorāsān, NE Iran
Sachsen 72 D4 Eng. Saxony, Fr. Saxe. State E Germany
Sachs Harbour 15 E2 Banks Island, Northwest Territories, N Canada
Sacramento 25 B5 state capital California, W USA
Sacramento Mountains 26 D2 mountain range New Mexico, SW USA
Sacramento River 25 B5 river California, W USA
Sacramento Valley 25 B5 valley California, W USA
Şa'dah 99 B6 NW Yemen
Sado 109 C5 var. Sadoga-shima. Island C Japan
Sadoga-shima see Sado
Safad see Ẕefat
Safed see Ẕefat
Säffle 63 B6 Värmland, C Sweden
Safford 26 C3 Arizona, SW USA
Safi 48 B2 W Morocco
Safīd Kūh, Selseleh-ye 100 D4 Eng. Paropamisus Range. Mountain range W Afghanistan
Sagaing 114 B3 Sagaing, C Myanmar
Sagami-nada 109 D6 inlet SW Japan
Sagan see Żagań
Sāgar 112 D4 prev. Saugor. Madhya Pradesh, C India
Saghez see Saqqez
Saginaw 18 C3 Michigan, N USA
Saginaw Bay 18 D2 lake bay Michigan, N USA
Sagua la Grande 32 B2 Villa Clara, C Cuba
Sagunt see Sagunto
Sagunto 71 F3 var. Sagunt, Ar. Murviedro; anc. Saguntum. País Valenciano, E Spain
Saguntum see Sagunto
Sahara 46 B3 desert Libya/Algeria
Sahara el Gharbîya 50 B2 var. Aş Şaḥrā' al Gharbīyah, Eng. Western Desert. Desert C Egypt
Saharan Atlas see Atlas Saharien
Sahel 52 D3 physical region C Africa
Sāḥilīyah, Jibāl as 96 B3 mountain range NW Syria
Sāhīwāl 112 C2 prev. Montgomery. Punjab, E Pakistan
Şaḥrā' Rabyanāh see Rabyanāh, Ramlat
Saïda 97 A5 var. Şaydā, Sayida; anc. Sidon. W Lebanon
Saidpur 113 G3 var. Syedpur. Rajshahi, NW Bangladesh
Saigon see Hô Chi Minh
Sai Hun see Syr Darya
Saimaa 63 E5 lake SE Finland
St Albans 67 E6 anc. Verulamium. E England, UK
Saint Albans 18 D5 West Virginia, NE USA
St Andrews 66 C4 E Scotland, UK
Saint Anna Trough see Svyataya Anna Trough
St.Ann's Bay 32 B4 C Jamaica
St.Anthony 17 Gmm3 Newfoundland, Newfoundland and Labrador, SE Canada
Saint Augustine 21 E3 Florida, SE USA
St Austell 67 C7 SW England, UK
St-Brieuc 68 A3 Côtes d'Armor, NW France
St. Catharines 16 D5 Ontario, S Canada
St-Chamond 69 D5 Loire, E France
St.Clair, Lake 18 D3 Fr. Lac à L'Eau Claire. Lake Canada/USA
St-Claude 69 D5 anc. Condate. Jura, E France
Saint Cloud 23 F2 Minnesota, N USA
St Croix 33 F3 island S Virgin Islands (US)
Saint Croix River 18 A2 river Minnesota/Wisconsin, N USA
St David's Island 20 B5 island E Bermuda
St-Denis 57 G4 dependent territory capital (Réunion) NW Réunion
St-Dié 68 E4 Vosges, NE France
St-Egrève 69 D5 Isère, E France
Saintes 69 B5 anc. Mediolanum. Charente-Maritime, W France
St-Étienne 69 D5 Loire, E France
St-Flour 69 C5 Cantal, C France
Saint Gall see Sankt Gallen
St-Gaudens 69 B6 Haute-Garonne, S France
St George 20 B4 N Bermuda
Saint George 127 D5 Queensland, E Australia
Saint George 22 A5 Utah, W USA
St.George's 33 G5 country capital (Grenada) SW Grenada
St-Georges 37 H3 E French Guiana
St-Georges 17 E4 Quebec, SE Canada
St George's Channel 67 B6 channel Ireland/Wales, UK
St George's Island 20 B4 island E Bermuda
Saint Helena 47 B6 UK dependent territory C Atlantic Ocean
St.Helena Bay 56 B5 bay SW South Africa
St Helier 67 D8 dependent territory capital (Jersey) S Jersey, Channel Islands
Saint Ignace 18 C2 Michigan, N USA
St-Jean, Lac 17 E4 lake Quebec, SE Canada
Saint Joe River 24 D2 river Idaho, NW USA
Saint John 19 H1 river Canada/USA
Saint John 17 F4 New Brunswick, SE Canada
St John's 33 G3 country capital (Antigua and Barbuda) Antigua, Antigua and Barbuda
St.John's 17 H3 Newfoundland, Newfoundland and Labrador, E Canada
Saint Joseph 23 F4 Missouri, C USA
St Julian's 80 B5 N Malta
St Kilda 66 A3 island NW Scotland, UK
Saint Kitts and Nevis 33 F3 off. Federation of Saint Christopher and Nevis, var. Saint Christopher-Nevis. Country E West Indies
St-Laurent-du-Maroni 37 H3 var. St-Laurent. NW French Guiana
St.Lawrence 17 E4 Fr. Fleuve St-Laurent. River Canada/USA
St.Lawrence, Gulf of 17 F3 gulf NW Atlantic Ocean
Saint Lawrence Island 14 B2 island Alaska, USA
St-Lô 68 B3 anc. Briovera, Laudus. Manche, N France
St-Louis 68 E4 Haut-Rhin, NE France
Saint Louis 23 G4 Missouri, C USA
Saint Louis 52 B3 NW Senegal
Saint Lucia 33 E1 country SE West Indies
Saint Lucia Channel 33 H4 channel Martinique/Saint Lucia
St-Malo 68 B3 Ille-et-Vilaine, NW France
St-Malo, Golfe de 68 A3 gulf NW France
St Matthew's Island see Zadetkyi Kyun
St.Matthias Group 122 B3 island group NE PNG
St-Maur-des-Fossés 68 E2 Val-de-Marne, N France
St.Moritz 73 B7 Ger. Sankt Moritz, Rmsch. San Murezzan. Graubünden, SE Switzerland
St-Nazaire 68 A4 Loire-Atlantique, NW France
St-Omer 68 C2 Pas-de-Calais, N France
Saint Paul 23 F2 state capital Minnesota, N USA
St-Paul, Île 119 C6 var. St.Paul Island. Island NE French Southern and Antarctic Territories
St Peter Port 67 D8 dependent territory capital (Guernsey) C Guernsey, Channel Islands
Saint Petersburg see Sankt-Peterburg
Saint Petersburg 21 E4 Florida, SE USA
St-Pierre and Miquelon 13 E5 Fr. Îles St-Pierre et Miquelon. French territorial collectivity NE North America
St-Quentin 68 C3 Aisne, N France
Saint Vincent 33 H4 island N Saint Vincent and the Grenadines
Saint Vincent and the Grenadines 33 H4 country SE West Indies
Saint Vincent Passage 33 H4 passage Saint Lucia/Saint Vincent and the Grenadines
Saipan 120 B1 island country capital (Northern Mariana Islands) S Northern Mariana Islands
Sajama, Nevado 39 F4 mountain W Bolivia
Sajószentpéter 77 D6 Borsod-Abaúj-Zemplén, NE Hungary
Sakākah 98 B4 Al Jawf, NW Saudi Arabia
Sakakawea, Lake 22 D1 reservoir North Dakota, N USA
Sakata 108 D4 Yamagata, Honshū, C Japan
Sakhalin see Sakhalin, Ostrov
Sakhalin, Ostrov 93 G4 var. Sakhalin. Island SE Russian Federation
Sakhon Nakhon see Sakon Nakhon
Şäki 95 G2 Rus. Sheki; prev. Nukha. NW Azerbaijan
Sakishima-shotō 108 A3 var. Sakisima Syotō. Island group SW Japan
Sakisima Syotō see Sakishima-shotō
Sakiz see Saqqez
Sakiz-Adasi see Chíos
Sakon Nakhon 114 D4 var. Muang Sakon Nakhon, Sakhon Nakhon. Sakon Nakhon, E Thailand
Saky 87 F5 Rus. Saki. Respublika Krym, S Ukraine
Sal 52 A3 island Ilhas de Barlavento, NE Cape Verde
Sala 63 C6 Västmanland, C Sweden
Salacgrīva 84 C3 Est. Salatsi. Limbaži, N Latvia
Sala Consilina 75 D5 Campania, S Italy
Salado, Río 42 C3 river C Argentina
Salado, Río 40 D5 river E Argentina
Şalālah 99 D6 SW Oman
Salamá 30 B2 Baja Verapaz, C Guatemala
Salamanca 70 D2 anc. Helmantica, Salmantica. Castilla León, NW Spain
Salamanca 42 B4 Coquimbo, C Chile
Salamīyah 96 B3 var. As Salamīyah. Ḥamāh, W Syria
Salang see Phuket
Salantai 84 B3 Kretinga, NW Lithuania
Salavan 115 D5 var. Saravan, Saravane. Salavan, S Laos
Salavat 89 D6 Respublika Bashkortostan, W Russian Federation
Sala y Gomez 131 F4 island Chile, E Pacific Ocean
Sala y Gomez Fracture Zone see Sala y Gomez Ridge
Sala y Gomez Ridge 131 G4 var. Sala y Gomez Fracture Zone. Tectonic feature SE Pacific Ocean
Šalčininkai 85 C5 Šalčininkai, SE Lithuania
Saldus 84 B3 Ger. Frauenburg. Saldus, W Latvia
Sale 127 C7 Victoria, SE Australia
Salé 48 C2 NW Morocco
Salekhard 92 D3 prev. Obdorsk. Yamalo-Nenetskiy Avtonomnyy Okrug, N Russian Federation
Salem 24 B3 state capital Oregon, NW USA
Salem 110 C2 Tamil Nādu, SE India
Salerno 75 D5 anc. Salernum. Campania, S Italy
Salerno, Golfo di 75 C5 Eng. Gulf of Salerno. Gulf S Italy
Salihorsk 85 C7 Rus. Soligorsk. Minskaya Voblasts', S Belarus
Salima 57 E2 Central, C Malawi
Salina 23 E5 Kansas, C USA
Salina Cruz 29 F5 Oaxaca, SE Mexico
Salinas 25 B6 California, W USA
Salinas 38 A2 Guayas, W Ecuador
Salisbury 67 D7 var. New Sarum. S England, UK
Sallyana see Salyan
Salmon River 24 D3 river Idaho, NW USA
Salmon River Mountains 24 D3 mountain range Idaho, NW USA
Salo 63 D6 Länsi-Suomi, W Finland
Salon-de-Provence 69 D6 Bouches-du-Rhône, SE France
Salonta 86 A3 Hung. Nagyszalonta. Bihor, W Romania
Sal'sk 89 B7 Rostovskaya Oblast', SW Russian Federation
Salt see As Salṭ
Salta 42 C2 Salta, NW Argentina
Saltash 67 C7 SW England, UK
Saltillo 29 E3 Coahuila de Zaragoza, NE Mexico
Salt Lake City 22 B4 state capital Utah, W USA
Salto 42 D4 Salto, N Uruguay
Salton Sea 25 D8 lake California, W USA
Salvador 41 G3 prev. São Salvador. Bahia, E Brazil
Salween 102 C2 Bur. Thanlwin, Chin. Nu Chiang, Nu Jiang. River SE Asia
Salyan 113 E3 var. Sallyana. Mid Western, W Nepal
Salzburg 73 D6 anc. Juvavum. Salzburg, N Austria
Salzgitter 72 C4 prev. Watenstedt-Salzgitter. Niedersachsen, C Germany
Salzwedel 72 C3 Sachsen-Anhalt, N Germany
Šamac see Bosanski Šamac
Samakhixai 115 E5 var. Attapu, Attopeu. Attapu, S Laos
Samalayuca 28 C1 Chihuahua, N Mexico
Samar 117 F2 island C Philippines
Samara 92 B3 prev. Kuybyshev. Samarskaya Oblast', W Russian Federation
Samarang see Semarang
Samarinda 116 D4 Borneo, C Indonesia
Samarqand 101 E2 Rus. Samarkand. Samarqand Wiloyati, C Uzbekistan
Samawa see As Samāwah
Sambalpur 113 F4 Orissa, E India
Sambava 57 G2 Antsirañana, NE Madagascar
Sambir 86 B2 Rus. Sambor. L'vivs'ka Oblast', NW Ukraine
Sambre 68 D2 river Belgium/France
Samfya 56 D2 Luapula, N Zambia
Saminatal 72 E2 valley Austria/Liechtenstein
Samnān see Semnān
Sam Neua see Xam Nua
Samoa 123 E4 off. Independent State of Samoa, var. Sāmoa; prev. Western Samoa. Country W Polynesia
Samoa Basin 121 E3 undersea feature W Pacific Ocean
Samobor 78 A2 Zagreb, N Croatia
Sámos 83 E6 prev. Limín Vathéos. Sámos, Dodekánisos, Greece, Aegean Sea
Sámos 83 D6 island Dodekánisos, Greece, Aegean Sea
Samosch see Someş
Samothráki 82 C4 anc. Samothrace. Island NE Greece
Samothráki 82 D4 Samothráki, NE Greece
Sampit 116 C4 Borneo, C Indonesia
Samsun 94 D2 anc. Amisus. Samsun, N Turkey
Samtredia 95 F2 W Georgia
Samui, Ko 115 C6 island SW Thailand
Samut Prakan 115 C5 var. Muang Samut Prakan, Paknam. Samut Prakan, C Thailand
San 77 E5 river SE Poland
San 52 D3 Ségou, C Mali
Şan'ā' 99 B6 Eng. Sana. Country capital (Yemen) W Yemen
Sana 78 B3 river NW Bosnia and Herzegovina
Sana see Şan'ā'
Sanae 132 B2 South African research station Antarctica
Sanaga 55 B5 river C Cameroon
San Ambrosio, Isla 35 A5 Eng. San Ambrosio Island. Island W Chile
Sanandaj 98 C3 prev. Sinneh. Kordestān, W Iran
San Andrés, Isla de 31 F3 island NW Colombia
San Andrés Tuxtla 29 F4 var. Tuxtla. Veracruz-Llave, E Mexico
San Angelo 27 F3 Texas, SW USA
San Antonio 27 F4 Texas, SW USA
San Antonio 30 B2 Toledo, S Belize
San Antonio 42 B4 Valparaíso, C Chile
San Antonio Oeste 43 C5 Río Negro, E Argentina
San Antonio River 27 G4 river Texas, SW USA
Sanaw 99 C6 var. Sanaw. NE Yemen
San Benedicto, Isla 28 B4 island W Mexico
San Benito 30 B1 Petén, N Guatemala
San Benito 27 G5 Texas, SW USA
San Bernardino 25 C7 California, W USA
San Blas 28 C3 Sinaloa, C Mexico
San Blas, Cape 20 D3 headland Florida, SE USA
San Blas, Cordillera de 31 G4 mountain range NE Panama
San Carlos see Quesada
San Carlos 26 B2 Arizona, SW USA
San Carlos 30 D4 Río San Juan, S Nicaragua
San Carlos de Bariloche 43 B5 Río Negro, SW Argentina
San Carlos del Zulia 36 C2 Zulia, W Venezuela
San Clemente Island 25 B8 island Channel Islands, California, W USA
San Cristobal 122 C4 var. Makira. Island SE Solomon Islands
San Cristóbal see San Cristóbal de Las Casas
San Cristóbal 36 C2 Táchira, W Venezuela
San Cristóbal de Las Casas 29 G5 var. San Cristóbal. Chiapas, SE Mexico
San Cristóbal, Isla 38 B5 var. Chatham Island. Island Galapagos Islands, Ecuador, E Pacific Ocean
Sancti Spíritus 32 B2 Sancti Spíritus, C Cuba
Sandakan 116 D3 Sabah, East Malaysia
Sandanski 82 C3 prev. Sveti Vrach. Blagoevgrad, SW Bulgaria
Sanday 66 D2 island NE Scotland, UK
Sanders 26 C2 Arizona, SW USA
Sand Hills 22 D3 mountain range Nebraska, C USA
San Diego 25 C8 California, W USA
Sandnes 63 A6 Rogaland, S Norway
Sandomierz 76 D4 Rus. Sandomir. Świętokrzyskie, C Poland
Sandoway 114 A4 Arakan State, W Myanmar
Sandpoint 24 C1 Idaho, NW USA
Sand Springs 27 G1 Oklahoma, C USA
Sandusky 18 D3 Ohio, N USA
Sandvika 63 A6 Akershus, S Norway
Sandviken 63 C6 Gävleborg, C Sweden
Sandy Bay 71 H5 bay E Gibraltar
Sandy City 22 B4 Utah, W USA
Sandy Lake 16 B3 lake Ontario, C Canada
San Esteban 30 D2 Olancho, C Honduras
San Felipe 36 D1 Yaracuy, NW Venezuela
San Felipe de Puerto Plata see Puerto Plata
San Félix, Isla 35 A5 Eng. San Felix Island. Island W Chile
San Fernando 70 C5 prev. Isla de León. Andalucía, S Spain
San Fernando 36 D2 var. San Fernando de Apure. Apure, C Venezuela
San Fernando 24 D1 California, W USA
San Fernando 33 H5 Trinidad, Trinidad and Tobago
San Fernando de Apure see San Fernando
San Fernando del Valle de Catamarca 42 C3 var. Catamarca. Catamarca, NW Argentina
San Fernando de Monte Cristi see Monte Cristi
San Francisco 25 B6 California, W USA
San Francisco del Oro 28 C2 Chihuahua, N Mexico
San Francisco de Macorís 33 E3 C Dominican Republic
San Gabriel 38 B1 Carchi, N Ecuador
San Gabriel Mountains 24 E1 mountain range California, W USA
Sangir, Kepulauan 117 F3 var. Kepulauan Sangihe. Island group N Indonesia
Sāngli 110 B1 Mahārāshtra, W India
Sangmélima 55 B5 Sud, S Cameroon
Sangre de Cristo Mountains 26 D1 mountain range Colorado/New Mexico, C USA
San Ignacio 30 B1 prev. Cayo, El Cayo. Cayo, W Belize
San Ignacio 28 B2 Baja California Sur, W Mexico
San Ignacio 39 F3 Beni, N Bolivia
San Joaquin Valley 25 B7 valley California, W USA
San Jorge, Golfo 43 C6 var. Gulf of San Jorge. Gulf S Argentina
San Jorge, Gulf of see San Jorge, Golfo
San José see San José del Guaviare
San Jose 25 B6 California, W USA
San José 30 B3 var. Puerto San José. Escuintla, S Guatemala
San José 39 G3 var. San José de Chiquitos. Santa Cruz, E Bolivia
San José 31 E4 country capital (Costa Rica) San José, C Costa Rica
San José de Chiquitos see San José
San José de Cúcuta see Cúcuta
San José del Guaviare 36 C4 var. San José. Guaviare, S Colombia
San Juan 33 F3 dependent territory capital (Puerto Rico) NE Puerto Rico
San Juan see San Juan de los Morros
San Juan 42 B4 San Juan, W Argentina
San Juan Bautista 42 D3 Misiones, S Paraguay
San Juan Bautista Tuxtepec see Tuxtepec
San Juan de Alicante 71 F4 País Valenciano, E Spain
San Juan del Norte 31 E4 var. Greytown. Río San Juan, SE Nicaragua
San Juan de los Morros 36 D2 var. San Juan. Guárico, N Venezuela
San Juanito, Isla 28 C4 island C Mexico
San Juan Mountains 26 D1 mountain range Colorado, C USA
San Juan River 26 C1 river Colorado/Utah, W USA
San Julián see Puerto San Julián
Sankt Gallen 73 B7 var. St.Gallen, Eng. Saint Gall, Fr. St Gall. Sankt Gallen, NE Switzerland
Sankt-Peterburg 88 B4 prev. Leningrad, Petrograd, Eng. Saint Petersburg, Fin. Pietari. Leningradskaya Oblast', NW Russian Federation
Sankt Pölten 73 E6 Niederösterreich, N Austria
Sankuru 55 D6 river C Dem. Rep. Congo
Şanlıurfa 95 E4 prev. Sanli Urfa, Urfa, anc. Edessa. Şanlıurfa, S Turkey
San Lorenzo 38 A1 Esmeraldas, N Ecuador
San Lorenzo 39 G5 Tarija, S Bolivia
San Lorenzo, Isla 38 C4 island W Peru
Sanlúcar de Barrameda 70 C5 Andalucía, S Spain
San Luis 28 A1 var. San Luis Río Colorado. Sonora, NW Mexico
San Luis 30 B2 Petén, NE Guatemala
San Luis 42 C4 San Luis, C Argentina
San Luis Obispo 25 B7 California, W USA
San Luis Potosí 29 E3 San Luis Potosí, C Mexico
San Luis Río Colorado see San Luis
San Marcos 30 A2 San Marcos, W Guatemala
San Marcos 27 G4 Texas, SW USA
San Marino 74 D1 off. Republic of San Marino. Country S Europe
San Marino 74 E1 country capital (San Marino) C San Marino
San Martín 132 A2 Argentinian research station Antarctica
San Mateo 37 E2 Anzoátegui, NE Venezuela
San Matías 39 H3 Santa Cruz, E Bolivia
San Matías, Golfo 43 C5 var. Gulf of San Matías. Gulf E Argentina
San Matías, Gulf of see San Matías, Golfo
Sanmenxia 106 C4 var. Shan Xian. Henan, C China
Sânmiclăuş Mare see Sânnicolau Mare
San Miguel 28 D2 Coahuila de Zaragoza, N Mexico
San Miguel 30 C3 San Miguel, SE El Salvador
San Miguel de Ibarra see Ibarra
San Miguel de Tucumán 42 C3 var. Tucumán. Tucumán, N Argentina
San Miguelito 31 G4 Panamá, C Panama
San Miguel, Río 39 G3 river E Bolivia
Sannār see Sennar
Sânnicolaul-Mare see Sânnicolau Mare
Sânnicolau Mare 86 A4 var. Sânnicolaul-Mare, Hung. Nagyszentmiklós; prev. Sânmiclăuş Mare, Sînnicolau Mare. Timiş, W Romania
Sanok 77 E5 Podkarpackie, SE Poland
San Pablo 39 F5 Potosí, S Bolivia
San Pedro 28 D3 var. San Pedro de las Colonias. Coahuila de Zaragoza, NE Mexico
San Pedro 30 C1 Corozal, NE Belize

Shantarskiye Ostrova – Somerset Island

Shantarskiye Ostrova 93 G3 *Eng.* Shantar Islands. *Island group* E Russian Federation
Shantou 106 D6 *var.* Shan-t'ou, Swatow. Guangdong, S China
Shantung *see* Shandong
Shanxi 106 C4 *var.* Jin, Shan-hsi, Shansi, Shanxi Sheng. Admin. region *province* C China
Shan Xian *see* Sanmenxia
Shanxi Sheng *see* Shanxi
Shaoguan 106 C6 *var.* Shao-kuan, *Cant.* Kukong; *prev.* Ch'u-chiang. Guangdong, S China
Shao-kuan *see* Shaoguan
Shaqrā *see* Shuqrah
Shaqrā' 98 B4 Ar Riyāḍ, C Saudi Arabia
Shar 130 D5 *var.* Charsk. Vostochnyy Kazakhstan, E Kazakhstan
Shari *see* Chari
Shari 108 D2 Hokkaidō, NE Japan
Shark Bay 125 A5 *bay* Western Australia
Shashe 56 D3 *var.* Shashi. *River* Botswana/Zimbabwe
Shashi *see* Shashe
Shatskiy Rise 103 G1 *undersea feature* N Pacific Ocean
Shatt al-Hodna *see* Hodna, Chott El
Shaṭṭ al Jarīd *see* Jerid, Chott el
Shawnee 27 G1 Oklahoma, C USA
Shchadryn 85 D7 *Rus.* Shchedrin. Homyel'skaya Voblasts', SE Belarus
Shchëkino 89 B5 Tul'skaya Oblast', W Russian Federation
Shchors 87 E1 Chernihivs'ka Oblast', N Ukraine
Shchuchinsk 92 C4 *prev.* Shchuchye. Severnyy kazakhstan, N Kazakhstan
Shchuchyn 85 B5 *Pol.* Szczuczyn Nowogródzki, *Rus.* Shchuchin. Hrodzyenskaya Voblasts', W Belarus
Shebekino 89 A6 Belgorodskaya Oblast', W Russian Federation
Shebeli 51 D5 *Amh.* Wabē Shebelē Wenz, *It.* Scebeli, *Som.* Webi Shabeelle. *River* Ethiopia/Somalia
Sheberghān 101 E3 *var.* Shibarghān, Shiberghan, Shiberghān. Jowzjān, N Afghanistan
Sheboygan 18 B2 Wisconsin, N USA
Shebshi Mountains 54 A4 *var.* Schebschi Mountains. *Mountain range* E Nigeria
Shechem *see* Nablus
Shedadi *see* Ash Shadādah
Sheffield 67 D5 N England, UK
Shekhem *see* Nablus
Shelby 22 B1 Montana, NW USA
Sheldon 23 F3 Iowa, C USA
Shelekhov Gulf *see* Shelikhova, Zaliv
Shelikhova, Zaliv 93 G2 *Eng.* Shelekhov Gulf. *Gulf* E Russian Federation
Shendi 50 C4 *var.* Shandī. River Nile, NE Sudan
Shengking *see* Liaoning
Shenking *see* Liaoning
Shenshi *see* Shaanxi
Shensi *see* Shaanxi
Shenyang 106 D3 *Chin.* Shen-yang, *Eng.* Moukden, Mukden; *prev.* Fengtien. Liaoning, NE China
Shepetivka 86 D2 *Rus.* Shepetovka. Khmel'nyts'ka Oblast', NW Ukraine
Shepparton 127 C7 Victoria, SE Australia
Sherbrooke 17 E4 Quebec, SE Canada
Shereik 50 C3 River Nile, N Sudan
Sheridan 22 C2 Wyoming, C USA
Sherman 27 G2 Texas, SW USA
's-Hertogenbosch 64 C4 *Fr.* Bois-le-Duc, *Ger.* Herzogenbusch. Noord-Brabant, S Netherlands
Shetland Islands 66 D1 *island group* NE Scotland, UK
Shibarghān *see* Sheberghān
Shiberghān *see* Sheberghān
Shibetsu 108 D2 *var.* Sibetu. Hokkaidō, NE Japan
Shibh Jazīrat Sīnā' *see* Sinai
Shibushi-wan 109 B8 *bay* SW Japan
Shigatse *see* Xigazê
Shih-chia-chuang *see* Shijiazhuang
Shihezi 104 C2 Xinjiang Uygur Zizhiqu, NW China
Shihmen *see* Shijiazhuang
Shijiazhuang 106 C4 *var.* Shih-chia-chuang; *prev.* Shihmen. Hebei, E China
Shikārpur 112 B3 Sind, S Pakistan
Shikoku 109 C7 *var.* Sikoku. *Island* SW Japan
Shikoku Basin 103 F2 *var.* Sikoku Basin. *Undersea feature* N Philippine Sea
Shikotan, Ostrov 108 E2 *Jap.* Shikotan-tō. *Island* NE Russian Federation
Shilabo 51 D5 E Ethiopia
Shiliguri 113 F3 *prev.* Siliguri. West Bengal, NE India
Shilka 93 F4 *river* S Russian Federation
Shillong 113 G3 E India
Shimbir Berris *see* Shimbiris
Shimbiris 50 E4 *var.* Shimbir Berris. *Mountain* N Somalia
Shimoga 110 C2 Karnātaka, W India
Shimonoseki 109 A7 *var.* Simonoseki; *hist.* Akamagaseki, Bakan. Yamaguchi, Honshū, SW Japan
Shinano-gawa 109 C5 *var.* Sinano Gawa. *River* Honshū, C Japan
Shīndand 100 D4 Farāh, W Afghanistan
Shingū 109 C6 *var.* Singû. Wakayama, Honshū, SW Japan
Shinjō 108 D4 *var.* Sinzyô. Yamagata, Honshū, C Japan
Shinyanga 51 C7 Shinyanga, NW Tanzania
Shiprock 26 C1 New Mexico, SW USA
Shīrāz 98 D4 *var.* Shīrāz. Fārs, S Iran
Shivpuri 112 D3 Madhya Pradesh, C India
Shizugawa 108 D4 Miyagi, Honshū, NE Japan
Shizuoka 109 D6 *var.* Sizuoka. Shizuoka, Honshū, S Japan
Shklow 85 D6 *Rus.* Shklov. Mahilyowskaya Voblasts', E Belarus
Shkodër 79 C5 *var.* Shkodra, *It.* Scutari, *SCr.* Skadar. Shkodër, NW Albania
Shkodra *see* Shkodër
Shkubinit, Lumi i 79 C6 *var.* Shkumbî, Shkumbin. *River* C Albania
Shkumbî *see* Shkubinit, Lumi i
Shkumbin *see* Shkubinit, Lumi i
Sholāpur *see* Solāpur
Shostka 87 F1 Sums'ka Oblast', NE Ukraine
Show Low 26 B2 Arizona, SW USA
Shpola 87 E3 Cherkas'ka Oblast', N Ukraine
Shreveport 20 A2 Louisiana, S USA
Shrewsbury 67 D6 *hist.* Scrobesbyrig'. W England, UK
Shu 92 C5 *Kaz.* Shū. Zhambyl, SE Kazakhstan
Shuang-liao *see* Liaoyuan
Shumagin Islands 14 B3 *island group* Alaska, USA
Shumen 82 D2 Shumen, NE Bulgaria
Shumilina 85 E5 *Rus.* Shumilino. Vitsyebskaya Voblasts', NE Belarus
Shuqrah 99 B7 *var.* Shaqrā. SW Yemen
Shwebo 114 B3 Sagaing, C Myanmar
Shyichy 85 C7 *Rus.* Shiichi. Homyel'skaya Voblasts', SE Belarus
Shymkent 92 B5 *prev.* Chimkent. Yuzhnyy Kazakhstan, S Kazakhstan
Shyshchytsy 85 C6 *Rus.* Shishchitsy. Minskaya Voblasts', C Belarus
Si *see* Syr Darya
Siam, Gulf of *see* Thailand, Gulf of
Sian *see* Xi'an
Siang *see* Brahmaputra
Siangtan *see* Xiangtan
Šiauliai 84 B4 *Ger.* Schaulen. Šiauliai, N Lithuania
Sibay 89 D6 Respublika Bashkortostan, W Russian Federation
Šibenik 116 B4 *It.* Sebenico. Šibenik-Knin, S Croatia
Siberia *see* Sibir'
Siberut, Pulau 116 A4 *prev.* Siberoet. *Island* Kepulauan Mentawai, W Indonesia
Sibetu *see* Shibetsu
Sibi 112 B2 Baluchistān, SW Pakistan
Sibir' 93 E3 *var.* Siberia. *Physical region* NE Russian Federation
Sibiti 55 B6 La Lékoumou, S Congo
Sibiu 86 B4 *Ger.* Hermannstadt, *Hung.* Nagyszeben. Sibiu, C Romania
Sibolga 116 B3 Sumatera, W Indonesia
Sibu 116 D3 Sarawak, East Malaysia
Sibut 54 C4 *prev.* Fort-Sibut. Kémo, S Central African Republic
Sibuyan Sea 117 E2 *sea* C Philippines
Sichon 115 C6 *var.* Ban Sichon, Si Chon. Nakhon Si Thammarat, SW Thailand
Sichuan 106 B5 *var.* Chuan, Sichuan Sheng, Ssu ch'uan, Szechuan, Szechwan. Admin. region *province* C China
Sichuan Pendi 106 B5 *depression* C China
Sichuan Sheng *see* Sichuan
Sicilia 75 C7 *Eng.* Sicily; *anc.* Trinacria. *Island* Italy, C Mediterranean Sea
Sicilian Channel *see* Sicily, Strait of
Sicily *see* Sicilia
Sicily, Strait of 75 B7 *var.* Sicilian Channel. *Strait* C Mediterranean Sea
Sicuani 39 E4 Cusco, S Peru
Sidári 82 A4 Kérkyra, Iónioi Nísoi, Greece, C Mediterranean Sea
Sidas 116 C4 Borneo, C Indonesia
Siderno 75 D7 Calabria, SW Italy
Sîdi Barrâni 50 A1 NW Egypt
Sidi Bel Abbès 48 D2 *var.* Sidi bel Abbès, Sidi-Bel-Abbès. NW Algeria
Sidirókastro 82 C3 *prev.* Sidhirókastron. Kentrikí Makedonía, NE Greece
Sidley, Mount 132 B4 *mountain* Antarctica
Sidney 22 D1 Montana, NW USA
Sidney 22 D4 Nebraska, C USA
Sidney 18 C4 Ohio, N USA
Sidon *see* Saïda
Sidra *see* Surt
Siedlce 76 E3 *Ger.* Sedlez, *Rus.* Sesdlets. Mazowieckie, C Poland
Siegen 72 B4 Nordrhein-Westfalen, W Germany
Siemiatycze 76 E3 Podlaskie
Siena 74 B3 *Fr.* Sienne; *anc.* Saena Julia. Toscana, C Italy
Sieradz 76 C4 Łódzkie, C Poland
Sierpc 76 D3 Mazowieckie, C Poland
Sierra de Soconusco *see* Sierra Madre
Sierra Leone 52 C4 *off.* Republic of Sierra Leone. *Country* W Africa
Sierra Leone Basin 44 C4 *undersea feature* E Atlantic Ocean
Sierra Leone Ridge *see* Sierra Leone Rise
Sierra Leone Rise 44 C4 *var.* Sierra Leone Ridge, Sierra Leone Schwelle. *Undersea feature* E Atlantic Ocean
Sierra Leone Schwelle *see* Sierra Leone Rise
Sierra Madre 30 B2 *var.* Sierra de Soconusco. *Mountain range* Guatemala/Mexico
Sierra Madre *see* Madre Occidental, Sierra
Sierra Nevada 25 C6 *mountain range* W USA
Sierra Pacaraima *see* Pakaraima Mountains
Sierra Vieja 26 D3 *mountain range* Texas, SW USA
Sierra Vista 26 B3 Arizona, SW USA
Sífnos 83 C6 *anc.* Siphnos. *Island* Kykládes, Greece, Aegean Sea
Sigli 116 A3 Sumatera, W Indonesia
Siglufjördhur 61 E4 Nordhurland Vestra, N Iceland
Signal Peak 26 A2 *mountain* Arizona, SW USA
Signan *see* Xi'an
Signy 132 A2 *UK research station* South Orkney Islands, Antarctica
Siguatepeque 30 C2 Comayagua, W Honduras
Siguiri 52 D4 Haute-Guinée, NE Guinea
Siilinjärvi 62 E4 Itä-Suomi, C Finland
Siirt 95 F4 *var.* Sert; *anc.* Tigranocerta. Siirt, SE Turkey
Sikandarabad *see* Secunderābād
Sikasso 52 D4 Sikasso, S Mali
Sikeston 23 H5 Missouri, C USA
Sikhote-Alin', Khrebet 93 G4 *mountain range* SE Russian Federation
Siking *see* Xi'an
Siklós 77 C7 Baranya, SW Hungary
Sikoku *see* Shikoku
Sikoku Basin *see* Shikoku Basin
Šilalė 84 B4 Šilalė, W Lithuania
Silchar 113 G3 Assam, NE India
Silesia 76 B4 *physical region* SW Poland
Silifke 94 C4 *anc.* Seleucia. İçel, S Turkey
Siling Co 104 C5 *lake* W China
Silinhot *see* Xilinhot
Silistra 82 E1 *var.* Silistria; *anc.* Durostorum. Silistra, NE Bulgaria
Silistria *see* Silistra
Sillamäe 84 E2 *Ger.* Sillamäggi. Ida-Virumaa, NE Estonia
Šilutė 84 B4 *Ger.* Heydekrug. Šilutė, W Lithuania
Silvan 95 E4 Dıyarbakır, SE Turkey
Silverek 95 E4 Şanlıurfa, SE Turkey
Simanggang *see* Sri Aman
Simanichy 85 C7 *Rus.* Simonichi. Homyel'skaya Voblasts', SE Belarus
Simav 94 B3 Kütahya, W Turkey
Simav Çayı 94 A3 *river* NW Turkey
Simeto 75 C7 *river* Sicilia, Italy, C Mediterranean Sea
Simeulue, Pulau 116 A3 *island* NW Indonesia
Simferopol' 87 F5 Respublika Krym, S Ukraine
Simitli 82 C3 Blagoevgrad, SW Bulgaria
Şimleu Silvaniei 86 B3 *Hung.* Szilágsomlyó; *prev.* Şimlăul Silvaniei, Şimleul Silvaniei. Sălaj, NW Romania
Simonoseki *see* Shimonoseki
Simpelveld 65 D6 Limburg, SE Netherlands
Simplon Pass 73 B8 *pass* S Switzerland
Simpson *see* Fort Simpson
Simpson Desert 126 B4 *desert* Northern Territory/South Australia
Sīnā' *see* Sinai
Sinai 50 C2 *var.* Sinai Peninsula, *Ar.* Shibh Jazīrat Sīnā', Sīnā'. *Physical region* NE Egypt
Sinaia 86 C4 Prahova, SE Romania
Sinai Peninsula *see* Sinai
Sinano Gawa *see* Shinano-gawa
Sincelejo 36 B2 Sucre, NW Colombia
Sind 112 B3 *var.* Sindh. Admin. region *province* SE Pakistan
Sindelfingen 73 B6 Baden-Württemberg, SW Germany
Sindh *see* Sind
Sindi 84 D2 *Ger.* Zintenhof. Pärnumaa, SW Estonia
Sines 70 B4 Setúbal, S Portugal
Singan *see* Xi'an
Singapore 116 A1 *off.* Republic of Singapore. *Country* SE Asia
Singapore 116 B3 *country capital* (Singapore) S Singapore
Singen 73 B6 Baden-Württemberg, S Germany
Singida 51 C7 Singida, C Tanzania
Singkang 117 E4 Sulawesi, C Indonesia
Singkawang 116 C3 Borneo, C Indonesia
Singora *see* Songkhla
Singû *see* Shingū
Sining *see* Xining
Siniscola 75 A5 Sardegna, Italy, C Mediterranean Sea
Sinj 78 B4 Split-Dalmacija, SE Croatia
Sinkiang *see* Xinjiang Uygur Zizhiqu
Sinkiang Uighur Autonomous Region *see* Xinjiang Uygur Zizhiqu
Sinnamarie *see* Sinnamary
Sinnamary 37 H3 *var.* Sinnamarie. N French Guiana
Sînnicolau Mare *see* Sânnicolau Mare
Sinoie, Lacul 86 D5 *prev.* Lacul Sinoe. *Lagoon* SE Romania
Sinop 94 D2 *anc.* Sinope. Sinop, N Turkey
Sinsheim 73 B6 Baden-Württemberg, SW Germany
Sint Maarten 33 G3 *Eng.* Saint Martin. *Island* N Netherlands Antilles
Sint-Michielsgestel 64 C4 Noord-Brabant, S Netherlands
Sint-Niklaas 65 B5 *Fr.* Saint-Nicolas. Oost-Vlaanderen, N Belgium
Sint-Pieters-Leeuw 65 B6 Vlaams Brabant, C Belgium
Sintra 70 B3 *prev.* Cintra. Lisboa, W Portugal
Sinujiif 51 E5 Nugaal, NE Somalia
Sinus Aelaniticus *see* Aqaba, Gulf of
Sinyang *see* Xinyang
Sinzyô *see* Shinjō
Sion 73 A7 *Ger.* Sitten; *anc.* Sedunum. Valais, SW Switzerland
Sioux City 23 F3 Iowa, C USA
Sioux Falls 23 F3 South Dakota, N USA
Siping 106 D3 *var.* Ssu-p'ing, Szeping; *prev.* Ssu-p'ing-chieh. Jilin, NE China
Siple, Mount 132 A4 *mountain* Siple Island, Antarctica
Siquirres 31 E4 Limón, E Costa Rica
Siracusa 75 D7 *Eng.* Syracuse. Sicilia, Italy, C Mediterranean Sea
Sir Darya *see* Syr Darya
Sir Edward Pellew Group 126 B2 *island group* Northern Territory, NE Australia
Siret 86 C3 *var.* Siretul, *Ger.* Sereth, *Rus.* Seret, *Ukr.* Siret. *River* Romania/Ukraine
Siret *see* Siret
Siretul *see* Siret
Sirikit Reservoir 114 C4 *lake* N Thailand
Sīrjān 98 D4 *prev.* Sa'īdābād. Kermān, S Iran
Sirna *see* Sýrna
Şırnak 95 F4 Şırnak, SE Turkey
Síros *see* Sýros
Sirte *see* Surt
Sirte, Gulf of *see* Surt, Khalīj
Sisak 78 B3 *var.* Siscia, *Ger.* Sissek, *Hung.* Sziszek; *anc.* Segestica. Sisak-Moslavina, C Croatia
Siscia *see* Sisak
Sisimiut 60 C3 *var.* Holsteinborg, Holsteinsborg, Holstenborg, Holstensborg. S Greenland
Sissek *see* Sisak
Sistema Penibético *see* Béticos, Sistemas
Siteía 83 D8 *var.* Sitía. Kríti, Greece, E Mediterranean Sea
Sitges 71 G2 Cataluña, NE Spain
Sitía *see* Siteía
Sittang 114 B4 *var.* Sittoung. *River* S Myanmar
Sittard 65 D5 Limburg, SE Netherlands
Sittoung *see* Sittang
Sittwe 114 A3 *var.* Akyab. Arakan State, W Myanmar
Siuna 30 D3 Región Autónoma Atlántico Norte, NE Nicaragua
Siut *see* Asyût
Sivas 94 D3 *anc.* Sebastia, Sebaste. Sivas, C Turkey
Sivers'kyy Donets' *see* Donets
Siwa 50 A2 *var.* Sīwah. NW Egypt
Sīwah *see* Siwa
Six-Fours-les-Plages 69 D6 Var, SE France
Siyäzän 95 H2 *Rus.* Siazan'. NE Azerbaijan
Sizuoka *see* Shizuoka
Sjar *see* Sääre
Sjælland 88 *Eng.* Zealand, *Ger.* Seeland. *Island* E Denmark
Sjenica 79 D5 *Turk.* Seniça. Serbia, SW Serbia and Montenegro (Yugo.)
Skadar *see* Shkodër
Skagerak *see* Skagerrak
Skagerrak 63 A6 *var.* Skagerak. *Channel* N Europe
Skagit River 24 B1 *river* Washington, NW USA
Skalka 62 C3 *lake* N Sweden
Skarżysko-Kamienna 76 D4 Świętokrzyskie, C Poland
Skaudvilė 84 B4 Tauragė, SW Lithuania
Skegness 67 E6 E England, UK
Skellefteå 62 D4 Västerbotten, N Sweden
Skellefteälven 62 C4 *river* N Sweden
Ski 63 B6 Akershus, S Norway
Skíathos 83 C5 Skíathos, Vóreioi Sporádes, Greece, Aegean Sea
Skidal' 85 B5 *Rus.* Skidel'. Hrodzyenskaya Voblasts', W Belarus
Skierniewice 76 D3 Łodzkie, C Poland
Skiftet 84 C1 *Fin.* Kihti. *Strait* Gulf of Bothnia/Gulf of Finland
Skíros *see* Skýros
Skópelos 83 C5 Skópelos, Vóreioi Sporádes, Greece, Aegean Sea
Skopje 79 D6 *var.* Üsküb, *Turk.* Üsküp; *prev.* Skoplje, *anc.* Scupi. *Country capital* (FYR Macedonia) N FYR Macedonia
Skoplje *see* Skopje
Skovorodino 93 F4 Amurskaya Oblast', SE Russian Federation
Skuodas 84 B3 *Ger.* Schoden, *Pol.* Szkudy. Skuodas, NW Lithuania
Skye, Isle of 66 B3 *island* NW Scotland, UK
Skýros 83 C5 *var.* Skíros. Skýros, Vóreioi Sporádes, Greece, Aegean Sea
Skýros 83 C5 *var.* Skíros; *anc.* Scyros. *Island* Vóreioi Sporádes, Greece, Aegean Sea
Slagelse 63 B7 Vestsjælland, E Denmark
Slatina 86 B5 Olt, S Romania
Slatina 78 C3 *Hung.* Szlatina, *prev.* Podravska Slatina. Virovtica-Podravina, NE Croatia
Slavonska Požega *see* Požega
Slavonski Brod 78 C3 *Ger.* Brod, *Hung.* Bród; *prev.* Brod, Brod na Savi. Brod-Posavina, NE Croatia
Slavuta 86 C2 Khmel'nyts'ka Oblast', NW Ukraine
Slawharad 85 E7 *Rus.* Slavgorod. Mahilyowskaya Voblasts', E Belarus
Sławno 76 C2 Zachodniopomorskie, NW Poland
Sléibhte Chill Mhantáin *see* Wicklow Mountains
Slēmānī *see* As Sulaymānīyah
Sliema 80 B5 N Malta
Sligeach *see* Sligo
Sligo 67 A5 *Ir.* Sligeach. NW Ireland
Sliven 82 D2 *var.* Slivno. Sliven, C Bulgaria
Slivnitsa 82 B2 Sofiya, W Bulgaria
Slivno *see* Sliven
Slobozia 86 C5 Ialomiţa, SE Romania
Slonim 85 B6 *Pol.* Słonim, *Rus.* Slonim. Hrodzyenskaya Voblasts', W Belarus
Slovakia 77 C6 *off.* Slovenská Republika, *Ger.* Slowakei, *Hung.* Szlovákia, *Slvk.* Slovensko. *Country* C Europe
Slovak Ore Mountains *see* Slovenské rudohorie
Slovenia 73 D8 *off.* Republic of Slovenia, *Ger.* Slowenien, *Slvn.* Slovenija. *Country* SE Europe
Slovenské rudohorie 77 D6 *Eng.* Slovak Ore Mountains, *Ger.* Slowakisches Erzgebirge, Ungarisches Erzgebirge. *Mountain range* C Slovakia
Slov"yans'k 87 G3 *Rus.* Slavyansk. Donets'ka Oblast', E Ukraine
Slowakisches Erzgebirge *see* Slovenské rudohorie
Słubice 76 B3 *Ger.* Frankfurt. Lubuskie, W Poland
Sluch 86 D1 *river* NW Ukraine
Słupsk 76 C2 *Ger.* Stolp. Pomorskie, N Poland
Slutsk 85 C6 *Rus.* Slutsk. Minskaya Voblasts', S Belarus
Smallwood Reservoir 17 F2 *lake* Newfoundland and Labrador, S Canada
Smara 48 B3 *var.* Es Semara. N Western Sahara
Smarhon' 85 C5 *Pol.* Smorgonie, *Rus.* Smorgon'. Hrodzyenskaya Voblasts', W Belarus
Smederevo 78 D4 *Ger.* Semendria. Serbia, N Serbia and Montenegro (Yugo.)
Smederevska Palanka 78 D4 Serbia, C Serbia and Montenegro (Yugo.)
Smila 87 E2 *Rus.* Smela. Cherkas'ka Oblast', C Ukraine
Smiltene 84 D3 *Ger.* Smilten. Valka, N Latvia
Smøla 62 A4 *island* W Norway
Smolensk 89 A5 Smolenskaya Oblast', W Russian Federation
Snake 12 B4 *river* Yukon Territory, NW Canada
Snake River 24 C3 *river* NW USA
Snake River Plain 24 D4 *plain* Idaho, NW USA
Sneek 64 D2 Friesland, N Netherlands
Sněžka 76 B4 *Ger.* Schneekoppe. *Mountain* N Czech Republic
Śniardwy, Jezioro 114 D2 *Ger.* Spirdingsee. *Lake* NE Poland
Snina 77 E5 *Hung.* Szinna. Prešovský Kraj, E Slovakia
Snowdonia 67 C6 *mountain range* NW Wales, UK
Snyder 27 F3 Texas, SW USA
Sobradinho, Represa de 41 F2 *var.* Barragem de Sobradinho. *Reservoir* E Brazil
Sochi 89 A7 Krasnodarskiy Kray, SW Russian Federation
Société, Archipel de la 123 G4 *var.* Archipel de Tahiti, Îles de la Société, *Eng.* Society Islands. *Island group* W French Polynesia
Society Islands *see* Société, Archipel de la
Socorro 26 D2 New Mexico, SW USA
Socorro, Isla 28 B5 *island* W Mexico
Socotra *see* Suquṭrā
Soc Trăng 115 D6 *var.* Khanh. Soc Trăng, S Vietnam
Socuéllamos 71 E3 Castilla-La Mancha, C Spain
Sodankylä 62 D3 Lappi, N Finland
Sodari *see* Sodiri
Söderhamn 63 C5 Gävleborg, C Sweden
Södertälje 63 C6 Stockholm, C Sweden
Sodiri 50 B4 *var.* Sawdirī, Sodari. Northern Kordofan, C Sudan
Sofia *see* Sofiya
Sofiya 82 C2 *var.* Sophia, *Eng.* Sofia; *Lat.* Serdica. *Country capital* (Bulgaria) Sofiya-Grad, W Bulgaria
Sogamoso 36 B3 Boyacá, C Colombia
Sognefjorden 63 A5 *fjord* NE North Sea
Sohâg 50 B2 *var.* Sawhāj, Suliag. C Egypt
Sohar *see* Şuḥār
Sohm Plain 44 B3 *undersea feature* NW Atlantic Ocean
Sohrau *see* Żory
Sokal' 86 C2 *Rus.* Sokal. L'vivs'ka Oblast', NW Ukraine
Söke 94 A4 Aydın, SW Turkey
Sokhumi 95 F1 *Rus.* Sukhumi. NW Georgia
Sokodé 53 F4 C Togo
Sokol 88 C4 Vologodskaya Oblast', NW Russian Federation
Sokółka 76 E3 Białystok, NE Poland
Sokolov 77 A5 *Ger.* Falkenau an der Eger; *prev.* Falknov nad Ohří. Karlovarský Kraj, W Czech Republic
Sokone 52 B3 W Senegal
Sokoto 53 F4 *river* NW Nigeria
Sokoto 53 F3 Sokoto, NW Nigeria
Sokotra *see* Suquṭrā
Solāpur 102 B3 *var.* Sholāpur. Mahārāshtra, W India
Solca 86 C3 *Ger.* Solka. Suceava, N Romania
Sol, Costa del 70 D5 *coastal region* S Spain
Soldeu 69 B7 NE Andorra
Solec Kujawski 76 C3 Kujawski-pomorskie, C Poland
Soledad, Isla *see* East Falkland
Soledad 36 B1 Anzoátegui, NE Venezuela
Solikamsk 92 C3 Permskaya Oblast', NW Russian Federation
Sol'-Iletsk 89 D6 Orenburgskaya Oblast', W Russian Federation
Solingen 72 A4 Nordrhein-Westfalen, W Germany
Sollentuna 63 C6 Stockholm, C Sweden
Solok 116 B4 Sumatera, W Indonesia
Solomon Islands 122 C3 *prev.* British Solomon Islands Protectorate. *Country* W Pacific Ocean
Solomon Islands 122 C3 *island group* PNG/Solomon Islands
Solomon Sea 122 B3 *sea* W Pacific Ocean
Soltau 72 B3 Niedersachsen, NW Germany
Sol'tsy 88 A4 Novgorodskaya Oblast', W Russian Federation
Solwezi 56 D2 North Western, NW Zambia
Sōma 108 D4 Fukushima, Honshū, C Japan
Somalia 51 D5 *off.* Somali Democratic Republic, *Som.* Jamuuriyada Demuqraadiga Soomaaliyeed, Soomaaliya; *prev.* Italian Somaliland, Somaliland Protectorate. *Country* E Africa
Somali Basin 47 E5 *undersea feature* W Indian Ocean
Sombor 78 C3 *Hung.* Zombor. Serbia, NW Serbia and Montenegro (Yugo.)
Someren 65 D5 Noord-Brabant, SE Netherlands
Somerset 20 A5 *var.* Somerset Village. W Bermuda
Somerset 18 C5 Kentucky, S USA
Somerset Island 15 F2 *island* Queen Elizabeth Islands, Nunavut, NW Canada
Somerset Island 20 A5 *island* W Bermuda

Sýros – Thrissur

Sýros 83 C6 *var.* Síros. *Island* Kykládes, Greece, Aegean Sea
Syvash, Zatoka 87 F4 *Rus.* Zaliv Syvash. *Inlet* S Ukraine
Syzran' 89 C6 Samarskaya Oblast', W Russian Federation
Szamos *see* Someş
Szamotuły 76 B3 Wielkopolskie, C Poland
Szczecin 76 B3 *Eng./Ger.* Stettin. Zachodniopomorskie, NW Poland
Szczecinek 76 B2 *Ger.* Neustettin. Zachodniopomorskie, NW Poland
Szczeciński, Zalew 76 A2 *var.* Stettiner Haff, *Ger.* Oderhaff. *Bay* Germany/Poland
Szczytno 76 D3 *Ger.* Ortelsburg. Olsztyn, NE Poland
Szechuan *see* Sichuan
Szechwan *see* Sichuan
Szeged 77 D7 *Ger.* Szegedin, *Rom.* Seghedin. Csongrád, SE Hungary
Székesfehérvár 77 C6 *Ger.* Stuhlweissenberg; *anc.* Alba Regia. Fejér, W Hungary
Szekszárd 77 C7 Tolna, S Hungary
Szenttamás *see* Srbobran
Szeping *see* Siping
Sziszek *see* Sisak
Szlatina *see* Slatina
Szolnok 77 D6 Jász-Nagykun-Szolnok, C Hungary
Szombathely 77 B6 *Ger.* Steinamanger; *anc.* Sabaria, Savaria. Vas, W Hungary
Szprotawa 76 B4 *Ger.* Sprottau. Lubuskie, W Poland

T

Table Rock Lake 27 G1 *reservoir* Arkansas/Missouri, C USA
Tábor 77 B5 Budějovický Kraj, S Czech Republic
Tabora 51 B7 Tabora, W Tanzania
Tabrīz 98 C2 *var.* Tebriz; *anc.* Tauris. Āžarbāyjān-e Khāvarī, NW Iran
Tabuaeran 123 G2 *prev.* Fanning Island. *Atoll* Line Islands, E Kiribati
Tabūk 98 A4 Tabūk, NW Saudi Arabia
Täby 63 C6 Stockholm, C Sweden
Tachov 77 A5 *Ger.* Tachau. Plzeňský Kraj, W Czech Republic
Tacloban 117 F2 *off.* Tacloban City. Leyte, C Philippines
Tacna 39 E4 Tacna, SE Peru
Tacoma 24 B2 Washington, NW USA
Tacuarembó 42 D4 *prev.* San Fructuoso. Tacuarembó, C Uruguay
Tademaït, Plateau du 48 D3 *plateau* C Algeria
Tadmor *see* Tudmur
Tadmur *see* Tudmur
Tādpatri 110 C2 Andhra Pradesh, E India
Taegu 107 E4 *off.* Taegu-gwangyŏksi, *var.* Daegu, *Jap.* Taikyū. SE South Korea
Taejŏn 107 E4 *off.* Taejŏn-gwangyŏksi, *Jap.* Taiden. C South Korea
Tafassâsset, Ténéré du 53 G2 *desert* N Niger
Tafila *see* Aṭ Ṭafīlah
Taganrog 89 A7 Rostovskaya Oblast', SW Russian Federation
Taganrog, Gulf of 87 G4 *Rus.* Taganrogskiy Zaliv, *Ukr.* Tahanroz'ka Zatoka. *Gulf* Russian Federation/Ukraine
Taguatinga 41 F3 Tocantins, C Brazil
Tagus 70 C3 *Port.* Rio Tejo, *Sp.* Río Tajo. *River* Portugal/Spain
Tagus Plain 58 A4 *undersea feature* E Atlantic Ocean
Tahat 49 E4 *mountain* SE Algeria
Tahiti 123 H4 *island* Îles du Vent, W French Polynesia
Tahlequah 27 G1 Oklahoma, C USA
Tahoe, Lake 25 B5 *lake* California/Nevada, W USA
Tahoua 53 F3 Tahoua, W Niger
T'aichung 106 D6 *Jap.* Taichū; *prev.* Taiwan. C Taiwan
Taieri 129 B7 *river* South Island, NZ
Taihape 128 D4 Manawatu-Wanganui, North Island, NZ
Tailem Bend 127 B7 South Australia
T'ainan 106 D6 *Jap.* Tainan; *prev.* Dainan. S Taiwan
T'aipei 106 D6 *Jap.* Taihoku; *prev.* Daihoku. *Country capital* (Taiwan) N Taiwan
Taiping 116 B3 Perak, Peninsular Malaysia
Taiwan 106 D6 *off.* Republic of China, *var.* Formosa, Formo'sa. *Country* E Asia
T'aiwan Haihsia *see* Taiwan Strait
Taiwan Haixia *see* Taiwan Strait
Taiwan Strait 106 D6 *var.* Formosa Strait, *Chin.* T'aiwan Haihsia, Taiwan Haixia. *Strait* China/Taiwan
Taiyuan 106 C4 *prev.* T'ai-yuan, T'ai-yüan, Yangku. Shanxi, C China
Ta'izz 99 B7 SW Yemen
Tajikistan 101 E3 *off.* Republic of Tajikistan, *Rus.* Tadzhikistan, *Taj.* Jumhurii Tojikiston; *prev.* Tajik S.S.R. *Country* C Asia
Tak 114 C4 *var.* Rahaeng. Tak, W Thailand
Takao *see* Kaohsiung
Takaoka 109 C5 Toyama, Honshū, SW Japan
Takapuna 128 D2 Auckland, North Island, NZ
Takhiatosh 100 C2 *Rus.* Takhiatash. Qoraqalpoghiston Respublikasi, W Uzbekistan
Takhtakŭpir 100 D1 *Rus.* Takhtakupyr. Qoraqalpoghiston Respublikasi, NW Uzbekistan
Takikawa 108 D2 Hokkaidō, NE Japan
Takla Makan Desert *see* Taklimakan Shamo
Taklimakan Shamo 104 B3 *Eng.* Takla Makan Desert. *Desert* NW China
Takow *see* Kaohsiung
Takutea 123 G4 *island* S Cook Islands
Talachyn 85 D6 *Rus.* Tolochin. Vitsyebskaya Voblasts', NE Belarus
Talamanca, Cordillera de 31 E5 *mountain range* S Costa Rica
Talara 38 B2 Piura, NW Peru
Talas 101 F2 Talasskaya Oblast', NW Kyrgyzstan
Talaud, Kepulauan 117 F3 *island group* E Indonesia
Talavera de la Reina 70 D3 *anc.* Caesarobriga, Talabriga. Castilla-La Mancha, C Spain
Talca 42 B4 Maule, C Chile
Talcahuano 43 B5 Bío Bío, C Chile
Taldykorgan 92 C5 *Kaz.* Taldyqorghan; *prev.* Taldy-Kurgan. Almaty, SE Kazakhstan
Taldy-Kurgan/Taldyqorghan *see* Taldykorgan
Ta-lien *see* Dalian
Taliq-an *see* Tāloqān
Tal'ka 85 C6 *Rus.* Tal'ka. Minskaya Voblasts', C Belarus
Tallahassee 20 D3 *prev.* Muskogean. *State capital* Florida, SE USA
Tall al Abyaḍ *see* At Tall al Abyaḍ
Tallinn 84 D2 *Ger.* Reval, *Rus.* Tallin; *prev.* Revel. *Country capital* (Estonia) Harjumaa, NW Estonia
Tall Kalakh 96 B4 *var.* Tell Kalakh. Ḥimṣ, C Syria
Tallulah 20 B2 Louisiana, S USA
Talnakh 92 D3 Taymyrskiy (Dolgano-Nenetskiy) Avtonomnyy Okrug, N Russian Federation
Tal'ne 87 E3 *Rus.* Tal'noye. Cherkas'ka Oblast', C Ukraine
Taloga 27 F1 Oklahoma, C USA
Tāloqān 101 E3 *var.* Taliq-an. Takhār, NE Afghanistan
Talsi 84 C3 *Ger.* Talsen. Talsi, NW Latvia
Taltal 42 B2 Antofagasta, N Chile
Talvik 62 D2 Finnmark, N Norway
Tamabo, Banjaran 116 D3 *mountain range* East Malaysia
Tamale 53 E4 C Ghana
Tamana 123 E3 *prev.* Rotcher Island. *Atoll* Tungaru, W Kiribati
Tamanrasset 49 E4 *var.* Tamenghest. S Algeria
Tamar 67 C7 *river* SW England, UK
Tamar *see* Tudmur
Tamatave *see* Toamasina
Tamazunchale 29 E4 San Luis Potosí, C Mexico
Tambacounda 52 C3 SE Senegal
Tambov 89 B6 Tambovskaya Oblast', W Russian Federation
Tambura 51 B5 Western Equatoria, SW Sudan
Tamchaket *see* Tâmchekket
Tâmchekket 52 C3 *var.* Tamchaket. Hodh el Gharbi, S Mauritania
Tamenghest *see* Tamanrasset
Tamiahua, Laguna de 29 F4 *lagoon* E Mexico
Tamil Nādu 110 C3 *prev.* Madras. *State* SE India
Tam Ky 115 E5 Quang Nam-Đa Năng, C Vietnam
Tampa 21 E4 Florida, SE USA
Tampa Bay 21 E4 *bay* Florida, SE USA
Tampere 63 D5 *Swe.* Tammerfors. Länsi-Suomi, W Finland
Tampico 29 E3 Tamaulipas, C Mexico
Tamworth 127 D6 New South Wales, SE Australia
Tana 62 D2 *var.* Tenojoki, *Fin.* Teno, *Lapp.* Deatnu. *River* Finland/Norway *see also* Teno
Tana 62 D2 Finnmark, N Norway
Tanabe 109 C7 Wakayama, Honshū, SW Japan
T'ana Hāyk' 50 C4 *Eng.* Lake Tana. *Lake* NW Ethiopia
Tanais *see* Don
Tanami Desert 124 D3 *desert* Northern Territory, N Australia
Ţăndărei 86 D5 Ialomiţa, SE Romania
Tandil 43 D5 Buenos Aires, E Argentina
Tanega-shima 109 B8 *island* Nansei-shotō, SW Japan
Tane Range 114 B4 *Bur.* Tanen Taunggyi. *Mountain range* W Thailand
Tanezrouft 48 D4 *desert* Algeria/Mali
Ṭanf, Jabal aṭ 96 D4 *mountain* SE Syria
Tanga 47 E5 Tanga, E Tanzania
Tanga 51 C7 *region* E Tanzania
Tanganyika, Lake 51 B7 *lake* E Africa
Tangeh-ye Hormoz *see* Hormuz, Strait of
Tanger 48 C2 *var.* Tangiers, Tangier, *Fr./Ger.* Tangerk, *Sp.* Tánger; *anc.* Tingis. NW Morocco
Tangerk *see* Tanger
Tanggula Shan 104 C4 *var.* Dangla, Tangla Range. *Mountain range* W China
Tangier *see* Tanger
Tangiers *see* Tanger
Tangla Range *see* Tanggula Shan
Tangra Yumco 104 B5 *var.* Tangro Tso. *Lake* W China
Tangro Tso *see* Tangra Yumco
Tangshan 106 D3 *var.* T'ang-shan. Hebei, E China
T'ang-shan *see* Tangshan
Tanimbar, Kepulauan 117 F5 *island group* Maluku, E Indonesia
Tanna 122 D4 *island* S Vanuatu
Tannenhof *see* Krynica
Tan-Tan 48 B3 SW Morocco
Tan-tung *see* Dandong
Tanzania 51 C7 *off.* United Republic of Tanzania, *Swa.* Jamhuri ya Muungano wa Tanzania; *prev.* German East Africa, Tanganyika and Zanzibar. *Country* E Africa
Taoudenit *see* Taoudenni
Taoudenni 53 E2 *var.* Taoudenit. Tombouctou, N Mali
Tapa 84 E2 *Ger.* Taps. Lääne-Virumaa, NE Estonia
Tapachula 29 G5 Chiapas, SE Mexico
Tapajós, Rio 41 E2 *var.* Tapajóz. *River* NW Brazil
Tapajóz *see* Tapajós, Rio
Ţarābulus 49 F2 *var.* Ţarābulus al Gharb, *Eng.* Tripoli. *Country capital* (Libya) NW Libya
Ţarābulus *see* Tripoli
Ţarābulus al Gharb *see* Ţarābulus
Ţarābulus ash Shām *see* Tripoli
Taraclia 86 D4 *Rus.* Tarakilya. S Moldova
Taranaki, Mount 128 C4 *var.* Egmont, Mount. *Mountain* North Island, NZ
Tarancón 71 E3 Castilla-La Mancha, C Spain
Taranto 75 E5 *var.* Tarentum. Puglia, SE Italy
Taranto, Golfo di 75 E6 *Eng.* Gulf of Taranto. *Gulf* S Italy
Tarapoto 38 C2 San Martín, N Peru
Tarare 69 D5 Rhône, E France
Tarascon 69 D6 Bouches-du-Rhône, SE France
Tarawa 122 D2 *atoll* Tungaru, W Kiribati
Taraz 92 C5 *prev.* Aulie Ata, Auliye-Ata, Dzhambul, Zhambyl. Zhambyl, S Kazakhstan
Tarazona 71 E2 Aragón, NE Spain
Tarbes 69 B6 *anc.* Bigorra. Hautes-Pyrénées, S France
Tarcoola 127 A6 South Australia
Taree 127 D6 New South Wales, SE Australia
Tarentum *see* Taranto
Târgovişte 86 C5 *prev.* Tîrgovişte. Dâmboviţa, S Romania
Târgu Jiu 86 B4 *prev.* Tîrgu Jiu. Gorj, W Romania
Târgul-Neamţ *see* Târgu-Neamţ
Târgu Mureş 86 B4 *prev.* Oşorhei, Tîrgu Mures, *Ger.* Neumarkt, *Hung.* Marosvásárhely. Mureş, C Romania
Târgu-Neamţ 86 C3 *var.* Târgul-Neamţ; *prev.* Tîrgu-Neamţ. Neamţ, NE Romania
Târgu Ocna 86 C4 *Hung.* Aknavásár; *prev.* Tîrgu Ocna. Bacău, E Romania
Târgu Secuiesc 86 C4 *Ger.* Neumarkt, Szekler Neumarkt, *Hung.* Kezdivásárhely; *prev.* Chezdi-Oşorheiu, Târgul-Săcuiesc, Tîrgu Secuiesc. Covasna, E Romania
Tarija 39 G5 Tarija, S Bolivia
Tarīm 99 C6 C Yemen
Tarim Basin 102 C2 *basin* NW China
Tarim He 104 B3 *river* NW China
Tarma 38 C3 Junín, C Peru
Tarn 69 C6 *cultural region* S France
Tarn 69 C6 *river* S France
Tarnobrzeg 76 D4 Podkarpackie, SE Poland
Tarnów 77 D5 Małopolskie, S Poland
Tarragona 71 G2 *anc.* Tarraco. Cataluña, E Spain
Tàrrega 71 F2 *var.* Tarrega. Cataluña, NE Spain
Tarsus 94 C4 İçel, S Turkey
Tartu 84 D3 *Ger.* Dorpat; *prev. Rus.* Yurev, Yur'yev. Tartumaa, SE Estonia
Ţarţūs 96 A3 *Fr.* Tartouss; *anc.* Tortosa. Ţarţūs, W Syria
Ta Ru Tao, Ko 115 B7 *island* S Thailand
Tarvisio 74 D2 Friuli-Venezia Giulia, NE Italy
Tashi Chho Dzong *see* Thimphu
Tashkent *see* Toshkent
Tash-Kumyr 101 F2 *Kir.* Tash-Kömür. Dzhalal-Abadskaya Oblast', W Kyrgyzstan
Tashqurghan *see* Kholm
Tasikmalaya 116 C5 *prev.* Tasikmalaja. Jawa, C Indonesia
Tasman Basin 120 C5 *var.* East Australian Basin. *Undersea feature* S Tasman Sea
Tasman Bay 129 C5 *inlet* South Island, NZ
Tasmania 127 B8 *prev.* Van Diemen's Land. *State* SE Australia
Tasmania 130 B4 *island* SE Australia
Tasman Plateau 120 C5 *var.* South Tasmania Plateau. *Undersea feature* SW Tasman Sea
Tasman Sea 120 C5 *sea* SW Pacific Ocean
Tassili-n-Ajjer 49 E4 *plateau* E Algeria
Tatabánya 77 C6 Komárom-Esztergom, NW Hungary
Tathlīth 99 B5 'Asīr, S Saudi Arabia
Tatra Mountains 77 D5 *Ger.* Tatra, *Hung.* Tátra, *Pol./Slvk.* Tatry. *Mountain range* Poland/Slovakia
Ta-t'ung *see* Datong
Tatvan 95 F3 Bitlis, SE Turkey
Ta'ū 123 F4 *var.* Tau. *Island* Manua Islands, E American Samoa
Tau *see* Ta'ū
Taukum, Peski 101 G1 *desert* SE Kazakhstan
Taumarunui 128 D4 Manawatu-Wanganui, North Island, NZ
Taungdwingyi 114 B3 Magwe, C Myanmar
Taunggyi 114 B3 Shan State, C Myanmar
Taunton 67 C7 SW England, UK
Taupo 128 D3 Waikato, North Island, NZ
Taupo, Lake 128 D3 *lake* North Island, NZ
Tauragė 84 B4 *Ger.* Tauroggen. Tauragė, SW Lithuania
Tauranga 128 D3 Bay of Plenty, North Island, NZ
Tauris *see* Tabrīz
Tavas 94 B4 Denizli, SW Turkey
Tavira 70 C5 Faro, S Portugal
Tavoy 115 B5 *var.* Dawei. Tenasserim, S Myanmar
Tavoy Island *see* Mali Kyun
Tawakoni, Lake 27 G2 *reservoir* Texas, SW USA
Tawau 116 D3 Sabah, East Malaysia
Ţawkar *see* Tokar
Tawzar *see* Tozeur
Taxco 29 E4 *var.* Taxco de Alarcón. Guerrero, S Mexico
Taxco de Alarcón *see* Taxco
Tay 66 C3 *river* C Scotland, UK
Taylor 27 G3 Texas, SW USA
Taymā' 98 A4 Tabūk, NW Saudi Arabia
Taymyr, Ozero 93 E2 *lake* N Russian Federation
Taymyr, Poluostrov 93 E2 *peninsula* N Russian Federation
Taz 92 D3 *river* N Russian Federation
T'bilisi 95 G2 *Eng.* Tiflis. *Country capital* (Georgia) SE Georgia
T'bilisi 90 B4 *international airport* S Georgia
Tchien *see* Zwedru
Tchongking *see* Chongqing
Tczew 76 C2 *Ger.* Dirschau. Pomorskie, N Poland
Te Anau 129 A7 Southland, South Island, NZ
Te Anau, Lake 129 A7 *lake* South Island, NZ
Teapa 29 G4 Tabasco, SE Mexico
Teate *see* Chieti
Tebingtinggi 116 B3 Sumatera, N Indonesia
Tebriz *see* Tabrīz
Techirghiol 86 D5 Constanţa, SE Romania
Tecomán 28 D4 Colima, SW Mexico
Tecpan 29 E5 *var.* Tecpan de Galeana. Guerrero, S Mexico
Tecpan de Galeana *see* Tecpan
Tecuci 86 C4 Galaţi, E Romania
Tedzhen 100 C3 *Turkm.* Tejen. Akhalskiy Velayat, S Turkmenistan
Tedzhen *see* Harīrūd
Tees 67 D5 *river* N England, UK
Tefé 40 D2 Amazonas, N Brazil
Tegal 116 C4 Jawa, C Indonesia
Tegelen 65 D5 Limburg, SE Netherlands
Tegucigalpa 30 C3 *country capital* (Honduras) Francisco Morazán, SW Honduras
Teheran *see* Tehrān
Tehrān 98 C3 *var.* Teheran. *Country capital* (Iran) Tehrān, N Iran
Tehuacán 29 F4 Puebla, S Mexico
Tehuantepec 29 F5 *var.* Santo Domingo Tehuantepec. Oaxaca, SE Mexico
Tehuantepec, Golfo de 29 F5 *var.* Gulf of Tehuantepec. *Gulf* S Mexico
Tehuantepec, Gulf of *see* Tehuantepec, Golfo de
Tehuantepec, Isthmus of *see* Tehuantepec, Istmo de
Tehuantepec, Istmo de 29 F5 *var.* Isthmus of Tehuantepec. *Isthmus* SE Mexico
Tejen *see* Harīrūd
Te Kao 128 C1 Northland, North Island, NZ
Tekax 29 H4 *var.* Tekax de Álvaro Obregón. Yucatán, SE Mexico
Tekax de Álvaro Obregón *see* Tekax
Tekeli 92 C5 Almaty, SE Kazakhstan
Tekirdağ 94 A2 *It.* Rodosto; *anc.* Bisanthe, Raidestos, Rhaedestus. Tekirdağ, NW Turkey
Te Kuiti 128 D3 Waikato, North Island, NZ
Tela 30 C2 Atlántida, NW Honduras
Telanaipura *see* Jambi
Tel Aviv-Jaffa *see* Tel Aviv-Yafo
Tel Aviv-Yafo 97 A6 *var.* Tel Aviv-Jaffa. Tel Aviv, C Israel
Teles Pirés *see* São Manuel, Rio
Telish 82 C2 *prev.* Azizie. Pleven, NW Bulgaria
Tell Abiad *see* At Tall al Abyaḍ
Tell Abyad *see* At Tall al Abyaḍ
Tell Kalakh *see* Tall Kalakh
Tell Shedadi *see* Ash Shadādah
Telšiai 84 B3 *Ger.* Telschen. Telšiai, NW Lithuania
Teluk Irian *see* Cenderawasih, Teluk
Teluk Serera *see* Cenderawasih, Teluk
Temerin 78 D3 Serbia, N Serbia and Montenegro (Yugo.)
Temirtau 92 C4 *prev.* Samarkandski, Samarkandskoye. Karaganda, C Kazakhstan
Tempio Pausania 75 A5 Sardegna, Italy, C Mediterranean Sea
Temple 27 G3 Texas, SW USA
Temuco 43 B5 Araucanía, C Chile
Temuka 129 B6 Canterbury, South Island, NZ
Tenasserim 115 B6 Tenasserim, S Myanmar
Ténenkou 52 D3 Mopti, C Mali
Ténéré 53 G3 *physical region* C Niger
Tenerife 48 A3 *island* Islas Canarias, Spain, NE Atlantic Ocean
Tengger Shamo 105 E3 *desert* N China
Tengréla 52 D4 *var.* Tingréla. N Côte d'Ivoire
Tenkodogo 53 E4 S Burkina faso
Tennant Creek 126 A3 Northern Territory, C Australia
Tennessee 20 C1 *off.* State of Tennessee; *also known as* The Volunteer State. *State* SE USA
Tennessee River 20 C1 *river* S USA
Teno *see* Tana
Tenojoki *see* Tana
Tepelena *see* Tepelenë
Tepelenë 79 C7 *var.* Tepelena, *It.* Tepeleni. Gjirokastër, S Albania
Tepeleni *see* Tepelenë
Tepic 28 D4 Nayarit, C Mexico
Teplice 76 A4 *Ger.* Teplitz; *prev.* Teplice-Šanov, Teplitz-Schönau. Ústecký Kraj, NW Czech Republic
Tequila 28 D4 Jalisco, SW Mexico
Teraina 123 G2 *prev.* Washington Island. *Atoll* Line Islands, E Kiribati
Teramo 74 C4 *anc.* Interamna. Abruzzo, C Italy
Tercan 95 E3 Erzincan, NE Turkey
Terceira 70 A5 *var.* Ilha Terceira. *Island* Azores, Portugal, NE Atlantic Ocean
Teresina 41 F2 *var.* Therezina. *State capital* Piauí, NE Brazil
Termia *see* Kýthnos
Términos, Laguna de 29 G4 *lagoon* SE Mexico
Termiz 101 E3 *Rus.* Termez. Surkhondaryo Wiloyati, S Uzbekistan
Termoli 74 D4 Molise, C Italy
Terneuzen 65 B5 *var.* Neuzen. Zeeland, SW Netherlands
Terni 74 C4 *anc.* Interamna Nahars. Umbria, C Italy
Ternopil' 86 C2 *Pol.* Tarnopol, *Rus.* Ternopol'. Ternopil's'ka Oblast', W Ukraine
Terracina 75 C5 Lazio, C Italy
Terrassa 71 G2 *Cast.* Tarrasa. Cataluña, E Spain
Terre Adélie 132 C4 *disputed region* SE Antarctica
Terre Haute 18 B4 Indiana, N USA
Territoire du Yukon *see* Yukon Territory
Terschelling 64 C1 *Fris.* Skylge. *Island* Waddeneilanden, N Netherlands
Teruel 71 F3 *anc.* Turba. Aragón, E Spain
Tervel 82 E1 *prev.* Kurtbunar, *Rom.* Curtbunar. Dobrich, NE Bulgaria
Tervueren *see* Tervuren
Tervuren 65 C6 *var.* Tervueren. Vlaams Brabant, C Belgium
Teseney 50 C4 *var.* Tessenei. W Eritrea
Tessalit 53 E2 Kidal, NE Mali
Tessaoua 53 G3 Maradi, S Niger
Tessenderlo 65 C5 Limburg, NE Belgium
Tessenei *see* Teseney
Testigos, Islas los 37 E1 *island group* N Venezuela
Tete 57 E2 Tete, NW Mozambique
Teterow 72 C3 Mecklenburg-Vorpommern, NE Germany
Tétouan 48 C2 *var.* Tetouan, Tetuán. N Morocco
Tetovo 79 D5 *Alb.* Tetova, Tetovë, *Turk.* Kalkandelen. Razgrad, N Bulgaria
Tetuán *see* Tétouan
Tevere 74 C4 *Eng.* Tiber. *River* C Italy
Teverya 97 B5 *var.* Tiberias, Tverya. Northern, N Israel
Te Waewae Bay 129 A7 *bay* South Island, NZ
Texarkana 20 A2 Arkansas, C USA
Texarkana 27 H2 Texas, SW USA
Texas 27 F3 *off.* State of Texas; *also known as* The Lone Star State. *State* S USA
Texas City 27 H4 Texas, SW USA
Texel 64 C2 *island* Waddeneilanden, NW Netherlands
Texoma, Lake 27 G2 *reservoir* Oklahoma/Texas, C USA
Teziutlán 29 F4 Puebla, S Mexico
Thaa Atoll *see* Kolhumadulu Atoll
Thai Binh 114 D3 Thai Binh, N Vietnam
Thailand 115 C5 *off.* Kingdom of Thailand, *Th.* Prathet Thai; *prev.* Siam. *Country* SE Asia
Thailand, Gulf of 115 C6 *var.* Gulf of Siam, *Th.* Ao Thai, *Vtn.* Vinh Thai Lan. *Gulf* SE Asia
Thai Nguyên 114 D3 Bắc Thai, N Vietnam
Thakhèk 114 D4 *prev.* Muang Khammouan. Khammouan, C Laos
Thamarīd *see* Thamarīt
Thamarīt 99 D6 *var.* Thamarīd, Thumrayt. SW Oman
Thames 67 B8 *river* S England, UK
Thames 128 D3 Waikato, North Island, NZ
Thanh Hoa 114 D3 Vinh Phu, N Vietnam
Thanintari Taungdan *see* Bilauktaung Range
Thar Desert 112 C3 *var.* Great Indian Desert, Indian Desert. *Desert* India/Pakistan
Tharthār, Buḥayrat ath 98 B3 *lake* C Iraq
Thásos 82 C4 *island* E Greece
Thásos 82 C4 Thásos, E Greece
Thaton 114 B4 Mon State, S Myanmar
Thayetmyo 114 A4 Magwe, C Myanmar
The Crane 33 H2 *var.* Crane. S Barbados
The Dalles 24 B3 Oregon, NW USA
The Flatts Village *see* Flatts Village
The Hague *see* 's-Gravenhage
Theodosia *see* Feodosiya
The Pas 15 F5 Manitoba, C Canada
Therezina *see* Teresina
Thérma 83 D6 Ikaría, Dodekánisos, Greece, Aegean Sea
Thermaïkós Kólpos 82 B4 *Eng.* Thermaic Gulf; *anc.* Thermaicus Sinus. *Gulf* N Greece
Thermiá *see* Kýthnos
Thérmo 83 B5 Dytikí Ellás, C Greece
The Rock 71 H4 E Gibraltar
The Six Counties *see* Northern Ireland
Thessaloníki 82 C3 *Eng.* Salonica, Salonika, *SCr.* Solun, *Turk.* Selânik. Kentrikí Makedonía, N Greece
The Valley 33 G3 *dependent territory capital* (Anguilla) E Anguilla
The Village 27 G1 Oklahoma, C USA
Thiamis *see* Thýamis
Thibet *see* Xizang Zizhiqu
Thief River Falls 23 F1 Minnesota, N USA
Thienen *see* Tienen
Thiers 69 C5 Puy-de-Dôme, C France
Thiès 52 B3 W Senegal
Thimbu *see* Thimphu
Thimphu 113 G3 *var.* Thimbu; *prev.* Tashi Chho Dzong. *Country capital* (Bhutan) W Bhutan
Thionville 68 D3 *Ger.* Diedenhofen. Moselle, NE France
Thíra 83 D7 *prev.* Santorin, Santoríni, *anc.* Thera. *Island* Kykládes, Greece, Aegean Sea
Thíra 83 D7 Thíra, Kykládes, Greece, Aegean Sea
Thiruvanathapuram *see* Trivandrum
Thitu Island 106 C8 *island* NW Spratly Islands
Tholen 64 B4 *island* SW Netherlands
Thomasville 20 D3 Georgia, SE USA
Thompson 15 F4 Manitoba, C Canada
Thonon-les-Bains 69 D5 Haute-Savoie, E France
Thorlákshöfn 61 E5 Sudhurland, SW Iceland
Thornton Island *see* Millennium Island
Thouars 68 B4 Deux-Sèvres, W France
Thracian Sea 82 D4 *Gk.* Thrakikó Pélagos; *anc.* Thracium Mare. *Sea* Greece/Turkey
Three Kings Islands 128 C1 *island group* N NZ
Thrissur *see* Trichūr

Ţurayf – Viborg

Ţurayf *98 A3* Al Ḩudūd ash Shamālīyah, NW Saudi Arabia
Turbat *112 A3* Baluchistān, SW Pakistan
Turda *86 B4 Ger.* Thorenburg, *Hung.* Torda. Cluj, NW Romania
Turek *76 C3* Wielkopolskie, C Poland
Turfan *see* Turpan
Turin *see* Torino
Turkana, Lake *89 C6 var.* Lake Rudolf. *Lake* N Kenya
Turkish Republic of Northern Cyprus *80 D5 Ger.* Dependent territory, *disputed territory.* Cyprus
Turkestan *92 B5 Kaz.* Türkistan. Yuzhnyy Kazakhstan, S Kazakhstan
Turkey *94 B3 off.* Republic of Turkey, *Turk.* Türkiye Cumhuriyeti. *Country* SW Asia
Turkmenbashi *100 B2 prev.* Krasnovodsk. Balkanskiy Velayat, W Turkmenistan
Turkmenistan *100 B2 off.* Turkmenistan; *prev.* Turkmenskaya Soviet Socialist Republic. *Country* C Asia
Turkmenskiy Zaliv *100 B2 Turkm.* Türkmen Aylagy. *Lake gulf* W Turkmenistan
Turks and Caicos Islands *33 E2 UK dependent territory* N West Indies
Turlock *25 B6* California, W USA
Turnagain, Cape *128 D4 headland* North Island, NZ
Turnhout *65 C5* Antwerpen, N Belgium
Turnov *76 B4 Ger.* Turnau. Liberecký Kraj, N Czech Republic
Turnu Măgurele *86 B5 var.* Turnu-Măgurele. Teleorman, S Romania
Turon Pasttekisligi *see* Turan Lowland
Turpan *104 C3 var.* Turfan. Xinjiang Uygur Zizhiqu, NW China
Turpan Pendi *104 C3 Eng.* Turpan Depression. *Depression* NW China
Tŭrtkŭl *100 D2 Rus.* Turtkul'; *prev.* Petroaleksandrovsk. Qoraqalpoghiston Respublikasi, W Uzbekistan
Turuga *see* Tsuruga
Turuoka *see* Tsuruoka
Tuscaloosa *20 C2* Alabama, S USA
Tusima *see* Tsushima
Tuticorin *110 C3* Tamil Nādu, SE India
Tutrakan *82 D1* Silistra, NE Bulgaria
Tutuila *123 F4 island* W American Samoa
Tuvalu *123 E3 prev.* Ellice Islands. *Country* SW Pacific Ocean
Ţuwayq, Jabal *99 C5 mountain range* C Saudi Arabia
Tuxpán *29 F4 var.* Tuxpán de Rodríguez Cano. Veracruz-Llave, E Mexico
Tuxpan *28 D4* Jalisco, C Mexico
Tuxpan *28 D4* Nayarit, C Mexico
Tuxpán de Rodríguez Cano *see* Tuxpán
Tuxtepec *29 F4 var.* San Juan Bautista Tuxtepec. Oaxaca, S Mexico
Tuxtla *29 G5 var.* Tuxtla Gutiérrez. Chiapas, SE Mexico
Tuxtla *see* San Andrés Tuxtla
Tuxtla Gutiérrez *see* Tuxtla
Tuy Hoa *115 E5* Phu Yên, S Vietnam
Tuz Gölü *94 C3 lake* C Turkey
Tuzla *78 C3* Federacija Bosna I Hercegovina, NE Bosnia and Herzegovina
Tver' *88 B4 prev.* Kalinin. Tverskaya Oblast', W Russian Federation
Tverya *see* Teverya
Twin Falls *24 D4* Idaho, NW USA
Tychy *77 D5 Ger.* Tichau. Śląskie, S Poland
Tyler *27 G3* Texas, SW USA
Tympáki *83 C8 var.* Timbaki; *prev.* Timbákion. Kríti, Greece, E Mediterranean Sea
Tynda *93 F4* Amurskaya Oblast', SE Russian Federation
Tyne *66 D4 river* N England, UK
Tyôsi *see* Chōshi
Tyre *see* Soûr
Týrnavos *82 B4 var.* Tírnavos. Thessalía, C Greece
Tyrrhenian Sea *75 B6 It.* Mare Tirreno. *Sea* N Mediterranean Sea
Tyumen' *92 C3* Tyumenskaya Oblast', C Russian Federation
Tyup *101 G2 Kir.* Tüp. Issyk-Kul'skaya Oblast', NE Kyrgyzstan
Tywyn *67 C6* W Wales, UK
Tzekung *see* Zigong
T,ơng Đ,ơng *114 D4 var.* Tuong Buong. Nghê An, N Vietnam

U

Uanle Uen *see* Wanlaweyn
Uaupés, Rio *see* Vaupés, Río
Ubangi *55 C5 Fr.* Oubangui. *River* C Africa
Ubangi-Shari *see* Central African Republic
Ube *109 B7* Yamaguchi, Honshū, SW Japan
Úbeda *71 E4* Andalucía, S Spain
Uberaba *41 F4* Minas Gerais, SE Brazil
Uberlândia *41 F4* Minas Gerais, SE Brazil
Ubol Rajadhani *see* Ubon Ratchathani
Ubol Ratchathani *see* Ubon Ratchathani
Ubon Ratchathani *115 D5 var.* Muang Ubon, Ubol Rajadhani, Ubol Ratchathani, Udon Ratchathani. Ubon Ratchathani, E Thailand
Ubrique *70 D5* Andalucía, S Spain
Ucayali, Río *38 D3 river* C Peru
Uchiura-wan *108 D3 bay* NW Pacific Ocean
Uchquduq *100 D2 Rus.* Uchkuduk. Nawoiy Wiloyati, N Uzbekistan
Uchtagan, Peski *100 C2 Turkm.* Uchtagan Gumy. *Desert* NW Turkmenistan
Udaipur *112 C3 prev.* Oodeypore. Rājasthān, N India
Uddevalla *63 B6* Västra Götaland, S Sweden
Udine *74 D2 anc.* Utina. Friuli-Venezia Giulia, NE Italy
Udintsev Fracture Zone *132 A5 tectonic feature* S Pacific Ocean
Udipi *see* Udupi
Udon Ratchathani *see* Ubon Ratchathani
Udon Thani *114 C4 var.* Ban Mak Khaeng, Udorndhani. Udon Thani, N Thailand
Udorndhani *see* Udon Thani
Udupi *110 B2 var.* Udipi. Karnātaka, SW India
Uele *55 D5 var.* Welle. *River* NE Dem. Rep. Congo
Uelzen *72 C3* Niedersachsen, N Germany
Ufa *89 D6* Respublika Bashkortostan, W Russian Federation
Ugāle *84 C2* Ventspils, NW Latvia
Uganda *51 B6 off.* Republic of Uganda. *Country* E Africa
Uglovka *88 B4 var.* Okulovka. Novgorodskaya Oblast', W Russian Federation
Uhuru Peak *see* Kilimanjaro
Uíge *56 B1 Port.* Carmona, Vila Marechal Carmona. Uíge, NW Angola
Uinta Mountains *22 B4 mountain range* Utah, W USA
Uitenhage *56 C5* Eastern Cape, S South Africa
Uithoorn *64 C3* Noord-Holland, C Netherlands
Ujelang Atoll *122 C1 var.* Wujlān. *Atoll* Ralik Chain, W Marshall Islands
Ujungpandang *117 E4 var.* Macassar, Makassar; *prev.* Makasar. Sulawesi, C Indonesia
Ujung Salang *see* Phuket
Ukhta *92 C3* Respublika Komi, NW Russian Federation
Ukiah *25 B5* California, W USA
Ukmergė *84 C4 Pol.* Wiłkomierz. Ukmergė, C Lithuania
Ukraine *86 C2 off.* Ukraine, *Rus.* Ukraina, *Ukr.* Ukrayina; *prev.* Ukrainian Soviet Socialist Republic, Ukrainskaya S.S.R. *Country* SE Europe
Ulaanbaatar *105 E2 Eng.* Ulan Bator. *Country capital* (Mongolia) Töv, C Mongolia
Ulaangom *104 C2* Uvs, NW Mongolia
Ulan Bator *see* Ulaanbaatar
Ulanhad *see* Chifeng
Ulan-Ude *93 E4 prev.* Verkhneudinsk. Respublika Buryatiya, S Russian Federation
Ulft *64 E4* Gelderland, E Netherlands
Ullapool *66 C3* N Scotland, UK
Ulm *73 B6* Baden-Württemberg, S Germany
Ulsan *107 E4 Jap.* Urusan. SE South Korea
Ulster *67 B5 cultural region* N Ireland
Ulungur Hu *104 B2 lake* NW China
Uluru *125 D5 var.* Ayers Rock. *Rocky outcrop* Northern Territory, C Australia
Ulyanivka *87 E3 Rus.* Ul'yanovka. Kirovohrads'ka Oblast', C Ukraine
Ul'yanovsk *89 C5 prev.* Simbirsk. Ul'yanovskaya Oblast', W Russian Federation
Uman' *87 E3 Rus.* Uman. Cherkas'ka Oblast', C Ukraine
Umán *29 H3* Yucatán, SE Mexico
Umanak *see* Uummannaq
Umanaq *see* Uummannaq
Umbro-Marchigiano, Appennino *74 C3 Eng.* Umbrian-Machigian Mountains. *Mountain range* C Italy
Umeå *62 C4* Västerbotten, N Sweden
Umeälven *62 C4 river* N Sweden
Umiat *14 D2* Alaska, USA
Umm Buru *50 A4* Western Darfur, W Sudan
Umm Durmān *see* Omdurman
Umm Ruwaba *50 C4 var.* Umm Ruwābah, Um Ruwāba. Northern Kordofan, C Sudan
Umm Ruwābah *see* Umm Ruwaba
Umnak Island *14 A3 island* Aleutian Islands, Alaska, USA
Um Ruwāba *see* Umm Ruwaba
Umtali *see* Mutare
Umtata *56 D5* Eastern Cape, SE South Africa
Una *78 B3 river* Bosnia and Herzegovina/Croatia
Unac *78 B3 river* W Bosnia and Herzegovina
Unalaska Island *14 A2 island* Aleutian Islands, Alaska, USA
'Unayzah *98 B4 var.* Anaiza. Al Qaşīm, C Saudi Arabia
Uncía *39 F4* Potosí, C Bolivia
Uncompahgre Peak *22 B5 mountain* Colorado, C USA
Ungarisches Erzgebirge *see* Slovenské rudohorie
Ungava Bay *17 E1 bay* Quebec, E Canada
Ungava, Péninsule d' *16 D1 peninsula* Quebec, SE Canada
Ungheni *86 D3 Rus.* Ungeny. W Moldova
Unimak Island *14 B3 island* Aleutian Islands, Alaska, USA
Union *21 E1* South Carolina, SE USA
Union City Tennessee, S USA
United Arab Emirates *99 C5 Ar.* Al Imārāt al 'Arabīyah al Muttaḩidah, *abbrev.* UAE; *prev.* Trucial States. *Country* SW Asia
United Kingdom *67 B5 off.* UK of Great Britain and Northern Ireland, *abbrev.* UK. *Country* NW Europe
United States of America *13 B5 off.* United States of America, *var.* America, The States, *abbrev.* U.S., USA. *Country*
Unst *66 D1 island* NE Scotland, UK
Ünye *94 D2* Ordu, W Turkey
Upala *30 D4* Alajuela, NW Costa Rica
Upata *37 E2* Bolívar, E Venezuela
Upemba, Lac *55 D7 lake* SE Dem. Rep. Congo
Upernavik *60 C2 var.* Upernivik. C Greenland
Upernivik *see* Upernavik
Upington *56 C4* Northern Cape, W South Africa
Upolu *123 F4 island* SE Samoa
Upper Klamath Lake *24 A4 lake* Oregon, NW USA
Upper Lough Erne *67 A5 lake* SW Northern Ireland, UK
Upper Red Lake *23 F1 lake* Minnesota, N USA
Uppsala *63 C6* Uppsala, C Sweden
Ural *90 B3 Kaz.* Zayyq. *River* Kazakhstan/Russian Federation
Ural Mountains *see* Ural'skiye Gory
Ural'sk *92 B3 Kaz.* Oral. Zapadnyy Kazakhstan, NW Kazakhstan
Ural'skiye Gory *92 C3 var.* Ural'skiy Khrebet, *Eng.* Ural Mountains. *Mountain range* Kazakhstan/Russian Federation
Ural'skiy Khrebet *see* Ural'skiye Gory
Uraricoera *40 D1* Roraima, N Brazil
Urbandale *23 F3* Iowa, C USA
Uren' *89 C5* Nizhegorodskaya Oblast', W Russian Federation
Urganch *100 D2 Rus.* Urgench; *prev.* Novo-Urgench. Khorazm Wiloyati, W Uzbekistan
Urgut *101 E3* Samarqand Wiloyati, C Uzbekistan
Uroševac *79 D5 Alb.* Ferizaj. Serbia, S Serbia and Montenegro (Yugo.)
Ŭroteppa *101 E2 Rus.* Ura-Tyube. NW Tajikistan
Uruapan *29 E4 var.* Uruapan del Progreso. Michoacán de Ocampo, SW Mexico
Uruapan del Progreso *see* Uruapan
Uruguai, Rio *see* Uruguay
Uruguay *42 D4 off.* Oriental Republic of Uruguay; *prev.* La Banda Oriental. *Country* E South America
Uruguay *42 D3 var.* Rio Uruguai, Río Uruguay. *River* E South America
Uruguay, Río *see* Uruguay
Urumchi *see* Ürümqi
Urumqi *see* Ürümqi
Ürümqi *104 C3 var.* Tihwa, Urumchi, Urumqi, Urumtsi, Wu-lu-k'o-mu-shi, Wu-lu-mu-ch'i; *prev.* Ti-hua. *Autonomous region capital* Xinjiang Uygur Zizhiqu, NW China
Urumtsi *see* Ürümqi
Urup, Ostrov *93 H4 island* Kuril'skiye Ostrova, SE Russian Federation
Urziceni *86 C5* Ialomiţa, SE Romania
Usa *88 E3 river* NW Russian Federation
Uşak *94 B3 prev.* Ushak. Uşak, W Turkey
Ushuaia *43 B8* Tierra del Fuego, S Argentina
Usinsk *88 E3* Respublika Komi, NW Russian Federation
Üsküb *see* Skopje
Üsküp *see* Skopje
Usmas Ezers *84 B3 lake* NW Latvia
Usol'ye-Sibirskoye *93 E4* Irkutskaya Oblast', C Russian Federation
Ussel *69 C5* Corrèze, C France
Ussuriysk *93 G5 prev.* Nikol'sk, Nikol'sk-Ussuriyskiy, Voroshilov. Primorskiy Kray, SE Russian Federation
Ustica, Isola d' *75 B6 island* S Italy
Ust'-Ilimsk *93 E4* Irkutskaya Oblast', C Russian Federation
Ústí nad Labem *76 A4 Ger.* Aussig. Ústecký Kraj, NW Czech Republic
Ustka *76 C2 Ger.* Stolpmünde. Pomorskie, N Poland
Ust'-Kamchatsk *93 H2* Kamchatskaya Oblast', E Russian Federation
Ust'-Kamenogorsk *92 D5 Kaz.* Öskemen. Vostochnyy Kazakhstan, E Kazakhstan
Ust'-Kut *93 E4* Irkutskaya Oblast', C Russian Federation
Ust'-Olenëk *93 E3* Respublika Sakha (Yakutiya), NE Russian Federation
Ustrzyki Dolne *77 E5* Podkarpackie, SE Poland
Ust Urt *see* Ustyurt Plateau
Ustyurt Plateau *100 B1 var.* Ust Urt, *Uzb.* Ustyurt Platosi. *Plateau* Kazakhstan/Uzbekistan
Ustyurt Platosi *see* Ustyurt Plateau
Usulután *30 C3* Usulután, SE El Salvador
Usumacinta, Río *30 B1 river* Guatemala/Mexico
Utah *26 A1 off.* State of Utah; also known as Beehive State, Mormon State. *State* W USA
Utah Lake *22 B4 lake* Utah, W USA
Utena *84 C4* Utena, E Lithuania
Utica *19 F3* New York, NE USA
Utrecht *64 C4 Lat.* Trajectum ad Rhenum. Utrecht, C Netherlands
Utsunomiya *109 D5 var.* Utunomiya. Tochigi, Honshū, S Japan
Uttar Pradesh *113 E3 prev.* United Provinces, United Provinces of Agra and Oudh. *State* N India
Utunomiya *see* Utsunomiya
Uulu *84 D2* Pärnumaa, SW Estonia
Uummannaq *60 C3 var.* Umanak, Umanaq. C Greenland
Uummannarsuaq *see* Nunap Isua
Uvalde *27 F4* Texas, SW USA
Uvaravichy *85 D7 Rus.* Uvarovichi. Homyel'skaya Voblasts', SE Belarus
Uvea, Île *123 E4 island* N Wallis and Futuna
Uvs Nuur *104 C1 var.* Ozero Ubsu-Nur. *Lake* Mongolia/Russian Federation
'Uwaynāt, Jabal al *88 A3 var.* Jebel Uweinat. *Mountain* Libya/Sudan
Uyo *53 G5* Akwa Ibom, S Nigeria
Uyuni *39 F5* Potosí, W Bolivia
Uzbekistan *100 D2 off.* Republic of Uzbekistan. *Country* C Asia
Uzhhorod *86 B2 Rus.* Uzhgorod; *prev.* Ungvár. Zakarpats'ka Oblast', W Ukraine
Užice *78 D4 prev.* Titovo Užice. Serbia, W Serbia and Montenegro (Yugo.)

V

Vaal *56 D4 river* C South Africa
Vaals *65 D6* Limburg, SE Netherlands
Vaasa *63 D5 Swe.* Vasa; *prev.* Nikolainkaupunki. Länsi-Suomi, W Finland
Vaassen *64 D3* Gelderland, E Netherlands
Vác *77 C6 Ger.* Waitzen. Pest, N Hungary
Vadodara *112 C4 prev.* Baroda. Gujarāt, W India
Vaduz *72 E2 country capital* (Liechtenstein) W Liechtenstein
Váh *77 C5 Ger.* Waag, *Hung.* Vág. *River* W Slovakia
Väinameri *84 C2 prev.* Muhu Väin, *Ger.* Moon-Sund. *Sea* E Baltic Sea
Valachia *see* Wallachia
Valday *88 B4* Novgorodskaya Oblast', W Russian Federation
Valdecañas, Embalse de *70 D3 reservoir* W Spain
Valdepeñas *71 E4* Castilla-La Mancha, C Spain
Valdés, Península *43 C6 peninsula* SE Argentina
Valdez *14 C3* Alaska, USA
Valdia *see* Weldiya
Valdivia *43 B5* Los Lagos, C Chile
Val-d'Or *16 D4* Quebec, SE Canada
Valdosta *21 E3* Georgia, SE USA
Valence *69 D5 anc.* Valentia, Valentia Julia, Ventia. Drôme, E France
Valencia *24 D1* California, W USA
Valencia *36 D1* Carabobo, N Venezuela
Valencia *71 F3* País Valenciano, E Spain
Valencia, Golfo de *71 F3 var.* Gulf of Valencia. *Gulf* E Spain
Valencia, Gulf of *see* Valencia, Golfo de
Valenciennes *68 D2* Nord, N France
Valera *36 C2* Trujillo, NW Venezuela
Valga *84 D3 Ger.* Walk, *Latv.* Valka. Valgamaa, S Estonia
Valira *69 A8 river* Andorra/Spain
Valjevo *78 C4* Serbia, W Serbia and Montenegro (Yugo.)
Valjok *see* Válljohka
Valka *84 D3 Ger.* Walk. Valka, N Latvia
Valkenswaard *65 D5* Noord-Brabant, S Netherlands
Valladolid *70 D2* Castilla-León, NW Spain
Valladolid *29 H3* Yucatán, SE Mexico
Vall d'Uxó *71 F3* País Valenciano, E Spain
Valle de La Pascua *36 D2* Guárico, N Venezuela
Valledupar *36 B1* Cesar, N Colombia
Vallejo *25 B6* California, W USA
Vallenar *42 B3* Atacama, N Chile
Valletta *75 C8 prev.* Valetta. *Country capital* (Malta) E Malta
Valley City *23 E2* North Dakota, N USA
Válljohka *62 D2 var.* Valjok. Finnmark, N Norway
Valls *71 G2* Cataluña, NE Spain
Valmiera *84 D3 Est.* Volmari, *Ger.* Wolmar. Valmiera, N Latvia
Valozhyn *85 C5 Pol.* Wołożyn, *Rus.* Volozhin. Minskaya Voblasts', C Belarus
Valparaíso *18 C3* Indiana, N USA
Valparaíso *42 B4* Valparaíso, C Chile
Valverde del Camino *70 C4* Andalucía, S Spain
Van *95 F3* Van, E Turkey
Vanadzor *95 F2 prev.* Kirovakan. N Armenia
Vancouver *14 D5* British Columbia, SW Canada
Vancouver *24 B3* Washington, NW USA
Vancouver Island *14 D5 island* British Columbia, SW Canada
Van Diemen Gulf *124 D2 gulf* Northern Territory, N Australia
Vänern *63 B6 Eng.* Lake Vaner; *prev.* Lake Vener. *Lake* S Sweden
Vangaindrano *57 G4* Fianarantsoa, SE Madagascar
Van Gölü *95 F3 Eng.* Lake Van; *anc.* Thospitis. *Salt lake* E Turkey
Van Horn *26 D3* Texas, SW USA
Van, Lake *see* Van Gölü
Vannes *68 A3 anc.* Dariorigum. Morbihan, NW France
Vantaa *63 D6 Swe.* Vanda. Etelä-Suomi, S Finland
Vanua Levu *123 E4 island* N Fiji
Vanuatu *122 C4 off.* Republic of Vanuatu; *prev.* New Hebrides. *Country* SW Pacific Ocean
Van Wert *18 C4* Ohio, N USA
Varakļani *84 D4* Madona, C Latvia
Vārānasi *113 E3 prev.* Banaras, Benares, *hist.* Kasi. Uttar Pradesh, N India
Varangerfjorden *62 E2 fjord* N Norway
Varangerhalvøya *62 D2 peninsula* N Norway
Varannó *see* Vranov nad Topľou
Varaždin *78 B2 Ger.* Warasdin, *Hung.* Varasd. Varaždin, N Croatia
Varberg *63 B7* Halland, S Sweden
Vardar *79 E6 Gk.* Axiós. *River* FYR Macedonia/Greece *see also* Axiós
Varde *63 A7* Ribe, W Denmark
Varėna *85 B5 Pol.* Orany. Varėna, S Lithuania
Varese *74 B2* Lombardia, N Italy
Vârful Moldoveanu *86 B4 var.* Moldoveanul; *prev.* Vîrful Moldoveanu. *Mountain* C Romania
Varkaus *63 E5* Itä-Suomi, C Finland
Varna *82 E2 prev.* Stalin, *anc.* Odessus. Varna, E Bulgaria
Varnenski Zaliv *82 E2 prev.* Stalinski Zaliv. *Bay* E Bulgaria
Vasilikí *83 A5* Lefkáda, Iónioi Nísoi, Greece, C Mediterranean Sea
Vasilishki *85 B5 Pol.* Wasiliszki, *Rus.* Vasilishki. Hrodzyenskaya Voblasts', W Belarus
Vaslui *86 D4* Vaslui, C Romania
Västerås *63 C6* Västmanland, C Sweden
Vasyl'kiv *87 E2 Rus.* Vasil'kov. Kyyivs'ka Oblast', N Ukraine
Vaté *see* Efate
Vatican City *75 A7 off.* Vatican City State. *Country* S Europe
Vatnajökull *61 E5 glacier* SE Iceland
Vättern *63 B6 Eng.* Lake Vatter; *prev.* Lake Vetter. *Lake* S Sweden
Vaughn *26 D2* New Mexico, SW USA
Vaupés, Río *36 C4 var.* Rio Uaupés. *River* Brazil/Colombia *see also* Uaupés, Rio
Vava'u Group *123 E4 island group* N Tonga
Vavuniya *110 D3* Northern Province, N Sri Lanka
Vawkavysk *85 B6 Pol.* Wołkowysk, *Rus.* Volkovysk. Hrodzyenskaya Voblasts', W Belarus
Växjö *63 C7 var.* Vexiö. Kronoberg, S Sweden
Vaygach, Ostrov *88 E2 island* NW Russian Federation
Veendam *64 E2* Groningen, NE Netherlands
Veenendaal *64 D4* Utrecht, C Netherlands
Vega *62 B4 island* C Norway
Veisiejai *85 B5* Lazdijai, S Lithuania
Vejer de la Frontera *70 C5* Andalucía, S Spain
Veldhoven *65 D5* Noord-Brabant, S Netherlands
Velebit *78 A3 mountain range* C Croatia
Velenje *73 E7 Ger.* Wöllan. N Slovenia
Veles *79 E6 Turk.* Köprülü. C FYR Macedonia
Velho *see* Porto Velho
Velika Morava *78 D4 var.* Glavn'a Morava, Morava, *Ger.* Grosse Morava. *River* C Serbia and Montenegro (Yugo.)
Velikaya *91 G2 river* NE Russian Federation
Velikiye Luki *88 A4* Pskovskaya Oblast', W Russian Federation
Veliko Tŭrnovo *82 D2 prev.* Tirnovo, Trnovo, Tŭrnovo. Veliko Tŭrnovo, N Bulgaria
Velingrad *82 C3* Pazardzhik, C Bulgaria
Vel'ký Krtíš *77 D6* Banskobystrický Kraj, C Slovakia
Vellore *110 C2* Tamil Nādu, SE India
Velobriga *see* Viana do Castelo
Velsen *see* Velsen-Noord
Velsen-Noord *64 C3 var.* Velsen. Noord-Holland, W Netherlands
Vel'sk *88 C4 var.* Velsk. Arkhangel'skaya Oblast', NW Russian Federation
Velsk *see* Vel'sk
Velvendos *see* Velvendós
Velvendós *82 B4 var.* Velvendos. Dytikí Makedonía, N Greece
Velykyy Tokmak *see* Tokmak
Vendôme *68 C4* Loir-et-Cher, C France
Venezia *74 C2 Eng.* Venice, *Fr.* Venise, *Ger.* Venedig; anc.Venetia. Veneto, NE Italy
Venezuela *36 D2 off.* Republic of Venezuela; *prev.* Estados Unidos de Venezuela, United States of Venezuela. *Country* N South America
Venezuela, Golfo de *36 C1 Eng.* Gulf of Maracaibo, Gulf of Venezuela. *Gulf* NW Venezuela
Venezuelan Basin *34 B1 undersea feature* E Caribbean Sea
Venice *see* Venezia
Venice *20 C4* Louisiana, S USA
Venice, Gulf of *74 C2 It.* Golfo di Venezia, *Slvn.* Beneški Zaliv. *Gulf* N Adriatic Sea
Venlo *65 D5 prev.* Venloo. Limburg, SE Netherlands
Venta *84 B3 Ger.* Windau. *River* Latvia/Lithuania
Ventimiglia *74 A3* Liguria, NW Italy
Ventspils *84 B2 Ger.* Windau. Ventspils, NW Latvia
Vera *42 D3* Santa Fe, C Argentina
Veracruz *29 F4 var.* Veracruz Llave. Veracruz-Llave, E Mexico
Veracruz Llave *see* Veracruz
Vercelli *74 A2 anc.* Vercellae. Piemonte, NW Italy
Verdalsøra *62 B4* Nord-Trøndelag, C Norway
Verde, Costa *70 D1 coastal region* N Spain
Verden *72 B3* Niedersachsen, NW Germany
Veria *see* Véroia
Verkhoyanskiy Khrebet *93 F3 mountain range* NE Russian Federation
Vermillion *23 F3* South Dakota, N USA
Vermont *19 F2 off.* State of Vermont; also known as The Green Mountain State. *State* NE USA
Vernal *22 B4* Utah, W USA
Vernon *27 F2* Texas, SW USA
Véroia *82 B4 var.* Veria, Vérroia, *Turk.* Karaferiye. Kentrikí Makedonía, N Greece
Verona *74 C2* Veneto, NE Italy
Vérroia *see* Véroia
Versailles *68 D1* Yvelines, N France
Verviers *65 D6* Liège, E Belgium
Vesdre *65 D6 river* E Belgium
Veselinovo *82 D2* Shumen, NE Bulgaria
Vesoul *68 D4 anc.* Vesulium, Vesulum. Haute-Saône, E France
Vesterålen *62 B2 island group* N Norway
Vestfjorden *62 C3 fjord* C Norway
Vestmannaeyjar *61 E5* Sudhurland, S Iceland
Vesuvio *75 D5 Eng.* Vesuvius. *Volcano* S Italy
Veszprém *77 C7 Ger.* Veszprim. Veszprém, W Hungary
Vetrino *82 E2* Varna, E Bulgaria
Veurne *65 A5 var.* Furnes. West-Vlaanderen, W Belgium
Vexiö *see* Växjö
Viacha *39 F4* La Paz, W Bolivia
Viana de Castelo *see* Viana do Castelo
Viana do Castelo *70 B2 var.* Viana de Castelo; *anc.* Velobriga. Viana do Castelo, NW Portugal
Vianen *64 C4* Zuid-Holland, C Netherlands
Viangchan *114 C4 Eng./Fr.* Vientiane. *Country capital* (Laos) C Laos
Viangphoukha *114 C3 var.* Vieng Pou Kha. Louang Namtha, N Laos
Viareggio *74 B3* Toscana, C Italy
Viborg *63 A7* Viborg, NW Denmark

INDEX

White Nile – Zarafshon

White Nile *50 B4 var.* Bahr el Jebel. *River* S Sudan
White River *22 D3 river* South Dakota, N USA
White Sea *see* Beloye More
White Volta *53 E4 var.* Nakambé, *Fr.* Volta Blanche. *River* Burkina faso/Ghana
Whitianga *128 D2* Waikato, North Island, NZ
Whitney, Mount *25 C6 mountain* California, W USA
Whitsunday Group *126 D3 island group* Queensland, E Australia
Whyalla *127 B6* South Australia
Wichita *23 F5* Kansas, C USA
Wichita Falls *27 F2* Texas, SW USA
Wichita River *27 F2 river* Texas, SW USA
Wickenburg *26 B2* Arizona, SW USA
Wicklow *67 B6 Ir.* Cill Mhantáin. *Cultural region* E Ireland
Wicklow Mountains *67 B6 Ir.* Sléibhte Chill Mhantáin. *Mountain range* E Ireland
Wieliczka *77 D5* Małopolskie, S Poland
Wieluń *76 C4* Łódzkie, C Poland
Wien *73 E6 Eng.* Vienna, *Hung.* Bécs, *Slvk.* Vídeň, *Slvn.* Dunaj; *anc.* Vindobona. *Country capital* (Austria) Wien, NE Austria
Wiener Neustadt *73 E6* Niederösterreich, E Austria
Wierden *64 E3* Overijssel, E Netherlands
Wiesbaden *73 B5* Hessen, W Germany
Wight, Isle of *67 D7 island* S England, UK
Wijchen *64 D4* Gelderland, SE Netherlands
Wijk bij Duurstede *64 D4* Utrecht, C Netherlands
Wilcannia *127 C6* New South Wales, SE Australia
Wilhelm, Mount *122 B3 mountain* C PNG
Wilhelm-Pieck-Stadt *see* Guben
Wilhelmshaven *72 B3* Niedersachsen, NW Germany
Wilkes Barre *19 F3* Pennsylvania, NE USA
Wilkes Land *132 C4 physical region* Antarctica
Willard *26 D2* New Mexico, SW USA
Willcox *26 C3* Arizona, SW USA
Willebroek *65 B5* Antwerpen, C Belgium
Willemstad *33 E5 dependent territory capital* (Netherlands Antilles) Curaçao, Netherlands Antilles
Williston *22 D1* North Dakota, N USA
Wilmington *19 F4* Delaware, NE USA
Wilmington *21 F2* North Carolina, SE USA
Wilmington *18 C4* Ohio, N USA
Wilrijk *65 C5* Antwerpen, N Belgium
Winchester *67 D7 hist.* Wintanceaster, *Lat.* Venta Belgarum. S England, UK
Winchester *19 E4* Virginia, NE USA
Windhoek *56 B3 Ger.* Windhuk. *Country capital* (Namibia) Khomas, C Namibia
Windorah *126 C4* Queensland, C Australia
Windsor *19 G3* Connecticut, NE USA
Windsor *126 D1* New South Wales, SE Australia
Windsor *16 C5* Ontario, S Canada
Windsor *67 D7* S England, UK
Windward Islands *33 H4 island group* E West Indies
Windward Islands *see* Barlavento, Ilhas de
Windward Passage *32 D3 Sp.* Paso de los Vientos. *Channel* Cuba/Haiti
Winisk *16 C2 river* Ontario, S Canada
Winisk *16 C2* Ontario, C Canada
Winnebago, Lake *18 B2 lake* Wisconsin, N USA
Winnemucca *25 C5* Nevada, W USA
Winnipeg *15 G5* Manitoba, S Canada
Winnipeg, Lake *15 G5 lake* Manitoba, C Canada
Winnipegosis, Lake *16 A3 lake* Manitoba, C Canada
Winona *23 G3* Minnesota, N USA
Winschoten *64 E2* Groningen, NE Netherlands
Winsen *72 B3* Niedersachsen, N Germany
Winston Salem *21 E1* North Carolina, SE USA
Winsum *64 D1* Groningen, NE Netherlands
Winterswijk *64 E4* Gelderland, E Netherlands
Winterthur *73 B7* Zürich, NE Switzerland
Winton *126 C4* Queensland, E Australia
Winton *129 A7* Southland, South Island, NZ
Wisconsin *18 A2 off.* State of Wisconsin; also known as The Badger State. *State* N USA
Wisconsin Rapids *18 B2* Wisconsin, N USA
Wisconsin River *18 B3 river* Wisconsin, N USA
Wisła *76 C2 Eng.* Vistula, *Ger.* Weichsel. *River* Śląskie, S Poland
Wismar *72 C2* Mecklenburg-Vorpommern, N Germany
Wittenberge *72 C3* Brandenburg, N Germany
Wittlich *73 A5* Rheinland-Pfalz, SW Germany
Wittstock *72 C3* Brandenburg, NE Germany
W.J. van Blommesteinmeer *37 G3 reservoir* E Suriname
Władysławowo *76 C2* Pomorskie, N Poland
Włocławek *76 C3 Ger./Rus.* Vlotslavsk. Kujawsko-pomorskie, C Poland
Włodawa *76 E4 Rus.* Vlodava. Lubelskie, E Poland
Wlotzkasbaken *56 B3* Erongo, W Namibia
Wodonga *127 C7* Victoria, SE Australia
Wodzisław Śląski *77 C5 Ger.* Loslau. Śląskie, S Poland
Wōjjā *see* Wotje Atoll
Woking *67 D7* SE England, UK
Wolf, Isla *38 A4 var.* Wenmen Island. *Island* W Ecuador
Wolfsberg *73 D7* Kärnten, SE Austria
Wolfsburg *72 C3* Niedersachsen, N Germany
Wolgast *72 D2* Mecklenburg-Vorpommern, NE Germany
Wollaston Lake *15 F4* Saskatchewan, C Canada
Wollongong *127 D6* New South Wales, SE Australia
Wolvega *64 D2 Fris.* Wolvegea. Friesland, N Netherlands
Wolverhampton *67 D6* C England, UK
Wŏnsan *107 E3* SE North Korea
Woodburn *24 B3* Oregon, NW USA
Woodland *25 B5* California, W USA
Woodruff *18 B2* Wisconsin, N USA
Woods, Lake of the *16 A3 Fr.* Lac des Bois. *Lake* Canada/USA
Woodville *128 D4* Manawatu-Wanganui, North Island, NZ
Woodward *27 F1* Oklahoma, C USA
Worcester *67 D6 hist.* Wigorna Ceaster. W England, UK
Worcester *19 G3* Massachusetts, NE USA
Worcester *56 C5* Western Cape, SW South Africa
Workington *67 C5* NW England, UK
Worland *22 C3* Wyoming, C USA
Worms *73 B5 anc.* Augusta Vangionum, Borbetomagus, Wormatia. Rheinland-Pfalz, SW Germany
Worms *see* Vormsi
Worthington *23 F3* Minnesota, N USA
Wotje Atoll *122 D1 var.* Wōjjā. *Atoll* Ratak Chain, E Marshall Islands
Woudrichem *64 C4* Noord-Brabant, S Netherlands
Wrangel Island *see* Vrangelya, Ostrov
Wrangel Plain *133 B2 undersea feature* Arctic Ocean
Wrocław *76 C4 Eng./Ger.* Breslau. Dolnośląskie, SW Poland
Września *76 C3* Wielkopolskie, C Poland
Wuchang *see* Wuhan
Wuday 'ah *99 C6* Najrān, S Saudi Arabia
Wuhai *105 E3* Nei Mongol Zizhiqu, N China
Wuhan *106 C5 var.* Han-kou, Han-k'ou, Hanyang, Wuchang, Wu-han; *prev.* Hankow. Hubei, C China
Wuhsi *see* Wuxi
Wuhsien *see* Suzhou
Wuhu *106 D5 var.* Wu-na-mu. Anhui, E China
Wujlan *see* Ujelang Atoll
Wukari *53 G4* Taraba, E Nigeria
Wuliang Shan *106 A6 mountain range* SW China
Wu-lu-k'o-mu-shi *see* Ürümqi
Wu-lu-mu-ch'i *see* Ürümqi
Wu-na-mu *see* Wuhu
Wuppertal *72 A4 prev.* Barmen-Elberfeld. Nordrhein-Westfalen, W Germany
Würzburg *73 B5* Bayern, SW Germany
Wusih *see* Wuxi
Wuxi *106 D5 var.* Wuhsi, Wu-hsi, Wusih. Jiangsu, E China
Wuyi Shan *103 E3 mountain range* SE China
Wye *67 C6 Wel.* Gwy. *River* England/Wales, UK
Wyndham *124 D3* Western Australia
Wyoming *22 B3 off.* State of Wyoming; also known as The Equality State. *State* C USA
Wyoming *18 C3* Michigan, N USA
Wyszków *76 D3 Ger.* Probstberg. Mazowieckie, C Poland

X

Xaafuun, Raas *50 E4 var.* Ras Hafun. *Headland* NE Somalia
Xaçmaz *95 H2 Rus.* Khachmas. N Azerbaijan
Xaignabouli *114 C4 prev.* Muang Xaignabouri, *Fr.* Sayaboury. Xaignabouli, N Laos
Xai-Xai *57 E4 prev.* João Belo, Vila de João *Bel.* Gaza, S Mozambique
Xalapa *29 F4 var.* Jalapa, Jalapa Enríquez. Veracruz-Llave, SE Mexico
Xam Nua *114 D3 var.* Sam Neua. Houaphan, N Laos
Xankändi *95 G3 Rus.* Khankendi; *prev.* Stepanakert. SW Azerbaijan
Xánthi *82 C3* Anatolikí Makedonía kai Thráki, NE Greece
Xátiva *71 F3 var.* Jativa; *anc.* Setabis. País Valenciano, E Spain
Xauen *see* Chefchaouen
Xeres *see* Jeréz de la Frontera
Xiaguan *see* Dali
Xiamen *106 D6 var.* Hsia-men; *prev.* Amoy. Fujian, SE China
Xi'an *106 C4 var.* Changan, Sian, Signan, Siking, Singan, Xian. Shaanxi, C China
Xian *see* Xi'an
Xiangkhoang *see* Pèk
Xiangtan *106 C5 var.* Hsiang-t'an, Siangtan. Hunan, S China
Xiao Hinggan Ling *106 D2 Eng.* Lesser Khingan Range. *Mountain range* NE China
Xichang *106 B5* Sichuan, C China
Xieng Khouang *see* Pèk
Xieng Ngeun *see* Muong Xiang Ngeun
Xigaze *see* Xigazê
Xigazê *104 C5 var.* Jih-k'a-tse, Shigatse, Xigaze. Xizang Zizhiqu, W China
Xi Jiang *102 D3 var.* Hsi Chiang, *Eng.* West River. *River* S China
Xilinhot *105 F2 var.* Silinhot. Nei Mongol Zizhiqu, N China
Xilokastro *see* Xylókastro
Xin *see* Xinjiang Uygur Zizhiqu
Xingkai Hu *see* Khanka, Lake
Xingu, Rio *41 E2 river* C Brazil
Xingxingxia *104 D3* Xinjiang Uygur Zizhiqu, NW China
Xining *105 E4 var.* Hsining, Hsi-ning, Sining. *Province capital* Qinghai, C China
Xinjiang *see* Xinjiang Uygur Zizhiqu
Xinjiang Uygur Zizhiqu *104 B3 var.* Sinkiang, Sinkiang Uighur Autonomous Region, Xin, Xinjiang. Admin. region *autonomous region* NW China
Xinpu *see* Lianyungang
Xinxiang *106 C4* Henan, C China
Xinyang *106 C5 var.* Hsin-yang, Sinyang. Henan, C China
Xinzo de Limia *70 C2* Galicia, NW Spain
Xiqing Shan *102 D2 mountain range* C China
Xixón *see* Gijón
Xizang *see* Xizang Zizhiqu
Xizang Gaoyuan *see* Qingzang Gaoyuan
Xizang Zizhiqu *104 B4 var.* Thibet, Tibetan Autonomous Region, Xizang, *Eng.* Tibet. Admin. region *autonomous region* W China
Xolotlán *see* Managua, Lago de
Xuddur *51 D5 var.* Hudur, *It.* Oddur. Bakool, SW Somalia
Xuwen *106 C7* Guangdong, S China
Xuzhou *106 D4 var.* Hsu-chou, Suchow, Tongshan; *prev.* T'ung-shan. Jiangsu, E China
Xylókastro *83 B5 var.* Xilokastro. Pelopónnisos, S Greece

Y

Ya'an *106 B5 var.* Yaan. Sichuan, C China
Yabēlo *51 C5* C Ethiopia
Yablis *31 E2* Región Autónoma Atlántico Norte, NE Nicaragua
Yablonovyy Khrebet *93 F4 mountain range* S Russian Federation
Yabrai Shan *105 E3 mountain range* NE China
Yafran *49 F2* NW Libya
Yaghan Basin *45 B7 undersea feature* SE Pacific Ocean
Yahotyn *87 E2 Rus.* Yagotin. Kyyivs'ka Oblast', N Ukraine
Yahualica *28 D4* Jalisco, SW Mexico
Yakima *24 B2* Washington, NW USA
Yakima River *24 B2 river* Washington, NW USA
Yakoruda *82 C3* Blagoevgrad, SW Bulgaria
Yaku-shima *109 B8 island* Nansei-shotō, SW Japan
Yakutat *14 D4* Alaska, USA
Yakutsk *93 F3* Respublika Sakha (Yakutiya), NE Russian Federation
Yala *115 C7* Yala, SW Thailand
Yalizava *85 D6 Rus.* Yelizovo. Mahilyowskaya Voblasts', E Belarus
Yalong Jiang *106 A5 river* C China
Yalova *94 B3* Yalova, NW Turkey
Yalpuh, Ozero *86 D4 Rus.* Ozero Yalpug. *Lake* SW Ukraine
Yalta *87 F5* Respublika Krym, S Ukraine
Yalu *103 E2 Chin.* Yalu Jiang, *Jap.* Oryokko, *Kor.* Amnok-kang. *River* China/North Korea
Yamaguchi *109 B7 var.* Yamaguti. Yamaguchi, Honshū, SW Japan
Yamaguti *see* Yamaguchi
Yamal, Poluostrov *92 D2 peninsula* N Russian Federation
Yambio *51 B5 var.* Yambiyo. Western Equatoria, S Sudan
Yambiyo *see* Yambio
Yambol *82 D2 Turk.* Yanboli. Yambol, E Bulgaria
Yamdena, Pulau *117 G5 prev.* Jamdena. *Island* Kepulauan Tanimbar, E Indonesia
Yam HaMelaḥ *see* Dead Sea
Yam Kinneret *see* Tiberias, Lake
Yamoussoukro *52 D5 country capital* (Côte d'Ivoire) C Côte d'Ivoire
Yamuna *112 D3 prev.* Jumna. *River* N India
Yana *93 F2 river* NE Russian Federation
Yanbu 'al Baḥr *99 A5* Al Madīnah, W Saudi Arabia
Yangambi *55 D5* Orientale, N Dem. Rep. Congo
Yangchow *see* Yangzhou
Yangiyŭl *101 E2 Rus.* Yangiyul'. Toshkent Wiloyati, E Uzbekistan
Yangon *114 B4 Eng.* Rangoon. *Country capital* (Myanmar) Yangon, S Myanmar
Yangtze *see* Chang Jiang
Yangtze Kiang *see* Chang Jiang
Yangzhou *106 D5 var.* Yangchow. Jiangsu, E China
Yankton *23 E3* South Dakota, N USA
Yannina *see* Ioánnina
Yanskiy Zaliv *91 F2 bay* N Russian Federation
Yantai *106 D4 var.* Yan-t'ai; *prev.* Chefoo, Chih-fu. Shandong, E China
Yan-t'ai *see* Yantai
Yaoundé *55 B5 var.* Yaunde. *Country capital* (Cameroon) Centre, S Cameroon
Yap *122 A1 island* Caroline Islands, W Micronesia
Yapanskoye More *see* Japan, Sea of
Yapen, Pulau *117 G4 prev.* Japen. *Island* E Indonesia
Yap Trench *120 B2 var.* Yap Trough. *Undersea feature* SE Philippine Sea
Yap Trough *see* Yap Trench
Yapurá *see* Caquetá, Río
Yapurá *see* Japurá, Rio
Yaqui, Río *28 C2 river* NW Mexico
Yaransk *89 C5* Kirovskaya Oblast', NW Russian Federation
Yarega *88 D4* Respublika Komi, NW Russian Federation
Yarkant *see* Shache
Yarlung Zangbo Jiang *see* Brahmaputra
Yarmouth *see* Great Yarmouth
Yarmouth *17 F5* Nova Scotia, SE Canada
Yaroslavl' *88 B4* Yaroslavskaya Oblast', W Russian Federation
Yarumal *36 B2* Antioquia, NW Colombia
Yasyel'da *85 B7 river* SW Belarus
Yatsushiro *109 A7 var.* Yatusiro. Kumamoto, Kyūshū, SW Japan
Yatusiro *see* Yatsushiro
Yaunde *see* Yaoundé
Yavarí *see* Javari, Rio
Yaviza *31 H5* Darién, SE Panama
Yavoriv *86 B2 Pol.* Jaworów, *Rus.* Yavorov. L'vivs'ka Oblast', NW Ukraine
Yazd *98 D3 var.* Yezd. Yazd, C Iran
Yazoo City *20 B2* Mississippi, S USA
Yding Skovhøj *63 A7 hill* C Denmark
Ýdra *83 C6 var.* Ídhra. *Island* S Greece
Ye *115 B5* Mon State, S Myanmar
Yecheng *104 A3 var.* Kargilik. Xinjiang Uygur Zizhiqu, NW China
Yefremov *89 B5* Tul'skaya Oblast', W Russian Federation
Yekaterinburg *92 C3 prev.* Sverdlovsk. Sverdlovskaya Oblast', C Russian Federation
Yelets *89 B5* Lipetskaya Oblast', W Russian Federation
Yell *66 D1 island* NE Scotland, UK
Yellowknife *15 E4 territory capital* Northwest Territories, W Canada
Yellow River *see* Huang He
Yellow Sea *106 D4 Chin.* Huang Hai, *Kor.* Hwang-Hae. *Sea* E Asia
Yellowstone River *22 C2 river* Montana/Wyoming, NW USA
Yel'sk *85 C7 Rus.* Yel'sk. Homyel'skaya Voblasts', SE Belarus
Yelwa *53 F4* Kebbi, W Nigeria
Yemen *99 C7 off.* Republic of Yemen, *Ar.* Al Jumhūrīyah al Yamanīyah, Al Yaman. *Country* SW Asia
Yemva *88 D4 prev.* Zheleznodorozhnyy. Respublika Komi, NW Russian Federation
Yenakiyeve *87 G3 Rus.* Yenakiyevo; *prev.* Ordzhonikidze, Rykovo. Donets'ka Oblast', E Ukraine
Yenangyaung *114 A3* Magwe, W Myanmar
Yendi *53 E4* NE Ghana
Yengisar *104 A3* Xinjiang Uygur Zizhiqu, NW China
Yenierenköy *see* Agialoúsa
Yenisey *92 D3 river* Mongolia/Russian Federation
Yenping *see* Nanping
Yeovil *67 D7* SW England, UK
Yeppoon *126 D4* Queensland, E Australia
Yerevan *95 F3 var.* Erevan, *Eng.* Erivan. *Country capital* (Armenia) C Armenia
Yeriho *see* Jericho
Yerushalayim *see* Jerusalem
Yeu, Île d' *68 A4 island* NW France
Yevlax *95 G2 Rus.* Yevlakh. C Azerbaijan
Yevpatoriya *87 F5* Respublika Krym, S Ukraine
Yeya *87 H4 river* SW Russian Federation
Yezd *see* Yazd
Yezyaryshcha *85 E5 Rus.* Yezerishche. Vitsyebskaya Voblasts', NE Belarus
Yiannitsá *see* Giannitsá
Yichang *106 C5* Hubei, C China
Yıldızeli *94 D3* Sivas, N Turkey
Yinchuan *106 B4 var.* Yinch'uan, Yin-ch'uan, Yinchwan. Ningxia, N China
Yinchwan *see* Yinchuan
Yin-hsien *see* Ningbo
Yining *104 B2 var.* I-ning, *Uigh.* Gulja, Kuldja. Xinjiang Uygur Zizhiqu, NW China
Yíthion *see* Gýtheio
Yogyakarta *116 C5 prev.* Djokjakarta, Jogjakarta, Jokyakarta. Jawa, C Indonesia
Yokohama *109 D5* Aomori, Honshū, C Japan
Yokohama *108 A2* Kanagawa, Honshū, S Japan
Yokote *108 D4* Akita, Honshū, C Japan
Yola *53 H4* Adamawa, E Nigeria
Yonago *109 B6* Tottori, Honshū, SW Japan
Yong'an *106 D6 var.* Yongan. Fujian, SE China
Yonkers *19 F3* New York, NE USA
Yonne *68 C4 river* C France
Yopal *36 C3 var.* El Yopal. Casanare, C Colombia
York *67 D5 anc.* Eboracum, Eburacum. N England, UK
York *23 F4* Nebraska, C USA
York, Cape *126 C1 headland* Queensland, NE Australia
Yorkton *15 F5* Saskatchewan, S Canada
Yoro *30 C2* Yoro, C Honduras
Yoshkar-Ola *89 C5* Respublika Mariy El, W Russian Federation
Youngstown *18 D4* Ohio, N USA
Youth, Isle of *see* Juventud, Isla de la
Yreka *24 B4* California, W USA
Yssel *see* IJssel
Ysyk-Köl *see* Issyk-Kul', Ozero
Yu *see* Henan
Yuan *see* Red River
Yuan Jiang *see* Red River
Yuba City *25 B5* California, W USA
Yucatan Channel *29 H3 Sp.* Canal de Yucatán. *Channel* Cuba/Mexico
Yucatan Peninsula *13 C7 peninsula* Guatemala/Mexico
Yuci *106 C4* Shanxi, C China
Yue *see* Guangdong
Yueyang *106 C5* Hunan, S China
Yugoslaiva *see* Serbia and Montenegro
Yukhavichy *85 D5 Rus.* Yukhovichi. Vitsyebskaya Voblasts', N Belarus
Yukon *14 C2 river* Canada/USA
Yukon *see* Yukon Territory
Yukon Territory *14 D3 var.* Yukon, *Fr.* Territoire du Yukon. Admin. region *territory* NW Canada
Yulin *106 C6* Guangxi Zhuangzu Zizhiqu, S China
Yuma *26 A2* Arizona, SW USA
Yumen *106 A3 var.* Laojunmiao, Yümen. Gansu, N China
Yun *see* Yunnan
Yungki *see* Jilin
Yung-ning *see* Nanning
Yunjinghong *see* Jinghong
Yunki *see* Jilin
Yunnan *106 A6 var.* Yun, Yunnan Sheng, Yünnan, Yun-nan. Admin. region *province* SW China
Yunnan *see* Kunming
Yunnan Sheng *see* Yunnan
Yuruá, Río *see* Juruá, Rio
Yushu *104 D4* Qinghai, C China
Yuty *42 D3* Caazapá, S Paraguay
Yuzhno-Sakhalinsk *93 H4 Jap.* Toyohara; *prev.* Vladimirovka. Ostrov Sakhalin, Sakhalinskaya Oblast', SE Russian Federation
Yuzhou *see* Chongqing
Yylanly *see* Il'yaly

Z

Zaanstad *64 C3 prev.* Zaandam. Noord-Holland, C Netherlands
Zabaykal'sk *93 F5* Chitinskaya Oblast', S Russian Federation
Zabern *see* Saverne
Zabīd *99 B7* W Yemen
Ząbkowice *see* Ząbkowice Śląskie
Ząbkowice Śląskie *76 B4 var.* Ząbkowice, *Ger.* Frankenstein, Frankenstein in Schlesien. Wałbrzych, SW Poland
Zábřeh *77 C5 Ger.* Hohenstadt. Olomoucký Kraj, E Czech Republic
Zacapa *30 B2* Zacapa, E Guatemala
Zacatecas *28 D3* Zacatecas, C Mexico
Zacatepec *29 E4* Morelos, S Mexico
Zacháro *83 B6 var.* Zaharo, Zakháro. Dytikí Ellás, S Greece
Zadar *78 A3 It.* Zara; *anc.* Iader. Zadar, SW Croatia
Zadetkyl Kyun *115 B6 var.* St. Matthew's Island. *Island* Mergui Archipelago, S Myanmar
Zafra *70 C4* Extremadura, W Spain
Żagań *76 B4 var.* Zagań, Żegań; *Ger.* Sagan. Lubuskie, W Poland
Zagazig *50 B1 var.* Az Zaqāzīq. N Egypt
Zágráb *see* Zagreb
Zagreb *78 B2 Ger.* Agram, *Hung.* Zágráb. *Country capital* (Croatia) Zagreb, N Croatia
Zāgros, Kūhhā-ye *98 C3 Eng.* Zagros Mountains. *Mountain range* W Iran
Zagros Mountains *see* Zāgros, Kūhhā-ye
Zaharo *see* Zacháro
Zāhedān *98 E4 var.* Zahidan; *prev.* Duzdab. Sīstān va Balūchestān, SE Iran
Zahidan *see* Zāhedān
Zaḥlah *see* Zahlé
Zahlé *96 B4 var.* Zaḥlah. C Lebanon
Záhony *77 E6* Szabolcs-Szatmár-Bereg, NE Hungary
Zaire *see* Congo
Zaječar *78 E4* Serbia, E Serbia and Montenegro (Yugo.)
Zakháro *see* Zacháro
Zākhō *98 B2 var.* Zākhū. N Iraq
Zākhū *see* Zākhō
Zákinthos *see* Zákynthos
Zakopane *77 D5* Małopolskie, S Poland
Zakota Pomorskiea *see* Danzig, Gulf of
Zákynthos *83 A6 var.* Zákinthos, *It.* Zante. *Island* Iónioi Nísoi, Greece, C Mediterranean Sea
Zalaegerszeg *77 B7* Zala, W Hungary
Zalău *86 B3 Ger.* Waltenberg, *Hung.* Zilah; *prev. Ger.* Zillenmarkt. Sălaj, NW Romania
Zalim *99 B5* Makkah, W Saudi Arabia
Zambesi *see* Zambezi
Zambeze *see* Zambezi
Zambezi *56 D2 var.* Zambesi, *Port.* Zambeze. *River* S Africa
Zambezi *56 C2* North Western, W Zambia
Zambia *56 C2 off.* Republic of Zambia; *prev.* Northern Rhodesia. *Country* S Africa
Zamboanga *117 E3 off.* Zamboanga City. Mindanao, C Philippines
Zambrów *76 E3* Podlaskie, E Poland
Zamora *70 D2* Castilla-León, NW Spain
Zamora de Hidalgo *28 D4* Michoacán de Ocampo, SW Mexico
Zamość *76 E4 Rus.* Zamoste. Lubelskie, E Poland
Zancle *see* Messina
Zanda *104 A4* Xizang Zizhiqu, W China
Zanesville *18 D4* Ohio, N USA
Zanjān *98 C2 var.* Zenjan, Zinjan. Zanjān, NW Iran
Zante *see* Zákynthos
Zanthus *125 C6* Western Australia
Zanzibar *51 C7 Swa.* Unguja. *Island* E Tanzania
Zanzibar *51 D7* Zanzibar, E Tanzania
Zaozhuang *106 D4* Shandong, E China
Zapadna Morava *78 D4 Ger.* Westliche Morava. *River* C Serbia and Montenegro (Yugo.)
Zapadnaya Dvina *88 A4* Tverskaya Oblast', W Russian Federation
Zapadno-Sibirskaya Ravnina *92 C3 Eng.* West Siberian Plain. *Plain* C Russian Federation
Zapadnyy Sayan *92 D4 Eng.* Western Sayans. *Mountain range* S Russian Federation
Zapala *43 B5* Neuquén, W Argentina
Zapiola Ridge *45 B6 undersea feature* SW Atlantic Ocean
Zapolyarnyy *88 C2* Murmanskaya Oblast', NW Russian Federation
Zaporizhzhya *87 F3 Rus.* Zaporozh'ye; *prev.* Aleksandrovsk. Zaporiz'ka Oblast', SE Ukraine
Zapotiltic *28 D4* Jalisco, SW Mexico
Zaqatala *95 G2 Rus.* Zakataly. NW Azerbaijan
Zara *94 D3* Sivas, C Turkey
Zarafshon *100 D2 Rus.* Zarafshan. Nawoiy Wiloyati, N Uzbekistan

INDEX